DICKENS

A LIFE

DICKENS

A LIFE

NORMAN AND JEANNE MACKENZIE

'Genius always pays for the gift'

HENRY JAMES

Oxford   New York   Toronto   Melbourne

OXFORD UNIVERSITY PRESS

1979

Oxford University Press, Walton Street, Oxford OX2 6DP

OXFORD LONDON GLASGOW
NEW YORK TORONTO MELBOURNE WELLINGTON
KUALA LUMPUR SINGAPORE JAKARTA HONG KONG TOKYO
DELHI BOMBAY CALCUTTA MADRAS KARACHI
IBADAN NAIROBI DAR ES SALAAM CAPE TOWN

British Library Cataloguing in Publication Data

MacKenzie, Norman, b. 1921
  Dickens.
  1. Dickens, Charles—Biography 2. Authors,
  English—19th century—Biography
  I. MacKenzie, Jeanne
  823'.8   PR4581   78-40833

ISBN 0-19-211741-6

*Printed in Great Britain by
Butler & Tanner Ltd., Frome and London*

For Daniel Aaron
In Friendship

Contents

Contents

PART THREE

A FEARFUL MAN 1851–1859

PART FOUR

THE NATIONAL SPARKLER 1859–1870

Illustrations

Acknowledgements

THIS biography owes a great debt to the Pilgrim Edition of the Dickens Letters. This splendid work of scholarship, so ably conducted by the late Madeline House, Graham Storey, and Kathleen Tillotson, contains a wealth of fresh material on Dickens and his contemporaries. We are grateful to the editors and to Mr. Christopher Dickens for permission to quote extensively from the four volumes of letters so far published—and for our constant delight in consulting them and their supporting notes. In the quarter-century since Professor Edgar Johnson published his comprehensive work on Dickens, which set the context for so much subsequent research, a number of important specialist studies have been added to the large and ever-growing Dickens bibliography. Professor Philip Collins has published four substantial works—*Dickens and Crime*; *Dickens and Education*; *Dickens: The Critical Heritage*; and *Charles Dickens: The Public Readings*—as well as a number of valuable articles and reviews. Professor K. J. Fielding, the author of indispensable contributions to the *Dickensian* and other journals, produced a notable volume on *The Speeches of Charles Dickens*. The files of the *Dickensian* itself have been a regular source for new information and the correction of old errors of fact. And the collection of books, pictures, and other Dickensiana at Dickens House has been a delight to the eye and a pleasure to use. We appreciate the assistance of its trustees and staff.

We are also grateful to Professor Tillotson for advice and help; to the staffs of the public libraries in Chatham and Broadstairs; to the Dickens Museum in Broadstairs; to the staffs of the British Library, the library of the University of British Columbia, and the library of the University of Sussex. We express our thanks to Catharine Carver, for her helpful comments on the first draft of this book; to Margaret Ralph and Betty ffrench-Beytagh, who typed much of the manuscript; to George Spater, who read it with such care; and to Diana Encel, who prepared the index. The editorial staff at Oxford University Press have been the kindest and most diligent of colleagues since this new one-volume biography was first conceived.

PART ONE

———

THE MAKING OF BOZ
1812–1842

1

A Child of Singular Abilities

THE Dickens family were always on the move. On Midsummer Day 1817 they arrived in Chatham where John Dickens had just been appointed as a pay clerk in the navy dockyard. He was thirty-two, his wife Elizabeth was twenty-eight, their eldest daughter Fanny was seven, their son Charles was five, and the second daughter Letitia was a baby. The widowed sister of Mrs. Dickens, Mary Allen, was also part of the household, and there were two servants—Mary Weller, who was the nursemaid, and Jane Bonny, a general domestic. On a salary of £200 a year, with some perquisites, John Dickens could afford a genteel address, and he rented 2 Ordnance Terrace, one of a set of four houses on the hill above the town. One neighbour was a naval officer on half pay and another was a retired London tailor in easy circumstances. And the house itself, a narrow brick-built property with two rooms on each of its three floors and a kitchen outhouse at the rear, was a marked improvement on the London lodgings in which the Dickens family had spent the past three years.

The terrace had acquired its name during the Napoleonic wars, when the hillside had been used for the storage of cannon, and the chalk downland behind the houses was still used for military exercises by the local garrison. In front of the terrace, across a hayfield, the ground dropped steeply away into the tangled streets of Chatham, sited where the River Medway took a great loop through hills covered with corn and orchards before it ran out into the marshlands of the Thames estuary. Just out of view, tucked under a curve of the hill, was the famous dockyard, where the Royal Navy built and repaired its ships—*Victory* had been launched there in 1765—fitted them with guns, powder, and stores, sent the crews abroad to fight the King's wars and paid them off when they came home again. The long war against France had been over for two years when John Dickens took his place in the Pay Office and the navy was being run down, but the dockyard was still busy. With the larger bases at Portsmouth and Plymouth it had to keep a fleet at sea and provide all the trades and services that task required; and its defences guarded the approach to London, which handled most of the nation's trade. The ten thousand inhabitants of Chatham therefore lived by and for the sea. They were carpenters and sailmakers, ship-chandlers and provision-merchants. They ran taverns and brothels, slop-shops for the seamen and outfitters for the officers. And it seemed to Charles Dickens, as a boy, that the town was always full of men—scores, hundreds, thousands of them, ranks, files, companies, and detachments, soldiers in red, pigtailed sailors, and convicts from one of the prison hulks moored in the river who clanked along dismally with numbers on their backs.[1]

Chatham was a lively place, where things were made and done, and men went to and from the corners of the world. Only a mile up the river, where a bridge carried the Dover Road past the Norman castle and cathedral, its twin town of Rochester slumbered in the past. Each night at 12.15 the down coach from London stopped at the post office in the High Street. At 1.45 a.m. the up coach came by, carrying mail and passengers from the Channel packets and vessels waiting in the Downs for a change of wind. Then the town went back to sleep. In the cathedral close the bishop presided over a decaying diocese, and in the guildhall the aldermen jobbed the town's offices and quarrelled about its charities.

In twenty minutes a boy could walk from one century to another.

That contrast had its counterpart within the Dickens family, for in fact John Dickens had to earn a living as a government clerk while he fancied himself as an eighteenth-century gentleman. For all his limited means he tried to dress stylishly, and he talked with a condescending verbosity that was an attempt at wit; he liked his wine, and convivial company; and he had the ingratiating charm of the habitual sponger, much needed to compensate for his fecklessness. He was a resilient man, with a gift of exclamatory self-renewal which enabled him to avoid the realities of life, and when his improvidence led to a crisis he was always confident that someone or something would turn up to rescue him.

John Dickens had learned these lordly manners at close quarters, for his parents spent their lives as upper servants of the aristocracy. His father, William Dickens, was the steward at Crewe Hall in Cheshire, a splendid country house designed by Inigo Jones in the seventeenth century; and his mother Elizabeth, formerly lady's maid to the wife of the Lord Chamberlain, became the housekeeper on her marriage. She was a competent woman, formidable but kind-hearted, and the children in the Crewe household remembered her as an inimitable storyteller.[2] After her husband died in 1785, the year in which John Dickens was born, she kept her post, bringing up the baby and his elder brother William as genteel copies of the upstairs people. Crewe Hall was both elegant and lively. Its owner was John Crewe, the staunch Whig M.P. for the county for almost fifty years, who was rewarded with a peerage in 1806; and his wife Frances was a fashionable beauty, the friend of such politicians as Charles James Fox, Burke, and Canning, of the painter Sir Joshua Reynolds and the playwright Richard Sheridan. John Crewe, moreover, was a generous man, arranging for the education of his housekeeper's fatherless sons and using his influence to get them a reasonable start in life. As John Dickens grew up his mother realized that he had a weak and dependent personality. She called him a lazy fellow and complained that he was always hanging about the house and touching her for money. Yet he was not incapable when he chose to exert himself, and when Crewe found him a post in the navy Pay Office at Somerset House on an annual salary of £80 he did well and after four years he could afford to marry.

His small and pertly pretty wife, Elizabeth Barrow, was twenty when they married at St. Mary-le-Strand on 13 June 1809, and he had been courting her for about two years. It seemed a good match. She was one of ten children, and one of her brothers was Thomas Culliford Barrow, who had been a friend and fellow clerk of John Dickens since they had joined the Pay Office on the same April day in 1805; and her father, Charles Barrow, who came from a comfortable family of musical instrument-makers and had himself taught music, held a senior post in the Pay Office as Chief Conductor of Moneys in Town on the respectable salary of £350 a year. Elizabeth was an agreeable girl, well-intentioned and easy-going. She had all the accomplishments, with a particular gift for mimicry, and she shared her husband's taste for songs and recitations. She also had weaknesses of character that became more marked with the years. She was inconsequentially garrulous, somewhat spoilt, more than a little vain and trivially snobbish, and her social pretensions were a hindrance to managing a house on a limited income.

The marriage began with good prospects, for John Dickens had been promoted to a better post in the dockyard at Portsmouth. Soon after the wedding he and Elizabeth took the stage-coach down to near-by Portsea and set up in a tidy little house at 387 Mile End Terrace. The rent of £35 a year was on the high side, but John Dickens was now earning almost £180 a year and he could afford this degree of elegance if he kept a careful eye on his domestic expenses. He seems, however, to have lived well up to his means; he was a hospitable man, who disdained penny-pinching and turned casually to credit and borrowing, and when Fanny was born a year after the marriage the young couple took on the additional cost of a nursemaid. Money was already becoming tight and the strain was intensified by a disaster in the Barrow family. In February 1810 Elizabeth's father was unmasked as an embezzler. He had held a position of trust in the Pay Office in which he could obtain large amounts of cash on his own signature, and when the authorities became suspicious they discovered that he had been stating false balances since 1803 and had stolen a total of £5,689. 3s. 3d. Barrow admitted his guilt, pleaded ill health and the burden of his large family as mitigating circumstances, and asked for time to visit his brother in Bristol in an attempt to raise money and repay the loss. That bid for help was a failure, and as Barrow was about to be arrested he fled abroad and never returned. Although the family was sold up, its effects realizing £499. 3s. 0d., neither John Dickens nor Thomas Barrow was professionally affected by the disgrace, and Thomas Barrow went on to make a very good career in the Pay Office which his father had swindled.

A year later Elizabeth Dickens became pregnant again. She was a sociable, pleasure-loving woman, who had gone about in company all through her pregnancy, and on the evening of 6 February 1812 she was at a dance in the Beneficial Societies Hall when her labour pains began. In the early hours of 7 February 1812 her son was born, and on 4 March he was christened Charles John Huffam Dickens, 'Huffam' after his godfather.[3]

By this time John Dickens had drifted into the financial muddle which blighted the remainder of his life. In June 1812, in the first of many such attempts to make ends meet, the family moved to 18 Hawke Street. Though the house was in a respectable neighbourhood, where rooms were let to 'superior naval persons', it was a cheap brick box, directly on the street, with a small garden at the rear. Charles had some vague memories of the place in later years—or, perhaps, of a house in Wish Street where the family lived in 1814—but he was only two when his father was recalled to London and took the family to live in lodgings at 10 Norfolk Street, near the Middlesex Hospital. With the ending of the war against Napoleon the work at Portsmouth dockyard had fallen off, and John Dickens was fortunate to have secure employment in the Pay Office in Somerset House. Prices were high, work was hard to come by, and the country was troubled by riots and political agitation. The factory system had already begun to change English society and the war had accelerated the process. It had made some men rich; it had also made many poor, and behind the bright stucco façade of the Regency the masses lived in squalor and misery. For those like the Dickens family, living on the margins of respectability, it was only a short step from solvency to social collapse.

John Dickens somehow managed to weather his immediate difficulties, and for the first four years at Ordnance Terrace after the move to Chatham in 1817 his finances were reasonably buoyant. His new post paid another £20 a year, he seems to have borrowed money from his mother, and he undoubtedly had several loans from Richard Newnham, the retired tailor who lived next-door-but-one and treated both John Dickens and his children with friendly generosity.[4] This period of relative prosperity was the peak of the family fortunes, and Charles Dickens always looked back upon it as the golden age of his childhood. The house had a cheerful rhythm, for John Dickens was a jovial man when times were good and he encouraged his children to enjoy themselves. The boy next door, George Stroughill, had a magic lantern which fascinated Charles; and Lucy Stroughill, a pretty girl on whom Charles doted, seemed to lead a life of birthdays and to be brought up entirely on cake, wine, and presents. There were, indeed, parties for all the occasions—Christmas and Twelfth Night and Guy Fawkes Day—and outings to the circus and the pantomime which seasonally rolled into town in great wagons filled with properties. Sometimes, as a special treat, Charles was taken on the *Chatham*, the high-sterned old yacht on which his father sailed round to Sheerness on business. And as he grew older there were walks into the countryside, with John Dickens telling stories along the way and a pause for refreshment at the Leather Bottle in Cobham or some other alehouse on the fringe of the marshes.

There were stories, too, from Mary Weller. The family nursemaid, with an occupational bent towards midwives and undertakers, had a ghoulish taste. She took her charges to lyings-in, which Dickens recalled so vividly that he jocularly wondered how he had 'escaped from becoming a professional martyr to them in after life', and she told the small children tales of horrors and hauntings. She took 'a fiendish enjoyment' in frightening them, Dickens said, dramatically beginning a tale 'by clawing the air with both hands and uttering a long low hollow groan'.[5] After this sepulchral overture she brought on her stock characters—Captain Murderer, who made his wives into meat pies; a shipwright who sold himself to the devil; indestructible rats; and many other grisly images which, forced into the dark corners of a child's mind and touching a nerve of morbid fear, became a spring of never-forgotten nightmares. And as Charles grew up he began to spin tales for himself, and tell them to his sisters and his friends, for he was a clever boy with a remarkable memory, and he had his mother's talent for mimicry and music. With his sister Fanny, who played the piano well, he soon developed a repertoire of comic recitations and songs which attracted the kind of flattery which makes precocious children vain. His delivery of 'The Voice of the Sluggard', Mary Weller said, was given with great effect: 'such *action* and such *attitudes*'.[6] There was always something theatrical about John Dickens, and he admiringly encouraged these parlour performances. He not only paraded his children before his guests at home: he also took them down to the Mitre Inn where, using a table as an impromptu stage, they sang duets of popular songs and sea-shanties, and were rewarded by a snack of salmon or fowl and given a tip for their efforts.

The theatre itself was not far away. On Star Hill in Rochester stood the little Theatre Royal, a plastered front and portico giving on to a wooden auditorium which smelt of orange-peel, lamp-oil, and sawdust. Sometimes a star such as the tragedian Macready or the great clown Grimaldi trod its boards, but for the most part the farces and melodramas were given by seedy travelling companies in which the actors doubled the parts. In one production of *Macbeth*, Dickens recalled, King Duncan 'couldn't rest in his grave, but was continually coming out of it and calling himself something else'.[7] From the age of eight he went fairly often to the theatre, taken by James Lamert, the son of an army surgeon who successfully proposed to the widowed sister of Elizabeth Dickens. Both the Lamerts had a taste for amateur dramatics, getting up private performances in the Ordnance Hospital, and the Dickens children became accustomed to the business of make-believe, the glamour of the costumes, and the clinging odour of grease-paint.

In later years Dickens had clear and nostalgic memories of all these childhood treats and excitements, and yet he described himself as 'a very small and not-over-particularly-taken-care-of boy'.[8] It is true that he was puny, and that he was plagued by violent bouts of renal colic and migraine-like attacks which came on when he was particularly anxious. Long before he was an adult he had slipped into the family habit of self-centred complaint. He was not so much neglected by his parents as spoiled and put aside like a plaything as the whim took them. Both John and Elizabeth Dickens seem to have been confusingly irresponsible in their treatment of their children, putting sentiment in place of love and carelessness in place of authority. Charles undoubtedly grew up with feelings of emotional uncertainty and a sense of neglect. In his formative years, moreover, there were other sources of confusion. John Dickens saw himself as the victim of circumstances over which he had no control. One episode in his picaresque life succeeded another without apparent cause, and fortunate coincidences were as likely as an adverse turn of fate. It was all magically bewildering to a child. And as each year passed there was an increasing gap between the manner in which John and Elizabeth Dickens actually lived and the style in which they aspired to live. The uneasy ambivalence of shabby-genteel existence consists of functioning in a shabby way while pretending to genteel values. As the Dickens family discovered, such a life is haunted by the fear of being found out in the shifts necessary to keep up appearances and by the ever-present threat of ruin.

After four years in Ordnance Terrace the pretence was beginning to wear thin. Although two more children had been added to the family (Harriet Ellen, who was born in 1819, died while a child, and Frederick was born in 1820),[9] John Dickens should have managed his affairs without difficulty, for it was a period of falling food prices and in 1820 he was given a very sizeable increase in salary to £350. He felt flush enough to give two guineas to a fund for victims of a fire which destroyed many houses in March 1820. He was treasurer of the relief committee and wrote the report of the disaster which appeared in *The Times* on 4 March. Before long, however, he had to repeat the pattern of retrenchment set at Portsea. On 25 March 1821 he moved down the hill to 18 St. Mary's Place.

The family could now manage with a smaller house, for Mary Allen had married Dr. Matthew Lamert and gone off to Ireland, taking Jane Bonny with her as her maid. But there was a marked difference between Ordnance Terrace and the cramped cottage close to the parish church and the dockyard entrance. It stood in a mean thoroughfare called The Brook, which only twenty years before had been a desirable area; but the stream which ran down the lane had become a ditch of sewage, dependent on the rain to flush it, and The Brook was now full of taverns—the Bell, the Golden Lion, the Three Cups, and the King's Head—beer-shops and lodging-houses. Next door to the Dickens home the Providence Baptist Chapel stood four-square like an outpost of propriety, and from his attic room Charles looked down into its graveyard. It was a room in which he came to spend much of his time, reading. Mary Weller remembered that he was always 'a terrible boy to read'.[10] Elizabeth Dickens had taught him well, using primers with 'fat black letters' cast in a series of roles that Dickens never forgot. ' "A was an archer, and shot at a frog." Of course he was. He was an apple-pie also, and there he is! He was a good many things in his time, was A, and so were most of his friends, except X, who had so little versatility that I never knew him to get beyond Xerxes or Xantippe.'[11] At the age of six Charles was sent to a dame-school over a dyer's shop in Rome Lane, run by a vinegary old woman dressed in black bombasine who frightened him and knuckled facts into his head to painful effect. He stayed there two years, and about the time that the family moved down to The Brook he and Fanny were sent to the 'Classical, Mathematical and Commercial School' round the corner in Rhode Street. This school was run by William Giles, an intelligent young graduate from Oxford who was the son of the minister of the near-by Zion Chapel. John and Elizabeth Dickens, nominally Anglicans, were friends of the father and occasionally took their children to the chapel where the earnest evangelical catechized them with lumbering jocularity and bored them with his prolix sermons. Charles was more fortunate in the son, who took to his bright pupil. Though he was small, Miss Giles remembered, he was 'a very handsome boy, with long curly hair of a light colour', and 'an amiable disposition' which made him 'capital company even then'.[12]

Charles liked the school and enjoyed his friendships, although he was not robust enough to be good at games and preferred to watch the other boys at play. His recollection of those years gave an impression of detachment. 'When I think of it', he wrote in an autobiographical passage, 'the picture always arises in my mind of a summer evening, the boys at play in the churchyard, and I sitting on my bed, reading as if for life.' In one of his impulsive moods John Dickens had subscribed to 'a glorious host' of reprints, including *Roderick Random, Tom Jones, Robinson Crusoe, The Vicar of Wakefield, Don Quixote*, and other classics, besides volumes of the *Tatler*, the *Spectator*, Johnson's *Idler*, Goldsmith's *Citizen of the World*, and theatrical farces. It was these books, Dickens later said, which 'kept alive my fancy, and my hope of something beyond that place and time', creating a private world into which he increasingly withdrew as he sat reading on his bed, taking imaginary voyages and dreaming of exotic adventures; he ran off with Tom Jones, tilted at windmills, and scrambled over Crusoe's island. His impersonations had a peculiarly vivid quality, almost more compelling than life, and he fused what he read with the impressions of his sharp eye and his marvellously quick ear. 'Every barn in the neighbourhood, every stone in the church, every foot of the churchyard', he wrote later, 'had some association of its own, in my mind, connected with those books, and stood for some locality made famous in them.'[13] By the time he was ten he had learned to let his imagination run outward to experience, and transform it; to find release from loneliness and tension in wandering through Chatham and watching the drama of its noisy streets; and to allow feelings provoked but not satisfied at home to fix these images of childhood.

Late in 1822 the spell was broken. John Dickens was called back to work in the head office at Somerset House. Despite his improved salary he had got his finances into such a state that he had to sell some of the family's effects before the move: Mary Weller, who was getting married and whose place was taken by an orphan from the Chatham workhouse, bought the parlour chairs. After the family departed Charles was left on his own for the first time, to finish his term with Mr. Giles, and it was a gloomy wet morning near Christmas when he was packed off to London—perhaps cheaply in a carrier's cart, for he recalled that he was padded like game in damp straw and consigned carriage-paid to Cheapside.

John Dickens had now come down to a four-roomed house, with a basement and a garret, into which he squeezed his family of eight (another son, Alfred, had been born in 1822), together with the orphan maid and James Lamert, who had boarded with the Dickens household in Chatham and come on to London while he awaited a commission in the army. The house at 16 Bayham Street in Camden Town was one of a row of forty run up by a speculator on the northern edge of London. Fields still stretched away to the heights of Hampstead and Highgate, but much of the area was a scruffy waste—the dust heaps where contractors piled the scavengings of London were not far away—and although the house was only ten years old it was already seedy. A washerwoman lived next door and there was a Bow Street runner across the road.

Charles was upset by the change. Soon after the move, early in 1823, his sister Fanny escaped with a boarding scholarship to the newly founded Royal Academy of Music off Hanover Square, but Charles was kept at home to run errands, clean boots, look after the younger children, and generally make himself useful.[14] He was chagrined and depressed. His father, he afterwards complained, 'appeared to have utterly lost at this time the idea of educating me at all'. What he charitably called 'ease of temper' in John Dickens was more wounding than 'the straitness of his means'; the indifference, the actual neglect, seemed all the worse when he recalled 'as kindhearted and generous a man as ever lived' from the happier days at Chatham. 'As I thought in the little back garret in Bayham Street, of all I had lost in losing Chatham,' he said in later life, 'what would I have given, if I had had anything to give, to have been sent back to any other school, to have been taught something anywhere!'[15]

There were some fragments of the old pattern which could be pieced together even if there was no school. James Lamert made him a toy theatre. His uncle, Thomas Barrow, lodged with a bookseller's widow in Soho who lent Charles books when he called. Sometimes he went across London to visit his godfather, Christopher Huffam, who had a boat-rigging business in Limehouse, and encouraged the boy to show off his repertoire of comic songs. The wharfs and the flow of sailing craft and steamers on the Thames reminded him of Chatham. And there were all the new sights and sounds of London to absorb. Dressed in white cord breeches, a green coat, and a beaver hat that had been the uniform at his Chatham school, Charles began to wander about the town. He was, he said, like a child in a dream inspired by a mighty faith in the marvellousness of things. He went to St. Paul's and the Mansion House, loitering through huddled streets and crooked short-cuts, past taverns, churches and coffee-rooms, lumbering stage-coaches and loaded wagons, peering at hawkers, lamplighters, shivering beggars, chimney-sweeps, barbers, muffin-men, and ostlers, pausing at pie-stalls and pastry-cooks', and gazing aghast at the prodigies of wickedness, want, and beggary he saw in the slums off the Oxford Road. One night he got lost, and went to a low theatre; and afterwards he drifted through the rain until in the small hours he gave himself up to a watchman who sent for his father. By the age of twelve he had come to know the twisted

geography of London and the clipped cadences of cockney speech as well
as any street-boy.

It was a sad time for the Dickens family, with debt and death in the house
after little Harriet died. John Dickens had made a temporary composition
with his creditors, but he was finding it hard to make the payments promised
in the 'Deed' which set out the settlement. There was a trade depression
and money was tight. Even the prosperous Christopher Huffam had gone
bankrupt, and after another sale of household effects had brought only a
brief respite John Dickens knew that unless he raised funds from his mother
or other relatives he was headed for a debtor's prison—and the likely loss
of his pensionable post. Everyone in the family felt the grip of anxiety.
Charles reacted with a fresh bout of feverish spasms. Mrs. Dickens, hoping
to save her home from collapse, opened a school. The enterprise was typically unrealistic, and its failure made matters worse. She had no experience
of teaching, apart from her own small children, no social connections which
might have brought her pupils, and no capital. There was scarcely enough
cash in the house to pay for the handbills which Charles and the maid distributed in the neighbourhood of 4 Gower Street North—the much more pretentious house impetuously rented to provide both home and premises—
or to meet the cost of the imposing brass plate which adorned the door of
'Mrs. Dickens's Establishment'. No one came to it. 'Nor', said Dickens,
'do I recollect that anybody ever proposed to come, or that the least preparation was made to receive anybody.'[16]

The callers at the house, on the contrary, were importunate tradesmen
who wanted payment for their bills. The Dickens family had sunk to
the point where men hung about the steps and shouted abusive taunts
through the door. There was no delicacy about bilked creditors and debt-
collectors. John Dickens responded with postures of remorse and despair,
but he had already acquired the furtive habits of the near-insolvent, hiding
away when the duns were about and slipping out quickly when the street
seemed clear. Every week something had to be pawned or sold. For
Charles the cruellest sacrifice was the sale of his treasured books, which
he had to carry off to a drunken bookseller in the Hampstead Road to
get a few shillings. The household was soon down to little more than its
beds, a kitchen table, and some chairs. Catastrophe could no longer be
avoided.

On his twelfth birthday Charles faced the unpalatable fact that he was
to go out to work two days later. He was quite unprepared for the shock
for he had been brought up with expectations of something better. The
Dickens family had been sliding steadily from shabbiness to ruin, but John
and Elizabeth Dickens refused to accept the reality of their decline. The

worse things had become, indeed, the more John Dickens seems to have hoped that the ghost of his respectability would effect a magical rescue at the last minute. When there was an offer to take Charles off his hands he was as pleased, Dickens bitingly recalled, as 'if I had been twenty years of age, distinguished at a grammar school, and going to Cambridge'. Humiliation and anger were converted into an enduring self-pity. 'It is wonderful to me', he wrote when he finally brought himself to speak of this moment of shame, 'how I could have been so easily cast away at such an age ... no one had compassion enough on me—a child of singular abilities: quick, eager, delicate, and soon hurt, bodily or mentally—to suggest that something might have been spared, as certainly it might have been, to place me at any common school.'[17]

He was going to work in a factory which made paste-blacking for boots and fire-grates. The offer of a job came from James Lamert, who had left the household before the move from Camden Town. Tired of waiting for his army appointment Lamert had gone into business. He had become a partner with a relative who had purchased the blacking factory, the lesser of two firms with the same name of Warren founded by brothers who had quarrelled; and in an effort to help his distressed friends he found a place for Charles in the ramshackle rat-ridden warehouse which stood between the Strand and the river at Hungerford Stairs. Charles was to work twelve hours a day, wrapping and labelling the pots of blacking. Lamert promised to ease the blow by giving Charles lessons in the lunch-hour and allowing him to do his work in a corner of the counting-house, but the lessons were soon forgotten in the press of business, and the little saving mark of status was lost when Charles was moved down to the workroom. He had at last fallen into the pit. The other boys were a rough lot. One of them had a sister who played imps in pantomime and another—a lad named Bob Fagin who was particularly protective when Charles suffered another attack of spasms—was the brother of a Thames waterman. They may have teased him for his couth speech and manners, but they were kindly and his connection with their employer no doubt secured him a shadow of deference; he was called 'the young gentleman'. He was willing, besides, to work hard on equal terms, and pride made him conceal his despair. 'No words can express the secret agony of my soul as I sunk into this companionship,' he later confessed; 'compared these every day associates with those of my happier childhood; and felt my early hopes of growing up to be a learned and distinguished man crushed in my breast. The deep remembrance of the sense I had of being utterly neglected and hopeless; of the shame I felt in my position; of the misery it was to my young heart to believe that, day by day, what I had learned, and thought, and delighted in, and raised my fancy and my emulation up by, was passing away from me, never to be brought back any more; cannot be written.'[18]

There was worse to come. On Friday 20 February, eleven days after Charles started work, a James Karr sent a bailiff to arrest John Dickens for a debt of £40. He spent the week-end in the bailiff's sponging-house, where debtors were held while they tried to raise the due amount, as the family turned unavailingly to relatives and friends for help. Charles remembered how he tearfully ran from one to another with begging messages. On the Monday John Dickens was transferred to the Marshalsea, the frowzy debtor's prison across the river in the borough. Orotund to the last, as he passed through the gate he histrionically declared that the sun had set on him for ever. These melodramatic words were terrifying. 'I really believed at the time', Dickens said, 'that they had broken my heart.'[19]

For the next month Charles continued to live with his mother and the other children in spartan conditions. They were able to stay on in the Gower Street house because the rent had been paid in advance to the March quarter-day, but the family was sold up and the bailiffs left only the legal minimum of beds and chairs. Even the spoons were pawned in the last desperate days. The law stipulated, moreover, that a debtor and his family could retain clothing and personal effects only to a total of £20, and when Charles was sent to an appraiser he stood apprehensively hoping that the man would not hear the ticking of his grandfather's silver watch in his pocket. On 21 March Mrs. Dickens took the younger children off to join her husband in the Marshalsea. John Dickens had a urinary complaint, and by the device of a medical certificate which stated that he was unfit for duty he was able to continue drawing his salary; he had hopes that he could arrange to resign and draw the pension earned by nearly twenty years of service before he forfeited his rights through insolvency. In the meanwhile, like other debtors who could pay for the privilege, he lodged his family in the prison. It was a gloomy barrack with a wall around it, but there was no penal regime. The debtors were merely detained, and they were free to run their wretched community as they pleased. Before long John Dickens had made such a high-falutin impression on the other prisoners that they elected him chairman of the committee which took charge of their petty affairs, and Charles remembered the pathetic and comical occasion when his father organized a petition begging for a royal bounty so that the inmates might drink the King's health on the royal birthday. 'Their different peculiarities of dress, of face, of gait, of manner, were written indelibly upon my memory,' he wrote. 'I would rather have seen it than the best play ever played; and I thought about it afterwards, over the pots of paste-blacking, often and often.'[20] He was soon familiar with every detail of the prison for

he went each day to see his family; there was no restraint upon visitors so
long as they were out of the gate before it was locked at night, and even
the little orphan maid lodged near by and went in daily.

Charles was now on his own, boarded out to a family acquaintance named
Mrs. Roylance who took in homeless boys at 37 Little Cottage Street in
Camden Town. His rent was paid by his father, but everything else had
to be found out of his meagre wage. Once more it was the sense of aban-
donment that hurt him. Just as the shock of going to work at Warren's factory
had been worse than the actual hardship, so the loneliness of his new situation was harder to bear than the penury. He had been cast into premature
manhood and hankered for the childhood he had so traumatically lost. Thus
undertaking, as he said, 'the whole charge of my own existence', he had
to eke out his wages, making a separate shilling serve each day and going
on Sunday to share the family's dinner at the Marshalsea. Even a small boy
needs more than bread and milk for breakfast, bread and cheese for supper,
with lunch a choice between a stale pastry, a saveloy, or a flabby currant
pudding. 'When I had no money', Dickens said, 'I took a turn in Covent
Garden and stared at the pineapples.' It was a rare treat to go into a coffee-
room or to stand himself a pot of cheap ale. 'I know that I have lounged
about the streets, insufficiently and unsatisfactorily fed,' he added. 'I know
that, but for the mercy of God, I might easily have been, for any care that
was taken of me, a little robber or a little vagabond.'[21]

The strain soon told on him. He was separated from his family, and miserably impressed by the stigma of its imprisonment. He worked long hours,
ate little, suffered bouts of painful colic, and returned each night to the
'miserable blank' of his shared room in Camden Town. To a boy of twelve,
the vista of drudgery seemed endless. One Sunday at the Marshalsea he
told his father 'pathetically and with so many tears' that he could not go
on in this way. A back attic was then found for him in Lant Street, close
enough to the prison for him to take breakfast and supper with the rest of
the family. 'When I took possession of my new abode', he wrote, 'I thought
it was Paradise.'[22]

His father's prospects were also improving. On 5 May, after John Dickens
had been in the Marshalsea three months, he began to pass through the
slow procedures of the Insolvency Act which were to lead to a new arrangement with his creditors and his release on 28 May. Meanwhile his aged
mother had died on 26 April and left him £450—a lesser sum than his elder
brother received because, his mother wrote in her will, he had been advanced
'several sums of money some years ago'; the will was not proved until 4
June, after John Dickens had left the prison, and the money was eventually
a bonus to his creditors. As a discharged debtor who had come into property

he was obliged to apply his legacy to his schedule of debts, and payments were made on 2 November 1825 and again on 13 November 1826. The family went straight from the Marshalsea to stay with Mrs. Roylance, and in June moved on to a poor little house at 29 Johnson Street in Somers Town. John Dickens was still negotiating about his pension and for the time being he returned to work at the Pay Office.

Charles assumed that this turn for the better would also free him from the blacking factory, and although he 'had not the same difficulty in merely living' once the family was reunited, he was bitterly disappointed when nothing was done for him. 'I never ... heard a word of being taken away,' he wrote, 'or of being otherwise than quite provided for.'[23] His feelings of resentment and envy were intensified by Fanny's comparatively fortunate lot. She was now being taught by Ignaz Moscheles, a pupil of Beethoven, and she had just won a silver medal as the second piano prize at the Royal Academy. Charles went with his mother to see Princess Augusta preside at the prize-day on 29 June, and he was desperately upset. 'I could not bear to think of myself—beyond the reach of all such honourable emulation and success,' he recalled. 'The tears ran down my face ... I prayed, when I went to bed that night, to be lifted out of the humiliation and neglect in which I was. I never had suffered so much before.'[24] He was still setting off each morning to trudge down to the factory, now installed in better premises in Chandos Street. He and Bob Fagin now worked at a window visible from the street, and they made such a performance of their dexterity in wrapping and labelling that passers-by would stand to watch them. 'I saw my father coming in at the door one day when we were very busy', he wrote, 'and I wondered how he could bear it.'[25]

John Dickens may have been touched by the sight. Soon afterwards he had a tiff with James Lamert about Charles, as a result of which he was asked to take his son away. Charles left, he said, 'with a relief so strange that it was like oppression'. Mrs. Dickens felt differently. She did not put pride before a few shillings a week and she did her best to smooth things over. She managed to appease Lamert, who offered to employ Charles again. But this time he refused to go, feeling dreadfully and irrevocably betrayed by his mother's desire to return him to his menial occupation, and his father at last supported him. Charles, he conceded, should go back to school.

For Charles, however, this grudging release from bondage came too late to ease his feelings of injustice. 'I had never done harm to anyone,' he wrote;[26] and still, for all his innocence, he felt that fate had put the mark of Cain upon him and that he had become an outcast. His parents, pretentious to the last, never acknowledged these humiliating experiences; and this denial intensified the burden of guilt. The domestic disaster was both unforgettable and unmentionable. As Dickens grew up he became eager for success and security, and he quickly acquired the manners of a gentleman. Yet he remained compulsively fascinated by this suppressed experience. It had forged an indissoluble bond of sympathy, even of identity, with the homeless, the friendless, the orphans, the hungry, the uneducated, and even the prisoners of London's lower depths. His childhood had been lost there and all his wanderings were a search for it.

2

Rising Hopes

WELLINGTON House Academy, where Dickens went in June 1824, was a one-storey timber building in the garden of its proprietor's house in the Hampstead Road. This 'Clerical and Commercial Academy' was considered to be a superior sort of school, one of the best in that part of London. It catered for the sons of aspiring tradespeople, publicans, and prosperous shopkeepers; the father of one pupil was a soap boiler. In retrospect, Dickens did not think much of the place. He later described the headmaster, William Jones, as a 'thrasher', as 'by far the most ignorant man I have ever had the pleasure to know', and 'one of the worst-tempered men perhaps that have ever lived, whose business it was to make as much out of us and to put as little into us as possible'.[1] Not surprisingly it was badly run by Jones and its reputation depended upon the talents of its ushers. Mr. Taylor, 'a bony, gentle-faced, clerical-looking young man in rusty black', taught English and mathematics: he looked after the business of the school and cultivated the parents. The Latin master, Mr. Manville, 'a colourless doubled-up near-sighted man with a crutch' who suffered from colds and deafness, was a good scholar and 'took great pains where he saw intelligence and a desire to learn': all the same he was monotonously feeble, 'having had the best part of his life ground out of him in a Mill of boys'. There was also a brisk little French teacher and a fat dancing master 'who came in a gig and taught hornpipes to the more advanced'.[2]

Although Dickens was not particularly distinguished at school, he did well enough to scrape a Latin prize and before he left three years later had become first boy. His peculiar independent experience of the world had not, however, equipped him for an academic career and he was remembered as sharp rather than thoughtful. But he was, as he said, a child of singular abilities.[3] Since he learned easily, was already well-read and could write with facility, had an acute ear, a sharp eye, and a remarkable memory, he benefited from the school in his own way. For once he could be a boy in a boy's world, having fun, playing games, and keeping white mice hidden in the desks. He was an avid reader of a penny weekly, the *Terrific Register*, which described itself as a 'Record of Crimes, Judgements, Providences and Calamities', all of which it reported in gory detail. Mary Weller's bedtime stories in Chatham and his own frightening experiences had given him a taste for tales that made the flesh creep. He started to write short tales of his own and entertained the other boys with them, and sometimes his excitement escalated to the verge of hysteria, giving way to bursts of uncontrollable laughter. His sense of drama and comedy also found an outlet at Wellington House. He played in a melodrama called *The Miller and His Men*, which ended with the mill collapsing in a crackle of fireworks; he knew the play by heart, often quoted it, and when he was grown up went eagerly to a revival. A friend named Beverley, moreover, had a knack for building toy theatres of the kind James Lamert had made. Dickens wrote childish playlets for Lamert's theatre when he was eight, and he was now more ambitious. In 1825, when Fanny was given a book called *Elizabeth, or the Exiles of Siberia* as a prize at the Academy, he condensed the story for his tiny stage.

Although Dickens later criticized the teaching at Wellington House, at the time he was very glad to be going there. It was not merely a matter of schooling. Education was a mark of gentility, if not of the gentleman. At the age of twelve Dickens was painfully aware of the difference between a schoolboy and a warehouse slavey whose father was in prison, and Wellington House was just the place to recover his nerve and respectability. It was not surprising that one of his friends should remember that 'he usually held his head more erect than lads ordinarily do, and there was a general smartness about him'. He wore a pepper-and-salt suit but 'instead of the frill which most boys at his age wore then, he had a turn-down collar, so that he looked less youthful'. Smart bright clothes were one way of concealing the past. His personality, too, belied it: he was remembered as having 'more than usual flow of spirits, inducing to harmless fun, seldom if ever to mischief'.[4]

This phase of relative stability in the family's affairs was one of the few, short periods of his childhood in which Dickens felt reasonably carefree, but his father's new-found respectability was still precarious. In the spring of 1825, a year after John Dickens had become an insolvent debtor, he was retired from the navy Pay Office and in recognition of his twenty years of service he was given a generous pension of £145. 16s. 3d. a year. Now, at the age of forty-one, he had to make a new career. Though he was financially incompetent John Dickens was not indolent. One acquaintance said that he was like a cork; pressed under in one place, he cheerfully bobbed up in another. He did odds and ends of journalism, and made himself master of Gurney's difficult shorthand system. In September and October 1826, turning his knowledge of the maritime world to good account, he wrote nine articles in the *British Press* supporting the Lloyd's underwriters against some speculative rivals in the insurance business. Unfortunately the *British Press* collapsed before John Dickens received his due, and he wrote to the committee of Lloyd's asking for compensation for his 'serious pecuniary inconvenience'. He was paid ten guineas, but this small sum brought only temporary relief to his accumulating difficulties. In March 1827 the family was evicted from the house in Johnson Street for non-payment of rates. The first move was to the Polygon in near-by Somers Town, and there were then a series of hasty removals over the next few years—to George Street off the Adelphi, to Margaret Street off Cavendish Square, to North End in Hampstead, 15 Fitzroy Street, and 18 Bentinck Street in Marylebone. From time to time John Dickens lived apart from his family. It was one way of evading pressing creditors.

Both Fanny and Charles felt the continuing financial strain. John Dickens had always found it difficult to pay her fees at the Royal Academy. On 6 October 1825, less than five months after he was discharged from the Marshalsea, he sent the Academy a money order from the navy Pay Office for £32. 11s. 11d. asking that this portion of his pension should be held as an earnest of his intention to pay up arrears. 'A circumstance of great moment to me will be decided in the coming term', he wrote in a veiled reference to his expectations, 'which I confidently hope will place me in comparative affluence, and by which I shall be ready to redeem the order before the period of Christmas Day.' He failed to do so, and by the following summer there was £53. 18s. 0d. owing to the Academy, in addition to 'the bill from Christmas last'.[5] He next proposed to pay off £10 a quarter. When that promise was broken Fanny was asked to leave the Academy in June 1827. She had, however, done well enough to attract notice and in August she was taken on as an assistant teacher at seven shillings for a two-hour session three times a week. She had also begun to receive a few professional engagements; her first concert was on 29 May 1827. John Dickens was almost certainly in similar trouble over the fees for Wellington House, for Charles was taken away from school before the summer term had ended and sent to work. Once again his parents relied upon a connection to place him. Mrs. Dickens had an aunt who took in lodgers, one of whom was the junior partner in Ellis and Blackmore, a firm of solicitors in Gray's Inn. This lodger, Edward Blackmore, was prevailed upon to employ Charles as a salaried clerk, starting at 10s. a week in May 1827, with two subsequent increases to 13s. 6d. and 15s. He disliked it from the start: the slow and stuffy ways of a law office frustrated him. With his eager temperament he was on the look-out for a more lively occupation. His father's journalistic contacts had enabled him, while still at school, to place small news items at a penny a line; and he soon followed John Dickens in struggling with the 'vagaries that were played

Charles Dickens, painted by Daniel Maclise in 1839

Elizabeth Dickens and John Dickens. These lithographs of the parents of Charles Dickens were the work of Edwin Roffe

by circles' in Gurney's shorthand system.[6] He was a natural reporter, and a born mimic. George Lear, a fellow clerk, remembered how 'he could imitate, in a manner I have never heard equalled, the low population of the streets of London in all their varieties'.[7] The lower depths fascinated and frightened him. He was drawn into the street life and yet held himself aloof from it. He was an outsider who looked, and listened: dramatizing it in jaunty gossip with his fellow clerks was one way of coping with its grimmer reality.

There was much to catch the reporter's eye and ear. Though London now had a population of about two million it was still in most respects the squalid but vital town that Hogarth had drawn a century before. Its tenements had little water, poor drains and smelt, like its streets, of sweat and ordure; disease was rife. Many of its inhabitants lived by begging, scavenging, street-trading, and thieving—each Monday there were bodies dangling from the gibbet at Newgate. On the western fringe the prosperous were, at the same time, making a new London. The line of imposing buildings pushed along Pall Mall and the Mall towards the new Buckingham Palace. There were new squares off Oxford Street and Nash was planning his terraces around Regent's Park. But old London had scarcely moved out of the eighteenth century.[8] One could walk out of it to the country beyond in forty minutes and quickly get to know it, as Dickens did, from Bow to Brentford. He had started to explore what William Cobbett had called 'the Great Wen' while his parents were in prison. Now, living with them in cramped and comfortless lodgings, he still wandered until this restless habit of walking and watching became a necessity. London, as yet little affected by the Industrial Revolution, provided him with a model of society that he never forgot.

By the time he was sixteen Dickens was alternating his prowls around London with visits to the theatre. There was little good drama in London, for until the Theatres Act of 1843 only Drury Lane and the Haymarket were licensed for 'legitimate' performances; but there was much popular entertainment, from cabarets and low music-halls to melodrama, conjuring shows, and circuses like the famous Astley's in Westminster Bridge Road. And there were cheap 'private' theatres, where broken-down actors and equally dubious promoters invited stage-struck copying-clerks and youths from counting-houses to join them and play a part for a fee. Modest roles in a Shakespeare play cost from a couple of shillings to a couple of pounds, according to length. The female performers were often women with no reputation. Dickens knew such seedy houses well, training himself to theatrical manners and sometimes performing himself. He soaked up the plots of lost inheritances, villainous relatives, and family mysteries; he learned the business and the rhetoric of the stage, the knack of verbal characterizations, and the punctuating effect of comic turns.

Reporter or actor? Both careers were means of withdrawing from the world while representing it—adult versions of the choice between the *Terrific Register* and the toy theatre; and both were familiar in the Dickens family, with his father and several relations in the newspaper line and his sister on the fringes of the stage. The streets and the boards alike were a vivid apprenticeship and either might offer a quick way out of the mundane life of a junior clerk, perched on a stool in a fusty office and clubbing with his fellows for a round of saveloys and porter. Dickens stayed with Ellis and Blackmore for eighteen months, moving in November 1828 to work for Charles Molloy, another lawyer with offices in Lincoln's Inn.

One of Molloy's articled clerks was Thomas Mitton, who was the same age as Dickens. Mitton, a kind, eccentric, and reliable young man, was the son of a publican in Somers Town and Dickens had first met him when their families lived as neighbours in the Polygon. They became friends. Dickens soon fell into the habit of letting Mitton handle his business affairs, and Mitton also helped with small advances when money was tight.[9] Dickens, however, did not stay long in Lincoln's Inn. Another family connection of his mother, Thomas Charlton, who reported in the Consistory Court in Doctors' Commons, offered Dickens a share of his rented cubicle. He had now worked up his shorthand to a point where he was competent enough to become a freelance legal reporter, and he had come into a little legacy which encouraged him to take the risk. There he sat, day by day, waiting for a proctor to engage him to take down a case. He had made a move, whereby he had more independence and could exercise his reporting skill—but he was still confined within the legal world, and he did not like it.

The experience left him with an abiding distaste for the frustrations of the law and the pomposity of lawyers. He was already familiar, as a clerk, with the maze of legal offices and courts which sprawled between the Thames and Holborn. He had run errands to many of the offices with such archaic names as Alienation, Exigenters, Protonotaries, Sixpenny Receivers, Filazer, Pell, and the Clerk of the Outlawry. He was now obliged to follow the sinuous path of cases through a series of courts which were the legacy of centuries of unreformed civil and ecclesiastical law, each with a special jurisdiction and its peculiar inheritance of precedent. Doctors' Commons, near St. Paul's, was a dark quaint-looking apartment used among others by the Admiralty Court, the Lord Chancellor's Court, the provincial court of the Archbishop of Canterbury, and the Consistory Court of the Bishop of London, in which Dickens mainly worked. It was a place, he recalled, where they granted marriage licences to love-sick couples and divorces to unfaithful ones, registered the wills of people who had any property to leave, and punished hasty gentlemen who called ladies by unpleasant names. At first he had time on his hands to read and look around him. His favourite haunt was one of the new Metropolitan Police Courts, recently established by Sir Robert Peel—with a run of thieves, wife-beaters, drunks, and murderers to observe.[10] By the time he was eighteen, early in 1830, he could qualify for a ticket to the British Museum and use some of his spare time burrowing in English literature and history.

All through the spring months of 1830 there was a sense of change in the air. George IV was so unpopular that his death on 26 June was received with relief rather than regret. William IV came to the throne when the country was ready for political reforms to match the changes that flowed from the Industrial Revolution, and the July outbreak in Paris—in which the middle classes evicted Charles X and installed the bourgeois Louis Phillipe—acted as a spur to change in England. At the general election in August 1830 the Whig opponents of the Duke of Wellington gained ground and, with a new government formed under Lord Grey which was pledged to 'peace, retrenchment and reform', the two-year struggle for the Reform Bill had begun. When the Bill was thrown out in March 1831, Parliament was dissolved and it was the single issue in the stormy election that followed, with the slogan 'The Bill, the Whole Bill, and Nothing but the Bill'. It was then rejected by the House of Lords, and there were riots and outbreaks of arson all over the country to remind the politicians of the restlessness of the masses. 'Haystacks and cornstacks burning all over the South and the middle of England!' Thomas Carlyle wrote in *Sartor Resartus* as a warning against the social chaos caused by industrialization. 'Where will it end? Revolution on the back of revolution for a century yet?' Before Christmas a new Reform Bill was introduced and under the threat that enough peers would be created to carry it, the Lords passed the Bill by a bare majority.

The contrast between these excitements and the fusty warrens of the law had an unsettling effect on Dickens. Casual work at Doctors' Commons seemed even more of a backwater when his father moved into political journalism. John Dickens had been helped to a start in newspaper work by another brother-in-law, John Henry Barrow, an accomplished scholar, a facile poet, and a competent editor. Barrow, now in his middle thirties, had begun as a legal reporter in the 'lazy old nook' of Doctors' Commons, and he had studied law to such effect that he was called to the Bar in 1828. In the same year he launched the *Mirror of Parliament* in an attempt to compete with *Hansard* as a report of the debates. In 1830, as a fraternal gesture, he found a place for John Dickens; and soon afterwards Charles began to pick up assignments from the paper.[11]

Dickens also wanted more money because he had fallen in love and had romantic aspirations towards marriage. He had become friendly with a bank clerk named Henry Kolle, and they went about town together, dining, and visiting theatres. Kolle was courting Anne Beadnell, one of the three daughters of George Beadnell, who held a responsible post in the Smith, Payne and Smith Bank at 1 and 2 Lombard Street, just by the Mansion House; and in 1829 or early 1830 Kolle introduced Dickens to the Beadnell family. In the autumn of 1831 Dickens declared that it was 'Twelve Months ago from last May' that he had lost his heart to Maria, the youngest of the three girls. She was two years older than Dickens, a pretty young woman with dark hair and bright eyes whose 'pettish manner' and playful flirtatiousness added to her attractions. The Beadnells were hospitable, and though Dickens was still a youth with no particular prospects they often received him at Lombard Street where they lived on the bank premises. He had charm. He was clever. And he was not bashful about his talents as a singer and recitationist, which came in useful on the social evenings when Maria played the harp and her sister sang. At one of the Beadnell parties he delivered a ballad called 'The Bill of Fare'—a set of rhyming couplets in the manner of Goldsmith's *Retaliation* which jestingly characterized the members of the Beadnell family and their friends.[12]

He enjoyed such evenings, and he took the lead in similar entertainments at home. For one occasion he wrote a musical travesty called *O'Thello*. His turn for histrionics, indeed, was becoming more than a parlour hobby. He took it seriously, and modelled himself on Charles Mathews, a popular comedian noted for his imitations; and he was toying with the idea that one way to make money, or as he put it, 'a great splash', was to join the profession himself. It was not then a respectable occupation, likely to appeal to the conventional Beadnells; nor was it easy to make a marriageable income from it. But Dickens had an itch of unrealized talent, a special kind of brashness which made him hungry for success. Writing to George Bartley, who was manager for Mathews at the Lyceum, to ask for an audition, he claimed that he had 'a strong perception of character and oddity, and a natural power of reproducing' what he perceived.[13] When the audition was offered he had a bad cold and excused himself until the following season.

By then Dickens had settled for a different career. He had already done some freelance reporting of Parliament for John Barrow when the *True Sun* was launched as a new evening paper, at the beginning of March 1832, and he was recruited as one of its parliamentary staff in time to cover the crucial stages of the Reform Bill debate. The paper never flourished: by July 1832 he was forced to write to Henry Kolle that 'The Sun is so obscured that I intend living under the planet no longer'.[14] He then moved to the *Mirror of Parliament*, to work with his father and under his uncle, who employed him as a sub-editor as well as a reporter; he often walked out to Norwood, where John Barrow had set up an irregular establishment after leaving his wife, and he owed much at this critical point in his career to his uncle's professional coaching and encouragement.

He quickly became an admirable shorthand-writer; he was accurate as well as quick at transcription, and he needed both qualities for his exacting work under uncomfortable conditions. 'I have worn my knees by writing on them in the old back row of the old gallery of the old House of Commons,' he remembered, 'and I have worn my feet by standing to write in a preposterous pen in the old House of Lords where we used to be huddled together like so many sheep.'[15] The work paid well, but he found the pressure and the late hours irksome—for a time he took lodgings off the Strand to be nearer Parliament. Though politically sympathetic to the parliamentary spokesmen for the Reform Bill he found them tedious and unconvincing. He disparaged Lord Grey for 'his style of speaking, his fishy coldness, his uncongenial and unsympathetic politeness, and his insufferable though most gentlemanly artificiality'.[16] The House of Commons, he wrote scathingly, was a political pantomime 'particularly strong in clowns. ... Night after night they twist and tumble about, till two, three and four o'clock in the morning; playing the strangest antics, and giving each other the funniest slaps on the face that can possibly be imagined, without evincing the smallest tokens of fatigue. The strangest noises, the confusion, the shouting and roaring, amid which all this is done, would put to shame the most turbulent sixpenny gallery that ever yelled through a boxing night.'[17]

In his disillusionment with politicians he saw them as prisoners of their own rhetoric, just as the lawyers he had watched in Doctors' Commons had appeared to lose the substance of their cases in a fog of precedent. There was something personal in this distaste. His rambling and pompous father, a demagogue of the domestic hearth, was a caricature of a politician who found excuses for doing nothing today while promising a better and brighter tomorrow. At an impressionable age Dickens had felt the effects of his futile good intentions as well as the impersonal cruelty of the law. Rage against his parents for abandoning him to the blacking factory had fused with contempt for a system that broke up his family and carried his father off to the Marshalsea. It was a double exclusion of the kind that makes a man into a rebel or a criminal. It certainly made Dickens into an outsider, restlessly impatient with government and all its works.

While Dickens sought to prove himself by earning a man's income—and in some weeks he earned a good deal more than the five pounds a week which was the regular rate for an experienced journalist—he discovered that his efforts were not enough to persuade the Beadnell family that he was an eligible suitor. Mrs. Beadnell in particular disapproved of him, and the Beadnells had probably learned that John Dickens was a bankrupt. They certainly tried to keep Dickens at a distance from Maria. In the summer of 1832 the young couple were reduced to using Kolle as a courier for their letters. And then Mr. Beadnell sent Maria back to Madame Martinez, who ran a finishing school in the rue de Berry in Paris which Maria had already attended: 'my whole being', Dickens recalled, 'was blighted by the Angel of my soul' being suddenly dispatched to France.[18]

Her absence was painful, but Dickens was more upset on her return when she proved teasingly fickle. She went to his twenty-first birthday party in February 1833, but she was not part of the scheme that spring to produce J. H. Payne's operetta *Clari, The Maid of Milan*, and two farces in which Charles, his sisters, and some friends took leading parts. It was an elaborate enterprise which he tackled with characteristic verve. 'The family are busy,' he told Kolle, who was helping with the scenery; 'the *Corps dramatique* are all anxiety . . . the machinery is finished, the Curtain hemmed, the Orchestra complete—and the manager *grimy*.'[19] Maria went to the performance on 27 April but was cruelly condescending. 'Our meetings of late have been little more than so many displays of heartless indifference on the one hand while on the other they have never failed to prove a fertile source of wretchedness,' he had written to her on 18 March.[20] He complained about her 'encouragement one day and a total change of conduct the next' and in tones of injured innocence contrasted his 'utter desolation' and honourable conduct to her teasing inconstancy. He returned her gifts and letters.

After the performance he still wrote to her as though the breach were not final and argument might change her mind. On 14 May he blamed their misunderstanding on Maria's jealous friend, Mary Anne Leigh, and railed at the 'duplicity' of the two girls in gossiping about him. He picked on trifles that had humiliated him and tried to extract a confession of guilt and apology from Maria. 'If you had ever felt for me one hundredth part of my feeling for you there would have been little cause of regret, little coldness, little unkindness between us,' he insisted, declaring that 'I have borne more from you than I do believe any creature breathing ever bore from a woman before'.[21] The following day he sent a sarcastic reproof to Mary Anne Leigh and a cold covering letter to Maria with a copy. Knowing that he was to meet Maria publicly at Kolle's wedding to her sister on 22 May, when he was to be best man, he then sent a last appeal through Kolle, at whose bachelor dinner on 17 May he had drowned his sorrows. No 'feeling of pride', he wrote to Maria on 19 May, would prevent him saying 'that there is nothing I have more at heart, nothing I more sincerely and earnestly desire than to be reconciled. . . . I have never loved and I never can love any human creature breathing but yourself . . . and the Love I now tender you is as pure, and as lasting as at any period of our former correspondence.'[22] The plea was in vain. Their separation, the Beadnells' discouragement, Maria's flightiness, and his imperious manner of courting had broken the idyll of happiness. Dickens had counted heavily upon it, and invested much emotion in it. His pride was hurt; characteristically he felt that he was the aggrieved party; he became chary of expressing his affections; and the idealized lost love stayed with him as a bitter memory.

The Dickens household was a school for resilience in adversity. Where John Dickens waited for a turn of fortune, his son was convinced that little comes to him who waits. Even if he was not to be married his 'natural wish . . . to enlarge the field of my exertions' was as strong as ever, and he had 'many strong inducements' for wishing to avoid idleness when the courts were in recess that summer, as he told the civil servant Richard Earle in a letter asking for commissions as a shorthand-writer.[23] He was still dependent on freelance assignments, which sometimes paid well, and he seems to have done some police-court work for both the *Morning Chronicle* and *The Times*. In July he had some hopes of a full-time post on the *Morning Chronicle*, and his uncle John Barrow tried to help by inviting him to dinner with J. P. Collier, a member of the *Chronicle* staff who was later unmasked as a notable literary forger. It was a jolly evening, at which Dickens did his party-turns, including a comic song called 'Sweet Betsey Ogle' which he had written himself. Yet nothing came of the introduction.

Nevertheless the prospects for a young journalist with talent and connections were reasonably good. There was a growing middle-class readership, and a shift in taste which raised a crop of new magazines to cater to it. The first and most influential was the *Edinburgh Review*, started early in the century by the witty and radical clergyman Sydney Smith and edited by his friend Francis Jeffrey. *Fraser's Magazine* was launched in 1830 as a rival to *Blackwood's* and other promoters copied its formula; some older publications, such as the *New Monthly Magazine*, which Edward Bulwer began to edit in 1831, were revamped to suit the new public. A number of them sympathized with the wave of political reform; others were little more than miscellanies of sketches and stories. Editors were hungry for copy, especially if they could get it cheap or free. *The Thief*, for example, was launched by Henry Mayhew in 1832 and true to its name, it printed nothing but articles taken from other magazines. Then in 1832, came *Chambers's Edinburgh Journal*, a pioneer of the more popular periodical. Another journal, the *Monthly Magazine*, avowedly radical, had started in 1796 and in 1833 it was struggling along on a circulation of about 600, selling at 2s. 6d. It was this magazine that Dickens tried that autumn of 1833 with a short sketch called 'A Dinner at Poplar Walk': it was a comic piece in which he gibed at the corn-chandling father of Mary Anne Leigh. He said that he dispatched it 'with fear and trembling', and he waited until the December issue was due, buying a copy from William Hall's bookshop.[24] Two days later, when he wrote cheerfully to Kolle to say his article was printed, he added a postscript: 'I am so dreadfully nervous, that my hand shakes to such an extent as to prevent my writing a word legibly.'[25] A week later he found the sketch pirated in *The Thief* (still so called though it had lately changed its name to the *London Weekly Magazine*). The editor of the *Monthly*, moreover, wrote asking for more sketches; though, as Dickens told Kolle, the paper was 'rather backward in coming forward with the needful',[26] he produced eight fresh pieces in the next few months, all of them worked up from his own sharp observation of the lower-middle-class milieu in which he worked and spent his leisure. At first they were unsigned, but in August 1834, he added the pseudonym 'Boz' to the second half of 'The Boarding House'. It was a shortening of his pet name for his small brother Augustus (born in 1827), whom he had called Moses 'in honour of the *Vicar of Wakefield*; which being facetiously pronounced through the nose, became Boses, and being shortened, became Boz'.[27]

In the same month Dickens was given an even better chance, and once again it was through a lucky connection. His father had been taken on to the *Morning Herald*, where he had become friendly with a journalist named Thomas Beard, a diffident man, quiet to the point of taciturnity. Beard soon became a close friend of the family and was a guest at the twenty-first birth-day party for Dickens and the amateur production of *Clari*. When he moved to the *Morning Chronicle* in 1834—it had changed hands and under its new owners was to become the leading anti-Tory paper, second only to *The Times* in circulation—he spoke for Dickens, five years his junior, who joined him as a political reporter.[28]

Free at last of the cramped gallery in the House of Commons, Dickens began to discover what England was like beyond the narrow alleys of London. In September 1834 he and Beard sailed to Scotland to report the cere-mony at which Edinburgh made Earl Grey a freeman of the city; in November he was off to Birmingham, 'the town of dirt, ironworks, radicals, and hardware',[29] to report a Liberal meeting in the town hall. That winter, after the coalition which had put through the Reform Act collapsed, there was a general election in which the Tories under Peel came back to form a short-lived government. Dickens was sent off to report from Essex and

Suffolk, notoriously one of the more corrupt areas. From Chelmsford he wrote to Beard in January 1835, 'I wish of all things that you were with me ... I wish to God you could have seen me tooling in and out of the banners, drums, conservative Emblems, horsemen and go-carts with which every little Green was filled.'[30] He was stimulated by new scenes and occasions which he described with irony; and, despite the discomfort, he acquired a taste for travel. 'There never was anybody connected with news-papers', he said years later, 'who had so much express and post-chaise experience as I.' He recalled charging for 'damage of a great-coat from the drippings of a blazing wax-candle, in writing through the smallest hours of the night in a swift-flying carriage and pair'.[31] His knack of scribbling in any inconvenient place, picked up in the parliamentary gallery, was a great asset to a reporter eager to make his deadline, 'galloping through a wild country, and through the dead of night, at the then surprising rate of fifteen miles an hour'.[32]

The travels were fun, but he had not forgotten London's streets as a source of copy. His editor John Black, a jovial eccentric, thought Dickens was wasted as a reporter. He gave him a chance to write occasional theatre criticisms—he covered productions at the Adelphi and the Coliseum—and he urged him to write sketches for the *Chronicle*. He was, Dickens said, 'my first hearty out-and-out appreciator'.[33] The first of these pieces appeared in September 1834, and before long other papers were quoting from them and speculating on the identity of 'Boz'. At the age of twenty-three Dickens had made a mark, and he was earning at the rate of nearly £300 a year.

Money, as always, was needed in the Dickens family. His father was once again sliding towards the debtor's prison. One evening at the end of November 1834 Dickens went home to find the family 'in great tribula-tion'.[34] John Dickens had gone out to raise money to pay the landlord, who refused to wait another day. He neither returned nor sent a message, and next morning Dickens discovered that his father was in Sloman's sponging-house on Cursitor Street, Chancery Lane, taken up on a debt to the wine-merchants Shaw and Maxwell. He scraped together enough cash to meet the immediate crisis and get his father released; he feared that he too might be taken up by a tipstaff and at one point in the next fortnight was so pressed that with embarrassment he asked Mitton to lend him four shillings. He also had to resettle his mother and the younger children, for his father had 'gone to the winds' until the creditors were appeased, rooming with a laun-dress in Hampstead. To save money the family were moved into cheaper lodgings at 21 George Street, Adelphi, where they had perched during an earlier period of difficulty.

When Dickens was at Doctors' Commons he briefly set up in rooms at

Cecil Street, the Strand: but he had not found the cheap bachelor life agreeable, and he returned to share the apartments and the enforced removals
of his parents. He now asserted his independence. In December 1834 he
moved into modest quarters in Furnival's Inn at £35 a year. His younger
brother Frederick went with him. The family's troubles had left him so short
of cash that he had to ask both Mitton and Beard for money; even so, he told
Beard, he had '*no dishes*, no curtains and no french polish'.[35] As the American
journalist Nathaniel Parker Willis found when he visited Dickens soon
after he and young Fred were installed, the apartment was 'an uncarpeted
and bleak-looking room, with a deal table, two or three chairs and a few
books, a small boy' with 'Mr. Dickens for the contents'.[36] Caught by surprise, Dickens was in a shabby coat: outdoors he had already begun to dress
smartly and new acquaintances thought him something of a dandy, given
to coloured waistcoats and an elegant cloak. For all the trouble caused by
his father's fecklessness he was in good spirits. 'We have much more cause
for cheerfulness than despondency,' he wrote to Beard in the middle of the
upheaval: 'I for one am determined to see everything in as bright a light
as possible, having thank God little at present to fear on my own score.'[37]
What he called 'those little screws of existence—pounds, shillings and pence'
had come so loose in his family's life that he was determined not to let his
own life fall apart for lack of them.

3

The Pilot Balloon

IN January 1835 Dickens was given a chance to lift himself beyond the rank of a run-of-the-mill reporter. The *Evening Chronicle*, a new thrice-weekly paper owned by the proprietors of the *Morning Chronicle*, was to begin publication at the end of the month; and George Hogarth, who was to be one of the editors, invited Dickens to contribute to it from the first issue. He eagerly accepted the invitation, suggesting a series in the same style as the miscellanies which he had written as 'Boz' for the *Chronicle* during the previous autumn, and politely asking Hogarth whether he would then have a 'claim to *some* additional remuneration'.[1] The *Chronicle* agreed and raised his pay from five to seven guineas a week.

Dickens had known Hogarth for several months, for they had both been working at the *Chronicle* since September 1834, and Dickens had also been socially introduced to the Hogarths by a colleague in the parliamentary press gallery who lived next door to them in York Place, a terrace of modest houses on the south side of the Fulham Road. Hogarth was an agreeable, easy-going man in his early fifties. He had begun life as a lawyer in Edinburgh, where he had been professionally involved in the ruinous partnership between the printer James Ballantyne (to whom he was related by marriage) and Sir Walter Scott. In 1830 Hogarth himself had run into money troubles and given up the law for journalism. He edited the *Western Luminary* in Exeter; then he went to edit the *Halifax Guardian* in Yorkshire; and when the *Morning Chronicle* was reorganized he moved south to join its staff. He was a good musician. He played the 'cello, wrote books on music, and composed a number of songs, and late in life he became secretary of the London Philharmonic Society. His wife Georgina, whose father had published the songs of Robert Burns and other Scottish poets, was also musical, and the couple tried to keep up cultivated appearances on a modest income in a house that was always full of children. The eldest was Catherine, called Kate, who was nineteen when Dickens began to visit York Place, and there were at least three other daughters—Mary, fifteen, Georgina, eight, and the baby Helen, just two years old. Dickens fascinated them all with his vitality, his charm, his knack for mimicry, recitations, and practical joking. One evening he entered by a window dressed as a sailor, and danced a hornpipe before the startled family; and he was never at a loss when it came to parlour tricks and entertainments. In the early weeks of 1835, however, the motive for his interest in the Hogarth family became clear: he was attached to Kate. On 11 February, after she went with her parents to his birthday party, she wrote to her cousin Mary Scott Hogarth, telling her that 'it was a delightful party, I enjoyed it very much. Mr. Dickens improves very much on acquaintance, he is very gentlemanly and pleasant.'[2] He was soon accepted as her suitor.

Kate was rather plump, but she was pretty and high-coloured, with a small mouth and a slightly *retroussé* nose. An acquaintance who knew her as a young woman said that she had a genial expression with a sleepy look in her slow-moving eyes, and she was kindly and generally placid by nature.[3] Like Maria Beadnell she was spoilt and self-indulgent; unlike Maria, who had tormented the lovesick Dickens by her vivacious teasing, Kate was shy, and she became peevishly withdrawn when her feelings were hurt. She seemed an unlikely partner for such an ebullient personality as Dickens, yet he found her childishness appealing and her passivity—the necessary antithesis to his dominating vigour—put him at an emotional advantage from the start. There was no sign of the romantic infatuation which had marked his adolescent attachment to Maria. Even before he was formally engaged to Kate in May Dickens had shown that he was less an impetuous lover than a prospective husband who intended that marriage should be on his terms. He regarded their courtship, indeed, as a kind of apprenticeship in which Kate had to earn the right to be idealized. She was not to manipulate him with feminine wiles or pettish moods, he anxiously insisted in his letters; and when he reproved her she was expected to admit her faults and seek to mend her ways.

The prospect of a close relationship made Dickens so uneasy that from the start he hedged it with constraints. Three weeks after their engagement he sent Kate a minatory letter complaining of her attitude. 'The sudden and uncalled for coldness with which you treated me just before I left last night, both surprised and deeply hurt me,' he wrote, 'surprised, because I could not have believed that such sullen and inflexible obstinacy could exist in the breast of any girl in whose heart love had found a place; and hurt me, because I feel for you more than I have ever professed, and feel a slight from you more than I care to tell.... If a *hasty* temper produces this strange behaviour, acknowledge it when I give you the opportunity.... If three weeks or three months of my society has wearied you, do not trifle with me, using me like any other toy as suits your humour for the moment; but make the acknowledgement to me frankly at once—I shall not forget you lightly, but you will need no second warning.'[4] After a little conversation he unbent, giving his 'ever dearest Kate' his 'repeated and solemn assurances of . . . a love which nothing can lessen—an affection which no alteration of time or circumstance can ever abate'.[5]

In June Dickens took lodgings for the summer months at 11 Selwood Place, near the Hogarth house, so that he and Kate could meet more conveniently. His work as a parliamentary reporter, with its irregular hours, made it difficult for him to see as much of Kate as he wished and his new lodging made it easier for him to call on her at odd moments. 'Will you indulge me by making breakfast for me this Morning? It will give me pleasure; I hope will give you no trouble,'[6] he wrote after returning home at dawn one Saturday morning. It was, however, never a carefree courtship. They occasionally found time to go to the opera or the theatre, but throughout his engagement Dickens was hard pressed. Apart from his regular duties at the House of Commons, and the street sketches which demanded much prowling round the odder corners of London to find copy, he was also sent off by his paper to cover political events in the provinces. Travel was often miserably uncomfortable and he had to work hard on arrival. In May he went down to Exeter to report meetings addressed by Lord John Russell, who was standing for South Devon. In the pouring rain he scribbled shorthand while 'two good-natured colleagues . . . held a pocket handkerchief over my notebook, after the manner of a state canopy in an ecclesiastical procession'.[7] Then there was the rush to get his report back to London by horse express, beating his competitor on *The Times*: 'we had a *much much* longer account than any other paper', he wrote exultantly to Thomas Beard, 'and the whole affair is considered one of "complete and signal success" and has been noticed as a feat by the *Spectator* and another Sunday Paper'.[8]

Dickens liked the sense of movement and the stimulus of haste. By the time he was twenty-three he was already showing signs of the anxious urgency which made him such a stimulating but exhausting person; in his work, and in his pleasures and his domestic affairs, there was a drive to achievement—and a need to cap each fresh achievement with another. Difficulties seemed to bring out the best of his talents, and he often created the very pressures of which he complained and with which he afflicted his colleagues and his family. In the summer of 1835 this ambitious trait had driven Dickens to the verge of exhaustion, and his letters to Kate revealed the strains under which he laboured. 'I am very tired my dearest',[9] he wrote one July morning at 4 a.m., and a few days later he told her that 'excessive fatigue prevents my saying more than a very few words'.[10] 'I am too tired and dispirited', he confessed in an August letter, 'to write more than a very brief note.'[11] In addition to his journalism he was also correcting the manuscript of *Two Journeys through Italy and Switzerland*, written by Kate's uncle William Thomson. This book was being published by a young man named John Macrone, who had come to London in 1833, briefly taken over the *Monthly Magazine* which had printed the first Dickens sketch, and then set up his own book business in September 1834.

At the beginning of October, when Dickens was back at his lodgings in Furnival's Inn, both Kate and her mother were stricken with scarlet fever. He called frequently, and he sent Kate affectionate letters. 'My dearest Kate,' he wrote one morning. 'It is very hard to preach consolation when one stands in no small need of it one's self but let me entreat you ... to keep up your spirits.'[12] His own health was beginning to suffer from persistent overwork and insufficient sleep. He was afflicted by bad headaches, attacks of dizziness, and pains in his side which recalled his childhood 'spasms', and he sought relief by having himself bled.

On 20 August 1835 Dickens published the last of his 'Boz' sketches for the *Evening Chronicle*, though over the signature of 'Tibbs' he wrote another dozen 'Scenes and Characters' for *Bell's Life in London* before the end of the year. He had begun by using acquaintances as models; then, gaining confidence, he extended his range over the whole shabby-genteel world in which he had grown up. It was a world that stretched from Richmond to the fair at Greenwich and the steamers running down the Thames to Margate, from the slums of Seven Dials to the vulgar gaiety of Vauxhall Gardens and Astley's Circus. It was, Dickens said, his 'magic lantern', and he marshalled its jostling images into word-pictures as vividly exuberant as a Rowlandson cartoon. It was this quality of exuberance that distinguished his work from the start. There was little fresh in his material—Pierce Egan, Leigh Hunt, and other essayists had found colourful copy in the streets; his characters were conventional and commonplace; his jokes were aimed at such familiar butts as henpecked husbands, fat men, spinsters, and tiresome mothers-in-law; and even his more elaborate sketches—'The Tuggs at Ramsgate', for instance, and 'A Passage in the Life of Mr. Watkins Tottle'—used situations from stock comedy. What made them different was his energy, which bubbled through every personation, and the dry wit which ridiculed the pretentions of the age.

By the summer of 1835 his wanderings through the margins of London had brought Dickens to the border between fact and fancy. He was still unsure how to cross it, uncertain whether the sketches led towards literature or towards the theatrical career which so appealed to him. But the sketches were winning him a reputation in print, and as they were talked about 'Boz' began to strike up useful friendships with some of the younger critics and authors—with W. Harrison Ainsworth, for instance, who met him in the

Morning Chronicle office one day early in the autumn of 1835. Ainsworth was barely thirty and had just done well with *Rookwood*, a historical romance featuring the highwayman Dick Turpin which had been published by John Macrone. He had left his native Manchester in 1824 to study law at the Temple, given up his legal ambitions to set up as a bookseller in Old Bond Street, and then begun his career as a novelist. He was known as the 'Adonis of Booksellers' for his elegant physique, and the fashionable flamboyance of his clothes—he liked to wear a coat with a gothic-arched collar, a black satin stock, a bright waistcoat, tightly strapped trousers, and adorned himself with rings and gold chains.[13] He had quickly made a mark in London's literary Bohemia, which was an open society in the mid-1830s, welcoming to talented and engaging newcomers. Loosely composed of a series of overlapping cliques of editors, artists, novelists, and some actors, its members met informally in the salons of such hostesses as Lady Holland and Lady Blessington, and clustered round a forceful publisher or a successful magazine; they were, in fact, informal clubs.

One such group was the 'Fraserians', associated with the influential *Fraser's Magazine*. Ainsworth was one of the set which turned the back parlour of *Fraser's* office in Regent Street into a dining club where such contributors as Thomas Carlyle, Robert Southey, and the artist Daniel Maclise met with the caustic editor, William Maginn, to talk 'picturesquely on everything that occurred', especially politics and literature. 'We condemned most liberally all persons who differed with us in either,' Maclise wrote, 'and with equal liberty extolled our friends ... and no small quantity of the time, not occupied in the natural business of filling and emptying glasses, was past in the divine pastime of song.'[14]

Private dinners in this set were conducted in much the same style, as Dickens discovered when he was invited to Kensal Lodge, in the Harrow Road, where Ainsworth had set up with his cousin's widow after separating from his wife in 1835. Ainsworth had taken a liking to him, for he had a way of making good company and could appreciate another man's talent. Dickens, for his part, was glad to be taken up by Ainsworth and his cronies, assuming the manners of a dashing young man about town, dining out and going to the theatre—usually at the reduced price for half-time entry, just before the main item in a long and varied bill.

Another regular guest at Kensal Lodge was John Macrone, Ainsworth's publisher, for whom Dickens had already worked when he prepared William Thomson's travel book for the printer. After one dinner in October 1835 Dickens and Macrone walked back into town together and on the way Macrone offered him another commission. He invited Dickens to collect and publish two volumes of his articles under some such title as *Bubbles from the Bwain of Boz.* Dickens thought about the idea, became excited by it, and then wrote to Macrone to suggest the more modest title of *Sketches by Boz*. He said that he had already begun to collect the printed pieces, and he assured Macrone that 'if the whole collection fell something short of the two volumes ... I will be ready with two or three new sketches to make weight'.[15] One of these, he proposed, should be about Newgate, notorious as one of the worst jails in the country and a veritable nursery of criminals. At the beginning of November he took Macrone along to Newgate and to the House of Correction at Coldbath Fields. Dickens was more fascinated than shocked. He had, he told Kate, 'lots of anecdotes to tell you of both places when I see you tomorrow—some of them rather amusing: at least to me, for I was intensely interested in everything I saw'.[16] In his sketch, 'A Visit to Newgate', he described the chilling sight of the condemned ward, filled with convicts of all ages, the condemned pew in the chapel, and the condemned cells where the prisoners about to die spent their final hours.

Dickens had scarcely time to digest this macabre experience than he was assigned to report a presentation banquet for Lord John Russell at Bristol: 'I never regretted anything in my life so much as I do the unpleasant circumstance ... of my having to start for Bristol this morning' he told Macrone early in November. The distraction was thoroughly 'aggrawatin'.[17] Macrone intended that the sketches should be illustrated by George Cruikshank, the most popular illustrator in London, and Dickens was introduced to him when he returned from Bristol. Cruikshank was a small man with a hooked nose, but for all that he was rather a buck, with a fast reputation as one of the gayest blades in London. He was a convivial and hearty drinker, though he later became a fierce advocate of temperance, and Maclise appropriately sketched him sitting on a barrel. His good-humoured and bibulous friendliness made him such excellent company that he was generally known as 'good old George'. Very early in his career he had become one of the finest masters of etching, similar to the great Gillray in style; by 1820, when Cruikshank was only twenty-eight, he was already so popular—especially for his political satires on the Prince Regent—that when his latest prints went on sale crowds gathered round the windows where they were displayed. He and Dickens were ideal collaborators. They were both enthusiasts for the theatre—a passion which made them see the characters of London's streets as comics and grotesques—and Cruikshank's appealing knack for pathos in his drawings was exactly the match for the sentimental streak in Dickens.

The plan was to publish the sketches by Christmas 1835, and Dickens was just as eager as Macrone to meet this deadline. But there were too many

explanation, an apology or an assurance intended to mollify her. 'I am most happy to hear that you have not been "coss",' he told her on 18 December, 'though I perceive you have not yet subdued one part of your disposition— your distrustful feelings and want of confidence. However this may be, you may rest satisfied that I love you dearly—far too well to feel hurt by what in anyone else would have annoyed me greatly.'[25] On occasion she was more amiable, regretting her complaints. He replied to one such letter that if she would show the same 'affection and kindness' when she felt disposed to be ill-tempered he would have 'no one solitary fault to find'. 'Your asking me to love you "once more", he insisted, 'is quite unnecessary—*I have never ceased to love you for one moment, since I knew you; nor shall I.*'[26] But that love was continually undermined by mutual anxiety and self-indulgence, clashing in a conflict which was never resolved.

For all the friction Dickens was eager to set a date for the wedding, although the Hogarths made it clear that he must first find a suitable home. This was not easy, for he was far from flush. On a visit to Cruikshank at the end of November some houses in the new streets around Pentonville caught his eye. He thought them extremely dear at £55 a year plus taxes: 'the houses themselves are very pretty,' he told Kate, 'but this is too much'.[27] In December he settled for a larger set of rooms in Furnival's Inn.

He was really too busy for house-hunting. The manuscript of the *Sketches* had no sooner gone off to Macrone than he turned to a new project. His delight in theatricals still made the stage as rewarding an outlet as print, and he had been writing theatrical reviews in the *Morning Chronicle* for some time. The composer John Hullah, who had been a pupil at the Royal Academy with Fanny Dickens and married her friend Caroline Foster in 1838, had suggested that Dickens might write the libretto for a Venetian operetta to be called 'The Gondolier'. He turned his hand to it at once, but he could do nothing with the idea, coming back with a simple rural story and persuading Hullah of 'the increased ease and effect with which we could both work on an English Drama where the characters would act and talk like people we see and hear of every day'.[28] Although he sensibly chose to write about the world he knew best and was well aware of what would appeal to the audience he wished to reach, the idea came more easily than the execution. The artificiality of the current stage conventions forced the comic naturalism of his style into an insipid piece of theatricalism quite unlike the vitality of his newspaper articles. But he was as enthusiastic about it as he was about the rest of his work.

Dickens called the operetta *The Village Coquettes*, and he was busy with it through most of January 1836, again with apologetic letters to Kate. 'Is it my fault that I cannot get out tonight?' he wrote to her on 21 January.

difficulties and delays. Dickens had to go down to Hatfield at the beginning of December to report a fire at Hatfield House, telling Kate that he had left town at 'only three hours notice and being previously out of bed until three o'Clock'.[18] On his return he arranged another visit to Coldbath Fields but then decided not to include that prison in his collection of sketches. 'You cannot throw the interest over a years imprisonment, however severe, that you can cast around the punishment of death,' he told Macrone. 'The Tread-Mill will not take the hold on men's feelings that the Gallows does.'[19] In mid-December he set off for Kettering to cover a brutally rowdy election which did nothing to change his already jaundiced view of politics. The place was dull, the weather cold; and when Kate complained that his letter was stiff and formal he explained that the noise and confusion on the first day of polling was so great 'that my head is actually splitting'.[20]

Insatiably eager for work, he took on so much that he could not fulfil all his commitments. On 9 December, for instance, he chided Macrone because he had received 'neither specimen page nor proofs',[21] but when the proofs did arrive he was away at Kettering and George Hogarth had to read them for him. On 22 December he thought Cruikshank had not completed his promised illustrations and he wrote tartly to Macrone, 'Will you have the kindness to write to Cruikshank on this subject and apply the spur?'[22]

Kate was neither sophisticated nor ambitious, and she was jealous of the creative talent which kept Dickens at work and away from her for so much of the time. Sometimes he had to cancel an arrangement to spend an evening with her and at the last minute send his brother Fred in his place. It was, he explained to her in mid-November, 'necessity and necessity alone' that forced him to forgo the pleasure of her company: 'my pursuits and labours such as they are are not more selfish than my pleasures ... your future advancement and happiness is the mainspring of them all'.[23] Though she was pettily possessive and resentful of what she felt was his neglect he repeatedly begged her not to blame him. 'You may be disappointed—I would rather you would—at not seeing me; but you cannot feel vexed at my doing my best with the stake I have to play for—you and a home for both of us,' he wrote on 25 November, explaining his style of work. 'You know I have frequently told you that my composition is peculiar; I can never write with effect—especially in the serious way—until I have got my steam up, or in other words until I have become so excited with my subject that I cannot leave off; and hoping to arrive at this state tonight, I have, after a great deal of combating my wish to see you, arrived at the determination I have just announced—I hope to do a good deal.'[24]

Almost every letter Dickens sent Kate during the winter months was an

'I must work at the Opera from the moment I have finished my dinner, until one or two o'Clock in the morning, or I shall be fearfully behind hand.'[29] But the pace at which he worked was affecting his health. He told Kate the next day: 'I am so ill this morning that I am unable to work, or do anything. I wrote till 3 o'Clock this morning (I had not done with the paper till 8) and passed the whole night ... in a state of exquisite torture from the spasm in my side far exceeding anything I ever felt ... I have not had so severe an attack since I was a child.'[30] He was, however, rewarded for his labours. George Hogarth commended the operetta to John Braham, England's most popular tenor, who had built the St. James's Theatre the year before. He told him that it was by the same author who had written so eulogistically in that day's *Chronicle* about Braham's current performance in *The Waterman*, and soon afterwards introduced Dickens himself. Dickens then eagerly pressed the connection. He was able to compensate Kate for his neglect by telling her on 18 January: 'We will have the Office Ticket and go to Braham's next week as soon as the Dramatic portion of the Opera is done, as I should very much like you to see a place and a set of people in which we are likely to be so much interested.'[31] At the beginning of February he told Cruikshank triumphantly that Braham had accepted the opera 'with the most flattering encomiums; and an assurance that it *must* succeed'.[32]

This cheerful news came when the *Sketches* were at last due to appear, but copies were still slow to come to hand and Dickens fretted all through the week. Although they were advertised as being ready on 4 February 1836 the first copies were not available until four days later. Even then Dickens was chivvying Macrone about review copies. 'We are losing time fearfully in getting the Notices,' he wrote on 9 February.[33] The first review, easily arranged beforehand, was by George Hogarth in the *Morning Chronicle*, on 11 February. It was, Dickens thought, a 'beautiful notice'.[34] Hogarth declared the *Sketches* were 'evidently the work of a person of various and extraordinary intellectual gifts ... a close and acute observer of character and manners, with a strong sense of the ridiculous. ... He has the power, too, of producing tears as well as laughter.'[35] Hogarth did his best for his future son-in-law, and although other reviews came in more slowly—Macrone was again reproved for his dilatory dispatch of review copies on 14 February— they were full of praise. 'Boz is a kind of Boswell to society—and of the middle ranks especially,' declared the *Court Journal*, and it called the two volumes 'the merriest of the season'.[36] Several reviewers commented on the connection between the tales and contemporary theatrical comedy. 'Have you read Boz?' became a familiar question. By the end of the month what Dickens had called in the preface his 'pilot balloon' was lifting to warm applause. He had already put his fee for future sketches in· the *Monthly Magazine* at eight guineas per sheet.

It was not merely the praise for the *Sketches* which made Dickens set a stiff price for his work. He had also been encouraged by a visit he received on 10 February from William Hall. It was from Hall, then running a bookshop in the Strand, that he had bought a copy of the *Monthly Magazine* containing his first article in December 1833, and he considered Hall's re-appearance a happy omen. Hall had been in partnership with Edward Chapman since 1830 as booksellers and periodical publishers and had only recently launched into book publishing.[37] They were full of new schemes— one was a periodical called the *Library of Fiction*, to be published monthly from April 1836—and were on the look-out for fresh talent. Both Chapman and Hall had been attracted by Dickens's stories in the *Monthly Magazine* and they naturally had him in mind as a contributor to their *Library of Fiction*. Dickens provided them with 'The Tuggs of Ramsgate' for their first number. But the purpose of this surprise visit from Hall was to make Dickens a different proposition. 'They ... have made me an offer of £*14 a month* to write and edit a new publication they contemplate, entirely by myself, to be published monthly and each number to contain four wood cuts,' he wrote to Kate that same day. 'The work will be no joke, but the emolument is too tempting to resist.'[38]

At the time it seemed little more than a humdrum assignment. The shil-ling number had no status, being regarded as mere literary ephemera. 'My friends told me it was a low, cheap form of publication by which I should ruin all my rising hopes,' Dickens recalled.[39] In any case the expected circu-lation was only about 400 copies. The new commission seemed to be little more than hack work which could be squeezed in somehow between report-ing and writing new sketches for a second series, and even making a start on a large historical tale, somewhat like Ainsworth's *Rookwood*, which he had had in mind since 1834. No one realized at the time, least of all Dickens, that he was involved in something much more important—a new kind of fiction and a new kind of publishing.[40]

In any event, the text was not considered the main attraction. Dickens was to provide 12,000 words for each number to accompany four illustrations by the misanthropic Robert Seymour, already well known for his sardonic sketches. The social pretensions of tradesmen rising in the world were a butt of current satire and Seymour, who had recently made a hit with a similar set of *Humorous Sketches*, had offered Chapman and Hall a series of drawings depicting the adventures of a 'Nimrod Club' of Cockney sportsmen. What the publishers expected from Dickens was a set of Boz-like anecdotes to exemplify Seymour's comic pictures. In their formal letter to Dickens on 12 February, they said that they planned a book 'illustrative of manners and life in the Country'. Dickens proposed to interpret that commission as broadly as possible. He disliked the notion of sporting sketches, telling Hall that he had no personal taste for hunting, shooting, or fishing, and that he thought that line of humour had been overdone; and he was unwilling to confine his imagination to the frame of Seymour's illustrations. This response left Chapman and Hall in the dark. But they were pressed for time, for they planned to launch the series in March and needed copy a month in advance. As Dickens had made such an impression of competence, they were willing to accept his conditions and make the disgruntled Seymour comply with them. Within a few days of Hall's visit Dickens had thought of his main character and was hard at work. 'Pickwick is at length begun in all his might and glory,' he wrote exultantly to Chapman and Hall on 18 February. 'The first chapter will be ready tomorrow.'[41]

Dickens had dashed at *The Posthumous Papers of the Pickwick Club*, though he found time in the course of the week to move to 15 Furnival's Inn, where in preparation for his marriage in April he had taken three third-floor rooms and a basement kitchen at a rent of £50 a year. As he hurried off the first part to clinch his bargain with his publishers he had no idea where the serial would lead. At the outset, indeed, he did not think of the book as a novel. He had written his *Sketches* on anything that caught his eye or excited his fancy; they were, so to speak, a walker's view of London. He now planned to complement it with a stage-coach traveller's view of the country, exposing Mr. Pickwick—that amiable, somewhat bewildered but resilient innocent abroad—to 'a constant succession of characters and incidents'.[42] That was certainly what Chapman and Hall had in mind when they placed their advertisement in the *Athenaeum* on 26 March. 'High-roads and by-roads, towns and villages, public conveyances and their passengers, first-rate inns and road-side public houses, races, fairs, regattas, elections, meetings, market days' would all, they promised in a catalogue of subjects which was a rural counterpart to the urban *Sketches*, be 'visited and beheld, by the ardent Pickwick and his enthusiastic followers'.

The episodic form in which Dickens cast his picaresque tale permitted such a jumble of impressions, and it also allowed him to treat the serial as a vast scrapbook into which he could insert memories of his own journeys about England, odd stories, references to current events, and fragments of public gossip. Such material could easily be padded or cut to fit a chapter as required. What was designed as a convenience, however, came to serve a larger purpose. This apparent chaos, Dickens said on more than one occasion, was 'real life', at least as he—and Mr. Pickwick—experienced it; and both author and character moved through it in the same restless, seemingly aimless and wondering fashion. *Pickwick Papers* was becoming another report on what Dickens saw in his 'magic lantern', and its superficial brightness was soon offset by darker images. As early as the third chapter Dickens used 'The Stroller's Tale' to describe the miserable death of an actor broken down by drink; three chapters later 'The Convict's Return' told of a dissolute man who drives his son to crime; and Dickens used other morbid interpolations, such as the account of a madman who marries and murders an heiress, to punctuate the junketings of Mr. Pickwick and his friends. It was really quite a short step from comedy to social comment.

Once Dickens had thought of Mr. Pickwick, so like a prosperous John Dickens, he immediately sent him down into familiar territory in Kent. 'I have at this moment, got Pickwick, and his friends, on the Rochester Coach', he told Kate on 21 February, 'and they are going on swimmingly, in company with a very different character from any I have yet described, who I flatter myself will make a decided hit. I want to get them from the Ball, to their Inn, before I go to bed—and I think that will take me until one or two o'Clock, *at the earliest*. The Publishers will be here in the Morning, so you will readily suppose I have no alternative but to stick at my Desk.'[43] Kate was still inclined to be 'coss' at the demands of the writing life, but Dickens remained adamant with her: 'I like the *matter* of what I have done today, very much, but the *quantity* is not sufficient to justify my coming out tonight. If the representations I have so often made to you, about my working as a duty, and not as a pleasure, be not sufficient to keep you in the good humour, which you, of all people in the world should preserve—why then, my dear, you must be out of temper, and there is no help for it.'[44] Despite his strictures, however, he too regretted their separation. 'I should like to have you by me—*so* much,' he wrote on 21 February, and a few days later 'God bless you dearest Pig. How long it is, since I saw you! Never mind—it will soon be over.'[45]

It was not only *Pickwick* which kept them apart. Dickens was attending the long debate in the House on the Irish Corporations Bill which went on into the small hours: he was writing more sketches as well as supervising the furnishing arrangements for Furnival's Inn. 'I have bought today, a pair of quart Decanters, and a pair of pints, a crystal Jug and three brown dittos with plated tops, for beer and hot water, a pair of Lustres, and two *magnificent* china Jars—all, I flatter myself, slight bargains,' he told Kate on 10 March.[46] But for the most part he remained 'chained to my table' even when his seemingly boundless energy began to wilt. 'I am tired and worn out today, mind and body,' he wrote to Kate one Sunday evening in March. 'I did not get to bed till 3 o'Clock this morning; and consequently could not begin to write until nearly one.'[47]

Dickens and Kate were married at St. Luke's Church in Chelsea on Saturday 2 April 1836. 'It was altogether a very quiet piece of business,' said Thomas Beard,[48] who was best man and, with Macrone, the only guest outside the family. Henry Burnett, a singer who had trained with Fanny Dickens at the Royal Academy and was to marry her the following year, recalled that Kate, dressed simply and neatly, looked bright and pleasant. After a wedding breakfast at the Hogarth house the young couple went down to a cottage at Chalk, a village near Gravesend in the Kent countryside Dickens had known and loved in his childhood. That one week's honeymoon was one of the rare periods in which they were alone together: thereafter there were always friends, relatives, and children in their home.

Young Frederick Dickens had lived with Charles in Furnival's Inn and he remained with them after Dickens and Kate were married. In May they had another visitor, for Kate's young sister Mary Hogarth came to stay for a 'delightfully happy month' in their new rooms. 'They have furnished them most tastefully and elegantly,' Mary wrote to a cousin, 'the drawing-room with Rose-wood the dining-room with Mahogany furniture.' Kate, she declared, 'makes a most capital housekeeper and is as happy as the day is long. I think they are more devoted than ever since their Marriage if that be possible.' Her brother-in-law, she reported, 'is such a nice creature and so clever he is courted and made up to by all the literary Gentlemen'.[49] Dickens was already fond of Mary, who had often been Kate's companion and chaperon during the year-long engagement, and her visit increased his attachment. At fifteen Mary was pretty, warm-hearted, spontaneous, and young enough to express innocent love and admiration, and Dickens—who could be equally affectionate and uninhibited in a fraternal relationship—found her so perfect that she became his ideal image of young womanhood. She was asked back to Furnival's Inn, and asked again, and before long she had almost become part of the household.

'PICKWICK TRIUMPHANT' Dickens wrote to Macrone after he returned to London.[50] The first number had received little notice and the sales had run to a modest 400 copies, but Dickens was full of enthusiasm. He wrote to Seymour on 14 April: 'I am happy to be able to congratulate you, the publishers, and myself, on the success of the undertaking, which appears to have been most complete.' They had not yet met and Dickens now asked Seymour 'to take a glass of grog' on Sunday evening to discuss an alteration to the illustration for 'The Stroller's Tale'. 'I think it extremely good, but still, it is not quite my idea ... I shall feel personally obliged, if you will make another drawing.'[51] Seymour was sensitive and overworked; an illegitimate child from a poor background, he had done well but he was aware of his social deficiencies and had suffered a mental breakdown five years before. The brief call at Furnival's Inn on Sunday 17 April did nothing to cheer him, and two days later, after an unsatisfactory attempt to change one of the drawings, he went into his garden and shot himself.

Chapman and Hall had lost the originator of their part-work before it was truly launched: Seymour had done only seven etchings and before the June issue they had to find Dickens a new collaborator. They thought of employing Cruikshank, but he had too much work in hand: they turned instead to another well-known illustrator, R. W. Buss, who accepted the offer although he had little experience in etching. With the death of Seymour, Dickens's share of the collaboration increased: the plates were reduced from four to two in each issue and the text was increased to thirty-two pages, eight more than before, bringing his payment to £18 for each number. Dickens took this opportunity to suggest making it up to £20. 'If the Work should be very *successful*,' he hopefully hinted to Chapman and Hall on 27 April, 'I apprehend you would have no objection to go a little further.'[52]

Neither marriage nor the extra work on *Pickwick* distracted Dickens from his other commitments. He had to make changes in *The Village Coquettes*, for plans for its production were now in hand and John Hullah was anxious to present it that autumn. At the end of July Dickens and Kate gave their first party, inviting a few friends to hear Dickens read over the libretto and to try out the music. They were, he told John Braham, 'enthusiastic in praise of the whole affair, from beginning to end',[53] and at the end of the first act Macrone wanted to buy the publishing rights. Although his interest was clearly on his own creative work, Dickens was still employed by the *Chronicle*. At the end of May he went off to Ipswich to report a series of political meetings and he continued to cover court cases for the paper.

Despite all these claims on his time and energies Dickens eagerly took on new tasks. In May he accepted an offer of £200 from Macrone for a three-volume novel he called *Gabriel Vardon, the Locksmith of London*, to be ready by November that year and he was also planning a second series of *Sketches*. In June he wrote a pamphlet—'Sunday Under Three Heads'—under the pseudonym of Timothy Sparks, attacking the killjoy provisions of a Sabbath Observance Bill. He took every opportunity to advance his reputation and income, for what he wanted most in the summer of 1836 was an assurance of enough income to become a full-time writer and give up the wearing attendance at the House of Commons. At the end of July he told Macrone that 'I devoutly hope 'ere next Session I may make some arrangements which will render its sittings a matter of indifference to me—as the story books say "for ever after".'[54]

Such a hope seemed reasonable after the success of *Sketches by Boz* and the contract for *Pickwick Papers*. From being a piece of hack work, *Pickwick* had become the test of his ability to hold and improve his new-found reputation. It had taken time for Chapman and Hall's new format to catch on; Seymour's death worried them, for it came at the moment when they had to decide whether to put more capital into the scheme and gamble for higher sales; and Buss proved an unsatisfactory successor to Seymour. It was clear by the third issue of *Pickwick* that his work would not suit and Dickens cast about for a replacement. One possibility was William Makepeace Thackeray, a journalist with a talent for sketching who was looking for whatever opening came his way. Thackeray was six months older than Dickens, a striking young man, over six feet tall with a flat, round face and a broken nose. He was very much a man-about-town with what he himself called 'a lazy epicurean nature'. After giving up his studies at Cambridge he drifted into a dissipated life around the edges of the London literary scene. Cruikshank gave him help and advice, but Thackeray was uncertain of himself and had no fixed purpose. When his inheritance was lost in 1834 he went off to Paris and worked as a correspondent for a newspaper owned by his stepfather. In August 1836 he married; back in London he tried to pick up commissions as an illustrator, and approached both Ainsworth and Dickens.[55] But Ainsworth chose Cruikshank for his new novel, *Crichton*, and Dickens decided to settle for Hablôt Knight Browne, a young engraver employed by Chapman and Hall as an illustrator of the *Library of Fiction*; it was he who was doing the illustrations for the pamphlet 'Sunday Under Three Heads' which Chapman and Hall were publishing.

Browne was a shy young man of twenty-one who had an appealing turn of humour. Dickens was already showing his preference for pliable colleagues and Browne was a quick, reliable worker who was willing to take his brief from the author. Dickens, moreover, had such a keen visual perception of what he wanted from his illustrator that he could conceive the drawing as a dramatic whole and describe the effect he wanted as graphically as in stage directions. They quickly learnt to work together and Browne, as an engraver, had technical skills that Buss had lacked. He made himself so much part of the scheme that, after signing his first illustrations as 'Nemo', he rechristened himself 'Phiz' to make a more euphonious pair with 'Boz'— and it was over this signature that he made his subsequent career.

The outlook for *Pickwick* had now greatly improved and Dickens developed it throughout the summer, quickly acquiring the knack of transposing his journalistic experience into fiction. On 22 June he attended the sensational divorce case in which the Hon. George Norton accused Lord Melbourne of adultery with his wife, and he drew on this for the comic trial of Bardell *v*. Pickwick which appeared in the fifth number in July. Everyone caught the topical reference and it appealed at once to the public's curiosity and good humour. He had also just introduced in the fourth number the engaging Cockney servant, Sam Weller, whom everyone seemed to like. Develop Sam Weller to the utmost, the journalist William Jerdan advised. Dickens was beginning to see the great advantage of serial writing which could easily be attuned to the public response. Advertisements were scarcely needed, for reviewers in the newspapers commented on each fresh adventure of Mr. Pickwick and his companions, and each instalment became a popular talking point. With the fifth number in July it was clear that Dickens had an audience. By August he was already being described as 'Boz the Magnificent'.[56]

Pickwick Papers began a revolution in publishing. Chapman and Hall had tried out a new formula without much idea of where it might lead, and stumbled upon a means of reaching a huge reading public with an author exactly to their liking. The middle-class reading public of the 1830s was small: possibly no more than fifty thousand would pay sevenpence for a newspaper, half a crown for a magazine and £1. 11s. 6d. for the three-volume novels then beginning their seventy-five year domination of the respectable fiction market. There was, however, another and larger public served by a host of cheapjack publishers who lived from hand to mouth and produced sensational tales and romances, books sold door-to-door or in markets, cheap periodicals and serials scribbled by Grub Street hacks at ten shillings a number. The reputation of such popular fiction was as low as its quality, and this was the reason why friends like Ainsworth were so disapproving when Dickens told them he was to write a book in parts. Few people had yet realized that there was a growing readership which lay between the extremes. It was, in a sense, the class from which Dickens himself had come and about which he wrote in his sketches—reasonably literate, with a taste for comedy and pathos, formed by the conventions of the popular theatre and raised on the visual metaphors of the cartoonists. The sales of *Pickwick* in 1836 tapped this great reservoir of new readers.

There was a very small profit on each shilling number, and success therefore depended on a big sale. This, in turn, meant that Chapman and Hall needed much capital to launch the venture and that they had to find a way of distributing a large number of copies each month. It was relatively easy to arrange this in London, where there was a well-developed network of booksellers, but it was much more difficult to open the provincial market, where the first issue sold poorly. Chapman and Hall, unsure what to do, followed the advice of another bookseller and shipped off large bundles of copies on sale or return. The risk was worth while. Within a matter of months, as sales rose to tens of thousands, the *Pickwick* scheme became a major part of their business and set a precedent that other publishers soon followed.[57]

Chapman and Hall had to face the economic implications of the triumph of *Pickwick*. For Dickens the matter was more complicated, for he did not immediately appreciate that his success had overtaken his more conventional literary plans. His first reaction was merely to make the most of his suddenly enhanced bargaining power. Early in August he was negotiating an advance of £100 from Thomas Tegg, a cheap publisher, on a children's Christmas book, *Solomon Bell, the Raree Showman*, but by the end of the month he had a much more attractive offer. This came from Richard Bentley, an opportunist with an eye for new talent who was already launched on a spectacular career in publishing. He was a short, pink-faced man, with large side-whiskers; he was a fluent talker, and so effusive that people considered him affected. He had been introduced to Dickens in March by George Hogarth, and he very soon realized that the young man's stock was rising fast. Bentley made an offer for two novels of £400 each. It was only a week since Dickens had made his agreement with Tegg, but as *Pickwick* boomed he began to raise his sights and he replied to Bentley's offer on 17 August. 'I have spoken to some confidential friends, on the subject of our yesterday's Interview,' he wrote. 'They concur in thinking, and strongly advise me, that for the *copyright* of a Novel in Three Volumes, I should have Five Hundred Pounds.' He told Bentley that he had no wish to drive a hard bargain, but considering 'the time, the labour, the casting about, in every direction, for materials: the anxiety I should feel to make it a work on which I might build my fame and the great probability of its having a very large sale (we are justified in forming our judgment upon the rapid sale of *everything* I have yet touched) I think you will not object to raising your terms thus far'. He added a final flourish: 'Recollect that you are dealing with an Author not quite unknown, but who, so far as he has gone, has been most successful.'[58] After Bentley had reluctantly given way, conceding an additional £100 after the sale had reached 1,450 copies, Dickens signed the contract on 22 August. He had now taken on more than he could possibly deliver and he had to shed some of his commitments. The agreement he had made with Macrone as recently as May now seemed trivial, and he secured an ambiguous verbal agreement to cancel the *Gabriel Vardon* contract on the strength of his undertaking to produce the second series of Boz sketches. He never wrote the comic book commissioned by Tegg.

At the end of August he and Kate went down to a cottage at Petersham, near Richmond, for a short holiday. Even there Dickens did not really relax; he had projects in hand before he turned to the first of the novels promised to Bentley. He had bought a horse for himself—'so I can be in town in no time', he told Thomas Fraser of the *Morning Chronicle*.[59] *The Village Coquettes* was soon to go into rehearsal and he was still working with Hullah on the finishing touches. Copying the style he had given Jingle in *Pickwick Papers*, he invited Hullah down to Petersham: 'Beautiful place—meadow for exercise—horse for your riding—boat for your rowing—room for your studying—anything you like.'[60] Dickens was as excited by *The Village Coquettes* as he had been by *Pickwick*, and he was getting the same kind of encouragement from his friends. When John Pritt Harley, the leading comedian at the St. James's Theatre, added his voice to the chorus of praise, Dickens was delighted and flattered; he wrote in a special part for Harley and dedicated this 'dramatic bantling' to him.[61] As soon as the text was complete he offered it to Bentley, suggesting that it might sell rewardingly as 'Boz's first play',[62] and Bentley published it in December 1836. Dickens was rather nervous about this simple tale of rural courtship, with characteristic misunderstandings and reconciliations, and in a preface he reminded his readers that it was 'a mere vehicle for the music' and was not to be judged 'by those strict rules of criticism which would be justly applicable to a five-act tragedy'. Nevertheless the enthusiasm of stage people such as Braham and Harley made him believe that he should continue to try his hand as a light dramatist. Down at Petersham he converted the sketch called 'The Great Winglebury Duel' into *The Strange Gentleman*. Braham paid him £30 for the copyright of this elopement farce in two acts, which also had a part written with Harley in mind. A production was planned for the end of September.

Dickens still thought of *Pickwick* as a form of journalism, very different from the three-volume novel which was the mark of the serious writer of fiction. Yet as *Pickwick* progressed from month to month its unique quality became clear to its author, his publishers, the critics, and the public. He had fused the regularity of journalism with the emotional engagement of fiction. His readers were amused, but they were also involved, because Mr. Pickwick and his friends were figures in a folk-tale made up of the sights and sounds of daily experience. Set in the England of the 1820s it appealed to everyone's youthful memories, which nostalgia made jollier and more carefree. Readers were flattered, too, for Dickens wrote from their standpoint and with their values—a marked change from the heroics of historical novels, the sugary sentiment of romances, and the stock comics carried over into fiction from the stage. Publication in parts positively strengthened the illusion that Mr. Pickwick might be met in the Strand or that the Fat Boy lurked around the next corner. By the winter sales had gone up to 14,000. Enthusiasts, the publisher Henry Vizetelly recalled, 'flattened their noses against the booksellers' windows, eager to secure a good look at the etchings, and peruse every line of the letter-press that might be exposed to view, frequently reading it aloud to admiring bystanders'.[63] In November the young artist W. P. Frith wrote to his mother: 'I just glanced at the eighth number of the "Pickwick Club" as I passed a shop window the other day, and I laughed fit to split my sides.'[64] By the end of its run the print order turned up towards its sensational peak of 40,000 a number, and the reprintings needed to meet the demand for back issues so wore the copper plates of the etchings that Phiz had to make new ones, taking the chance to improve them to reflect the spirit he himself had now caught from the exuberant prose of Dickens.

The public response by the end of 1836 revealed how successfully Dickens was insinuating his characters into popular consciousness: the *Metropolitan Magazine*, in fact, kept a running account of his success. In May 1836 he was 'a rising writer'; by August he was 'making for himself a standard fame', and in September Boz was marching on 'triumphantly'. In the early months of 1837 the journal was even more enthusiastic. The world, it declared in January, 'never saw drollery and wit offered to them before in a form so singular' and in April it reported that the numbers 'grow more uproarious in their fun'.[65] Pickwick chintzes began to appear in drapers' shops and Weller corduroys in the advertisements of breeches-makers. Imitators were at work too. Pickwick had not finished its run before the flood of copies and continuations began to come on the market, and it was to become the most plagiarized book of its time. By November 1836 a farce called *The Peregrinations of Pickwick* was playing at the Adelphi, for in days of loose copyright no permission was needed from an author for such dramatizations. But it was all a reflection of the way in which the public had fallen in love with the Pickwickians—and with their creator, Boz. For Dickens, too, it was a kind of love affair; he was building a curiously close relationship with the public which was to affect everything he was to write thereafter. 'It is needless for me to say how cordially I am interested in its success, or how proud I am of it,' he wrote happily to Chapman and Hall on 1 November. 'If I were to live a hundred years, and write three novels in each, I should never be so proud of any of them, as I am of Pickwick, feeling as I do, that it has made its own way, and hoping, as I must own I do hope, that long after my hand is withered as the pens it held, Pickwick will be found on many a dusty shelf with many a better work.'[66]

4

Asking for More

ON 2 November 1836 Dickens received an offer which quite changed his plans. Bentley asked him to edit a new magazine which he proposed to call *The Wits Miscellany*, offering Dickens £20 a month as editor and an additional twenty guineas for sixteen pages of his own writing. This was a better rate than Chapman and Hall paid for the *Pickwick* parts and much more than his salary as a reporter for the *Chronicle*. Dickens agreed to the proposal at once, subject to a guarantee of a year's engagement, and by 4 November he had signed an agreement with Bentley.[1]

This attractive offer meant that Dickens could at last throw up his connection with the *Chronicle*. Throughout the autumn he had found it difficult to meet all the demands on him, and when J. P. Collier pressed him for a sketch he replied that he was 'over head and ears in work'.[2] Though he had started a new series of sketches for the *Morning Chronicle*, by 1 November he had to tell its owner, John Easthope, why Number Five of his new series of sketches had not been done: 'I have been labouring under one of those severe colds which bring with them a state of semi-stupefaction, and have been wholly unable to set pen to paper for some days past.'[3] He was also explaining delays in *Pickwick* to Chapman and Hall: 'spirits are not to be forced up to *Pickwick* point, every day'.[4] It was in part his theatrical ambition that continued to distract him. *The Strange Gentleman* was staged on 29 September. Eager to have everything just right, Dickens told Bentley that he was superintending its production 'morning, noon and night'[5] and confidently expected that it would go well. When Cruikshank saw it, however, he thought it was badly acted: 'very like my own impression',[6] Dickens declared. In the event the farce went quite well, running for over fifty performances. Dickens then transferred his optimism and his energies to *The Village Coquettes*, telling Cruikshank on 18 November that 'I hope you and Mrs Cruikshank will accompany us, on the first night of the opera— next Monday fortnight. I am sanguine about that.'[7]

Dickens wasted no time in handing in his resignation to the *Chronicle*, which he did on 5 November, the day after he signed the agreement with Bentley. He wrote a gracious letter to Easthope explaining that he had been offered 'less burdensome and more profitable employment'[8] and promising to deliver the sketches for which he had already been paid. Easthope, in his chagrin at losing this talented reporter, sent an angry answer, accusing Dickens of leaving without a personal farewell and without supplying the promised sketches. Dickens was provoked by the charge of sharp practice, and went on from a reasonable explanation of his actions to defend his whole career at the *Chronicle*. He had done his 'difficult and harassing duty' as a reporter, 'on many occasions at a sacrifice of health, rest and personal comfort, I have again and again ... done what was always before considered impossible'. He told Easthope of his resentment that 'my reward at last would be a regret that I had ever enjoyed a few weeks' rest, and a fear lest at the close of two years, I should have received six pound six, too much'. If Easthope wished to inspire his staff to extra exertion and attract competent successors, he concluded, 'this is not the way to do it'.[9]

Dickens was also at odds with Macrone, and if any charge of sharp practice was to be made against him a stronger case could be made about his dealings with the young publisher. The two families had been on close social terms all summer: Dickens was hoping that Macrone might give Fred a start in his office, and he had negotiated for a second series of 'Boz' sketches to be published in December. Although he casually assumed that Macrone had released him from the *Gabriel Vardon* contract in August, when he signed with Bentley for two unspecified novels on more favourable terms, it was not until November that Macrone realized what had happened. When Ainsworth heard of the situation he told Macrone on 12 November that the loss of Dickens was 'a serious misfortune ... I look upon him as unquestionably a writer of the first order'. It was small consolation to Macrone to be told that even Bentley's generous terms were not 'at all adequate' to the worth of Dickens, and Ainsworth added that he could not 'blame Mr. Bentley or any other spirited Publisher for patronising rising talent'. All he could suggest to Macrone, when he wrote again on 14 November, was that he put the matter in the hands of a lawyer.[10]

Macrone had the legal advantage and was determined to keep Dickens to his promise. As a provocative reminder he continued to advertise *Gabriel Vardon* as a forthcoming novel under his imprint, even trying to place advertisements in the *Pickwick* parts and in the first number of Bentley's *Miscellany*. For several weeks the haggling went on. On 5 January 1837 a compromise was reached: if Macrone would return the agreement for *Gabriel Vardon*, Dickens agreed to let him have the copyrights for both of the series of *Sketches* for £100 instead of the £250 which he had originally wanted. In his hurry to settle everything and exploit his advantageous agreement with Bentley, Dickens had little option but to accept this arrangement or to pay damages to Macrone. It was a stiff price to pay to clear the field for the Bentley contract. Outright copyrights were valuable properties, for a publisher could go on making money from new and cheap editions without any additional payment to the author. That was the point which Dickens sought to make two years later when he estimated that the *Sketches* had by then earned £400 for himself and £4,000 for Macrone.

Dickens had rushed at Bentley without realizing that the publisher made a better first impression than a lasting one. Bentley had a gift for picking literary winners, and backed his hunches with generous offers—though this streak of commercial brashness which attracted ambitious authors usually became a liability once they were established. At first, though, Dickens and Bentley were on excellent terms. Bentley put on dinners in his offices at New Burlington Street to introduce possible contributors to the *Miscellany*—now renamed *Bentley's Miscellany*—and proposed Dickens for membership of the newly formed Garrick Club. Dickens in turn presented Bentley with tickets for the first performance of *The Village Coquettes* at the St. James's Theatre on 6 December, the night on which *The Strange Gentleman* reached its fiftieth performance. 'I am so worried with it just now', he told Bentley the day before the first night, 'that I have hardly time to write this hasty note.'[11] He was busy at the theatre attending to last-minute details with Harley and taking care that the main critics had copies of the libretto.

G. A. Sala, then a boy of ten, was backstage on the first night. He recalled the 'very young gentleman with long brown hair falling in silky masses over his temples', fashionably dressed, and with a face 'full of power and strong will, and with a touching expression of sweetness and kindliness' who fussed anxiously in the wings.[12] At the final curtain Dickens appeared on the stage after persistent calls for 'Boz'. The critics disliked the innovation of the librettist taking a curtain call: the *Morning Herald* was 'utterly amazed', the *Literary Gazette* considered it 'ridiculous nonsense', and the *News* thought him 'extremely ill-advised' to come forward. It seemed like an attempt to bolster a feeble text with the reputation of Boz. The papers liked Hullah's music and the staging of the operetta but attacked the libretto. Dickens wrote to Hullah on 11 December telling him that the reviews 'blow their little trumpets against unhappy me'.[13] The *Weekly Despatch* declared that 'he will most probably blast his reputation as a periodical writer by attempting to become a dramatist'.[14] He was, nevertheless, still bent on making his mark in the theatre, and though *The Village Coquettes* ran for only sixteen nights, he was not discouraged.

'Have you seen the *Examiner?*' Dickens wrote in his letter to Hullah. 'It is *rather* depreciatory of the Opera, but like all their inveterate critiques against Braham, so well done that I cannot help laughing at it, for the life

Georgina Hogarth, painted by Frank Stone

Catherine Dickens, painted by Daniel Maclise about 1846

The four elder children of Charles and Catherine Dickens,
drawn by Daniel Maclise

and soul of me.' The critic for the *Examiner* was John Forster, a friend of Ainsworth's; and in his review he had gone out of his way to express his 'great respect' for 'Boz'. When he and Dickens met during that winter they took an immediate liking to each other. Although his background was more stable and prosperous, Forster's career had followed a parallel course to that of Dickens. He too was born in 1812, the son of a butcher in Northumberland, and he had been educated with the help of his uncle at the Grammar School in Newcastle and University College, London. In 1828 he entered the Inner Temple as a law student, but this 'raw oddly-dressed, energetic, impetuous youth from the provinces',[15] as he was then described, found the legal world as distasteful as Dickens was finding it at Ellis and Blackmore. He was more interested in the theatre and literature, writing a play and planning a biography of Cromwell. He soon made literary friends, such as Leigh Hunt, Charles Lamb, Robert Browning, and Walter Savage Landor. By 1832 he had become the dramatic critic of the *True Sun* when Dickens was working there; in the following year he went on to the *Examiner*, where he took over the literary page, and by 1835 had become its sub-editor. By the time Dickens met him he was already established on the London literary scene with comfortable bachelor rooms at 58 Lincoln's Inn Fields. He was a stocky man, with a combative manner; he was abrasive, jealous, opinionated, and unable to bear contradiction. Robert Browning said he laughed like a rhinoceros, Carlyle called him a most noisy man, and Thackeray once remarked that a dinner at which Forster did not say a single rude thing during the whole evening was an event. Yet his qualities more than compensated for his failings. He was a man of taste, integrity, and energetic loyalty who devoted himself to promoting the interests of literature in general and of his friends in particular. Even while he was making his own career he tried to find a publisher for Browning's *Sordello*, got up a subscription edition of the impoverished Hunt's poems, and sought out authors to write suitable tragedies for the notable actor William Macready. Never an easy companion, he won respect for his judgement and helpfulness. He was immensely supporting, offering reassurance and practical advice based on his legal training. At a time when there were no literary agents Forster played a unique role, part business adviser, part personal confidant, part critic, still finding time for his own work as editor and biographer. It was not surprising that he soon earned himself the nickname of 'The Beadle of the Universe', and some saw him as another Samuel Johnson.[16] Dickens warmly responded to Forster's overtures, expressing 'his desire to cultivate and avail himself of a friendship which has been so pleasantly thrown in his way',[17] for Forster was just the man that Dickens needed to complement his own anxious impulsiveness.

At the beginning, however, Dickens had his attention fixed on domestic affairs. Kate was expecting their first child and he resolved to spend more time with her—a resolve that weakened when he was caught up in a round of seasonal parties. From one of these, just before Christmas, he told Thomas Beard, 'he arrived home at one o'Clock this morning dead drunk, and was put to bed by my loving missis'.[18] On 6 January 1837 Kate gave birth to a son after what had been to Dickens 'a day and night of watching and anxiety':[19] they called him Charles Culliford Boz after her uncle.

Although Dickens had told Easthope when he gave up the *Chronicle* in November 1836 that his new work would be 'less burdensome', in the first months of 1837 he was as hard pressed as ever. He was still writing *Pickwick*, as it had been agreed from the beginning that there should be twenty numbers; there was the new miscellany to put together; and each month he had to write sixteen pages of original material as well. It was understandable that he should tell Cruikshank in February, 'I really am so driven for time that I know not where to turn.'[20]

The *Miscellany* was the first chance for Dickens to try his hand as editor, and he went at the task with his characteristic enthusiasm. When the first number appeared in January it sold well, and the magazine soon had more than six thousand subscribers. It was an eclectic publication carrying comic tales, ghost stories, biographical notes, and verses, and to fill its pages with such diverse material Dickens had to seek out an equally diverse set of contributors. This was no chore for a man with such an appetite for new acquaintances, and many of those who were attracted to the magazine were already well known in the literary and artistic world: the contributors included such men as William Jerdan, who was editor of the *Literary Gazette*; Gilbert à Beckett, a playwright and barrister who wrote for *Fraser's* and other journals; and Francis Mahony, an Irish priest who had become a professional writer under the pseudonym of 'Father Prout'. It was Mahony who brought in Daniel Maclise, who had already made a mark as a portrait painter and illustrator and a regular member of the group round *Fraser's* for which he had been doing portrait sketches since the magazine began. This handsome young man was six years older than Dickens; despite his humble origins he had studied art at the academy in Cork—where he had been born—and then at the Royal Academy schools. His work was brilliant from the first, and by 1829 he was already exhibiting at the Royal Academy. Maclise was a convivial bachelor. In 1836 he succeeded Benjamin Disraeli as the lover of Lady Sykes, and in the following year was the centre of a public scandal when her husband surprised the lovers. He had an engaging but erratic disposition, exaggerating his poor health with hypochondria, and he sometimes found company distressing. But when he was in good spirits he was most likeable, and he and Dickens soon became close friends.

Dickens was busy with the second issue when he wrote to Bentley in the middle of January: 'I am very happy to say that I think the next No. will be an exceedingly good one. I have bestowed great pains and time upon it, and shall consider the arrangement well. Moreover, I think I have hit on a capital notion for myself, and one which will bring Cruikshank out.'[21] This 'capital notion' was *Oliver Twist* and the first instalment appeared in the February issue of the *Miscellany*. The original intent of the story was in part to ridicule the Poor Law Amendment Act which had been passed in 1834 when Dickens was still a parliamentary reporter. He was a Radical in politics, like so many of the young journalists and writers with whom he spent his time, and he had been employed by papers which championed the cause of reform. Yet he was something more. He was sympathetic to such a preacher as Carlyle, who attacked contemporary reformers for worshipping the Body Politic rather than the Soul Politic—for an obsession with 'external combinations and arrangements' which heartlessly put institutions before people. This was why Dickens reacted so strongly against the new Poor Law which had been introduced in an effort to make the treatment of paupers more efficient and economical.

The ramshackle methods of relief, dating from the days of Queen Elizabeth, had broken down. Under the old system relief was distributed locally by each parish. The burden of the cost fell on the ratepayers who supplemented starvation wages by doles, proportionate to the rise in the price of bread, which was unduly high because of the prohibition on imported corn. The result was that wages were depressed, the poor rates were excessive and the working people were pauperized. The reformers, eager for administrative tidiness, and guided by utilitarian economics, had attempted to replace this easy-going system by a uniform plan under national control. This well-intentioned idea had led to unforeseen misery. To save the ratepayers and to prevent the degradation of the labourer, outdoor relief was cut back and the paupers were driven into the workhouses, soon to become known as 'Bastilles', where families were broken up and virtually imprisoned under near-penal conditions. To ensure that no one shirked at public expense conditions in the workhouse were set below the wages of the poorest labourer. This idea of deterrence corrupted the entire system; fear of pampering the able-bodied degenerated under the petty tyranny of self-important and parsimonious parish officials into near starvation for the sick, the aged, and the children. Logic had triumphed over humanity.[22]

Dickens felt bitter about the change and the opening chapters of *Oliver Twist* were shot through with sarcastic derision: 'since the new system of feeding has come in', he wrote savagely, 'the coffins are something narrower and more shallow than they used to be'. The topical impact of the story intensified as a severe winter, a trade depression, and food shortages drove more and more people into the harsh grip of the unpopular Poor Law.

'I have thrown my whole heart and soul into *Oliver Twist*,' Dickens feelingly told Bentley. He had had an idea of a workhouse story for some time and as he worked out the fable of an innocent but rejected child struggling for survival—'the best subject I ever thought of'—he touched buried feelings, so powerfully upsetting that they obliged him to put his writing aside for a few days. He reported to Bentley that he was suffering 'a violent attack of God knows what, in the head', and feeling so sick and depressed that he had dosed himself with 'about as much medicine as would be given to an ordinary-sized horse'.[23] His own childhood miseries had in reality been short-lived and far less frightening than those to which he subjected Oliver, but they were still so vivid that he could scarcely bear to remember them consciously let alone speak of them directly; and the nightmarish experiences of the wretched Oliver were the first translation of those remembrances into the healing release of fiction. Oliver was the first Dickens hero to express his creator's own flight from the terrors of despair. He is always running away, threatened from birth by the twin fears of suffocation and isolation— of dying unloved, or of being an outcast without identity if he lives. He is a wanderer in the mazes of London; he is imprisoned, contaminated by low company in the rat-ridden warehouses along the river, afflicted by puzzling changes of circumstance; he is a boy in desperate need of parents, wronged and misunderstood. And then, at the end of the story, he comes into his rights and is educated, entering such a fantasy of bliss that he might as well be a cherub.

There was nothing new in the idea of a lost child who eventually comes into his true inheritance. 'The Parish Boy's Progress', as Dickens summarized it in his sub-title, was typical of the cartoon series made famous by Hogarth and other eighteenth-century satirists, and it was a staple plot in romantic tales and stage melodrama. Nor was the description of London's criminal milieu a surprise: 'Newgate novels' had been popular since the time of Henry Fielding. All the same, *Oliver Twist* was a startling and risky break from the predominantly humorous works which had so quickly made Dickens a reputation. It was startling because its tone was ambivalent. It was ostensibly a moral homily on the triumph of good over evil, and Dickens gave it the emotional energy of his own escape into respectability. It also evoked a nether world with fascinated vigour. Though Dickens saw Fagin as a devil, his gang of boys as attendant demons, Nancy as a fallen angel, and Sikes as a monster, he nevertheless felt drawn to these outcasts. It was an ambiguity which he never resolved, but it was masked by his prurient stance as a reformer, attacking 'the haunts of hunger and disease ... the foul and frowsy dens' which were so dangerously close to the middle-class parlours in which his books were read. 'I had', he said, 'no faith in the delicacy which could not bear to look upon them.' Therein lay the risk. Such social criticism could well antagonize subscribers who did not care for this 'low debasing view of mankind'—as Lord Melbourne put it in an irritated phrase. 'I don't *like* those things,' Melbourne added: 'I wish to avoid them: I don't like them *in reality* and therefore I don't wish them represented.'[24]

It proved to be a risk worth taking. Dickens had a gift for involving his readers in the emotions of a story, whether they were humour, pathos, or tragedy, and it had worked marvellously with *Pickwick*. In *Oliver Twist* he proved that he could repeat the success with a very different kind of tale. It was not simply a matter of brilliant narration and descriptive power, of varying the balance between comedy and excitement, and of working up to an appropriate point of suspense at the end of each part in order to bring the purchaser back a month later. Dickens had already grasped those essentials in *Pickwick*. His genius lay in his capacity to reach out to his readers, like a great actor holding his audience across the footlights as much by the projection of his own personality as by his impersonation of the characters he plays. When Dickens read an instalment of *Pickwick* or *Oliver Twist* to Kate he was satisfying a performer's need for a positive response; a direct confirmation of the dramatic effect of what had to go out as the written word.

In the first weeks of the year, however, Kate was not able to offer much encouragement; the new baby was an anxiety and Kate was slow to recover, Dickens telling Bentley a fortnight after the birth that she was still 'in a very low and alarming state'.[25] Her sister Mary, staying with them over the confinement, gave a more intimate account in a letter to their cousin Mary Scott Hogarth on 26 January 1837. 'Kate has not gone on so well as her first week made us hope she would,' Mary reported; 'it was discovered she was not able to nurse her Baby so she was obliged with great reluctance ... to give him up to a stranger. Poor Kate! It has been a dreadful trial for her. Every time she sees her Baby she has a fit of crying and keeps constantly saying she is sure he will not care for her now she is not able to nurse him.' And she added that Dickens was 'kindness itself' to his wife, 'constantly studying her in everything'.[26] Early in February, in fact, he took Kate down to the cottage at Chalk where they had spent their honeymoon, and Mary Hogarth went as a companion to her sister during several weeks of convalescence.

'Between the anxieties of my private affairs, and the distractions of my public engagements,' Dickens wrote to J. P. Harley on 21 January 1837, 'I have not yet got over Pickwick and the Miscellany and consequently can admit no "other lodger" to my brain at this moment.'[27] All the same he was pleased that Harley was pressing him for another farce, and he deprecatingly offered him a one-acter about a bored husband and a nagging wife, called *Cross Purposes*, which he had written long before. He worked on this at Chalk to turn it into a comic burletta entitled *Is She His Wife?* which was performed in March at the St. James's with Harley in the leading role. Coming up to London for business appointments, Dickens took the opportunity to look about for a new home. The rooms in Furnival's Inn were not suitable for a family and, although he was so short of ready cash that he had to ask Bentley for an advance of £100 to cover moving expenses, he felt that he could now afford something better. Before long he settled on 48 Doughty Street, a terrace house in Bloomsbury with three main floors, attics, and a large basement, for which he was asked an annual rent of £80 on a three-year lease.

With the move to Doughty Street it was possible for Dickens to entertain in some kind of style. It was a much more respectable property than anything his family had occupied; there was even a gate at the end of the road and a liveried attendant to keep unwanted callers and street-arabs away. And the kitchen quarters were ample for the servants he now had to employ. Bentley was one of the first to be invited, going to a family dinner on the last Saturday in April and joining John Dickens, George Hogarth and other relations at what he described as 'a right merry entertainment'.[28] Dickens did imitations of prominent actors, sang some songs and did his favourite party piece—a patter song called 'The Cat's Meat Man'; and there was plenty of brandy and water to keep up the high spirits. There were public dinners, too, now that Dickens was a notable man of letters. On 8 April the first birthday of *Pickwick* was celebrated by Chapman and Hall with a banquet at which they presented Dickens with a bonus cheque for £500. On 3 May he was the guest of honour at the Literary Fund dinner when it celebrated its forty-eighth anniversary. It was a grand occasion at the Freemasons' Tavern, with the Duke of Somerset in the chair, and in his first significant appearance as a public speaker Dickens replied to the toast of 'The Health of Mr. Dickens and the Rising Authors of the Age'. In little more than a year the tide of success had carried him from anonymous journalism to this triumph. The whole family was pleased and excited: 'his literary career gets more and more prosperous every day', Mary Hogarth wrote to her cousin in Scotland, 'and he is courted and flattered on every side by all the great folks of this great city'.[29]

Suddenly, three days after the Literary Fund dinner, the spell was disastrously broken. Mary Hogarth collapsed, and died a few hours later.

There was no warning of ill health. She had been among the ladies in the gallery to hear Dickens make his speech at the dinner. Then, on Saturday 6 May, she went with Kate, Dickens, and his parents in a family party to the St. James's Theatre where *Is She His Wife?* was running with *The Eagle Haunt*, in which Dickens's brother-in-law Henry Burnett was singing. They arrived home late and Mary went off to bed in 'her usual delightful spirits' only to collapse as soon as she reached her room on the third floor. A doctor who was hurriedly fetched could do nothing for this unexpected heart attack, and she died the following afternoon.

Dickens was overwhelmed by the tragedy. It was a shattering loss. 'For her who is dead I can feel no sorrow,' he wrote, 'for I know that before a single care of life had wounded her poor heart, she has passed quietly away to an immortality of happiness and joy.'[30] His pain rang through all the letters which he wrote to break the news to relatives and friends. 'Since our marriage,' he wrote, 'she has been the grace and life of our home—the admired of all for her beauty and excellence—I could have better spared a much nearer relation or an older friend, for she has been to us what we can never replace, and has left a blank which no one who ever knew her can have the faintest hope of seeing supplied.'[31] He told Edward Chapman on the eve of the funeral that 'it will be no harder time to anyone than myself',[32] and other letters were full of the same misery. 'Thank God she died in my arms,' he wrote to Thomas Beard, 'and the very last words she whispered were of me.'[33] He had idealized the young Mary to the point where her death was traumatic. 'I have lost the dearest friend I ever had,' he told one of the *Miscellany* contributors.[34] 'I solemnly believe that so perfect a creature never breathed,' he assured Beard. 'I knew her inmost heart and her real worth and value. She had not a fault.'[35] For her gravestone he composed an appropriate inscription: 'Young, beautiful and good, God in His Mercy numbered her with his angels at the early age of seventeen'; and he bought a double plot in the Kensal Green cemetery in the hope that he could one day be buried beside her.

The tragedy put the whole family into a state of shock. Mrs. Hogarth was in a coma for several days and Kate's distress brought on a miscarriage. 'Oh Mary, is it not dreadful to think that she has left us for ever,' Kate wrote to Mary Scott Hogarth; 'if ever there was an angel it was she. She was only too good for this world ... my dear Husband loved her as much as I did. ... We have often said we had too much happiness to last, for she was included in all our little schemes and pleasures.'[36]

'I have been so unnerved and hurt,' Dickens wrote to Harrison Ainsworth after the funeral, 'that I have been compelled for once to give up all idea of my monthly work, and to try a fortnight's rest and quiet.'[37] He and Kate went to recuperate at Collins's Farm, on the north slope of Hampstead Heath. But time did not help him to forget Mary. He kept the unsullied image he had of her constantly fresh and preciously vivid in his mind, enclosing it with all the symbols of sentiment. A month after Mary died he visited her grave, telling a friend that 'the grass around it was as green and the flowers as bright, as if nothing of the earth in which they grew could ever wither or fade'.[38] He treasured other reminders. 'I have never had her ring off my finger by day or night,' he wrote to Mrs. Hogarth when she sent him a lock of Mary's hair that autumn, and for months he dreamed of her.[39]

The crisis of Mary's death forced Dickens to pause for the first time since he began his fast climb to fame. He normally eased the pressure of work in his own way, by walks, convivial evenings, and outings, but even these forms of relaxation were part of a compulsively busy pattern and often put to some use by providing professional contacts or copy for his writing. Now, he was forced to stop writing. Both *Pickwick* and *Oliver Twist* would have to miss a number and the tragic reason for it was explained to the disappointed readers, serving to strengthen his personal bond with them.

Cut off from the normal hurried rhythm of London life and his writing obligations, the desperate need for consolation made his friends more welcome than ever. 'You cannot think how glad I should be to see you just now,'[40] Dickens told Ainsworth on 17 May and he wrote the same day to Beard saying, 'I hope you will join us in the old way.'[41] One visitor to Collin's Farm was John Forster, who had written to say how much he had been affected by *Oliver Twist*. His admiration for the work of Dickens was now translated into friendship. In his unhappy mood Dickens was 'more than ordinarily susceptible ... to all kindliest impressions', Forster noted: 'his heart opened itself to mine'. Forster left Hampstead 'as much his friend and as entirely in his confidence, as if I had known him for years'.[42]

A single conversation had put the relationship on a basis of trust which lasted a lifetime. For all his brusqueness Forster evoked that kind of reaction. 'I cannot explain the secret of his influence over people,' Ainsworth remarked. 'He had the knack of making people do as he liked, whether they liked it or not.'[43] And though the impetuous Dickens was not easily tamed, Forster had the skills and the personality to complement his genius. He supplied what was so notably lacking in the Dickens family—common sense, patience, and a capacity to act responsibly.

As soon as Dickens returned to London in June he was to call on precisely those qualities in his new friend, and it was not long before Forster was playing the role of business agent for him. Macrone was running into financial difficulties, partly because he had borrowed money to purchase the Boz copyrights from Dickens; and he therefore needed to exploit these valuable properties to the full. He proposed to issue the *Sketches* in a form which deliberately imitated the popular green cover of the monthly parts of *Pickwick*. Dickens was furious and determined to recover the copyrights. Chapman and Hall also wanted them; a serial version of the *Sketches* would suit them very well as a stable companion for *Pickwick*, and cement their ties to Dickens. He appealed to Forster, telling him the details of the publishing arrangements he had made with Macrone, Bentley, and Chapman and Hall. He was beginning to realize that he had made some impetuous decisions: 'I fear in my desire to avoid present vexations, I have laid up a bitter store for the future,' he told Forster.[44] Macrone's price was high: he wanted £2,000 for the Boz copyrights or 'apples of discord'[45] as Dickens called them, and Forster advised his friend to keep quiet for a time. Dickens was too impatient for such advice, particularly when Chapman and Hall decided that even at such a price they might be able to publish the *Sketches* in sufficient numbers in monthly parts to make a profit. An agreement was duly signed on 17 June in which Macrone handed over to Chapman and Hall the copyrights for the *Sketches*, the remaining copies of the first and second series, and Cruikshank's plates for £2,250. 'I was glad,' Forster remarked, 'to have been no party to a price so exorbitant.'[46]

Although Forster's advice on this occasion was disregarded, he had proved his value as a man of affairs as well as a friend, and Dickens eagerly pursued the relationship. He pressed manuscripts on Forster, asked him to read proofs, and consulted him on money matters. Forster responded to this gush of intimacy by drawing Dickens into his own circle of friends. On 16 June Forster took Dickens to see William Macready play in *Othello* at the Haymarket Theatre. Forster was already a close friend of Macready, and after the play he introduced Dickens to the famous actor. Macready was then forty-four, and since the death of Kean in 1833 he had been the leading tragedian on the English stage. He had achieved his success more by willpower and talent than by choice. He was the son of a dissolute itinerant actor and had grown up with such distaste for the disreputable aspects of the profession that he had wished to become a lawyer. But when his father went bankrupt and was put in the debtors' prison, Macready reluctantly took over his company. Once committed to a stage career he was determined to make the best of it, for he was always driven by anxiety to make a decent living. Besides the needs of his own growing family he had to meet the claims of the illegitimate brothers and sisters who were part of his inheritance. Even at the peak of his reputation he looked forward to the day when he could leave the boards for ever, and he said that he would rather see a son of his in a coffin than on a stage.[47]

This disdainful attitude made Macready unpopular with other actors, and his difficulties were accentuated by his severe manner and sharp temper. He found writers and artists more congenial and collected a kind of Cabinet of cronies who wrote for him, designed his productions, and provided cultivated companionship. Forster was already in this group of odd fellows. So was the aristocratic Edward Bulwer (later known as Bulwer-Lytton), a singular figure already famous for his Gothic romances, whose friendship with Macready had stimulated him to write plays. Robert Browning was another member of this theatrical set, and so was Thomas Noon Talfourd, a fashionable barrister and politician who was also making a name for himself as a man of letters. Talfourd prided himself on his liberal opinions, claiming that he had played some part in the abolition of the pillory, and he was equally proud of his connection with advanced writers. He had helped Bulwer edit Hazlitt's papers; he was Charles Lamb's literary executor; and while he was still young he had become the dramatic critic of the *New Monthly*. After he was elected to the House of Commons he combined all his talents in a vigorous campaign for a bill to give authors copyright protection, and at the same time he turned playwright, writing a florid tragedy called *Ion* in which Macready scored a success in 1836. He was an agreeable and social man, who put himself out to help the less fortunate; but he was anxious by temperament and given to fits of self-commiseration—a noticeable trait among this group of friends. Dickens met him in 1837, soon after he took up the cause of copyright in Parliament, and became a frequent visitor to his large house in Russell Square.[48]

Dickens felt quite at home in this freemasonry of talent. It was only a few days after meeting Macready that he was inviting the great actor to join Phiz, Forster, and Cattermole on a visit to Coldbath Fields House of Correction and a tour of Newgate. The outing had disquieting undertones. Macready and Dickens both had uncomfortable memories of a debtors' prison; and Dickens had now carried Mr. Pickwick's increasingly sombre adventures to the point where he had been outwitted by legal shysters and incarcerated in the Fleet for debt. Mr. Pickwick had been progressively instructed in the injustices and disorders of the world, and the fate of people cast loose in it without money, rights, or a settled place. 'I have seen enough,' he cried, as he looked at the miseries around him. 'My head aches with these scenes, and my heart too.' And Dickens felt the same. On the tour of Newgate, the horror of this gloomy human depository was etched in his mind for use in the last pages of *Oliver Twist*, and the condemned cells—in one of which sat an old acquaintance of Macready, the painter, forger, and poisoner Thomas Wainewright—evoked the morbid fantasies of Fagin's death on the gallows. Yet Dickens could recover quickly from such gruesome impressions, saving them for his prose and allowing his natural high spirits to take over. The party went back from Newgate to have dinner at Doughty Street and, Macready noted, 'our evening was very cheerful'.[49] Dickens and Macready had taken to each other from their first meeting and the friendship then begun grew steadily in warmth and intimacy.

At the beginning of July Dickens went off with Kate and Phiz for his first trip abroad, spending a week visiting Ghent, Antwerp, and Brussels. While he was travelling his mind was really on a drawn-out battle with Bentley. After the incident with Macrone over copyrights he began to believe that he was being exploited. The flattery of reviewers and friends made him regret even more his earlier bargains and he was now encouraged by Forster to ask a stiffer price for his new work and to get better control over his copyrights. He was beginning to feel that unless he could retain an interest in subsequent editions of his books his success would make his publishers rich at his expense; he therefore proposed to revise the agreement he had made with Bentley the previous August.

On 2 July 1837 Dickens opened his campaign for better terms with a letter reminding Bentley of 'the great alteration of circumstances which has occurred' since the agreement was made. What, in view of 'the increased popularity of my works', would Bentley now offer?[50] Bentley wanted to know what Dickens had in mind. Dickens suggested £600 for an edition of 3,000 copies of *Barnaby Rudge* (the new title for *Gabriel Vardon*) and £700 for a similar printing of *Oliver Twist*, less the payments already made for the instalments which had appeared in the *Miscellany*. Dickens admitted to Bentley that the publisher had the power to hold him to his original agreement, but he went on to remind Bentley that as editor of the *Miscellany* he also had his rights: 'I shall abide by the strict letter of my agreement respecting the *Miscellany*, and arrange my future plans with reference to it, accordingly.'[51] Bentley had now replaced Macrone as the villainous exploiter. When Bentley took his time to reply Dickens wrote to Forster early in August to say 'No news as yet from the "infernal, rich, plundering, thundering old Jew"',[52] quoting his own description of Fagin. A week later Bentley went to Doughty Street to discuss the matter but was received by Dickens with 'an air of coldness and restraint'. Bentley in fact agreed to pay the larger sums for the two novels but refused to make any other conditions as he had already made an agreement for the entire copyrights of both books. In any case, he claimed, he already possessed the *Oliver Twist* copyright by virtue of the part-publication in the *Miscellany*. Dickens responded to Bentley with 'considerable irritability, threatening amongst other in-temperate expressions that he would not write the novel at all. His object was evidently to provoke me,'[53] Bentley afterwards recalled.

Dickens, determined to put Bentley in the wrong, agreed to negotiate, but he had no intention of giving way. Forster was all the time at hand to give moral support. 'A note has arrived from the Robber,' he wrote to Forster in August.[54] Bentley understood that Dickens 'proposed to refer the matter to the arbitration of Mr. Sergeant Talfourd',[55] but in the event Dickens simply sent his friend Thomas Beard to speak for him. In briefing Beard he said that he had no intention of departing from his point: 'as any reason-able man will feel convinced that my proposal is a most fair and moderate one, I merely want to concede this to him for the sake of appearances'.[56] Bentley, in turn, asked his solicitor John Gregory to represent him but this action only served to fuel Dickens's indignation. He sent off a letter to Bent-ley, jeering at the idea of a solicitor as 'the disinterested, unprejudiced, pri-vate friend who you were to select with so much care'.[57] He claimed that Bentley had been guilty of an act of bad faith, and he now refused to com-municate with him except through a third party.

At the beginning of September Dickens took Kate and her mother to Broadstairs for a holiday. It was a small and charming watering-place on the Kent coast, and they lodged at 12 High Street just back from the cliff-top esplanade which ringed the sandy bay. Dickens was poorly when they arrived, and could not get on with the next number of *Pickwick*. He had been so queer, he told Forster on 3 September, 'that I have been compelled for four-and-twenty mortal hours to abstain from porter or other malt liquor!! I done it though—really.'[58] They did not stay more than a few days, because they were called back to London to deal with a robbery at Doughty Street, but Dickens was greatly taken with the bracing air and fine prospects of the seaside village.

George Cruikshank, concerned about his own work on *Oliver Twist*, also tried to resolve the dispute with Bentley. He found Dickens as adamant as ever, and advised Bentley that he would be wise to give way. After Dickens returned to London he found a new grievance. On the eve of his departure he had arranged the contents for the next issue of the *Miscellany*. In his absence at Broadstairs, he wrote angrily to Bentley on 16 September, he found that Bentley had interfered with his plans. 'By these proceedings I have been actually superseded in my office as Editor of the *Miscellany*,' he fulminated; 'they are in direct violation of my agreement with you, and a gross insult to me ... henceforth I decline conducting the *Miscellany* or con-tributing to it in any way.'[59] Bentley replied that he had no choice but to consult his legal advisers and affirmed his determination to hold Dickens to his agreement. Dickens now sent his own solicitor, Thomas Malloy, to talk to Bentley and Gregory.

It was difficult to find common ground. Dickens understandably wanted to escape from a contract made before *Pickwick* had raised the price of his work, and he was touchy about his independence as an editor. Bentley had the law on his side, he wanted some control over the magazine which bore his name, and he felt browbeaten by the pressures Dickens had used in this round of graceless haggling. Finally, Forster worked out a settlement. On 28 September Dickens signed a new agreement which increased his salary on the *Miscellany* to £30 a month but left Bentley with a power of veto over proposed articles. He was given £500 for the remainder of *Oliver Twist* and £700 for *Barnaby Rudge* and after three years half the copyright in both books was to revert to him.[60]

He had won a satisfying victory: the final terms were better than his original demands. As a sweetener, moreover, Bentley threw in an additional assignment. Joseph Grimaldi, the greatest of the English clowns, had died in May 1837 and Bentley had acquired the draft of his memoirs from the hack dramatist Thomas Wilks. He now asked Dickens to edit the text for £300 and a half-share of profits. Although Dickens was a pantomime enthusiast, and had a shadowy memory of seeing Grimaldi on the stage, he disliked the idea of knocking the 'dreary twaddle' of Wilks into shape, and he did little but cut it and write a perfunctory introduction and conclusion which were decked out with illustrations by Cruikshank.

Dickens had settled with Bentley but he still had his deadlines to meet. He was particularly harassed during the autumn as he was writing a double number of *Pickwick* to celebrate the end of the story. Mr. Pickwick was now a more chastened figure than the plump and comic tradesman whom Dickens had taken over from Seymour's first drawings; he had become serious, and curiously educated by the sardonic wit of Sam Weller; and at the last he found comfort in the society of his friends, in a domestic retreat where he had become a gentleman, protected against the evils of the world by his money and his benevolent feeling.

While Dickens was bringing Mr. Pickwick to this happy conclusion he had to forgo invitations to dine and to ride. He told Talfourd in October that the 'two Pickwicks for the month are so heavy a task, and it is so important that they should be out of my hands this week, that I am obliged in violation of my established usage to write this evening'.[61] On one such evening, his brother-in-law Henry Burnett recalled how Dickens declared that he would be more sociable and brought his writing-table into the sitting-room and went on working while people chattered around him. It was fascinating, Burnett said, 'to watch, upon the sly, the mind and the muscles working (or, if you please, playing) in company, as new thoughts were being dropped upon the paper. And to note the working brow, the set of the mouth, with the tongue tightly pressed against the closed lips.'[62] When the special number of *Pickwick* was set by the printer Dickens showed the proofs to Forster: it was the beginning of a practice which he maintained all through his life. 'There was nothing written by him after this date,' Forster claimed, 'which I did not see before the world did.'[63] And once the work which had brought him fame and fortune was finished Dickens took Kate off to Brighton to enjoy a few days in a fine bay-windowed apartment on the seafront. By now the habit of work was so strong that he found it difficult to adjourn. 'I have had great difficulty,' he wrote to Forster, 'in keeping my hands off Fagin and the rest of them in the evenings, but as I came down for rest, I have resisted the temptation and steadily applied myself to the labour of being idle.'[64]

The recriminatory feud with Bentley was in marked contrast to the amiable feelings between Dickens and Chapman and Hall. It was characteristic of Dickens to see his relationships in extreme terms. While he was vilifying Bentley he was acclaiming Chapman and Hall for their 'honourable and generous treatment', and their 'delicate and warm-hearted feeling';[65] to mark the completion of *Pickwick* they gave a banquet at the Prince of Wales tavern in Leicester Square on 18 November. Dickens was surrounded by admiring friends—Ainsworth, Phiz, Forster, Cruikshank, Macready, Jerdan, and Talfourd—at what Ainsworth described as 'a capital dinner, with capital wine and capital speeches'.[66] Talfourd, to whom the bound volumes of *Pickwick* were dedicated, proposed the toast and the restaurant owner capped the feast with 'a glittering temple of confectionary' within which stood a model of Mr. Pickwick. Chapman and Hall did even better. They gave Dickens a cheque for £750. He used most of it to open his first bank account at Coutts in the Strand.

Unlike Bentley, who had tried to hold Dickens to his original terms, Chapman and Hall were more generous. They owned the copyright of *Pickwick* and were under no obligation to pay more out of the very large profits it had brought them: the £14,000 it had earned floated them into a leading position among Victorian publishers. Yet they had paid Dickens bonuses which totalled over £2,000 and under Forster's persuasion they now agreed to give him a one-third share in the rights after five years. On the day of the banquet they signed a new contract which increased the resentment Dickens felt against Bentley's parsimony. He was bound to finish *Oliver Twist* and *Barnaby Rudge* for a few hundred pounds apiece: as soon as he could begin to clear that commitment he was promised £3,000 by Chapman and Hall for a serial to succeed *Pickwick*.

In August 1837 Thomas Talfourd told Dickens that he was 'the most genial delineator of human manners'[67] since Fielding. The hard bargaining during that summer and autumn had shown that he was much less genial when it came to matters of business. Although fiction welled out of him in an inspired flow, he had learned that it was a valuable commodity. Henceforth he would deal with his associates like a rising entrepreneur.

5

Hard Bargains

'INCREASED reputation and means—good health and prospects,' Dickens noted in the diary he began to keep on 1 January 1838.[1] Still a month short of his twenty-sixth birthday, he had remarkably good reasons to count his blessings. In less than three years, with only two complete books published, he had pushed through to the front rank of fiction. There was an air of confidence and authority about his style of life, and he liked nothing more than to share his good fortune with his friends. There was a christening party on 9 December for little Charley; Dickens, writing invitations for the occasion, called him the 'Infant Phaenomenon'[2] and the 'living wonder'.[3] Just before Christmas Chapman and Hall sent him three 'extra Super' bound volumes of *Pickwick* and he at once sent one apiece to Ainsworth and Forster as the 'most comprehensive expression of my warmest friendship and esteem'.[4] It was a happy time, but for one flaw—the vivid memory of Mary Hogarth.

On such anniversaries he keenly felt her loss and in this respect he noted that it was a 'sad New Year's Day'. If only she were living and 'sympathising with all my thoughts and feelings more than anyone I knew ever did or will,' he confessed, 'I think I should have nothing to wish for, but a continuance of such happiness'.[5] The nerve of grief was easily pricked. Just before Christmas 1837 Dickens had been much moved when the critic Leigh Hunt made a gracious comment on his inscription for Mary's gravestone. At New Year Mrs. Hogarth sent him Mary's penwiper as a memento and he advised her not to give way to unavailing grief—advice he needed quite as much for himself. On 6 January, when he finally gave up the lease of his old rooms in Furnival's Inn, he was further upset by remembrances. 'I shall never be so happy again as in those Chambers three Stories high,' he wrote in his diary, 'never if I roll in wealth and fame.'[6] A week later he copied Walter Scott's comments on the death of his wife into the diary because they expressed 'thoughts which have been mine by day and night, in good spirits and bad, since Mary died'. And early in February when he was away in Yorkshire he told Kate that he dreamed constantly of her dead sister: 'I should be sorry to lose such visions for they are very happy ones.'[7]

Dickens was able to accept the physical fact of Mary's death once the immediate grief had passed. It was the sense of emotional loss that persisted. As he harped on the happiness of the dead he seemed to be speaking of something even closer to himself than Mary's translation into eternal bliss. He was glad, he told William Bradbury a year later, in 'being always able to think of her as a young and promising girl, and not as one whom years and long sorrow and suffering had changed'.[8] The image of unchanging perfection, frozen like an immortelle upon a grave, was also an image of lost childhood—a companion in memory expressing a desperate need to hold on to something forever beyond recall.

The themes of betrayed innocence, lost childhood, and fraternal affection underlay the new serial, *Nicholas Nickleby*, which Chapman and Hall planned to bring out on 31 March. He was running a risk by starting it before *Oliver Twist* was finished. It was hard enough to manage one serial; two running at the same time left him no safety margin if his energy or invention flagged. 'I no sooner get myself up, high and dry,' he wrote to Bentley when *Oliver Twist* was slipping into arrears, 'than up come the waves of each month's work, and drive me back again into a sea of manuscript.'[9] To press on with a third story, the *Barnaby Rudge* promised to Bentley, was to court disaster. His output was already provoking comment from the critics. 'Mr. Dickens writes too often and too fast,' a critic complained in the *Quarterly Review* for October 1837: 'it requires no gift of prophecy to foretell his fate—he has risen like a rocket and will come down like a stick.' Yet Dickens was undeterred.[10] He was eager for acclaim, hungry for money, and used to working under pressure. The serial system met all three needs. He appeared before his public as regularly as an actor, each month bringing a fresh round of applause. He was paid twice for the same work, once for the serial version and again for the bound book published when all the parts were finished. And he needed deadlines to concentrate his effort. Part-publication was not a method which diverted his genius but the precise set of conditions which fostered it; the serial story was simply a vehicle, a literary stage-coach, which carried his characters about while Dickens invented experiences for them and filled out a rambling tale with melodramatic episodes and comic low-life sketches. The element of genius lay not in the construction but the effect. 'The truth is,' Ainsworth wrote to his friend Crossley that spring, 'to write for the mob we must not write too well. The newspaper level is the true line to take ... as Dickens departs from this he will decline in popular favour.... I think, however, he has so much tact that he will ... become bad enough to suit all tastes.'[11]

Ainsworth's cynical comment contained a measure of truth. Dickens was becoming a man of letters, but at this stage in his career he could produce literature only in the format and by the techniques of journalism. One reason for his delay in starting *Barnaby Rudge* was the feeling that he was committed to a 'novel'. To bring off a conventional three-decker without the stimulating discipline of a serial was somewhat daunting. The project hung over him, he told Forster in February 1838, 'like a hideous nightmare'.[12]

The impress of journalism showed in other ways. Dickens had a gift for sensing shifts in the public mood and trimming his writing to them. Though his stories were never crudely topical, they usually echoed some current concern. He had, too, the reporter's appetite for copy. No idea or impression was beneath notice. He picked up anecdotes, incidents in coaches and inns, the quirks of fellow travellers, folk-tales, songs, comic and tragic situations in the theatre. And like a reporter he did research for a story—not so much as to bury a tale in fact, but enough to give him the authentic feel of his subject. All his early tales depended more upon his power to conjure up circumstances than upon their creaking plots and their superficial characterization.

It was this need to sample a situation that sent him northwards with Phiz at the end of January 1838 on a mission through the snow. He wanted to get an impression of the ill-reputed cheap schools in the wild countryside of north Yorkshire where boys were boarded under miserable conditions. Charging between £14 and £100 a year, and ominously advertising 'no vacations', the principals of such schools were in the market for unwanted children—with no questions asked. Visiting Bowes, where the notorious William Shaw ran his academy, Dickens noted the graves of twenty-five pupils in the churchyard. He and Phiz saw a little of Shaw and his school, looked about some neighbouring academies to get local colour, and were off back home. They had quickly found what they needed.

On his twenty-sixth birthday Dickens began to write his story. 'I have been ... seduced from Nicholas by a thousand blandishments,' he wrote to Chapman and Hall two weeks later, 'but the first chapter is ready, and I mean (God willing) to begin in earnest tomorrow night, so you can begin to print as soon as you like.' Once Dickens was geared into his deadlines the rhythm of composition took hold. 'The sooner you begin,' he added to his publishers, 'the faster I shall get on.'[13]

Oliver Twist had opened in a workhouse. The hero of *Nicholas Nickleby* was soon caught in a school that was a similarly venal place of detention for defenceless children. Nicholas meets Mr. Squeers at the Saracen's Head, in the grim shadow of Newgate, and that shadow of crime and revenge lies over the whole narrative: Squeers, the cruel prison-keeper of Dotheboys Hall, abetted by sadists and perjurers, is eventually transported; Ralph Nickleby is a swindling usurer who hangs on a makeshift gallows, and his crony Gride is a fraudulent fortune-hunter; and even the release of the 'flogged and starved down' inmates of Dotheboys Hall reads like a triumphant jail-delivery, the fall of a minor Bastille. And there were other echoes between the two books, which Dickens was writing almost in parallel. Oliver had to run for his life, and Nicholas and his pitiful shadow Smike must do the same. As a character, indeed, Nicholas is really a grown-up Oliver, 'a young man of impetuous temper' who has been deprived of his patrimony, who feels himself 'to have committed no fault, and yet to be so entirely alone in the world'.

Nickleby became a sprawling drama in which, as in *Pickwick* and *Oliver Twist*, Dickens's habit of breaking up the action into sketch-like episodes was encouraged by serial publication. Sketches, moreover, provided a convenient stage for his cast—a point neatly underlined by the way in which Vincent Crummles and his troupe of touring actors perform a *Hamlet*-like parody of the story. For the theatrical conventions, so freely used in *Nickleby*, allowed Dickens to indulge his powerful range of comic, somewhat deranged and actively malevolent characters without totally upstaging the distressed gentlefolk of the Nickleby family and stock parts like Sir Mulberry Hawk and Sir Frederick Verisopht. He almost concluded his melodrama with a fantasy of Nicholas and his sister walking hand in hand through the years in blissful but unmarried companionship, but in the end he allowed the Cheeryble brothers to arrange equally stagy marriages for them both.

Dickens always set out to entertain his readers in terms they understood, and he carried his fast-growing public with him from *Pickwick* and *Oliver Twist*; but, as *Oliver Twist* had plainly shown, he was also a preacher, and the new novel a tract. He had a relatively simple view of human nature. He assumed that a child had inborn innocence which was later corrupted by neglect or cruelty, and that the only saving response to the evils of society was to attack the worst abuses and to rely upon personal kindness to redress the harm they caused. He therefore used *Nickleby* to deride the education of his day for its failure to make the most of the child's wondering interest, for its harsh disciplines, and for its fatuous definitions of knowledge. He was at pains to deny the charge that he had exaggerated a few bad cases. 'Mr. Squeers and his school', he insisted, 'are faint and feeble pictures of an existing reality.' Most schoolmasters, he went on, were 'blockheads and imposters', and the infamous Yorkshire schools were simply 'the lowest and most rotten' part of a structure which 'for absurdity and a magnificent *laissez-aller* neglect, has rarely been exceeded in the world'.[14] He had begun to unfold a canvas which portrayed a callous, incompetent, and humanly destructive social system. *Oliver Twist* had become an indictment of poverty and the way in which the Poor Law dealt with it; *Nickleby* became a polemic against the waste and perversion of a child's birthright.

The serial had twenty months to run, into the autumn of the following year. But before Dickens could settle seriously to the critical early chapters he had to get over the domestic distraction of Kate's second confinement. On 6 March 1838 he wrote to Bentley to announce 'an instalment of posterity in the shape of a daughter'.[15] With little Charley just over a year old, and with a miscarriage coming between his birth and that of Mary, Kate had been almost continuously pregnant since her marriage, and this imposed severe constraints upon her social life. Though there were months in which she could give dinners, visit, and go to the theatre, Dickens commonly sought his entertainment with male friends in bachelor style. Few of his regular companions had domestic ties. Ainsworth's wife, who died in the first week of March, had been separated from him for three years; Forster, Maclise, and Hablôt Browne were all unmarried. They were easily on call when Dickens wanted someone to walk, ride, or share a chop with him, and this was an important factor in his choice of friends, for he could not bear to be inactive and alone. 'Come and give *me* a call, and let us have a "bit o' talk",' he scribbled to Forster one evening when Kate was out. 'Come and sit here and read, or work, or do something, while I write the *last* chapter of *Oliver* which will be arter a lamb chop.'[16] It was to Forster that he turned most often. They took rides and walks together. 'You don't feel disposed, do you, to muffle yourself up,' he wrote to him in January 1838, 'and start off with me for a good brisk walk over Hampstead Heath? I knows a good 'ous there where we can have a red hot chop for dinner, and a glass of good wine. All work and no play makes Jack a dull boy. I am as dull as a Codfish.'[17] He was compulsively gregarious. Apart from private dinners there was the Garrick Club and the Parthenon; and Dickens was a regular attender at the new Shakespeare Club which met every Saturday evening at the Piazza Coffee House in Covent Garden to read plays and give papers. Dickens was soon on good terms with its secretary, the self-taught artist Frank Stone, who had given up cotton broking in Manchester for painting. He was twelve years older than Dickens and had exhibited notable portraits at the Royal Academy.

It was, however, the theatre which provided the main distraction for Dickens. On 13 March he asked Macready, who had taken over as actor-manager at Covent Garden in the previous October, to put his name down on the stage-door list. 'I have passed ... fifty times this season,' he wrote, 'but as the porter was not particularly sober last night, and exceedingly insolent, I should like to have right upon my side.'[18] Like Macready's other close friends he was also welcomed to rehearsals—Bulwer's *Lady of Lyons* was staged in February and *Coriolanus* followed in March. Macready, Dickens told Forster, was trying to restore to the stage the association of good literature and intellectual enjoyment. With such aspirations he was finding it hard to make Covent Garden productions pay; the audiences were often too thin for profit and the newspaper critics depressed him. When he read the reviews of *Coriolanus* in March he regretted that he had ever striven 'to win the opinions of such profligate, ignorant and bad men'.[19] Later in the year Dickens offered to dramatize *Oliver Twist* for Macready. It was a reasonable idea, even if the story was not so high-toned as the dramas that Macready took from Browning, Bulwer, and Talfourd: a pirated version of *Oliver Twist* was already running at the St. James's Theatre in March before the serial was completed, and four other unauthorized versions were put on before Frederick Yates staged one at the Adelphi, in February 1839, with the approval of Dickens. Macready was more choosy than the producers of such pot-boilers. 'Nothing could be kinder than this generous intention of Dickens,' he wrote in his diary, 'but I fear it is not acceptable.'[20] He was equally unresponsive to another proposal that autumn. Dickens wrote an astrological farce, *The Lamplighter*, and sent this and the text of his earlier comedy, *The Strange Gentleman*, to Macready: 'if I had as much time as I have inclination,' he told him, 'I would write on and on, and on, farce after farce and comedy after comedy, until I wrote you something that would run'.[21] Macready did not like disappointing him (that same month Dickens had resigned from the Garrick Club in protest against another member's apparent slight on the touchy Macready) and when Dickens went over the play Macready remarked that 'he reads as well as an experienced actor would—he is a surprising man'. He thought the plot meagre and the play 'went flatly'. He suspected that Forster, 'the most *indiscreet* friend that ever allied himself to any person', had 'goaded' Dickens to write the play and 'would *drive* it upon the stage',[22] but he controlled his tetchiness in telling Dickens frankly that the play would not do—an opinion which Forster in fact shared. Dickens took the rebuff with dignified good spirits. His only disappointment, he replied to Macready, lay in 'not having been able to be of some use to you'.[23] Such an answer, Macready observed, was 'high-minded and warm-hearted'. He added that 'Dickens and Bulwer have been certainly to me noble specimens of human nature'[24] and he asked Dickens to stand as godfather to his son, who had been born in December.

Dickens was indeed high-minded and warm-hearted; and he did like to be of use to people. It was when he felt himself crossed or snubbed that he revealed a fierce temper and wilful determination. He had been infuriated with Macrone about the copyright of *Sketches by Boz*, but when he discovered that Macrone's death had left his widow in poverty Dickens promoted a benefit volume of stories called *The Pic-Nic Papers* to help her and the children. He had a gracious turn of phrase in letters to authors and actors whom he admired, a quick humour with his intimates, and a decent modesty in formal correspondence. In a very few years, with few marks of his rough-and-tumble youth upon his manners, he had acquired the style of a cultivated man. He sat for Samuel Laurence, noted for his portraits of writers, and the work was lithographed and put on sale to the public. In June, in an astonishing tribute to his fast-grown reputation, he was one of a number of men 'known for their scientific or literary attainments' elected to the Athenaeum. Among those selected with the youthful Dickens were Charles Darwin, the eminent historian Grote, and the social reformer Edwin Chadwick—as well as Macready, who had been rejected three years earlier. Such recognition made an impression. In June, at one of the receptions which made Holland House the liveliest place in London, Lady Holland asked Bulwer 'if Boz was presentable'; Bulwer felt she was 'condescending with a man of genius, a thing not to be forgiven; so I growled and snapped'.[25] She then asked Thomas Talfourd to bring Dickens to the house. When he went with Talfourd on 12 August he was found socially acceptable. Lady Holland's sister considered him dandified, conceding that he had a beautiful face, 'because blended with his intelligence there is such an expression of goodness'. Lord Holland thought him 'very unobtrusive, yet not shy, intelligent in countenance, and altogether prepossessing'.[26]

It was a summer of success. *Grimaldi* was finished. '*1700 Grimaldis have been already sold, and the demand increases daily!!!!*' he exclaimed to Forster.[27] *Nickleby* came out on 31 March. At the Star and Garter hotel at Richmond, where Dickens had taken Kate to recuperate after her difficult confinement, they celebrated their second wedding anniversary, the twenty-sixth birthday of Forster who had joined them, and the 50,000 sale of the first number of *Nickleby*. In June and July the family spent most of its time at a rented house on the river at Twickenham, though they came up to watch the young Queen's coronation procession on 28 June. Dickens had his parents, brothers, and sisters down for visits; Ainsworth was there, and Talfourd, Bentley, Hullah, and of course Forster. Ballooning was a current fad and Dickens invented a balloon club for the children—'the Gammon Aeronautical Balloon association for the encouragement of Science and the Consumption of Spirits of Wine'[28]—with Forster as its president and supplier of toy balloons.

These jollifications took their toll of time. Dickens was in such arrears with *Oliver* that, much embarrassed, he had to ask Bentley if he might miss a month's instalment. He took Kate off to the Isle of Wight for a week in September 'for *Oliver* purposes'.[29] When he returned to London he pretended to be away and left his letters unopened. He had not time for callers, for the last number was still unwritten and *Oliver Twist* was due to appear in hard covers on 9 November. In the second week of October he reached the death of Sikes. Fagin's fate was still unsettled: 'not having yet disposed of the Jew who is such an out and outer that I don't know what to make of him',[30] Dickens reluctantly told Forster that work must come before riding. Forster indeed recalled that he never knew Dickens to work so frequently after dinner or to such late hours as during the final months of *Oliver Twist*. He was intensely caught up in his story. At the beginning of October he wrote to Forster: 'Hard at work still. Nancy is no more. I shewed what I have done to Kate last night who was in an unspeakable "*state*", from which and my own impression I augur well.'[31]

It was 20 October before Dickens sent 'the last portion of this marvellous tale' round to George Cruikshank for illustration. In the final hectic days he had been immensely encouraged by a long article in the *Edinburgh Review* which surveyed his whole career from *Sketches* and *Pickwick* to the still unfinished serials. 'It is all even *I* could wish,' he wrote to Forster on 2 October, 'and what more can I say!'[32] A month later, with the book version of *Oliver* reinforcing the triumph of the serial, Ainsworth wrote to his friend Hugh Beaver: 'I need not enlarge on the merits of Mr. Dickens as by common consent he has been installed in the throne of letters vacated by Scott.'[33] Early in the following year Queen Victoria gave it royal approval. She found *Oliver Twist* 'excessively interesting' and commended it to her Prime Minister, Lord Melbourne.[34]

As soon as *Oliver* had gone to the printer Dickens took Hablôt Browne off on a ten-day whirl of sightseeing. Travelling by post-chaise, in daily stages of about seventy miles, they worked their way up through the Midlands to North Wales—where they were joined by Forster—and back by way of Manchester. The expenses which Dickens noted in his diary were typical of the coaching age—Hostler 1s., Mulled Wine at Birmingham 4s., Turnpikes 1s. 6d., Posting, dinner & gates £1. 0s. 0d., hotel bill at Stratford £2. 10s. 0d., at Llangollen £1. 10s. 6d. It was an age nearing its sudden end. When Forster came after Dickens and Browne he travelled by train: the line to Birmingham had been opened only a month before. The contrast between traditional and industrial England was equally marked. Dickens was enchanted by Kenilworth, thinking that it might make a good resort for the following summer, and fascinated by Warwick and Stratford: beyond Birmingham he travelled through cold fog, 'through miles of cinder-paths and blazing furnaces and roaring steam engines, and such a mass of dirt gloom and misery as I never before witnessed'.[35] He almost abandoned the journey at Stratford. The strain of completing *Oliver Twist* had brought on a painful spasm in his left side which he eased by taking a powerful dose of a narcotic. He was welcomed at Manchester by friends of Ainsworth, meeting the amiable brothers William and Daniel Grant whom he used as models for the benevolent Cheeryble partners in the latter part of *Nickleby*.

Dickens had to return before he had seen as much of Manchester as he planned. He was worried about mistakes in *Oliver Twist*, especially in Cruikshank's plates; Forster wrote to Bentley on 8 November demanding that two of them, drawn while Dickens was away on his tour, be omitted from the next printing. They were, Forster insisted, 'a vile and disgusting interpolation on the sense and bearing of the tale'.[36] He also instructed Bentley to insert a new title-page. For the first time 'Charles Dickens', rather than 'Boz', appeared as the author.

He had been much affected by his first and fleeting glimpse of the industrial districts of the Midlands and Lancashire. 'I went', he wrote to Edward Fitzgerald at the end of December, 'and saw the *worst* cotton mill. And then I saw the *best*. ... There was no great difference between them.' In mid-January 1839 he proposed to return briefly to Manchester, where Ainsworth and he were to be guests of honour at a banquet, and this prospect made him feel that he was going 'into the enemy's camp, and the very head-quarters of the factory system advocates'. To Fitzgerald, who was acting as an intermediary between Dickens and the great reformer Lord Ashley (later the Earl of Shaftesbury), he made no secret of his antipathy to a system which exploited and brutalized its workpeople, especially the children. He did not need much more evidence, he told Fitzgerald. 'So far as seeing goes, I have seen enough for my purpose, and what I have seen has disgusted and astonished me beyond all measure. I mean to strike the heaviest blow in my power for these unfortunate creatures, but whether I shall do so in the "Nickleby", or wait some other opportunity, I have not yet determined.'[37]

Dickens did not plan his early serials in detail. He had a feeling for background—something like a series of stage sets—a cast of characters and an overall view of the kind of story he proposed to write. The division into parts and the minor climaxes of plot that these divisions required were tackled as they arose. This meant that he was able to assimilate new ideas and turn the plot as he went along: in the end it did not suit him to use *Nickleby* for an attack on mill-owners and the Manchester school of economists—though he left that option open for several instalments by locating the business of the Cheerybles in Lancashire. He could grasp enough of the Yorkshire academies for his purpose on a flying visit. Factories, however, were not so easily transformed into manageable copy. Although they were visually exciting, and Dickens was always quickened by human suffering and always seeking human causes for it, he could not dramatize what was wrong. He had struck at cruelty in workhouses by attacking Mr. Bumble, at sadistic parsimony in boarding-schools by pillorying Squeers; it was difficult to fasten responsibility for the wretchedness of the new proletariat on similar figures of calumny. The essence of the industrial system was its abstract inhumanity—it was controlled, the economists of the day asserted, by laws of the market and not by individuals who could be called to account. Dickens glossed over the sources of the Cheeryble wealth and kept the amiable twins and Nicholas down in a counting-house set in the familiar alleys of the City: paternalism was more comprehensible and acceptable than political economy.

As *Oliver Twist* ran out Bentley became anxious about the delivery of its successor. He annoyed Dickens by advertising that *Barnaby Rudge* would appear 'forthwith' in the *Miscellany* when none of it was actually written. On 4 January 1839 Dickens told Forster 'I *have* begun', but it was a forced and false beginning.[38] On 21 January he sent Forster a despairing letter to explain an enclosed message to Bentley asking for a delay of six months. 'I *cannot* write this tale ... until I have had time to breathe; and until the intervention of the summer, and some cheerful days in the country, shall have restored me to a more genial and composed state of feeling.' Exhaustion was one cause of his difficulty. Another was his lack of enthusiasm for the story. It had become an embarrassing commitment which he did not wish to fulfil—and certainly not on the conditions he had agreed with Bentley. It was resentment against Bentley, indeed, that filled the splenetic letter to Forster. Bentley was making 'immense profits' from *Oliver Twist*: 'I have still the slavery and drudgery of another work on the same journeyman-terms ... my books are enriching everybody connected with them but myself. ... I, with such a popularity as I have acquired, am struggling in old toils, and wasting my energies in the very height and freshness of my fame, and the best part of my life, to fill the pockets of others.' The contract against which Dickens was fulminating had actually been drafted at his request, and after substantial concessions from Bentley. In his present irritation he simply ignored that fact. 'I hold myself released from such hard bargains as these,' he fumed, 'after I have done so much for those who drove them.' He was suffering from an attack of financial claustrophobia in which the desire to escape was stronger than professional pride or obligation. 'This net that has been wound about me', he told Forster, 'so chafes me, so exasperates and irritates my mind, that to break it at whatever cost—*that* I should care nothing for—is my constant impulse.'[39]

Bentley replied three days later. He offered to postpone *Barnaby Rudge* if Dickens agreed to do nothing for six months except finish *Nickleby*. 'I trust', Bentley added with a hint of sarcasm, 'the recreation you promise yourself will tend to the improvement of your health and strength.'[40] Dickens was enraged. 'I have dreamt of Bentley all night, and am fierce,' he wrote to Forster next morning.[41] Writing to Bentley 'as one who is enriching you at the expence of his own brain, and for a most paltry and miserable pittance', Dickens refused to give such a pledge: 'if you presume to address me again in the style of offensive impertinence which marks your last communication, I will from that moment abandon at once and for ever all conditions and agreements that may exist between us, and leave the whole question to be settled by a jury'.[42] There was an element of guilt in this outburst. Dickens had not only promised to edit the benefit volume of *Pic-Nic Papers* for Mrs. Macrone. He had also agreed—without Bentley's knowledge—to write a comic book which Chapman and Hall proposed to publish the following Christmas.

During the quarrel with Bentley in the summer of 1837 Dickens had threatened to give up the editorship of the *Miscellany*. He now completely broke that tie. Bentley tried for a compromise. Dickens could write the comic annual and have £40 a month for the use of his name on the *Miscellany*, on condition he did not edit another journal. Dickens refused, and gave Bentley something like an ultimatum. If Bentley took on Harrison Ainsworth as editor, on the same salary, Dickens would write a gracious article commending his successor and regard it as a point of honour neither to edit nor write for any other magazine for the remainder of 1839. The scheme was devised so impulsively that Ainsworth knew nothing of it until a messenger from Dickens roused him from his bed with a message to go immediately to Bentley and agree to take over the magazine. 'I have burst the Bentleian bonds', Dickens wrote jubilantly to Thomas Talfourd,[43] and he celebrated his triumph with an impromptu dinner on his twenty-seventh birthday—'only my own folks, Leigh Hunt, Ainsworth and Forster' he told Harley in asking him to join in the ' "conwiviality" of the meeting'.[44] Negotiations were now in hand for two new agreements which were to be signed on 27 February. One released Dickens from the *Miscellany*. The other gave him until 1 January 1840 to deliver *Barnaby Rudge* and again raised the price for the much-delayed novel. He was to get a minimum of £2,000, and twice as much if the sales reached 15,000.[45] With good reason he noted in his diary that his birthday marked the end of 'a most prosperous and happy year, for which and all other blessings I thank God with all my heart and soul'.[46]

One of the reasons Dickens was so anxious about money was the weight of responsibility which he carried. His father's incompetence had made him the effective head of his family and he proposed to conduct its affairs very differently. In November he was obliged to pay off an old debt for John Dickens. 'And so it always is,' he wrote with resignation to Forster, 'directly I build up a hundred pounds, one of my dear relations comes and knocks it down again.'[47] But success toughened him and there was some limit to filial patience. In February, soon after his birthday dinner, he discovered that his father's incurable fecklessness was embarrassingly out of control. Apart from the debts to tradesmen, which John Dickens ran up as easily as a gentleman of means, he was also trading shadily on his son's reputation. For more than two years he had been extracting money from Chapman and Hall. In February 1837 he had asked them to consider 'how much your interests are bound up with those of my son' and added the blackmailing hint of 'fatal consequences' if they refused a loan: neither his publishers nor Dickens could afford to see his father back in the debtor's prison. The threat was more explicit on another occasion. If 'a man is placed in the situation in which I have placed myself, all but subjected himself to the laws of his country', John Dickens wrote to the obliging partners, 'he will snatch at a straw to save himself not from drowning, but a scarcely milder sentence'. For a long time he concealed this petty extortion. At the end of 1837 he had unctuously thanked Chapman and Hall for conniving at this secrecy. Were Charles to know, he wrote, 'it could have led to a breach of a most distressing nature'.[48]

By the early weeks of 1839, after he had been reduced to peddling letters and other Dickens manuscripts to collectors, John Dickens had come to the point where there was no escape. The rent on his rooms in King Street was in arrears; and he was only a writ's length from the sponging house. Dickens decided to get his parents and his youngest brother, Augustus, out of town. 'This promptitude is *necessary*,' he wrote hurriedly to Forster on 1 March, 'and worth a thousand prospective resolutions.'[49] Three days later he took the coach down to Exeter. The next morning he rented Mile End Cottage at Alphington, just out of the city, reporting to Kate that it was 'in the most beautiful, cheerful, delicious rural neighbourhood I was ever in'.[50] Delighted to find such 'a jewel of a place' he sent money and instructions for his parents to follow him; meanwhile, he attended to the furnishing, fitting up the whole establishment for about £70. Cottage rent and furniture, however, were only part of the cost of resettling his parents, for their debts had also to be cleared. 'I hope and believe', Dickens wrote to Kate in the evening of his hectic day, 'that these three or four hundred pounds will come back to us one-day in three or four hundred thousand recollections which nothing else could buy.'[51]

He had been astonishingly considerate of his parents. He had made no snobbish attempt to keep them secluded from his smart new friends. Even in his exasperation, when he was driven summarily to exile them to Devon, he did his best to save his father from humiliation. Instructing Thomas Mitton to settle some of the debts and to ensure that John Dickens was dispatched by coach, he added: 'you are supposed not to know the *cause* of all this'.[52] His parents showed no appreciation for his tact or generosity. They resented being bundled into the country and sent complaining letters, full of self-pity. In mid-July a plaintive note from his mother made Dickens expostulate to Forster: 'I do swear that I am sick at heart with both her and father too, and think this *is* too much.'[53]

What Dickens described to Thomas Beard as 'arrangements concerning the settling-down for life of the governor'[54] were scarcely completed before he had to settle-down Forster and Ainsworth, who were at cross-purposes. One source of friction was Forster's severe review of Ainsworth's sensational novel, *Jack Sheppard*. Another was a suspicion that Ainsworth was colluding with Bentley, as Dickens put it in a long and stiff letter to Ainsworth on 26 March, to place 'a mutual friend of ours in a false position'. Bentley, Dickens said, was putting it about that Forster had goaded him into breaking his agreements and 'entangled and entrapped the innocent and unsuspecting bookseller'. This was untrue, and Dickens complained that Ainsworth had done nothing to stop the gossip though he knew it to be false. 'Forster must and shall be set right. ... I wish to know distinctly from you who shall do so, *without the delay of an instant*—You or I.' The imperious demand for a 'friendly and manly avowal of feeling' had an immediate effect.[55] Ainsworth exonerated Forster and extracted a grudging letter from Bentley which mollified Dickens without conceding that Forster was blameless.

It was some time before Dickens again felt easy in Ainsworth's company. Ainsworth, hitherto treated as an intimate, was notably missing from the list of friends asked down to Petersham, where Dickens had again taken Elm Cottage for June and July. It was a good warm summer and he was in jocular good humour, dispatching comical invitations for river sports and outings. 'You haven't a notion of the glories we have been working,' he wrote to Maclise at the end of June: 'Come down—and that without loss of time— and leave the rest to me, and I'll warrant y⸱u good health for 12 months at least.'[56] Dickens was delighted with the portrait Maclise had just completed, 'which all people say is astonishing',[57] and was waiting eagerly for the engraver William Finden to produce copies of it. It was 'perfectly amazing' in its likeness, Thackeray said: 'a looking-glass could not render a better facsimile...the real identical man...the inward Boz as well as the outward'.[58]

Dickens went up to London when obliged, or for pleasure. Macready's term at Covent Garden was ending, a financial failure though an artistic success. Looking forward to the last night on 16 July, Dickens told Laman Blanchard, 'I verily believe I shall cry.'[59] And at the grand testimonial dinner for Macready four days later he proposed the toast to the Covent Garden company. Most of the summer, however, he was out of town. In late August 1839, he took the family off to stay for a month at Albion Street in Broadstairs while he finished off *Nickleby* and Kate waited out the last week of yet another pregnancy. 'It is a *house*—not a lodging', he wrote proudly to Forster, announcing that its amenities included 'the most beautiful view of the sea from its bay-windows that you can imagine ... surprisingly clean beds, and a costively inconvenient water-closet'.[60] As soon as he was settled he sent off invitations to friends to come down, giving them instructions to catch the Ramsgate steamer from London Bridge wharf and, provided the weather was calm, to go ashore on the boat which would put out from Broadstairs to meet it. And there were other acquaintances already in residence. J. P. Harley was staying in the next street, the publisher Thomas Longman had put up at the library with his wife and baby, and the long-lived poet Samuel Rogers, who had known Samuel Johnson, was at the Albion Hotel next door.

The cadaverous Rogers, who looked rather like Voltaire, was then seventy-six. He had long been a figure of note in the London literary world though he had only a minor talent as a poet. As the son of a banker, with an income of £5,000 a year, he could afford to lay himself out to society and to indulge his tastes as a critic, collector, and connoisseur; and although he had a bitter tongue, he was a lively host and generous in his help to other writers. Dickens had met him at Lady Holland's receptions—Macaulay called him 'The Oracle of Holland House'—and now came to know him better as a neighbour in Broadstairs.

Nickleby was finished on 20 September 1839 and a 'Nicklebeian fete' was planned for 5 October at the Albion in Aldersgate. Although it was lavish— '*too* splendid' Macready noted misanthropically—it was not a large banquet, and only a score of friends were there to see Chapman and Hall present the portrait of Dickens which they had commissioned from Maclise. Bradbury and Evans were present as the printers of *Nickleby*; so were Forster, Phiz, Talfourd, Beard, and the artists George Cattermole, Sir David Wilkie, and Clarkson Stanfield. The last of these was another member of the Macready circle, whom Dickens had met at Covent Garden in December 1837 when he painted the diorama for Macready's pantomime. Dickens became greatly attached to 'Stanny', whom he later described as 'the soul of frankness, generosity and simplicity, the most loving and most lovable of men'.[61] Stanfield, eighteen years older than Dickens, had been press-ganged into the navy during the Napoleonic wars, and his gift as a painter had been discovered by Douglas Jerrold, the radical journalist, then serving as a midshipman; when Jerrold had got up some amateur theatricals on board H.M.S. *Namur* the scenery was painted by Stanfield, and before long he left the sea and found similar employment ashore. By the time he met Dickens he had given up scene-painting, except to oblige his friends, and had embarked on a successful career as a painter of large canvases of seascapes, battles, and public ceremonials.

Almost all those who attended the dinner were men who, like Dickens and Stanfield, had come up in the world from hard or humble beginnings and knew the seamier side of life as well as they knew success. When Macready proposed the toast he took this into account. He did not dwell on the light-hearted humour of *Pickwick* but pointed the moral of *Oliver Twist* and *Nickleby*. He spoke of Dickens, he noted afterwards in his diary, 'as one who made the amelioration of his fellow-men the object of all his labours'.[62]

All summer Dickens had been thinking hard about the nature of serial writing, and how it fitted into his life. Already and reluctantly committed to *Barnaby Rudge*, he was afraid that yet another story in instalments might weary his public. He also wanted some relief from the creative strain of spinning out a serial and some form that was less restricting than the set lengths of monthly parts. On 14 July he asked Forster to approach Chapman and Hall, to discover 'what they meant to do at the conclusion of *Nickleby*', to encourage them to do 'something handsome—even handsomer perhaps than they dreamt of doing', and to drop a hint that Dickens might consider other tempting offers. If, he added, 'they wish to secure me and perpetuate our connection, now is the time for them to step gallantly forward and make such proposals as will produce that result'.[63] With this brief went a detailed proposal which Forster was to unveil to Chapman and Hall if they seemed amenable.

When they went to Forster's rooms in Lincoln's Inn Fields to open negotiations the partners were dazzled, but game. Dickens proposed that they should publish a threepenny weekly—something like a literary club whose members would 'write amusing essays on the various foibles of the day ... take advantage of all passing events ... and vary the form of the papers by throwing them into sketches, essays, tales, adventures, letters from imaginary correspondents and so forth'. He seemed to be promising a new *Pickwick*. He intended, explicitly, to revive Mr. Pickwick and Sam Weller as characters in the new work, and that alone was enough to make his publishers happy with the 'very rough and slight outline of the project' which Forster had been instructed to give them. It was actually far from slight, for Dickens had crammed sufficient ideas for at least three such ventures into his proposal. There were also to be 'stories and descriptions of London as it was many years ago, as it is now, and as it will be many years hence'—sketches, so to speak, by a time-travelling Boz. And for good measure Dickens added the notion of something like a new *Gulliver's Travels*, as well as travelogues which he would himself work up from summer journeys to Ireland and America. If Chapman and Hall agreed to suitable terms the first issue would be ready for what, after *Pickwick* and *Nickleby*, Dickens believed was his lucky publication date—31 March in the following year.

It was an extraordinary proposition. Its chances of success, Dickens coolly suggested, were 'great, very great; indeed, almost beyond calculation, or I should not seek to bind myself to anything so extensive'.[64] In fact he seems to have done no editorial calculation. The scheme was no more than a set of loosely conceived and potentially attractive ideas, bound up into a package designed to extract the best possible offer from Chapman and Hall; and when the detailed discussion of the contract began Dickens spent far more time working out its financial implications, checking every aspect of the venture with papermakers and printers, than he devoted to the nature of the magazine he was intending to produce. By 25 July there was agreement in principle, although the contract was not signed until just before the publication of the first issue.

The principle was staggering, and unique. Dickens had effectively reversed the balance between author and publisher. He was to have an additional £1,500 for *Nickleby*. As editor of the new magazine he was to receive £50 a week, and half the profits on each number. Chapman and Hall would have to meet all the costs of printing and advertising out of their half-share, and carry the loss if any number failed to pay its way. If the magazine reached a circulation of 50,000, Dickens estimated, he would make £10,000 profit and his publishers would only make half that amount. None of his contemporaries could have driven such a bargain. It ensured that his income rose with sales, that he was guaranteed against loss, and that he would receive the greater share of the profits. It was, he told Thomas Mitton in confidence, 'as good as could be. . . . I don't despair of making a decent thing out of some one of my works yet.'[65]

With such an assuring prospect ahead Dickens had even less incentive to grind away at *Barnaby Rudge*. As soon as *Nickleby* was finished he turned, with a groan of duty, to the task. The deadline for Bentley was only two months away and nothing was written except the first few pages. He had even squandered some of his time—and broken his promise to Bentley that he would do nothing but *Nickleby*—by producing an anonymous pot-boiler for Chapman and Hall called *Sketches of Young Couples*. In December, with the unfulfilled contract looming over him, Dickens saw a chance of escape: Bentley might be provoked into invoking the last clause in their agreement which gave him the right to cancel it if any other work by Dickens was written or advertised before it. What Bentley had devised as a safeguard could be used against him.

The excuse on which Dickens seized for a new quarrel with Bentley was an advertisement announcing that *Barnaby Rudge* was 'preparing for publication' and referring to *Pickwick* and *Nickleby*. Bentley, Dickens complained in virtuous tones to his solicitors on 16 December, was using his name and some of his writings in 'an unwarrantable manner ... hawking them about in a manner calculated to do me serious prejudice'.[66] There were other complaints about Bentley's publishing policy to spice the letter. Its substantial point, however, was simple. Dickens did not intend to deliver *Barnaby Rudge* on New Year's Day. He had devoted himself to another work—the scheme which he had put up to Chapman and Hall in July—and Bentley was therefore entitled to invoke the cancellation clause in their contract.

Over the year's end, nevertheless, the battle raged. 'War to the knife, and with no quarter on either side, has commenced with the Burlington Street Brigand,' Charles wrote to Thomas Beard on 17 December.[67] 'The Brigand is sleeping,' he told Edward Chapman ten days later, 'but I suspect with one eye open. Whether he is ogling the Vice-Chancellor with it, or not, time will show.'[68] At each stage in the protracted quarrel about *Barnaby Rudge* he had dared Bentley to sue him—either by a Chancery suit forcing him to write the novel or by an action for damages because he refused to write it. It was a reasonable bluff. It was unlikely that a Chancery court would try to compel an author to work; and an attempt to extract damages could well cost Bentley more than he won, as well as discrediting him in the literary world.

The expectations aroused by the new venture with Chapman and Hall had encouraged Dickens to defy Bentley. They had also enabled him to move out of Doughty Street. Two days after the birth of his second daughter, Kate, on 29 October 1839, he was house-hunting. He first looked at an attractive property in Kent Terrace, near the Hanover Gate of Regent's Park, but Macready, who once lived there, told him that the stench from the stables was 'a decided and insurmountable objection'. Mrs. Dickens, who had been brought up from Devon for Kate's confinement, was dispatched to look at other possibilities. 'I begin', Charles wrote to Thomas Mitton, 'to droop and despair.'[69] Three days later he was fizzing with excitement, telling Forster that a house of 'great promise' and 'excessive splendour' was in view.[70] This was 1 Devonshire Terrace, on the Marylebone Road and near the York Gate of Regent's Park, which he took at an annual rental of

George Cruikshank, drawn by Daniel Maclise

William Charles Macready. An engraving by Posselwhite from a miniature painted by Robert Thorburn in 1843

Daniel Maclise, painted by Edward Matthew Ward in 1846

£160 from 1 December, paying £800 premium for the twelve years remaining of the lease. The 'agonies of house-letting, house-taking, title proving and disproving, premium paying, fixture valuing, and other ills too numerous to mention'[71] were in themselves enough to ensure that no progress was made with *Barnaby Rudge*, and on 16 December Dickens decided to break the contract with Bentley. With Kate still recovering from the birth of her daughter, he had to supervise all the domestic as well as the legal details of the removal, making 'appointments with carpenters, bricklayers, upholsterers and painters'.[72] When he had moved into Doughty Street he had needed to watch what was spent. He could now afford to do things in a style to match the imposing, bow-windowed, white-stuccoed Georgian house which confirmed his improved social position. There was a fine library on the ground floor, with windows giving on to the garden and a prospect past the carriage-house to the park; its lining shelves were soon stocked with a collection of over 2,000 volumes whose titles reflected his eclectic interests and his literary friendships, and there was space left on the walls for engravings of Carlyle and Tennyson. The whole house, indeed, was to be furnished in the solid but fussy taste of a prosperous Victorian family—mahogany and rosewood furniture, elaborate gilding to set off the heavy damask curtains, heavily framed paintings by Maclise, Stanfield, Frith, Wilkie, and Landseer, mirrors everywhere, ornaments to clutter the rooms, and a stuffed bird and a marble bust to embellish the entrance hall. Dickens was a stickler for domestic detail. To complete his preparations he called in Thomas Chapman, a surveyor in the City who was the elder brother of his publisher and 'a genius in houses', to make suggestions 'relative to the Watercloset'.[73]

The four years since Christmas 1835, when Dickens had been courting Kate and trying to finish off *Sketches by Boz* for Macrone, had been a breathless rush to the freedom and prestige that money could buy—to the gentlemanly life of which his father had been a walking caricature. To mark the occasion John Dickens was summoned up from Devon for the family Christmas in the new house. He arrived, Dickens told Forster, 'both sore and sorely bruised'.[74] The 'Defiance', on which he was coaching up from Exeter, had been turned over along the way. John Dickens had always had high hopes and bad luck.

6

Flourishing Exceedingly

IN 1840 Dickens rolled buoyantly on fortune's wave. He was full of confidence and high spirits. The Christmas festivities in the new house had been prolonged—he thanked Bradbury and Evans for a turkey of 'astonishing capabilities'[1]—and in the New Year he enjoyed a long break from the daily grind. Early in February there were public celebrations for the Queen's marriage to Prince Albert. Maclise had been asked to paint the Queen as a secret present for the Prince, and this royal favour set Dickens off in a transport of joky jealousy. He went down to Windsor with Forster and Maclise; the three men, Dickens wrote to Thomas J. Thompson, prowled about the castle 'with a hopeless passion whose extent no tongue can tell ... we wear marriage medals next to our hearts'. Maclise, he said, was 'raving with love for the Queen' while Forster 'counterfeits a passion too, but *he does not love her*'.[2] This light-hearted romp brought Dickens closer to Maclise, who had now replaced Ainsworth to make a trio with Forster and Dickens. They were in constant communication and scarcely a day passed when they did not meet for dinner, a walk, or a ride. On the day of the wedding they all went to Thompson's chambers to watch the royal procession. Dickens had come to know Thompson through Charles Smithson, who was his brother-in-law and the partner of Thomas Mitton. A very wealthy widower of the same age as Dickens, Thompson lacked a particular occupation and made himself an available companion.

Dickens was so exuberant that new acquaintances were easily drawn into his humours. The elaborate jest about Queen Victoria, for instance, was spun out over several days and Dickens told it to many of his friends. It was visited upon the elderly Walter Savage Landor, the poet and critic whom Dickens had recently met at Lady Blessington's house. Landor, hot-headed but kindly, an enemy of humbug and an enthusiast for liberty, recently returned from a twenty-year residence in Florence to settle at Bath, was just the kind of person to appeal to Dickens. He in turn thought Dickens 'truly extraordinary ... a good as well as a delightful man', telling Forster that Dickens 'has drawn from me more tears and more smiles than are remaining to me for all the rest of the world, real or ideal'.[3]

Dickens liked to draw his talented friends into work as well as play; and during the first months of 1840 he was struggling to make something of the project he had so boisterously sold to Chapman and Hall six months earlier. His general idea was for a new miscellany of tales to be published weekly: 'I am sure I can make a good thing of this opening' he told Forster. It would begin with an old man—Master Humphrey—in a strange house telling his own tale. 'Then I mean to tell how that he has kept odd manuscripts' in a 'quaint queer-cased clock', and how a club of friends 'by reason of their punctuality and his regard for this dumb servant' took the name of 'Master Humphrey's Clock' for their proceedings.[4] Dickens planned to write old Humphrey's papers himself and to commission other authors to contribute the articles by the club members. It was a tortuous description of a clumsy literary device; the idea was like a combination of *Sketches* and *Pickwick*, and it was not surprising that Dickens found it difficult to get started. 'I am thinking awfully,' he again wrote to Forster, 'but not writing, as I intend (Please God) to start tomorrow.'[5] Three days later this half-risen notion had been inflated into an important innovation in fiction. Inviting George Cattermole to become one of the regular illustrators for the new weekly, he told him that 'the plan is a new one' and he begged Cattermole to keep the venture 'a profound secret'. *Pickwick*, *Oliver Twist*, and *Nickleby* had all been plagiarized whilst the serials were still running, and Dickens feared that if the secret got out 'there would be fifty Humphreys in the field'. His unbroken run of successes had made him so confident that he cheerfully assured Cattermole that he was 'justified by past experience in supposing that the sale would be enormous, and the popularity very great'.[6]

Dickens was fortunate in his illustrators. Cruikshank had helped to establish him with the *Sketches* and *Oliver Twist*; Phiz had played his part with *Pickwick* and *Nickleby*; and now he had recruited a prominent antiquarian painter whose woodcuts would fit the gothic mood of his current work. George Cattermole, who had been introduced to Dickens by Forster, was one of the Gore House set, and in 1839 he had married a connection of the Barrow family and settled in Clapham. He was nervous and self-effacing, like Phiz, and the two managed to work well together in meeting the exacting demands that Dickens made upon them.[7]

Dickens was still in high spirits as the publication day of 4 April approached. Two days before he went to Richmond with Forster and Maclise for the now customary 'launching' dinner, and then he took Kate off to Birmingham to visit his brother Alfred, who was there training to become an engineer. Forster arrived after the weekend with the cheering news that *Master Humphrey's Clock* had sold almost 70,000 copies of the first issue, and the party celebrated to such effect that Dickens and Forster had to pawn their gold watches to pay their return train fares. Back in London, Dickens crowed happily to William Hall: 'The Clock goes gloriously indeed. What will the wiseacres say to weekly issues *now*? And what will they say to any of those ten thousand things we shall do together to make 'em wink, and stagger in their shoes? Thank God for this great hit. I always had a quiet confidence in it, but I never expected *this*, at first.'[8]

In a matter of days Hall discovered that Dickens had wildly miscalculated. Anxious for relief from the monthly treadmill of serial writing, Dickens had persuaded himself that his public was equally eager for a change. He was quite wrong. The first number had done so well merely because his readers expected a successor to *Oliver Twist* and *Nickleby*; they fell away disappointed when they discovered that they were offered a desultory miscellany. Sales sagged alarmingly in the second week and disastrously in the third. Thackeray wrote to his mother that 'Dickens is sadly flat with his old *Clock* but still sells 50,000',[9] though that was barely enough, on the tight budget of weekly parts, to keep the *Clock* ticking. 'How Dickens, with his talents and experience, could have suffered such a *thing* to go forth under the sanction of his name', the *Monthly Review* asked in May, 'is to us a matter of unfeigned marvel.' The material was weak; the ideas—which had flowed so freely when Dickens first put the proposal to his accommodating publishers—were strained and poorly executed; and, as the poet and critic Thomas Hood pointed out later in the year, the main fault of the work was in its construction. 'The truth is', he said, 'the Author is rather too partial to one of the most unmanageable things in life or literature, a Club';[10] his readers plainly agreed with Hood.

For all his ebullience Dickens had half sensed that there was something wrong with the *Clock*. In March, a fortnight before the first number appeared, he realized that 'I must write it *all*, if we are to hope for that great success which we expect'. He had to tell his old friend Thomas Beard from the *Morning Chronicle*, to whom he had all but promised a post of assistant editor, that there was no place for him as there would be 'nobody to write to or transact business with, but me'.[11] But he had not expected such a fiasco; and neither he nor his publishers could afford a failure, for he now had a reputation at risk, and they stood to lose a great deal of money under the tough contract which was finally signed only four days before publication. Something had to be done at once to stop the mass desertion of disillusioned subscribers.

The first step was to revive Sam Weller and Pickwick as stop-gaps while the original plans for the *Clock* were scrapped and something else was found to replace them. There was no doubt what that should be. As soon as possible

Dickens had to produce another serial of the kind his readers so plainly wanted.

The breakdown of the *Clock* thus faced Dickens with greater problems than those he had sought to avoid. He had not wanted to start a new long-running tale and he was tired of meeting monthly deadlines. Now he had to devise a story at short notice, to begin writing it without any lead time to accumulate copy, and to send copy to the printer every week. He could not even fall back upon the much-planned *Barnaby Rudge*, for he was still arguing about that with Bentley. He reacted like a professional. He did not recriminate about the failure of the *Clock*, or complain about this fresh burden upon his imaginative energies. He created the story of Little Nell.

The idea had already come to him before the crisis. In February, when he and Forster visited Landor at Bath, he had conceived a 'little child-story'[12] which he thought might do for the third number of the *Clock*. The more he considered it the more he liked it. It was another variant on the theme of the betrayed innocent: in fusing the memory of Mary Hogarth with his own introspection, he realized that he could do much with a tale he first called *The Old Curiosity Dealer and the Child*. As quickly and as spontaneously as he had converted Seymour's sporting portfolio into *Pickwick*, and without even the minimal planning that he had put into *Oliver Twist* and *Nickleby*, Dickens expanded the simple sketch to meet his urgent need for a longer story. The first chapter appeared in the *Clock* on 25 April under the simpler title of *The Old Curiosity Shop*. It was immediately popular, and by June he was so confident about it that he abandoned his ambitious schemes for the *Clock* and gave the magazine over to the serial originally designed to save it from collapse.

The story which Dickens cobbled together in this emergency had little obvious merit. It was a weak and rambling tale about the ruin of a doting old gambler and his subsequent flight through the English countryside with his ailing and angelic grandchild; it was, indeed, a reversal of the plot of *Oliver Twist*, for Oliver rises to fortune while Little Nell declines to her fate. It read like a melodrama, complete with a villainous moneylender and other roles cast straight from the stage; it was padded out with comic turns and set-pieces; it was mawkish, it moralized about the greed for gold, and it hinted crudely at lust and sexual cruelty. Dickens was hard put to convert his stock parts into such vivid characters as Dick Swiveller, the Marchioness, Mrs. Jarley, Sally, and Sampson Brass, and to furnish them with patches of brilliant dialogue. In settling upon a pubescent girl for his heroine, however, Dickens had carried over from *Oliver Twist* the secret of its success— the curiously compelling, almost magical evocation of the bewilderment and fears of childhood; and as he described the confusing changes of scene and mood in the odyssey of Little Nell the story became more like a child's half-remembered dream populated by such nursery figures as Punch and Judy men, freaks, and waxworks. Once Dickens had translated his readers into that twilight world on the borders of memory and fairyland he held them there week after week, entranced by the struggle between the monstrous Quilp, a bogyman of restless destructiveness, and Little Nell, the spirit of goodness personified. Like Mary Hogarth, in dying at the threshold of adult life Little Nell became immortal, victorious over the terrors of night and the powers of evil.

In the first months of 1840 Dickens was in energetic good humour, and neither the fiasco of the *Clock* nor the need to press on with the bitter-sweet tragedy of *The Old Curiosity Shop* cramped his style. He was eager and busy, involved in life at every turn; and a recognized figure in the social scene. In May the Maclise portrait was shown at the Royal Academy. Bulwer and other men of standing invited him to dinner. Richard Monckton Milnes, the Tory M.P. and man of letters, asked him to breakfast—a fashion led by Samuel Rogers, whose morning occasions were admired for their brilliant talk and their influence on critical fashion. 'I never went out to breakfast in my life', Dickens replied, 'and am afraid to try how one feels under such circumstances; but I will be with you next Friday at eleven o'Clock for the purposes of small talk.'[13] He was more at ease now and a frequent attender at the very different salons of Lady Holland and Lady Blessington.

Lady Holland, an imperious, outspoken *grande dame* who had been 'cut' by respectable society because she had lived with the gentle Lord Holland before they were married, had long established her own distinguished circle. She had made Holland House the centre of wit and culture and her hospitality had acquired immense prestige. Marguerite Blessington was a flamboyant Irishwoman who had put herself outside respectability by her unconventional liaison with Alfred, Count d'Orsay, the handsome Frenchman who had been briefly married to her young stepdaughter; Thomas Carlyle called him the 'Phoebus Apollo of dandyism'. She was a dozen years older than d'Orsay and had been married twice. Her first husband was killed when he fell in a drunken state from a window in the King's Bench prison; her second, the Earl of Blessington, was immensely rich, with an annual income of £30,000. In 1829 he died in Paris and Lady Blessington soon returned to London. On a reduced income of £2,000 a year she set up an extravagant and Bohemian establishment at Gore House, Kensington, where d'Orsay eventually joined her. She supplemented her means by writing novels and editing gossipy beauty magazines. She was kindly and talented—as was d'Orsay, a competent artist who painted the last portrait of the Duke of Wellington and sketched Dickens in 1841—and together they entertained a brilliant group of politicians, painters, novelists, playwrights, and poets. Wellington was there, and so were the *émigré* Prince Louis Napoleon, Benjamin Disraeli, the witty Sydney Smith, Ainsworth, Bulwer, Forster, Monckton Milnes, Talfourd, and Landor.[14]

Dickens found them all thoroughly congenial, but much as he enjoyed sophisticated company, his happiest moments were spent with more intimate friends. He bombarded Beard, Maclise, and Forster with proposals for outings—dinners, steamer trips to Gravesend, an evening at Astley's circus. In May he amusingly described to Leigh Hunt an expedition with Maclise to Eel Pie Island, on the Thames at Twickenham, 'eating lamb chops, and drinking beer, and laughing like a coal-heaver'.[15] He was at the first night of Talfourd's gloomy new play, *Glencoe*—'Rehearsal yesterday, and cannot keep away today' he told Talfourd, '. . . what will become of *Humphrey's Clock*, I don't know'.[16]

On 1 June he took the family to Broadstairs, this time staying at 37 Albion Street. Within two hours of his arrival, he reported to Thomas Beard, 'the dining-parlour closet already displays a good array of bottles . . . the Spirits labelled "Gin", "Brandy", "Hollands", in autograph character—and the wine tasted and approved. The castors already boast mushroom ketchup, harvey, cayenne, and such like condiments; the writing table is set forth with a neatness peculiar to your estimable friend; and the furniture in all the rooms has been entirely re-arranged by the same extraordinary character. The sea is rolling away, like nothing but the sea, in front of the house, and there are two pretty little spare bedrooms waiting to be occupied.'[17] The next day he wrote to Maclise 'come to the bower which is shaded for you . . . COME!'[18] He was hoping to make headway with *The Old Curiosity Shop* and he was encouraged to hear from Forster that he thought well of it. 'I feel the story extremely myself, which I take to be a good sign; and am already warmly interested in it.'[19] He worked well and by 16 June he was writing to Thomas Mitton: 'We are flourishing exceedingly, and as brown as berries. I am up every morning at 7, and usually finish work for the day, before 2.'[20] Sometimes he drove himself harder. One day he told Forster that he had been writing for nearly eight hours and 'really dried myself up into a condition which would almost justify me in pitching off the cliff, head first'. But he was pleased with what he had done: 'if I had read it as anybody else's writing, I think I should have been very much struck'.[21]

Dickens was equally buoyed up by the prospect of a final release from his entanglements with Bentley. In February Bentley was still threatening legal action—either to compel him to deliver *Barnaby Rudge* or for damages if he failed to do so. 'The law,' Dickens told Macready, who felt that Dickens was in the wrong and was urging him to patch things up with Bentley, 'bad as it is, is more true and more to be trusted than such a hound. . . . If I were a builder or a stone-mason I might fulfil my contract with him, but write for him I really cannot unless I am forced and have no outlet for escape.'[22] He was fairly safe in his defiance. Bentley's lawyers thought poorly of the publisher's chances in court, and under their advice another attempt was made to settle the dispute through intermediaries—this time Forster spoke for Dickens and Bentley was represented by William Jerdan, editor of the *Literary Gazette*. An agreement was signed on 2 July. Once again Chapman and Hall had to find the money to finance a complicated scheme: their desire to become the sole publisher of Dickens was so strong that the expense seemed justified. Dickens was to pay Bentley £1,500 for his share of *Oliver Twist* and for releasing all rights in anything Dickens had published through him during their uneasy association. For another £750 Dickens was to get the Cruikshank plates and a thousand unsold copies of *Oliver Twist*. The money to buy out Bentley was to be loaned by Chapman and Hall and set off against a £3,000 advance for a six-month copyright on the still un-written *Barnaby Rudge*.[23]

Dickens thus wrenched himself free from the commitment to Bentley at no cost, for in the long run the copyrights he recovered were worth much more than he paid for them. And by this time Bentley was glad to see the back of him, though he knew that he was losing his most profitable author and that Dickens had evaded both his legal and moral obligations. The trouble between them had been as much a matter of personality as of law and publishing policy, for the two men had some of their worst traits in common. Both were proud, strong-willed, easily offended, and prone to self-justification; both were anxious about money and suspicious of being cheated. Dickens liked to patronize his publishers—Chapman and Hall had to provide balm for his ego as well as cheques for his bank—and Bentley wanted to patronize his authors. They were incompatible, and though Bentley held the contracts Dickens held the cards. He played them well, though scarcely with credit, and Bentley was at last beaten. Dickens was well aware of the debt he owed to Forster in conducting the tricky negotiations and he marked his appreciation when the agreement was signed by sending him a silver-mounted claret jug. 'Take it from my hand', Dickens wrote, '—filled to the brim and running over with truth and earnestness.'[24]

On his return to London at the beginning of July, Dickens was quickly drawn into the excitement over the hanging of Courvoisier at Newgate on 6 July. The case of Courvoisier, a Swiss valet who had murdered his master Lord William Russell, was tried at the Old Bailey in the middle of June and attracted considerable attention; Dickens had himself written a pseu-donymous letter to the *Morning Chronicle* while he was down at Broadstairs, protesting at the way in which the defence lawyer had handled the case and suggesting that he had maligned the character of innocent witnesses, even attempting to blame a female fellow servant. He was disgusted by the legal claptrap, and held no brief for Courvoisier, but in the general excitement he succumbed to curiosity and went off with his brother-in-law Henry Burnett and Maclise to rent a window overlooking the scaffold. The street was packed long before dawn: among the hawkers and pickpockets Dickens saw Thackeray and Monckton Milnes. 'I came away', Thackeray wrote in *Fraser's Magazine* next month, 'with a disgust for murder, but it was for *the murder I saw done.*' Thackeray felt 'ashamed and degraded at the brutal curiosity'[25] which took him to Newgate, and Dickens reacted in much the same way. Years later he vividly recalled the 'odious' crowd: 'No sorrow, no salutary terror, no abhorrence, no seriousness; nothing but ribaldry, debauchery, levity, drunkenness, and flaunting vice.' The effect on him and his friends was one of disgust and even pity for a vicious murderer: 'It was so loathsome, pitiful, and vile a sight, that the law appeared to be as bad as he, or worse; being very much the stronger, and shedding round it a far more dismal contagion.'[26]

The sight of Courvoisier's grim death helped to make Dickens a vigorous critic of capital punishment. Yet the impulse to watch Courvoisier drop was not a passing whim; he described the fascination of the gruesome business. The death penalty, he wrote, 'engenders a diseased sympathy—morbid and bad, but natural and often irresistible—among the well-conducted and gentle'.[27] He had often felt the perverted appeal of that emotion. It had lured him to the condemned cells of Newgate as a young reporter seeking copy for *Sketches by Boz.* It made him an addict to reports of murder cases in the newspapers. Its shadow fell so darkly across *Oliver Twist* that in January 1840 a magazine critic put him in the 'gallows-school' of novelists. And Thackeray noted in the February issue of *Fraser's* the emotional tones in which Dickens wrote about the underworld. The reader, Thackeray declared, was led 'breathless to watch all the crimes of Fagin, tenderly to deplore the errors of Nancy, to have for Bill Sikes a kind of pity and admiration, and an absolute love for the society of the Dodger'. Dickens was aware of this ambivalence, which ran like a dark vein through his fiction and his journalism. He called it 'the attraction of repulsion'. He knew it was a pathology; and he seems to have sensed its origins in fear, hostility, and guilt. Yet for all his declared distaste he was intrigued by it and he exploited it. Within a few months of the judicial murder of Courvoisier he brought the violence of *Barnaby Rudge* to its climax outside the same gate of Newgate, with the public hangman himself dangling in the noose.

Dickens was fascinated by crime. He was also attracted that summer by a psychic underworld, to which the new fad of mesmerism opened the door. One of the chief exponents of this hypnotic technique was Macready's doctor, Dr. John Elliotson, who was professor of medicine at the University of London. Elliotson was well qualified and competent, but his interest in the esoteric fringes of his profession—in mesmerism, phrenology, and abnormal psychology—made him suspect in the eyes of his more conventional colleagues. He began to practise hypnosis on his ward patients in the summer of 1837, and he was soon convinced that by this means he could relieve both physical and mental symptoms. In the following year he gave public exhibitions in the theatre of University College Hospital, and the interest these aroused led to talk of a 'mesmeric mania' among the educated public—and to growing opposition from the medical establishment, which thought hypnosis both fraudulent and improper. In September 1838 the *Lancet* denounced Elliotson's two most successful subjects as imposters, and he was instructed to abandon his demonstrations. By December the opposition was strong enough to force his resignation; and he thenceforth supported himself by private practice and authorship, continuing his demonstrations at his own house.[28]

Dickens went to one of these occasions with Macready, Cruikshank, and Ainsworth. He was always drawn to conjurers and impersonators, and he expected to find mesmerism a somewhat sensational form of parlour entertainment. It was, he discovered, something more. Elliotson claimed to reveal 'human nature in a new state', and Dickens found such a claim irresistible. He was soon on friendly terms with Elliotson: 'I should be untrue, both to him and myself, if I should shrink for a moment from saying that I am a believer', he wrote of Elliotson's work, 'and that I became so against all my preconceived opinions.'[29] When Elliotson was attacked for insulting public decency Dickens turned on the gossips who impugned his integrity: the criticism in the newspapers, he angrily told Macready, came fròm 'every rotten-hearted pander who has been beaten, kicked, and rolled in the kennel, yet struts it in the Editorial We once a week'.[30] And as evidence of his confidence he adopted Elliotson as his own doctor, referred friends to him for advice and help, and began to study hypnosis under his guidance.

In the summer of 1840 Elliotson invited Dickens to dinner to meet the Reverend Chauncy Hare Townshend, an accomplished poet and art collector who had published *Facts in Mesmerism* earlier that year. Townshend was anxious to hypnotize Dickens; but Dickens refused, for reasons he repeated in the following year, when Townshend asked him again. 'I am horribly hard at work', he said, 'and dare not be mesmerised, lest it should damage me at all. Even a day's headache would be a serious thing just now.'[31]

With Dickens work always came first, much as he enjoyed social distractions. Sometimes, however, unforeseen crises upset his schedule. 'I must go hard to work to make up what I have lost by being dutiful and going to see my father,' he told Cattermole in August, pressing him to speed up delivery of his illustrations.[32] In June he had received a complaining letter from John Dickens and, despite the discomforts and tedium of the journey, he decided to go down with Kate at the end of July. The 'Telegraph' to Exeter, he told Forster, was a 'monstrously dangerous coach. Coming down, we were *twice* as nearly over as you can conceive. The hills are very steep and the pace tremendous.' He found the house he had taken for his parents as enchanting as ever. When he saw the 'perfect little doll's house ... in the best possible order', he could not understand his father's complaints and wondered 'more than ever how he had the heart to write as he did'. Both parents, he told Forster, '*seem* perfectly contented and happy'.[33]

Although the family was annoying and irresponsible, Dickens was always anxiously loyal to his parents and his brothers, and he did all he could to help them settle in suitable jobs: he took particular care of Fred, who had just been appointed as a junior clerk in the Treasury. He dealt with close friends in the same warm-hearted style, even when they irritated him. During the summer of 1840 Macready was a frequent and welcome guest at the Dickens table while his wife and family were spending the summer down at Broadstairs. 'We hope that until we go to Broadstairs you will dine with us every Sunday when you are not better engaged. Is it a bargain?' he wrote to Macready.[34] On Sunday 12 August Macready, Maclise, and Forster were all dining at Devonshire Terrace. 'Forster got on to one of his headlong streams of talk', Macready noted in his diary, 'and waxed warm.'[35] Dickens was angered, Kate was reduced to tears, and Forster was asked to leave the house. He was detained at the door by Macready. Dickens, who 'could not answer for his temper under Forster's provocations', got himself under control and confessed that 'he had spoken in passion', but Forster could neither bring himself to leave nor accept this limited apology. He stood, in Macready's phrase, 'skimbling-skambling a parcel of unmeaning words', and then grudgingly and boorishly agreed to remain. 'I am very much grieved, and yet I am not penitent,' Dickens wrote to Macready next day. 'With all the regard I have for Forster ... there is no man, alive or dead, who tries his friends as he does.'[36] There was, moreover, no man on whom Dickens so heavily depended, and he was learning to take the rough side of Forster with the smooth. He was back at the dinner table on the following Sunday, and two days later as one of the many guests for the christening party of baby Kate. It was, Macready said, 'rather a noisy and uproarious day', though 'not so much *comme il faut* as I could have wished'.[37]

Dickens loved these large family parties and used any excuse for larks and celebrations. Seaside holidays were perfect occasions for jolly gatherings. At the end of August the household moved back to Broadstairs for five weeks. It was difficult to find a house to rent: 'the place is very full indeed', Dickens wrote to Thomas Mitton, 'and the people wildly rapacious and rearing up on their hind legs for money'.[38] As soon as he had found a place to stay—this time he took Lawn House, an attractive property right above the little harbour—he sent off invitations. 'Come down for a week ... come down for a month,' he told Maclise. 'It's charming, and the house a most brilliant success—far more comfortable than any we have had.'[39] Mitton's partner Charles Smithson had taken a neighbouring house and the two family parties played guessing games and charades, walked, danced, and bathed together. Dickens was in exuberant form. One evening they danced a quadrille at the end of the jetty at dusk, and Dickens, 'possessed with the demon of mischief', held the nineteen-year-old Eleanor Emma Picken in the rising tide until the salt water spoiled her silk dress. He pretended to be lovelorn for the older Amelia Thompson, conducting a semi-jocular and 'wholly nonsensical' flirtation with her. Then, with a sudden change of mood, his eyes would be like 'danger lamps' and the girls would run out of his way.[40] Dickens was stimulated to such merriment by visits from friends such as Mitton and Angus Fletcher. Mitton's good humour and laughter was infectious and he easily brought out the liveliest side of Dickens. Fletcher, who had been introduced by Macrone, was an eccentric Scots sculptor for whom Dickens had sat for a bust shown at the Academy in 1839. Fletcher's antics were even wilder than the heavy jocularity and practical joking of Dickens. He committed 'all manner of absurdities', Dickens told Maclise. 'Such a devil—such a bald, howling, fearful devil' who bathed in the buff and 'splashed like a fleet of Porpoises'.[41] He sometimes persuaded gullible bystanders that he was Dickens. His 'insane gambollings', Dickens believed, were one reason for the fast-running rumour that the novelist had become 'raving mad' and was confined to St. Luke's or Bedlam; Dickens was so upset by this report, indeed, and so determined publicly to assert that he was sane, that he insisted on publishing a denial in the preface to the bound half-yearly volume of *Master Humphrey's Clock*. Forster and his publishers with difficulty persuaded him to tone down the jocosely complicated text.

This half-yearly volume, yet another publishing innovation, came out at the beginning of October and Dickens dedicated it to Samuel Rogers, commending the 'generous and earnest feeling' of a man whose life showed 'active sympathy with the poorest and humblest of his kind'.[42] It was a landmark that Dickens invariably used as an excuse for a party. He had been hard put to meet the deadline, for he was suffering from an attack of facial neuralgia: 'I am as bad as Miss Squeers,' he told Chapman and Hall, 'screaming out loud all the time I write.'[43] Yet he had recovered in time to summon the 'Clock Corps'—the designers, printers, wood-cutters, and publishers—to dinner at Devonshire Terrace on 20 October. There were so many toasts that evening that Forster, who had made a prompt list before the evening began, simply rounded it off with the words 'And then Everybody proposes Everything'.[44]

The completion of *The Old Curiosity Shop*, however, was a less jolly business. Dickens had been persuaded by Forster that it was artistically necessary for Little Nell to die; but this was a closely guarded commercial secret; and as the eager readers were drawn on to the ending the circulation rose to over 100,000. The approach to the final scene was harrowing for him as well as for his public. 'You can't imagine (gravely I write and speak) how exhausted I am with yesterday's labours,' he told Forster. 'I went to bed last night utterly dispirited and done up. All night I have been pursued by the child; and this morning I am unrefreshed and miserable. I don't know what to do with myself.... I think the close of the story will be great.'[45] Dickens also recruited Maclise to do a suitable illustration, driving out to Hampstead with him to read the chapter and to walk: 'For Heaven's sake let us range the fields and get some freshness if it's only fresh rain.'[46]

Meanwhile, with misgivings, he had agreed to a dramatization at the Adelphi which gave nothing away. Frederick Yates, who had put on dramatic versions of *Oliver Twist* and *Nickleby*, was playing the demonic Quilp in a two-act burletta. Dickens told Macready that he hoped to prevent Yates 'making a greater atrocity than can be helped',[47] and he even devised comic business for the characters of Codlin and Short—played by acrobats— and a happy ending in which Quilp was routed and Nell married Dick Swiveller. Dickens hadn't the heart to go on the opening night; Fred took Kate instead. 'The thing may be better than I expect,' he told Thomas Mitton, 'but I have no faith in it at all.'[48] His name now had such pulling power that even this patent travesty of his unfinished tale was a success with the critics and the public.

By the end of November Dickens had worked himself into a morbid mood and communicated it to his readers. He told Chapman and Hall that he was 'inundated with imploring letters recommending poor Little Nell to mercy'.[49] And the surge of sentiment, he told Forster in a letter seeking to patch up the quarrel with Ainsworth, had reminded him 'of many old kindnesses' and made him regret that 'men who really liked each other should waste life at arm's length'.[50] Except for a necessary break over Christmas, and a New Year's Eve party 'with forfeits and such like exercises',[51] he shunned distractions. The last episode 'is such a painful task to me that

I must concentrate myself upon it tooth and nail', he told William Harness.[52] And he said much the same to Forster: 'I am afraid of disturbing the state I have been trying to get into, and having to fetch it all back again.'[53]

Dickens was so caught up in the lachrymose fantasy that he was surprisingly ungenerous about a real tragedy. On 25 November Macready's three-year-old daughter Joan died suddenly of the consumption that afflicted his whole family. Forster, who was the child's godfather, was striken with sorrow and spent the week mourning with the disconsolate Macready. 'I vow to God that if you had seen Forster last night', Dickens wrote on 27 November to Maclise, 'you would have supposed our Dear Friend was dead himself—in such an amazing display of grief did he indulge.'[54] Dickens, however, was equally indulgent about his own feelings. 'I am breaking my heart over this story,' he told Cattermole at the end of December when he sent his instructions for the final illustrations, 'and cannot bear to finish it.'[55] A few days later he told Macready: 'I am slowly murdering that poor child, and grow wretched over it. It wrings my heart. Yet it must be.'[56] Macready, still deeply upset by his own loss, begged Dickens to spare Little Nell. 'I never have read printed words that gave me so much pain,' he wrote in his diary on 22 January. 'I could not weep for some time. Sensation, sufferings have returned to me, that are terrible to awaken....'[57] And as Dickens brought his tale to its sentimental close he found his emotions about Nell evoking memories of Mary Hogarth. 'Nobody will miss her like I shall,' he wrote to Forster in almost the same terms as he had written when Mary died. 'It is such a very painful thing to me, that I really cannot express my sorrow. Old wounds bleed afresh when I only think of the way of doing it. Dear Mary died yesterday when I think of this sad story.'[58] The catharsis was deliberate. 'I resolved to try and do something which might be read by people about whom Death had been,' he told Forster, 'with a softened feeling, and with consolation.'[59]

Dickens finished *The Old Curiosity Shop* in the middle of January 1841, writing on until four in the morning. 'It makes me very melancholy to think that all these people are lost to me forever, and I feel as if I never could become attached to any new set of characters,'[60] he told Forster. The final drama of *The Old Curiosity Shop* touched the emotions of his readers to release feelings which often remained unexpressed. Macready, returning home from the theatre where he was playing in Bulwer's new comedy *Money*, saw Cattermole's print of Nell on her deathbed in a bookseller's window and broke down. Dickens himself was moved to write his appreciation to Cattermole: 'Believe me that this is *the very first time* any designs for what I have written have touched and moved me, and caused me to feel that they expressed the idea I had in my mind.'[61] When Forster read the final chapter he wrote next day to say how moved he was: 'I think it is your literary master-piece.' He felt Nell's death 'as a kind of discipline of feeling and emotion which would do me lasting good ... if anything could have increased my affection for you, this would have done it'.[62]

Some critics were cynical. Edward Fitzgerald thought it 'sham pathos'; a religious reviewer felt the subject of child mortality was so familiar to 'half the families of England' that it should not be exploited for 'a work of amuse-ment, and amid dreamy sentiment'.[63] Yet Dickens had achieved the effect he intended. Dr. Elliotson wrote to say that he 'cried a deluge ... we all agreed that you must be a good man to be able to write thus'.[64] Captain Basil Hall, the author and traveller, described the reading of the last number to his assembled family: 'All the party were in deep affliction—weeping and sobbing as if their hearts were breaking.'[65] Bulwer wrote to tell Forster that 'it perfectly fascinated me. I think it contains patches of the most exquisite truth and poetry.'[66] Dickens had known since *Pickwick* that he could make his readers laugh and since *Oliver Twist* that he could make them cry. With the final parts of *The Old Curiosity Shop* he achieved something more. He made his readers respond like converts at a revival meeting, sharing the preacher's emotional experience. 'I think I shall always like it better than anything I have done or may do,' he wrote in retrospect.[67]

With the strains of winding up the tale of Little Nell behind him, Dickens was able to relax again. He began going to Cattermole's house at Clapham for the dinners of a group which called itself the 'Portwiners'—the familar set of Forster, Thackeray, Macready, Maclise, and also Bulwer, the fashion-able painters Charles and Edwin Landseer, and the playwright Mark Lemon. Apart from family occasions Kate played almost no part in this lively social life for she was again pregnant. 'Our third child can't walk yet, and here is a fourth upon her heels,'[68] Dickens wrote to Basil Hall. On 8 February 1841, after a difficult confinement, she gave birth to 'a jolly boy',[69] as he told Mitton. They called him Walter Landor after one of his godfathers. Dr. Elliotson was the other.

Dickens now settled down to *Barnaby Rudge* in earnest, but it was still far from easy going. All his interest remained with the characters of *The Old Curiosity Shop*, Kate was still unwell, and he was distracted by pressing social engagements. He confided his difficulties to Forster: 'I didn't stir out yesterday, but sat and *thought* all day; not writing a line. . . . I was unutterably and impossible-to-form-an-idea–of–ably miserable.' But he was generally in good spirits and optimistic that he would make something of the new work. 'I have gone to work this morning in good twig, strong hope, and cheerful spirits,' he told Forster.[70] As soon as Kate was well enough to travel he took her down to the Old Ship at Brighton, 'getting out of harm's way',[71] as he told Forster, to grind on at the tale. When they returned at the beginning of March he had family problems. He failed to persuade the New Zealand Company to take on his younger brother Alfred as a surveyor now that he had finished his apprenticeship. And he also failed to induce his father to live abroad on a remittance.

John Dickens had lately been running into debts to such an extent that Dickens was driven publicly to repudiate him. On 8 March he published an advertisement in all the main newspapers which described 'certain persons bearing, or purporting to bear the surname' of Dickens who had been issuing promissory notes payable at Devonshire Terrace or at the office of Chapman and Hall. Henceforth, 'Charles Dickens will not discharge ... any debt ... save those of his own or of his wife's contracting'. Then in March his pet raven died and, suspicious that it had been poisoned by a malicious butcher, he arranged a post-mortem on the bird. A merry social gathering, however, always helped to dispel worries of this kind, and in April he arranged a *Clock* dinner for the half-yearly volume. There would be 'songs breaking out in unexpected places—and many other moral Vesuviuses of that nature', Dickens promised in his invitation to Edward Majoribanks, the partner in Coutts Bank who looked after his financial affairs.[72]

In April he entertained Lord Jeffrey, the Scots judge and famous editor of the *Edinburgh Review*, who had long been an admirer of his work and had been reduced to tears by *The Old Curiosity Shop*. Although Francis Jeffrey was nearly seventy and belonged to a different literary generation, a warm friendship sprang up between the two men, Jeffrey persuading Dickens to visit Scotland in the summer and offering to take the chair himself at a civic dinner on 25 June. Dickens wrote at once to tell Angus Fletcher of the invitation. 'In the matter of the dinner', he wrote, 'I feel bound to say—stop nothing. You know my "quiet ways", but coming Northward really as an acknowledgement of the kind opinion of the Northern people ... I would not for the world reject any compliment they, or any of them, sought to offer me.'[73]

There was much excitement about the visit to Edinburgh. Kate 'will be mad to see the house she was born in', Dickens told Angus Fletcher, and he declared that he was 'on the highest crag of expectation'.[74] They travelled by rail as far as Darlington and posted on from there. 'The hotel is perfectly besieged,' he wrote to Forster the day after their arrival, describing the Scottish notabilities who had called.[75] He reported the civic dinner as 'the most brilliant affair you can conceive' and wrote ecstatically to Forster, Chapman and Hall, to Cattermole, and other friends.[76] On 29 June the town council voted him the freedom of the city. Lunches, dinners, and receptions for the best of Edinburgh society crowded on him thickly, and although he enjoyed being lionized he was beginning to feel by the end of the month that 'there is no place like home; and that I thank God most heartily for having given me a quiet spirit, and a heart that won't hold many people. I sigh for Devonshire-terrace and Broadstairs, for battledore and shuttlecock.'[77]

He was delighted with his triumph, but he did not forget that he had work to do. 'I am a poor Slave of the Lamp,' he reminded Lord Jeffrey, who had been too ill to chair the dinner, 'and tomorrow it will have been rubbed thrice, with no response from me.... I must fly for my life—or for my living, which is the same thing.'[78] With Angus Fletcher for a guide Dickens and Kate escaped for a short tour of the Highlands; the necessary instalment of *Barnaby Rudge* was completed along the way and dispatched to Forster, together with long accounts of the eccentric Fletcher—whom he had found disconcerting at Broadstairs but of service in the bleak mountain inns—and anecdotes of their travels through the misty scenery. Dickens, now homesick for his intimates, refused a public dinner in Glasgow and hurried on to London. 'The only thing I felt at the Edinburgh Dinner', he wrote to Maclise from Inveraray on 12 July, 'was that except for Kate there was nobody I cared for there to see.'[79]

Dickens was quick to resume work after his Scottish trip. 'I must stick to it, like wax, pitch, glue, cement,' he wrote to Forster on 26 July. 'Pity and protect The Slave.'[80] There was, all the same, time for a long-promised expedition with Kate, the Macreadys, Stanfields, Forster, Maclise, and Cattermole; the party went off for the day in two carriages to visit the house and grounds of Belvedere, down the Kent bank of the Thames, and returned to dine at Greenwich with other friends, including Elliotson.

At the beginning of August, before Dickens left for the family holiday at Broadstairs, he had a touchy exchange with Chapman and Hall with whom he had always been on cordial terms. Their solicitor had sent him a peremptory letter asking for a formal deed, rather than the personal letter in which he acknowledged his debt for the money advanced to buy out Bentley's interest. Sensitive on the matter of deeds and personal honour, he refused to sign it; even when he was induced to endorse a modified version he still felt so aggrieved that he wrote a curt letter to his publishers asking for the return of the original letter in which he had warmly thanked them for the loan. But as soon as Chapman and Hall sent a mollifying letter, offering to return the offending bond, Dickens unbent: 'my sentiments have undergone a complete change', he wrote with pleasure on 3 August. The 'spirit of confidence', shaken by a legalism that had reminded him of the way Bentley clung to the letter of the law, had been restored.[81]

'I am warming up very much about *Barnaby*,' Dickens wrote to Forster from Broadstairs.[82] He had at last worked through the first part of the novel, so long planned and so delayed, producing a gloomy prologue shot through with repressed hatred and containing an unsolved murder, two lovers kept apart by a bitter family feud, mysterious strangers, a half-witted hero, and other melodramatic devices in the style of Scott and Ainsworth; and he was now caught by the excitement of the anti-Catholic disorders of 1780, which provided the spectacular climax to the plot. 'I think I can make a better riot than Lord George Gordon did,' he wrote, and as he loosed anarchy and arson on to the streets of London he seemed to feel himself part of these wild events. 'I have just burnt into Newgate,' he told Forster early in September, when he had come to the passage in which that grim prison is stormed like the Bastille, 'and am going in the next number to tear the prisoners out by the hair of their heads.'[83] Always fascinated as well as frightened by violence, and tempted by fantasies of revenge, Dickens could not condemn the rioters out of hand—he saw them as victims, manipulated by sinister figures in the shadows, whose religious bigotry was 'begotten of intolerence and persecution ... senseless, besotted, inveterate and unmerciful'.[84] He even showed some sympathy for the maligned leader of the mob. 'Say what you please of Gordon,' Dickens replied when Forster compained that he was too favourable to the fanatic Protestant who gave his name to the disorders, 'he must have been at heart a kind man, and a lover of the despised and rejected, after his own fashion. ... He always spoke on the people's side, and tried against his muddled brains to expose the profligacy of both parties.'[85] And although the novel ends with the restoration of order—after the troops have been called in—Dickens is characteristically scornful of the politicians and judges; and nominates Dennis the public hangman, who ends upon his own gallows, as the morbidly ironic spokesman for the constitutional proprieties.

In this rebellion of forty thousand outcasts, gaolbirds, and fugitives from Bedlam, the characters of the novel are whirled away like corks in a flood to a variety of miserable fates—even the grotesques lack real humour. The melancholic Haredale sees his house burnt down, and after killing the villainous Sir John Chester in a duel he flees to Europe and dies in a monastery. Chester's natural son Hugh, one of the leaders of the riot, is hanged; so is Rudge, the father of the half-witted Barnaby, who himself only gets a last-minute reprieve; Sim Tappertit loses both his legs, Joe Willet comes back from the American Revolution without an arm, and the stony-hearted Miggs becomes a female turnkey at the Bridewell prison. Emma Haredale and Edward Chester, a pallid pair of lovers, survive to marry and emigrate; and only the charming Dolly Varden and her bluffly honest father Gabriel— whom Dickens had originally intended as the central personage of the story—lead sane and kindly lives. It was not so much a sad story as a dark and angry one; much of its action, indeed, takes place at night and Dickens used his nocturnal knowledge of London to great effect. And it is instinct with powerful hatreds which lead to personal ruin and public havoc. 'Down with everybody,' the rioters cry, 'down with everything!' They are blindly demanding 'an altered state of society'.

That was the moral of those dreadful days for Dickens. He did not know much history, but he had a sense of events. He had gone to the British Museum for background material, and he probably drew upon an earlier book by Thomas Gaspey, who had worked on the *Evening Chronicle*. But he had also been influenced by the dramatic scenes in Carlyle's *French Revolution*, which had appeared in the years since he first planned this novel; and in any case the riots he was describing had happened only sixty years before, almost within common memory. All these sources had been woven into a stark analogy. Gordon had lived, Dickens said, in a politically wicked time, and his anti-Catholic agitation had been the focus of a dozen discontents, from squalor and corruption to the stresses caused by the American War of Independence; and such an outbreak could happen again, in the distressed decade that became known as the Hungry Forties. There was already a new wave of anti-Catholic feeling, stirred by evangelical Protestants and appealing directly to workingmen; and 'No Popery', as one character in *Barnaby* mistakenly shouts, might well become a cry of 'No Property!' There had lately been Chartist riots in Sheffield and Birmingham; at Newport there had been an abortive rising to free Chartist prisoners; and as Dickens wrote there were much publicized strikes and Poor Law disorders in the industrial north. The novel that he had first conceived as a historical romance had become a blazing tract on what Thomas Carlyle called the Condition of England question.

Carlyle, indeed, had helped to shape that question in the mind of Dickens. A dour, indignant puritan, Carlyle had made his reputation with his criticisms of commercial society in *Sartor Resartus* and his brilliant use of *The French Revolution* to preach a message of doom and regeneration. Though he had thought little of *Pickwick*—a 'thinner wash ... was never offered to the human palate'[86]—when he met Dickens at dinner in March 1840 he was more generous. Dickens, he noted, was 'a quiet, shrewd-looking, little fellow, who seems to guess pretty well what he is and what others are'.[87] Dickens already admired him, and shared his hatred of hypocrisy and his feeling that society must be restored by moral passion rather than economic principles. From Carlyle's *Chartism*, which argued that the agitation for the People's Charter was a just reaction to cruelty, injustice, and incompetence, Dickens caught the political mood which underlay *Barnaby*, and led him to the same conclusion—there might have to be an apocalyptic cleansing of the old world before reason and righteousness could make a new beginning.

'By Jove how radical I am getting,' he exclaimed to Forster in August 1841. 'I wax stronger and stronger in the true principles every day.'[88] In that mood he had just written three rhymed lampoons, published in the *Examiner*, which attacked the Tories. 'The Fine Old English Gentlemen', one of them ran, garnished their laws 'with gibbets, whips and chains ... fine old English penalties, and fine old English pains.'[89]

Dickens was radically inclined by conviction and temperament, but he was no party man; and he had little confidence in a party system that he thought was dominated by reactionaries, self-seekers, and time-servers, while public-spirited men in both the Commons and the Lords were doomed to frustration. In May, when the fall of Lord Melbourne's government led to a general election and the return of the Tories under Sir Robert Peel, Dickens was himself asked to stand as the running-mate of his friend Talfourd in the double-member seat at Reading. He refused on the grounds that he could not afford the heavy expenses. It was hinted that the outgoing administration so valued his name that the money might be found. He again declined: such support would compromise his independence.

He strongly approved, for instance, the refusal of Lord Ashley to take office under Peel because the new Prime Minister would not commit himself to legislation protecting children in mines and factories. In August 1840 Ashley had persuaded the government to set up a four-man commission to investigate the horrifying conditions in which children were employed. When Dickens read Ashley's speech he told Dr. Southwood Smith, the sanitary reformer who was one of the commissioners, that 'I could not forbear ... cursing the present system and its fatal effects in keeping down thousands upon thousands of God's images.'[90] It was a theme that much appealed to him and he promised 'a most striking and remarkable' article on it to Macvey Napier, who had succeeded Francis Jeffrey as editor of the *Edinburgh Review*. On 8 August, however, he had to tell Napier that the report was delayed and that its sensational revelations were confidential until it had been presented to Parliament. When it was debated Ashley noted thankfully in his diary that there was deep public disgust at 'such a mass of sin and cruelty'.[91]

The Dickens family spent all August and September at Broadstairs, and as usual relatives and friends filled up the spare beds or roomed near by; Dickens even brought his errant father and mother up from Devon for the holiday. Fanny and her husband were also invited; and so was his other sister, Letitia, who in 1837 had married Henry Austin, a public-spirited civil engineer whom Dickens had known as long ago as the days when they were both callers at the Beadnell house. Dickens was a most open-handed man with such invitations, energetic at organizing walks, sailing trips, party games, and dancing; there was nothing he enjoyed better than the role of master of ceremonies, and no outlet for his exuberant drive to dominate all around him that he found more satisfying than the entertainment of friends.

He was in a cheerful mood all through the long holiday, though the sales of the *Clock* had fallen away as *Barnaby Rudge* followed *The Old Curiosity Shop*. The critics were disappointed, comparing his historical novel unfavourably with the work of Scott. When John Ruskin saw the advertisement for *Barnaby Rudge* he wrote that he hoped for better things from it than from the 'diseased extravagance' of *The Old Curiosity Shop*, but afterwards he declared that it was 'a stupid novel'.[92] Edgar Allan Poe, who was interested in the murder mystery, complained that the riots were an unnecessary distraction and that Dickens had not done the book 'so thoroughly well as his high and just reputation would demand'.[93] And Forster conceded that the story had serious narrative defects. Dickens himself was more concerned by the collapse of the original scheme for the *Clock*, underlined by Cattermole's defection on the grounds that illustrations detracted from his serious work without bringing much financial reward, and he had realized that the weekly numbers were too much of a strain. 'I cannot bear these jerky confidences which are no sooner begun than ended,' he told his readers.[94] The obvious remedy was to revert to a conventional serial in monthly parts, and on 20 August he went up to London to see Forster and his publishers.

It was provisionally agreed that the new work should be launched by Chapman and Hall in March 1842. The next day, as Dickens walked round Lincoln's Inn with Forster before they dined with Chapman and Hall, he confessed that he was afraid that he might spoil his success by repetition. Scott had ruined his best work, he told Mitton, *'because he never left off'*. Would it not be better to allow a pause and then come out with a complete three-decker a year later which might 'put the town in a blaze again'?[95] That evening Forster had to break the new proposal to the partners, who were cheerfully expecting some indication of the new serial, and to ask them how much they would give for the half-copyright in addition to an allowance of £500 every quarter. They were dumbfounded. When Chapman reflected, he said he thought that in the short run Dickens was wrong but he might well be right in the long run. Hall still hoped for a new run of monthly parts rather than a complete novel at the end of the proposed sabbatical. Forster was uneasy about the new plan, feeling that Dickens, with his restless nature, needed a firmer arrangement.

During the next three weeks there was more discussion. On 7 September the new contract was signed. It was agreed that Dickens could have a break from writing, but Hall had also carried his point: the new work would be a serial, starting in the following November; during the next fourteen months Dickens was to receive £150 a month as an advance on a three-quarters share of the profits; and as soon as publication began he was to get £200 a month—and these payments were to count as an expense to be met before profits were calculated.[96] It was an even better bargain than before. Dickens was delighted, telling Mitton that 'for a year I am a free man',[97] and the prospect of release induced a holiday spirit. 'I am in an exquisitely lazy state,' he told Forster, 'bathing, walking, reading, lying in the sun, doing everything but working.'[98]

When Dickens first planned the *Clock* he had casually proposed that he would go to America and write some travel notes. He had always found the democratic temper of the New World an appealing prospect, and his curiosity had been aroused by reports from visitors to the United States who ridiculed its oddities and extravagances, and exposed the brash promotions of its frontier. In 1837, for instance, a Boston speculator named Darius B. Holbrook had drawn many English investors into his fraudulent Cairo City and Canal Company—a land scheme on a mosquito-ridden swamp of the Mississippi.[99] In 1838 Dickens had informed an inquiring American publisher that he hoped to go over 'before long'.[100] 'Have a passage taken ready for 'Merrika', Tony Weller had said to Sam in a revealing topical reference in *Pickwick Papers*, 'and then let him come back and write a book about the 'Merrikans as'll pay all his expenses and more, if he blows 'em up enough.' By 1841 Dickens had found the time and money to do so. 'I am still haunted by visions of America, night and day,' he told Forster while he was finally making up his mind.[101] He had been greatly encouraged by an agreeable correspondence with Washington Irving, who had sent a letter in April which warmly praised his work. 'There is no living writer', he told Irving, 'whose approbation I should feel so proud to earn,'[102] and he felt the flattering notice of such an eminent American was a good augury. Irving, he told William Hall on 14 September after another exchange of letters, 'writes me that if I went, it would be such a triumph from one end of the States to the other, as was never known in any Nation'.[103]

During the next few days Dickens weighed the prospects against the problems, and by 19 September the matter was settled. 'I HAVE MADE UP MY MIND (WITH GOD'S LEAVE) TO GO TO AMERICA' he wrote to Forster.[104] Kate was reluctant; when he first mooted the idea he reported to Forster that she 'cries dismally if I mention the subject',[105] and she still persisted in her objections. She did not want him to go alone; she did not wish to go and leave the children; and she did not like the idea of transporting the whole family across the Atlantic. Uncertain what to do, Dickens decided to consult Macready as a family man who had been to America. He was, he wrote to his friend on 21 September, 'sorely tossed and tumbled on a moral ocean' of doubt.[106] Macready advised him not to take the children, but Dickens needed to talk it over and he at once went up from Broadstairs and called that night on Macready. 'The American preliminaries are necessarily startling', he explained to Forster, 'and, to a gentleman of my temperament, destroy rest, sleep, appetite, and work, unless definitely arranged.'[107] Macready wrote Kate a warm and encouraging letter urging her to accept what '*is a duty and must be a source of happiness*', and promised 'every duty of friendship in our care for and attention to your children'.[108]

Kate liked and respected Macready and his kind advice reconciled her to the idea. She even talked about it 'quite gaily' Dickens told Fred, who was to look after things while they were away. And once she had agreed he went ahead with his plans. They were to travel with only one servant, Kate's maid Anne Brown, whom Dickens described to Macready as 'a moral cork jacket'.[109] They were to cross the Atlantic in a small steamer in midwinter, sailing from Liverpool on 4 January. 'I can hardly believe I am coming,' Dickens wrote to Washington Irving on 28 September.[110] His study, a visiting American journalist noticed that autumn, was 'blazing with highly-coloured maps of the United States',[111] and he became an avid reader of such travellers' tales of the New World as Fanny Trollope's *Domestic Manners of the Americans*, Captain Marryat's diary, and Harriet Martineau's prosy *Society in America*. Kate, meanwhile, asked Maclise to make a drawing of the children to carry with them, and since arrangements had been made to let Devonshire Terrace, she lodged them in Osnaburgh Street under the supervision of Fred and near to the Macreadys. There were also letters to write, introductions to be arranged, and a £5,000 insurance to be effected. The Eagle Insurance Company, Dickens told Thomas Mitton, 'were very particular in requiring an emphatic contradiction of the mad story'.[112]

The insurance company was less particular about the operation on 8 October when Dickens had a fistula removed. The surgeon, Frederick Salmon, was a specialist of such skill and reputation that his assurance of a complete recovery was sufficient. It was a painful experience—'the cutting out root and branch of a disease caused by working over much', Dickens wrote to Thomas Beard four days after this 'cruel operation'.[113] The last pages of *Barnaby Rudge* had yet to be written and the surgeon's knife, Dickens told Lady Blessington, 'is a bad sharpener of the pen'.[114]

He was still poorly when Kate's brother George died on 24 October, and he felt obliged to offer the Hogarth family the space next to Mary's grave which he had reserved for himself. 'The desire to be buried next her is as strong upon me now, as it was five years ago,' he confided to Forster; 'and *I know* (for I don't think there ever was love like that I bear her) that it will never diminish.' And when the grave was opened he went to the cemetery to look again at her coffin: 'coming so suddenly, and after being ill, it disturbs me more than it ought'.[115] Forster later described these few weeks as 'the greatest trial of his life ... when illness, sorrow and the writing of a novel coincided'.[116] The episode had so vividly awakened the memory of Mary, Dickens confessed to Forster, that it seemed 'like losing her a second time'.[117] After three weeks of misery he went down to the White Hart at Windsor to recuperate and finish off *Barnaby Rudge*.

By the middle of November Dickens was getting 'stout and hearty'[118] and was able to walk about Windsor Park as vigorously as ever. The prospect of the American tour was a tonic, and he reported to Forster at the end of November that he was back in trim, 'bolt upright, staunch at the knees, a deep sleeper, a hearty eater, a good laugher'.[119] Before he left he went to Drury Lane, where Macready opened in *The Merchant of Venice* with 'a brilliant triumph' on 27 December. 'I have always expected one, as you know,' he wrote the next day, 'but nobody could have imagined the reality.'[120] Once again Macready was launched upon a management, like that at Covent Garden, which combined Shakespearian splendour and financial disaster.

In the preface to the *Clock* Dickens confided his plans to his readers as though they were personal friends. 'I have decided, in January next, to pay a visit to America. The pleasure I anticipate from this realization of a wish I have long entertained ... is subdued by the reflection that it must separate us for a longer time than other circumstances would have rendered necessary.' It was clearly hard for him to leave his public, but he promised 'another tale of English life and manners' on his return. It was harder still to leave his children and such intimates as Forster, Macready, and Maclise. For the first time in his life he was going away from home for a long time and for an immense distance. And yet the feeling of impending change and the prospect of new sensations buoyed him up. 'I cannot describe to you the glow into which I rise', he wrote to Gaylord Clark, the editor of the American *Knickerbocker Magazine*, 'when I think of the wonders that await us, and all the interest I am sure I shall have in your mighty land.'[121]

7

A Kind of Queen and Albert

DICKENS and Kate sailed for Boston on the *Britannia* on 4 January 1842. Steam was still as much a novelty at sea as on the land: only two other British paddle-steamers had crossed the Atlantic before the maiden voyage of the *Britannia* in 1840. They were small—the *Britannia* was only 1,135 tons—and the mixture of sails and steam meant a risk of fire. The crossing was hazardous at any time, and dangerous in mid-winter; but if all went well it was fast. The steamers could make over eight knots and reach Boston in about eighteen days.

A lively party went up to Liverpool to see the *Britannia* sail. Forster was there, of course; so were Angus Fletcher and Fanny Burnett. Dickens was aglow with excitement and anticipation, and even the reluctant Kate was in 'glorious spirits'[1] despite an attack of toothache. Forster was impressed by her cheerfulness about the whole thing. 'Never saw anything better,' he reported to Maclise. 'She deserves to be what you know she is so emphatically called—the Beloved.'[2] The day before sailing they all went on board to inspect the ship and then to a farewell dinner at the Adelphi Hotel. The advertisements had given Dickens an impression of spaciousness and he was taken aback when he saw the tiny cabin. Telling Maclise of its 'wild absurdity', he compared it unfavourably to a cab. 'There are two horse-hair seats in it, fixed to the wall. . . . Either would serve for a kettle holder. The beds . . . might both be sent to you per post, with one additional stamp. The pillows are no thicker than crumpets.'[3] The saloon, which had to cater for eighty-six passengers, was little better. It was like 'a gigantic hearse with windows in the sides' and 'a melancholy stove'[4] at one end. But Dickens was in such a good mood that he saw the comic side of this cramped accommodation, telling Mitton that he 'laughed so much at its ludicrous proportions, that you might have heard me all over the ship'.[5]

'The luggage is all aboard: and tomorrow at 2 will be the saddest goodbye I have ever said in my life,'[6] Forster wrote to Maclise. Next day Dickens went ashore for a last carouse at the hotel. The ship was ready to sail before the jolly boat drew alongside and the group of friends had a stirrup cup with the captain before the last goodbye.

The officers, Dickens wrote to his brother Fred before sailing, expected a very fine passage: 'God send they may be right.'[7] They were wrong, for the *Britannia* ran into the worst storm they had experienced. 'I never expected to see the day again, and resigned myself to God as well as I could,' Dickens reported to Forster. It was a miserable voyage. The tiny cabin was uncomfortable but the saloon was worse; 'the noise, the smell, and the closeness being quite intolerable'. Card-playing was one of the few distractions, but 'we are all flung from our seats, roll out at different doors, and keep on rolling until we are picked up by stewards';[8] winners at whist, Dickens reported, stuck their tricks in a pocket to save the cards from scattering. There was worse to come. As the ship ran into Halifax harbour at night it struck on a mudbank with breakers all round. Some of the crew began to strip to swim ashore—the lifeboat had been smashed during the storm—and distress flares were burnt. It was three in the morning before the excitement died down. Kate, who was suffering badly from toothache and seasickness, wrote to Fanny about their 'dreadful' voyage: 'I was nearly distracted with terror, and don't know what I should have done had it not been for the great kindness and composure of my dear Charles.'[9]

During the brief stay in Halifax Dickens went ashore with the ship's doctor for fresh oysters and was waylaid by a breathless man who announced himself as the Speaker of the House of Assembly. A carriage was sent to fetch Kate, and Dickens was taken to visit the Governor, Lord Falkland, and brought on to the legislature. 'I wish you could have seen the crowds cheering the inimitable in the streets,' Dickens wrote to Forster next day. 'I wish you could have seen judges, law-officers, bishops and law-makers welcoming the inimitable. I wish you could have seen the inimitable shown to a great elbow-chair by the Speaker's throne....'[10]

Dickens was flattered and amused by such a reception. He was only thirty but he was clearly a celebrity, received as clamorously in the cold provincial streets of Nova Scotia as in Scotland. He was surprised by such acclaim, but he was quite taken aback by the frenzied excitement of his welcome in Boston two days later. It was in the afternoon of Saturday 22 January that the *Britannia* worked itself into the narrow Cunard pier in Boston. 'No sooner was it known that the steamer with Dickens on board was in sight', the poet R. H. Dana Sr. wrote to a friend, 'than the Town was pouring itself out upon the wharf.'[11] Before the ship was moored, Dickens reported to Forster, 'a dozen men came leaping on board at the peril of their lives', and he was astonished to discover they were newspaper editors, anxious to interview him 'and beginning to shake hands like madmen'.[12] One from the *Boston Transcript*, a Dr. Palmer, learnt that Dickens had no hotel reservations and he ran off at once to order rooms and dinner at the Tremont

House, the finest hotel in Boston—'a trifle smaller than Finsbury-Square'[13] was Dickens's description. All the hackneys on the wharf wanted the patronage of Boz. They were disappointed. Francis Alexander, the portrait painter for whom Dickens had already promised to sit, had a cab waiting to carry the English visitors to the hotel.

One of those who saw Dickens arrive was James Fields, a young Boston publisher. 'He ran, or rather flew up the steps of the hotel, and sprang into the hall,' Fields recalled. 'Here we are,' he shouted when several gentlemen came forward to greet him. 'He seemed on fire with curiosity and alive as I never saw mortal before. From top to toe every fibre of his body was un-restrained and alert.' That evening Dickens refused other invitations and supped alone with the young Earl of Mulgrave, a fellow passenger who was staying in Boston a few days on his way to join his regiment in Canada, and at midnight they set out to explore Boston. Fields and his friends fol-lowed. It was a freezing night with a full moon. Dickens, muffled up in a shaggy fur coat, ran over the shining snow and 'kept up one continual shout of uproarious laughter as he went rapidly forward, reading the signs on the shops, and observing the "architecture" of the new country into which he had dropped as if from the clouds'.[14]

Boston, some sixty years after the War of Independence, was a prosperous city of 150,000 people. The arrival of Dickens was treated as a public gala: everyone was curious to meet the celebrated Boz, and the hotel was besieged with callers. He had been given letters of introduction by Edward Everett, a leading Bostonian who was then American Minister in England, but they were scarcely needed. After a quiet week-end—an invitation to hear the well-known Unitarian minister Dr. William Ellery Channing was declined because of 'the fatigues of the Voyage' and 'no change of dress: our luggage being still on board'[15]—Dickens was plunged into a continual social whirl. Charles Sumner, then a rising young lawyer and a spokesman of anti-slavery sentiment in Boston, was one of the first to meet Dickens. 'We are on tiptoe to see who shall catch the first view of Dickens above the wave,' he had written to Lord Morpeth a few days before his arrival.[16] Sumner took it upon himself to show Dickens the sights of Boston and to introduce him to some of its dignitaries. On that first Monday he and the British consul, T. C. Grattan, took Dickens off to the State Capitol. In the evening there was a visit to the Tremont Theatre where Joseph Field, a leading play-wright and actor, presented scenes from *Nicholas Nickleby* and his own dramatic tribute, *Boz: A Masque Phrenologic*. In his dedication of the manu-script Field unwittingly touched on a sensitive nerve, saying that he had taken the liberty of 'making Boz hint at the "International Copyright" ques-tion'.[17] Dickens had strong feelings on the subject, but for the moment he let the controversial point pass: he did not even mention it in his letter of thanks. He was plainly anxious to make a good impression on his hosts.

The sittings for the portrait in Alexander's studio began at ten on the morning of Tuesday 26 January. As a newspaper had announced the time and place, the entrance was crammed with people waiting to see Boz pass in and out, and the ante-room was filled with those who had come in the hope of an introduction. Dickens was literally hemmed in by enthusiasts. The sculptor Henry Dexter, who was working on a bust, had to do his modelling while Dickens ate his breakfast and read his letters. And each day there was a pile of fresh invitations from eager Bostonians, as well as proposals for dinners and civic receptions along his intended route to the south. To ease the strain Alexander introduced one of his students, G. W. Putnam, to act as secretary. By the end of the first week Dickens had employed Putnam for the whole tour at a salary of ten dollars a month and expenses. He was, Dickens informed Forster, 'most modest, obliging, silent, and willing; and does his work *well*'.[18]

On 26 January there was a welcoming ball at Boston's grandest assembly rooms, Papanti's Hall. On the next evening Dickens and Kate were received at the home of Francis Gray on Beacon Street, where they met W. H. Prescott, at work on his great history of Mexico; Richard Henry Dana Jr., the author of *Twenty Years Before the Mast*; and Jared Sparks, the historian who edited the *North American Review*. They went on to the house of another eminent historian, George Bancroft, and the evening closed with a party. 'We are constantly out two or three times in the evening,' Kate wrote home to Fanny.[19]

The people of Boston had welcomed Dickens warmly because they admired his writings for their humour, sympathy, and democratic spirit; and as they came to know him they found him charming and good-natured. His easy sociability made a quick impression on Americans. Sumner called one day to introduce Longfellow, the Professor of Modern Languages at Harvard and already known as a poet. The three men met again on Sunday 30 January for a sightseeing trip round Boston. Their ten-mile walk included a visit to the battlefield of Bunker Hill and a sermon from the famous preacher Father Taylor at the Seamen's Bethel. 'Dickens is a glorious fellow,' Longfellow wrote to his father that same day. 'He is a gay, free and easy character ... and withal a slight dash of the Dick Swiveller about him.' And he found Kate 'a good-natured—mild, cosy young woman—not beautiful, but amiable'.[20]

It was R. H. Dana Sr. who caught the quality which so enchanted every one who met Dickens. 'He is full of life,' the elder Dana wrote to the poet and journalist William Cullen Bryant. 'I never saw a face fuller of vivid action, or an eye fuller of light. And he is so freely animated—so unlike *our folks*. He is plainly enough a most hearty man and a most kind hearted one. People do not seem to crowd about him as to see a lion, but from downright love of him.'[21] His son, Richard Henry Dana Jr., had been more critical. Four days before Dickens arrived he wrote in his diary: 'Nothing talked of but Dickens' arrival. The town is mad. All ... calling on him.' When he called himself he was disappointed with Dickens, noting his 'hearty, off-hand manner, far from well-bred and a rapid, dashing way of talking ... full of cleverness.... You admire him and there is a fascination about him which keeps your eyes on him, yet you cannot get over the impression that he is a low-bred man.' Yet after an evening in the company of Dickens he was forced to abandon his condescending attitude, saying that 'you can't bear to leave him'. Dickens, he confessed, was 'perfectly natural and unpretending. He could not have behaved better. He did not say a single thing for display.'[22]

It was not until the week-end that Dickens had time to write home about his own impressions. 'How can I give you the faintest notion of my reception here,' he wrote to Forster, 'of the crowds that pour in and out the whole day; of the people that line the streets when I go out; of the cheering when I went to the theatre; of the copies of verses, letters of congratulations, welcomes of all kinds, balls, dinners, assemblies without end?' Even this catalogue, he claimed ecstatically, gave no notion of 'the cry that runs through the whole country'. He was so carried away by the wonder of his reception as to claim that 'deputations from the Far West ... have come from more than two thousand miles distance: from the lakes, the rivers, the back-woods, the log-houses, the cities, factories, villages and towns'. It was all summed up, he told Forster, by Dr. Channing's declaration that 'there never was, and never will be, such a triumph'.[23] Similar descriptions went into every letter he sent back to England. 'There never was a King or Emperor upon the Earth, so cheered, and followed by crowds,' he wrote to Thomas Mitton on 31 January.[24] Kate put the matter simply in her letter to Fanny. 'The people are most hospitable', she wrote, 'and we shall both be killed by kindness.'[25]

Dickens liked his hosts—'noble fellows' he told Forster—and he liked Boston. 'There is no man in this town, or in this State of New England, who has not a blazing fire and a meat dinner every day of his life.'[26] He was equally impressed by the government—'their Institutions I reverence, love and honor', he told Macready.[27] Sumner and the Mayor of Boston, Jonathan Chapman, took him to see Dr. Samuel Howe's work at the Perkins Institute for the Blind, and he was delighted to see that there were 'no charity uniforms ... in that blind school'. He visited the Lawrence mills at Lowell and approved of the admirable provision for the working girls, which included such luxuries as a piano, a library, and their own periodical. He thought the State Hospital for the Insane and the House of Correction, which had replaced the treadmill by useful work, were humane institutions; and after a visit to Harvard he concluded that American universities were free of bigotry. 'I have a book already,' he was able to tell Forster at the beginning of February.[28]

The climax of the visit was a banquet at Papanti's Hall on 1 February organized by the Young Men of Boston—a set of lawyers, journalists, and literary figures which included the young James Russell Lowell and Oliver Wendell Holmes—who brought together all the eminent townspeople to honour Dickens. 'Were ever heard such cheers before?' James Fields recalled. 'And when Dickens stood up at last to answer for himself, so fresh and so handsome, with his beautiful eyes moist with feeling, and his whole frame aglow with excitement, how we did hurrah, we young fellows.'[29]

There was much in the speech to evoke applause. Dickens made a graceful allusion to the Tree of Liberty and said that he had long dreamed 'of setting foot upon this shore, and breathing this pure air'. He spoke movingly of his own purposes as an author, of his wish to increase the common stock of cheerfulness and enjoyment, and of his belief that the meanest and most unfortunate of creatures 'are moulded in the same form and made of the same clay'. This eulogy of the rights of man was what the proper Bostonians wished to hear from Dickens. His closing remarks on the rights of authors were scarcely noticed among the multitude of toasts and jollification. He simply said that he hoped before long American authors would receive some profit in England from their labours and that the same would be true of English writers in America. 'I would rather have the affectionate regard of my fellowmen than I would have heaps and mines of gold', he said, but he thought they were not incompatible—'nothing good is incompatible with justice'.[30] Some people felt that it was not good manners to introduce the vulgar question of earnings at a testimonial dinner, or to imply that one's hosts tolerated an injustice: Boston had given Dickens a royal welcome and was a little surprised to hear him talking like a man of business. But all went well for the last few days, although Dickens was clearly tiring. The lawyer William W. Story observed that he was 'rather unwell from excitement'.[31] On the evening after the dinner he sent an apology to his hosts, Mr. and Mrs. James Paige, half an hour after he was due to arrive at their house. 'Poor man, he's literally used up' was one comment.[32]

Cheering crowds saw Dickens and Kate off to Worcester on 5 February where they stayed the week-end with the Governor of Massachusetts. They went on to Hartford, where four days of sightseeing and levees began with a lavish banquet for some seventy guests on 8 February.

Dickens was still brooding over copyright. It was a subject with which he had long been concerned. Two years before, on 14 April 1840, he had written to Gaylord Clark of the *Knickerbocker Magazine* in New York saying that the subject 'is one of immense importance to me, for at this moment I have received from the American Editions of my works—fifty pounds'.[33] He added that it was also important to Americans if they were to have a literature of their own. Clark, like Washington Irving, wanted a change in the law to protect the property rights of authors, but American literary opinion was divided on the issue. George Bancroft, for instance, took the opposite and high-minded view that creations of the mind were above the law since they were the property of humanity. James Fenimore Cooper agreed with him. Others, such as the New York journalist Cornelius Mathews and the 'Young America' group, thought that stricter control of copyright would keep out British works and allow native authors to flourish. Apart from principle there was a practical problem. There had been a depression in the American book trade for the previous five years and this had led to a rash of cheap periodicals which survived by pirating British authors in supplements. There were thus a number of publishers and newspapers which, doing well out of piracy, were motivated by crude self-interest; and there were more reputable editors, like Horace Greeley, who deplored intellectual robbery but felt obliged to pirate as vigorously as their competitors. Dickens, excited and impressed by his Boston welcome, misjudged this confused situation. He began, in effect, to treat American publishers as he had treated Bentley—to use his soaring reputation as a means of extracting better terms.

By the time that Dickens rose to speak at the Hartford banquet he had worked himself into a combative mood and this time he broached the thorny subject with a touch of cockney bravado. 'I have made a kind of compact with myself', he confided to his listeners, 'that I never will while I remain in America omit an opportunity' of referring to international copyright. 'I do not see', he argued, 'why fame... should not blow out of the trumpet a few notes of a different kind from those with which she has hitherto contented herself', and he went on dramatically to conjure up the deathbed of Sir Walter Scott 'crushed in body and mind' by financial difficulties from which a copyright law might have saved him; 'from the land in which his own language was spoken', Dickens exclaimed, not 'one grateful dollar-piece' came 'to buy a garland for his grave'.[34]

These forthright words brought a sharp response. 'We want no advice on this subject', wrote the Hartford *Daily Times*, 'and it will be better for Mr. Dickens if he refrains from introducing the matter hereafter.' Other newspapers quickly took the same line. The *New World* even declared that his business in visiting America at such an unseasonable time was to help a copyright law through Congress.³⁵ Such comments made matters worse, for Dickens was easily provoked. In his headlong rush to fame he had not learned the art of being famous, and he found it as difficult to cope with the flattery he liked as with the criticism he resented. On the copyright issue he allowed his impetuous emotions to run away with him—the question of manners seemed trivial when a principle was at stake and he felt that he had right on his side—and there was no friend at hand in America to offer him cooler counsel. He poured out his feelings of self-justification in a letter to Forster: 'I wish you could have heard how I gave it out. My blood so boiled as I thought of the monstrous injustice that I felt as if I were twelve feet high when I thrust it down their throats.'³⁶ His indignation at the criticism of his behaviour even spilled out in letters to American friends. 'I have never in my life been so shocked and disgusted, or made so sick and sore at heart, as I have been by the treatment I have received here (in America I mean) in reference to the International Copyright question', he told Jonathan Chapman, the Mayor of Boston, complaining that the newspapers attacked him in 'terms of vagabond scurrility' not fit even for a murderer.³⁷

On the way from Hartford to New York Dickens stopped overnight at New Haven, where the press of people anxious to meet him and shake his hand was so great that the throng filling the passages had to be kept at bay by a cordon of porters and it was nearly midnight before Dickens could retire, after shaking hands with 'considerably more than five hundred people'.³⁸ There was, however, a growing undercurrent of feeling that his reception was overdone. 'We hope our folks will treat him like a gentleman and not like a show,' one New Haven paper remarked; 'this sickening flattery', another commented, 'is doubtless as contemptible in his eyes as it is derogatory to us'.³⁹ Dickens was in a mixed temper when he and Kate arrived in New York by steamer on Saturday 12 February. Once more there was the heartening welcome from a dense crowd on the wharf and as he passed through, he wrote to Maclise, people were 'screwing small dabs of fur out of the back of that costly great coat I bought in Regent Street!'⁴⁰ He was beginning to feel that his reception was turning into a torment, and the press was aware of his displeasure. The New York *Tribune* commented that there had been very little annoyance from the crowd as he proceeded to the Carlton House Hotel on Broadway, where he was left in peace over the week-end.

Installed in 'a very splendid suite of rooms', Dickens was soon meeting some of the people he had come to see. On the first evening Washington Irving came, 'with open arms'.⁴¹ Dickens was particularly anxious to meet him; he admired Irving's work, and it was Irving who had encouraged him

John Forster, painted by Daniel Maclise

Mark Lemon as Falstaff

An engraving from the *Illustrated London News* of 24 May 1851, showing Dickens and his company at Devonshire House performing Bulwer-Lytton's *Not So Bad As We Seem* before Queen Victoria and Prince Albert

to visit America. They saw much of each other. Dickens told Forster what a '*great* fellow' Irving was—'just the man he ought to be'—and how 'we have laughed most heartily together'.[42] There were other visitors—William Cullen Bryant, Clark of the *Knickerbocker* and the poet Fitz-Greene Halleck, who found Dickens 'a thorough good fellow'.[43] Dickens was particularly glad to have the company of Cornelius Felton, a Harvard classicist who had been so taken with Dickens in Boston that he joined him on the journey to New York. In the midst of so much public pomp Dickens enjoyed the informality of spontaneous friendship with Felton. Samuel Ward wrote to Longfellow to tell him how the grave professor and the theatrical Boz had 'walked, laughed, talked, eaten oysters and drunk champagne together' like Siamese twins.[44] Such 'roistering and oystering' punctuated a daily round of visits—to the theatre, and to such customary tourist sights as the Lunatic Asylum, the Alms House, and the gloomy Toombs prison, where Dickens was intrigued by an ingenious means of hanging a man by dragging him into the air instead of dropping him. In the miserable Five Points, where he was taken for a night's prowl by two police officers, he saw the brothels and thieves' dens which supplied the prison with convicts as profusely as the stews of London's Seven Dials provided inmates for Newgate.

One of the highlights of the New York visit was the Boz Ball, two days after his arrival. It was a grand affair of lavish splendour held at the Park Theatre. Three thousand people turned out in full dress. Dickens was in black with a gay vest, and Kate 'in a white, figured Irish tabinet trimmed with mazarine blue flowers'.[45] She had a wreath of the same colour round her head, with pearl necklace and ear-rings, and her hair was curled in long ringlets. They were received by the Mayor and then paraded round the enormous ballroom. Between the dances there were *tableaux vivants* of scenes from *Pickwick* and the other novels. It was an extraordinary festival—'quite unparalleled here', Dickens told Forster—'the light, glitter, glare, show, noise, and cheering, baffle my descriptive powers'.[46] The New York *Herald* brought out a special number devoted to the event. 'If he does not get his head turned by all this, I shall wonder at it,' wrote Philip Hone, one of the organizers, and there were some who disapproved. 'The whole transaction was such an offence against the laws of decorum that ... I felt in common with many others the blood tingling in my cheeks,' the New York lawyer William Watson wrote to R. H. Dana Sr. in Boston.[47] Dickens took it all in good part and was amused by suggestions in the press that he had never before been received in such high society.

After four days in bed with a sore throat Dickens prepared himself for a dinner at the City Hotel on 18 February. Some 230 eminent male guests sat down to the banquet while Kate and other lady visitors looked on from the stage. Washington Irving, who was the obvious choice as chairman, was such a diffident man that a public speech threw him into a state of 'tragi-comical distress', and he was able to do little more than to introduce Dickens briefly as 'the literary guest of the nation'.

'Gentlemen,' Dickens began, 'I don't know how to thank you—I really don't know how.' The charm of his graceful speech, Halleck remarked, was not so much in his words but in his manner of saying them. Much of it was a fulsome tribute to Irving. 'I do not go to bed two nights out of seven', Dickens said, 'without taking Washington Irving under my arm.' Once more he included a good-humoured reminder of his views on 'a question of universal literary interest'.[48] He gave Forster the impression that he alone, in the face of vilification, had championed the cause: 'every man who writes in this country is devoted to the question, and not one of them *dares* to raise his voice and complain of the atrocious state of the law'. And he reported that the organizing committee for the dinner had begged him not to pursue the subject, '*although they every one agreed with me*'.[49] In fact, there was such agreement that the main toast of the evening was 'International Copyright', proposed by Irving himself, and in a long reply Cornelius Mathews defended the right of Dickens to speak his mind. In the press, too, Dickens had support. Horace Greeley's *Tribune*, for instance, welcomed him to New York with an editorial urging Americans to be first just, then generous. In seeking justice for authors, Greeley declared, Dickens spoke 'the frank round truth'.[50] Dickens had, indeed, made a new and dramatic point in asserting that an author had a *right* to copyright protection—though his intervention, some sympathizers complained, did the cause as much harm as good. It was too easy to dismiss his case as the special pleading of a man who hoped to make money out of the change.

Dickens, aware that he was in a vulnerable position, asked Forster to organize a sympathetic letter of support from other English men of letters, declaring that 'it would be a thousand pities if we did not strike as hard as we can, now that the iron is so hot'.[51] He was becoming a man with a mission; and as the criticism of his copyright campaign increased so the lustre began to fade on all things American. He began a letter to Forster on 24 February with a sweeping attack: 'I believe there is no country, on the face of the earth, where there is less freedom of opinion on any subject in reference to which there is a broad difference of opinion.' The letter ended with a dark reservation about the national character. 'I tremble for a radical coming here,' Dickens wrote, 'unless he is a radical on principle, by reason and reflection, and from the sense of right. I fear that if he were anything else, he would return home a tory.'[52]

Disagreements over copyright and the strains of public life were beginning to tell on him. A petulant note now rang through his letters in place of the good-humoured enjoyment with which he had described the first days of his visit. 'I am sick to death of the life I have been leading here—worn out in mind and body—and quite weary and distressed', he wrote to Jonathan Chapman after ten days in New York, telling him that 'I have declined all future Invitations of a public nature'.[53] He explained to Forster two days later that 'I can do nothing that I want to do, go nowhere where I want to go, and see nothing that I want to see ... I have no rest or peace, and am in a perpetual worry.'[54] And to Maclise he poured out all his feelings of homesickness: 'Oh for Jack Straw's! ... Oh for Charley, Mamey, Katey—the study, the Sunday's dinner, the anything and everything connected with our life at Home! How cheerfully would I turn from this land of freedom and spittoons—of crowds, and noise, and endless rush of strangers—of every-thing public, and nothing private—of endless rounds of entertainments, and daily levees to receive 500 people—to the lightest, least-prized pleasure of "Den'ner Terrace"! I turn my eyes towards the picture ... and yearn for Home ... Oh Mac, Mac!'[55]

Some of his acquaintances realized that he was peculiarly distressed. Dickens, Samuel Ward wrote to Longfellow on 22 February, was 'so perse-cuted that he will run into misanthropy or Americano-phobia. I saw a manifest wildness in his eye yesterday.' And three days later when Dickens had cancelled a second invitation from Ward he wrote again to Longfellow expressing his displeasure: 'I know that the persecutions to which he is a martyr justify him in his defensive system. But ...'[56] Kate, too, was home-sick, and unwell with a throat infection. To make matters worse, the steamer *Caledonia*, which they had expected to bring news of the family, had been delayed by storms and was feared lost. All they could do was to put off their departure for Philadelphia for six days until 6 March and while they were in New York they booked their passage home on a sailing-packet in early June.

The six-hour journey to Philadelphia was the first stage of a 'dash' to the backwoods. Without some such escape, Dickens explained to Forster, 'I can never be a free agent, or see anything worth the telling.'[57] In his speech in New York he had publicly declared his intention to avoid public occasions—'to shake hands with Americans, not at parties but at home'. This was easier said than done. He did have two agreeable conversations with Edgar Allan Poe, who had thought so highly of *The Old Curiosity Shop*, and attended a pleasant party given by the publisher Henry Carey, who opposed a copyright law but had voluntarily paid royalties to Scott and other authors. But the public handshaking went on. There was no official reception in Philadelphia and instead Dickens agreed to meet a committee of local dignitaries. He expected a few people in his private apartment. Instead, a local politician, Colonel Florence, advertised in the press that Dickens would receive admirers that morning: more than five hundred people turned up in front of the United States Hotel. Fearing a riot if Dickens refused to hold an impromptu reception, the landlord persuaded him to greet them. Dickens undertook his task of shaking hands philosophically but was rather taken aback when the landlord presented him with a bill for meals as well as the rooms that had not been taken because of their delayed arrival. He felt unable to protest, he indignantly told Forster, in case he aroused 'the sacred wrath of the newspapers'.[58]

There was another reason for indignation in Philadelphia. Dickens was taken to visit the Eastern Penitentiary, well known for its unique system of solitary confinement. 'It is wonderfully kept, but a most dreadful, fearful place,' he wrote to Forster after he had spent most of a day in this gloomy bastille, going from cell to cell and talking to the prisoners. 'I never shall be able to dismiss from my mind, the impressions of that day ... I looked at some of them with the same awe as I should have looked at men who had been buried alive, and dug up again.'[59] Dickens was very much affected by what he saw and told his official hosts—'extremely kind and benevolent men'—that nothing could justify such cruel punishment. As the journey went on, indeed, he was becoming increasingly outspoken and critical about the things he disliked. The atmosphere in Washington, where he and Kate arrived on 9 March, was calmer and less fuss was made in the press about his visit, but there were other causes of complaint. 'We are now in the regions of slavery, spittoons, and senators—all three are evils in all countries,' he told Charles Sumner,[60] and he had written to Forster in February that the fierce debates going on in Congress over slavery made him feel 'repelled by the mere thought' of approaching Washington.[61] He also confided his feelings to Felton: 'There are very interesting men in this place ...—but it's not a comfortable place; is it?'[62]

The Capitol was one of the first places of call the day after their arrival. Kate sat in the gallery while Dickens went on the floor of both houses and was introduced to Congressmen and senators. He readily warmed to such distinguished figures as the ageing former President, John Quincy Adams, the former Vice-President and senator from South Carolina, John Calhoun, and the senator from Kentucky, Henry Clay, who had been trying to change the international copyright law since 1837. It was to Clay that Dickens brought a new petition from American writers. He met, too, some 'noble specimens' from the West. 'Splendid men to look at, hard to deceive, prompt to act, lions in energy ... Indians in quickness of eye and gesture, Americans in affectionate and generous impulse,' he told Forster.[63] He was not, however, greatly impressed by Congress—but, as he later assured the readers of his *American Notes*, he was not a man who was 'moved to tears of joyful pride by the sight of any legislature'.⁶⁴

Dickens, quick to censure others, was himself guilty of some odd errors of taste—as if he had, quirkily, to assert his independence. He was invited to dinner at the White House by President Tyler, but he declined, contenting himself with a dry exchange in a private audience. When he and Kate went to lunch with John Quincy Adams they arrived late and left the ex-President's table early, because they had to dress for a formal dinner with Robert Greenhow, a translator in the State Department—'a particularly funny idea' commented a fellow guest, Philip Hone. Another remarked that Dickens 'seemed rather to prefer dining with reporters and newspaper men than with persons in official position' and noted a brusque waywardness 'which led him to put on airs in the company of men entitled to his respect'.⁶⁵ Though he refused a number of invitations and wisely avoided speech-making, he went as the guest of honour to a men's dining club. In the course of the evening of songs and story-telling Kate sent word that the letters from home, so long delayed on the *Caledonia*, had at last arrived. Dickens at once excused himself to go back and read them with Kate. They felt, he reported to Cornelius Felton, 'as if the prodigal father and mother had got home again'.⁶⁶

The finale of the Washington visit was the President's levee on 15 March when the city turned out to greet the two honoured guests, Dickens and Washington Irving, who was on his way to Spain as American Minister there. 'The greatest lion among the men was Boz, the never-ending Boz,' reported one correspondent. 'Wherever he moved it was like throwing corn among hungry chickens.'⁶⁷ The President's daughter-in-law, who was present, was condescendingly critical. He 'wears entirely too much jewelry, very English in his appearance, and not the best English. . . . Poor fellow, he seemed horribly bored by the crowd pressing around.'⁶⁸

Each letter that Dickens sent home revealed that the gap between him and his American hosts was widening. He was careful to make a measured appraisal, cataloguing their admirable qualities. A typical set of adjectives— 'naturally courteous, good-tempered, generous, warmhearted and obliging'—was included in a letter to Lady Holland.⁶⁹ Yet he had now quite made up his mind that their disagreeable habits outweighed their virtues. There was the universal habit of spitting of which he complained in one letter after another. 'I can bear anything but filth,' he told Albany Fonblanque, the editor of the *Examiner*. 'I would be content even to live in an atmosphere of spit, if they would but *spit clean*; but when every man ejects from his mouth that odious, most disgusting, compound of saliva and tobacco, I vow that my stomach revolts . . . they flood the carpet while they talk to you.' There were spit-boxes in hospitals, prisons, law-courts; in stage-coaches, railroad cars—the 'flashes of saliva' on the windows 'looked as though they were ripping open feather beds inside, and letting the wind dispose of the feathers'—and even beside the President's chair in the White House.[70]

Slavery, of course, was brought into the indictment. Spittle physically nauseated Dickens; slavery morally sickened him. 'My heart is lightened as if a great load had been taken from it', he wrote to Forster when they left the South, 'when I think that we are turning our backs on this accursed and detested system.' He had seen a slave's wife and children sold away from him, and collected horrifying stories of maiming, manacling, beating, and branding. He hated being asked his opinion of the peculiar institution. 'They *will* ask you what you think of it', he complained, 'and *will* expiate on slavery as if it were one of the greatest blessings of mankind.'[71] Even in the West it was inescapable, and the cant of slave owners and their apologists drove him to outbursts of bitter sarcasm. 'I don't like the country,' he concluded in a letter to Forster, 'I would not live here, on any consideration. It goes against the grain with me ... I think it impossible, utterly impossible, for any Englishman to live here, and be happy.'[72]

Dickens and Kate left Washington on 16 March, travelling by steamer down the Potomac and on by stage to Richmond, where he was again warmly entertained. Mr. Gales Seaton was one of those introduced to Dickens at Richmond and in a letter to his father he expressed the feelings which so many experienced after meeting the novelist: 'I do feel very sorry that he has gone,' he wrote. 'I have never seen a man in whom, in so brief a period, I was so greatly interested. His likenesses certainly flatter him, but they cannot give the charm of his face, his rich expression of humour and merriment when he laughs—his whole face lights up.'[73]

The original plan to go further south to Charleston had now been abandoned. Dickens instead turned north again to Baltimore before starting on a trip to the West, by train, canal boat, and river steamer. In Baltimore he met Washington Irving again: they dined together and shared a mint julep 'wreathed with flowers' which Dickens said lasted them 'far into the night'.[74] Dickens was now in a calmer mood, even writing to the wealthy New York merchant Charles Davis on 4 April that 'we enjoyed Washington very much'.[75] There was a lighter tone in the letters which went off to friends in England, but the jollity was all in personal references which intimates such as Maclise and Macready understood, or in amusing cameos. 'Imagine Kate and I—a kind of Queen and Albert—holding a Levee every day,' he wrote to Maclise on 22 March.[76] Talfourd, Lord Jeffrey, Thomas Mitton, Samuel Rogers, and Forster all received lively letters written on that day.

But there was no change in his basic view. There was a special comment for Macready, who liked America and thought Dickens was unfairly misjudging it. Dickens explained that he had burned his last letter rather than send it, because it might seem 'an ill-considered word of disappointment'. Still he added, 'I *am* disappointed. This is not the Republic I came to see. This is not the Republic of my imagination.... In everything of which it has made a boast—excepting its education of the people, and its care for poor children—it sinks immeasurably below the level I had placed it upon.' England, 'bad and faulty as the old land is', was so much better than the 'new love'; and 'yearning after our English customs and English manners', he bought a concertina and nostalgically played 'Home Sweet Home' on it every night.[77]

The plan was to travel to Pittsburgh and sail down the 900-mile length of the Ohio river to its mouth and then up the Mississippi as far as St. Louis. As they left Pittsburgh on the steamboat *Messenger* a 'most ardently looked-for packet of letters' from England caught up with them.[78] The pleasure and heartache were a compensation for the company. One fellow traveller, Dickens complained, was 'perhaps the most intolerable bore on this vast continent'. Others wanted him to 'magnetize' a phrenologist on board. He refused, but reporting this request to Forster he added that in Pittsburgh he had mesmerized Kate on a dare from his host. It was his first attempt and his success rather alarmed him: 'In six minutes, I magnetized her into hysterics, and then into the magnetic sleep.'[79]

As they pushed west, through thinly settled country, travelling became more uncomfortable. They were 'handsomely lodged' in Cincinnati and he was received without fuss. Dickens liked the town—'the prettiest place I have seen here, except Boston. It has risen out of the forest like an Arabian-night city,' he told Forster. They stopped again at Louisville and at Cairo—the site of the notorious land swindle—started on the final stage up the Mississippi to St. Louis. It was hard going, through scenery of dismal swamps and unwholesome vegetation. 'It is well for society that this Mississippi, the renowned father of waters, had no children who take after him. It is the beastliest river in the world.'[80]

It was April when Dickens and Kate arrived in St. Louis. After weeks of travelling and continuous social engagements, they were very weary. Although the social graces were maintained, Dickens was often visibly bored and even an expedition to the prairie did not arouse his enthusiasm. Like America as a whole, it fell short of his preconceived idea. He told Forster that it was 'a sea without water' and Salisbury Plain was decidedly more impressive. To say 'that the sight is a landmark in one's existence', he told Forster, 'is sheer gammon'. But he concluded that it was worth the ride, and he managed to warm himself into a state of 'surpassing jollity' with the 'friendly companionable party', although the society of St. Louis generally, he reported, was 'pretty rough, and intolerably conceited'.[81] On 14 April he turned gladly towards home—by steamboat back to Cincinnati, stage-coach to Sandusky, and steamboat again across Lake Erie to Niagara Falls.

It was rough going at times, especially on the corduroy roads of logs across swampy ground, which were 'like nothing but going up a steep flight of stairs in an omnibus'. Dickens was now in a mood where he grudged good words. The people of Ohio were 'morose, sullen, clownish, and repulsive . . . destitute of humour . . . I have not heard a hearty laugh these six weeks, except my own; nor have I seen a merry face on any shoulders but a black man's.' When the boat stopped at Cleveland sightseers peered through the cabin window while Dickens was washing and '*Kate lay in bed*', and he was so incensed that he refused to see the Mayor, on the dock to greet him. He was full of praise for Kate's fortitude and patience during their travels; she had accommodated herself cheerfully to the arduous conditions and 'proved herself perfectly game'. She had, however, displayed her customary clumsiness, which Dickens described with mock exasperation: 'She falls into, or out of, every coach or boat we enter; scrapes the skin off her legs; brings great sores and swellings on her feet . . . and makes herself blue with bruises.'[82]

The rest at Niagara Falls was a relief for them both. Writing the address at the head of a letter to Forster from the Falls, Dickens wrote '(upon the *English* Side)', and told Thomas Mitton that it was the 'most wonderful and beautiful' place in the world.[83] He had now received the 'very manly' letter drafted by Edward Bulwer-Lytton and signed by other literary friends which supported his copyright campaign. Bulwer, sending the letter to Forster for onward transmission, was somewhat cynical. Only Dickens and Ainsworth would benefit much from a change in the American copyright law, Bulwer wrote, so Dickens was probably right 'to jeopardize an idle popularity for the probability of advancing a cause which may put so many dollars into his pocket!'[84] Dickens kept up his attacks on 'Monstrous and Wholesale Injustice' until he sailed for home, provoked by a publishers' convention in Boston at the end of April which urged a tax on foreign books as well as opposing a copyright law—and urged on by a letter from Thomas Carlyle which compared literary pirates to cattle-thieves. It was no use, he wrote to Cornelius Felton, 'to clutch these robbers in any other part of their ungodly persons but the throat . . . meaning to let my indignation loose when I get home, I do not choose to curb it here'.[85]

The side-trip to Montreal became a pleasurable diversion from this press-ing anger. Lord Mulgrave, with whom they had crossed in the *Britannia*, drew them into garrison theatricals and Dickens worked himself into a better mood by his energetic services as Stage Manager and Universal Director, 'urging impracticable ladies and impossible gentlemen on to the very confines of insanity'.[86] For ten days he worked at every detail, securing costumes, ordering scenery, and sending off to New York for a special wig. Three plays were performed before the Governor-General and a private audience, and repeated with professional actresses at a public performance; Dickens played in all three—a comedy, an interlude, and a farce—and everything 'went with a roar'. He told Forster that 'I was very funny' and that Kate played 'devilish well'.[87]

Back in New York, Dickens and Kate were taken up the Hudson to visit a Shaker village which he left 'with a hearty dislike of the old Shakers and a hearty pity for the young ones'.[88] There were farewells to make to friends and parting letters to others whom they had come to like. Engagements went on until the last moment; even on the day of departure there was a breakfast party at a country house outside New York. Yet, as the time for leaving drew near, Dickens told Forster, 'we get FEVERED with anxiety for home ... oh home—home—home—home—home—home—HOME!!!!!!!!!!!'[89]

The *George Washington* sailed out through the Narrows on Tuesday 7 June and in good weather the packet reached Liverpool in three weeks. Dickens was in a hilarious mood throughout the voyage. He got up a comical musical troupe, which he called the United Vagabonds, in which he played the accordion, another passenger the violin, and a third the bugle. 'We were really very merry, all the way,' he afterwards wrote to Felton.[90] Reaching London on 29 June, a day sooner than expected, he went at once to Macready's house. 'I was lying on the sofa when a person entered abruptly,' Macready noted in his diary. 'Who was it but dear Dickens holding me in his arms in a transport of joy. God bless him!'[91] Then he went on to find Forster who was dining out. Forster leaped into the carriage and began crying as they drove off to call on Maclise. The children, who had not enjoyed the 'gloomy austerity' of Macready's guardianship, also wept with joy and excitement as they were collected from their lodgings and returned to Devonshire Terrace. Charley was attacked by 'alarming convulsions' which had been brought on 'with the surprise and joy of our return'.[92] As to the pleasures of home itself 'they are unspeakable', Dickens assured Jonathan Chapman. 'I never in my life felt so keenly as on the night of our reaching it.'[93]

PART TWO

CAROL PHILOSOPHIES

1842–1851

8

Coxcombry and Cockneyism

DICKENS returned from America in a belligerent mood and he found ample material for his pent-up moral indignation in the condition of England. The labouring men of England, he reported to the American historian W. H. Prescott at the end of July 1842, were 'badly off and worse disposed'.[1] In the Hungry Forties the country was fast being industrialized, but at a terrible price. Seven people in every hundred were registered paupers living under the grinding misery of the Poor Law, and many who worked had scarcely enough to eat; in some towns the population was decimated by outbreaks of cholera, and scarlet fever, diphtheria, tuberculosis, and other killer diseases were endemic in the insanitary tenements in which millions of people were now herded. In February 1842 Carlyle had written to his brother that the 'distress of the people in Britain this winter, I believe, excels all that they have ever known before ... here at Chelsea, for the first time, I notice the garden palings torn up this winter and stolen for fuel'.[2]

In their desperation the poor turned against the Corn Laws which kept up the price of bread, the Poor Law, and the factory system itself. The countryside was alight with burning ricks; in the industrial towns broken machines, demonstrations, and mutterings of political revolt were suppressed by widespread arrests and shows of military force. In these miserable days the cry was still for the People's Charter, and when a national petition with four million signatures was presented in May 1842 the floor of the House of Commons looked as though it had been snowing paper. But such numbers were nothing to a Parliament strong for property and resolute against further political reform; its members were more concerned about the income tax of sevenpence in the pound recently introduced by Sir Robert Peel than about the state of the people.

Although Dickens had no desire to be a radical politician he had a strong inclination to be a radical editor. When his feelings were touched by injustice, in fact, he always turned back to journalistic styles, either in a letter or an article, or in a passage in his fiction which was plainly editorial. He had a gift for vituperative prose and the leader-writer's knack of finding a target for the attacks that spilled from his pen. No sooner was he home than he again rallied behind Lord Ashley's campaign to exclude women and girls from the mines. Before his visit to America he had promised an article on that subject to the *Edinburgh Review*, but in the event he preferred to express his opinions in a more popular context, sending a savage letter of support for Ashley's Bill to the *Morning Chronicle* on 25 July. According to the titled colliery owners, Dickens wrote sarcastically, the miners led 'such rollicking and roystering lives that it is well they work below the surface of the earth, or society would be deafened by their shouts of merriment'. Lord London-derry and other coal-owning peers seemed more upset by the disgusting drawings in the evidence, which they feared would inflame the minds of the public, than by the disgusting conditions they portrayed. The gulf between rich and poor, Dickens concluded, 'grows broader daily' though each of 'these two great divisions of society' was dependent upon the other 'for its strength and happiness and the future existence of this country, as a great and powerful nation'.[3]

An occasional article of this kind was not sufficient release for what Dickens felt. As soon as he reached London he learned that the *Courier*, once a Whig newspaper, had fallen into Tory hands and then gone out of business. He wrote at once to Lady Holland regretting that he had missed the chance to save the paper by throwing his reputation and his talents into the breach. 'I am strongly inclined', he continued, 'to establish a new evening paper, on the right side, in its place';[4] and he proposed to bid for the premises and equipment if such powerful Liberal leaders as Lord Lans-downe and Lord Melbourne would back the project. Within three days Lady Holland had told him he could not expect financial support: 'in such ques-tions', Dickens replied sadly, 'the Liberal party have very seldom made a mistake on the Bold side'. There was a sense of professional as well as politi-cal regret. 'The notion of this newspaper was bred in me by my old training,' Dickens explained. 'I always feel when I take up a paper now ... that the subjects which all the writers leave unhandled ... are exactly the questions which interest the people most.'[5]

This was just one of the concerns which led Dickens to tell Cornelius Felton three weeks after his return that he had faced 'stupendous' demands on his time. He wrote of the 'dinners I have had to eat, the places I have had to go to, the letters I have had to answer, the sea of business of business and business of pleasure in which I have been plunged'. Another task was the campaign on American copyright. 'I am bent upon striking at the Piratical newspapers with the sharpest edge I can put upon my small axe,' he told Felton.[6] He had scarcely settled at home again before he was telling the publisher Thomas Longman that he was 'fresher for the fray than ever, will battle it to the death, and die game to the last'.[7] On 7 July he sent a circular letter to British authors and journals summarizing his complaints against American publishers—for not paying writers their due and for altering their books to suit the American taste. It was a system 'of piracy and plunder'. He would neither send early proofs, he declared, nor take any profits from such a source.[8] He was particularly concerned about the huge weekly papers, the *New World* and *Brother Jonathan*, which printed English works which had appeared in magazines like *Fraser's* and *Bentley's*. The *New World* serialized English novels—*The Old Curiosity Shop* and *Barnaby Rudge* had appeared in its pages—and then sought to compete with the pirates who published in book form by bringing out complete versions themselves. This manifesto had a good reception in England, but Dickens had no illusions that anything would come of it: 'we may cry "Stop Thief" nevertheless— especially as they wince and smart under it'.[9] In America, understandably, it was poorly received. Dickens had made so much fuss on the issue that even some of his sympathizers, such as Horace Greeley, were cooling towards him.

Dickens was revelling in being home again and picking up the threads of his old life. 'Here I am in my old room,' he wrote to Charles Sumner on 31 July, 'with my books, and pen and ink and paper—battledores and shuttlecocks—bats and balls—dumbbells—dog—and Raven!'[10] He was enjoying playing games with the children, seeing old friends like Beard, Landor, Ainsworth, and Mitton, and, best of all, indulging in 'some gentlemanly piece of vagabondism with Maclise and Forster'.[11] There was a grand reunion dinner at Greenwich on 9 July with Forster, Maclise, Cattermole, Stanfield, Ainsworth, Cruikshank, and other cronies. 'They were', Dickens wrote to Felton, 'very jovial', drinking with 'fearful vigor and energy'. Cruikshank was 'perfectly wild at the reunion ... singing all manner of maniac songs ... coming home (six miles) in a little open phaeton of mine, *on his head*—to the mingled delight and indignation of the Metropolitan Police'.[12] He dined with Rogers and Lady Holland, who was entertaining again at Holland House, closed since Lord Holland's death in 1841. He went to see Lady Blessington, who was now in her fifties. She 'wears brilliantly', Dickens told Sumner, 'and has the gloss upon her, yet'.[13] Since 1841 d'Orsay had been confined to the house, except on Sundays, 'by a severe attack of the bum-bailiffs';[14] all the same he was 'not an atom the worse in temper, health, looks, or spirits'. Dickens went to the theatre—the Austrian conjurer Ludwig Dobler was performing at the St. James's—and to the Academy exhibition. Maclise, who had been ill and depressed while Dickens had been away, was arousing considerable interest with his painting of the play scene in *Hamlet*. It was 'a *tremendous* production', Dickens told Sumner. 'He is a great fellow.'[15]

There were parties again at Devonshire Terrace. Macready, arriving late on 12 July, found that 'Dickens had been mesmerizing his wife and Miss Hogarth, who had been in violent hysterics',[16] and he needed much persuasion before agreeing to submit to the magnetic force of his friend. Macready was referring to Kate's younger sister, Georgina Hogarth, then fifteen. She had seen much of the children while their parents were away and they liked her. She was carried off with the family for the usual holiday at Broadstairs and then in the autumn, and at the same age that Mary Hogarth had gone to stay with the Dickens family, she became part of the household. She was a helpful companion for Kate, and Dickens found her presence peculiarly appealing. Her likeness to the lost Mary was so strong, he wrote to her mother early in 1843, that 'I seem to think that what has happened is a melancholy dream from which I am just awakening'. So much of Mary's spirit 'shines out in this sister, that the old time comes back again at some seasons, and I can hardly separate it from the present'.[17]

For all the excitement of his return, Dickens was soon 'working like a dray-horse'[18] and four chapters of *American Notes* were drafted before the family left for Broadstairs at the beginning of August. He began on a challenging note. The introductory chapter, he wrote in the middle of July, 'may seem to prepare the reader for a much greater amount of slaughter than he will meet with; but it is *honest* and *true*. Therefore my hand does not shake.'[19] The chapter defensively explained why he had not allowed his friendly reception in America to blind him to the country's defects. At the end of July he showed it to Macready, who noted '*I do not like it*'.[20] Forster had the same reaction and, just before the book was printed, he persuaded Dickens to omit it.

Dickens was delighted to be back in Broadstairs again and at his old lodgings in Albion Street. 'This place is most beautiful just now,' he wrote to Beard on 4 August urging him to come, 'the weather being past all descriptive powers. Heavens, how crisp the water is—I bathed yesterday.'[21] There were visits from Forster, Maclise, and Cruikshank, as well as local diversions. The Ranelagh Gardens, Dickens wrote pressingly to Beard, were 'exulting in the proprietorship of a family of Tumblers, called "The Five Patagonians"—the Theatre open at Margate—all manner of breeziness, freshness, and waviness going on'.[22] Nevertheless he made good headway with *American Notes*. The work moved along quickly and was easily written, for on this subject Dickens could deploy his old skills as a reporter; and he was also able to incorporate long passages from the letters he had sent to Forster and other friends during the trip.

While he was working on the book at Broadstairs he learnt that the New York *Evening Tattler* had published a spurious text of the letter which he had written to British authors about copyright. Abuse had been written into the paragraphs of the genuine circular, and it was damagingly reprinted in papers all over the United States. Dickens was not surprised by it. 'Nothing but Honesty or common sense would startle me, from such a quarter,' he wrote to the British consul in Boston.[23] But he was pained by it. 'It exasperated me (I am of rather a fierce turn, at times) very much,' he told Longfellow, 'and I walked about for a week or two, with a vague desire to take somebody by the throat and shake him—which was rather feverish.'[24] Although Dickens complained that it was as 'foul a forgery as ever felon swung for', it kept the agitation against him hot in the popular American press, and did nothing to curb the sharpness of his own pen.[25]

As the summer advanced there were more visitors to Broadstairs. Rogers was staying hard by; and Eleanor Emma Picken (who had frolicked with Dickens on the seashore two years before) was down again, lately married to Edward Christian. By this time Dickens had cooled to Eleanor Christian but Fred, who was down for a visit, was more friendly and they all danced together at the Tivoli Gardens. There was a regatta to enjoy and Talfourd's play *The Athenian Captive* was on at the Margate theatre. At the end of September, with the book almost finished and the autumn gales beginning to blow up the Channel, Dickens and the family returned to London.

'There is great curiosity afloat in all directions, about the book,' Dickens wrote to Mitton on 21 September.[26] He was pleased with what he had done but he still wrote of it with a defensive tone as if he had to ward off potential criticism. 'I have spoken very honestly and fairly,' he wrote to Longfellow on 28 September, 'and I know that those in America for whom I care, will like me better for the book.' His treatment by the American newspapers had made him also realize that some would 'make a Devil of me, straightway'.[27] As with the serials, the chapters were set in type as they were written and the book appeared on 19 October, less than a fortnight after Dickens had finished it.

Longfellow came to stay with Dickens at Devonshire Terrace just before the publication of the book, and after reading the proofs he wrote to Charles Sumner to say that it was 'jovial and good-natured' and 'at times very severe'.[28] In fact the veneer of pleasantries was very thin and the animus was obvious both to English and American readers. Macaulay, who had asked to review it for the *Edinburgh Review*, sent the book back when he looked through it. 'I cannot praise it; and I will not cut it up,' he wrote to Macvey Napier. 'It is written like the worst parts of *Humphrey's Clock*. ... I pronounce the book in spite of some gleams of genius, at once frivolous and dull.'[29]

American critics took much the same view. Emerson considered it a readable book, but nothing more. 'Truth is not his object for a single instant', he wrote in his journal, 'but merely to make good points in a lively sequence. ... As a picture of American manners nothing could be falser.' He thought the book 'makes a poor apology for its author, who certainly appears in no dignified or enviable position'.[30] Poe, who had taken a liking to Dickens when they met, decided that it was 'one of the most suicidal productions, ever deliberately published by an author, who had the least reputation to lose'.[31] And, as Dickens had predicted, the American press was mostly vituperative. The New York *Herald* said the book was the product of 'the most coarse, vulgar, impudent and superficial' writer ever to visit America. The *New Englander* called the book 'a compound of egotism, coxcombry and cockneyism'.[32] Though friends in America were loyal, many who had given Dickens hospitality and shown him round their institutions were surprised and hurt by what he wrote. There were also English readers who thought Dickens guilty of bad taste and bad temper—even Macready feared that he was spoiling for a fight. Dickens stood his ground, insisting to Felton that in Britain *American Notes* had been 'a most complete and thoroughgoing success'.[33] By the end of the year it had run through four printings and earned him £1,000. The American public, irritably curious, was even more eager to read what Dickens had written. One publisher, who had secured proofs by bribing a printer in London and whisking them across the Atlantic, set up and ran off 24,000 copies within the first couple of days after publication. Several other firms followed suit. One pirate, serializing the work to his own advantage, self-righteously attacked Dickens for money-grubbing. Yet for all the financial success of *American Notes* it did nothing for his reputation. It seemed to confirm the 'rowdyism' of his personality which had been the commonest note of criticism in America; and Richard Henry Dana Jr., who had condescended to Dickens when he first arrived in Boston, was confirmed in his initial impression. 'He is not a gentleman,' he wrote in his journal. 'His journey to America has been a Moscow expedition for his fame.'[34]

The American expedition could equally be compared to a failed love affair, beginning with impetuous hopes and declining through misunderstanding into mutual acrimony. Why had it gone so sadly wrong? It had been a failure on both sides. Americans had been agog for Boz—as a humorist and a sentimental novelist, it is true, but also as a spirited and humane radical, a man of the people with no humbug about him. From the start he had been idealized as well as idolized. Boz, in turn, had been eager to discover similar qualities in America. He had set out expecting to refute previous travellers such as Mrs. Trollope and Harriet Martineau, who had reported on the defects of

America, but before he reached New York he found himself beginning to agree with them. The Americans were also disappointed. They had expected a genial Boz who would be flattered and grateful for their adulation: instead they had to deal with a flashy young man of coarser cut whose criticism was as impetuous as his flattery.

There were many reasons why the initial fantasy dissolved into disagreeable fact. Dickens listed some of them in his lengthening catalogue of grievances. But the fundamental failure was emotional. In quarrelling with the Americans he was in a sense arguing with his own shadow. He saw them as bumptious and aggressive; they had a thrusting ambition; they were given to self-righteousness; they loved to drive a hard bargain and crow about it afterwards; though they were hospitable they were touchily proud and resentful of criticism; and, having come up in the world, insecurity made them crave admiration. At the heart of his angry discontent lay a strong element of self-deception.

As soon as *American Notes* had gone to press, Dickens rushed Forster and Longfellow off to Rochester to see his childhood haunts. On another occasion they went to look at the wretched lodging-houses of the Old Mint area of the borough, occupied by tramps and thieves. Maclise, who accompanied them, was so upset and sick that he had to remain outside in the care of the police. There was a visit to Bath to call on Landor, before Dickens saw off Longfellow next day at Bristol. Back in London he prepared for the 'vagabondism' with Forster, Maclise, and Clarkson Stanfield which had been planned as a special celebration of his homecoming. He was thinking of opening his next novel in 'some terribly dreary iron-bound spot'[35] on the Cornish coast, he had told Forster in September, and he wanted to see the lie of the land. The four men travelled partly by rail—the Great Western line had now reached Taunton—and partly in an open carriage. Primed by bottles 'distracting in their immense varieties of shape' the party rollicked round the sights of Cornwall—Tintagel, Land's End, St. Michael's Mount. It was an expensive eight-day jaunt—£88 for the four of them—but worth while. 'I do believe there never was such a trip,' Dickens gasped to Felton, 'I never laughed in my life as I did on this journey.'[36]

Plotting the new tale of 'English Life and Manners', which Chapman and Hall were to publish in monthly parts from 1 January 1843, was a much less jolly business. It was the serial he had promised his readers before going to America, but it had been delayed by *American Notes* and now he was under pressure to have it ready. 'I am in the agonies of a new harness just now,' he wrote to Thomas Hood on 12 November 1842, 'and walk up and down the house smiting my forehead dejectedly.'[37] He was loath to get started; on the same day as he wrote to Hood he was offering to write a prologue for *The Patrician's Daughter*, the new play which Macready was putting on at Drury Lane in December, and he started at once to write it. In his uncertainty he could not decide where to set the new novel or what to call it. 'I have been working feebly all day,' he wrote to Maclise on 15 November, 'and between that and the weather, am damnably hipped. Shall we repair to some Saloon tonight?'[38] He finally decided to shift the opening scene from Cornwall to a Wiltshire village. He ran through a declension of names—Sweezlewag, Chuzzleboy, Chuzzlewig—before he hit on Martin Chuzzlewit for his hero. By 26 November the first advertisements had appeared for the story of Chuzzlewit's 'family, friends and enemies. . . . The whole forming a complete key to the house of Chuzzlewit.'

It was also a key to the house of Dickens, who knew from his own experience how selfishness could corrupt a family and how anxiety about money could destroy affection. A Dickens hero soon learns that he is alone in the world and cannot count upon his relations. Like Oliver and like Nicholas, the young Martin Chuzzlewit is denied his birthright; maligned and misunderstood, he also becomes a wandering exile. This arbitrary change in his fortunes is a profound shock. 'I have been bred up from childhood with great expectations', Martin says in a self-commiserating tone, 'and have always been taught to believe that I should be, one day, very rich.' And he is chastened by one tribulation after another. Cheated by the hypocritical Mr. Pecksniff, who steals his work as an architect, he emigrates to America; swindled out of his remaining assets by the land speculators in the Mississippi settlement of Eden, he nearly dies of swamp fever. Only a magical turn of events can rescue him, and to round out the novel the miserly old Martin Chuzzlewit relents and restores him to favour in a general round of punishments and rewards. The fate of Martin, it seems, depends as much upon the whims of his grandfather as the fate of a child depends on apparently irrational shifts of mood and circumstance in its parents.

At the time that Dickens was launching *Chuzzlewit* he had been driven to reflect on the disposition to selfishness and even to fraud exhibited by his own family, especially his father. John Dickens was energetically selfish without any sense of shame, and he had acquired the experienced debtor's knack of living from day to day without any thought of detection. While Dickens had been away in America he had gone back to his old habit of raising money from his son's friends and business associates without his knowledge. He managed to get £20 from Macready, but a letter sent to 'Miss Coutts & Co' in March 1842 requesting a loan of £25 was refused; 'contemporaneous events', he wrote to the bankers, 'place me in a difficulty which without some anticipatory pecuniary effort I cannot extricate myself from'.[39] Dickens, however, had asked Mitton to send his father a regular allowance. 'How long he is, growing up to be a man!'[40] Dickens had written to Mitton in April when he heard that John Dickens was in trouble again; soon he was fobbing off some of his creditors by presenting them with pages from the manuscript of *O'Thello*, the farce which Dickens had written for family entertainment years before. By the summer of 1842 any hopes of keeping John Dickens in Devon were beginning to fade. He had already let the lease of the Alphington cottage lapse and moved temporarily into the neighbouring house which he rented furnished at twelve shillings a week; and by February 1843 he was back in London, living out on the Kent road at Lewisham. Dickens was exasperated. 'The thought of him besets me, night and day,' he wrote to Mitton on 20 February 1843, 'and I really do not know what is to be done with him. It is quite clear that the more we do, the more outrageous and audacious he becomes.' In the words of Sam Weller he declared that his father 'has gone ravin' mad with conscious willany'.[41]

Wretched though Dickens felt about his father's behaviour, he was resiliently cheerful and determined that his own home should be run on very different lines. He made sure that he was in control of things. The fussy manner in which he had treated Kate as her suitor was hardening into a habit as a husband, and as a father. He was full of fun and affection for his children, but he kept them at a distance; games were to be played in his way to enable him to shine as master of the revels. On Twelfth Night 1843 at the customary party to celebrate Charley's birthday there was a magic lantern show and a conjuring act to amuse the children. Yet Dickens, inspired by the professional performance he had seen the previous summer, was equally anxious to perform before 'some children of a larger growth' including the painter Edwin Landseer, Leigh Hunt, and Captain Marryat. He and Forster had bought the stock-in-trade of a conjurer, he reported to Felton, 'the practice and display whereof is entrusted to me'.[42] The magic and the posture of command appealed to Dickens and the role became a part of his social repertoire for years to come.

After so long a rest from fiction Dickens found it difficult to recover the rhythm of the serial. He was also missing the constant support of Forster, who was ill for much of the year with rheumatic fever. 'I am in a difficulty', Dickens wrote to the invalid in February, 'and am coming down to you sometime today or tonight. I couldn't write a line yesterday; not a word, though I really tried hard. In a kind of despair I started off at half-past two with my pair of petticoats to Richmond; and dined there!!'[43] A few days later, when *Chuzzlewit* was moving more easily, he declared to Forster that the opening out of the characters was 'one of the most surprising processes of the mind in this sort of invention. Given what one knows, what one does not know springs up; and I am as absolutely certain of its being true, as I am of the law of gravitation.'[44] By the end of the month he had set up a working routine. 'My plan now is to keep myself strictly at home (with the exception of a long country walk or ride every day) during one half of the month,' he told Lady Holland; 'and I find it a capital one, both for health and pleasant authorship.'[45]

At the end of March 1843 Dickens took rooms at Cobley's Farm at Finchley, staying for at least a month to get on with his novel; and the convalescent Forster joined him there and talked over the problems of writing it. He worked at it steadily throughout the spring, and although he was pleased with some of it the story was not going as well as he hoped or as well as his publishers expected by way of sales. By the end of April the subscription had fallen to about 20,000 copies, a fifth of *The Old Curiosity Shop* at its peak and half of *Nickleby*. Forster thought it had been a mistake to revert to monthly parts. Someone else suggested that the interval since the last novel had been too long. And the general depression in trade did not help. To stimulate the market Dickens decided to dispatch Martin Chuzzlewit to America.

The adverse reception also created difficulties between Dickens and his publisher. By midsummer the serial was scarcely paying its way, and when Dickens called on William Hall one afternoon in June the publisher not only complained about the poor sales but hinted that the firm might invoke the penalty clause in the contract. This stipulated that if the profits were not enough to meet the monthly advance of £200 the publisher might deduct £50 from it. The hint was enough to send Dickens storming away to complain to Forster. The next day, still fuming, he told Forster that he was so irritated 'that a wrong kind of fire is burning in my head, and I don't think I *can* write'.[46] As recently as October 1842 he had recommended Chapman and Hall to W. H. Prescott as 'perfectly truthful, reliable and honorable men in all their dealings'.[47] Now, when Hall suggested that hard times might require them to claim their contractual rights, Dickens fell into intemperate abuse and declared that he would break with these 'scaly-headed vultures' as he had broken with Bentley. The first disdainful step was to force the money into their 'reduced mouths' although Dickens himself was currently hard up and borrowing from Mitton. 'I am bent on paying Chapman and Hall *down*,' he informed Forster. 'And when I have done that Mr. Hall shall have a piece of my mind.'[48] The second step was to open negotiations with a printer. Dickens resented the prosperity of his publishers and for some time he had been toying with the idea of handling his books himself. Bradbury and Evans seemed a likely prospect. They had printed *American Notes* and were running off *Chuzzlewit*. In 1842 the firm had taken over the radical *Punch*, founded a year before as a weekly of 'wit and whim, cuts and caricature' by Mark Lemon and Henry Mayhew. Forster was now instructed to make a confidential approach to Bradbury. Dickens was about to move on again.

The theatre was one relief from these irritations. For all the success of Macready's productions at Drury Lane, he had failed to make the venture pay and he decided to make a tour in America. Dickens gladly organized a testimonial for his friend, which was to be presented by the Duke of Cambridge at the end of Macready's season, and he was at the farewell performance of *Macbeth* on 14 June when the great tragedian was greeted by his audience with 'mad acclaim'. Such fervent approval impressed Dickens and encouraged him to revive his old daydreams of becoming a playwright. He had already responded to a light-hearted letter from Douglas Jerrold about a competition with a prize of £500 for a new comedy sponsored by the dramatist Benjamin Webster. 'Chuzzlewit be damned. High Comedy and five hundred pounds are the only matter I can think of,' he told Jerrold. 'I walk up and down the street at the back of the Theatre every night, and peep in at the Green Room Window—thinking of the time when "Dick-Ins" shall be called for.... Then I shall come forward and bow—once—twice–thrice—Roars of approbation—Brayvo—Brarvo—Hooray—Hoorar —one cheer more.'[49]

Dickens enjoyed the flattery of applause and he was familiar with it as a public speaker. It was yet another role in which he excelled and he was constantly in demand for meetings in support of good causes and for dinners on behalf of worthy institutions. On 17 May he presided at a meeting called to form a Society of Authors, intended to protect the interests of authors, publishers, printers, and booksellers and to work for copyright protection.

On 20 May he excused himself from Talfourd's birthday party on account of 'a horrible engagement' for a dinner of the Deaf and Dumb Society. Complaining of the 'nuisance of these things' he swore that this would be the year's 'final appearance on the London Tavern Stage'.[50] Nevertheless he turned out for the Printers' Pension Society, the Actors' Benevolent Fund, the Hospital for Consumptives, and a dinner in June, with Lord Ashley in the chair, to support the sanatorium which the noted health reformer Dr. Southwood Smith had recently opened opposite the Dickens house in Devonshire Place. He was equally energetic in personal charities, raising money for hard-up theatrical people and embarrassed men of letters. He was, for instance, the chairman of the subscription got up for the penniless children of the actor Edward Elton, drowned in the North Sea in July 1843, and devoted himself to the matter on and off for several months.

His relatives were another set of charitable concerns, though he found these 'blood petitioners' a growing strain on his temper and his purse. The most persistent claimant, of course, was his father, an unremitting source of worry and irritation. John Dickens was still in debt, and still sponging. In July he wrote to Chapman and Hall. 'As I am to be an independent Gentleman,' he saucily inquired, 'how am I to get rid of my time?' And he went on to suggest that they should pay the five-guinea yearly cost of a steamer ticket up the Thames from Greenwich so that he could divert himself at the British Museum.[51] He also sent Dickens 'a threatening letter, before God', complaining that more should be done for Alfred—although Dickens had planned to take on his brother as a paid secretary when he could not find work as a trained engineer. Dickens, as he confessed to Mitton, was impatiently dispirited by the 'audacity' of his father's ingratitude. 'He, and all of them, look upon me as a something to be plucked and torn to pieces for their advantage. They have no idea of, and no care for, my existence in any other light. My soul sickens at the thought of them.'[52]

It was a time of distress and strong reactions. In April, with much approval from Dickens, Thomas Carlyle published *Past and Present*, and its passionate setting of the poor against the rich was so powerful that it frightened moderate reformers and angered the ruling classes. Carlyle's teasing friend, the poet and politician Richard Monckton Milnes, declared that the book 'would be very dangerous if turned into the vernacular and generally read'. At Christmas, *Punch* came out with Thomas Hood's attack on sweated labour in his poem 'The Song of the Shirt', and again Dickens warmly endorsed its bitter sentiments. The new magazine was in the forefront of the reform movement from the beginning and, although Dickens did not write for it himself, he was soon on the friendliest terms with its staff. Its portly editor, Mark Lemon, was witty, warm-hearted, full of clownish good humour, and such a free spender that he was always in trouble about money. He was three years older than Dickens, and though he had lost his father when he was young he had grown up in comfortable circumstances, until the failure of a family business had cut off his income and forced him to support himself for a spell by tavern-keeping. He published some papers and verses in *Bentley's Miscellany* while Dickens was editing it, and before that—by an odd turn of events—in April 1836 the Strand Theatre had put on Lemon's first farce, which was based on Stamper Jingle, the man who wrote the rhyming advertisements for Warren's Blacking. In the next few years Lemon produced a run of burlettas and melodramas (in 1842 he wrote the Christmas pantomime for Covent Garden) and after he launched *Punch* in the summer of 1842 the paper was at first kept afloat by subsidies from his stage income. His sense of fun, his sentimental radicalism, and his love of the theatre all appealed to Dickens, and by the spring of 1843 Mark and Nelly Lemon were regular guests at Devonshire Terrace.[53]

John Leech, who was the leading cartoonist at *Punch*, was also recruited into the Devonshire Terrace group. Tall, handsome, and melancholy, he was quick and prolific, and his eye for contemporary style was so sharp that women living in the provinces were said to use his cartoons as a guide to London fashion. Thackeray, too, was now back in London working as a freelance journalist and writing regularly for *Punch*. He had been through a troubled time. After the birth of his daughter Harriet in 1840 his wife had succumbed to a mental illness and they had moved to Paris to be near her family. When her condition deteriorated she was confined to a nursing home, leaving Thackeray to care for his two young daughters and to resume his career. He was not an easy colleague. 'I never felt quite at home with him,' Mark Lemon confessed; 'he was always so infernally wise. He seemed too great for ordinary conversation.'[54] Yet his cynical humour suited *Punch*, his contributions were popular, and he was soon taken up by the literary set. Forster was a particular friend. 'When anybody is in a scrape we all fly to him for refuge,' Thackeray said of his characteristic helpfulness. 'He is omniscient and works miracles.'[55] And though Thackeray's cool temperament held off the familiarity with which Dickens liked to envelop his intimates he was welcomed at Devonshire Terrace. In April 1843 he spent a jolly day at the house; there was riding in the afternoon and card games over claret after dinner.

Alfred Tennyson, then beginning to make his formidable reputation, was a fellow guest on that occasion. His *Poems*, which had appeared in the previous year, proclaimed a 'vision of the world and all the wonder that might be' with an expansive sweep which caught the imagination of energetic Victorians. Though Dickens was attracted by such buoyant rhetoric, he was politically more sympathetic to the fiery-tempered radicalism of Douglas Jerrold which set the tone of *Punch*. Jerrold was a man of striking appearance, for he had a large head with a swept mane of hair on a slight body; he was given to puns with a sharp, aggressive edge—he once saluted Forster in his club with the words 'Well, Forster, they tell me Dickens pays the dog-tax for you', and he was given to making quips at Thackeray's expense. Having struggled to educate himself and tried the navy, printing, and journalism for a living, Jerrold had a base of hard experience for his sympathy with the poor. His combative posture appealed to Dickens, who told Jerrold on one occasion that he shared 'the exact spirit' of *Punch* and hated 'the Power of the Purse'. He could let himself go to Jerrold, to whom he wrote after a charity dinner on 1 May 1843, describing the City aldermen as 'slobbering, bow-paunched, overfed, apoplectic, snorting cattle' who made him feel 'degraded and debased'.[56]

Dickens was just as indignant about sacerdotal clergymen and he was disturbed by the High Church movement, led by Pusey, Newman, and Keble, which he thought reactionary and obsessed with dogma and ritual. He wrote to Cornelius Felton in March 1843 that he was disgusted with 'our Established Church, and its Puseyisms, and daily outrages on common sense and humanity'.[57] In June he sent an unsigned leader for the *Examiner* to the same effect. 'Good God,' he exclaimed to Albany Fonblanque, 'to talk in these times of most untimely ignorance among the people, about what Priests shall wear and whither they shall turn when they say their prayers!'[58] Dickens preferred the Unitarians, a sect to which Forster belonged because they '*would* do something for human improvement, if they could'.[59] In November 1842 he had gone to the nearby Unitarian Chapel in Little Portland Street to hear a sermon by its minister, the Revd. Edward Tagart. He was so taken by Tagart's views that he rented a pew and the family became regular attenders. To ensure that his son Charley should not 'get hold of any conservative or High Church notions', he told Jerrold, he had begun to write a history of England for children.[60]

As a break from 'powdering away' at *Martin Chuzzlewit* Dickens took Kate for a holiday at the beginning of July to stay near Malton in Yorkshire.[61] Their host was Charles Smithson, who had private means and had retired from his partnership with Thomas Mitton before he was forty. He and his wife, the sister of T. J. Thompson, were old friends of the Dickens family—Dickens was godfather to their daughter, and his mother had gone to help at the birth earlier in the year. 'We performed some madnesses there', he wrote to Felton, 'in the way of forfeits, pic-nics, rustic games, inspections of ancient monasteries at midnight when the moon was shining.'[62] By the middle of July he was back in London 'very brown in the face from Northern toasting', and in good spirits ready for the annual expedition to Broadstairs at the beginning of August.[63] He found it as 'bright and beautiful' as ever but was disturbed by music next door. 'I have been here six years, and have never had a Piano next door,' he wrote to Angela Burdett Coutts. 'I was driven into such a state of desperation on Saturday that I thought I must have run away and deserted my family.'[64]

Dickens was pleased with his progress on *Chuzzlewit*. 'I have great confidence in the story,' he told Mitton in July;[65] and from Broadstairs he reported, 'I have nearly killed myself with laughing at what I have done of the American No.—though how much comicality may be in my knowledge of its Truth, I can't say.'[66] He did not, however, manage to make his American readers laugh; he made them angry. Reports of its reception were beginning to come in and they were far from favourable. Dickens had repeated the posture of *American Notes* in an exaggerated fictional form without the saving expression of friendship. 'I have a strong spice of the

Devil in me,' Dickens had written to the Scots author David Moir on 19 May; 'and when I am assailed, as I think falsely or unjustly, my red hot anger carries me through it bravely.'[67] Even friends who had stood by him over *American Notes* found it hard to accept *Chuzzlewit*, and it cost him the respect of such American acquaintances as Irving, Halleck, and W. C. Bryant. Longfellow now thought that Dickens was 'living in a strange hallucination about this country'.[68] Some readers in England again criticized Dickens for bad manners. Elizabeth Barrett complained that he had 'used all this honor to dishonor himself—he is an ungrateful, an ungrateful man!'[69] Macready commented when he read the American number: 'It will not do Dickens good, and I grieve over it.'[70] Carlyle was one of the few who approved. 'The last *Chuzzlewit* on Yankee-doodledodum is capital,' he wrote to Forster. 'We read it with loud assent, loud cachinnatory approval!'[71]

Dickens was not abashed by the criticism. 'Martin has made them all stark staring raving mad across the water,' he told Forster, but he felt obliged to meet the charge of discourtesy. He asked Forster whether it would be wise to announce 'that as soon as I began to have any acquaintance with the country, I set my face against any public recognition whatever but that which was forced upon me to the destruction of my peace and comfort—and made no secret of my real sentiments'.[72] In August he spoke at a splendid dinner given at the Star and Garter at Richmond on the eve of Macready's departure for America. But he was eager to spare his friend embarrassment and he refrained from going to Liverpool as planned with Forster, Maclise, and Stanfield to see Macready on board the steamer; 'after the last *Chuzzlewit*', he wrote to Macready, that would be '*fatal* to your success, and certain to bring down upon you every species of insult and outrage'.[73] And so he stayed at Broadstairs 'pegging away, tooth *and nail*, at *Chuzzlewit*', until the middle of September, when he went up to London to look into an unusual philanthropic enterprise.[74]

An appeal for help had appeared in *The Times* in February 1843 for the Ragged Schools, a religiously inspired movement which had begun some years before to give the elements of instruction to some of the poorest waifs in London. Dickens was understandably intrigued. The Report on Child Employment which had just been published had already turned his mind to the notion of writing a cheap pamphlet on the plight of the poor man's child. And the Ragged Schools touched the same nerve. At the instance of Miss Coutts, who had been asked to give financial support to the venture, he arranged to visit the school at Field Lane, Saffron Hill, on 14 September. He was appalled by what he saw; it reminded him of Fagin's den. Stanfield went with him and was overcome by the foulness of the place. 'I have very seldom seen, in all the strange and dreadful things I have seen in London and elsewhere,' Dickens told Miss Coutts, 'anything so shocking as the dire neglect of soul and body exhibited in these children.' He had no doubt that the experiment was 'most worthy of your charitable hand'. In his description of the plight of the slum children—'who know nothing of affection, care, love, or kindness of any sort'—he objected to the canting 'viciousness of insisting on creeds and forms in educating such miserable beings', and remarked appreciatively on the willingness of Miss Coutts to provide a larger schoolroom and baths rather than uplifting tracts. 'I know you to be very, very far-removed, from all the Givers in all the Court Guides between this, and China.'[75]

Dickens had known Miss Coutts for about four years—he had met her through one of the partners of Coutts & Co., where he had banked since he began to make money from *Pickwick*—and he was becoming a friend to whom she turned for advice in her charitable undertakings. 'I have no doubt she will do whatever I ask her in the matter,' Dickens told Forster after his visit to Saffron Hill. 'She is a most excellent creature ... and I have a most perfect affection and respect for her.'[76] There was an odd story behind her fortune. She was the sixth child of Sir Francis Burdett, the passionate and eccentric radical who represented Westminster in the House of Commons and had twice been imprisoned for his opinions. Burdett was the son-in-law of Thomas Coutts, the great banker, who left his fortune to an actress he had married in old age; and she in turn passed it on to Angela Burdett, who was required to assume the family name. In 1837, when Angela Burdett Coutts came into her vast inheritance (it was said that if her capital were turned into gold sovereigns the line would stretch for twenty-four miles, and her annual income was variously set at sums of up to £100,000), she was twenty-three, and she had been brought up in a round of spas and watering-places. She was plain with a poor complexion, but she was agreeable, quiet, and strong-minded. With the support of Hannah Meredith, her one-time governess and lifelong companion, she proved capable of managing her wealth and devoting it to pious and charitable ends, often anonymously. She founded bishoprics and built churches, supported missionaries, patronized scientists, and encouraged education.[77]

At first Dickens was somewhat overawed by her wealth and social standing. A dinner invitation for 15 August 1840 to meet a royal duke and duchess had made him apprehensive, not least about the prospect of looking ridiculous in court dress. Early in 1841, however, he was on sufficiently close terms to make Miss Coutts one of the six persons to whom he revealed in advance that Little Nell would die, and in the late summer he wrote a jolly letter from Broadstairs about her dinner invitations that had followed him round the country. He kept in regular touch with her. By the end of 1843, after both Miss Coutts and her companion had been ill—and their drunken nurse had provided a model for Mrs. Gamp—Dickens dedicated *Martin Chuzzlewit* to her.

On 16 September 1843, two days after Dickens visited the Ragged School, he suggested to Macvey Napier that he should write an article about the outcast children for the *Edinburgh Review*. Its purpose, he explained, would be 'to come out strongly' against a system of education 'based exclusively upon the principles of the Established Church'. What he called the 'Dangerous Classes of Society' were in such a miserable state 'that their very nature rebels against the simplest religion'.[78] Napier was uneasy and thought it bad policy to hit the Church unnecessarily.[79] In the event the article was never written. A few weeks later, at the instigation of his sister Fanny who had moved to Manchester in 1841, Dickens went up to speak in the Free Trade Hall with Disraeli and Cobden. The occasion was a soirée to raise money for the Athenaeum, an educational institution for workingmen, which had run into debt as a result of the trade depression. It was a suitable occasion to talk of the abolition of poverty by the abolition of ignorance and while he was there Dickens had the idea of turning his experience at the Ragged School into fiction. By mid-October he had begun to write *A Christmas Carol*. The outcast children who reminded Dickens of Fagin's gang had provided the emotional spring which drove on the story. There was also a more mundane motive for writing it. *Chuzzlewit* was not doing well and he needed money. In the summer he had borrowed £70 from Mitton so as not to overdraw his account. Now he set about working from morning till night until the Christmas story was completed at the beginning of December. He told Felton that he excited himself 'in a most extraordinary manner' when he was writing it; he 'wept and laughed, and wept again', he wrote, 'and thinking whereof he walked about the black streets of London fifteen and twenty miles many a night when all sober folks had gone to bed'.[80]

Dickens had not yet broken with Chapman and Hall, but with the *Carol* he went half-way towards a separation. He designed the book, employed John Leech to illustrate it (Phiz was busy with the illustrations for *Chuzzlewit*) and met the production costs himself. Chapman and Hall were reduced to publishing it on commission. When it was done Dickens showed it to his friends. 'I have never seen men, personally and mentally opposed to each other, so unanimous in their predictions, or so hot in their approval,' he wrote as he hastened the manuscript off to meet the Christmas market.[81] It was on sale by 19 December, but the booksellers were at first obstructive. 'There is a dead set against it I suspect in the trade,' Thomas Hood told Dickens, 'for not a showboard is to be seen nor will they put it in their windows.'[82] Dickens blamed Chapman and Hall. 'Can you believe that with the exception of Blackwood's, *the Carol is not advertised in One of the Magazines*,' he wrote to Mitton on 4 December; 'nothing but a tremendous push can possibly atone for such negligence.'[83] Even so, the first printing of 6,000 copies was sold out at once, and by March 1844 it was into its sixth edition. Dickens sent off copies to Cornelius Felton and Macready in America; 'by every post, all manner of strangers write all manner of letters', he told Felton, 'about their homes and hearths, and how this same *Carol* is read aloud there, and kept on a very little shelf by itself. Indeed it is the greatest success as I am told, that this Ruffian and Rascal has ever achieved.'[84] It was far better in its 'genuine goodness', declared Lord Jeffrey, 'than caricaturing American knaveries';[85] and Thackeray wrote enthusiastically in *Fraser's* that, if such an evocation of Christmas sentiment had appeared a fortnight sooner, 'all the prize cattle would have been gobbled up in pure love and friendship, Epping denuded of sausages, and not a turkey left in Norfolk'.[86]

A Christmas Carol was a 'prodigious success', and Dickens was quick to celebrate. 'I broke out like a Madman,' he told Felton. 'Such dinings, such dancings, such conjurings, such blindmans-buffings, such theatre-goings, such kissings-out of old years and kissings-in of new ones, never took place in these parts before.'[87] Macready was much missed during this jolly Christmas, particularly at the madcap party at his house. Forster and Dickens conjured bravely. 'A hot plum pudding was produced from an empty saucepan, held over a blazing fire, kindled in Stanfield's hat, without damage to the lining', Dickens told Macready, and 'a box of bran was changed into a live Guinea Pig, which ran between my God child's feet, and was the cause of such a shrill uproar and clapping of hands that you might have heard it (and I daresay did) in America.'[88] Jane Carlyle was one of the guests who was swept up by the gaiety of 'us little knot of blackguardist literary people' at 'the *very* most agreeable party that I was ever at in London'. Dickens, she wrote, was 'the *best* conjurer I ever saw', and he worked so extravagantly with Forster at his effects that 'they seemed *drunk* with their efforts'. After 'the pulling of crackers, the drinking of champagne, and the making of speeches', Forster seized her by the waist and whirled her away into a country dance.[89] Dickens was so taken up with his new role that he asked Fred to hire a magician's costume for the Twelfth Night party—'a black cloak with hieroglyphics on it ... a grave black beard—and a high black sugar-loaf hat—and a wand with a snake on it'. Forster ordered a similar set of garments in fiery red.[90]

With the *Carol* Dickens recovered and enhanced his popularity. Writing *American Notes* and *Martin Chuzzlewit* had done nothing, however, to dispel his feelings about America. He was as vitriolic in his language as ever, describing its leaders as 'the human lice of God's creation' and telling Macready that 'I never knew what it was to feel disgust and contempt 'till I travelled in America'.[91] But with the *Carol* he reasserted his radicalism in the sentimental form which was more appealing than sarcasm and anger. 'GOD BLESS HIM,' wrote Thackeray in the mood of the *Carol* itself. 'What a feeling is this for a writer to be able to inspire, and what a reward to reap!'[92]

9

Shadows in the Waters

'IF I had made money, I should unquestionably fade away from the public eye for a year,' Dickens told Forster in November 1843.[1] The completion of *Chuzzlewit* would mean a period of freedom and he did not know what to do with it. Dickens was eager for more success of the kind which he had so amply enjoyed in the ten years since *Pickwick* had made him a literary phenomenon; he had now become, as the *Westminster Review* remarked, 'the form and pressure of the age'.[2] At the same time he felt a need to escape. His American visit had taught him that a public role as 'the Inimitable Boz' could be irksome and exhausting as well as flattering. He also wanted some relief from the treadmill of serial composition. 'I am afraid of putting myself before the town as writing tooth and nail for bread, headlong, after the close of a book taking so much out of one as *Chuzzlewit*,' he wrote to Forster in explanation of his reluctance to tackle another book. 'I am afraid I could not do it, with justice to myself.' He thought he might temporarily revert from fiction to journalism, for he had not abandoned his idea of editing a newspaper or magazine and he knew that Bradbury and Evans were keen to invest in such a venture; but he was deterred by the economic depression. 'I am afraid of a magazine—just now,' he admitted to Forster. 'I don't think the time a good one or the chances favourable.'[3] He opted instead for a series of travel sketches of the kind he had written about America; and before the year was out he had decided to let the house in Devonshire Terrace and take his 'whole menagerie' to Europe.[4]

Forster was startled by the news. He did not want Dickens to go and urged him to give it more thought, believing that Dickens would be ready to write again after a break of two or three months. Dickens, however, said it was not rest enough after so many years never 'leaving off'. 'It is impossible to go on working the brain to that extent for ever,' he declared.[5] Forster suggested he should wait until the proposed cheap edition of his work had brought in more money. Although Dickens knew that Bradbury and Evans were keen to do business with him, he thought their scheme for a cheap reissue of all his books as premature as the plan to launch a newspaper: 'it would damage me and damage the property *enormously*',[6] he observed to

Forster. At the same time he was unwilling to make any new arrangement with Chapman and Hall, whom he now dismissed as 'preposterously ignorant of all the essentials of their business'.[7] Dickens stuck resolutely to his plan, convinced that a period abroad would cut his expenses by half.

One of the causes for his financial anxiety and the desire to get away was the 'unreasonable and unjust' cadging of his parents.[8] Back in Lewisham they were a great embarrassment and more expense than ever; 'anything like the damnable Shadow which this father of mine casts upon my face, there never was—except in a nightmare', Dickens told Mitton in February 1844, when he had been infuriated by yet another dun from his father.[9] To add to his familial obligations a fifth child was born to Kate on 15 January 1844. The boy was named Francis Jeffrey after the Scots judge and critic. Dickens was relieved when it was all over; he told Lady Holland afterwards that Kate had been 'exceedingly depressed and frightened', and with this latest pregnancy he began to feel that he had made sufficient contribution to the country's population.[10] Two days after the birth he eagerly responded to an invitation to dine with Forster, Stanfield, and Maclise at Richmond, even though he facetiously joked to Forster about leaving such 'delights of private life' as 'nurses wet and dry; apothecaries; mothers-in-law; babbies'.[11] A month after Kate's confinement Dickens wrote to T. J. Thompson to say that though Kate and the baby were doing well, 'I decline (on principle) to look at the latter object'.[12] Another child only added to his growing burden of responsibility and in his original plans for his European visit he proposed to leave the infant behind with Kate's mother.

Dickens was counting on the sales of the *Carol* to put his accounts straight and, unwilling in the meantime to become more indebted to his publishers, he overdrew two months' income from Coutts Bank and borrowed £200 from Thomas Mitton to tide him over Christmas. 'In March or so, please God, I shall be as rich as (a very moderate) Jew,' he had told Mitton in December.[13] He was in for a disappointment. When the accounts for the *Carol* were made up in February 1844 he discovered that so much had been spent on a lavish production selling for a mere five shillings that much of the expected income had been lost. 'Such a night as I have passed!' he complained to Forster. 'The first six thousand copies show a profit of £230! And the last four will yield as much more. I had set my heart and soul upon a Thousand, clear. What a wonderful thing it is, that such a great success should occasion me such intolerable anxiety and disappointment!'[14] Dickens had now so little regard for Chapman and Hall, he told Mitton, that 'I have not the least doubt that they have run the expences up, anyhow, purposely to bring me back, and disgust me with charges'. The result was that he was not only on his beam ends 'but tilted over on the other side'.[15]

Dickens was determined to get away but, money apart, it was not easy to decide where to settle. 'I have made up my mind to "see the world", and mean to decamp, bag and baggage, next midsummer for a twelvemonth!' he wrote to Lady Blessington on 10 March. 'I have got it into my head that Nice would be a favorable spot for Headquarters ... I am anxious to have the benefit of your kind advice.'[16] Lady Blessington recommended Italy, suggesting Pisa; then Dickens heard that Byron's old house at Albaro near Genoa might be rented, and he decided to write to his old friend Angus Fletcher, then living in Italy, asking his help.

As his plans developed through the spring he was beset by a fresh irritation. A flagrant plagiarism of *A Christmas Carol* in a twopenny weekly called *Parley's Illuminated Library* so incensed him that he instructed Thomas Talfourd to secure an injunction. 'If these Vagabonds can be stopped,' he angrily declared to Mitton, 'they must be.' Dickens had long suffered from plagiarists in England as well as pirates in America. *Pickwick* indeed was the most plagiarized book of the century, appearing in so many versions that after an unsuccessful attempt in 1838 to secure an injunction against an imitator Dickens concluded that he could do nothing but ignore 'dishonest dullards' who copied his work. Now he was in different mood. 'Let us be *sledge-hammer* in this', he went on to Mitton, 'or I shall be beset by hundreds of the same crew when I come out with a long story.'[17] His case was so strong that on 18 January the judge granted the injunction without even hearing Talfourd's carefully prepared argument, much to his chagrin. 'The pirates', Dickens crowed to Forster, 'are bruised, bloody, battered, smashed, squelched, and utterly undone.'[18] He soon discovered that the cry of triumph was premature. With Talfourd's encouragement he brought six separate actions—those against the printers and the booksellers he agreed to settle for an apology and costs—to find that the disreputable publishers went bankrupt to avoid the claim for damages. The more Dickens pursued the case through the maze of the law the more complicated and expensive it became. Finally he had to withdraw from the proceedings and meet the total cost of over £700. 'I shall not easily forget the expense, and anxiety, and horrible injustice,' he wrote two years later; 'asserting the plainest right on earth, I was really treated as if I were the robber instead of the robbed.' The case had reopened the wounds of the equally unsuccessful campaign against the American pirates, and when the same publishers plagiarized him again with saucy impunity, he responded with bitter resignation. 'It is better to suffer a great wrong', he told Forster, 'than to have recourse to the much greater wrong of the law.'[19]

The 'horrible injustice' of the *Carol* case confirmed Dickens in the contempt he had acquired in his youthful work as a law reporter and in his dislike of the established order; his disposition to exaggerate what he liked and disliked was beginning to harden into prejudice. 'I declare,' he told Forster in March, 'I never go into what is called "society" that I am aweary of it, despise it, hate it, and reject it. The more I see of its extraordinary conceit, and its stupendous ignorance of what is passing out of doors, the more certain I am that it is approaching the period when, being incapable of reforming itself, it will have to submit to be reformed by others off the face of the earth.'[20] And when he felt slighted he found comfort in radical rhetoric which identified him with other victims. 'I have great faith in the poor,' he wrote early in the year: 'to the best of my ability I always endeavour to present them in a favourable light to the rich; and I shall never cease, I hope, until I die, to advocate their being made as happy and wise as the circumstances of their condition, in its utmost improvement, will admit of their becoming.'[21]

It was in this spirit that he agreed to go to Liverpool in late February to preside at a soirée for the Mechanics' Institute and, although he could not accept all such invitations, promised to go on to a lavish conversazione at Birmingham in support of its Polytechnic Institute. He was in a jolly mood. Fanny and her husband came over from Manchester to see him. The *Britannia* on which Dickens had crossed to America, was in the Mersey and Dickens was delighted to go on board again and to take 'champagne and biscuits' with Captain Hewitt. 'I am very sorry indeed (and so was he) that you didn't see the old Ship,' Dickens wrote to Kate. The soirée was a huge success. Greeted by 'See the Conquering Hero Comes' on the organ, Dickens spoke to a packed hall of 1,300 people. He gave, he wrote facetiously to Kate, 'a vigorous, brilliant, humourous, pathetic, eloquent, fervid and impassioned speech' which was wildly applauded.[22] One of the items in the entertainment that followed was a piano solo by Christiana Weller, the daughter of T. E. Weller, a clerk in the Dublin Steam Packet Co. who knew Captain Hewitt; Weller was also an amateur music and drama critic who had written to Dickens a year before. Dickens amused his Liverpool audience by a punning reference to Christiana's family name, calling for his 'god-child', and he was clearly much taken by this frail nineteen-year-old beauty in a fur-trimmed green dress. She bore a striking resemblance to Mary Hogarth. Next day he sent Captain Hewitt to Weller, inviting himself to lunch, and afterwards he sent Christiana a lightly flirtatious piece of doggerel as a keepsake: 'I love her dear name which has won me some fame, but Great Heaven how gladly I'd change it!' He left next day for Birmingham after a lively costume ball which ended with 'Sir Roger de Coverley' at three in the morning.[23]

T. J. Thompson had been with Dickens in Liverpool and after the

Birmingham meeting Dickens wrote to tell him that the town hall was crammed to the roof, and that 'when Dick showed himself the whole company stood up, rustling like the leaves of a wood'. Dickens, who had been 'horribly nervous', when he arrived was delighted with the affair: 'Tarnation grand, it was, and rather unbalancing (especially after Sir Rogers and brandys-and-waters), but Dick with the heart of a lion dashed in bravely and made decidedly the best speech I ever heard him achieve. Sir, he was jocular, pathetic, eloquent, conversational, illustrative, and wise—always wise.' Though Dickens was in such a buoyant mood his second thoughts on Christiana were more sober. 'I cannot joke about Miss Weller', he told Thompson, 'for she is too good; and interest in her (spiritual young creature that she is, and destined to an early death, I fear) has become a sentiment with me. Good God what a madman I should seem, if the incredible feeling I have conceived for that girl could be made plain to anyone!'[24] He had reacted spontaneously to Christiana, endowing her with an ethereal appearance and childlike charm, and his first impulse was to protect and encourage her. As soon as he reached London he wrote to Mr. Weller enclosing his own two-volume set of Tennyson's *Poems* for Christiana, marking the items 'calculated to give her a good impression of the Poet's Genius'; and he said 'that she started out alone from the whole crowd the instant I saw her, and will remain there always in my sight'.[25]

Ten days later Dickens received a letter from Thompson saying that he had fallen in love with Christiana. 'I felt the blood go from my face to I don't know where, and my very lips turn white,' Dickens replied at once. 'I never in my life was so surprised, or had the whole current of my life so stopped, for the instant, as when I felt, at a glance, what your letter said.' Dickens confessed that he had been looking forward to Thompson's return in order to discuss Christiana's 'wonderful endowments' with him, and he went on to set out his complicated reactions to Thompson's news. 'If I had all your independent means', he said, 'I would not hesitate, or do that slight to the resolution of my own heart which hesitation would imply. But would win her if I could, by God.' Dickens admitted in the same letter that he was 'an excitable and headstrong man', and this flow of vicarious courtship swept him away. Always susceptible to an image of early death he had persuaded himself that Christiana was likely to be 'lost to this sad world' if her father pressed her to continue her musical career: 'I saw an angel's message in her face that day that smote me to the heart.' In phrases which directly recalled the last hours of Mary Hogarth he insisted that 'I could bear better her passing from my arms to Heaven than I could endure the thought of coldly turning off into the World again to see her no more.' But Christiana could be saved from her father's ambitions and her fate, he told

Thompson in emotional tones: 'a foreign climate would be, in a springtime like hers, the dawning of a new existence'. And he dreamed 'of the quiet happiness we might enjoy abroad, all of us together, in some delicious nook. ... Such Italian Castles, bright in sunny days and pale in moonlight nights, as I am building in the air!'[26]

Dickens seemed to feel no embarrassment or jealousy about Thompson's courtship. It clearly offered him a means of indirectly expressing his own feelings, and a month later he was urging Thompson to be forward in his suit. 'As to the father, I snap my fingers,' he wrote on 13 March. 'I would leap over the head of the tallest father in Europe, if his daughter's heart lay on the other side, and were worth having.'[27] As he began to promote Thompson's cause, indeed, his own fascination with Christiana passed. When he wrote to her on 8 April he was cheerfully avuncular. He had encouraged Thompson, he said, 'for I had that amount of sympathy with his condition, which, but that I am beyond the reach—the lawful reach—of the Wings that fanned *his* fire, would have rendered it the greatest happiness and pleasure of my life to have run him through the body'.[28] Dickens was writing from Malton in Yorkshire, where he had again seen Thompson at the funeral of his brother-in-law Charles Smithson who had died suddenly; at this meeting he learned that Christiana had depressed her suitor by telling him he was 'premature' and that there were 'other footprints in the field'. Writing in his most agreeable style he sought to tease Christiana into a more pliant mood; and before she married Thompson in October 1845 he was again called on to help—once, in June 1844, to secure Christiana a musical engagement at the Hanover Rooms, and several times to help the couple get over their difficulties with Mr. Weller.[29]

Dickens talked airily about the Italian skies, but during the early months of 1844 he was more short of cash than ever. Borrowing another £100 from Thomas Mitton he explained that 'my father's debts, two quarters income tax, etc., coming all at once, drive me, sailing so near the wind by not drawing any profits from C. and H., into a most uncomfortable corner'.[30] For all his urgent need to settle his affairs with Chapman and Hall the negotiations dragged on all through the spring; eventually the publishers were told that Dickens proposed to be done with them after the bound volume of *Chuzzlewit* appeared in July, and that he would repay the money he owed them for unearned advances. He reached this decision in June, when the situation took a marked turn for the better because Bradbury and Evans put up £1,500 to pay off the debt to Chapman and Hall and gave Dickens himself £1,300. This total advance of £2,800 was to be set against a quarter of what Dickens wrote over the next eight years, and it was to be interest free and without any conditions beyond an understanding that he would write a successor to the *Carol* for Christmas 1844. He had at last raised the money he needed to finance his year abroad.

The final instalment of *Martin Chuzzlewit* appeared on 1 July. The novel had provoked a great deal of critical comment in both England and America during the course of its appearance. In January 1844, the *Critic* noted that it was now 'the rage to decry Dickens, by pronouncing his *Chuzzlewit* a failure', and the sales had gone badly. When the critics assessed the novel as a whole, however, they generally took a more favourable view, and Sairey Gamp was universally regarded as one of his best creations. Both Laman Blanchard and Forster recognized that it marked a technical advance in his work. 'His characters have been more agreeable', Forster declared, 'but never so full of meaning thoroughly grasped and understood, or brought out with such wonderful force and ease.'[31] Not only did he regard it as the best novel Dickens had written, but he saw it as a turning point in his career. Dickens himself had believed in it from the beginning. 'I think "Chuzzlewit" in a hundred points immeasurably the best of my stories. That I feel my power now more than I ever did,' he told Forster. 'That I have a greater confidence in myself than I ever had. That I *know*, if I have health, I could sustain my place in the minds of thinking men, though fifty writers started up tomorrow.'[32] Although *Chuzzlewit* had a creaking plot, oscillated between relentless satire and aimless pathos, and lacked a single character for whom the reader might feel the kind of sympathy excited by Oliver or Little Nell, it was ambitious in its scale and social purpose. The clue to it lay in the biblical text which Dickens quoted in a preface: 'As we sow, we reap'. And he explained his intention. 'What is substantially true of families in this respect,' he wrote, 'is true of a whole commonwealth.' The novel was thus a deliberate homily on the failings of human nature after English and American society had done with it—a calendar of social evils from humbug, impersonation, and marital cruelty, to murder and suicide. Men might be born free, his moral ran, but everywhere they were 'bred for misery and ruin'.

'On the first of July—the first of July!—Dick turns his head towards the orange groves,'[33] Dickens told Thompson excitedly, though he still had to make all the practical arrangements to transport himself, Kate, Georgina, five small children, three women servants, and the dog Timber across France to Italy. It was not easy to decamp with such a large 'caravan', but he soon came up with an original solution. He decided to buy a 'good old shabby devil of a coach' for £45 from a relative of George Cattermole. It was, he told Forster, 'about the size of your library; with night-lamps and day-lamps and pockets and imperials and leathern cellars, and the most extra-ordinary contrivances'.[34] It was a cumbersome but convenient means of travelling, and to superintend all the arrangements along the way Dickens recruited a jovial French courier named Louis Roche, who turned out to be a 'perfect gem'.[35]

The last weeks in London were hectic. The family had to move out of Devonshire Terrace at the end of May to make room for their tenant and to set up an 'encampment' in Osnaburgh Street near by. On 4 June Dickens spoke at a dinner to assist Dr. Southwood Smith's sanatorium, and then on 19 June there was a grand farewell dinner at Greenwich which included among the forty guests such close friends as Maclise, Forster, Ainsworth, Stanfield, Hablôt Browne, Jerdan, Fonblanque, Jerrold, Thackeray, Stone, and Cruikshank. Carlyle declined. 'I truly love Dickens', he told Forster, 'and discern in the inner man of him a tone of real Music,' but the prospect of 'leg-of-mutton eloquence' at Greenwich in the dog-days was too much for him.[36] There was another, more private dinner given by Forster the day before the party left London, and on 2 July the Dickens family crossed the Channel at Dover.

The coach was taken across to Boulogne. It rumbled and swayed to Paris, and then three days down the road to Chalon-sur-Saône where it was hoisted aboard a barge, and the family went on by boat to Lyons and on to Avignon. From there the travellers rode to Aix and Marseilles, boarded the steamer *Marie Antoinette*, and sailed overnight to Genoa. Angus Fletcher, eager to help and comically incompetent, had been unable to rent Byron's house as it had fallen into disrepair, and as an alternative he had taken a three-months lease on the near-by Villa di Bella Vista. The party arrived on the evening of 16 July 1844. For all its splendid situation looking out over the bay, Dickens was at first taken aback and disappointed; he complained to Forster that this 'ghostly, echoing, grim, bare house' was set in 'the most perfectly lonely, rusty, stagnant old staggerer of a domain that you can possibly imagine'. The kitchens were like 'alchemical laboratories', and the stables were so full of vermin and swarmers 'that I always expect to see the carriage going out bodily, with legions of industrious fleas harnessed to and drawing it off'. He was soon calling the place the Pink Jail.[37]

He realized that Fletcher had made a poor bargain, for he soon discovered that a better house could have been taken at a quarter of the price. But he was committed for only three months and his natural buoyancy, encouraged by the Italian ambience, persuaded him to make the best of things: 'the sea breeze blows away all objections to it', he told Mitton.[38] Dickens was enchanted by the Italian light and colour, and he was soon writing to tell his friends and inviting them to visit. The sea was so bright, he wrote to Maclise, that it seemed as if a draught of it 'would wash out everything else, and make a great blue blank of your intellect'. While the children played in the vineyard he idled through the hot days doing little but 'eat and drink and read'.[39] It took time to acclimatize. The sirocco, he said, was 'like a gigantic oven out for a holiday'. Walking was out of the question and he felt the deprivation very much; instead, he told Stanfield, he went swimming each day among the rocks below the house 'like a fish in high spirits'.[40] As the days cooled he began to explore the 'extraordinary alleys and by-ways' lying between the crumbled palaces of Genoa, and he fell easily into his London habit of wandering about and watching. He looked into churches, noted Jesuit priests 'slinking noiselessly about in pairs, like black cats', poked about the markets and lounged about the harbour quays.[41] He went to the opera, the theatres, and the fascinating marionettes; and he set about learning Italian, astonished at the 'audacity with which one begins to speak when there is no help for it'.[42] Before the end of July Dickens was telling Maclise that they had 'fallen into a pretty settled easy track. We breakfast about halfpast nine or ten—dine about four—and go to bed about eleven. We are much courted by the visiting people, of course; and I very much resort to my old habit of bolting from callers, and leaving their reception to Kate.'[43] It was a pleasant, easy life. 'I never knew what it was to be lazy before,' Dickens wrote to d'Orsay.[44] He had not yet begun to work. There was so much to see and do and his writing materials did not arrive until the middle of August. 'I have got my paper and inkstand and figures now', he told Forster, 'and can think—I have begun to do so every morn-ing—with a business-like air, of the Christmas book.' He wrote from the best bedroom with its cheerful peaceful view, looking out 'at the sea, the mountains, the washed-out villas, the vineyards'.[45]

And yet he could not settle to write. For one thing, he was distracted by an accident; hurrying home one night after a reception at the palace of Byron's friend the Marquis di Negri he fell over a pole laid across the road, which brought on 'unspeakable and agonizing pain in the side' like that he had suffered as a boy.[46] For another, he had bouts of rheumatism; one night he was kept awake by a 'girdle of pain' round his waist. He was also homesick for his friends. 'Losing you and Forster is like losing my arms and legs,' he wrote to Maclise, 'and dull and lame I am without you.'[47] He invited Fred out for a fortnight's stay, offering to pay part of the cost; in early September Dickens went to meet him in Marseilles and brought him back along the difficult corniche road. They stopped the first night at Nice where, Dickens wrote to Forster, fleas 'of elephantine dimensions were gambolling boldly in the dirty beds; and the mosquitoes!—But here let me draw a curtain (as I would have done if there had been any). We had scarcely any sleep, and rose up with hands and arms hardly human.'[48] The morning after they arrived back in Genoa Fred was almost drowned while swimming in full view of the family 'all, crying, as you may suppose, like mad creatures'.⁴⁹ And when Fred left there was the further distraction of a move to new apartments in Genoa.

'There is not in Italy, they say (and I believe them) a lovelier residence than the Palazzo Peschiere,' Dickens wrote of the house to which he moved at the end of September.⁵⁰ It stood in imposing gardens, laid out in terraces with fountains and groves of oranges, lemons, roses, and camellias, with a view across the city to the sea. Dickens paid five guineas a week for the main apartment where the family could live in ducal style, with a real Spanish duke occupying the floor below. The grand *sala*, Dickens reported to Forster, was larger than the dining-room of the Academy; the frescoes on the walls and ceiling had been 'designed by Michael Angelo'; and the general effect, he told Angela Coutts, was like 'a Palace in a Fairy Tale'.⁵¹ Yet, despite its size and grandeur, he declared to Forster that 'the effect is not only cheerful but snug'.⁵²

Such style was enjoyable but scarcely conducive to work. He had an idea for his Christmas story but no title, and he seemed to need a working title before he could make a start. So he fretted. Frustration, he told Forster, 'has made my face white in a foreign land'.⁵³ It was the first time that he had tried to write away from his familiar surroundings, and he found the vivid Italian scene a distraction rather than a stimulus; he was homesick and his letters revealed it. 'Never did I stagger so upon a threshold before,' he complained to Forster. 'I seem as if I had plucked myself out of my proper soil when I left Devonshire Terrace; and could take root no more until I return to it.' If the fountains at the Peschiere played nectar, he added, 'they wouldn't please me half so well as the West Middlesex waterworks at Devonshire Terrace'.⁵⁴ Put down on Waterloo Bridge with freedom to roam the London streets, he wrote to Forster, 'I would come home, as you know, panting to go on' with his work.⁵⁵ And when he sent Macready a warm letter on 14 October to greet his return from America he said feelingly: 'My whole heart is with you *at home*.'⁵⁶ The perpetual tolling of the Genoa bells was particularly tiresome. He declared that they made his ideas 'spin round and round till they lost themselves in a whirl of vexation and giddiness and dropped down dead'.⁵⁷ They also had a numinous effect. At the end of September Dickens had a dream, almost as vivid as 'an actual Vision', in which 'poor Mary's spirit' spoke to him. 'I was not at all afraid,' he told Forster, 'but in a great delight, so that I wept very much, and stretching out my arms to it called it "Dear".' Affected, he thought, by the presence of an old altar in his bedroom, he talked to the ghostly figure in his dream about religion. 'You think, as I do, that the Form of religion does not so greatly matter, if we try to do good?—or,' Dickens believed he said, 'perhaps the Roman Catholic is the best? perhaps it makes one think of God oftener, and believe in him more steadily?' The Spirit, he told Forster, was 'full of such heavenly tenderness for me, that I felt as if my heart would break', and it replied, 'for *you*, it is the best!' He woke and at once repeated the dream to Kate 'that I might not unconsciously make it plainer or stronger afterwards'.[58]

Suddenly he realized that he could relieve his discomfort and put his nostalgia to creative use by indulging in a long reverie of London. The title came first. 'We have heard THE CHIMES at midnight, Master Shallow!' he exclaimed to Forster in a one-sentence note.[59] Though the bells might 'clash upon me now from all the churches and convents of Genoa, I see nothing but the old London belfry I have set them in.'[60] The contrast of misery and magnificence that lay all about him in Genoa was transposed to the familiar London streets and composed to point a moral. 'I like more and more my notion of making, in this little book, a great blow for the poor,' he told Forster on 8 October. And the nightmare of Mary's ghost both set the mood and provided a device for the plot. Trotty Veck, the broken-down messengerman, was more wretched than Bob Cratchit, and his seraphic daughter was as pathetically appealing as Tiny Tim. Veck, lacking even Cratchit's spark of manly independence, runs away from disagreeable realities by identifying with the rich and nodding agreement to their condescending quips against the poor. On New Year's Eve he seemingly dies, and his unhappy ghost has to watch the years of misfortune that afflict his daughter as the logical result of the cruel Malthusian arguments with which he has foolishly and obsequiously agreed. Then all this misery turns out to be nothing more than a bad dream. The bells, tolling out their judgement of failure in the Old Year and of hope for the New Year, have hallucinated Trotty Veck, and he wakes to realize that there is a greater truth in love than in the laws of political economy.

Dickens was at work upon a confused fantasy, in which the final effect depended upon a comforting stroke of magic even less convincing than Scrooge's conversion by Marley's ghost in *A Christmas Carol*. Yet he felt that it would repeat the earlier homily's success, and really move his readers by its telling and improving sentiments. 'If my design be anything at all,' he wrote, 'it has a grip upon the very throat of the time.'[61] Once he had started, indeed, he was much excited by the work. He sent a summary of the whole plot to Forster along with the first part of the story, telling him that he was 'in regular, ferocious excitement with the *Chimes*; get up at seven; have a cold bath before breakfast; and blaze away, wrathful and red-hot, until three o'clock or so'. He had seen how 'to work the bells' to echo his moral indignation. 'I am fierce to finish in a spirit bearing some affinity to those of truth and mercy, and to shame the cruel and the canting.'[62] He missed Forster, whom he always needed as a sounding-board, and he frankly admitted that 'with my steam very much up I find it a great trial to be so far off from you'.[63]

Throughout October he was totally absorbed in *The Chimes*. 'I have undergone as much sorrow and agitation as if the thing were real; and have wakened up with it at night,' he wrote to Forster, enclosing the third part. 'I was obliged to lock myself in when I finished it yesterday, for my face was swollen for the time to twice its proper size, and was hugely ridiculous.'[64] And when it was finished on 3 November he had 'what women call "a real good cry"!'[65] It had so deeply caught his emotions that even when it was done he could not settle. He had done his best in Genoa to repeat the London rhythm of work and play, but it was not enough. He missed his night-time marauding through the lively streets of London, the walks to Hampstead for a chop at Jack Straw's Castle, and the rides out to Richmond for a dinner. In the wild and wet Italian autumn he had to make do with the by-ways of the seaport, with long mountain walks in the rain, or a muleback expedition to take supper at a country inn. He apologized to Mitton for his failure to send a letter: 'None of my usual reliefs have been at hand; I have not been able to divest myself of the story . . . and am so shaken by such work in this trying climate that I am nervous as a man who is dying of Drink; and as haggard as a Murderer.' But he was pleased with his work. 'I believe I have written a tremendous Book', he told Mitton, 'and knocked the Carol out of the field.'[66]

The domestic background was superficially tranquil. Roche was running the household with great efficiency; the children were happy; and the family led a comfortable and agreeable life. Yet there were irritations. Macready's young sister-in-law Susan Atkins was staying and she was a tiresome guest. Although Dickens was anxious to reciprocate Macready's care for his children whilst he and Kate had toured America, and insisted that she should be treated kindly, the strain of her presence only increased his tension and he yearned to get away. He was almost desperate for the company of his London cronies, and longed for the stimulus of their reaction to *The Chimes*. 'I would give a hundred pounds (and think it cheap) to see you read it,' he told Forster.[67] It was not long before he had found the excuse of seeing the proofs through the press to justify a trip to London. When Forster objected that the trip would be costly and difficult with winter drawing on, Dickens insisted. It was 'not because the proofs concern me at all', he now confessed, 'but because of that unspeakable restless something which would render it almost as impossible for me to remain here and not see the thing complete, as it would be for a full balloon, left to itself, not to go up'. The only way he could find the necessary release was to go home and present the tale to his friends. 'I particularly want Carlyle above all to see it before the rest of the world,' Dickens wrote to Forster, knowing that the Sage of Chelsea would warmly praise his savage attack on heartless utilitarians; 'and I should like to inflict the little story on him and on dear old gallant Macready with my own lips and to have Stanny and the other Mac sitting by. Now, if you was a real gent, you'd get up a little circle for me, one wet evening, when I come to town.'[68]

Dickens had so far seen nothing of Italy beyond Genoa and he decided to take a sightseeing holiday before heading for England. Roche was to go with him: as they planned their tour to Parma, Venice, Verona, and Milan (where Kate and Georgina were to join him for a few days), he watched 'the brave courier measuring bits of maps with a carving-fork, and going up mountains on a tea-spoon'.[69] They left on 6 November in a coach which splashed through the mire at four miles an hour.

Although Dickens was so anxious to get away that he left three days after he finished *The Chimes*, he was bothered, he said, about leaving Kate behind like a baron's lady at the time of the Crusades. He knew that both Kate and Georgina were 'easily run away with . . . by the irritation and displeasure of the moment' and, still fearful of a scene over their troublesome guest which might upset Macready, he wrote from Parma to remind Kate of the rules of hospitality: 'do not let any natural dislike to her inanities, interfere in the slightest degree with an obligation so sacred'. He was clearly in an anxious state of mind. 'Keep things in their places,' he added. 'I can't bear to picture them otherwise.' And for all the distractions of the journey he felt lonely away from the family. 'It is dull work, this travelling alone,' he told Kate. 'My only comfort is, in Motion. I look forward with a sort of shudder to Sunday, when I shall have a day to myself in Bologna. . . . Never did anybody want a companion after dinner (to say nothing of after supper) so much as I do.'[70]

Venice, which he reached at night after five days on the road, delighted him and he wrote lyrically about it to Forster and Jerrold. 'Opium couldn't build such a place', he told Forster,[71] and he assured Jerrold that 'the sensation of that night and the bright morning that followed, is a part of me for the rest of my existence'.[72] Yet the brilliance was matched by darkness. He also described to Forster the sickening gloom of 'its awful prisons, deep below the water; its judgment chambers, secret doors, deadly nooks'.[73] The fearful implements of torture he had seen in a museum provoked a tirade against 'the good old days'. It was far better, he insisted to Jerrold, to live in a supposedly degenerate age when iron was being used to build a railway to Venice instead of making 'engines for driving screws into the skulls of innocent men'.[74]

It was a slow journey, punctuated by visits to Roman ruins, galleries, and palaces. The pace of the coach was often so tedious that Dickens would walk ahead for a couple of hours, giving himself exercise and the pleasure of conversation with the amiable Italians he met along the road. By 18 November, when he made his rendezvous with Kate and Georgina, he had shaken off his irritable mood; he looked healthier and he was sleeping better. Three days later he and Roche left for England.

Dickens planned to walk into the coffee-room of the Piazza Hotel in Covent Garden in time for dinner on Sunday 1 December. 'Now, you know my punctiwality,' he had written to Forster on 4 November. 'Frost, ice, flooded rivers, steamers, horses, passports, and custom-houses may damage it.'[75] All such hindrances came his way, but he was in increasing good spirits. He dragged Roche along on a moonlight crossing by foot of the Simplon Pass, up through the ice and snow and down to breakfast among the Swiss meadows. They went on to Basle and Strasburg, thence to Paris in a diligence that toiled for fifty hours through the mud, and straight on to Boulogne. He was a day early when he walked into the Piazza Hotel on Saturday evening and, seeing Forster and Maclise at their usual table by the fire, rushed across the room to embrace them.

The first of the eight days Dickens spent in London were taken up with revision of *The Chimes* manuscript to meet Forster's criticism that the satire on flint-hearted political economists was too extreme. Dickens complied, though he reminded Forster that the *Westminster Review* had considered Scrooge's present of a turkey to the Cratchit family as a breach of sound economic laws. On Monday, the text was taken to Bradbury and Evans for setting; as the firm was still no more than a printing house, Chapman and Hall were to distribute the book. Dickens was in such a benevolent mood that he agreed to this scheme without recalling his irritation at the way his old publishers had managed the *Carol* only a year before. He had Doyle and Leech to breakfast to discuss their illustrations for *The Chimes* and he wrote to Kate that 'with that winning manner which you know of' he had persuaded them to redraw one apiece.[76] He dined at Gore House with Lady Blessington and Count d'Orsay. On Tuesday 3 December at half past six, he went round to Forster's rooms in Lincoln's Inn Fields to read the story.

Maclise sketched the listening group—Forster, Stanfield, 'the grave attention' of Carlyle, Blanchard Jerrold, Laman Blanchard, the journalist W. J. Fox, the painter William Dyce, and the literary clergyman William Harness—and sent it off to Kate; 'there was not a dry eye in the house', he told her. 'We should borrow the high language of the minor theatre and even then not do the effect justice—shrieks of laughter—there were indeed—and floods of tears as a relief to them—I do not think that there ever was such a triumphant hour for Charles.'[77] Macready missed the reading, for he was about to leave for a Paris season, but Dickens gave him a private performance before he left. 'If you had seen Macready last night,' he told Kate, 'undisguisedly sobbing, and crying on the sofa as I read, you would have felt, as I did, what a thing it is to have Power.' It moved anyone who heard it, he said, 'in the most extraordinary manner'. When Forster read it to Gilbert A'Beckett, a member of the *Punch* staff, the man 'cried so much, and so painfully, that Forster didn't know whether to go on or stop'.[78] When he sent a copy to Angela Coutts, who was in a far from cheerful mood after losing both parents, Dickens told her, 'I am bent on making you cry.'[79] And it certainly made Lady Blessington weep. The book, she told Forster, would 'melt hearts and open purse strings. ... I was embarrassed to meet the eyes of my servants, mine were so red with tears.'[80]

The Chimes sold well. After the *Carol* the public was keen for a new seasonal tale from Dickens which would exemplify the sympathetic sentiment which they had come to look for in his work. Yet it had a mixed public reception. Dickens, *The Times* declared, had become 'the *serious* advocate of the humbler classes', and warned that 'there are some among the working classes who may find in it nourishment for discontent', but in the Chartist newspaper *Northern Star* he was hailed as the champion of the people. Other reviewers objected to the homiletic manner in which he crudely contrasted the heartlessness and greed of the rich to the virtues of the downtrodden. Such comments were understandable, for Dickens had fused sentiment and social criticism to make his gloomy parable appropriate for a Christmas in the Hungry Forties.

Although Dickens had made *The Chimes* an apocalyptic tract on the consequences of selfish individualism, he had no political remedies for the condition of the poor. He was essentially a moralist, and his habitual reaction to the general problems of poverty was much the same as his response to particular cases of distress. Both were a matter for compassion; and because he believed that circumstances and persons could be changed for the better by a change of heart he naturally tried to induce such changes by provoking indignation or evoking pity. This belief ran through everything he wrote, constraining the development of his characters and providing the moral of his plots, and it came out most crudely in the transformation-scene conclusions of the *Carol* and *The Chimes*. It also controlled his own behaviour, for he was a man of dominating temperament who was disposed to manipulate people in everyday life as if they were creatures of his imagination. He liked being generous, and he liked being appreciated; and both traits could be expressed more easily with unfortunates who were ready to submit to his patronage than with friends and relatives who were less tractable. He therefore made a more favourable impression of good-humoured benevolence in public than he did in private, where he was given to fits of irritation and annoyance with his dependents when they failed to live up to his expectations. He was much less tolerant of his father, for instance, than of the equally importunate John Overs, a tubercular cabinet-maker with literary aspirations, who had been his protégé since 1841.

Dickens had done a great deal for Overs, helping him to place his songs and stories, and just before leaving for Italy had written a preface to a collection of his work. He had sent him to Dr. Elliotson for treatment. He had even persuaded Macready to find the man a post at the theatre; and when the disgruntled Overs had attacked Macready's management and peevishly turned on Dickens for supporting Macready, Dickens contained his irritation and still tried to help Overs. When he made his brief visit to London at the end of 1844 Overs was dead, leaving his wife and six children in 'great distress and perplexity': the life which had produced the tragedy of Overs and the art which had spun the misery of Trotty Veck lay very close together. Before Dickens returned to Italy he busied himself on behalf of the Overs family. He did not manage to see Angela Coutts, but he wrote soliciting her help for them.[81]

He proposed to be back in Genoa for Christmas; on the way he spent three days in Paris with Macready, who was launching a Shakespeare season. Macready introduced him about the town, to the socialist Louis Blanc, to Victor Hugo, Alexandre Dumas, and Théophile Gautier. And in these crowded days Dickens also met Régnier, of the Théâtre-Français, the painter Delacroix, and the historian Michelet. The weather was terrible when he left Paris on 13 December, taking the stage through deep slush on the three-day journey to Marseilles. On arrival, he told Mrs. Macready, he was in such a torpid state that he 'was at first supposed to be luggage'. He almost missed his steamer, and wished he had; it ran into a fearful storm on the passage to Genoa. 'I should have made my Will if I had had anything to leave,' he reported, 'but I had only the basin; and I couldn't leave that, for a moment.'[82] Three days before Christmas Dickens was back with the family, ready for the round of celebrations which stretched from Christmas Eve to little Charley's birthday on Twelfth Night. For this occasion Angela Coutts had sent a cake weighing ninety pounds. It was, Dickens said, 'detained at the custom-house for Jesuitical surveillance!' and then, at the Swiss pastry-shop where it was sent for repairs to its decorations, it was displayed as an exotic marvel.[83]

Once the festivities were over Dickens proposed to go on his travels again. He had given up any notion of writing a novel at leisure, away from the tyranny of serial deadlines; he realized that he was not cut out for the life of the literary exile. It had been hard for him to start *The Chimes*, and he had been forced back to the London streets for his stimulus and to his London friends for the response he needed. Without something to write—or something which could absorb the psychic energy he poured into his work—he was restless. He liked the elegant life of the Palazzo Peschiere, but it bored him. On his way to London he wrote to Kate suggesting that they should visit the south of Italy on his return; and his mind was made up before he left London. 'Florence, Rome, Naples and Palermo lie before me,' he wrote to Angela Coutts on 8 December.[84] Once he was back in Genoa the scheme burgeoned into an elaborate itinerary which would absorb most of the six months for which Devonshire Terrace was still let and the Palazzo Peschiere was still taken. If he could do no serious work in that time he could at least collect the material for a book of traveller's impressions.

Dickens planned to start on his trip at the end of January. Meanwhile he enjoyed the company of friends in Genoa. Among those he had come to know was Angus Fletcher's friend, the Swiss banker Emile de la Rue, who lived in the splendid Palazzo Rosso with his attractive English wife Augusta and her mother. Madame de la Rue, who resembled Fanny Dickens, was a small dark lady with a cheerful nervy disposition; Dickens described her as a 'most affectionate and excellent little woman'.[85] She was, unfortunately, troubled with hysterical symptoms which ranged from headaches and insomnia to convulsions and hallucinations. Dickens had not lost his interest in mesmerism and he had already found that he could use his skill to relieve Kate's headaches. Now, with time on his hands and convinced that Madame de la Rue could be helped by hypnosis, he offered to try the effects of 'magnetic sleep'. On Boxing Day 1844 he sent a note to de la Rue assuring him that he would 'derive great happiness from being the fortunate instrument of her relief'.[86]

It was a daring proposal. Dickens was not a doctor; he was not even a quack. He was merely a parlour mesmerist presuming to a degree of intimacy with his friend's wife that broke all the conventions. Although mesmerism was now more respectable and more accepted than it had been when Elliotson had started to practise, in the public mind there was still an association between mesmerism and social scandal. Emile de la Rue was, however, a trusting man and the misery of his wife's afflictions made him agree to risk the experiment, and to allow Dickens to insist on 'her subservience' to his will. Daily mesmeric sessions soon began, and Dickens wrote detailed accounts of them for de la Rue. By the beginning of January he had become involved in an intense emotional relationship.

Madame de la Rue had a recurring delusion in which she found herself on a hillside, sometimes alone, sometimes in a crowd, where great stones were hurled down at her. She was haunted by a phantom figure, so fearful that she could not describe him. Dickens identified this shadowy figure as his antagonist, and he pursued it like a priest seeking to exorcize a devil. When he and Kate left Genoa on 19 January for their tour of southern Italy, Dickens arranged for Emile de la Rue to report regularly to him by letter. Dickens in turn would try to hypnotize the lady at a set hour each day, thus continuing to wage his campaign against the phantom by telepathy; on one occasion as he travelled along on the coach with Kate beside him, he claimed, his intense concentration put her into a hypnotic trance. Dickens also wrote long letters to de la Rue giving comfort and discussing his wife's condition; the 'devilish figure' continued to fascinate him. 'I cannot yet quite make up my mind', he told de la Rue, 'whether the phantom originates in shattered nerves and a system broken by Pain; or whether it is the representative of some great nerve or set of nerves on which her disease has preyed—and begins to loose its hold now, because the disease of those nerves is itself attacked by the inexplicable agency of the Magnetism.'[87]

It seems that this 'inexplicable' power offered Dickens some relief from his own anxieties. He was certainly abstracted and absorbed by it as he and Kate rolled through Tuscany and on to Rome, where they spent carnival week. The city was full of people and the streets alive with masked parades. 'At two each day, we sally forth in an open Carriage', Dickens wrote to Georgina, 'with a *large sack* of sugar plums and at least five hundred little Nosegays, to pelt people with.'[88] But his thoughts were still with Madame de la Rue. One night he woke up suddenly 'in a state of indescribable horror and emotion'; he was full of anxiety about her and felt so close to her, indeed, that he had 'a sense of her being somehow a part of me'.[89] From Rome he and Kate moved on to Naples where they were joined by Georgina coming by boat from Genoa and bringing news of the children. And with the same boat came the eagerly awaited letters from the de la Rues. They revealed that Augusta had regressed while Dickens was away and confirmed their plan to meet the Dickens family in Rome for Holy Week, when the treatment could be resumed. The phantom figure had regained its influence and Dickens now saw himself as the contender for the soul of Madame de la Rue in a struggle between the forces of good and evil. He wrote with optimistic enthusiasm to de la Rue about their meeting in Rome. 'When I think of all that lies before us,' he wrote, 'I have a perfect conviction that I could magnetise a Frying-Pan.'[90]

Meanwhile he continued his tour of Italy. The original plan had been to go as far south as Sicily, but the weather was unpleasant, getting colder as they went south. Fleas continued to be a problem, sowing themselves 'like self-acting mustard and cress, in my flannel dressing-gown', Dickens told de la Rue.[91] They visited Sorrento, Pompeii, and Herculaneum; they climbed Vesuvius, ice-capped and smoking. It was a dangerous venture with six saddle-horses, an armed soldier for a guard, and twenty-two guides. Dickens timed the trip, he explained to Mitton, to see the sunset as they climbed and 'night at the top, where the fire is raging'. Kate and Georgina were put into two litters and carried up most of the way, but at the top they had to struggle on foot—'they were thorough game and didn't make the least complaint'. Dickens and two of the guides climbed to the brink and looked down into the crater itself; it left them 'alight in half-a-dozen places and burnt from head to foot. You never saw such devils. And I never saw anything so awful and terrible.'[92] The return was more hazardous than the ascent; two of the guides were hurt and the ladies' clothes were 'literally torn off their backs, and hanging in Rags about them', he told de la Rue in a letter full of excited anticipation of their reunion in Rome on 10 March.[93]

By the time they met bad news from home had made Dickens all the more eager to help his distressed friends. Before he left Genoa he had heard that Forster's brother had died suddenly; any close bereavement always reminded him of the loss of Mary Hogarth that had made his own hearth 'cold and dark', and he quickly sent Forster a note of comfort. In Rome he heard that Laman Blanchard, who had been at the reading of *The Chimes*, had cut his throat in a depression brought on by the recent death of his wife and by his own ill health and poverty. There were children to be cared for and educated: Bulwer, Thackeray, the poet Bryan Proctor, and Charles Lever were already offering help. 'It says something for our pursuit', he wrote, 'that in the midst of all its miserable disputes and jealousies that the common impulse of its followers . . . is surely and certainly of the noblest.' In Rome, too, he heard of the death of Sydney Smith and that Thomas Hood was past all hope of recovery. 'No philosophy will bear these dreadful things', Dickens wrote to Forster, 'or make a moment's head against them, but the practical one of doing all the good we can, in thought and deed.'[94] At the Hotel Meloni in Rome his practical help was needed. The de la Rues had arrived, and every day Dickens gave Madame her treatment. Her condition was often worse at night, and when a fit seized her Emile would call Dickens whatever the hour. One night he was fetched at one o'clock to find her 'rolled into an apparently impossible ball'; on another night he sat with her until dawn. The lady was nevertheless well enough between times to join her husband and the Dickens family on sightseeing trips around Rome.

The odd relationship continued on the journey northward; 'wheresoever I went in Italy,' Dickens later recalled, 'she and her husband travelled with me, and every day I magnetised her; sometimes under olive trees, sometimes in vineyards, sometimes in the travelling carriage, sometimes at wayside inns during the midday halt'.[95] Such therapeutic attentions had a beneficial effect on Augusta de la Rue and they so absorbed Dickens that he thought of little else. 'We are exceedingly happy, and don't fight much,' he reported to Fletcher at the beginning of the journey back to Genoa.[96] The situation, however, was beginning to irritate Kate and her increasing resentment cast a blight over the journey northwards. The tension was broken by a stop in Florence; at Fiesole Dickens plucked an ivy leaf in the garden of Landor's house and asked Forster to send it to the old man. Among the English colony there he met Mrs. Trollope and her son Thomas, who thought Dickens a 'dandified, pretty-boy looking sort of figure, something of a whipper-snapper' yet with a laugh 'brimful of enjoyment ... when recounting or hearing anything absurd'.[97] Before the party arrived at Genoa jealousy had brought Kate to the point where she could not speak to the de la Rues, and in private she angrily complained that she was being neglected.

Kate was excusably upset. While Dickens devoted himself sympathetically to the emotional problems of his attractive friend he was stubbornly insensitive to the way in which he was upsetting his newly pregnant wife. It seems to have been thoughtlessness, rather than ill will, which made him neglect her, for he was not so much interested in Augusta de la Rue as in her intriguing mental state, and he was obviously captivated by the effect of his mesmeric activities. All through this strange hypnotic relationship, in fact, he apparently assumed that his actions were entirely reasonable and that Kate was wrong to criticize. When she asked him to abandon the private sessions with Madame de la Rue he refused, insisting that he could not give up his hope of a cure because the treatment sent his wife into jealous tantrums, and putting Kate at a further disadvantage by claiming that her protests were actually jeopardizing his efforts. Annoyed and embarrassed by such domestic discord he at first tried to excuse Kate's evident hostility to the de la Rues by telling them that she was suffering from a nervous breakdown; but the cause of her tearful pleas became so humiliatingly evident that he felt obliged to admit the painful truth even at the cost of his loyalty to his wife.

Although Dickens still wrote affectionately to Kate when they were separated, and referred warmly to her in letters to their friends, the sojourn in Italy had clearly brought out hidden stresses in their marriage, and the complicated involvement with their neighbours had caused additional strain. Dickens found some consolation in the warm Italian spring. 'I have been upon the Wing, now, full six months on end', he told Mitton in April, and he was glad to sit down again in his shady armchair 'among the Peschiere oranges'.[98] He was busy describing the 'shadows in the water' which he worked up into *Pictures from Italy*.[99] 'I have seen so many wonders', he wrote to Lady Blessington, 'and each one of them has such a voice of its own, that I sit all day listening to the roar they make, as if it were in a sea-shell.'[100]

Despite the pleasantries of life in Genoa—he gave a reading of the *Christmas Carol* to a select circle of friends—his thoughts turned to England. 'On Monday, the Ninth of next month we turn homewards,' Dickens told Maclise in May. 'I *can't* say how happy I am in the hope of speedily seeing you again.'[101] Forster had been ill but was now well enough to agree to meet Dickens in Brussels; in any case Dickens was 'impatient to renew our happy old walks and old talks in dear old home'.[102] *The Chimes*, he learnt, had been 'a most sweeping success'; the profit on the first 20,000 copies had come to over £1,400.[103] 'Bradbury and Evans are the Men for me to work with,' he declared to Mitton.[104] The books which Chapman and Hall still controlled had also brought in nearly £1,000. He thus felt sufficiently in funds to arrange for the Devonshire Terrace house to be redecorated in readiness for their return, sending Mitton instructions to make it 'cheerful and gay'. And while the household applied itself to packing, Dickens kept well clear of the 'miseries of moving', spending much of his time at the Palazzo Rosso with the de la Rues and passing on to Emile the elementary techniques of mesmerism. Although Madame de la Rue was much better, Dickens promised to continue the experiment in telepathic hypnosis by concentrating at a given hour each day after he returned to London.

The great travelling coach was at last ready and the party headed north over the St. Gotthard pass, only just open after the winter snow, where the road was 'like a geometrical staircase, with horrible depths beneath it'. Coming down was 'the most dangerous thing that a carriage and horses can do'; they 'slip and slide, and get their legs over the traces and are dragged up against the rocks'. Dickens and his courier Roche—the 'Brave', Dickens called him—were busy all the way extricating the whole concern from a tangle 'like a skein of thread' he explained to Forster.[105] In Brussels the party was met by Maclise and Jerrold as well as Forster—they had all been summoned for a week's jaunt in Flanders while the painters finished their work at Devonshire Terrace—and Dickens wrote to the de la Rues fondly recalling the good times they had enjoyed together.

By the end of June the family was home again. It had been a distracting year, for Dickens had never quite settled in Genoa, and his domestic situation had degenerated disagreeably in the final months. Nevertheless he had enjoyed much of it. 'I like the common people of Italy, very much,' he had written to Angela Coutts while he was away.[106] For all the oppression they suffered from princes and priests, he found them 'naturally well-disposed, and patient'. He would not easily forget, he told Forster, 'the beautiful Italian manners, the sweet language, the quick recognition of a pleasant look or cheerful word' that were left behind when he crossed the Alps on his way to 'dear old home'.[107]

10

Battle of Life

ON 19 October 1845 John Forster called on Macready for tea. He told him that Bradbury and Evans were planning to launch a new morning newspaper and that Dickens was to be its editor. 'I heard the news with a sort of dismay,' Macready noted in his diary. Two weeks later Forster called again and read Macready the prospectus that Dickens had prepared for the *Daily News*. 'It *increased* my apprehensions,' Macready decided. 'I feel that he is rushing headlong into an enterprise that demands the utmost foresight, skilful and secret preparation and qualities of a conductor which Dickens has not.'[1] Macready, with bitter memories of theatrical seasons that were critical successes and financial failures, knew the pitfalls of a new venture that demanded a large capital, patience, and the management of many not easily compatible professionals. His doubts were shared by Forster, who had already tried to dissuade Dickens from this potentially disastrous scheme.

Dickens had returned from Italy set on a new journalistic venture. He had been playing with some such idea since his return from America, and he had talked vaguely about a new journal with Bradbury and Evans before he first left for Italy. As soon as he was back in England he started on a different tack, asking Forster whether he liked the notion of a weekly magazine called *The Cricket* in which 'I would chirp, chirp, chirp away in every number until I chirped it up to—well, you shall say how many hundred thousand.... You know also exactly how I should use such a lever, and how much power I should find in it.' Dickens still hankered for the role of editor; it seemed much less demanding to work to the miscellany formula—what he called '*Carol* philosophy, cheerful views, sharp anatomization of humbug'[2]—than to write long works of fiction. Forster, less sanguine, discouraged the proposal, and Dickens subsequently reworked it into *The Cricket on the Hearth* as the Christmas story for 1845: making the cricket 'a little household god', silent in sorrow and loud at happy moments, seemed to Dickens 'a delicate and beautiful fancy'.[3]

He then came back to the plan for a daily paper. It had understandable attractions for him. For one thing, as he told Forster, it offered some security if it succeeded: 'I have, sometimes, that possibility of failing health or fading popularity before me, which beckons me to such a venture when it comes within my reach.'[4] For another, he had been a successful journalist, and the idea of commanding his own paper was undoubtedly attractive. In the last two years his reforming impulses had been much stimulated by events, and he wanted to write directly about poverty, humbug, flint-heartedness, and other evidences of social evil; in a year which Forster described as 'prodigal of excitement and disaster'[5] there was much to provide copy. It also seemed a propitious moment to establish a great newspaper to serve reform as *The Times* served reaction. Since Peel had taken office in 1841 he had been under increasing attack for protecting British agriculture from imported corn, and thus keeping food prices high and the factory populations desperately underfed. Reformers such as Lord Ashley and Dr. Southwood Smith campaigned for better conditions in the mines and factories, and for a Ten Hours Bill to limit the working day; Edwin Chadwick's followers in the sanitary movement agitated about the bad drains and poor water supplies which led to outbreaks of cholera, typhoid, and diphtheria. The future Tory leader Benjamin Disraeli began to write social novels, publishing *Coningsby* in 1844 and *Sybil*—denouncing the division of England into Two Nations—in the following year. Across the Irish Sea, to cap the misery of the poor, a very wet summer spoilt the harvest and blighted the potato crop: there was so little to eat in Ireland that a million peasants died in the Great Hunger. To meet such desperate times Peel was under pressure to reverse his policy and repeal the Corn Laws to allow the import of cheap grain.

By the summer of 1845 the idea of such a newspaper became financially more feasible because of the boom in railway speculation; there was capital available for such an investment and the added attraction of revenue from advertisements of new companies that were springing up. The link between the newspaper world and the railway interests was Joseph Paxton, who had begun life as a humble gardener employed by the Duke of Devonshire at Chatsworth and risen to be his confidant and friend. Paxton, who promoted a number of railway schemes and by 1845 had £35,000 invested in them, was also an old friend of the printer William Bradbury; he was involved in the world of journalism through his editorship of the *Magazine of Botany*; and he was on friendly terms with the staff of *Punch*. Paxton and Bradbury had already toyed with the idea of a new liberal-minded newspaper, and in 1845 they thought the time was ripe. While Forster regarded it as one of 'the wild and hazardous enterprises of that prodigious year',[6] Dickens himself was full of enthusiasm and energy. He had returned from Italy such a veritable emporium of intentions that he had no time that summer to take a long break at Broadstairs, where he went in the middle of August with Kate and Georgina to settle the children for the holidays.

Forster was much more enthusiastic about another idea which was exciting Dickens; it was an ambitious scheme of amateur theatricals. There had been talk of getting up a group to give private performances ever since Dickens came back to England to give his dramatic reading of *The Chimes*. As soon as he returned to Italy he asked Forster, 'ARE we to have that play???' and telling him of his youthful enthusiasm for the stage: 'I have often thought, that I should certainly have been as successful on the boards as I have been between them.'[7] Dickens clearly had a natural talent for the stage and it came out as strongly in everyday life as in his passion for theatrical entertainment. Forster was well aware of this love of acting. Dickens 'seemed to be always the more himself for being somebody else', he remarked, 'for continually putting off his personality'.[8] And Dickens made much the same impression on such casual acquaintances as the French journalist P. E. D. Forgues, who interviewed him for *L'Illustration* in 1844 and said that he might have been taken for 'an astute and wily barrister ... or simply the manager of a troupe of strolling players'.[9]

Within three weeks of his return Dickens had chosen the play. It was to be Ben Jonson's *Every Man in his Humour*, a comedy which Dickens felt congenial, for his own work was in the Jonsonian tradition in which the characters exemplified such 'humours' as melancholy, pride, greed, and vanity. He had also settled on the accompanying farce and he wrote to tell Macready that it would be *Two O'Clock in the Morning*, 'as performed by the Inimitable B' at Montreal.[10] The production, set for 20 September, was to be staged at the Royalty, a private theatre in Dean Street where the actress Frances Kelly ran a dramatic academy.

The parts were quickly allocated. Dickens was to play the braggart Bobadil, and he recruited his brothers Frederick and Augustus and his friend T. J. Thompson. Forster took the part of Kitely. Douglas Jerrold, who was one of the original enthusiasts for the play, brought in colleagues from *Punch*—John Leech, Gilbert A'Beckett, and Percival Leigh. Thackeray offered to enliven the proceedings by singing between the acts. The most valuable recruit was the editor himself, Mark Lemon. He proved to be as good an actor as he was a playwright. Dickens was delighted with him—'a most excellent actor', he declared, with 'instinctive discrimination'—and he took on the part of Brainworm.[11] Stanfield, invited to play Downright, excused himself and undertook to paint the scenery as his contribution. Dickens invited George Cruikshank, then Cattermole, to take his place, but they both declined. Dudley Costello, a journalist and author, finally played the part.

Maclise had been a doubtful collaborator from the start and he cried off before the rehearsals opened. Dickens was extremely fond of him, but was beginning to be irritated by his anxious temperament and his tendency to hypochondria. On one occasion, when Maclise claimed that his health kept him housebound, Dickens failed to pay an expected call on him; and this provoked a plaintive letter to Forster. Maclise asked whether Dickens was annoyed at his refusal to dine and insisted that because he was 'lowered to nothing' he had declined similar invitations from Stanfield, Talfourd, Stone, Cattermole, and other friends: 'I hate anybody to be offended with me as much as I never wish to offend anybody.'[12] Maclise, indeed, had become such a worrier that his affectionate friends were learning that they could no longer count on him to join a party or an outing.

Dickens turned his mind to the play as soon as he was settled again in Devonshire Terrace. 'My steam is up,' he told Stanfield on 15 July.[13] He was, it seemed to Forster, 'the life and soul of the entire affair. . . . He took everything on himself. . . . He was stage director, very often stage carpenter, scene arranger, property man, prompter and bandmaster. Without offending anyone, he kept everyone in order.'[14] He was enjoying himself hugely and fired the whole company with such enthusiasm as if it were 'the whole business of our lives'.[15] He took particular care to have the costumes just right, copying them from old pictures, and he engaged a tailor from the English Opera House for the job. '*Be very careful that the colours are bright; and that they will shew well by Lamplight*,' he wrote; 'I wish particularly to see the red, of which you propose to make Bobadil's breeches and hat. I want it to be a very gay, fierce, bright color.'[16] At the end of July 'merry rehearsals innumerable'[17] began. Macready, who was called upon to give professional advice, was not as enthusiastic as the players. All of them, he noted disparagingly after one of the performances, 'seemed to be under a perfect delusion as to their degree of skill and power in an art of which they do not know the very rudiments'.[18]

As the night of the performance approached, the excitement and tension mounted. 'Some of my company', Dickens wrote, 'begin to feel like used-up cab-horses—going perceptibly at the knees,' and Dickens declared himself 'half dead with Managerial work'.[19] He told Macready's sister that he never had to do 'with such an utterly careless and unbusiness-like set of dogs (with the exception of Stanfield and Brainworm) as my fellow actors. I don't except Forster: for so far as he is concerned, there is nothing in the World but Kitely—there is no World at all; only a something in its place that begins with a "K" and ends with a "Y".'[20] It was a part which Macready had played in his early days and Forster turned to his friend for help and advice to such effect that his whole performance savoured of Macready.

Jerrold's son, Blanchard Jerrold, noticed the 'great tragedian airs' which Forster adopted in the green room and throughout the rehearsals, even insisting on having the best dressing-room in the theatre. Forster, in his excess of zeal and his preoccupation with his own costume, clashed with Dickens in his managerial role, and there was a 'wordy encounter' during rehearsals, but tempers were restored for the performance.[21]

The oddity of the occasion, and the public reputation of the players, ensured a full house for what Forster described as 'one of the small sensations of the day'.[22] Each player invited about thirty friends. It was a distinguished gathering, although Jane Carlyle described the audience as '*a rum set*'. It included Lady Holland, Lady Blessington, Count d'Orsay, Talfourd, Alfred Tennyson, and the Duke of Devonshire. The production, Jane Carlyle wrote to her husband, was too professional for private theatricals and the amateur actors 'too insipid' by professional standards.[23] Robert Browning was better pleased, writing to Elizabeth Barrett that 'the performance was really good.... Forster's Kitely was very emphatic and earnest. ...Dickens' Bobadil *was* capital—with perhaps a little too much of the consciousness of entire cowardice.'[24] Another guest admired the 'supreme conceit and frothy pomp' that Dickens brought to the part. Macready, never given to light-heartedness, was grudging. 'Several of the actors were very fine as amateurs', he noted, but he thought the play was 'a very dull business'.[25] Jane Carlyle had the impression that there was 'a good deal of jealousy in Macreadydom on the subject of the amateur actors'; and Macready, suffering from a cold, did not stay long at the supper party which followed the performance.[26]

Dickens himself was delighted with the whole affair. 'Good Heaven, how I wish you could have been there! It really was a brilliant sight,' he told Augusta de la Rue, discoursing on the 'distinguished' audience, the splendid costumes, the enthusiastic reception. His own managerial skills confirmed him in his belief that his real *métier* was to be the manager of a theatre. 'There are whispers of Gold snuff-boxes for the indefatigable manager, from the Performers—Hem!'[27] Although it was a strictly private affair, word of it reached the press and *The Times*, generous in its praise, made the occasion seem exclusive. Those who felt left out were eager for Dickens and his colleagues to repeat the performance and they soon planned a benefit at the larger St. James's Theatre on 15 November, devoting the profits to Dr. Southwood Smith's sanatorium. 'Here's a pretty kettle of Fish!' Dickens exclaimed to Beard on 26 October on hearing that Prince Albert wished to attend;[28] and among the other celebrities who had hastened to take tickets were the Duke of Wellington, Prince George, and the Baron de Rothschild. 'Lord and Lady Lansdowne and the 'Tarnal Smash knows who' had also taken boxes, he told Stanfield on 26 October.[29] The performance earned a flattering notice in the *Illustrated London News*, which praised the intelligence of the acting and the perfection of the costumes. Not everyone agreed. Charles Greville thought the play 'intolerably heavy' and the audience 'as cold as ice'.[30] Lord Melbourne, who brought the notorious Mrs. Norton with him, was among the bored. 'I knew this play would be dull,' he said, 'but that it would be so damnably dull as this I did not suppose!'[31] The actors, however, were so pleased with themselves that they could not easily disband. They went on to promote another benefit night—this time for Frances Kelly herself for lending her theatre—and staged *The Elder Brother* by Massinger and Fletcher on 3 January as part of the New Year festivities. Soon afterwards these theatrical interests brought Dickens an invitation to preside over the first annual dinner of the General Theatrical Fund, a charity set up to provide pensions for actors.

Dickens had allowed himself to be much distracted by this playmaking and had fallen behind on his Christmas story. 'I am in the preliminary seclusion and ill-temper of the Christmas book,'[32] he told Bradbury and Evans on 29 September. He did not really get under way until mid-October; by then Kate was on the verge of her confinement. On 28 October she gave birth to what 'is usually called (I don't know why) a chopping Boy', Dickens remarked to Stanfield in the disparaging comic style which he had adopted at the birth of Francis Jeffrey. 'I am partial to girls', he added, 'and had set my heart on one—but never mind me.'[33] It was he, however, who chose the name, once more calling his son after illustrious friends—a habit which was attracting comment. Robert Browning sardonically reported to Elizabeth Barrett that the boy was to be christened Alfred d'Orsay Tennyson Dickens. 'Ay, Charlie, if this don't prove to posterity that you might have been a Tennyson and were a d'Orsay—why excellent labour will have been lost!' he wrote. 'You observe, "Alfred" is common to both the godfather and the—devil—father, as I take the Count to be!'[34] Edward Fitzgerald thought it the worst of 'Snobbishness and Cockneyism' to indulge in such pretensions. 'It is one thing to worship heroes', he remarked, 'and another to lick up their spittle.'[35]

Dickens was finding it hard to get on with his story, soon due at the printers. Tired with his theatrical efforts, bothered by the fusses of childbirth, and worried about the newspaper venture, he had to cry off a visit to a soirée of the Manchester Athenaeum at which Talfourd was to preside and his friends Stone and Jerrold were guest speakers. A few days earlier, in the middle of October, he had gone up to Chatsworth to see Paxton about the detailed financial arrangements of the newspaper and he was soon writing to Mitton to say that the 'venture is quite decided on; and I have made the Plunge'.[36] He was, however, still apprehensive about undertaking such responsibility. At the end of October he told Forster that he felt sick, bothered, and depressed. 'Visions of Brighton come upon me; and I have a great mind to go there to finish my second part, or to Hampstead,' he wrote. 'I never was in such bad writing cue as I am this week, in all my life.'[37] He was soon writing again to Forster to complain: 'I have been so very unwell this morning, with giddiness, and headache, and botheration of one sort or other, that I didn't get up till noon.' The demands on his time had interfered with his habit of taking long walks. 'It's the loss of my walks,' he told Forster, 'but I am as giddy as if I were drunk, and can hardly see.'[38] There was no let-up in November and Dickens had to cancel a long promised article for the *Edinburgh Review* on capital punishment. 'I have never in my life had so many insuperable obstacles crowded into the way of my pursuits,' he wrote to Macvey Napier.[39]

Forster tried once more to dissuade Dickens from the newspaper venture, but he had made up his mind and was already tackling the practical problems. The first was money. He liked journalism, he hoped the newspaper would be a powerful lever on public opinion, but above all he wanted a guaranteed income. On 3 November, when he wrote to Bradbury and Evans to say that he would become editor of the *Daily News*, he stressed the point: 'I will take that Post of Editor which is marked in the little statement as having a Salary of a Thousand Pounds attached to it—for double that Salary.'[40] To meet such a high figure, and to cover all the complicated costs of newspaper production, a great deal of capital was needed. Apart from Joseph Paxton—who 'has command of every railway and railway influence in England', Dickens told Mitton[41]—the initial backers were William Jackson, M.P., a leading Liberal in the north; and Sir Joshua Walmsley, the Mayor of Liverpool and a fierce campaigner against the Corn Laws, who had praised Dickens as the best friend to reform yet seen in English fiction. Dickens did not care much for Paxton's 'loose, flurried way' of conducting his business,[42] and he was a little shaken a few days after he accepted the editorship when two of his backers were involved in the failure of a City broker. 'But never say die is the Inimitable's motto', he told Beard on 4 November, 'and I have already pumped up as much courage as will set me going on my old tracks, Please God, in four and twenty hours.'[43] Nevertheless he began to fear that the paper would be stillborn or a monstrous failure. He sent Bradbury and Evans a depressing list of the difficulties facing him and telling them that he could not go on as he now had no faith in the venture—'it would always oppress me as a doomed thing'—and urging them to withdraw. 'I believe in my Soul', he told them, 'it would end in your Ruin.'[44] He called in Forster and they consulted with Beard. Though they all agreed that it was a great risk, now that confidence had been lost, the printers had stronger nerves and went on with their plans, putting up £22,500 to match £25,000 from Paxton, and £2,500 from Richard Seaton Wright, solicitor of Bradbury and Evans; and later Jackson and Walmsley brought in as much again. On 17 November the financial agreements were signed; Dickens was persuaded to withdraw his resignation, and he became the first editor of the *Daily News*.

The second problem was to find a suitable talented staff. At Forster's suggestion Dickens recruited William Henry Wills as his personal assistant. Wills, a patient and dependable man, had worked on *Punch* when it was founded and then moved on to Edinburgh as assistant editor to *Chambers's Journal*; Dickens soon came to like and trust him. He took on his friends Douglas Jerrold and Mark Lemon from *Punch* as regular contributors; for leader-writers he acquired Forster and Albany Fonblanque from the *Examiner*, and the literary Unitarian William J. Fox, well known as a speaker for the Anti-Corn-Law League; and the various departments—railways, clerical, commercial, military, foreign—were all assigned to experts. The post of music critic went to Kate's father, George Hogarth, at a modest rate of five guineas. Lady Blessington, who was appointed in January, was glad to be given almost twice as much to write social and literary gossip; she and d'Orsay had run deeply into debt through their flamboyant lifestyle. John Dickens, the prodigal father, was put in charge of the reporters, and he turned up each evening at eight to supervise the editing of copy for the printers. Now over sixty, he was described by one of his colleagues as 'obese, fond of a glass of grog, full of fun, never given to much locomotion...he was always hot whatever the weather might be'.[45] He was as feckless financially as ever, and at least one member of the reporting staff thought him a sloppy and inaccurate supervisor. A third relative—the John Henry Barrow who had given Dickens his start on the *Mirror of Parliament*—was sent out to India as a reporter, and Cornelius Felton was recruited as Boston correspondent.[46]

As news of the venture got about it provoked a good deal of curiosity; it also made rival editors apprehensive, for Dickens had collected together some of the best-known and ablest men in Fleet Street, and he proposed to pay the reporters so well that men left other newspapers to join him. The project was openly ambitious. One of those invited to contribute reported to John Blackwood that Dickens and his friends 'have hopes, modest men! of crushing *The Times*',[47] and Dickens himself told Paxton at the end of December: 'It is war to the knife, now, with *The Times*.'[48] All the same, there were other sceptics as well as Forster and Macready, who were not altogether sure that Dickens was the man for the job. 'Is Dickens fit for it?' Elizabeth Barrett wondered. In her view he lacked '*breadth* of mind enough for such work, with all his gifts'.[49]

Getting up a newspaper excited Dickens as much as getting up a play, and once the performance of *Every Man in his Humour* on 15 November was over he turned his mind to the task. The office of the new paper was a set of ramshackle and fusty rooms next to the Bradbury and Evans printing works off Fleet Street. 'They are not very business-looking chambers for appointments in their present condition', he complained to them, 'and are certainly not over-comfortable.'[50] By December Dickens was telling Paxton that 'I am regularly in harness now; and we are getting on, vigorously and steadily': the paper was publicly announced on 1 December as appearing early in the New Year.[51] While 'rounding off the few last chirpings of *The Cricket on the Hearth*'[52] Dickens was also driving the printers to chase Maclise, Stanfield, and Leech, who had already been advertised as the illustrators of the Christmas story. Edwin Landseer was drawn in at the last moment to contribute a woodcut. By 1 December all was ready and the printers began running off *The Cricket on the Hearth*.

The Christmas tale was a 'tremendous success'. Its sales soon doubled those for the *Carol* and the *Chimes*. 'It has beaten my two other Carols out of the field, and is going still like Wildfire,' Dickens wrote to Felton.[53] 'You hear talk of it in every company,' declared Thackeray.[54] By 20 December there was already a dramatization of it by Albert Smith at the English Opera House, and two weeks later some fourteen theatres were running dramatic versions of the story. Some of the critics shared the enthusiasm. The *Athenaeum* gave it lavish praise and the *Illustrated London News* preferred it to *The Chimes*. But there were critical voices. To one critic it was 'mawkish and maudlin'; another said that 'Mr. Dickens's reputation, some time since on the decline, will gain nothing by this little book.'[55] Thackeray, who now called Dickens the 'literary master of ceremonies for Christmas', felt that he had lost the simple engaging manner of his early tales.[56] And *The Times* gave it a savage notice, describing it as 'a twaddling manifestation of silliness almost from the first page to the last ... the babblings of genius in its premature dotage'.[57] No doubt *The Times* was affected by the knowledge that Dickens was about to launch a competitor. Macready certainly thought so. The review, he declared, was 'the heavy and remorseless blow of an enemy, determined to disable his antagonist', and he felt sorry for 'my poor dear friend Dickens'.[58] But Dickens did not seem to feel sorry for himself or his small book. *The Times*, he consoled himself, 'has done us a great deal of service' by such an attack.[59]

Dickens was driving himself hard—it was hardly surprising that Elizabeth Barrett was calling him 'Boz the universal'—and he did not want to be distracted by the poor reviews for *The Cricket*.[60] Neither did he wish to listen to Forster, who was still carping about the *Daily News*. Forster was piqued because his advice had been disregarded and their disagreement produced some bad feeling. 'I was sorry to hear of intemperate language between them,' Macready noted in his diary, 'which should neither have been given nor received.' Forster unburdened himself to Macready, telling him that Dickens was 'so intensely fixed on his own opinions and in his admiration of his own works' that Forster felt himself to be 'useless to him as counsel, or for an opinion on anything touching upon them'. Since Dickens refused to listen to criticism, Forster added, 'this partial passion would grow upon him, till it became an incurable evil'.[61] His imperious attitude was a trait which less sympathetic observers had already noted. 'He hates argument,' one acquaintance had observed two years before, 'in fact, he is unable to argue—a common case with impulsive characters who see the whole truth and feel it crowding and struggling at once for immediate utterance.'[62] The friendship of Forster, Macready, and Dickens had never been so strained, and the benefit performance of *The Elder Brother* which the amateur group put on in the New Year did little to improve morale or heal Macready's jealous feelings. On 2 January Macready called on Forster only to find Dickens there in his costume of doublet and hose; 'it is quite ludicrous the fuss which the actors make about this play', was his private comment. Next day he had a note from Forster '*pestering* me about his cloak—to "wear it, or not"—absurd'. When the play was finally performed he dismissed it as 'dull and dragging'; the reviewers shared his opinion.[63] But these irritations did not seriously mar such close friendships and Forster and Macready were both at the jolly Twelfth Night party at Devonshire Terrace. Captain Marryat, one of the many guests, reported it as 'lots of fun' with 'convivial songs', 'speeches', a 'ball and capital supper'.[64]

Although Macready was still as apprehensive as Forster about the new newspaper, he sent Dickens a few words 'by way of a starting cheer'.[65] By the middle of January the staff were set up in comfortable new offices in Whitefriars ready for the first issue of the paper on Wednesday 21 January 1846. 'Everything looks well for our Start,' Dickens told Paxton on 16 January. 'I can't sleep; and if I fall into a doze I dream of first numbers till my head swims.'[66] A dummy issue was printed the following night, but despite such careful preparations the first issue was disappointing. It consisted of eight pages, three of them given over to advertising, at a cost of fivepence. It was badly printed on poor paper and badly made up. 'They had engaged an incompetent printer and all our effort was nearly being floored at four O'clock this morning,' Paxton wrote to his wife. 'I never passed four hours in such a state of suspense in my life.'[67] Dickens immediately tried to take the edge off such weaknesses by writing an amusing letter signed 'Your Constant Reader' which complained of the many typographical errors.

The first leading article in the paper was a statement of policy by Dickens. The *Daily News*, he declared, would be based on the 'principles of progress and improvement, of education, civil and religious liberty' which 'the advancing spirit of the times requires'. Three of the leading articles were on free trade, and there were several accounts of meetings in support of that policy, including one brought by special train from Norwich, where Cobden had spoken. From a political point of view the *Daily News* was well timed. Sir Robert Peel had resigned early in December because he could not carry his party on the free trade issue. Lord John Russell, who had just announced his conversion to free trade, then failed to get his fellow Whigs to form a government and Peel tried again. It was known that Peel planned to announce the repeal of the unpopular duties on imported grains in a long speech on 27 January, and John Dickens unsuccessfully applied to Peel for an advance copy. Like other reporters, however, he was shown a draft and the *Daily News* managed to come out at 5 a.m. next morning with a verbatim report of a four-hour speech which Peel had only finished in the small hours. In a bid to win circulation by this achievement, John Dickens and his son Augustus took copies of this special edition down to Exeter and Plymouth by train, and returned the same night. 'Mr. Dickens is a gentleman of most enviable stamina,' the editor of the *Western Times* wrote admiringly on 31 January 1846. 'Time seems to have made no impression on him whatever.'[68]

Despite such achievements, and an improvement in the paper itself, it was not the challenge that other papers had expected. 'At the sight of the outer sheet, hope at once lighted up the gloom of Printing House Square, the Strand, and Shoe Lane,' wrote W. H. Russell, at that time one of the recruits to the *Daily News* and later the famous foreign correspondent of *The Times*.[69] Those who had expected something different from the new paper were disappointed. Elizabeth Barrett told Robert Browning that she thought the leading article was weak, merely giving support to the Anti-Corn-Law League and laying down no broad principles.[70] Macready was no better impressed. There was 'nothing very striking or startling in it,' he remarked, 'nothing, I think, to stimulate curiosity or excite expectation'.[71] He did not even care very much for the 'Travelling Letter' which Dickens had written as his first instalment of *Pictures from Italy*. Part of the trouble lay with Dickens himself. 'Dickens was not a good editor,' W. H. Russell remarked; 'he was the best reporter in London, and as a journalist he was nothing more.' He was certainly not an effective manager of a large staff or a complicated undertaking. While he had recruited able people, and harried them impatiently, he allowed them to produce slipshod work. He was, moreover, no longer accustomed to the discipline and long hours of a morning newspaper. One of his staff recalled that he often left the office early, not long after midnight, and that he took his duties rather lightly. 'There were frequent sounds of merriment, if not modest revelry, audible from the little room ... where the editor sat in conclave.'[72] Another colleague, noting how much Dickens relied on the 'very intelligent and industrious' Wills, felt that he did not have any clear policy for the paper he had founded; 'he was absent-minded and indisposed to say anything definite, and would never *discuss* any topic properly', J. T. Danson said; and he concluded that Dickens was 'a decidedly unhappy man' who was unfit for the post he had assumed.[73]

To make matters worse Dickens was soon at odds with his backers. By the end of January he was writing a sharp letter to Bradbury and Evans, warning them that the railway interests might taint the independence of the *Daily News*, and objecting to their interference with his appointment of a sub-editor. Some nameless authority had said that the man was incompetent. 'I wish to know from whom you learn this,' Dickens wrote indignantly. 'When I tell you, distinctly, that I shall leave the Paper immediately, if you do not give me this information, I think it but fair to add that it is extremely probable I shall leave it when you have done so.... I am thoroughly disgusted, and shall act accordingly.'[74] True to his word, he wrote to Forster, 'I have been revolving plans in my mind this morning for quitting the paper'; and he went on to say that he had the idea of 'going abroad again to write a new book in shilling numbers'.[75] As soon as he glimpsed the prospect of escape Dickens felt more cheerful. Escape depended, however, upon the co-operation of Forster. Dickens not only needed him in his usual roles as a confidant and as a man of business; he also needed him as his successor. The matter was quickly settled. After a birthday outing to his old haunts at Rochester with Forster and Jerrold as well as Kate and Georgina, Forster agreed to replace him. Forster seemed 'elated with his position and looked forward to improving the paper', Macready noted three days afterwards, but he doubted Forster's 'ability to do so sufficiently for success'.[76] On 9 February, after only seventeen issues of the *Daily News*, Dickens resigned.

Until matters were formally settled Dickens hung about in London. In the meantime he undertook to contribute some articles on social problems— one on crime and education had already appeared on 4 February—and to continue the extracts from his travel notes which had begun in the first issue. Always eager to shrug off responsibility, he blamed his resignation on his argumentative backers. At the end of February in a manner which recalled his objections to Bentley's interference in the *Miscellany*, he complained to Evans that Bradbury had interfered with 'almost every act of mine at the newspaper office'. Bradbury had also slighted John Dickens, and for once Dickens felt obliged to come to his father's defence, insisting that there was not 'a more zealous, disinterested, or useful gentleman attached to the paper'.[77] The *Daily News* was actually in real trouble. 'I find them all in a Mess at the *Daily News*,' Paxton wrote on 4 March, 'it must break down I do think.'[78] But Dickens had no patience with all 'the disputes and differences' and after the middle of March he made no more contributions from his Italian notes. He too believed that the paper was going to collapse, airily telling Madame de la Rue in April that Bradbury and Evans 'would be the ruin of what might otherwise have been made a very fine property'.[79]

Ever since Dickens decided to visit America he had been in an unsettled state of mind. In four years he had produced a controversial novel, two travelogues, and three Christmas stories—a marked contrast in both quantity and quality to the books with which he had so quickly made his reputation. Although he had gaily told Forster that he now intended to go abroad to write another novel he was in fact still undecided. One of the attractions of running the *Daily News* was that it provided a good regular income while enabling him to put his views before the public every day. Even after he had resigned he was reluctant to give up his ambitions as a social reformer and to see himself simply as a novelist, and he was still casting around uncertainly for some other way to change things.

He turned at first to the contributions he had promised to the *Daily News*, using the opportunity to write the long discussion of capital punishment originally promised to the *Edinburgh Review* before his visit to America. During the last decade the number of capital offences had been so reduced that few criminals apart from murderers were hanged, and the campaign to abolish capital punishment altogether was gaining ground. Douglas Jerrold had been an outspoken advocate of abolition, denouncing public executions from the early days of *Punch*. Now Dickens with carefully reasoned argument condemned the obscene 'ever-haunting, ever-beckoning' shadow of the gallows, recalling in graphic detail the execution of Courvoisier. The 'Punishment of Death', he insisted, was a morbid stimulant to crime rather than a deterrent, corrupting the society which enforced it.[80]

While his mind was occupied with this theme in the spring of 1846, Dickens thought he might become a paid magistrate and thus combine— as Henry Fielding had done a century before—an obsession with London's underworld, a career as a novelist, and a role as a social reformer. When he wrote to a member of the government inquiring about his chances of appointment to the bench nothing came of the idea. He then turned his mind to the philanthropic plans of Angela Coutts to establish a residential home for rehabilitating prostitutes in preparation for a new life in Australia.

This scheme had a peculiar appeal for him, for it touched his moral enthusiasms as well as his fascination with poverty and crime. He was more than familiar with the scale of prostitution in London from his early work as a reporter in the police courts, and from his nocturnal prowls around the shadier parts of the city; in any case, as Miss Coutts realized from the crowds of women soliciting all the way from Haymarket to the street before her own house overlooking Green Park, it was as flagrant a social disease as drunkenness. Miss Coutts thought she might set up a refuge for younger women who wished to escape this sordid life. In the spring of 1846 she consulted Dickens, who considered that there were risks to her reputation in such a scheme, and suggested that she was better occupied with Ragged Schools and the church she was building in Westminster. His interest, however, was soon caught and he came forward with ideas for the 'plan, management and expense' of a home for fallen women. 'I do not know whether you would be disposed to entrust me with any share in the supervision and direction of the Institution,' he asked Miss Coutts on 26 May. 'But I need not say that I should enter on such a task with my whole heart and soul.'[81]

While Dickens was casting around for new interests his thoughts turned to a new novel. 'I go wandering about at night into the strangest places', he told Lady Blessington on 2 March, 'according to my usual propensity at such a time—seeking rest, and finding none.'[82] He began to think that another long stay in Europe might be the best way to appease his restlessness. But he could not quite make up his mind, and in a letter to Madame de la Rue on 17 April he rehearsed his difficulties. He was still caught up with the problems of the *Daily News*. Its future was uncertain and until things were settled he felt he could not leave town. He was also nominally still a law student and if he stayed to be called to the Bar 'there are many little pickings to be got—pretty easily within my reach'. At the same time he was anxious to get the benefit of his popularity with the public: 'it might be a pity to run away from them, when they are so very kind'. On the other hand, if the *Daily News* did close he would rather not 'have to be questioned, and condoled with, and all sorts of things, in all kinds of society'.[83]

Long meetings about the future of the *Daily News* dragged on. 'As they cannot make up their minds,' Dickens wrote to Mitton on 20 April, 'I have made up mine—Abroad again!'[84] On 25 April it was decided that the *Daily News* would continue under the management of Charles Wentworth Dilke and at a reduced price of $2\frac{1}{2}d.$; Forster tried to dissuade Dickens from going. 'I don't think I *could* shut out the paper sufficiently, here, to write well,'[85] Dickens replied, and added that he would save money by another year abroad. He had already outlined his plans to Madame de la Rue. 'I need not tell you that I want to go to Genoa', he wrote, but 'Mrs. Dickens, who was never very well there, cannot be got to contemplate the Peschiere'. Mrs. Dickens was obviously unwilling to contemplate Madame de la Rue as a neighbour. Dickens therefore decided to take 'a middle course', and 'pitch my tent somewhere on the lake of Geneva—say at Lausanne, whence I should run over to Genoa immediately'.[86] Roche was once again engaged as courier and major-domo for the household.

It took a few weeks to let Devonshire Terrace and make plans for transporting the Dickens family to Switzerland. There was a round of jolly outings, family parties, and farewell dinners—for release from the *Daily News* and the prospect of travel had put Dickens into a brighter mood. At the beginning of April he took Kate, Georgina, Forster, Maclise, Stanfield, and Macready off to the Star and Garter at Richmond for a lively day; Macready remarked that it was 'a very merry—I suppose I must say *jolly* day—rather more tumultuous than I quite like'.[87] Later in the month Lady Blessington gave a dinner for close friends such as Forster, Landseer, Jerdan, and Macready, who had only just been told of the proposed move to Switzerland and was 'much distressed by it'. When the new baby was christened, Tennyson was invited to dinner as one of his godfathers. Dickens, Elizabeth Barrett reported to Browning, asked Tennyson to join the expedition to Switzerland. Tennyson, she said, laughingly declined: 'If I went I should be entreating him to dismiss his sentimentality and we should quarrel and part and never see one another any more.'[88]

Farewell dinners were given by Macready, Talfourd, and Forster in the last days of May. The Devonshire Terrace house was let for the year at £300. *Pictures from Italy*, with pretty woodcuts by Samuel Palmer (Stanfield, who had agreed to do them, cried off when the text offended his Catholicism), was published as Dickens left. The first edition of 6,000 was soon sold, but it did little to add to his reputation. 'We did not expect learning but we did look for fun,' *The Times* wrote bluntly. 'The book has been written as a task ... without love, without inspiration, and without the healthy motives that actuated Mr. Dickens in his earliest achievments.'[89] Macready loyally considered the review 'stern and unkind', but others said much the same.[90] Robert Browning, who knew Italy so well, thought he had 'expended his power on the least interesting places—and then gone on hurriedly seeing and describing less and less till at last the mere names of places do duty for pictures and at Naples he fairly gives it up'.[91] Dickens still sold well, but *The Chimes*, *The Cricket*, and the Italian travel notes were beginning to tarnish his literary glitter. Something fresh and impressive had to come out of the Swiss sojourn to refurbish it.

The family crossed to Ostend, where Dickens had hoped to see his brother Alfred, now working at York, who had married on 16 May and gone abroad for his honeymoon. He was disappointed, and they went to Cologne by train, steamed up the Rhine in easy stages to Strasburg, took another train to Basle, and finished their journey to Lausanne in a convoy of three coaches. The logistics of the journey intrigued Dickens and he set the directions out in detail in a letter to his brother Fred, urging him to visit. When the party reached Lausanne it put up temporarily at the ugly Hotel Gibbon on the waterfront, but after two days of house-hunting Dickens soon found an 'odd little house'. Rosemount stood, he wrote to Angela Coutts on 25 June, 'in the midst of beautiful grounds, on the slope of the Hill going down to the Lake—and the blue waters thereof, and the whole range of Mountains, lie in front of the windows'. It was smaller than the Peschiere (Dickens had a study upstairs 'something larger than a Plate Warmer'),[92] but it was convenient and attractive—'a kind of beautiful bandbox' at £10 a month.[93] Enough roses rambled over the balcony, Dickens told Forster, to 'smother the whole establishment of the *Daily News*'.[94] He was altogether enchanted with his new surroundings. He made no attempt to start the new novel or the planned Christmas story before his familiar writing materials and desk ornaments arrived, and there were also domestic details to arrange. He sent Charley to be 'imprisoned as a weekly Boarder' at a near-by school.[95] He found a governess for the girls. He sketched out a part of the simplified New Testament he was preparing for the children, and by the beginning of July the Christmas book was 'simmering over a slow fire'.[96] He started on regular ten-mile walks and he was going 'with great vigour at the French'.[97]

With all his new interests he had not forgotten the problems at home. He wrote to Lord John Russell about the Ragged Schools, and he was corresponding with Angela Coutts about her proposed asylum. Its aim, he suggested, must be to condition its inmates to a better life by a series of rewards and punishments; they must be given the chance to earn a new character and to emigrate to distant colonies where their marriage would be 'the greatest service to the existing male population'. Dickens thought there was little point in reminding a woman of her Debt to Society while she was 'full of affliction, misery, and despair to *herself*', and had still to regain her self-respect: 'Society had used her ill and turned away from her, and she cannot be expected to take much heed of its rights or wrongs.' The managers of the asylum, he argued, must appeal to a woman's pride, her sense of shame, her heart, her reason, and her interest; and they must be capable of the love which could keep hope alive and show the way to the penitence which was the emblem of moral recovery.[98]

The theme of the woman who has fallen, but who is not wholly lost, was consciously woven into the pattern of *Dombey and Son*, in which Dickens linked the traffic in bodies and souls to the values of the counting-house. Mr. Dombey, the purse-lipped City gentleman, buys his second wife into a loveless marriage; Carker, his confidential clerk and manager, ruins Mrs. Dombey's cousin and reduces her to prostitution. In both senses Dombey and Carker are in the same business. Dickens began this new novel in Lausanne on 27 June 1846, and on the following day he cheerfully told Forster that he had started with 'a plunge straight over head and ears into the story'.[99] It was the first time that he had planned his work in some detail and at the outset it ran swiftly. A month later he sent Forster the manuscript of four chapters and told him what was to follow. 'I design to show Mr. D. with that one idea of the Son taking firmer and firmer possession of him, and swelling and bloating his pride to a prodigious extent.... But the natural affection of the boy will turn towards the despised sister ... and when he is ill, and when he is dying, I mean to make him turn always for refuge to the sister still, and keep the stern affection of the father at a distance.' After the death of the pathetic Paul, Dickens went on, he proposed to change Mr. Dombey's indifference towards his daughter Florence into a positive hatred. Yet Florence, in the end, was to save her father by her self-sacrificing devotion. 'I mean to carry the story on ... through the decay and downfall of the house, and the bankruptcy of Dombey, and all the rest of it; when his only staff and treasure, and his unknown Good Genius always, will be this rejected daughter, who will come out better than any son at last, and whose love for him, when discovered and understood, will be his bitterest reproach.'[100]

The curse which had destroyed the House of Chuzzlewit was about to fall upon the House of Dombey, in which the getting of money has taken the place of the giving of love. Mr. Dombey runs his life as though it were a business and regulates his relationships by the rules of self-interest. 'Some philosophers', Dickens remarked in a parody of Dombey's commercial values which owed much to his recent experiences with the backers of the *Daily News*, 'tell us that selfishness is the root of our best loves and affections'; and he turned the novel into a balance sheet of Dombey's affairs to show how selfishness leads to emotional as well as to financial insolvency. Dombey, however, is not a wicked man. He is pathologically ill. 'A sense of injustice is within him, all along,' Dickens wrote of his resentment when, as Miss Tox puts it, Dombey and Son turned out to be a Daughter after all. 'The more he represses it, the more unjust he necessarily is.'[101] Thus flawed, Dombey is driven to one offence against human feeling after another, and everything he touches turns to dust; he even squanders the fortune which seemed so secure as the story began.

In all the novels after *Pickwick*, in fact, Dickens had explored how selfishness and greed corroded family ties, and in all of them he had used a deprived child to exemplify the consequences. All through *Dombey*, as Dickens released that forlorn sentiment, he kept coming back to the relation of parents and children. The chill gloom of the Dombey household is contrasted to the lively happiness of the railway stoker Toodles and his family, who have little money but love and enough to spare. The child-quelling qualities of Mr. Dombey are echoed in the schooldame Mrs. Pipchin, who is so sombre that 'gas itself couldn't light her up after dark', and Dr. Blimber, who is bent on blowing up his pupils with the abstractions that fill the vacuous speech of Mr. Toots. Solomon Gills serves as a substitute father for Walter Gay, and Captain Cuttle does the same for Florence when she is homeless. Mrs. Skewton and Mrs. Brown come from different levels of society, but they both play the pander to their daughters. 'Not an orphan in the wide world', Dickens wrote in *Dombey*, 'can be so deserted as the child who is an outcast from a living parent's love.'

Dickens made a good beginning with *Dombey*, but as the summer went on he slowed down. He was pleased with his new surroundings. The climate of Lausanne was more comfortable than that of Genoa, there were fewer Catholic churches and priests to irritate him, the house was clean and attractive, and there was congenial English company nearby. 'I do not think we could have fallen on better society,' he reported to Forster after only a few weeks.[102] One interesting new acquaintance was William Haldimand, a friend of Samuel Rogers, who had been a Member of Parliament for Ipswich before he settled in Lausanne. He was a philanthropic man, contributing to the English Church and establishing an asylum for the blind. He took Dickens off to see the asylum, the local jail, and other notable attractions; and on 29 June he gave a dinner to introduce the Dickens family to members of the English set. Among the guests were Haldimand's sister, Mrs. Marcet, William de Cerjat, de Cerjat's English wife—who had helped Haldimand set up his asylum—her sister, and her brother-in-law. And they were joined by Richard Watson and his wife Lavinia, also friends of Haldimand, who had reached Lausanne four days after Dickens. Like Haldimand, Watson had been a reforming member of the House of Commons, and owned an imposing estate at Rockingham Castle in Northamptonshire. 'Met Boz, Mrs. Dickens and her sister Miss Hogarth,' Watson noted in his diary. 'Like him altogether very much as well as his wife. He appears unaffected.'[103] Dickens was equally taken with Watson, whom he thought 'a very agreeable fellow', telling Forster that he was a 'thorough good Liberal' and that he had 'a charming wife, who draws well'.[104] The merry dinner was the beginning of a lively social season. Members of this little society dined with each other, gave whist parties, and put on musical evenings which Dickens reported were 'interrupted only by the occasional facetiousness of the Inimitable'.[105] Such congenial companions made Dickens think of theatricals, especially as there was 'not a bad little theatre' in the town. 'I should certainly have got it open with an amateur company', he told Forster, 'if we were not so few that the only thing we want is the audience.'[106]

He was soon taking trips with his new friends. It was a particularly hot summer and they sought out cool places to visit. At the end of July the group went to Chamonix, 'that glorious place', to see the glacier and Mont Blanc. Kate and Georgina, Dickens reported, were mounted on mules '*for ten hours at a stretch*', and they rode up and down 'the most frightful precipices'.[107] There were other outings to Vevey and the Château de Chillon, where Dickens was depressed by the dungeons, the torture chambers, and the stake: 'the greatest mystery in all the earth', he commented to Forster, 'is how or why the world was tolerated by its Creator through the good old times, and wasn't dashed to fragments'. There was a regatta at Ouchy with a rowing match by women which they all thought very funny, and a 'prodigious fête' in Lausanne.[108]

There was no shortage of visitors from home. Some were public personalities who called on Dickens as one notable to another, such as the great railway and steamship engineer Isambard Kingdom Brunel, the economist Nassau Senior, and the historian Henry Hallam. Some were friends. Harrison Ainsworth brought his daughter; he and Dickens had seen little of each other during the last year or so—'the unintelligible novelist', Dickens called him—and now they walked about all day 'talking of old days at Kensal-lodge'.[109] Tennyson, too, spent an evening over 'Rhine wine, and cigars innumerable'.[110] The Talfourds stayed for a week-end at the end of the summer. Elliotson came for a week or so and Dickens, busy again with mesmeric experiments, was pleased to report to Jerrold that Elliotson 'holds my magnetic powers in great veneration'.[111] At the beginning of August T. J. Thompson, at last married to Christiana Weller, took a house in Lausanne for eight months. Dickens now found Christiana to be 'a mere spoiled child' with 'a devil of a whimpering, pouting temper',[112] and he was far from pleased that his brother Fred wanted to marry her sister Anna; nevertheless, she and her husband joined the friendly circle at Lausanne.

An energetic social life provided some of the stimulus Dickens needed once he had begun a story, but there were problems. The weather was often too hot for work and he was worrying about the publishing arrangements of his new novel as well as its contents. His difficulties over the *Daily News* had done nothing to inspire his confidence in Bradbury and Evans and he suggested to Forster that Chapman and Hall might after all be better equipped to publish his new work. He was also finding it difficult to put his mind to a new novel and at the same time to start work on his Christmas story. 'What do you think, as a name for the Christmas book of THE BATTLE OF LIFE?' he asked Forster in July. 'If I can see my way, I think I will take it next and clear it off. If you knew how it hangs about me, I am sure you would say so too. It would be an immense relief to have it done.'[113] But he could make little headway. He found it hard to resist tempting expeditions with his friends. One day in the middle of August, for instance, he went with the Cerjats, the Watsons, and Haldimand to the Lac de Bret, twelve miles away in the mountains. Dickens was also trying to arrange a meeting with the de la Rues, who were in Switzerland—he suggested a 'joyful' day with them at Vevey at the end of August—but he was clearly bothered by the pressure from Forster and the printers who were anxious to have copy. 'I am set upon in all directions', he wrote on 17 August to de la Rue, 'and am not working with a very good will either.'[114] When the Watsons entertained Dickens, Kate, and Georgina a few days later, Watson noted 'Boz in a state of great animation'.

Dickens needed something more, as he explained to Forster at the end of August. 'The difficulty of going at what I call a rapid pace, is prodigious; it is almost an impossibility. I suppose this is partly the effect of two years' ease, and partly of the absence of streets and numbers of figures. I can't express how much I want these. It seems as if they supplied something to my brain, which it cannot bear, when busy, to lose ... the toil and labour of writing, day after day, without that magic lantern, is IMMENSE!!' This curious fact, he explained, was not a symptom of low spirits but a genuine discovery. 'My figures seem disposed to stagnate without crowds about them.'[115] A few days later, in another note to Forster, he returned to the point. 'The absence of any accessible streets continues to worry me, now that I have so much to do, in a most singular manner,' he said. 'It is quite a little mental phenomenon. I should not walk in them in the daytime, if they were here, I dare say: but at night I want them beyond description. I don't seem able to get rid of my spectres unless I can lose them in crowds.' Even in Genoa there had been 'two miles of streets, at least, lighted at night ... and a great theatre to repair to, every night'.[116]

Despite such difficulties Dickens was making headway with *Dombey* and he was pleased with the first number. 'I have taken immense pains,' he told Mitton on 30 August, 'and think it strong. Some of it made me laugh so, that I couldn't see the paper as I was writing.'[117] His friends in Lausanne were equally pleased when Dickens held a soirée to read it to them. It was an 'unrelateable success', he told Forster, and he declared that he would leave Lausanne in 'a brilliant shower of sparks' when he read them the Christmas book.[118] All the same he still found it easier to talk about the

Christmas book than to write it. There was another expedition at the beginning of September, and this took the Dickens family and their English friends to the convent of the Great St. Bernard—'a most serious hindrance to me just now', Dickens told Forster, 'but I have rashly promised'.[119] The visit made a vivid impression on him: it was 'the most distinct and individual place I have seen', where everything was 'iron bound and frozen up', an extraordinary place 'full of great vaulted passages'. Beside the convent was a little outhouse, containing the bodies of travellers found in the snow 'who have never been claimed and are withering away'. The monks, Dickens casually decided, were 'a lazy set of fellows' with a reputation built on 'sheer humbug'.[120]

The trip was a distraction, and when Dickens made a beginning with his story he soon ran into trouble. 'I never had to *begin* two stories together, before,' he told Mitton, 'and it is desperate work.'[121] At the end of September he dismally wrote to Forster that 'I fear there may be NO CHRISTMAS BOOK!'—although by then he had written a third of it. 'I am sick, giddy, and capriciously despondent,' he complained. 'I have bad nights; am full of disquietude and anxiety; and am constantly haunted by the idea that I am wasting the marrow of the larger book, and ought to be at rest.'[122] He took refuge in movement; he would sometimes walk for fifteen miles or so. At the end of September he set off for Geneva for a week. Kate was with him and they were soon joined by Georgina. The fate of the Christmas book was still unsettled and he was also worried about falling behind with *Dombey*, on which he was pinning his hopes. Torn between the two, he sent Forster a worried note. 'If I don't do it, it will be the first time I ever abandoned anything I had once taken in hand,' he wrote; 'and I shall not have abandoned it until after a most desperate fight.'[123] When he arrived in Geneva he had a bloodshot eye and a headache so painful that he felt he must be bled for relief. The pressure might well have been emotional as well as physical since the story that was causing so much trouble touched a painful nerve. *The Battle of Life* described a girl who gives up her sweetheart to her sister; the presence of Georgina as well as the memory of Mary was there to parallel that fantasy.

The liveliness of Geneva—on the verge of a popular revolution—helped to dispel his anxiety and he was soon at work. The 'rushing Rhone' and the noise in the streets 'seemed to stir my blood again', he told Forster. 'I am, I hope, greatly better.... I hope and trust, *now*, the Christmas book will come in due course!'[124] It was actually finished in the next two weeks, and once the crisis was over his spirits rose: he felt 'a little used up, and sick', he told Forster. 'But never say die!'[125] Forster, as usual, was asked for criticism and comfort. 'I trust to Heaven you may like it,' Dickens wrote.

Forster was also expected to suggest improvements, read proofs, and give advice on instalments of *Dombey*. It was not surprising that Dickens described him to Lord Jeffrey as 'my right hand and cool shrewd head'.[126] The publishers had already arranged for Leech and Richard Doyle to illustrate *The Battle*; Dickens brought in Stanfield; and Forster enlisted Maclise as a pleasant surprise for Dickens. Maclise had reluctantly agreed to help, for he was resentful that Dickens himself had not seen fit to invite his collaboration, and he was also annoyed by the quality of the engraving and the printing. Forster manfully attended to all these chores, though he had troubles of his own. Things had not gone well for him at the *Daily News*. Although the paper was now beginning to make headway, with sales up to nearly 20,000, Dickens believed that Forster felt uneasy about 'the confinement and drudgery';[127] when the price was put up to threepence, in fact, Forster protested and then resigned on 22 October.[128] This unfortunate experience, Macready observed, increased his general churlishness of manner, but Dickens sent him a warm-hearted and encouraging letter.

Things had gone better for *Dombey*. The first number had appeared on 1 October: 'The *Dombey* success is BRILLIANT!!!' Dickens told Forster. The first edition of 25,000 was quickly sold and ten days later another 5,000 were printed. 'I had put before me thirty thousand as the limit of the most extreme success,' he added. 'You will judge how happy I am!'[129] There was relief and applause from the critics when they realized that Dickens was back in more familiar form. 'The good ship Boz is righted and once more fairly afloat,' declared *Chambers's Edinburgh Journal*.[130] *The Economist* had no doubt that 'this great painter of English manners ... should bid adieu to politics and controversy—should cease to paint pictures of Italy—a land which he does not understand—and confine himself to London and Middlesex'.[131] Friends were no less pleased. Douglas Jerrold, who started his own *Weekly Newspaper* that summer, wrote that 'our author will again delight his tens of thousands'.[132] Macready wrote saying that the new book was 'full of genius and beauty',[133] and Lord Jeffrey was delighted with it. 'The Dombeys, my dear D!' he wrote, 'how can I thank you enough for them!'[134]

On 19 October, when the 'tea-cup revolution' in Geneva was over, Dickens returned to work on the third number of *Dombey*. Before he went he read the second number 'to the most prodigious and uproarious delight' of the circle of friends in Lausanne. The habit of reading his work aloud had given Dickens an idea. He thought, he told Forster, 'that in these days of lecturings and readings, a great deal of money might possibly be made (if it were not *infra dig*) by one's having Readings of one's own books. It would be an *odd* thing. I think it would take immensely. What do you say?'[135] And he speculatively suggested that Forster might consider leasing Miss Kelly's theatre or the St. James's for the purpose.

The tensions of the past weeks had left Dickens sick, over-wrought, and suffering from headaches and sleeplessness: 'the mental distress, quite horrible' was his summary to Forster.[136] In Geneva, however, 'a week of perfect idleness has brought me round again.'[137] There were a few souvenirs of the brief fighting, but Dickens was impressed by the fact that everyone had gone back to work and order was so quickly restored. There was, he concluded in a letter to Macready on 24 October, 'no country on earth ... in which a violent change could have been effected in the Christian spirit shewn in this place, or in the same proud, independent, gallant style. Not one halfpennyworth of property was lost, stolen or strayed. Not one atom of party malice survived the smoke of the last gun.' Such an ideal revolution was most attractive, and Dickens was delighted by the government addresses which expressed nothing but 'a regard for the general happiness, and injunctions to forget all animosities'.[138] Life did sometimes produce the same happy ending as one of his stories.

By the end of the month Dickens was again at work on *Dombey*, 'with good speed, thank God', despite what he called 'these bird-of-passage' circumstances.[139] Back in Lausanne, as he had promised, he read *The Battle of Life* as a gesture of farewell, for the family was about to leave for Paris. 'He read it with wonderful charm, and spirit,' Watson noted. 'Lavinia was quite overcome by it.'[140] As a mark of his affection for these new-found friends, Dickens dedicated the story 'To my English Friends in Switzerland'. There was a farewell dinner at Haldimand's on 15 November and everyone was sorry that the convivial visit was ending. 'I don't believe there are many dots on the map of the world where we shall have left such affectionate remembrances behind us, as in Lausanne,' Dickens wrote to Forster. 'It was quite miserable this last night.'[141] He had enjoyed that 'little society'. 'We have been thoroughly good-humoured and agreeable together, and I'll always give a hurrah for the Swiss and Switzerland.'[142] The Swiss, he remarked to Landor on 22 November, 'are a thorn in the sides of European despots, and a good wholesome people to live near Jesuit-ridden kings on the brighter side of the mountains'.[143]

For all his pleasure Dickens was ready to move on. He had not planned to stay longer in Lausanne than the late autumn, intending that the household should then decamp to Paris for the winter. Constant change, he admitted, 'is indispensable to me when I am at work: and at times something more than a doubt will force itself upon me whether there is not something in a Swiss valley that disagrees with me'.[144] During the stay at Lausanne, indeed, Dickens had become aware that he was the victim of a deep-seated but inexplicable malaise. It made him an anxious fidget, dissatisfied with his surroundings whatever they were, driving him with erratic impulses—into foreign travel, for instance, and into the launching of the *Daily News*—and depressing him to the point of physical illness. He asked himself what was amiss, but he found only trivial answers. He blamed the climate of Lake Leman, the location of the villa; he missed the stimulus of London streets, the vitality of his friends, the familiar routine of home. Whatever the cause, he realized that he was a driven man, a slave to his own relentless and exhausting energy.

On 16 November the family was packed into three coaches which climbed through the frost and fog of the Jura and headed for Paris, reaching the Hotel Brighton four days later. After the 'paroxysm' of house-hunting for another 'four mortal days', he took rooms at 48 rue de Courcelles—'the most preposterous house in the world'—and he told Richard Watson of its strange arrangement. 'The bedrooms are like opera boxes,' he wrote. 'The dining room is a sort of cavern painted (ceiling and all) to represent a Grove, with unaccountable bits of looking-glass sticking in among the branches of the trees.' The drawing-room was approached by 'a series of small chambers, like the joints in a telescope, which are hung with inscrutable drapery'. Dickens was intrigued by the oddity of his new apartments. 'The maddest man in Bedlam having the materials given him, would be likely to devise such a suite',[145] he wrote to Richard Watson on 27 November, and a few days later he reported to Forster that the decorations were commissioned by Bulwer's younger brother Henry who 'got frightened at what he had done, as well he might, and went away'. Dickens could not make the place comfortable, even when he had moved the furniture to suit his taste. The weather was bitterly cold, bursting water-jugs with frozen water; everything was dear, particularly fuel. For all the drawbacks, however, Dickens was glad of the change of scene. He confessed to Forster that he had become dreadfully depressed in Lausanne: 'when my spirits sunk so, I felt myself in serious danger.'[146]

On the night of his arrival Dickens set out to explore Paris and on that first week-end he took colossal walks about the city. He was amazed to see on a Sunday walk the 'dirty churches, and the clattering carts and waggons, and the open shops'.[147] Paris, he concluded, was a 'wicked and detestable place though wonderfully attractive'. Although he was relieved to be again in the streets of a city, he still could not settle to his work. No sooner had he arrived than he had disquieting news of his sister Fanny. She had broken down while singing at a party in Manchester and John Dickens had written to say that consumption was diagnosed. 'I am deeply, deeply grieved about it,' he wrote to Forster, and he cried off a visit to the theatre with Kate and Georgina when he heard the news.[148] He now thought he should return to London in the spring, three months sooner than he had planned. In the circumstances it was difficult to get on with *Dombey* and on 6 December he told Forster that he had been 'hopelessly out of sorts—writing sorts; that's all. Couldn't begin, in the strange place; took a violent dislike to my study.' He described how he tried to settle to his desk, going 'about and about it, and dodged at it, like a bird at a lump of sugar. In short, I have just begun.'[149]

Dickens was determined to keep his spirits up 'even under *Dombey* pressure' and he managed to create sufficient prose for the printer before he dashed across to London on a four-day excursion in freezing weather a week before Christmas. *The Battle of Life* was to be staged at the Lyceum Theatre. Dickens was pleased with the volume and delighted with the illustrations by his friends. 'Say everything to Mac and Stanny, more than everything! It is a delight to look at these little landscapes,' he told Forster. 'I have a perfect joy in them.'[150] He was less pleased, however, with the dramatic production. 'I really am bothered to death by this confounded dramatization,' he explained to Kate. 'Unless I had come to London, I do not think there would have been much hope of the Version being more than just tolerated,' he told her on 19 December, two days before the play opened. 'All the actors bad. All the business frightfully behind-hand.'[151] In this dissatisfied mood he called all the company to a reading of the parts at Forster's apartment in Lincoln's Inn Fields; and although he had a fierce cold he worked the actors until two in the morning. After the first night he reported to Kate that 'the play went, as well as I can make out, with great effect. There was immense enthusiasm at its close, and great uproar and shouting for me.'[152] The critics, however, did not care for the almost maudlin self-sacrifice of the tale, either on the stage or in print. Thackeray found it 'a wretched affair', *The Times* considered it '*the very worst*' of 'the deluge of trash' that was dumped on the market at Christmas. And the *London Magazine* summed up both versions in one sentence; the tale was 'condemned by the critics, pooh-poohed by the public, hissed at the Lyceum, and finally "dead and buried" by *The Times*'.[153] The loyalty of the public, however, was strong. Despite such criticism *The Battle of Life* sold well: '23,000 copies already gone!!!'[154] Dickens told Kate on publication day. It brought him a profit of nearly £1,300, and for another year he was assured of sufficient money to live in the open-handed style to which he had grown accustomed.

11

Good Samaritan

'PAUL is dead,' Dickens wrote to Angela Coutts on 18 January 1847. 'He died on Friday night about 10 o'clock, and as I had no hope of getting to sleep afterwards, I went out, and walked about Paris until breakfast time the next morning.'[1] Since his return from London in December Dickens had devoted himself to the fifth number of *Dombey*. It had been a hard struggle and his trip across the Channel, though cheering, had not eased his difficulties. He sent Forster almost daily reports on his state of mind: 'most abominably dull and stupid'; 'working very slowly'; 'very mouldy'. He was not helped by what he knew was a 'morbid susceptibility to exasperation'; he was annoyed by references to the bad review of his Christmas book in *The Times*. 'I see that the "good old *Times*" are again at issue with the inimitable B. Another touch of a blunt razor on B's nervous system,' he wrote to Forster. 'Disposed to go to New Zealand and start a magazine.' Dickens shared all his problems over the plot of *Dombey* with Forster, and eventually he was able to report that he was ploughing along. 'It is difficult; but a new way of doing it, it strikes me, and likely to be pretty.'[2]

Now that he was again settled into the familiar routine of serial writing he was able to develop a better rhythm of work, dividing the month into two fortnights, one given to the next instalment of *Dombey* and the other to relaxation. At the same time he put down a plan for each number before he began to write it. Forster came over for the unoccupied fortnight in January. When he had given up the *Daily News* in the autumn Dickens had written to him from Lausanne: 'we'll have, please God, the old kind of evenings and the old life again, as it used to be, before those daily nooses caught us by the legs'.[3] Now with that contentious issue behind them, they enjoyed Paris together. By 24 January Dickens was telling Lady Blessington that 'Forster has been cramming into the space of a fortnight every description of impossible and inconsistent occupation in the way of sight-seeing. He has been now at Versailles, now in the prisons, now at the opera, now at the hospitals, now at the Conservatoire, and now at the Morgue, with a dreadful insatiability.'[4] And Dickens introduced him to Dumas, the poet Lamartine, to Chateaubriand, the mystery writer Eugène Sue, the dramatist

Scribe, and to Victor Hugo, the French novelist to whom, in his democratic sentiments and belief that the novel was a means to social reform, Dickens felt most sympathetic. Dickens enjoyed Forster's visit with its hectic pace: 'away I was borne again, like an enchanted rider', he wrote to Edward Tagart, his Unitarian minister. 'I have had no rest in my play.'[5]

Forster went back to London at the beginning of February, taking the ten-year-old Charley with him to be enrolled at King's College School in preparation for his entry to Eton, where he was to go at the expense of Angela Coutts. Dickens himself would have preferred to send the boy to Bruce Castle at Tottenham, an experimental school set up by the reformer Rowland Hill and his brothers which emphasized moral and social training as much as pedagogy. 'I suppose, however, Miss Coutts is best,' Dickens told Forster.[6] He now turned to the next part of *Dombey* with the difficult task of shifting the focus of the story from the dead Paul to his sister Florence. 'I have taken the most prodigious pains with it,' he told Forster. 'May you like it! My head aches over it now (I write at one o'clock in the morning).'[7]

Before he left again for London Dickens knew he had made a hit. 'Paul's death has amazed Paris,' he wrote. 'All sorts of people are open-mouthed with admiration.'[8] And in London it was welcomed with a chorus of praise. Forster called this burst of pathos 'one of his greatest achievements', and public comment made it plain that after six years he had repeated the emotional impact of Little Nell's death. 'What a Number 5 you have now given us,' wrote Francis Jeffrey.[9] 'It is indeed most beautiful', Macready recorded in his diary.[10] Thackeray walked into Mark Lemon's office at *Punch* and put the passage in front of him. 'There's no writing against such power as this—one has no chance,' he declared, 'it is stupendous!'[11]

Thackeray's admiration was genuine, and so was his chagrin, for his own novel *Vanity Fair* had begun to appear in parts in January 1847. He had already made something of a mark with *Barry Lyndon* in *Fraser's Magazine*, but with *Vanity Fair* he had written a novel of great distinction. He was proud of it and after it had been running for a year he wrote to his mother. 'I am become a sort of great man in my way,' he told her, 'all but at the top of the tree: indeed there if the truth were known and having a great fight up there with Dickens.' He was fiercely competitive. His Christmas book for 1846, he wrote to his mother, was 'a great success—the greatest I have had—very nearly as great as Dickens'.[12]

English fiction had been dominated by Dickens in the fifteen years since the death of Sir Walter Scott. Now things were beginning to change. He had recently produced some inferior work which had disappointed the critics. It had even seemed possible that, like Ainsworth, he was beginning to fade after a brilliant start and that other novelists might overtake him.

In 1847, for instance, Charlotte Brontë had placed *Jane Eyre* with Smith and Elder, and her sister Emily published *Wuthering Heights*: both books, appearing under male pseudonyms, were greeted as masterpieces. But the main challenge came from Thackeray. It was not so much a race for readers, royalties, or even reputation, as a choice between two literary traditions, two views of society, and two concepts of human nature. Dickens was a writer of fairy-tales, full of terrors and wonders and magical changes of fortune; he had learned his humours from Jonson, his melodrama from Fielding and Smollett, his comedy and caricature from Hogarth and Gillray; and his characters smelt of lamp-oil and grease-paint. He used his prose to entertain; he exaggerated to make his readers laugh, or cry, or experience a change of sympathy; he created what John Ruskin later called 'a circle of stage fire' around a political moral, or a social tract.[13] He needed, like an actor or a lecturer, to tune his work to his audience as he went along, and for that purpose serial parts suited him admirably. And, marked from childhood as an outsider, all his work was held in a frame of social rage. By all these means he aimed at effect rather than at art, as Jane Austen and now Thackeray conceived it. For Thackeray, attempting to present a realistic novel of manners, thought his characters should be morally autonomous and that the plot should be the outcome of their relationships: he saw them as subjects rather than objects of society, and felt that they should evoke the sensibilities rather than the sensations of the reader. While he was less obviously compassionate than Dickens, and certainly much less of a moralist, he too had suffered; and the experience had made him more cynically tolerant of the failings and more charitably understanding of the faults of his fellow men. Where Dickens laid blame, like a child, for such faults, Thackeray saw them as the result of a human condition in which he shared adult responsibility for good and evil.

The fact that *Dombey* and *Vanity Fair* were running alongside each other in serial parts naturally invited such comparisons between the two books and the two authors, and the difference of assumptions was reflected in a struggle for the control of *Punch*. Although Dickens was not directly involved he supported his friend Douglas Jerrold, who thought satire should be a means of arousing the public conscience against social evils—what Dickens meant when, from time to time, he spoke of dealing 'sledgehammer' blows against cant and injustice. *Punch*, for Jerrold, had to be in radical earnest. Thackeray disagreed. Humour had its own intrinsic virtue, he believed, and ridicule was no respecter of parties or persons. He had for some time been a contributor to *Punch*, and the success of *Vanity Fair* increased his influence on the paper at Jerrold's expense. In April he started to write a set of parodies called *Punch's Prize Novelists*, and the first of these poked fun at the flatulent style of Edward Bulwer. This upset Forster, who was a friend of Bulwer, and he angrily told a mutual acquaintance that Thackeray was 'false as hell'. The remark was passed on and caused much bad feeling. Dickens tried to mediate; he gave a reconciliation dinner at Greenwich for Thackeray and Forster, which led to an uneasy truce. The quarrel also persuaded Bradbury and Evans that it was too risky to allow Thackeray to write a parody of Dickens, their most important author, in a magazine they owned. A year later Dickens jokingly complained to Thackeray about the 'injustice' of omitting him from a series of satirical articles, but he added that he thought men of letters demeaned themselves by sneering at each other. Thackeray, like Macready, valued his own work highly but thought little of his profession; he thought of himself as a gentleman who lived by writing, not as one of a company of authors upholding 'the dignity of literature'. Years later Dickens criticized him for his 'pretence of undervaluing his art'. The effect of such literary jests as the *Punch* articles, moreover, was to increase this alienation from his literary colleagues. While Thackeray realized what was happening—and he became more cut off as the years passed—he regretted it and tended to blame his friends for misunderstanding him.[14] 'Jerrold hates me,' he noted in the summer of 1847, 'Ainsworth hates me, Dickens mistrusts me, Forster says I am false as hell, and Bulwer curses me—he is the only one who has any reason... no end of quarrels in this wicked Vanity Fair.'[15]

Jerrold certainly disliked Thackeray's influence on *Punch*. 'I do not very cordially agree with its new spirit,' he wrote. 'I am convinced that the world will get tired (at least I hope so) of this eternal guffaw at all things. After all, life has something serious in it. It cannot all be a comic history of humanity.'[16] Dickens, less censorious and recognizing Thackeray's talent, concurred in thinking him facetious and cynical. 'I feel exactly as you do,' he told Jerrold. 'Such joking is like the sorrow of the undertaker's mute, reversed.'[17]

Dickens had planned to stay in Paris until the end of March, but he was no sooner back from his business trip to London than he had to leave again. Charley was ill with scarlet fever and in the care of Mrs. Hogarth. Leaving Georgina to look after the children, he and Kate hurried to London. Since Devonshire Terrace was let until the summer, he took a short tenancy on a house in Chester Place, off Regent's Street, to be near the Hogarths at Albany Street. Worry about Charley, house-hunting, and everyday distractions made it difficult for him to give *Dombey* the attention it needed at a critical stage of the plot and by 9 March he had written none of the next number. 'So far from having "got through my agonies" . . . I have not yet begun them,' he wrote to Georgina. 'My wretchedness, just now, is inconceivable.'[18] William Hall died soon after his return and Dickens felt able to go to his funeral at Highgate; he had now overcome the intemperate impulse that had made him part company with the publisher, whom he had known from the start of his career as a writer, and to whom he owed so much.

Although Charley's condition was improving, there was another good reason for Dickens and Kate to remain in London. Kate was again near a confinement and on 18 April, after a distressingly difficult delivery, she gave birth to their seventh child and fifth son, Sydney Smith Haldimand. Despite all the domestic upheaval Dickens managed to drive himself through the next 'convulsions of *Dombey*', but the number was scarcely in print before he too was incapacitated. He was bitten on the arm by a horse in his stable. He made light of it, saying that the horse was 'under the impression that I had gone into his stall to steal his corn, which upon my honor I had no intention of doing'. Yet the accident unnerved him, and he felt 'hideously queer' each morning. He was suffering, he told Chapman, from 'a low, dull, nervousness of a most distressing kind'.[19] He needed to recuperate as much as Kate and Charley, and also to get the next number of *Dombey* written in a hurry; and so they all went down to Brighton for a few days at the end of May.

While Dickens had been away in France he had kept in touch with Miss Coutts about the proposed refuge for prostitutes, and on his return he began to look about for a suitable property. His patron, however, had other things on her mind. In the course of the winter Miss Coutts had developed a close and curious relationship with the aged Duke of Wellington, and on 7 February she actually made the Duke an offer of marriage despite the disparity of their years. He sent an affectionate and charming refusal, but he continued to escort her to so many balls and other social affairs that the prospect of a match between them was the talk of the town and the subject of a joke in *Punch*. The Duke thought poorly of the plan for the women's asylum, insisting to Miss Coutts that 'there is but little if any hope of saving in this World that particular Class of Unfortunates to whom you have referred';[20] and though she was not deterred by this sceptical advice she was then so much involved with the Duke that she could give little time and attention to the scheme. On several occasions Dickens called at her house to consult her and was told that she was out. On one June evening, indeed, he and Kate were formally invited to a party. When they arrived they discovered that it had been cancelled without notice and they 'withdrew in melancholy splendor'.[21] Dickens, who had cast himself in the role of secretary-almoner, was therefore obliged to report his activities to Miss Coutts by letter. On 16 May he wrote to say that he had found a house in Lime

Grove, Shepherd's Bush, about two miles west of Marble Arch, and he asked her where she was and when he might see her. A week later he sent more details of the 'retired but cheerful' premises which he had taken on a long lease, and all through the summer he kept writing to seek her agreement to his plans and to keep her informed about the progress of the work.[22] In August he sent a hopeful letter to say that 'we shall be ready, very early in October, to shew you the Institution in perfect order'.[23]

He crammed each day with activity, as though anxiety might break through an unfilled moment. At the end of May, when Macready gave a grand dinner to grand people, Landor noticed that Dickens looked thin and poorly, and Dickens himself confessed that he was under strain. 'I have been so extremely busy', he wrote to Miss Coutts, 'that I have not had an hour by day (and not many by night) to call my own.'[24] One way and another it had been a demanding and difficult spring and as soon as the children were brought back from Paris they went down with whooping cough. At the end of June the family went off as usual to Broadstairs, again staying at 37 Albion Street. The weather was cold, wet, and windy.

In addition to his own burdens, Dickens now took it upon himself to raise a benefit fund for the charming and improvident Leigh Hunt. It had already been in his mind to revive the theatricals and now an occasion was provided by the needs of Hunt. Dickens, who had known Hunt from the early days of his career, found him a strange, pitiable, and lovable person. Jane Carlyle, who was a neighbour of the Hunts, called him the 'talking nightingale' and described the household as 'a poetical Tinkerdom, unparalleled even in literature'. Callers would find Mrs. Hunt asleep on cushions, with 'four or five beautiful, strange, gypsy-looking children running about in undress'.[25] Nevertheless, Dickens respected Hunt, saying that he should have received 'some enduring return from his country for all he had undergone and all the good he had done'.[26]

The amateur company which had staged *Every Man in His Humour* now prepared to present both that play and Shakespeare's *The Merry Wives of Windsor* in London, Manchester, and Liverpool; and to that end some new members were recruited, including G. H. Lewes, Augustus Egg, and George Cruikshank. Rehearsals at Miss Kelly's theatre had just started in June when Lord John Russell awarded Hunt a civil list pension of £200 a year. The change in Hunt's fortunes did not deter Dickens, who knew that he had debts that must be paid off, and that the old dramatist John Poole, who had written *Paul Pry* and other comic pieces, was in even more desperate need, and had 'no provision for the decline of his life'.[27] He dropped the London performance, however, gave up the plan to present *The Merry Wives of Windsor* on account of cost, and decided to share the profits between Hunt and Poole. Talfourd wrote a prologue for the Jonson play at Manchester on 26 July and Bulwer did the same for the Liverpool presentation two days later. As usual, Dickens drove his collaborators hard; when he went off to Broadstairs he kept at it by mail, sending off letters about rehearsals to Lemon, about dress to the costumier Nathan, about wigs to Wilson, to the actors, to the theatres, and to the hotels—in short, he told Thompson, he was in a whirlwind of managerial correspondence. Dickens kept his company at a keen pitch of excitement. Part comic and part impresario, he conducted the whole party by train, and exhausted himself in the production and his own performance. He spared nothing, certainly not expense. The two performances brought in over £900, but half the money was needed to meet the cost of the venture.[28] No sooner was Dickens settled again at Broadstairs than he came up with another idea to make up the disappointing profits. His notion was to devise a history of the jaunt, written in the character of Mrs. Gamp as if she were an eyewitness, and illustrated by some of the artists who had taken part. His colleagues, however, were not so energetic and the idea was abandoned after the first few pages were written.

'I am at a great loss for means of blowing my superfluous steam off, now the play is over', he wrote from Broadstairs on 11 August, 'and find myself compelled to tear up and down, between this and London, by express trains.'[29] There was an excursion to Canterbury, visits to local theatres, and friends were taken on long walks—Frank Stone was lamed on one seventeen-mile trek. An unusual guest that summer was Hans Christian Andersen, visiting England for the first time and being lionized by London society. 'I must meet Andersen,' declared Dickens, for he shared the general enchantment with Andersen's work, and when he did meet the Danish story-teller at one of Lady Blessington's receptions he at once invited him to meet the family down at Broadstairs. Andersen's arrival gave Dickens an excuse to invite Miss Coutts, who was then staying two miles away at Ramsgate to be near the Duke, in residence at near-by Walmer Castle; and she went over one evening for supper.

Dickens was normally restored by a visit to Broadstairs, but for once the town irritated him. 'I fear Broadstairs and I must part company in time to come,' he complained to Forster. 'I cannot write half an hour without the most excruciating organs, fiddles, bells or glee-singers.'[30] It was time to start thinking about the annual Christmas story. He confided to Forster, however, that as his thoughts were so full of *Dombey* he was in serious doubt whether to produce one that year though he was loath to forgo the money and unwilling 'to leave any gap at Christmas firesides which I ought to fill. In short I am ... BLOWED if I know what to do'.[31] He was glad to have possession again of his own house, and at the end of the summer the family settled once more at Devonshire Terrace. *Dombey* was doing well. 'The profits of the half-year are brilliant,' he told Forster in September. 'I have still to receive two thousand two hundred and twenty pounds, which I think is tidy. Don't you?'[32] Dickens had at last turned the corner, and thereafter he was never seriously short of cash.

Dombey was his main concern, but there was still much to occupy Dickens at the refuge for women, now named Urania Cottage. He was still unable to draw Miss Coutts into an active role. She took no part in the choice of a matron, and Dickens vainly asked her to watch from concealment while he selected the inmates from the Middlesex House of Correction who were to be 'tempted to virtue'. In any case, she soon left for a holiday in France and all the work had to go forward in the absence of its sponsor; as the opening date approached Dickens himself went to Shoolbred's in Tottenham Court Road to buy the household linen and to choose 'cheerful' dress material for the girls. And to the astonishment of starchier reformers he provided the house with a second-hand piano, invited his musical friend John Hullah to organize singing lessons, and persuaded Edward Chapman to supply a set of books. In all possible respects he wanted Urania Cottage to exemplify 'the *Carol* philosophy' of cheerfulness and redemption—he had written an 'Appeal' which was to be read to prospective inmates in which he urged them to take advantage of the new chance made possible by 'a great lady' who 'from the window of her house has seen such as you going past at night, and has felt her heart bleed at the sight'.[33] On 28 October he wrote to Miss Coutts to say that he hoped for a group of eight women to start the venture, 'and I have as much confidence in five of them as one *can* have in the beginning of anything so new'.[34] Disappointingly, Miss Coutts was still away when the Home opened in November; it was December before she and her companion Hannah, who had remained with her after marrying Dr. William Brown in 1844, drove out to Lime Grove to see what Dickens had done in her name. He had put much effort into a small-scale charity, and the scheme prospered; Urania Cottage, begun as a home for reclaimed prostitutes, became a general refuge for afflicted women, taking in girls from the Ragged Schools, starving needlewomen of good character, girls from ill-run workhouses, and domestic servants who had been seduced and lost their character. About half of the fifty-six women who passed through the house in the next six years were genuinely helped; a good many of them found a new life in Australia or other colonies where women were few.

Although Dickens had put his Christmas story aside until the following year he felt that he should make some public contribution in its place. He decided to use the Christmas season to help the new educational institutions which welcomed workingmen and encouraged self-help. At the beginning of December he went up to Leeds to address a soirée on behalf of the Mechanics' Institute, defending popular education against the charge that it would set class against class. Ignorance, he said, was 'a very dreadful power ... powerful to fill the prisons, the hospitals, and the graves—powerful for blind violence, prejudice and error'.[35] And after Christmas he took Kate up to Glasgow where he spoke to an audience of four thousand celebrating the first anniversary of the Glasgow Athenaeum. 'Unbounded hospitality and enthoozymoosy the order of the day,' he cheerily reported to Forster on 30 December.[36] Unfortunately Kate had a miscarriage on the train between Edinburgh and Glasgow, and was ill for some days. While they stayed in Scotland Lord Jeffrey told Dickens that the playwright James Sheridan Knowles, a friend of Macready, had become bankrupt. Dickens immediately conceived a scheme for helping Knowles; there had already been talk of buying Shakespeare's house at Stratford-upon-Avon, and Dickens decided that his 'splendid strollers'—as Maclise called them—should raise money to buy the house and establish Knowles as its paid curator. When Dickens returned to London he suggested the benefit for Knowles, but the group, which had already been amusing itself with rehearsals of Jonson's *The Alchemist*, could not agree upon a play and the project was delayed. Dickens was also busy with the final stages of *Dombey*. The serial reached its end in April 1848 and the bound volumes were published.

Dickens saw himself in the role of the Good Samaritan, caring for the outsiders and victims of Victorian society. This role was the antithesis of the life-denying system of Dombeyism which he pilloried in his novel. *Dombey* was the first book in which Dickens used a contemporary setting, rather than the older-fashioned England in which he had grown up. The House of Dombey was at the meeting-point of sail and steam, and the London in which its business affairs were conducted was being ripped apart by the explosive force of railway building. The whole tale was pervaded by a sense of insecurity and of potential violence. In its early stages Dickens had been exposed to the outbreak of revolution in Geneva, and before the book was finished the February revolution in Paris overthrew Louis Philippe in the first wave of the flood of revolutionary nationalism that spread across Europe in 1848. 'Vive la République,' Dickens exclaimed to Forster in an ecstatic letter written in French on 29 February 1848.[37] He told Emile de la Rue that the aristocracy in England would naturally dislike this 'noble republic', but added: 'All the intelligence, and liberality, I should say, are with it, tooth and nail.'[38] England, however, was more uneasy than Dickens implied. A cholera epidemic spread from Europe; and across the Irish Sea an outbreak of typhus added new horrors to the miseries of the potato famine. 'Our streets even here', Thomas Carlyle wrote to his wife in April, 'are getting encumbered with *Irish* beggars ... and in the manufacturing districts ... there hardly ever was greater misery.'[39] There were understandable fears that Britain might also be infected with the revolutionary temper from Europe. On 6 March there was a riot in Trafalgar Square, and the Chartist plan to present a monster petition to the House of Commons threw London's respectable classes into a panic. On 10 April, the day on which the Chartist demonstrators assembled in Kennington, troops were stationed at key points and thousands of special constables were sworn in to patrol the streets and prevent the Chartists forcing their way over the Thames bridges. 'I have not been special constabling myself to-day—thinking there was rather an epidemic in that wise abroad,'[40] Dickens told Edward Bulwer. Carlyle went into town to see what was happening. 'Piccadilly itself told how frightened the people were,' he noted: 'not a single fashionable carriage was on the street, not a private vehicle . . . not a gentleman to be seen.'[41] The intelligent and the liberals, whom Dickens described as supporting the revolution in France, may have been supporting the Chartists that day, but they showed no inclination to challenge the show of strength by the government; and the middle classes made it quite clear that they wanted order quite as much as reform. Dickens did not take it seriously. 'Chartist fears and rumours shake us, now and then,' he wrote in June, 'but I suspect the Government make the most of such things for their own purpose, and know better than anybody how little vitality there is in them.'[42]

There was no violence—the Chartist threat collapsed so easily that it seemed ridiculous, and so finally that it was obvious that April 1848 was a punctuation-point in British history. A new society was emerging. It was stable, though sharply divided between riches and poverty. It was increasingly prosperous, making money both from its burgeoning industry and its ramifying financial and commercial interests. It was regulated by the laws of political economy—free competition at home and free trade abroad—which appeared to be written by the Hand of Providence. And it was as cold-spirited as Mr. Dombey. The poor, Dickens realized as the democratic hopes of 1848 faded, were to be kept in their place: 'It is necessary', Mr. Dombey said, 'that the inferior classes should continue to be taught to know their positions, and to conduct themselves properly.'

Dombey had evoked unqualified praise in its early stages and it sold well. Now, as the book drew towards its close, feelings were mixed; there was a sense of disappointment. In October 1847 Ainsworth told his closest friend, James Crossley, that 'the last Dombeys are infernally bad—an opinion not confined to myself but shared by all the reading world', and six months later, as the parts came to an end, he repeated that it was 'disgust-ingly bad'.[43] Macready clearly felt much the same. 'I fear dear Dickens called to ascertain our feeling about the last number of *Dombey*,' he noted just before Christmas. 'I could not speak as I wished, and therefore did not allude to it.'[44] The critics for the most part gave it qualified praise. *Blackwood's* declared that the story was the 'greatest failure' of Dickens.[45] Thackeray was more generous, and on 8 January 1848 Dickens wrote to say that he was 'cut tenderly to the heart' by his praise. And Charles Kent, the editor of the *Sun*, declared that *Dombey and Son* was 'assuredly the masterpiece of Charles Dickens'[46]—a judgement which so delighted Dickens that he sent Kent the manuscript and thus began a close friendship. Dickens himself was not deterred by criticism. 'I must acknowledge that I have great faith in *Dombey*, and a strange belief that it will be remembered and read years hence,' he wrote to George Hogarth as he finished it in April. 'All through, I have bestowed all the pains and time at my command upon it—and I feel in the strangest of states, now that it is gone from me.'[47]

Dickens had gone down to Brighton with Kate to write the end of *Dombey*, and when the final copy had gone to the printer he dashed off to Salisbury with Forster, Lemon, and Leech, telling Kate that they had 'a most glorious expedition' on horseback across the Plain.[48] And a 'Dombey dinner' at Devonshire Terrace on 11 April completed the celebrations. 'Book yourself for that day and hour', Dickens instructed Beard, 'and for half a pint or so of the rosy.'[49]

Once *Dombey* was finished, Dickens could relax in his own hectic manner and he threw himself at once into theatricals. In association with Peter Cunn-ingham, the biographer, archivist, and treasurer of the Shakespeare Society—a genial and heavy drinker who ended by forging seventeenth cen-tury documents—Dickens revived the plan to establish Knowles as curator of the Shakespeare house, which Stratford Town Council had decided to buy, and to raise an endowment with his troupe. Cunningham looked after the non-theatrical business and Dickens laid his plans on a grand scale. The company was to repeat its Jonson play and finally settled on *The Merry Wives of Windsor* to alternate with it, and to add *Love, Law, and Physic* to *Animal Magnetism* as the supporting farces. Dickens was soon eagerly absorbed in 'the protracted agonies of management', selecting the music for the overtures and entr'actes, dealing with the costumiers, sending off notes to his actors and bringing them up to the mark at rehearsals in Miss Kelly's theatre.[50] There was a distinguished newcomer to the amateur group. Mary Cowden Clarke, a well-known Shakespearian scholar whom Dickens had met at Edward Tagart's, was recruited to play Mistress Quickly to Mark Lemon's Falstaff. By 10 May the rehearsals were moved to the Haymarket, where

the company was to open with *The Merry Wives of Windsor* on 15 May before
the Queen and Prince Albert. Dickens fussed about every detail, even devising a special way for numbering the seats. He would brook no obstruction
or delay. 'I have sent (through the Post) a small red hot poker for the stirring
up of those gentlemen,' he wrote in reference to the Shakespeare committee.[51] Mary Cowden Clake recalled the way he managed things.
'He was always there among the first arrivers at rehearsals, and remained
in a conspicuous position during their progress,' she wrote. 'He had a
small table placed rather to one side of the stage, at which he generally
sat.... On this table rested a moderately sized box, its interior divided
into convenient compartments for holding papers, letters, etc., and this
interior was always the very pink of neatness and orderly arrangement.
...He never seemed to overlook anything ... he asserted his authority
firmly and perpetually; but ... for no purpose of self-assertion or self-
importance.'[52]

The Shakespeare comedy was followed two nights later by the Jonson
play and the farce *Love, Law, and Physic*. Dickens as Flexible and Mark
Lemon as Lubin Log gave hilarious performances in the farce: the two men,
Mrs. Cowden Clarke recalled, 'were hand in glove in inventing liberties that
lifted the farce to heights of absurdity'. The audience was in an uproar and
even the cast could hardly refrain from laughing. From these successes
Dickens was at once caught up in the arrangements to perform *Every Man
in his Humour* at Manchester, Liverpool, and Birmingham in the first week
of June 1848. During this tour, said Mrs. Cowden Clarke, 'there was a positive sparkle ... of holiday sunshine about him; he seemed to radiate brightness and enjoyment'.[53] Back in London, when the triumph at Birmingham
led to demands for a return engagement with *The Merry Wives of Windsor*,
Dickens decided to put on the 'screaming afterpiece' called *Two O'Clock
in the Morning* in which he had acted at Montreal. In the train to Birmingham he and Lemon worked over the comic business and amused the rest
of the company with his 'Gampian' larks. Glasgow, too, wanted a performance, and Dickens therefore wrote on 10 June to Angus Fletcher telling him
of the 'unbounded satisfaction of the lieges' at the London and provincial
productions and asking if he could promote an appearance in Edinburgh.[54]
This 'amazing flood of botheration' was almost too much for even his rich
stock of energy. Two days later he wrote to Mark Lemon that 'between
the Scotch correspondence, the Birmingham ... the Leamington ... and
Shepherds Bush, I am like an over-driven Bull'.[55] Another farce, *Used Up*,
had now been added to the repertoire and this had to be rehearsed in the
two weeks between one performance and the next. Mark Lemon invented
a special laugh for his performance—a squeaking, hysterical giggle followed

by a suddenly checked gasp. Dickens loved it and begged Lemon to do it over and over again.

One of the problems of management was that some of the actors were dropping out. Leech, who was worried about his sick child and found it hard to remember his lines, thought of giving up. He could not make up his mind, and his havering drove an exasperated Dickens to write to Lemon: 'And now we cannot drivel about Leech, but must either have him in, or leave him out.' Leech, never an enthusiast, decided to leave the tour after the Birmingham performance in June. For a time Cruikshank also threatened to withdraw. When Lemon, dissatisfied with his own part, said he would like to take over from Cruikshank in *Used Up*, the impatient Dickens expostulated 'don't make a Jackass of yourself by coming out with such preposterous suggestions' and signed his reproof 'Inflexible'. But once the players were finally on the road Dickens was again the life and soul of the party. Each performance was climaxed by fun and frolics at the hotel, where the company had a roistering supper, drunk a punch made by Dickens, and indulged in guessing games and leapfrog. 'I never saw anything like those clever men,' declared one bystander, 'they're just for all the world like a parcel of boys!' By the time the series was finished, and topped off with a champagne supper in Glasgow, the takings amounted to £2,551. No one had enjoyed it more than Dickens: 'his was the brightest face, the lightest step, the pleasantest word', Forster remembered. 'There seemed to be no need for rest to that wonderful vitality.' Even when the expenses were deducted there was a handsome profit, though once again the government's hand had been forced by such public fund-raising and it had granted Knowles a pension. As there was no longer any need to make him curator of Shakespeare's house, Dickens simply gave him the profits.[56]

'I am very miserable,' Dickens wrote to Mrs. Cowden Clarke on 22 July in the blend of jocosity and half-truth he often used to cover his feelings. 'I loathe domestic hearths. I yearn to be a vagabond.... A real house like this is insupportable, after that canvas farm wherein I was so happy.'[57] And a few days later, in the same wistful mood, he recalled the carefree days in Switzerland. 'I should like to go somewhere, too, and try it all over again,' he wrote to Mrs. Watson. 'I don't know how it is, but the ideal world in which my lot is cast has an odd effect on the real one, and makes it chiefly precious for such remembrances. I get quite melancholy over them sometimes, especially when, as now, those great piled-up semi-circles of bright faces, at which I have lately been looking—all laughing, earnest and intent— have faded away like dead people. They seem a ghostly moral of everything in life to me.'[58] These comments, written within days of the ending of the tour, reflected a depressing sense of anticlimax. While the financial plight of Knowles had provided a charitable pretext for the theatricals, Dickens had engineered them for his own purposes as well. He needed company and action to keep up his spirits; he also enjoyed the jolly make-believe that he was the actor-manager of a group of travelling players. He worked like a serious-minded professional, pernickety about detail, making his cast work hard, preparing sets of rules for rehearsals, receiving friends afterwards in his dressing-room and issuing stage-door passes as Macready issued them to him.

It was not easy for him to step out of the glare of the gaslight and he clutched at any opportunity to sustain the illusion. In July there was a special Royal Command performance at Drury Lane to mark Macready's departure for the United States. Macready was now thinking of settling there and his visit was to raise money for his intended retirement. Dickens got himself appointed business manager for this occasion and made himself generally helpful. Macready, he told Lemon on 4 July, was 'all aghast at me, because I won't put on a Court dress and receive the Queen'.[59] A private farewell for Macready was much less formal. At a whitebait dinner at Greenwich before Kate and Georgina took the children down to Broadstairs in July, there were the usual group of friends. 'We were all very cheerful— very gay,' Macready noted; 'all was mirth unrestrained and delighted gaiety.'[60]

Dickens had a capacity to lift his mood for such parties even when he was troubled and depressed. In the summer of 1848 his sister Fanny was dying of the tuberculosis which had afflicted her for the past two years. She was staying with her sister Letitia at Hornsey for the country air and Dickens went frequently to visit her. Fanny had always been close to him, though he had seen little of her after the Burnetts moved to Manchester in 1841. She was a straightforward and cheerful woman, religious but without the affected piety that had made her husband withdraw from a stage career. One of her friends described her as a self-denying saint. By July she realized that she was near her end. Writing to Forster on 5 July, 'in the very pity and grief of my heart', Dickens described his long talk with Fanny about her approaching death and her concern for her children—especially the sickly and crippled Augustus who died not long after her. It was, he wrote, 'an affecting exhibition of strength and tenderness, in all that early decay'.[61] She lingered on, 'worn and wasted', and for the next fortnight he visited her daily until he joined the family at Broadstairs on 29 July.

Kate, as Dickens told Bulwer on 4 August when he refused a social invitation, was 'at present in that *un*interesting condition which makes visiting irksome to her'.[62] Four days later, returning from London, Dickens was walking from Margate to Broadstairs when he found Kate in the wreck of their pony chaise; the pony had bolted, the groom had jumped out, and Kate had luckily escaped with no more than a shaking.

It was pleasant and quiet at Broadstairs. Friends came down as usual—the Leeches, Mark Lemon, Augustus Egg, Frank Stone, and, of course, Forster. 'We are reasonably jolly,' Dickens put it in an invitation to Forster, 'but rurally so; going to bed o'nights at ten, and bathing o'mornings at half-past seven.'⁶³ Fanny's illness, however, saddened the whole summer, and at the end of August Dickens was hurriedly called to her deathbed. She died on 2 September 1848. At the same time Dickens learned that Roche, the amiable courier, was also fatally ill with heart disease: he looked, Dickens told Forster, 'like one with his face turned to the other world', and he took him out of his poor lodging and with the help of Miss Coutts installed the 'faithful, affectionate, and devoted man' in St. George's Hospital, where he died before the turn of the year.⁶⁴

The tragedies of Fanny and Roche put Dickens in a poor mood to listen to the importunities of his brother Fred, still bent on marriage to Anna Weller. Dickens was fond of Fred, for all his faults, and increasingly dubious about the Wellers. In October 1847 he wrote to Fred insisting that there was an impracticable streak in the family and arguing that weak parents had given Anna a character 'which can never come right'.⁶⁵ Fred had persisted in his courtship. He had a small income, but he was always in debt and as free as his father with unkept promises to pay. Dickens had offered to furnish a home for him, if he did marry, but Fred asked for cash as well; the day after Fanny died Dickens sent him a fierce letter refusing to throw more money 'into the unfathomable sea of such a marriage with debt upon its breast'.⁶⁶

Since Dickens completed *Dombey* he had been indulging himself. In six months he had written only nine short newspaper articles. 'I am all the better for my idleness no doubt,' he wrote to Forster at the end of the Broadstairs holiday; but he had yet to complete the Christmas story which he had put aside the year before. 'I must go to work, head foremost, when I get home.'⁶⁷ By the beginning of October he was absorbed in *The Haunted Man*.

12

Golden Harvest

'YOU have heard perhaps how that I now stand seized and possessed of six sons and two daughters,' Dickens wrote to Macready on 2 February 1849, telling him of the birth of Henry Fielding on 15 January and describing the Twelfth Night party at Devonshire Terrace. He had, as usual, put on a magic lantern show and done his conjuring tricks for the children. Katey and Mamie had taught him the polka, and after the absent Macready's health had been drunk Dickens had led off with Mrs. Macready—Kate being too close to her confinement—and they had danced the other couples off the floor in a couple of hours. The high jinks were faithfully reported, but there was a wistful note in the mock-pathetic sketch that Dickens gave of himself. There never was, he assured Macready, 'such an old man as I consider myself to be'. And he gave a touching report of the 'cosy little knot of us old patriarchs' sitting round after supper to talk 'of the days of our youth and the fashions of that remote period'.[1]

Dickens was still a young man, about to celebrate his thirty-seventh birthday, when he wrote this letter to Macready; yet he was at a new stage in his life and its changes brought back the long-buried events of his childhood. He was almost at the age at which his father had collapsed under his debts, broken up his home, and entered the Marshalsea, and the Twelfth Night party was to celebrate Charley's twelfth birthday—the age at which Dickens had been sent to the blacking factory. He had already been reminded of that old misery. In the spring of 1848 John Forster had casually mentioned that Charles Wentworth Dilke, now managing the *Daily News* and once a colleague of John Dickens at the navy Pay Office, had seen Dickens as a boy. Dilke, Forster reported, had remembered him sitting at Warren's window in the Strand with his blacking bottles and had given him half a crown. Dickens was embarrassed by the anecdote; jolted by such a sharp remembrance of the past he avoided an answer. He decided to confide in Forster, giving him an intimate account of his family and its tribulations. 'I am more at rest for having opened all my heart and mind to you,' Dickens wrote to Forster on 7 May 1848, noting that 'this day eleven years, poor dear Mary died'.[2] It was more than a coincidence. The springs of memory always mixed the pain of his childhood and his grief for Mary in a single sense of lost innocence.

The death of Fanny that autumn gave an added poignancy to those recollections. All through the summer of 1848, as she lay dying, Dickens thought a great deal about his boyhood—about experiences so disagreeable that he had never mentioned them even to Kate, about Hungerford Stairs, and about the streets leading to the Marshalsea, which had such unpleasant associations that for years he avoided them in his walks around London. Now he began to draft an autobiography. The first pages, describing those early days in London, he sent to Forster. The next part, in which he recalled the torments of his frustrated love for Maria Beadnell, was so distressing that he had to give it up altogether. It was destroyed and he got no further.

The surviving fragment, which recalled and repeated his misery, was not softened by adult understanding and it read like an articulate cry of pain from a boy of twelve. 'No one had compassion enough on me,' he wrote, 'a child of singular abilities.' He had, he cried, 'no advice, no counsel, no encouragement, no consolation, no support from anyone I can call to mind, so help me God.... How much I suffered, it is... utterly beyond my power to tell.' There was a measure of reprieve for John Dickens: his father, he wrote, had a 'kind nature' and had eventually and remorsefully removed him from the blacking factory. For his mother there was no such pardon. She had tried to patch up the quarrel between James Lamert and John Dickens and thus force Charles back into his miserable servitude. 'I do not write resentfully or angrily,' Dickens insisted, 'for I know how all these things have worked together to make me what I am; but I never afterwards forgot, I never shall forget, I never can forget, that my mother was warm for my being sent back.' Like an unjustly imprisoned man, free at last to arraign those who betrayed him, Dickens ran through the other counts of his indictment—the family's poverty, his father's imprisonment, the blighting of his educational hopes—and found his parents guilty upon them all.[3]

The feelings released by this attempt at autobiography flowed into his work. *The Haunted Man*, the Christmas story for 1848, had obvious similarities of thought and even phrase, and Dickens was much affected as he wrote it. 'I finished last night,'[4] he told Bradbury on 1 December, 'having been crying my eyes out over it.' Redlaw, a scientist whose worldly success conceals a self-pitying obsession with his youthful sufferings, also bears a grudge against his parents and cherishes the memory of a lost love. 'I bear within me a sorrow and a wrong,' he exclaims in a bitter attack upon his parents for selfishness, and for prematurely thrusting him upon the world. 'No mother's self-denying love, no father's counsel aided *me*.' Haunted by 'phantoms of past and present despondency', Redlaw invokes a spectre which grants him the power to obliterate all memory of past unhappiness—a power which he passes on to all around him. Such amnesia, he soon discovers, is terrifyingly destructive: freedom from sadness is also freedom from compassion, joy, and affection. He has been given a deadly Midas touch that kills all feeling, and he begs to return to a life where there is 'good and evil, happiness and sorrow, in the memories of men'.

In his autobiography Dickens could claim that he no longer felt bitter, just as he could bring Redlaw to realize that love must triumph over hate with one of the characteristic magical strokes by which in his Christmas stories he pointed that seasonal moral. Yet this adult will to forgiveness was not sufficient to dispose of the deeply ingrained childish feelings of self-pity and injustice, nor of the fantasies of revenge which lay behind them. It was a conflict which Dickens could not resolve in his own life, for all his good intentions, and his repeated attempts to do so in his fiction led him into mawkish sentimentality and theatrical solutions. To make human kindness prevail, when innocence was so weak and villainy so powerful, he had to resort to such tricks as changes of heart, quirks of fate and the avuncular figures, uncorrupted despite their wealth, who cast a glow of goodwill and gold over so many of his closing pages. Even Scrooge, for all his disagreeable demeanour, turns out to have a turkey under his arm and a pocket full of guineas. Something like a transformation scene at the end of a pantomime was always needed to get the clowns and devils off the stage and to bring on the final tableau of familial bliss.

Such a fantasy solution—the domestic paradise regained—was essentially Utopian, and like all Utopias it lay beyond the border of magic. Dickens provided such an artificial route to happiness in his novels because he knew no other. Caught emotionally at the threshold of adolescence, he kept transacting the unfinished business of his youth in his writings as if he might there discover some ending that had escaped him in ordinary life. The world he described was a child's world, bewildering, full of hidden terrors, inexplicable rejection, pathetic loyalties and lost loves, apparently senseless cruelty and unexpected benevolences. Seen through a child's eye, life is so episodic, so full of rich detail, so brimming with energy and yet seemingly so purposeless. The problems of adult life cannot be properly stated let alone understood and solved, even by the cleverest child. And even the cleverest adult cannot cope with them, maturely, when his vision of the world is shaped by the perspectives of childhood and coloured by its enduring resentments. 'No words can express the secret agony of my soul,' Dickens wrote in his autobiographical note almost a quarter of a century after the blacking factory episode. 'My whole nature', he added in the same self-commiserating tone that he used in *The Haunted Man*, 'was so penetrated

Angela Burdett Coutts at about the age of forty

Dr. John Elliotson, physician and mesmerist

Broadstairs from the pier. Fort House is the large building on the headland

with the grief and humiliation of such considerations, that even now, famous and caressed and happy, I often forget in my dreams that I have a dear wife and children; even that I am a man; and wander desolately back to that time of my life.'

Dickens now blended autobiographical fact with fiction in the novel he called *The Personal History, Experience and Observations of David Copperfield the Younger, of Blunderstone Rookery, which he never meant to be published on any account.* In its first lines he addressed himself to the central question which he had been revolving in his mind all through 1848— 'whether I shall turn out to be the hero of my own life'. Could he come to terms with his past?

Immediately after the Twelfth Night party in 1849 Dickens went off for a few days in East Anglia with Leech and Lemon. His ghoulish interest had been aroused by the sensational murder of the Recorder of Norwich and, as he was writing some unsigned articles for Fonblanque's *Examiner*, he had an eye to the prospects of copy. He went to Stanfield Hall, the scene of the crime, to the home of Rush the murderer, and to the site of the Norwich scaffold—a setting he thought 'fit for a gigantic scoundrel's exit'.[5] The three men then went on to Yarmouth. Dickens wrote to Forster, who had stayed behind because he was unwell, that the little fishing port was 'the strangest place in the world', with almost 150 miles of marsh between it and London. And during a long walk along the coast to Lowestoft and back he found the locale he needed for Copperfield's childhood in a village set among marshes which recalled his boyhood haunts on the tidal fringes of the Medway.

The novel was beginning to take shape. 'I shall certainly try my hand at it,' he wrote to Forster from Yarmouth on 12 January.[6] As usual he found it hard to get started. Kate's confinement was a preliminary distraction. Fearing that she would have difficulties, Dickens insisted that she be given the novel relief of chloroform. The doctors, he told Macready on 2 February, 'were dead against it, but I stood my ground, and (thank God) triumphantly ... she was to all intents and purposes, *well* the next day'.[7] Two weeks later he hurried down to Bath to celebrate Landor's seventy-fifth birthday, came back to find his father unwell, and was soon off again to Brighton with Kate and John Leech and his wife for company. The landlord and his daughter went berserk soon after their arrival and after Leech and Dickens had gone to the rescue of the doctor who was called to deal with them, the party moved to the Bedford Hotel. The exciting confusion of 'Mrs. Gamps, strait-waistcoats, struggling friends and servants', Dickens reported gaily to Forster, was 'quite in keeping with my usual proceedings'.[8] For all the anxiety about the new novel Dickens was in the jolliest of moods, and taking the tune of 'Lesbia hath a beaming eye' he dashed off a rhyme to Mark Lemon: 'Oh, my Lemon, round and fat / Oh, my bright, my right, my tight 'un / Think a little what you're at / Don't stay at home, but come to Brighton.' The verse was signed by all the party, and Dickens used one of his favourite pseudonyms, T. Sparkler.[9]

He had reported to Forster from Brighton that he felt 'deepest despondency, as usual, in commencing',[10] but back in London at the end of February he finally launched himself into *Copperfield* and in the middle of April he was at the end of the second chapter, well in hand for the start of the serial on 1 May. 'Though I know what I want to do,' he told Forster on 19 April, 'I am lumbering like a stage waggon.'[11] The letter was written in the aftermath of an excessively convivial dinner the night before, at which the aged Samuel Rogers and another guest had to be carried out. Dickens was settling into his necessary habit of hard work and hard play, and with his years of toil beginning to yield a golden harvest, he was now entertaining at Devonshire Terrace in a smart manner, adding titles and fashionable names to the familiar guest list of literary friends, artists, and actors. Jane Carlyle caustically remarked that it was unbecoming for a man of letters so to rely on ornament and grandeur. She noted the 'quantities of *artificial* flowers' and 'pyramids of figs, raisins, oranges—ach ... the very candles rose each out of an artificial rose!'[12] No occasion was missed for a celebration. On 3 January there had been a party for *The Haunted Man* and a grand dinner on 12 May (which was the occasion for Jane Carlyle's puritanical comment) marked the appearance of the first part of *Copperfield*. Thackeray, one of the after-dinner guests, was full of praise for the new novel: he thought it was 'beautiful' and showed signs that Dickens has been 'taking a lesson from *Vanity Fair*'.[13] Phiz was there too, and Forster, Jerrold, and Samuel Rogers, who ought—Jane Carlyle said—'to have been buried long ago, so old and ill-natured he is grown'.

Mrs. Carlyle was more generous to another guest, Elizabeth Gaskell, the wife of a Unitarian minister in Manchester, who had just made a success with her first novel, *Mary Barton*. She was, Mrs. Carlyle observed, 'a natural unassuming woman' whom 'they have been doing their best to spoil by making a lioness of her'.[14] Carlyle himself had been much impressed by Mrs. Gaskell's sympathetic account of working-class tribulations. He was now writing his *Latter Day Pamphlets*, full of sulphurous indignation against religion, railways, and political economy, and on 8 November 1848 he had told Mrs. Gaskell that her work deserved 'to take its place far above the ordinary garbage of novels'. She treasured this first mark of public recognition, and when she went to London in March she met the Carlyles, Dickens, and Forster, who had suggested to Edward Chapman that he should publish

Mary Barton. She had been somewhat piqued when Dickens had not acknowledged the copy sent to him on publication, though she told Chapman on 7 December 1848 that it had been dispatched 'more to satisfy my own feelings, than to receive thanks'. This first misunderstanding set the tone of their relationship. All the same, Dickens warmly welcomed her at Devonshire Terrace and told her later that when he read *Mary Barton* at Brighton he was 'most profoundly affected and impressed'. She, in turn, admired his work, shared his genuine concern for the unfortunate, and appreciated his professional encouragement. She corresponded with him about his efforts on behalf of fallen women at Urania Cottage—her novel *Ruth* was based upon one such girl and his Little Em'ly upon another—and enlisted his help in shipping a reclaimed prostitute to a new life in South Africa.[15]

Urania Cottage, indeed, had become a serious part-time occupation for Dickens, who made himself a kind of unpaid superintendent.[16] He reported regularly to Miss Coutts. He went to the committee meetings, fussed about the details of administration, and kept himself informed about the past lives, present behaviour, and future prospects of the women who came to the place. Even when he was away from London he expected to be kept in touch, telling Angela Coutts on one occasion that he was 'greatly mortified' to hear that one of the inmates had stolen a bonnet and shawl. It was, he commented, 'a great comfort to me that the girl is a new girl and not one in whom we have trusted and been long deceived'; and he told the housekeeper that, in speaking of the case to the other women, she was to stress that the offender had not 'had the benefit of the Home's institution and advice for any length of time'.[17]

Trust, for Dickens, was a positive influence on character. So was a wholesome environment. But what happened if trust was betrayed and a child was thrown into unwholesome company? He had asked that question, so painfully pertinent to his own upbringing, in *Oliver Twist*, and less dramatically in *Nicholas Nickleby*. Could such a child find himself? And by what means? And at what price? In his new novel, as in the autobiographical fragment, Dickens at last felt able to explore such questions with explicit reference to his own childhood. Writing to Forster on 10 July from Broadstairs, where he had gone to recover from a fall that affected his left kidney and to press on with *Copperfield*, he explained that he had fused his traumatic memories of the blacking factory into the tale of young David. 'I really think I have done it ingeniously', he wrote, 'and with a very complicated interweaving of truth and fiction.'[18] And having found the way to weave fact and fantasy from such emotionally sensitive material, he went on to do the same for other painful and almost suppressed memories, including the unsatisfied yearning to be the favourite, wanted child which he made the agony of David's boyhood. It took courage, and skill, to transpose his experience into *Copperfield*, and to endow the Micawbers with the facts of his own family's collapse into the debtor's prison; it took genuine insight and affection to convert his father's foibles into the charm, humour, and irresponsible optimism of Mr. Micawber, for there was real forgiveness in that portrait.

It was a much more complex matter for Dickens to translate the women in his life into the pages of *Copperfield*, and his female characters reveal the ambiguity of his feelings. Elizabeth Dickens was flighty to the point of silliness, and she was clearly unable to cope with domestic shipwreck. Although Dickens was distressed by her incompetence, he did not attack her for that failing. In the person of Mrs. Micawber he even gave it an endearing gloss. What he could not condone was the maternal weakness and thoughtlessness which he experienced as rejection—and burnt into the deficiencies of Mrs. Copperfield. He was similarly ambivalent in the way he drew upon his later experience of women. Maria Beadnell and Kate were both childish, petulant, and self-indulgent; Dora, like them, wished to be treated like a doll and to live in a doll's house. The virtues of Mary Hogarth and Georgina, idealized for their self-sacrifice, were enshrined in Agnes, a sexless image of the patient sister-companion whom Dickens found so necessary to his emotional balance. In setting up the antithesis between the child-wife and the child-martyr Dickens was presenting a choice between two types of women, neither of whom could properly grow to maturity, and dramatizing the poles of his own personality. In the early chapters of *Copperfield* he succeeded brilliantly in playing over the curtain-raiser to his own life. The remainder of the book was a dress rehearsal in fiction of a situation which Dickens was later to act out in reality.

The flow of the early chapters released so much that had been long repressed that Dickens fell into a lighter state of mind than he had known for some time. He was eager, with summer coming on, to find a congenial resort where the family could take a holiday and he could push on with the novel. He thought of Folkestone as an alternative to Broadstairs, but he learned that the bathing was poor and no suitable house was on offer. His friend James White, the literary clergyman, proposed to let the Dickens family have a house he owned next to his own property at Bonchurch, nestling snugly under the great cliff at Ventnor on the Isle of Wight. Dickens hurried down to look at it with John Leech, who took a near-by cottage. 'I think it is the prettiest place I ever saw in my life, at home or abroad,' he wrote cheerfully to Kate on 16 June. It was cool, airy, had private sea-bathing and 'everything delicious', including a waterfall in the grounds which Dickens at once commissioned a carpenter 'to convert into a perpetual shower-bath'.[19] In less than two weeks he was back. Thackeray, who had been staying on the island, was running for the ferry at Ryde, when he met 'the great Dickens with his wife his children his Miss Hogarth all looking abominably coarse vulgar and happy'.[20] As always with a new enthusiasm Dickens was lyrical at first. The views, he declared to Forster, 'are only to be equalled on the Genoese shore of the Mediterranean' and as usual the cohorts of friends were invited down—Talfourd, Phiz, Thomas Beard, Frank Stone, and Jerrold.[21] The rotund Mark Lemon, whom the children nicknamed 'Uncle Porpoise', was a great success in the races at the picnics which Dickens organized with customary zest, and Dickens put on his conjuring shows in the guise of an 'unparalleled necromancer Rhia Rama Rhoos'.[22] Talfourd, now a judge, recorded in his journal that he took 'a delightful dip in the sea, the prologue to a glorious walk with Dickens— through Ventnor—all the way talking as authors talk'.[23] Yet the attractions of Bonchurch soon began to pall. Dickens found it hard to get his writing done, though he closeted himself up until two in the afternoon each day. He found the air too balmy; it made him drowsy during the day and sleep restlessly at night. He felt depressed and bilious, and he developed a persistent cough. 'Of all the places I ever have been in,' he was telling Forster in September, 'I have never been in one so difficult to exist in, pleasantly ... I am quite convinced that I should die here, in a year ... the prostration of it is *awful*.'[24]

He had made reasonable progress with *Copperfield*, but the quality of the book, in which he had recaptured his best form, was not reflected in its sluggish sales. 'The accounts are rather shy, after *Dombey*,' he told Forster, though he put a brave face on the matter. 'I cannot bring myself to care much for what opinions people may form.... A steady twenty-five thousand, which it is now on the verge of, will do very well.'[25] By the middle of September he had made up his mind to move back to the bracing air of Broadstairs. Before he could leave, John Leech was knocked down by a wave, badly concussed, and put to bed, Dickens reported to Forster on 26 September, with 'twenty of his namesakes on his temples'. When Leech became restless with pain Dickens offered to mesmerize him. It was not easy to settle him, but Dickens wrote gleefully to tell Forster of his success. 'What do you think to my setting up in the magnetic line with a large brass plate?' he asked.[26] ' "Terms, twenty-five guineas per nap." ' As soon as Leech was plainly on the mend the Dickens family was shipped back to the Kent coast. The weather was appallingly wet. 'I somehow or other don't mind it much,' Dickens declared.[27] He was now able to sleep better and to write more easily. 'Veeve le Broadstairs,' he wrote to Leech.[28]

Dickens had such a fund of energy that the business of composition seemed actually to stimulate him to cast around for fresh distractions and new professional ventures. Before *Copperfield* was finished a new plan was forming in his mind. On 13 November 1849 George Manning and his wife were publicly hanged for the murder of their lodger. The macabre attraction of seeing the first hanging of a husband and wife for a century and a half drew a crowd of more than thirty thousand; Dickens, who had taken a close interest in the trial, was among them. John Leech, who produced a memorable and bitter cartoon for *Punch* entitled 'The Great Moral Lesson at Horsemonger Lane Gaol', had asked Dickens to go with him. 'The doleful weather, the beastly nature of the scene, the having no excuse for going (after seeing Courvoisier) and the constantly recurring desire to avoid another such horrible and odious impression', he wrote to Leech a week before, 'decide me to cry off.'[29] A few days later he changed his mind and took charge of the bizarre outing, renting the roof and back garden of a house near the prison 'for the extremely moderate sum of Ten Guineas' and arranging a special supper for the party at the Piazza Coffee House.[30] Dickens was both fascinated and appalled by the gruesome scene. Three years later his memory was haunted by the 'terrible impression' of 'the two forms dangling on top of the entrance gateway—the man's, a limp, loose suit of clothes as if the man had gone out of them; the woman's, a fine shape, so elaborately corseted and artfully dressed, that it was quite unchanged in its trim appearance as it slowly swung from side to side'.[31] On the evening of the execution he wrote a powerful letter to *The Times*. 'The horrors of the gibbet and of the crime which brought the wretched murderers to it', he explained, 'faded in my mind before the atrocious bearing, looks, and language of the assembled spectators. When I came upon the scene at midnight, the *shrillness* of the cries and howls that were raised from time to time . . . made my blood run cold. . . . I do not believe that any community can prosper where such a scene of horror and demoralisation as was enacted this morning outside Horsemonger Lane Gaol is presented at the very doors of good citizens, and is passed by unknown and forgotten.'[32]

After the hanging of Courvoisier in 1840 Dickens had echoed that grisly event in *Barnaby Rudge*, and had explicitly attacked capital punishment in his *Daily News* articles in 1846. But by 1849 he was more cautious; his attitude had begun to change—later he even came to defend execution in savage cases—and he had reduced his public case to a demand merely that such obscene proceedings should be conducted in private. Even this was too much for *The Times*, which argued that executions inside a prison would create a mystery and that the public should be able to see that both the rich and the poor were hanged. To this Dickens replied with a suggestion of a special jury of witnesses to testify to the fact of an execution. The idea of hanging still nauseated him, but he had concluded that it was tactically more sensible to demand an end to public executions than to attack the punishment of death on principle. Abolitionists, he now declared, might be 'good and pure in intention'; they were also 'unreasonable, and not to be argued with'.[33] This retreat from the abolitionist opinions Dickens had expressed only a few years before greatly upset Douglas Jerrold, who had long campaigned against the gallows in *Punch*. He seized every chance for mordant irony. On one occasion, when the wife of a public hangman was convicted of stealing potatoes, Jerrold sarcastically commented that she had lapsed despite 'the elevating benefits of a close companionship with such a national moralist'.[34] He sent a sad and reproving letter to Dickens about his apparent apostasy. 'I am grieved that the weight of your name, and the influence of your reputation', he wrote, 'should be claimed by such a party.... Sorry I am, my dear Dickens, to differ from any opinion of yours—most sorry upon an opinion so grave; but both of us are only the instruments of our convictions.'[35] For some months they were estranged, for all their previous intimacy. Then they found themselves dining back to back at the Garrick Club. Jerrold turned round in his chair, held out his hands to Dickens, and said warmly: 'For God's sake, let us be friends again! Life's not long enough for this!'[36]

Dickens had a strong taste for public argument. It was implicit in the reforming tone of his novels. It was explicit in his speeches and his journalism. And it was one of the reasons why he kept coming back to the notion of editing his own magazine, though he had scarcely made a success of Bentley's *Miscellany*, *Master Humphrey's Clock*, and the *Daily News*. He was a moralist and he wanted a pulpit for his homilies. Even before the controversy about the hanging of the Mannings he had been mulling over the idea of starting another paper. On 24 September 1849 he wrote to Forster from Bonchurch: 'The old notion of the Periodical, which has been agitating itself in my mind for so long, I really think is at last growing into form.' And he soon made it clear that he intended to launch a magazine early in 1850. 'I have already been busy, at odd half hours,' he told Forster, 'in shadowing forth a name and an idea.'[37] At this time his scheme was to evoke a Shadow, to play something of the same role as Master Humphrey; it would, he assured a sceptical Forster, be 'a cheerful, useful, and always welcome Shadow... it will represent common sense and humanity'.[38]

By the end of November Dickens had brought David Copperfield to the verge of manhood and he saw his way before him. He and Kate went down to Rockingham Castle in Northamptonshire to visit the Richard Watsons, the friends he had made during the Lausanne visit; young Charley, about to start at Eton, went with them. Parodying a book by the awe-struck American traveller Henry Colman, Dickens described himself to Forster as the denizen of an ancient castle, 'waited on by six-and-twenty servants; the slops (and wine-glasses) continually being emptied; and my clothes (with myself in them) always being carried off to all sorts of places'.[39] He revelled in such a style of entertainment, staying up till three in the morning when there was country dancing in the great hall, putting on his usual conjuring show and, of course, promoting some amateur theatricals. He struck up a jolly friendship with Mrs. Watson's niece, Mary Boyle, a thirty-nine-year-old spinster from a distinguished naval family. She was a tiny and attractive blue-eyed blonde, with a seraphically innocent face and a cultivated mind; she wrote three novels and a book of verse, had a passion for the theatre, dancing, and other lively pleasures, and she was an enthusiastic walker. Dickens found her a delightful companion and they were vivaciously flirtatious together. With her help he put on some scenes from *The School for Scandal* and a sketch based on the episode in *Nicholas Nickleby* in which the lunatic makes love over the wall to Mrs. Nickleby. The whole household, he told Forster with pride, was 'uncommonly merry' at his efforts. The only blight on the New Year jollifications was the death of Francis Jeffrey on 26 January; he had been, Dickens said, 'an affectionate and devoted friend to me'.[40]

He had, meanwhile, to keep *Copperfield* moving. Over Christmas, he told William de Cerjat, he had been thinking out Little Em'ly's runaway affair with Steerforth and its relevance to the work he supervised at Urania Cottage. Was the return to virtue of such girls cut off? He hoped, he said, 'in the history of Little Em'ly (who *must* fall—there is no hope for her), to put it before the thoughts of people in a new and pathetic way, and perhaps to do some good'.[41] And, at the same time, he was boiling up ideas and titles for the new magazine—a prospectus very similar in its profusion of suggestions to that which years before he had sent Chapman and Hall when proposing to launch the *Clock*. He tried 'The Robin' on Forster, then 'The Holly Tree', 'The Comrade', 'The Microscope', 'The Lever', and even 'Charles Dickens: A Weekly journal designed for the instruction and entertainment of all classes of readers: Conducted by Himself'. Trying to catch what 'ought to be the spirit of the people and the time', he ran through the domestic declension. 'The Household Voice' was followed by 'The Household Guest' and 'The Household Face'. Finally he settled on *Household Words*. He was to be its 'Conductor', at £500 a year; and, to avoid the disputes which had harassed his previous ventures, he was to be half-owner. Forster was allocated a one-eighth share to ensure that Dickens was clearly in control. Bradbury and Evans had to be content with a quarter of what was likely to be a very remunerative business. The remaining one-eighth went to William Henry Wills, whom Dickens had found such a useful assistant during his brief association with the *Daily News*. On 22 January 1850 Dickens invited Wills to head the magazine's staff. He was an efficient if prosaic editor, whom Dickens described as 'decidedly of the Nutmeg-Grater, or Fancy-Bread-Rasper School',[42] and he was to be paid £8 a week in addition to his share of the profits. *Household Words* also found a modest place for John Dickens and George Hogarth, and for Richard Henry Horne, whom Dickens had met through the *Daily News*. The small staff was accommodated in offices at 16 Wellington Street, close to the Gaiety Theatre in the Strand, and the first twopenny number was due to appear on 30 March 1850. In his 'Preliminary Word' Dickens declared his plan to fill the weekly with 'social wonders, good and evil', making it a popular educator and champion of moral and material progress. It was not conceived, he added, in a 'mere utilitarian spirit': it would 'cherish that light of Fancy which is inherent in the human breast'.

He began as he meant to go on. He enlisted his brother-in-law Henry Austin, who was now the secretary of the Sanitary Commission, to provide articles on water supplies, housing conditions, and other matters of public health. He told possible contributors that he wanted short stories whose 'general purpose' would call attention to suffering and injustice. And he commissioned Elizabeth Gaskell to contribute something in the radical vein of *Mary Barton*. 'I do honestly know', he wrote to her on 31 January, 'that there is no living English writer whose aid I would desire to enlist in preference to the authoress of *Mary Barton*', and he explained that his aim was 'the raising up of those that are down, and the general improvement of our social condition'.[43] Mrs. Gaskell sent back a depressing tale of a servant girl and her illegitimate child, entitled *Lizzie Leigh*, which appeared in the first three issues and so pleased Dickens that he immediately asked for more.

The paper prospered from the start. Unlike the uneasy situation at the *Daily News*, where Dickens was nominally in charge but was actually constrained by the urgencies of daily newspaper production and the pressures from his financial backers, at the new paper he was in complete command. The enterprise was small enough for him to keep everything under his direct control, and the principle of anonymity permitted him to reshape the articles to his taste. For no articles were signed in *Household Words*. When Jerrold protested that this was unfair to contributors, whether they already enjoyed a reputation or had yet to make one, Dickens replied that the whole paper was anonymous. Jerrold read out the words that ran across the top of each page—'Conducted by Charles Dickens'. Yes, said Jerrold, 'I see it is *mononymous* throughout.'[44]

The first issue showed the range of the magazine. Apart from the opening instalment of *Lizzie Leigh* it packed in an article by Dickens himself on the theatres patronized by the lower classes, a biographical sketch, a description of London's main post office, a couple of poems, and an article on Caroline Chisholm's scheme to dispatch free emigrants to the convict-colonies of Australia. It sold almost 100,000 copies, and in the middle of April, writing to Angela Coutts, Dickens reported that his paper was 'exceedingly well liked, and "goes" in the trade phrase, admirably.... The labor, in conjunction with *Copperfield*, is something rather ponderous; but to establish it firmly would be to gain such an immense point for the future (I mean my future) that I think nothing of that.'[45]

The circulation soon settled at about 40,000, and by the end of the year the paper was making a very satisfying profit for Dickens and his printer-publishers. Its success was to some extent due to a technical change. It was becoming much easier to produce and distribute a periodical. The printing trade was becoming mechanized, there were better methods of wholesaling, new roads and railways made it easier to carry what was printed all over the country—even the penny post was a valuable ally—and improved accounting brought in the money from sales more efficiently. Above all, houses were better lit, either with new types of oil-lamps or gas, and evening reading was no longer a matter of peering at print by the light of one or two candles. In all these respects the market had changed for the better since Dickens had launched *Master Humphrey's Clock*.

Yet the success was also due to his editorial policy. Dickens was at last managing to run a serial story and a genuine magazine in double harness without using one to prop up the other. It was a notable achievement, at which he had been aiming since he contracted to produce *Bentley's* in the style of the literary miscellanies which he had so liked as a boy. It allowed him to make the most of the novel as an independent venture. At the same time it offered him some insurance against a falling-off in his income from fiction; and it provided him with a public platform from which he could influence opinion directly. One of his first suggestions for a title for the paper, in fact, had been 'The Lever', and the contents reflected his enthusiasms and his causes. In May he persuaded the eminent scientist Michael Faraday to permit the conversion of his lectures to children into a series of educational articles; and this interest in fresh and improving knowledge was matched, as the paper established its distinctive style, by regular campaigns on sanitary reform, slum housing, popular education, the right of workingmen to form trade unions and to safer conditions of work. Dickens ensured a wide appeal by drawing upon such established storytellers as Bulwer, Charles Reade, and Charles Lever, and by bringing on such new talents as George Augustus Sala, Wilkie Collins and his brother Charles,

Sheridan Le Fanu, Lynn Linton, and Edmund Yates. He had a gift for sensing what his audiences wanted, whether he came before them as an editor, an author, or an actor. With *Household Words* added to *Copperfield* and his theatricals he had become the complete domestic instructor and family entertainer.

13

A Man of Parts

DICKENS gave his heart to the story of young David. For ten days in the middle of each month, he explained when he refused an invitation at Christmas time, he was 'the Slave of the Lamp called Copperfield'.[1] After *Household Words* was launched in March 1850 he told Angela Coutts that he had to get away to Brighton for a couple of weeks 'to pursue Copperfield in peace',[2] and he clearly proposed to give the novel pride of place until he had completed it in the autumn. The division of his efforts between the magazine and the serial was demanding, but he enjoyed the stimulus; and his excellent spirits bubbled up at home. He was pleased with Charley, whose tutor, he proudly told Angela Coutts, 'gave us yesterday a most brilliant account ... work is no trouble to him, and he always does it admirably ... he is fast becoming one of the most popular boys at Eton'.[3] The ten-year-old Walter, 'a patient capable child', was already being prepared for a military cadetship in India. And though Dickens felt burdened by the approaching birth of yet another child—Dora Annie, born on 16 August 1850 as her namesake was dying in *Copperfield*—he was cheerfully warm-hearted to Kate. As he waited for her confinement, he told Forster that the serial was 'in a very decent state of advancement domesticity notwithstanding',[4] and the day before the child was born he reported that 'Mrs. Micawber is still, I regret to say, in statu quo'.[5]

He was eagerly looking forward to his customary family holiday at the seaside. 'I hope to go down to that old image of Eternity that I love so much', he wrote on 11 June, telling Macready that he planned to finish *Copperfield* 'to its hoarse music'.[6] He had leased Fort House at Broadstairs. It stood by itself on a little promontory above the harbour, with cornfields beside it—'a good bold house on the top of a cliff, with the sea winds blowing through it and the gulls occasionally falling down the chimneys by mistake'.[7] He took Georgina and the children down in July, returning to London to wait with Kate and see to his business at *Household Words*. 'I have planned out the story for some time past, to the end, and am making out my purposes with great care,' he informed James White on 13 July. '*Household Words* goes on *thoroughly well*,' he added; 'it is taking a great and steady stand,

and I have no doubt already yields a good round profit.'[8] Hours after Dora was born he bustled back to Broadstairs, 'to my various children—real and imaginary',[9] and to all the pleasures of swimming, cricket, walks, and picnics. 'I am happy to think that you have named your day for coming down please God,' he wrote to Kate on 20 August. 'We all want you very much, and I think you will be thoroughly pleased with the house and gardens.'[10]

As usual, friends were invited. Forster arrived in a 'tip-top' state of amiability. There was a guest cottage for Frank Stone and Augustus Egg, while Wills and Horne were invited with their wives to stay at Fort House. For all the stream of visitors Dickens took the chance to get on with 'all manner of appointments and business discussions'.[11] He had, he wrote to Mary Boyle, 'my pen on the paper, my eye on *Household Words*, my head on Copperfield and my ear nowhere particularly'.[12] He needed such distraction and companionship even when he was hard pressed. 'Why do you try the feelings of your friends by prolonged absence?' he asked Thomas Beard on 15 September,[13] though on the same day he confessed to Forster that he was at the climax of his tale: 'eight hours at a stretch yesterday, and six hours and a half to-day, with the Ham and Steerforth chapter, which has completely knocked me over—utterly defeated me!'[14] Two days later he had to tell Wills that he could not stop to provide additional copy for the paper. 'I am in that tremendous paroxysm of *Copperfield*,' he declared, 'having my most powerful effect in all the Story on the Anvil—that you might as well ask me to manufacture a Cannon seventy-four pounder, as . . . do anything now.'[15] But a month later the serial was complete. 'I am within three pages of the shore,' he wrote to Forster from Broadstairs on 21 October, 'and am strangely divided, as usual in such cases, between sorrow and joy. Oh, my dear Forster, if I were to say half of what Copperfield makes me feel tonight, how strangely, even to you, I should be turned inside out! I seem to be sending some part of myself into the Shadowy World.'[16]

The book was a great success from the first. 'I think it is better liked than any of my other books,' Dickens had told Cerjat in December 1849, and he certainly liked it best of all. The critics also sensed the change of tone and warmed to *Copperfield*. One praised it for its 'easy originality' and called it a 'fresh, healthy book'; another declared it to be 'the best of all the author's fictions'. Childhoods were a staple currency of Victorian fiction and when Dickens told so much of his own beginnings he easily evoked a familial response. 'There is not a fireside in the kingdom where the cunning fellow has not contrived to secure a corner for himself as one of the dearest, and by this time one of the oldest friends of the family,' declared one reviewer in *Fraser's*. 'Most men would as soon think of dissecting a first cousin as of criticising Charles Dickens.'[17] Thackeray had also brought out an autobiographical novel, *Pendennis*, and many critics reviewed the two books together. 'The epic is greater than the satire,' *The Times* declared.[18]

Theatricals had by now become a regular event in Dickens's life and while he was still deeply involved with *Copperfield* he already had a new venture in view. The idea came from Edward Bulwer. In the summer of 1850, on his return from a year abroad, he asked Dickens to go with Macready and Forster on a visit to Knebworth, the family house in Hertfordshire which he had inherited in 1843. It was, Macready reported, 'a most finished specimen of a baronial seat', and quite in keeping with the patrician style of its owner, who on his mother's death had taken her maiden name of Lytton and styled himself Sir Edward George Earle Lytton Bulwer-Lytton. He was an aloof man, whose marriage had broken up when his wife became insanely jealous, and he devoted himself to writing and politics. Nine years older than Dickens, and already popular when *Pickwick* carried his young rival to the head of the literary world, he had been generous about his books— he wrote, for instance, to say how much he liked *Copperfield*—and their relationship was agreeable, but not intimate. It was Bulwer-Lytton's plan to give a dramatic festival at Knebworth, an idea which, Dickens wrote to Bulwer-Lytton in July, 'stirs my blood like a trumpet':[19] and in between times at Broadstairs that summer he was busy organizing his cast for yet another round of the Jonson play, first at Knebworth in mid-November and then in the New Year at Rockingham Castle for the Watsons.

As soon as Dickens was back at Devonshire Terrace he busied himself with the rehearsals at Miss Kelly's private theatre, and with the business of putting on a production at a country house. He fussed about the transport of a choremusicon to Knebworth, this hybrid of an organ and a piano serving in place of a small orchestra; he worried about the handbills, the colour of the drugget on the stage floor, anxiously calculated the number of gas lamps required, and arranged for a bed at a local public house for the man who went down to attend to the lighting. During the rehearsals Kate fell through a trapdoor, spraining her ankle so badly that Lemon's wife had to take over the small part Kate hoped to play—and the script was quickly expanded to include a topical quip about 'Lemon-aid'. 'My unfortunate other half (lying in bed) is very anxious that I should let you know that she means to break her heart, if she should be prevented from coming as one of the audience,' Dickens wrote to Bulwer-Lytton on 3 November, and he arranged for her to be taken in a special carriage for the first night on 18 November.[20] There were three brilliant performances to an audience of Bulwer-Lytton's smart friends and neighbours: 'everything', Dickens wrote to Mrs. Watson when they were all home again, 'has gone off in a whirl of triumph and fired the whole length and breadth of the county of Hertford-shire'. Georgina, who also had a part, had 'covered herself with glory'.[21]

Dickens was no sooner back, indeed, than he was busily corresponding with Mrs. Watson about the construction of the stage for the Rockingham performances. They were to do three plays, *A Day After the Wedding*, *Animal Magnetism*, and *Used Up*, and much ingenious carpentry was needed to position the special sets. It was a jolly party at Rockingham on 15 January 1851 with country dancing to top off the amateur dramatics, and Dickens flirted gaily with Mary Boyle, sending her 'teasing notes'—'the call of honor stands between me and my rest—baulks my inclination—beckons me from happiness'— and sealing his role of disconsolate lover with a demure kiss.[22]

Afterwards he relapsed into the state of dull anticlimax which always followed a theatrical spree. 'I feel a loss of oh! I can't say what exquisite foolery, when I lose a chance of being someone in voice, etc. not at all like myself,' he told Bulwer-Lytton on 5 January.[23] A few days later he wrote cryptically to Mrs. Watson. 'What a thing it is, that we can't always be innocently merry and happy with those we like best without looking out at the back windows of life,' he told her. 'Well, one day perhaps—after a long night—the blinds on that side of the house will be down for ever, and nothing left but the bright prospect in front.'[24]

The phrase about the 'back windows of life' reflected a subtle but significant change in circumstances. For one thing, the lease of Devonshire Terrace was running out and in the next few months he had to find a new London home for his large and still expanding household. For another, the circle of old friendships was showing signs of age and wear. There was, for example, friction with Maclise. Although Dickens had always been warmly affectionate to him, there was a self-commiserating side to his personality which marred his friendships, and the painter often felt disadvantaged by the dominating exuberance of Forster and Dickens. He had confessed as much to Kate Dickens in 1844: 'if ever a man has nulled me and made me void, Forster is that man', he wrote, and he had come to feel exactly the same about Dickens.[25] He made this comment when he sent Kate his sketch of Dickens and the group of friends as they listened to the reading of *The Chimes*. Maclise, indeed, linked some of his most sensitive work to his friendships. His sympathetic portrait of Dickens, although George Eliot described it as 'keepsakey', did in fact convey the romantic charm of Dickens as a successful young man, and he had also done pictures of Kate, Georgina, and the older children.

In the early months of 1850 Forster commissioned him to paint Macready in the title role of Byron's *Werner* and Macready took the picture with him on his last provincial tour. 'I hope this melancholy apparition of himself constantly rising up before him in strange places', Maclise wrote to Forster on 21 March 1850, 'will not drive Macready mad.'[26] Maclise, too shy to participate himself in the Dickens theatricals, also painted scenes from the productions, one showing Forster as Kitely in *Every Man in his Humour*. Dickens was always full of praise for the work of his friend and was delighted by his success. When his cartoon for the fresco for 'The Spirit of Chivalry' had been exhibited in Westminster Hall in May 1845 it was appropriately acclaimed and eventually chosen as the first of a series of historical frescoes in the newly built House of Lords—a task which caused Maclise much trouble and argument. 'It delights me to receive such accounts of Maclise's fresco', Dickens wrote to Lady Blessington on 9 May 1845, expressing the hope that he would 'give his magnificent Genius fair play';[27] and in Jerrold's new magazine he declared the mural to be one of the masterpieces of all time. 'Dear Dick,' wrote Maclise, 'how good he is—he sets me in a glow when I read his warm praise.'[28] Dickens took the oddities of his friends with good humour. 'Maclise is taken with one of his fits of seclusion', he told de la Rue when Maclise was working on the fresco, 'and is never beheld by Mortal Eye.... He says he wishes he was a Wild Man. Which I tell him is unreasonable and discontented; he being already something so very near it.'[29]

As his youthful enthusiasm gave way to depression Maclise became tetchily difficult with Dickens and other friends. He had done illustrations for *The Chimes* and *The Cricket on the Hearth* and when he came to the last of his collaborations with Dickens, in *The Battle of Life*, he complained dolefully to Forster. 'Dickens does not care one damn whether I make a little sketch for the book or not,' he wrote. 'I do this at your bidding—and not at all for D. and on the whole would prefer not engaging in the matter at all.' Although Dickens was grateful, the quirks of Maclise's temperament increasingly annoyed him. In June 1850 the two friends went to Paris, partly for a brief holiday, partly to see d'Orsay who had dramatically bolted from London in April 1849 to escape his creditors. Maclise wrote to Forster that he was 'truly unwell' there; he thought it might be 'Hypochondria, a return of my old complaint', and he undoubtedly found the extremely hot weather fatiguing.[30] But when he was nauseated by a mutilated corpse in the Paris Morgue, Dickens was more irritated by his sensitivity than understanding of his distress. 'Mac has been a little heavy since yesterday morning', he reported to Kate, 'and rather disposed to be cross—but don't say so, to Forster.'[31] While his national reputation as a painter continued, in his private life Maclise increasingly withdrew into a quiet domestic routine with his unmarried sister.

Macready, too, was retiring from London life. His original hope of making enough money to settle in America had been foiled by the jealousy of a rival actor, William Forrest, who set the crowds on him; and in June 1850 he gave up his house in Clarence Terrace and moved to the country at Sherborne in Dorset. On 1 March 1851, after a series of farewell performances— *King Lear* on 2 February and a last appearance at Drury Lane in *Macbeth* on 26 February—Dickens organized a testimonial dinner for him, with such old companions as Bulwer-Lytton, Forster, Lemon, and Jerdan among the six hundred guests. Dickens, said the young actor John Coleman, made a speech 'as florid as his costume'. He wore, Coleman noted, 'a blue dress coat, faced with silk and aflame with gorgeous brass buttons, a vest of black satin with a white satin collar, and a wonderfully embroidered shirt'. When he got up to speak, Coleman added, 'his long curly hair, his bright eyes and his general aspect of geniality and *bonhomie* presented a delightful picture'.[32] Thackeray put it more tartly: 'Yes, the beggar is as beautiful as a butterfly, especially about the shirt front.'[33]

In the speech which Dickens made that night he spelt out a new plan. It had all begun at Knebworth the previous autumn. 'This is a great power that has grown up about you, out of a winter-night's amusement,' Bulwer-Lytton had then said to Dickens, 'and do let us try to use it for the lasting service of our order.'[34] Bulwer-Lytton felt that penury detracted from the dignity of the profession of letters and he was keen for authors to provide collective support when one of them fell on hard times. A number of benevolent schemes had been mooted since the early 1830s, but none had come to anything. The only source of help was the Literary Fund, which was founded in 1790 and acquired royal patronage when Prince Albert presided in 1842. The Fund was run on the basis of patronage, and its charitable activities were administered by a body of well-meaning conservative philanthropists. The idea of the new scheme, by contrast, was that grants would be made not as a charity but as legitimate professional awards. It was Bulwer-Lytton's idea to set up an endowment scheme—a life insurance or friendly society similar to those then becoming common in other professions—which would be financed in the first instance by the performance of a play which he would write and the Dickens company would perform. Dickens was delighted with the idea. Not only did it provide a worthwhile opportunity to continue with the beloved theatricals, but the plan was in line with his own view of the literary profession. Although he was a member of the Royal Literary Fund and had never openly criticized it, he had long felt that more successful writers should do all they could to help their more needy colleagues. As well as his own benefit performances on behalf of Leigh Hunt, John Poole, and Sheridan Knowles, he had also pressed the government for pensions to assist them. At the end of 1850 he successfully negotiated with Lord John Russell about a grant to Poole, living miserably in Paris, and he had been at the forefront of schemes to help the widows and orphans of actors and authors alike. Before long Bulwer-Lytton's plan had become even more ambitious and all through 1851 Dickens was busy with it. There was to be a Guild of Literature and Art, and Bulwer-Lytton was to provide land on his Knebworth estate for it to build a group of houses for indigent authors and artists; the endowment fund would also pay a stipend both to established authors without means and to a number of young men of promise. 'I do devoutly believe that this plan carried', Dickens wrote enthusiastically to Bulwer-Lytton, 'will entirely change the status of the literary man in England, and make a revolution in his position.'[35]

Other writers were not so sure or so enthusiastic, and Thackeray was one outspoken critic of the scheme. He had already differed with Forster on a similar point in January 1850, after the publication of his autobiographical novel *Pendennis* which satirized the publisher Bentley, the group around *Fraser's*, and other cronies he had known earlier in his career. On that occasion the *Morning Chronicle* had attacked him for 'baneful prejudice' and Forster—whose recent *Life of Goldsmith* had revealed his identification with the eighteenth-century man of letters—had objected in the *Examiner* that Thackeray caricatured his fellow authors 'to gain the applause of the non-literary class'. Thackeray hit back with a sermon in the *Morning Chronicle* on 'The Dignity of Literature'. Unlike Forster (and Dickens), who thought that authors should boldly claim professional status, Thackeray believed that they should 'silently assume that they are as good as any other gentleman'. It was therefore not surprising that he reacted strongly when Dickens outlined his plans for the Guild at the Macready dinner. He had never liked the idea of theatricals to assist 'decayed literary men', regarding such efforts as 'unworthy and derogatory', and when he addressed a banquet of the Royal Literary Fund on 14 May 1851 he attacked the Guild as a form of self-pity which was bound to lower the public's esteem for men of letters. He asked Forster to tell Dickens privately 'that I'm not his enemy ... but we're on different sides of the house ... I don't believe in the Theatrical scheme. I think *that* is against the dignity of our profession.... Try to get it out of your head that I am a sneak and a schemer and to think I have a little heart.'[36]

Neither Dickens nor Thackeray wished to lead a literary faction against the other, but their supporters—and the critics—treated them like protagonists, comparing their respective merits and waiting eagerly for each new novel. In May, for instance, David Masson wrote a long article in the *North British Review* acclaiming both authors as 'friendly competitors for the prize of light literature' and compared Thackeray, 'a perfect master' of realism, to the romantic Dickens, whom he criticized for using his fiction to tilt at social abuses. Few men dominated by the artistic temperament, Masson wrote, 'have shewn so obvious an inclination as Mr. Dickens to step beyond the artist and exercise the functions of the social and moral critic'.[37] Thackeray felt the article was unjust to Dickens and he sent Masson a fervent letter extolling the merits of his rival.

Dickens himself was turning his attention to his role of actor-manager which he could now play on a grand scale and with eminent patrons. The trustees of the Guild included the Duke of Devonshire and Sir Charles Eastlake, the President of the Royal Academy, and as soon as Bulwer-Lytton had finished three acts of the play Dickens was busy seeking even more exalted sponsors. The Great Exhibition was to open in Hyde Park on 1 May 1851, and as a curtain-raiser Dickens proposed that a special performance be given to the Queen and Prince Albert. This would ensure, he wrote to Bulwer-Lytton, that the play would be 'the town talk before the country people and foreigners come'. He had already designed a special travelling stage, since he planned to take the play on tour, and he now approached the Duke of Devonshire to ask if the play could be put on for the Court at Devonshire House in Piccadilly. In two hours the Duke responded with lordly generosity: 'My services, my house, and my subscription will be at your orders.' His response, Dickens observed, 'is quite princely, I think, and will push us along as brilliantly as heart could desire'.[38]

After a five-day break in Paris in February with Leech, Dickens absorbed himself in the preparations. The play, a costume piece set in the early eighteenth century, was now finished and entitled *Not So Bad As We Seem*. Dickens liked it; it was, he told Bulwer-Lytton, 'full of character, strong in interest, rich in capital situations, and *certain to go nobly*'.[39] To make sure of success he felt obliged to push his amateur company hard. Frank Stone, he declared, was 'a Millstone';[40] Lemon was 'too farcical'; Richard Horne 'the very worst actor the world ever saw'; Forster, characteristically, was 'too loud and violent'.[41] On 10 February Dickens asked Wills to take a small part in the scheme, 'which is a very great and important one and which cannot have too many men who are steadily—not flightily, like some of our friends—in earnest'.[42] Wills declined, pleading that one of them should give his undivided attention to *Household Words*. Augustus Egg, who was painting the scenery with Clarkson Stanfield and David Roberts, then brought in a 'very desirable recruit'.[43] Wilkie Collins was only twenty-seven, small, short-sighted, with a prominent forehead, and Dickens thought him well suited to play the part of a valet.

Dickens had known his father, the painter William Collins, and had much admired his godfather, Sir David Wilkie; and in addition to Augustus Egg the young Collins and Dickens had a number of common acquaintances—including John Leech, Jerrold, Maclise, and Macready. Although Collins had begun as a clerk in a tea-broker's office and wanted to run away to sea, he had never known a struggle with the world. When his father died there was sufficient means to support him at Lincoln's Inn, where he was a desultory student of the law: his hedonistic and Bohemian tastes ran to good food, wine, racy talk, and women of easy virtue, and his driving ambition was to to be a writer of some kind and preferably a dramatist. He had already been involved in amateur theatricals, for in 1849 he had produced Goldsmith's *The Good-natur'd Man* with the painters John Millais and William Frith among the actors. He lived on the fringe of the Pre-Raphaelite set, for his brother Charles had been one of the original group with Millais, Dante Gabriel Rossetti, and Holman Hunt. He admired Dickens as a writer—in 1851, in strict imitation, he published a Christmas story with Bentley that was illustrated by Millais and Hunt—but he was at first personally suspicious. Bentley had been disparaging about him; and Dickens had made an odd and vitriolic attack on the Pre-Raphaelites in an article in *Household Words* on 15 June 1850. Dickens objected to the 'realistic' style of the Millais painting of 'Christ in the House of His Parents' and defended an Ideal Conception of the Virgin Mary. His onslaught was partly an expression of his distaste for the High Church religiosity of the Pre-Raphaelites, and partly an effusion of current opinion. *The Times* thought the picture 'plainly revolting' and the *Literary Gazette* described it as 'a nameless atrocity'. Dickens went even further. Jesus, he wrote, was 'a hideous, wry-necked, blubbery, red-haired boy in a nightgown', and his mother Mary was portrayed as a woman 'so horrible in her ugliness' that 'she would stand out from the rest of the company in the vilest cabaret in France'. Although this upset Wilkie Collins he was soon mollified. When he turned up at Forster's apartment in Lincoln's Inn on 3 March 1851 he found that Egg, Jerrold, and other friends were present, and everything went so easily that he was captivated by Dickens. When the company went to Manchester and Liverpool in the following year he was promoted to a bigger part, and the easy friendship was capped by the publication of his successful story 'A Terribly Strange Bed' in *Household Words*.

The work for the Guild came at a good time for Dickens. He had no novel in hand and he needed something to distract him from the series of personal troubles which made 1851 such a sad contrast to the successes of 1850. Early in February the first shadow fell across his enthusiasm. Dora was taken ill. The baby's condition, described as congestion of the brain, seemed so serious that she was hastily baptized. Within four weeks Kate also collapsed, with fits of giddiness and alarming confusion. The symptoms were not new.

Dickens thought he had seen signs of this affliction—'a nervous one and of a peculiar kind'—over several years;[44] he had noticed it most recently when Kate was under strain during the social visits to Knebworth and Rockingham Castle. He decided to consult his friend Dr. Southwood Smith about her. Smith shared his suspicion that Kate was suffering from psychological rather than physical illness, and suggested that she be sent to the spa at Great Malvern for the 'water cure' which had become a fashionable treatment for hysterical conditions—Tennyson, for instance, had gone there in 1847 when he was suffering from morbid depression. The cure, which combined a strict regimen of diet and rest with sessions in which the patient was packed in cold wet sheets to produce a physical reaction, was particularly associated with Dr. Gully—who was later involved in the scandalous Bravo murder case. Kate was entrusted to the care of Gully's colleague, Dr. James Wilson, and Dickens wrote to say that 'great caution' was needed. She was not, as Wilson proposed, to stay in the doctor's own house but 'in some cheerful cottage in the neighbourhood'. Dickens, basing his insistence on 'what I have lately observed when we have been staying in the country houses even of intimate friends', was adamant that Kate must be under her own roof.[45]

At the beginning of March Dickens took Kate and Georgina down to Malvern. It was, he reported to Forster, 'a most beautiful place' and he found the patients amusing. 'O Heaven, to meet the Cold Waterers (as I did this morning when I went out for a shower-bath) dashing down the hills, with severe expressions on their countenances, like men doing matches and not exactly winning!'[46] Kate, who had to cope with the demands of a large family as well as with the frenzied enthusiasms that Dickens generated, clearly found him exhausting company. If Dickens himself was not cracking under the strain, Kate was. Some of his friends, too, were critical of his grand schemes. On 23 March he defended himself energetically to Angela Coutts, who had suggested that theatricals were not quite the thing for a prominent literary man. 'I have perceived a dim shadow of your mysterious objection to my acting, before now,' he wrote. 'Yet I hope you will go to this Play, consoling your mind with the belief that we have on former occasions done a great deal of good by it, and that no such thing would ever be done but for me, and that there is no one else whom these men would allow to hold them together, or to whose direction they would good-humouredly and with perfect confidence yield themselves.'[47] This sense of indispensability, with a production before the Queen herself looming ahead, intensified the pressures upon him. 'The amount of business and correspondence that I have to attend to in connexion with the play', he wrote to Bulwer-Lytton on 23 March, 'is about . . . equal to the business of the Home Office.'[48] He managed to free himself from the rush of preparations for ten days, and then he left Kate at Malvern while he returned to London for rehearsals.

On arrival Dickens found that his father was desperately ill. John Dickens, he wrote to Kate, 'was in that state from active disease (of the bladder) which he had mentioned to nobody, that mortification and delirium, terminating in speedy death, seemed unavoidable'. A surgeon was called, 'who instantly performed (without chloroform) the most terrible operation known in surgery, as the only chance of saving him'. He bore the knife with great bravery, but Dickens was greatly affected when he went into the room and found it 'a slaughter house of blood'.[49] Yet John Dickens rallied, slept as well as anyone 'so cut and slashed' might expect, and seemed 'so wonderfully cheerful and strong-hearted' that Charles felt able to go back to Kate at Malvern.[50] Four days later he was back to sit through the night by his unconscious father before death came in the early hours of 31 March. Dickens went out to Highgate to arrange for the funeral. The old irritation had faded in the last years, and Dickens saw the comedy, affection, and professional skills which had enabled John Dickens to survive so many vicissitudes. The headstone he ordered was to testify to the old man's 'zealous, useful, cheerful spirit'.

There was, as Dickens now wrote to Kate, 'no end of trouble' beside the bereavement. 'I have been so worried and worn since I have been here', he told her on the day before he buried his father, 'that I have not even had the power of taking rest—having been up, now, three whole nights—and out and walking about, too.' He spent one night watching the comings and goings at Bow Street police station. For once he let slip a sigh of harried despair. 'I have sometimes felt, myself, as if I should have given up, and let the whole battle ride on over me.'[51] His febrile state was understandable. The Queen had set 30 April for the command performance, and much remained to be done.

Kate was now on her own after Georgina had returned from Malvern to Devonshire Terrace to mind the children, and Dickens, back in London, presided at the dinner of the General Theatrical Fund on 14 April. 'I never heard him to greater advantage,' Forster declared. It was indeed a poignant occasion, for just before Dickens began to speak of the actor's lot—'how often it is with all of us that in our several spheres we have to do violence to our feelings and hide our hearts in carrying on this fight for life'—Forster was called out of the room.[52] Little Dora, whom Dickens had just left in apparently good health and spirits, had been seized by convulsions and died. He decided to let Dickens deliver his speech, and then with Lemon's help broke the news. Lemon sat up all night with Dickens after this second bereavement in a fortnight, while Forster was sent off to fetch Kate from Malvern with a carefully-worded letter to cushion the shock. 'You must read this letter, very slowly and carefully', Dickens began with consideration for her fretted nerves. He told her the baby was seriously ill: 'I do not think her recovery at all likely.' And he prepared Kate to find her 'quietly asleep',[53] begging her to remain composed and to consider the other children. After her return he told Angela Coutts that Kate was 'as well as I could hope',[54] but he was more frank with such intimates as Beard and Mitton, saying Kate was very low and that he had decided to get away from Devonshire Terrace as soon as possible. He again took Fort House at Broadstairs from the middle of May and set about letting the London house until the end of his lease in September.

Under these grievous family circumstances even Dickens was forced to postpone the play; the Queen agreed to put off the performance until 16 May, and the rehearsals were soon resumed in the library at Devonshire House, where Dickens supervised the erection of the travelling theatre, which was an elaboration of the temporary stage he had ingeniously fitted into Rockingham Castle. He was, he reported to Angela Coutts, in a 'maze of bewilderment' with carpenters, painters, tailors, and wigmakers.[55] And he had to bring on his cast. They had begun by rehearsing for five hours twice a week; as the gala night approached he brought them in three times a week and kept at it all day. Forster, subduing himself, 'improved the part a thousand per cent'. Stone was 'inexpressibly better than I should have supposed possible', he wrote to Bulwer-Lytton on 28 April. 'All the points are gradually being worked and smoothed out with the utmost neatness all through the play.'[56] He was bothered because Richard Horne was playing a character who smoked a clay pipe and it was known that the Queen hated tobacco. Horne tried a herbal mixture, then a new pipe; then he put a swirl of cotton in the bowl of the pipe. Even then Dickens was uneasy. 'Her Majesty', he declared, 'would *think* she smelt tobacco, and that would be just as bad!'[57] He drove himself even harder than he harried his company. 'My legs swell so, with standing on the stage for hours together,' he told Beard three days before the performance, 'that my stockings won't come off. I get so covered with sawdust among the carpenters, that my Infants don't know me. I am so astonishingly familiar with everybody else's part, that I forget my own.'[58]

Despite such pressing commitments Dickens managed to cope with his public and domestic business. Six days before the royal evening he spoke at a brilliant affair at Gore House on behalf of the Metropolitan Sanitary Association. Lady Blessington, whom he had so often visited there, had followed d'Orsay to Paris in 1849 and died there soon afterwards, and the elegant house had been opened as a smart restaurant for the Exhibition year by the great chef, M. Soyer. The interest evoked by Soyer's 'Universal Symposium' gave Kate an idea. She decided to write *What Shall We Have for Dinner?*, a cookbook of her menus at Devonshire Terrace, which Bradbury and Evans put out over the signature of 'Lady Maria Clutterbuck'. The task was a distraction from her grief and condition. Though the recipes were uninspired—and reveal how much Dickens liked milk punch and toasted cheese—the book was kindly received. Before the performance, too, Dickens had to settle his living arrangements. While the family were down at Fort House, he proposed to convert two rooms in the *Household Words* office into a *pied-à-terre*, and before Kate left he took her about to see possible new houses for the autumn. One of them was Tavistock House, an eighteen-roomed mansion on the east side of Tavistock Square, where his friend Frank Stone had rented a studio. It was grander and more ornate than Devonshire Terrace, and the drawing-room was large enough to receive a party of up to three hundred. They decided to take it.

Dickens had been worried, as the royal evening approached, by threats from Bulwer-Lytton's estranged and hysterical wife Rosina that she would force her entrance in disguise and throw oranges at the Queen. In an abusive letter to Dickens she called the Queen sensual and pig-headed, denounced the actors as disreputable charlatans, and called her husband a ruffian and a scoundrel. Dickens took her seriously enough to engage a detective specially to watch the entrance to Devonshire House, but she did not appear. All, in fact, went very well. There was a dress rehearsal for friends of the cast on 14 May. Two nights later, the fashionable audience sat in the velvet-draped picture gallery while the Duke's private orchestra played a specially commissioned overture; and, after the play had been rapturously received, there was a splendid supper at which the Queen sat in a bower of roses, orchids, and other spring blossoms. The Duke, pleased with the social success of the evening and at the fact that it had brought in over £1,000 for the Guild, begged the company to repeat the play on 27 May before moving on to public performances. For this occasion Dickens decided to add a farce in which, he wrote to Macready, 'a distinguished amateur will sustain a variety of assumption-parts, and in particular, Samuel Weller and Mrs Gamp'.[59] He in fact appeared in six roles, and the comic business he worked up with Lemon in the ludicrous piece they called *Mr. Nightingale's Diary* was wildly successful, the hilarity merging into the supper party and ball which the Duke gave to celebrate the occasion.

'I am pining for Broadstairs,' Dickens told Macready while he was waiting for the second Devonshire House performance. 'I lurk from the sun, during the best part of the day, in a villainous compound of darkness, canvas, saw-dust, general dust, stale gas (involving a vague smell of pepper) and disenchanted properties.'[60] And when he got down to his 'airy nest' at Fort House he sent Forster a lyrical letter on 1 June: 'Corn growing, larks singing, garden full of flowers, fresh air on the sea—O it is wonderful!'[61] Yet the smell of sawdust and grease-paint still lingered. Writing to the Duke of Devonshire he repeated his happy description of Broadstairs, and then added that he was feeling 'the melancholy of having turned a leaf in my life'. It was so sad to see the curtain drop at Devonshire House 'that something of the shadow of the great curtain which falls on everything seemed . . . to be upon my spirits'.[62]

London was in a gay mood that summer, and the city full of visitors to the Great Exhibition. Yet Dickens, normally so responsive to festive occasions, did not catch on to the spirit of the affair. He visited it twice, telling Mrs. Watson on 11 July that he was 'used up' by the show in Hyde Park because 'so many things bewildered me'.[63] He had, he explained, 'a natural horror of sights', and he told Wills a fortnight later of his 'instinctive feeling against the Exhibition of a faint, inexplicable sort'.[64] He was much happier with private celebrations, like the Star and Garter dinner at Richmond which Talfourd organized in the middle of June to celebrate *Copperfield*, when Forster, Jerrold, Thackeray, and Tennyson were among the guests. 'I have rarely seen Dickens happier than he was amid the sunshine of that day,' Forster remarked.[65] In June he also went down to see Macready at Sherborne and there was a rain-drenched boating expedition with Charley at Eton which he described to Mrs. Watson at cheerful length. Most of his energies, however, were needed for the performances of the Bulwer-Lytton play at the Hanover Rooms on 18 June, 2 July, 21 July, and 4 August. He now had the added task of keeping his company in line, for some of them were becoming sated and regretting the demands on their time. Forster and Jerrold, in particular, were 'wet-blanketing' and objecting to the plan to take the play to the provinces. Dickens had to keep them all up to scratch for the tour to Bath and Bristol in November as well as making the arrangements to go to Manchester and Liverpool in February. 'No great thing ever was done (I suppose) without being hammered at with a sledge hammer,' he wrote to Bulwer-Lytton on 10 July 1851. 'At any rate I have taken mine in hand for this piece of work, and mean to keep it going.'[66]

Household Words also had to be kept going. At the end of July he dashed across to Dover one day in the hope of catching Wills on his way to Paris. 'It is no matter,' he wrote when he missed him; 'I had nothing of any moment to say—merely wished to pat you on the back.'[67] Sometimes a minute editorial point caught his eye. On 17 July, for instance, he sent Wills five possible titles for an article the latter had written on the Custom House, including 'The Dull End of the Broad Arrow' and 'Her Majesty's only Disagreeable Customs'. 'I want a great paper done on the distribution of Titles in England,' he instructed Wills on 22 August: 'ascertain what they were given *for*. How many chemists, how many men of science, how many writers, how many aldermen. How much intellect represented. How much imagination. How much learning. How much expression of the great progress of the country ... of improvements in machinery, of any sort of contribution to the happiness of mankind.'[68]

He was increasingly concerned that summer with what he described to Frank Stone as 'the great house question'. He had paid £1,450 for a forty-five year lease on Tavistock House and was pleased with it. 'Of the bow in the drawing-room and of the general air of the room, I cannot speak in terms of sufficient praise,' he wrote to Kate. 'I think it will be best for you in a week or so, to come up with me for a few hours and choose the paperings.'[69] At Broadstairs he fretted about the alterations and repairs. He drew up a plan for the garden, and ordered shrubs to be carried there from Devonshire Terrace. He altered the hall and the ground-floor rooms, insisted upon a separate water-closet, ordered a modern range for the kitchen, and commissioned furnishings 'on a scale of awful splendour and magnitude'.[70] At first he complained that the workmen had not yet started. When they did begin he wrote impatiently to his brother-in-law Henry Austin, whom he had asked to supervise the building work: 'I am perpetually wandering (in fancy) up and down the house and tumbling over the workmen. When I feel that they are gone to dinner I become low. When I look forward to their total abstinence on Sunday I become wretched. The gravy at dinner has a taste of glue in it. I smell paint in the sea.'[71] When he went up to London to inspect progress he felt equally frustrated. The workmen, he wrote to Beard, were 'always going up ladders apparently with no earthly object but that of staying there until dinner time, every day'.[72]

It was a fretful summer at Broadstairs, punctuated by his own visits to London and as usual by visits from friends. Forster, Wills, Stone, Egg, the Hornes, and Talfourd all went down to Fort House. The fuss about the house fused with anxiety about a new novel. 'I begin to be pondering afar off, a new book,' he wrote to Angela Coutts on 17 August. 'Violent restlessness and vague ideas of going I don't know where, I don't know why, are the present symptoms of the disorder.'[73] He told Forster that he had a sudden impulse to go to Switzerland: 'such a torment of a desire to be anywhere but where I am ... takes hold of me, that it is like being *driven away*'.[74] He did not go to the Alps, only as far as the Duke of Devonshire's great house in Derbyshire. 'I had such an affectionate note of invitation from the Duke', he explained to Wills on 29 September, 'that I can't help running down to Chatsworth however short the time I can spare for the purpose.'[75] He stayed only two days, writing to tell Kate of the grandeur of his bedroom and of the wonderful gardens—'the principal Fountain is just twice the height of the Great Horse Shoe Fall at Niagara'.[76]

He was, as he told Angela Coutts, 'three parts distracted and the fourth part wretched' until he was over 'the agonies of getting into a new house ... I *can not* work at my new book—having all my notions of order turned completely topsy-turvy'.[77] The agitation and the delay became intolerable as he waited for the paint to dry. 'Oh! if this were to last long,' he wrote desperately to Henry Austin: 'the distraction of the new book, the whirling of the story through one's mind, escorted by workmen, the imbecility, the wild necessity of beginning to write, the not being able to do so, the, O! I should go—O!'[78]

PART THREE

A FEARFUL MAN

1851–1859

14

The Romance of Discontent

'WE are beginning to be settled in our new house,'[1] Dickens reported to Angela Coutts in mid-November 1851. The family had moved back to London on 20 October, but the builders were still at work and Dickens was waiting for Maples and Shoolbreds to complete the ornate furnishings—lavish curtains, red plush, gilt, mirrors and all. He watched every detail of style and utility. For the false bookcases which concealed the door from his study to the drawing-room he invented comic titles, such as *Forty Winks at the Pyramids* and *The Quarrelly Review*; the satirical seven volumes of *The Wisdom of Our Ancestors*, subtitled Ignorance, Superstition, The Block, The Stake, The Rack, Dirt, and Disease, were set alongside the very small accompanying volume on *The Virtues of Our Ancestors*. He explained to the dubious Miss Coutts why he had installed a shower-bath. 'It is because my cut-out way of life obliges me to be so much up on the strain, that I think it is of service to me as a refresher,' he wrote, 'not as a taker out, but as a putter in of energy.'[2] His greatest delight in the house, however, was the discovery that the big schoolroom was large enough for a small stage, and it was soon christened the Theatre Royal and used for the first time to stage Albert Smith's burletta *Guy Fawkes* for the usual party to celebrate Charley's birthday on Twelfth Night.

Charley was now fifteen, Mamie was almost fourteen, Kate was twelve, and the younger brothers—Walter Landor, Francis Jeffrey, Alfred Tennyson, Sydney Smith, and Henry Fielding—tailed away at roughly two-year intervals. Dickens took a close interest in their upbringing as well as in their romps and pleasures. There was a governess for the girls and the smaller boys, but the education of the older ones was his main concern. Charley wanted to go into commerce, and Dickens was already planning to send him on to Germany for business training when he left Eton. And he had now begun to dictate to Georgina the chapters of *A Child's History of England* which was to appear in *Household Words* in January. The book had been in his mind since Charley was small. In August 1843 when the boy was still 'making fortifications in the sand with wooden spades', Dickens had written to Angela Coutts from Broadstairs of his plan to produce a revised version of English history for his son so that 'he may have tender-hearted notions of War and Murder, and may not fix his affection on wrong heroes'.[3] When he finally came to write the book, he let himself go and produced a radical, melodramatic, and wildly opinionated caricature of the standard Victorian textbook.

From the time of *A Christmas Carol* Dickens had increasingly appeared to his readers as the fount of the domestic virtues, and he had taken on the role of the Victorian patriarch at home. But he still had the youthful gaiety and pleasing appearance of a man of forty. 'His hair is not much grizzled and is thick although the crown of his head is getting bald,' the American historian John Lothrop Motley remarked after meeting him at dinner with Forster. 'His features are good, the nose rather high, the eyes largish, greyish and very expressive.' He was, Motley added, 'genial, sympathetic, agreeable, unaffected, with plenty of light easy talk and touch and go fun without any effort or humbug of any kind'.[4] Many of the people who met him reacted similarly to his charm and vitality. George Eliot, who met him in the spring of 1852, came to see him as 'a man one can thoroughly enjoy talking to—there is a strain of real seriousness along with his keenness and humour'.[5] Others noted that he never spoke in platitudes. Thomas Trollope declared that he 'warmed the social atmosphere whenever he appeared with that summer glow which seemed to attend him',[6] and Percy Fitzgerald said that 'the mere thrill of his wonderful voice had a magic of persuasion in it'.[7]

For all such qualities Dickens was justly admired and they account for his popularity. He was a lively and warm-hearted friend. Yet there were less appealing traits in his complex personality, and as he grew older they became more marked. He always had a short temper, as Bentley and other men who crossed him quickly discovered; he was resentful when he felt slighted, cocksure and overbearing when he was thwarted, and inclined to be censorious of those who could not live up to his own demanding standards. 'The society in which he mixed, the hours which he kept, the opinions which he held', Mrs. Lynn Linton recalled, 'were all settled by himself, not merely for himself, but for all those brought into connection with him.'[8] Even outsiders sensed the way he exerted power over other people. The Irish journalist Justin McCarthy felt it when he met Dickens on his arrival in London in 1852. 'Dickens rather frightened me,' he recalled. 'His manner was full of energy; there was something physically overpowering about it; the very vehemence of his cheery good humour rather bore me down.'[9]

The combination of his attractive and his dominating characteristics made Dickens an ambivalent figure in the family. He bewitched everyone in the

Charles Dickens, painted by William Powell Frith in 1859

Ellen Ternan as a young woman

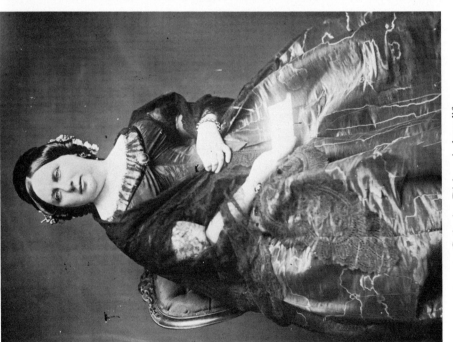

Catherine Dickens in later life

house with his vitality and yet, as his daughter Kate confessed, everyone was also rather afraid of him. The girls, who shared a room at the top of the house, could choose their own decorations, but they were required to keep everything in perfect order; 'he made a point of visiting every room in the house once each morning', Mamie Dickens recalled, 'and if a chair was out of place, or a blind not quite straight, or a crumb left on the floor, woe betide the offender!'[10] The same obsession with neatness and order, which made Dickens so fastidious about his personal appearance and the arrangement of his knick-knacks and the furniture, was increasingly directed against the whole family. It was necessary for him to have everything under his control. His family reacted in different ways. Catherine, as she was now called as little Kate grew up, was crushed by his overbearing presence and reacted with peevish complaint. 'My poor mother was afraid of my father,' Kate Dickens later recalled. 'She was never allowed to express an opinion— never allowed to say what she felt.'[11] The boys found it difficult to be manly and to develop freely under his pressure; it was not surprising that so many of them were sent off to careers in the armed services. Georgina and Mamie protected themselves by sycophancy. They were devoted to him, and took his side in domestic arguments, and were rewarded by his praise of their sisterly qualities. Georgina, Dickens said in a typically flattering phrase, had 'one of the most remarkable capacities I have ever known'.[12]

Georgina's position in the Dickens household was somewhat peculiar. She was a pretty and able young woman and she did not lack admirers, but when Augustus Egg proposed to her she refused him, making it plain that her preferred place was beside her admired brother-in-law and that her duty was to supervise his household and to bring up his children. Such a part in life was common for a maiden aunt in Victorian families, especially where the wife was an invalid or the husband a widower. What was uncommon in this case was the manner in which Georgina gradually assumed all the functions of a wife, except those of sexual partner, although the wife herself was still alive and well and living in her own home. The Victorian conventions made many men ambivalent about their sexuality; physical passion seemed a hidden and shaming thing, and in public they idealized womanhood and extolled chastity. One means of coping with this contradiction was the double standard, which made mistresses and prostitutes the price of domestic virtue. Dickens apparently found a different solution, which was echoed in one novel after another, and harked back to the triangular relationships of the short-lived idyll in Furnival's Inn—and possibly even to complex childhood feelings towards his mother and his sister Fanny. During the first year of his marriage his powerful attachment to Mary Hogarth enabled him to polarize his emotions. He was physically attracted to Catherine, whereas young Mary became the epitome of innocence. Her death not only shocked him, it also destroyed the balance of his emotional needs. He later declared that his troubles with Catherine began soon afterwards, at the time when Mamie was born. After Georgina joined the family and grew into the place that Mary had left vacant, the balance was to some extent restored.

This pattern persisted through the years in which Catherine was bearing children and Georgina was looking after them. But repeated pregnancies were exhausting Catherine's sexual role and, lacking the personality to keep her in favour with Dickens, she had no other. She only irritated him with her lethargy, nervousness, clumsiness, and complaints. She had long lost her physical charm. When Harriet Beecher Stowe met Catherine during a visit to England in 1853 she described her as 'a good specimen of a truly English woman; tall, large and well-developed'—a phrase which glossed over the fact that, as the years passed and she became more isolated and neglected, Catherine took little exercise and indulged herself in food and drink.[13]

Dickens was confused and angry with these changes in the family. He had solved David Copperfield's dilemmas by ending his story on the threshold of a new marriage, but his own problems were more intractable. It was not so much that he resented the fact that he was growing old but that he was having to accept a different, less congenial role. He had grown up in a family that was bewilderingly chaotic and now, as the children grew up, his own family was threatening to get out of control. The streak of self-righteousness which had come out in his youthful letters reproving Maria Beadnell and Catherine for their shortcomings, now hardened into a minatory dislike of any form of backsliding. He was quick to commend penitence: it was 'like the sun after a shower', one of his sons remarked. But he was hard on delinquency, whether the person who had failed to come up to the mark was one of his children, a printer, a friend pressed into his theatricals, or a girl at Urania Cottage.

He could not, however, take blame upon himself as easily as he imputed it to others; and Catherine often had to bear his displeasure in situations that were as much his responsibility as hers. He had long complained about her fertility, and the prospect of yet another child in the spring of 1852 threw him into a fit of irritated restlessness. 'Wild ideas are upon me', he wrote to Forster a week before the baby was born, 'of going to Paris—Rouen—Switzerland—somewhere—and writing the remaining two-thirds of the next No. aloft in some queer inn room.'[14] And after the birth on 13 March of Edward Bulwer-Lytton, Dickens sardonically told Miss Coutts that he had a seventh son 'whom I cannot afford to receive with perfect cordiality, as on the whole I could have dispensed with him'.[15] Dickens, in the habit of giving his children pet names, blessed this child with Plornish-maroontigoonter; and Plorn soon became a favourite.

His loudest complaints of irresponsibility, however, were directed at public men in general and the government in particular. He was so outspoken that one critic complained of *Household Words* that 'there is scarcely a work in the land that tends more to separate class from class, or to make the poor man feel oppressed and overborne by the rich, and that the laws and institutions, and authorities of the country, are *against him* and *for them*'. The article entitled 'The Last Words of the Old Year', which appeared on 4 January 1851, was the harangue of a man at odds with himself, and increasingly at odds with the world. 'I have been a year of ruin', it began, and Dickens went on to list its crimes and omissions—starving and illiterate children, blighted farmers, overcrowded slums, disease-producing sewers. It was a bleak indictment in the optimistic year of the Great Exhibition. To add to it he listed the dreary legacies to the New Year: 'I bequeath to my successor a vast inheritance of degradation and neglect in England, a general mismanagement of all public expenditure, revenues and property. I do give and bequeath to him, likewise, the Court of Chancery. The less he leaves of it to his successor, the better for mankind.'

The reference to Chancery was timely as it was the subject of considerable public interest throughout 1851. 'The Court of Chancery is a name of terror, a devastating gulf, a den whence no footsteps return,' declared *The Times*, adding its voice to the public demand for reform. By October 1851 a Chancery Reform Act had been introduced into the House of Commons. Dickens had so often been outraged by the ways of the law that he understandably chose the evils of Chancery as the theme of his new novel. By the end of November 1851, when he had recovered from the move to Tavistock Square, he started to write *Bleak House*.

The first number was published in March 1852. It was an instant success, and the regular sale of 35,000 copies was comfortably above the figure for *Copperfield*—though Forster later decided that with this book 'some want of all the freshness of his genius first became apparent'. He was right to notice that this novel differed significantly from its predecessors. Since childhood Dickens had been driven by a sense of unappeased grievance; in his fiction, as in his speeches and his journalism, the resulting anger had made him a champion of the weak and the foe of injustice. In *Bleak House* he went much further. As he traced 'the ten thousand stages of an endless cause' in the lawsuit of Jarndyce *v.* Jarndyce—which corrupted or ruined everyone involved in it, except the lawyers who swallowed up the whole estate in costs—he mapped a network of frauds and abuses: the criticism of society, once incidental to his stories, had become the dominant purpose of the new novel and all the characters were informed by it. 'The system! I am told on all hands it's the system,' cries Mr. Gridley, the perennial litigant, frustrated and ruined by legal entanglements, who thus justifies his murderous anger. 'I must have this vent under my sense of injury, or nothing could hold my wits together,' he declares in desperation. 'If I took my wrongs in any other way, I should be driven mad! It is only by resenting them, and by revenging them in my mind, and by angrily demanding the justice I can never get, that I am able to keep my wits together.' Like Carlyle, whose indictment of past mischiefs and present miseries in the condition of England rang through the pages of *Bleak House*, Dickens had become a polemical moralist, shaking off responsibility for the depressing wrongs of the world by proclaiming the need to reform them, asserting his innocence and releasing his anger. *Bleak House* was his apocalyptic response to the Crystal Palace, that glittering show-place of the utilitarian values which he and Carlyle rejected.

The plan for writing *Bleak House* stretched far ahead, to the end of August 1853, but Dickens had become so accustomed to the long rhythms of his serials that he could pace himself comfortably, fitting his family life and other interests into the intervals between the monthly parts. He had more trouble, in fact, with *Household Words*. 'I declare before God that your men are enough to drive me mad!'[16] he wrote petulantly to Evans when the printers made mistakes in his Christmas article for 1851. He complained to Wills that, for all its commercial success, the magazine was 'deficient in excellence' and that it needed an 'elegance of Fancy'.[17] Wills assured him that 'we come out brilliantly' by comparison with competitors. 'No one, not even yourself,' he added, 'can sparkle to order, especially writers who have only an occasional sparkle in them.' And Dickens, as editor, had to accept some responsibility for the defects. 'If you could regularly see and go over each sheet before it is put to press', Wills told him firmly, 'there would be a very thick sprinkling of the excellence in which you say *Household Words* is deficient.'[18]

Dickens did instruct his contributors and alter their articles, though the tone in which Wills wrote implied that he was often too rushed to edit *Household Words* with care. But some authors resented his editing. It was, for instance, a source of friction between him and Elizabeth Gaskell, from whom he had commissioned a number of somewhat morbid short stories after the success of *Mary Barton*. She was a hesitant author, but she objected to any alteration in her work and even to the need to tailor what she wrote to an editor's requirements; Dickens was too pressing and too flighty for her modest taste. 'My dear Scheherazade,' he addressed her on 25 October 1851, 'for I am sure your powers of narrative can never be exhausted in a single night, but must be good for at least a thousand nights and one.' The appeal for copy was on this occasion answered. Mrs. Gaskell had been staying in Knutsford for a rest and she sent him off a delightfully light-hearted sketch of the gossiping ladies of the town in which she had grown up. It became the first two chapters of *Cranford*, published in *Household Words* on 13 December 1851. 'I was so delighted', Dickens wrote to her as that issue went to press, 'that I put it first in the number.' He found it less easy to conjure the later instalments out of her, for all his good-humoured patter. She had once gossiped about the grand style in which he lived, and he now jokingly teased her about it. 'We have just bought a neat little dinner service of pure gold, for common use,' he wrote. 'It is very neat and quiet.' That kind of jest, which he tossed off casually in his notes to Macready or Forster, was not in Mrs.Gaskell's style. Nor was his jocular browbeating. 'O what a lazy woman you are,' he complained on 25 February 1852 in another effort to extract her overdue copy, 'and where is that article?'[19] He told Wills that she exasperated him. 'If I were Mr. G. Oh Heaven how I would beat her.'[20]

Dickens put much energy into *Household Words*, but his interest, as Wills tartly reminded him, was erratic. Wills had to keep the magazine running steadily while the nominal editor was off pursuing one of his other enthusiasms. In 1852, for example, he became absorbed in a scheme for model flats in Bethnal Green which Angela Coutts was promoting. But his main delight was the barnstorming for the Guild of Literature and Art. The tour to Bath and Bristol coincided with the removal to Tavistock House in November 1851, and Dickens had written to Catherine that he 'was continually thinking of the House in the midst of all the bustle but I trust it with such confidence to you that I am quite at my ease about it.'[21] He was able to crowd so much into his daily life because he had the knack of acquiring and using subordinates, provided that they unhesitatingly accepted his terms—as for instance, he controlled Georgina in domestic matters, Forster as his literary adviser and agent, Wills for the magazine, and Evans as his printer-publisher. In February 1852 Dickens carried his travelling company off to Manchester and Liverpool. At Manchester, Forster said, the audience was in a 'fury of delight'. 'I cannot go to bed without telling you what a triumph we have had,' Dickens wrote exultantly to Bulwer-Lytton on 15 February. 'I have been so happy in all this that I could have cried.'[22] He had already raised £3,000 and he now aimed at a total of £5,000. 'I am very much disposed to put it to the rest that we *must* go on while the great towns remain open to us,' he told Bulwer-Lytton. Some, like Jerrold—'who never in his life was true to anything', Dickens sourly remarked—had dropped out; others, such as Forster, were feeling the strain. Dickens himself found the tours exhausting, but exhilarating, telling Bulwer-Lytton that he was 'a giant refreshed'.[23] In May the group whirled off to Shrewsbury and Birmingham, accompanied by 'a perfect army of carpenters, gasmen, tailors, barbers, property-men, dressers and servants'.[24] In the space of a week in August the company played in Nottingham, Derby, Newcastle, Sunderland, and Sheffield, and the tour was wound up by final appearances in Manchester and Liverpool at the beginning of September. Dickens, as he had planned in February, had carried 'a perfect fiery cross through the North of England'.[25]

Theatricals on this scale released many talents in Dickens. He had to provide an unending flow of energy to keep his amateurs up to their tasks, to serve as the promoter, producer, tour manager, and publicity agent of their company, to entertain the sponsors and civic notabilities in each town, and to keep a general eye on the finances of the whole enterprise. What made all this effort worth while was the excited response of the audiences—to the company as a whole and in particular to Dickens himself. He revelled in his parts, especially in *Mr. Nightingale's Diary*, the farce which he and Mark Lemon had concocted to give themselves a sequence of comic characters. He had become a star, and the crowds rallied to the Free Trade Hall in Manchester and the Lyceum in Sunderland to see him and to applaud him. He had discovered a direct way to reach his public, and by the time he was forty-two he was better known by sight than any other author in England. The dream of being called for by 'excited hundreds', which he had confided to Jerrold years before, had now come true.

The Guild of Literature and Art was a worthy cause, and Dickens was in earnest about it. 'I have a more fervent hope than ever of setting right at last what is very wrong in my calling,' he wrote to Angela Coutts on 2 September as the tour came to its triumphant end.[26] Yet once the money was raised, and Dickens no longer had a plausible excuse for indulging his histrionic tastes, the urgency went out of the scheme. It took Bulwer-Lytton two years to persuade Parliament to grant the Guild a charter as a charity, and even then he had to accept a restrictive clause which prevented it '*from doing anything*', Dickens complained to Thackeray, for the next seven years. Thomas Babington Macaulay, who had shared Thackeray's scepticism about the project, had told Bulwer-Lytton at the outset that it would come to very little, because the best authors would either be self-supporting or receive government pensions. By the time that Dickens came to pay money out of the Guild, which he served as its chairman for the rest of his life, Macaulay's prediction seemed justified. There was little public interest, and few donations; and the beneficiaries were mostly mediocre journalists and illustrators.

In July 1852 Dickens rented a place in Dover for the summer, which was the family base for the next three months. 'We are very pleasantly situated here in a very cool house,' he informed Miss Coutts, but he did not care for Dover as much as Broadstairs.[27] It had too many bands, he told Mary Boyle, and was 'infinitely too genteel'.[28] Wilkie Collins, one of the holiday guests, described the family's life 'within a minute's walk of baths and bathing machines'. Breakfast was sharp at ten past eight, and Dickens then shut himself up to work until two, when he was 'available for every pleasant social purpose that can be imagined for the rest of the day', including his daily swim and a long walk in the country. Dinner was at half past five, often followed by card games for modest stakes, and bedtime was between ten and eleven. One evening Dickens read the opening chapters of *Bleak House*, 'making his audience laugh and cry with equal fervour'.[29]

Bleak House was 'a most enormous success', Dickens had told Cerjat in May, 'all the prestige of Copperfield . . . falling upon it, and raising the circulation above all my other books'; and the Guild theatricals were equally rewarding.[30] Yet Dickens still felt unsatisfied and restless. 'This is one of what I call my wandering days before I fall to work,' he wrote to Mary Boyle from Dover on 22 July. 'I seem to be always looking at such times for something I have not found in life, but may possibly come to a few thousands of years hence, in some other part of some other system. God knows.'[31] A few days later he was saddened by the news that his friend Richard Watson, who had been planning another bout of theatricals at Rockingham for the Christmas holidays, had died on his way to Switzerland. 'When I think of that bright house, and his fine simple honest heart, both so open to me, the blank and loss are like a dream,' Dickens wrote to Forster.[32] On 7 August Count d'Orsay died. 'It is a tremendous consideration that friends should fall around us in such awful numbers as we attain middle life,' Dickens exclaimed to Forster next day. 'What a field of battle it is!'[33] And on 18 September Macready's wife succumbed to the family disease of tuberculosis. 'This tremendous sickle certainly does cut deep into the surrounding corn,' Dickens again wrote to Forster when he heard the news. 'But *this* is all a Dream, maybe, and death will wake us.'[34] Macready had already seen several of his children die of consumption before it killed his wife, and Dickens sent a warm-hearted letter about 'the old cheerful times' they had spent together.[35]

At the beginning of October the children were sent back to London and Dickens took Catherine and Georgina across for a fortnight in Boulogne. He had an idea that it might make a good holiday place—quaint, cheap, easily reached from London in six hours, and with the sea air, cliffs, and country walks that he liked—and his stay convinced him; 'please God I shall be writing on these said ramparts next July', he wrote to Forster.[36] With the holidays and the theatricals behind him he was anxious to ginger up *Household Words.* 'Strengthen the number, pray, by anything good you may have,' he wrote to Wills from Boulogne on 13 October. 'It is a very dreary business as it stands.'[37] And when he got back to the office he busied himself with plans for the Christmas number, which was designed round one of his favourite images. It should, he wrote to James White inviting him to collaborate, 'consist entirely of short stories supposed to be told by a family sitting round the fire', and he persuaded Mrs. Gaskell to write one of them.[38] On Christmas Eve he complained bitterly to Wills, who was away ill, that the number had been an 'awful one' for correction, and he exploded at the 'imbecility, carelessness, slovenly composition, relatives without ante-cedents, universal chaos' which 'beats anything in print and paper I have ever "gone at" in my life'.[39]

On 14 September the Duke of Wellington died. Dickens sent a note of sympathy to Miss Coutts, and fetched Charley up from Eton to join the rest of the family at the office of *Household Words,* from which they watched the funeral procession pass on its way to St. Paul's. 'I consider it altogether a mistake, to be temperately but firmly objected to,' he told Mrs. Watson, and though he thought the military parade 'very fine' he attacked the ghastly folly of such occasions.[40] He disliked funerals, and morbid sightseeing— at its worst at public executions—always upset him and attracted him: he denounced profiteers who let their windows to onlookers, and mercenary ghouls who sold cheap souvenirs and bogus relics along the route.

The old Duke's death, nearly forty years after his victory at Waterloo, was a symbol of change in British politics. The general election of July 1852 had produced a minority Conservative government, thus delaying urgently needed measures of reform. The party was still recovering from the defection of so many Conservatives to the Whigs after Peel had reversed his policy on the Corn Laws. One of those defectors was William Ewart Gladstone, and on 17 December 1852 he made his first attack on the clever Tory Chan-cellor of the Exchequer, Benjamin Disraeli. New men, who were to dominate British politics through the decades of industrial and military supremacy, were coming to the fore.

Dickens could have been in that Parliament, like his friend Bulwer-Lytton who was elected as Conservative member for Hertfordshire, but he had again refused an invitation to join 'the bellowers and prosers of St. Stephen's'.[41] He was, he insisted, more useful and more happy in his own 'sphere of ser-vice', and when that was recognized he was indeed 'affected and gratified', as he told the Society of Artists when they proposed to present him with a silver salver and a diamond ring. He went down to Birmingham accompanied by Catherine on 6 January 1853 to receive the presentation and address a banquet. He spoke, he told Macready on 14 January in a letter of thanks for his congratulations, 'about the eternal duties of the arts to the people'.[42] He attacked the 'coxcombical idea of writing down to the popular intelligence': the ordinary reader, he argued, had liberated literature from 'the shame of the purchased dedication, from the scurrilous and dirty work of Grub Street, from the dependent seat on sufferance at my Lord Duke's table today, and from the sponging-house or Marshalsea tomorrow'.[43] There was a subscription for £20,000 to build an Industrial and Literary Institute in Birmingham, and Dickens offered to help by giving a series of public readings, based on *A Christmas Carol*, in the following December.

He was invariably generous to causes he had at heart, though such 'invitations to feasts and festivals' were one of the reasons for the exhaustion he felt through the winter and spring of 1853. In March, after spending two weeks at Brighton with Catherine and Georgina, he was back in London for the banquets of the Theatrical Fund and the Royal Academy; and on 2 May there was a Lord Mayor's dinner to celebrate Harriet Beecher Stowe for *Uncle Tom's Cabin*, which had just been published. His only relaxations were convivial outings and dinners with friends. 'Come alongside the Tavistock same day and hour, 'stead of *Owssel Words*,' he wrote to Clarkson Stanfield on 2 January 1853 with typical jocularity. 'Hail your shipmets, and they'll drop over the side and join you, like two new shillings a-droppin' into the purser's pocket.'[44] And in May he entertained Cornelius Felton, the Harvard Professor of Greek whom he had liked so much on his visit to America; 'not at all starry *or* stripey', he remarked to Stanfield when inviting him to join a party for dinner at Greenwich on 12 May.[45]

For all the show of cheerful nervous energy, however, Dickens was flagging. He was driving himself too hard. Forster noticed that his bursts of euphoria alternated with fits of depression and tetchiness. 'Not infrequently a complaint strange upon his lips fell from him', which Forster attributed to 'the overstrain of attempting too much'.[46] He was still tired from the theatrical ventures of 1852. He had written almost 200,000 words of *Bleak House* and dictated half as much for his *Child's History*. Urania Cottage still claimed some of his time; he was helping Miss Coutts with her plans to clear slums in Bethnal Green, Westminster, and Bermondsey and advising her about other claims on her purse from respectable causes and writers of begging letters. And there were constant invitations to public celebrations as well as the continuing task of editing and writing for *Household Words*. 'Hypochondriacal whisperings tell me that I am rather overworked,' he not surprisingly confided to Forster early that summer. 'The spring does not seem to fly back again directly, as it always did when I put my own work aside, and had nothing else to do.'[47] He was in fact close to a physical collapse, suffering from the painful kidney trouble which had afflicted him at intervals since childhood, and he took to his bed for a week. But he longed to get away: 'I really feel as if my head would split like a fired shell if I stayed here.'[48] His old friend and doctor, John Elliotson, encouraged him, and after spending a few days convalescing at Folkestone, the family moved across to Boulogne on 12 June 1853.

The Château des Moulineaux, set on a wooded hillside above the port, was an odd single-storeyed building. Dickens described it as 'the best place I have ever lived in abroad, except at Genoa', and he found the whole setting agreeable. With a military campsite on the top of the hill and the grounds dropping away to the river valley and the old port it was singularly like Ordnance Terrace on a grander scale. The 'doll's house of many rooms' was surrounded by flowers;[49] there were five summer-houses and at least a dozen goldfish ponds; and the garden was full of odd architectural features, many of them named after Napoleonic battles, erected by the eccentric owner. Dickens quickly took to his landlord, a dealer in cotton goods named M. Beaucourt who was endlessly obliging and comically engaging. In a good humour, and helped—as he wrote cheerfully to Frank Stone—'by far the best wine at tenpence a bottle that I have ever drunk anywhere', Dickens quickly recovered.[50] 'I believe you would never suppose to look at me that I had had that week or barely an hour of it,' he wrote to Wills soon after he arrived.[51]

Boulogne itself was picturesque and Dickens thought the old town as attractive as many more famous continental resorts. There was a weekly pig market which, he told Forster, was 'insupportable in its absurdity', an annual fair in august, and a theatre which naturally attracted him.[52] And there were fêtes, picnics, and outings to near-by towns such as Amiens and Beauvais. With so many diversions Dickens had to get up at dawn to work on the last part of *Bleak House*. By 27 August he could tell Angela Coutts that 'I have just finished my book (very prettily indeed, I hope) and am in the first drowsy lassitude of having done so'. It was, unfortunately, a poor summer. 'I should', he added, 'be lying in the sunshine by the hour together, if there were such a thing.'[53] All the same he had the compensation of visitors from London. Frank Stone took a house on the edge of the town. Wilkie Collins was put up in one of the garden pavilions to live 'with a delicate English graft upon the best French manner, and learn to get up early in the morning again'—an obsession with punctuality that Collins disliked, for Dickens made latecomers go without breakfast.[54] Leech and his wife went across; so did Wills and his wife, Peter Cunningham, and Thomas Beard. And at the end of the holiday, to celebrate the completion of *Bleak House*, there was the best dinner that Boulogne could provide for the publishers, the illustrators, Forster, and Lemon. The novel, Dickens wrote to Mrs. Watson on 27 August, had taken extraordinarily, 'beating dear old Copperfield by a round ten thousand or more'.[55]

He had certainly given his many readers a complex plot, using the depressing obscurities of the Chancery court as the setting for a series of mysteries— Esther Summerson's illegitimate birth, the cruelly interminable lawsuit which consumes the Jarndyce fortune and destroys the wretchedly hopeful Richard Carstone, the murder of the intriguing Mr. Tulkinghorn, and the family secrets which linked the great house at Chesney Wold to the disease-ridden tenements of Tom All Alone's. All these things, as Dickens said, were 'very curiously brought together' in the story; all of them, in fact, were riddles about parenthood, legitimacy, and identity. These were precisely the legal issues with which the Court of Chancery was formally concerned, for it served as the heartless guardian of widows, orphans, and lunatics, and its business was to deal in wills, disputed inheritances, and the tragic litigation which flowed from them. Dickens saw Chancery as a ghastly caricature of a family, pointing out that 'the Lord Chancellor, at his best, appeared so poor a substitute for the love and pride of parents'; and to emphasize the resemblance between the breakdown of social institutions and family failure, he presented a succession of inadequate and heartless parents. Lady Dedlock, who has lost the child of her love-match with Captain Hawdon, lives out her lie of a life with Sir Leicester while her lover dies in debt and misery; Mrs. Jellyby, a selfish fanatic for the rights of Africans, neglects her long-suffering husband and children; and the self-important Mr. Turveydrop actually persuades his exploited son to admire him. Even John Jarndyce, the one figure of unimpaired and warm-hearted strength in the gloomy story, is unable to protect the orphans for whom he is responsible. His protégée Esther Summerson is emotionally crushed by her sense of illegitimacy, temporarily blinded, and permanently scarred by the smallpox, and the engagement of his pathetic wards, Ada Clare and Richard Carstone, is driven to a disastrous end by Carstone's obsession with his dubious birthright. All the characters, in fact, are in some way victims, whose truth is half hidden in the swirling fog of guilt about their origins and doubt about their rightful places in the world. Dickens had repeatedly used that theme in the earlier novels which sprang from his childhood experience, but in *Bleak House* he broadened his focus to the parental mysteries and the testing problems of adult family life. There was not a normal or satisfactory marriage in the book, and not a single child was brought up to be independent, happy, and uninhibitedly affectionate.

It was a powerful but confusing novel. There was some praise for its political satire and its pathos, and most reviewers paid the now customary tribute to the genius of its author. 'Mr. Dickens has rarely if ever been happier than in *Bleak House*,' the *Athenaeum* curiously remarked of a book noteworthy for its pervading gloom. Yet more attention than usual was given to its shortcomings. The *Rambler* insisted that the novel was 'inferior to anything Dickens has written before', and other critics complained that the plot was weak, that the device of two distinct narrators made for muddled construction, and that the humour was deficient. Dickens was also criticized for his habit of exaggerating physical defects into points of character and for trying to discredit a whole class of persons by caricaturing the foibles of an individual—he hit at Low Church clergymen through Mr. Chadband, female reformers through Mrs. Jellyby, and lawyers through Mr. Tulkinghorn. 'He has added some new full-lengths to his dreaded gallery of the Denounced,' the *Illustrated London News* remarked. The *Spectator* suggested that his work had begun to pall: 'had his genius gone on growing and maturing, acquiring art by study and reflection,' it wrote, 'it would not be easy to limit the admiration and homage'. As it was, the magazine concluded, Dickens might amuse his readers 'without profoundly affecting their intellects or deeply stirring their emotions'.[56] Even Forster, who lyrically praised his friend, shared this widespread sense of disappointment and considered the latest story too much observed and lacking in imagination. 'It is the romance of discontent and misery', he wrote, 'with a very dissatisfied moral and is too much brought about by agencies disagreeable and sordid.'[57] Forster also felt that Dickens had overstepped the mark of friendly courtesy in using Walter Savage Landor as the model for the boisterous Squire Boythorn and, more painfully, in making the selfish sponger Harold Skimpole such a recognizable sketch of Leigh Hunt. Dickens had not intended to cause offence. In every one of his books he had worked up relatives, friends, and passers-by into his characters—when a woman wrote to complain that she was identifiable as the dwarfish Miss Mowcher in an early part of *Copperfield* he generously recast the role in a later instalment—and he had assured Forster as the proofs of *Bleak House* had come in that he would 'soften down words here and there'. He ended, in fact, by making substantial changes, yet Forster still complained that 'the radical wrong remained'.

Forster had sensed a change in Dickens. The darker side of his personality had always cast a shadow over his life and work; and yet he had seemed able to draw upon its hidden powers to complement his vivacity and humour. As he reached middle age, however, the shadow became the dominant aspect of that creative relationship, and he came more and more to depend upon its angry melancholy force for his energy. The change was reflected in the novels after *David Copperfield*. It affected his friendships, for he dropped away from the social habits of a man of letters and began to consort more with business cronies and such raffish young men as Wilkie Collins, which provoked Forster to irritation and jealousy. It showed in his family relationships, for the shadow fell ominously across his marriage, and there were no more gay holidays at Broadstairs; in his health, which had broken down significantly during the writing of *Bleak House*; and in his pessimistic attitude towards the doctrine of material progress and the smug bourgeois values of Victorian society. His desire to move on, the restless anger to escape, were symptoms of underlying dread and despair.

In January 1853 Dickens asked Collins to 'a bellyful of Gin Punch on Sunday next at 5 at the "Family Arms"' to discuss a jaunt across Europe when *Bleak House* was finished.[58] Augustus Egg was to make up the party. By the end of September Dickens was almost ready. He breezed through a pile of work with Wills to stock up *Household Words* in his absence, quickly finished off his *Child's History* at 1688, put Alfred and Frank into school at Boulogne, and arranged to get the rest of the family back to England. Before he left, the Guild of Literature and Art put on a dinner at the London Tavern which was 'a most amazingly gorgeous and brilliant affair... turtle cooked in six ways', which Dickens considered was almost perfect, spoilt only by Forster's obvious jealousy which made him 'a very uncomfortable and restless Chairman'.[59]

On 10 October the three men left Boulogne for Paris, where Miss Coutts had paused on a long holiday to recover from the annoying attentions of an insane Irish barrister who followed her about to press proposals of marriage. She entertained the travellers sumptuously, and they went on to Strasburg and Switzerland. From Lausanne Dickens wrote to Catherine to send news of their old friends William Haldimand, Cerjat, and Chauncy Hare Townshend, at whose house they had again dined with the travelling Miss Coutts. From Geneva they went to Chamonix, then over the Simplon Pass to Milan and Genoa. Both Collins and Egg found it difficult to keep pace with Dickens. Collins, who liked his creature comforts, was harangued by Dickens for complaining about the inns and the rapacity of innkeepers—a sore point because Dickens was in charge of the accounts and Collins, less well off, thought him too free-handed. Dickens also found Collins an irritating whistler. Yet they were, on the whole, a good-humoured trio. As their carriage rolled on through the Italian countryside Collins made notes for articles which he hoped to sell to Bentley for the *Miscellany*, Egg was studying Italian, and Dickens himself stared eagerly out of the window. The risk of brigands was so great on some parts of the road that when the travellers rode at night they tied strings from their wrists to their baggage on the roof so that they would be awakened by any attempt to rob them.

Dickens was now growing a moustache and beard, and Egg and Collins were imitating him, producing whiskers which he declared to Georgina were 'more given to wandering into strange places and sprouting up noses and dribbling under chins, than anything... since the Flood': to set a better example he impetuously shaved off his own beard.[60] He showed his companions the Palazzo Peschiere, now a school for girls, and sent home reports about acquaintances they had not seen for ten years. On the crowded steamer to Naples both Collins and Egg were accommodated in the store-room, sleeping among the pickles, fruits, and 'a very large double Glo'ster cheese'; Dickens slept in the steward's tiny cabin with the engine 'under the pillow'.[61] They made their way north to Rome. 'I am so restless to be doing,' Dickens wrote to Angela Coutts, 'always shall be, I think... that if I were to stay more than a week in any one city here, I believe I should be half desperate to begin some new story!!!'[62] At Rome there were two peevish letters from Forster, complaining that Wills was editing *Household Words* without any reference to him, but Dickens was now in too cheerful a mood to be upset by petty jealousies. 'We lead the most luxurious dandy-dilettante sort of life here,' Collins wrote to his mother from Venice. 'We live among pictures and palaces all day, and among Operas, Ballets and Cafés more than half the night.'[63] After a visit to hear Verdi's *Nabucco* Dickens described the procession led by Collins with 'incipient moustache, spectacles, slender legs, and extremely dirty dress gloves—Egg second, in a white hat, and a straggly mean little black beard—Inimitable bringing up the rear, in full dress and big sleeved great coat, rather considerably ashamed'.[64] He was by now looking forward to his return—'I miss you *very much*,' he wrote to Catherine from Rome on 14 November—but he felt the holiday had been an admirable change. 'I could not have done a better thing to clear my mind and freshen it up again.'[65]

A few days later Dickens wrote to Catherine from Turin to tell her that he had seen the de la Rues in Genoa on his way south. Except for a brief visit they had made to London in October 1851 to see the Great Exhibition he had not met them since the rendezvous in Vevey in 1846. He had again offered to mesmerize Madame de la Rue, but she had declined. All the same, he wrote to de la Rue after his visit on 28 October, that it was 'a great happiness to me to see her again, even for so short a time, and to see her looking so well and to find her in her old brave spirits'.[66] He was so touched by their warm-hearted messages to Catherine that he tried to restore good relations. He suggested, 'very seriously and affectionately', to Catherine that she should send Madame de la Rue a friendly note. 'I am perfectly clear that your position beside these people is not a good one—is not worthy of you at all.... If you could do this without any secret reservation in your own mind you would do an unquestionably upright thing.' He assured Catherine that she had been unreasonably suspicious in Genoa: his obsession with the treatment of Madame de la Rue was no more than a quirk of personality which made him pursue any enthusiasm as zealously. 'Whatever made you unhappy in the Genoa time had no other root, beginning, middle or end, than whatever has made you proud and honoured in your married life and given you station better than rank, and surrounded you with many enviable things.' He outlined the letter he wished her to send, complimenting Augusta de la Rue upon her cheerfulness despite her sufferings, and hoping that any reunion might be 'a friendly association without any sort of shadow upon it'.[67] The appeal was successful, and the letter was sent.

On the way home for Christmas the three friends were met in Paris by Charley, carrying a discouraging report from his instructor. He had now left Eton for commercial studies in Leipzig. Although he had made reasonable progress in German, he lacked the application to make a success of the course at the commercial school, 'His inclinations are all good', Dickens wrote sadly to Miss Coutts in terms very similar to those he used to describe Richard Carstone's 'indecision of character' in *Bleak House*, 'but I think he has less fixed purpose and energy than I could have supposed possible in my son. He is not aspiring or imaginative in his own behalf.' Dickens simply blamed his wife for the boy's shortcomings. 'With all the tenderer and better qualities which he inherits from his mother,' he concluded, 'he inherits an indescribable lassitude of character ... which seems to me to express the want of a strong compelling hand always beside him.'[68]

The hectoring attitude always flashed out of Dickens when he was disappointed. It was there in his reproofs to Kate when they were engaged, and in his reactions after they were married; it lay behind the irresponsible sarcasm with which he greeted each of her later pregnancies. The children felt it too, often with crushing force. Dickens wanted them to be charming, clever, and to show initiative. His letters were full of phrases extolling their virtues when they were small, and promising great things to come from each new member of the family. And yet he left them little emotional space in which to develop such qualities. They were expected to perform to his rules and to come up to his expectations. If they did so, they were entertained and spoiled by an indulgent father; and at any sign of failure they were made to feel guilty. Charley was the first to show the effects of this ambivalent attitude, but one boy after another grew up with the same anxious desire to please and lacking in self-confidence and independence.

Dickens revealed the same trait in his business dealings and in his work at Urania Cottage. He arrived home from Italy to find that a girl who had come from Petworth prison was threatening to bolt after a friend who had run away. When Dickens said she would be turned out, she broke down and begged to stay. 'I told Mrs. Morson', he reported to Miss Coutts, 'to give her no hope or relief all night.' When the girl's spirit was broken he relented, 'as it was the great forgiving Christmas time', but he improved the occasion by sending a message to all the inmates reminding them that the Home 'was *not* the place for those who audaciously slighted the shelter of the only roof interposed between them and the great black world of Crime and Shame'.[69] And his ambiguous feelings broke through again in his political attitudes. On the one hand he was emotionally attracted to dissenters, rebels, social freaks, and even criminal outcasts. On the other he was eager for order, strong for authority, and warm for those who sought to improve themselves by honest toil and education. On one occasion he decided 'to try my hand as prosecutor'. After being derided by a saucy young woman he asked a constable to 'take that girl into custody, on my charge, for using bad language in the streets'. The policeman had never heard of such a charge. 'I had,' Dickens insisted; 'so he took the girl and I went home for my Police Act.' The case came up next day before the magistrate, who somewhat incredulously asked, 'Do you really wish this girl to be sent to prison?' To which Dickens primly answered: 'If I didn't, why should I take the trouble to come here?' The girl was then fined ten shillings and told she would serve ten days in prison if she failed to pay.[70]

Dickens seemed to react in real life and in his fiction as if there were two poles to his personality. While he was travelling in Italy he told Angela Coutts that he was upset by reports of strikes at Preston and 'symptoms of rioting' at Blackburn, and he contrasted the strikers with the respectful workingmen he saw at literary institutes and lyceums. 'I wish you could come to Birmingham', he wrote to Miss Coutts, 'and see *those* working people on the night when I have so many of them together. I have never seen them collected in any number in that place, without extraordinary pleasure—even when they have been agitated by political events.'[71] They were, he felt, the best of the audience that packed the Birmingham town hall at the end of December 1853 when, accompanied by Frank Beard and Collins, he gave the first public readings from his books. On 27 December he read from *A Christmas Carol* for three hours; two nights later he gave extracts from *The Cricket on the Hearth*; and on 30 December he did the *Carol* again, most of the two thousand places being reserved for artisans and their families at reduced prices. 'They lost nothing, misinterpreted nothing, followed everything closely, laughed and cried,' he reported to Mrs. Watson, 'and animated me to that extent that I felt as if we were all bodily going up into the clouds together.'[72] The readings did much for the new educational Institute, bringing in over £400 for its endowment fund. They did more for Dickens. They proved, as he had for some time suspected, that public readings from his works could be popular and profitable; by this device he could fuse the kind of acclaim he had enjoyed in his theatrical ventures with the direct response he sought from the readers of his novels. The role of actor-manager, which he played with such vigour, was about to be transformed into that of author-actor. The impulse to perform, which his father had encouraged in his childhood songs and recitations, had become increasingly powerful over the years; when he was a young man, with a taste for theatrical entertainment, it had been no more than a pleasant hobby, but it was now breaking through into his professional life and changing it.

Back at Tavistock House, the actor-manager had an engagement for Twelfth Night. When he returned from Italy, he told Angela Coutts, 'I found the children getting up a dull charade.' He at once intervened, and characteristically took charge of the business himself. He adapted Fielding's *Tom Thumb* for the occasion, and the four-year-old Henry Fielding—'who has a remarkable ear for music'—was cast in the title role.[73] Dickens, billing himself as the 'Modern Garrick', played a ghost, Mark Lemon was a giantess, and there were parts for all the family. The Lemon children, too, were now old enough to take part, and as they lived close by in Gordon Street, there was much coming and going between the two houses. It was good fun and the jollity was infectious. Thackeray, who was one of the party guests, fell off his chair in a fit of laughter.

15

Black and White

IN January 1854, when Bradbury and Evans told Dickens that the sales of *Household Words* were declining, the publishers suggested a familiar restorative. Dickens should write a new serial for the magazine. Although he had so recently finished both *Bleak House* and his *Child's History* he agreed without much demur because he already had a theme in mind. The idea of a parable on the industrial system, he admitted later in the year, 'laid hold of me by the throat in a very violent manner'.[1] He had in fact been thinking of some such story since 1838, when he had been appalled by the Manchester mills at the time he was writing *Nickleby*; and he had always been disturbed by strikes and other outbreaks in the factory districts. While he had been away in Italy the weavers of Preston had been locked out after they had closed one mill after another in a running strike for a 10 per cent increase in wages; it was a bitter dispute, that dragged on for twenty-nine weeks, and Dickens came to the conclusion that it would provide the background for 'a story which has a direct purpose in reference to the working people all over England'.

At the end of January he took the train northwards to Lancashire, at the end of the newly built line, and he quickly collected impressions of the closed Preston cotton-mills and their idle operatives. It was less easy to marshal this grim material into a serial. When Dickens wrote *The Old Curiosity Shop* he had complained that weekly climaxes spoilt the effect; he still disliked the short rhythm imposed by publication in *Household Words*; and, to make matters worse, he had decided to compress the novel he called *Hard Times* into less than half the length of *Bleak House*. 'The difficulty of the space', he wrote to Forster as he began to map out his work, 'is CRUSHING.'[2] He persevered ('here I am with my armour on again', he wrote to Emile de la Rue in March) and the first part appeared on 1 April 1854.[3] Despite its depressing theme the story did what Bradbury and Evans wanted. The circulation of *Household Words* had doubled by June, and it continued to rise as the serial ran on to mid-August.

In addition to his weekly stint at the serial Dickens had to spend a good deal of effort on editing *Household Words* in the early months of 1854. Wills was still unwell, and in April he went off to Malvern to take the waters and rest. 'I am in a dreary state,'[4] Dickens wrote to Wills on 15 April, feeling that *Hard Times* was too much of a strain. As usual he sought relief in vigorous distractions. Spiritualism, a cult of the dead which had an easy appeal to a society so afflicted by bereavement and so given to religiosity as middle-class England, had come across the Atlantic. Dickens, already disposed to such a fad by his interest in mesmerism, was for a time much taken up with table-rapping. He was also, as he told Mark Lemon, 'on a regimen of fresh air'.[5] Lemon was walked off to a Thames-side tavern to see performing dogs: Wilkie Collins was taken up to Hampstead Heath, and then to Tunbridge Wells. There were convivial dinners at the Athenaeum and the Garrick, and down at Greenwich, and a delightful few days when Macready arrived in town.

On 13 March 1854 Sir Thomas Talfourd died as he was addressing the grand jury at the opening of the Stafford Assizes. In his unfinished address Talfourd was regretting the number of criminal offences which revealed 'that separation between class and class which is the great curse of British society'; and he had reminded his listeners that 'we have men and women growing up around us, ministering to our comforts, supplying our wants, and continual inmates of our dwellings, with whose affections and tempers we are as little acquainted as if they were the inhabitants of some other sphere'. Those words exactly expressed the spirit in which Dickens had decided to write *Hard Times*, and two weeks later in *Household Words* he underlined what he called a 'righteous warning' against each order of society 'holding itself aloof', as well as recalling Talfourd's early encouragement to the youthful Boz.

It was twenty years since Dickens had written the first of the sketches that launched his career, and in the early summer of 1854 he had another and happier reminder of his early days of success. Several of the novels had been dramatized by the actor Frederick Yates; his son Edmund, who had literary aspirations, now introduced himself at Tavistock House. When Dickens saw the young man he was struck by the likeness to his father; but Edmund Yates, who had grown up with the impression of Dickens formed by the Maclise portrait of 1839, was shocked to see a middle-aged man. 'His hair', Yates recalled, 'tho' long, was beginning to be sparse: his cheeks were shaved: a moustache and "door-knocker" beard. His eyes bright and piercing: his bearing hearty and somewhat aggressive.'[6]

When Yates called at the house Dickens was preparing to transport the family across to Boulogne again. Georgina had gone over in April to inspect a larger house owned by last year's landlord, M. Beaucourt; Dickens reported to Wills that it 'beats the former residence all to nothing'. Once again the congenial owner hovered about the family 'like a guardian genius',[7] and Dickens was delighted to find that in the Villa du Camp de Droite, which was much higher above the town with splendid views, there were even more 'wonderful inventions and contrivances' than in the house he had taken the previous summer—'and all for five guineas a week!'[8] On 22 June, four days after he arrived, Dickens reported to Wills that he had written only seventy-two words of *Hard Times*; but within a couple of weeks he was 'stunned with work',[9] and he told Forster that the 'perpetual rushing' at the book had left him 'three parts mad and the fourth part delirious'.[10] Three days later he had finished, and he carried the last pages across to London. He celebrated that night with Wilkie Collins at the Garrick; next day he went to the opera with Angela Coutts; and on the third night, after seeing the Spanish dancers at the Haymarket, he sat drinking gin slings with the manager until dawn. He had, he wrote to Georgina on 22 July, been living 'in a blaze of dissipation altogether and have succeeded (I think) in knocking the remembrance of my work out'.[11]

Hard Times, which Dickens had originally thought of calling 'Black and White' because he wished to dramatize its theme of confrontation, had proved a discomforting experience. In his previous book Dickens had satirized an archaic and corrupt system of laws which ruined people through its indifference to human needs and feelings. The anger which had fired *Bleak House* remained to drive the hammering prose of *Hard Times*, in which he attacked a different kind of system—the equally inhuman laws of political economy which took their name from Manchester—to point the same kind of moral. Preston was the epitome of that system. The masters and the operatives grinding harshly together belonged to the world of Fact, of markets and statistical averages and other abstractions, controlled by men whom Carlyle described as 'steam-engine intellects', always working and always learning as though the search for utility were the mainspring of life and factual knowledge the precise measure of its progress. And against that emotionally bleak society, whose spokesmen are Bounderby, Gradgrind, and M'Choakumchild, Dickens set another world of Fancy, filled with the fairy-tale people of the circus, who come and go on the fringes of Coketown like whisps of imagination in the smoke.

All the characters except the circus folk, indeed, are victims of a system which is impersonally destroying them by setting one against another. 'There is some love in the world,' the circus-master Sleary says, 'and it is not all self-interest.' But the iron laws of *laissez-faire* leave little room for affection and compassion. Stephen Blackpool, a workingman ground down by the principles of competition and miserably married to a drunkard, is rejected by his workmates because he refuses to join their union; and yet he is driven out of Coketown by his heartless employer, Bounderby, who is equally hard on him. Understandably Blackpool can make no sense of things and, before he dies by falling into a disused mine in the dark, he cries repeatedly that 'It's a' a muddle'. Louisa Gradgrind, who has had all but a spark of human feeling drilled out of her by her father's relentless indoctrination of utilitarian values, succumbs to a loveless match with Bounderby and is driven towards the abyss of social destruction which faced the Victorian adulteress. Her brother Tom, who takes the dogma of self-help literally, steals from Bounderby's bank and escapes appropriately to the penal settlements in Australia. And Harthouse, the cynical adventurer whose advances had touched Louisa's buried feelings, packs his bags and leaves when her conscience prevails. It was impossible, for once, for Dickens to bring himself to the happy ending his readers preferred, for in his all-or-nothing hatred of the system he had forced the logic of its rules to determine the end of the game. By the last pages every one of the characters has died, or fled from Coketown; or, like Bounderby and the frigid Mrs. Sparsit, is condemned to a living death; or is making the best of a sadly damaged life, like Louisa and her repentant father, the saintly Rachael who had befriended Blackpool, and Cissy Jupe, who came from the circus into this grey world and still mourns the broken-down father who abandoned her. The grimy townscape of Coketown, 'where grapes are gathered from thorns, and figs from thistles', has proved too arid for anything human to flourish.

The conclusion was deliberate, and political. Dickens had even worked in a reference to Parliament as the 'national dust-yard', where the 'national dustmen' engaged in noisy mock battles while the people starved. *Hard Times*, he told Carlyle in a letter asking if he might dedicate the book to him, 'contains nothing in which you do not think with me, for no man knows your books better than I'.[12] The attack on what Carlyle called 'the cash nexus' of Victorian England also appealed to John Ruskin, then at the peak of his reputation. Ruskin realized that Dickens had exaggerated for effect, but approved of his moralizing against selfishness and the corrupting power of money; and Ruskin concluded that 'his view was finally the right one, grossly and sharply told'.[13] The historian Macaulay, in contrast, dismissed the tale as 'sullen socialism' and its plot as 'disagreeable and over-strained'.[14] And other critics objected to its melodramatic tone and didactic radicalism. Dickens normally shrugged off criticism, except from such professional intimates as Forster and Collins, but on this occasion he replied with a denial that he was stirring up class conflict. What he desired, he said, was a coming together of men of goodwill to make life better for 'the hardest-worked people on whom the sun shines',[15] and he saw the possibility of meeting a penitent Mr. Gradgrind 'at some halfway house where there are flowers on the carpets, and a little standing-room for Queen Mab's chariot among the Steam Engines'.[16]

The novel done, Dickens began to idle. When the weather was sunny he drowsed with a book in a haystack; when it rained he went for long walks and got wet. He organized ball games and clay-pigeon shooting, and entertained his visitors—Beard and Mitton among his oldest friends, Evans, Wills, Collins and Egg among the newer ones. He gave a series of sittings to the painter E. M. Ward. And Thackeray was spending the summer at Boulogne with his family in a house on the Paris road. His daughters were close in age to Mamie and Kate, and had been frequent guests in London; they came to the Villa du Camp de Droite, where Lemon's daughters were also staying, for games of forfeits and 'buzz'.

There was a real military camp in the fields which gave the villa its name, for in March the British and French had put aside their long enmity to become allies against Russia: the forty-year peace which had lasted since the Congress of Vienna was broken by the ill-conceived and appallingly executed campaign in the Crimea. Dickens was fascinated by the military exercises just down the road; in September the Prince Consort sailed over to join Napoleon III in a review, and Dickens met the pair of them riding as he took his daily walk. All three celebrities raised their hats. When, to celebrate the review, Dickens illuminated the eighteen front windows of the villa with over a hundred candles, M. Beaucourt was so excited that he '*danced* and *screamed* on the grass'. Yet, as he told Mrs. Watson, he was 'full of mixed feeling about the war—admiration of our valiant men, burning desires to cut the Emperor of Russia's throat, and something like despair to see how the old cannon-smoke and blood-mists obscure the wrongs and sufferings of the people at home'.[17]

In this mood he accepted an even grimmer industrial novel than *Hard Times* to follow it in his magazine. He had greatly admired Mrs. Gaskell's new story, *Ruth*, which dealt sympathetically with a fallen woman and caused something of a stir, and he was delighted when she offered him the chance of serializing *North and South*. It was not a fortunate arrangement. Mrs. Gaskell was always slow to make a start, she disliked being pressed for copy, she found it almost impossible to shape her plots to meet the dramatic demands of a weekly serial, and she was most recalcitrant about corrections. On every point Dickens had to assert his editorial needs against her. 'It is perfectly plain to me that if we put in more, every week, of North and South than we did of Hard Times', he wrote anxiously to Wills in a letter from Boulogne which berated the printers for underestimating the length of Mrs. Gaskell's manuscript, 'we shall ruin Household Words.'[18] He was, he added, 'unspeakably vexed by all this needless trouble'.[19] When the first section of the novel appeared in the issue of 2 September it was clear that Dickens had been right to worry: by October the sales had fallen markedly. 'I am not surprised,' Dickens responded to this bad news from Wills. 'Mrs. Gaskell's story, so divided, is wearisome in the last degree.... Never mind! I am ready to come up to the scratch on my return, and to shoulder the wheel.'[20]

He had, meanwhile, startled his readers with a passionate article on 7 October. Addressed 'To Working Men', it was an outburst against the slum conditions in the industrial towns; all that summer a cholera epidemic had been sweeping through the country, and killed over twenty thousand people. Dickens himself had a severe shock in September when Mamie collapsed with 'English Cholera'—a severe but seldom fatal infection; happily, his friend Dr. Elliotson was staying in Boulogne and he assisted Dickens in treating the attack. Dickens, with a house full of young children, was alarmed, and his fright intensified his anger. Cholera came out of the slums, and in his article he urged the workers to demand 'Homes, instead of polluted dens'. They could expect little from Parliament. It was full of 'sharking mountebanks ... contesting for places, power, and patronage'. He hoped, he told Forster in a gloss on this article, 'to have made every man in England feel something of the contempt for the House of Commons that I have'.[21] And his loosely worded appeal to the workingmen to sweep away 'the Indifferents and the Incapables' and bring in a new government by Christmas seemed to threaten more than reform. Miss Coutts certainly took it as provocation to violence, for she wrote to protest that such rhetoric was dangerous when the workers had no votes. Dickens sent her an ambiguous reply. The 'worthless government', he insisted, would do nothing until sanitary reforms 'are made election questions and the working people unite to express their determination to have them'. The war, he dolefully predicted, 'will be made an administrative excuse for all sorts of shortcomings ... nothing will have been done when the cholera comes again'. He concluded with an apocalyptic prophecy that there could come 'such a shake in this country as was never before seen on Earth since Samson pulled the Temple down upon his head'.[22]

In the autumn of 1854 his public language was violent. The war had accentuated the anxious feelings which afflicted him when he finished a novel. 'I have had dreadful thoughts of getting away somewhere altogether by myself,' he told Forster in October. 'I have visions of living for half a year or so, in all sorts of inaccessible places, and opening a new book therein. ... *Restlesssness*, you will say. Whatever it is, it is always driving me and I cannot help it. I have rested nine or ten weeks, and sometimes feel as if it had been a year—though I had the strangest nervous miseries before I stopped. If I couldn't walk fast and far, I should just explode and perish.'[23]

That tense state of mind persisted after the family returned to Tavistock House in mid-October. Dickens had no book in hand to absorb his energies, and he had to content himself with planning the Christmas festivities. He decided to give more readings from *A Christmas Carol*, since the experiment had been so successful in Birmingham the previous year. The first, at Reading on 19 December 1854, was in memory of his old friend Talfourd, who had been the town's Member of Parliament. On the next day he read at Sherborne, where Macready had helped to promote a literary institute. And on 28 December he read to almost four thousand people in Bradford on behalf of the Mechanics' Institute. Meanwhile, at Tavistock House, work was in hand for the customary Twelfth Night play on the schoolroom stage, for which Dickens adapted *Fortunio and His Seven Gifted Servants* by the prolific English dramatist James Planché. There were parts for all—Mark Lemon and Marcus Stone and their families, Wilkie Collins, and all the Dickens children—including the baby 'Mr. Plornishmaroontigoonter (who has been kept out of bed at a vast expence)' and Charley, specially billed as back from his German engagements. Dickens joked about Charley, and worried about him. His eldest son, he fretfully confessed to Angela Coutts, was very anxious to make a beginning: 'And so, indeed, is his father.'[24] But the boy clearly lacked aptitude for a commercial career, and Dickens unsuccessfully canvassed his business and banking friends for a suitable opening. Meanwhile Charley filled in time in the office of *Household Words*.

The war news provided a grim background to the holiday season, and Dickens had no hesitation in using his magazine to express his critical opinions. After the battle of Balaclava on 25 October, and the bloody victory of the outnumbered British infantry at Inkerman on 5 November, winter and disease struck the troops in the Crimea. According to John Roebuck, the Radical M.P. for Sheffield, by Christmas more than two-thirds of the 54,000 men were dead of wounds, typhoid, cholera, frostbite, and general neglect; and the ensuing scandal brought down the government of Lord Aberdeen. Even in England it was an unusually cold winter—on his birthday Dickens walked from Gravesend to Rochester between walls of snow—and the army was not equipped for the Russian climate. The wretched soldiers, Dickens believed, were as much victims of political economy as the workers he had described in *Hard Times*—victims of men who calculated in 'figures and averages, and nothing else . . . addled heads who would take the average of cold in the Crimea during twelve months as a reason for clothing a soldier in nankeens on a night when he would be frozen to death in fur'. Since such bureaucrats apparently controlled the War Office, and all the other offices upon which the miserable army depended for its supplies, the mere change of government would make little difference. In a parody of the

Arabian Nights, which Dickens wrote for *Household Words* after Aberdeen's defeat, he was just as scathing about the new Prime Minister, describing Lord Palmerston as the 'Twirling Weathercock'. And he resented public apathy as much as official complacency. 'I have a dreadful belief that the army will be virtually no more in another six weeks,' he wrote to Miss Coutts on 25 January 1855, as one scandal followed another. 'I have made up my mind', he told her, 'that what one can do in print to wake the sleepers, one is bound to do at such a serious juncture.'[25] As a more practical form of help he commissioned, on her behalf, an elaborate drying apparatus for use in Florence Nightingale's hospital at Scutari. 'The Machine', a doctor who saw it in operation reported to Dickens, 'does great credit to Miss Coutts's philanthropy and also to your engineering.'[26] Dickens himself claimed that the device was 'the only solitary "administrative" thing, connected with the war, that has been a success!'

Theatricals had been one distraction in this unhappy winter, the cause of the suffering soldiery another: yet neither sufficed to shake Dickens out of what he described to Forster as his 'dishevelled state of mind'. He could not explain what he felt was wrong, but he referred ominously to 'miseries of an older growth threatening to close upon me'. He had another impulse to run away—to Bordeaux, this time, or the Pyrenees—and he was brooding again about his childhood feelings of deprivation. 'Why is it', he asked, 'a sense comes always crushing on me now, when I fall into low spirits, as of one happiness I have missed in life, and one friend and companion I have never made?'[27] It was not clear to Forster what he meant. But the style—the romantic, self-commiserating nostalgia with which David Copperfield spoke of his past—was unmistakable; and the anguished question hinted at the deep sense of deprivation which so closely underlay his exuberance. The unknown happiness and the undiscovered friend were pursued through life as idealized images of unfulfilled desire.

For a time in his youth Dickens thought he had found that complementary emotion in Maria Beadnell, and though he had lost touch with her the memory of that disappointed love had remained astonishingly fresh. On 10 February 1855, the morning before he was due to leave with Wilkie Collins on a week's jaunt to Paris in the hope of raising his spirits, Dickens recognized the handwriting on one of an otherwise uninteresting delivery of letters. It was from Maria. 'Three or four and twenty years vanished like a dream', he wrote to her at once, 'and I opened it with the touch of my young friend David Copperfield when he was in love.' Maria, married to a City merchant named Henry Winter, was now forty-four and the mother of two daughters, but Dickens still saw her with the eyes of youth. 'It is impossible to be spoken to out of the old times', he wrote to her, 'without a softened emotion'; and in that nostalgic mood he told her that he hoped that she and her husband would come to a quiet dinner on his return from Paris.[28]

The holiday with Collins was enjoyable. Dickens wrote to Wills on 16 February saying that he was staying at the Hotel Meurice as 'a free and easy sort of superior vagabond',[29] and Collins described their 'delightful apartment, looking out on the Tuileries, gorgeously furnished drawing-room, bedrooms with Turkey carpets, reception-room, hall, cupboards, passages—all to ourselves'.[30] They dined well, and went to the theatre every evening. Yet Dickens continued to moon over his memories of Maria, and he wrote to her again. 'I have never been so good a man since, as I was when you made me wretchedly happy,' he told her; *David Copperfield* had shown how dearly he had loved her and how vividly he remembered that 'the most innocent, the most ardent, and the most disinterested days of my life had you for their Sun'.[31] Maria replied in kind, encouraging him to more sentimental recriminations. 'Though it is so late to read in the old hand what I never read before I have read it with great emotion, and with the old tenderness softened to a more sorrowful remembrance than I could easily tell you,' he wrote. 'How it all happened as it did, we shall never know this side of Time; but if you had ever told me then what you tell me now, I know myself well enough to be thoroughly assured that the simple truth and energy which were in my love would have overcome everything.'

The flow of romantic fantasies was so strong that it swept reality aside. 'You ask me to treasure what you tell me, in my heart of hearts,' Dickens replied to Maria. 'O see what I have cherished there, through all this time and all these changes!'[32] He took no notice of her insistence that she was now 'toothless, fat, old and ugly'. 'My entire devotion to you, and the wasted tenderness of those hard years which I have ever since half loved, half dreaded to recall, made so deep an impression on me that I refer to it a habit of suppression which now belongs to me, which I know is no part of my original nature, but which makes me chary of showing my affections, even to my children, except when they are very young.'[33] He then seized on her suggestion that they should have a private meeting before the proposed family dinner. By this, he wrote, 'you open the way to a confidence between us which still once more, in perfect innocence and good faith, may be between ourselves alone'. Could she call at Tavistock House on Sunday afternoon 25 February, 'asking first for Catherine and then for me?' It was almost a certainty that he would be alone. 'Remember,' he added eagerly, 'I accept all with my whole soul, and reciprocate all.'[34]

The meeting was not simply an anticlimax: it was a severe shock, shatter-ing the evocative dreams in which Dickens had indulged for the past two weeks. Maria was indeed fat; her teasing laugh had degenerated into a giggle;

her run of charming chatter had become a stream of affected verbosity; and her intimate manner had become an embarrassing familiarity. He confessed his disappointment and distress to Forster, who thought he was exaggerating. Dickens insisted that his love for Maria had shaped his life: it had so steeled his ambition with suffering 'that to see the mere cause of it all, now, loosens my hold upon myself'. The pain had been great when he remembered his youth to write *Copperfield*. 'And, just as I can never open that book as I open any other book, I cannot see the face (even at four-and-forty), or hear the voice, without wandering away over the ashes of all that youth and hope in the wildest manner.'[35] The shock of seeing Maria had a strange effect on Dickens. It did not help him to bear the pain of reality: it only made him turn away from it with greater desperation. It seemed that he had been in love with his own dreams rather than Maria Beadnell. He nevertheless managed to fulfil some of the practical obligations of his impetuosity. The dinner with her husband and Catherine on 7 March had to be borne; Maria came with a sniffling cold which Dickens caught, and there was an uncomfortable similarity between her unattractive domesticity and Catherine's appearance and manner. That prosaic evening, he decided, must be an end to the matter, though Maria continued to press him for more meetings. She proposed to call one Sunday afternoon with one of her children. Dickens made sure he was out, and when she called again he sent her a kindly explanation. 'A necessity is upon me now—as at most times,' he wrote, 'of wandering about in my own wild way, to think. I could no more resist this on Sunday or yesterday, than a man can dispense with food, or a horse can help himself from being driven.'[36] All the same, Maria called a few more times at Tavistock Place; Dickens once went with Catherine to call on her at home, and noticed that she took brandy in her tea, and he sent her a kind note when her baby died in June. But from the moment he had first laid eyes on her again at the end of February he had been seeking an inoffensive way of disentangling himself. The episode had disorientated him, leaving him more than ever frustrated and angry.

He also broke out irritably on public issues. The first of his targets was the Royal Literary Fund. He had joined it in 1837, had been elected to its general committee in 1839, and although he seldom attended a meeting he had sat on its council until 1854. By that time he had become critical of its old-fashioned style of patronage, which seemed part of the system of jobbery which had led to the disasters of the Crimean War; and his criticism was intensified when his scheme for the Guild of Literature and Art had been put into suspense for seven years. He busied himself, with Forster, Charles Wentworth Dilke, and other friends, in organizing a reform faction with the aim of getting control of the Fund and merging it with the Guild.

They launched their attack at the annual meeting of the Fund on 14 March 1855. The Fund, they argued, was extravagant and self-indulgent, devoting too much of its income to the upkeep of its own comfortable premises in Great Russell Street and too little on authors who needed help; and they objected to the manner in which the constitution reduced the council to a cypher and put all the power into the hands of the committee. At the meeting Dickens called for a new charter, attacked the official list of candidates, and declared that the Fund should be controlled by literary and scientific men rather than by philanthropic notabilities. He had strong arguments, but men of letters were a minority of the membership and the clique which ran the Fund was again returned. He had spoken so eloquently, however, that the meeting was persuaded to appoint a Special Committee to look into the question of a new charter, and Dickens, Forster, and Dilke were appointed to it as the spokesmen of the reform group. 'I wish you could have seen your servant last Wednesday beleaguer the Literary Fund,' Dickens wrote gleefully to Collins. 'They got so bothered and bewildered that I expected to see them all fade away under the table; and the outsiders laughed so irreverently whenever I poked up the chairman that it was quite a facetious business. Virtually, I consider the thing done.'[37] And *The Times* supported his campaign against 'our old enemy, routine ... flunkeyism and worship of rank'.

The Special Committee proposed that the council should be given more advisory powers and that the Fund should be able to award loans and annuities as well as the traditional charitable gifts; it also made the more radical suggestion that the fine premises should be made a club for authors, providing meeting and library facilities, and opening its doors to literary men from other countries. On 30 May Dickens and Forster put these suggestions to the general committee, which decided to call a special meeting of the membership to consider them. Before that meeting was convened at Willis's Rooms on 16 June it was clear that Dickens had been too quick to claim a victory. The old guard, resenting the criticism of their conduct of the Fund, had drummed up their supporters, and the reformers had proposed so many changes that they had scared off many who had originally sympathized with them. Dickens spoke smoothly of his goodwill. 'How *can* I want to work against them in so gallant a cause—if we can but work together,' he wrote to Whitwell Elwin, who edited the *Quarterly*. But he was privately devising other means of putting pressure on his opponents. He told Mark Lemon that he was waiting for the report to be printed to take it to Colonel Phipps, hoping to enlist the Queen in his campaign, 'even to the withholding of her annual subscription should they refuse to be refounded'.

At the special meeting Dickens moved the report and he was seconded by Forster. He made an amusing speech, asserting that the Fund should be run by authors for the benefit of their profession. The Fund, he declared, 'had overslept itself by a great number of years, and it was absolutely necessary to knock it up; and, please God, they would get it out of bed by some means or other'. Bulwer-Lytton also spoke, assuring the members that if the motion were carried the Guild of Literature would hand over its money. But the members carried an amendment from Monckton Milnes, rejecting the report on the grounds that it would radically alter the nature of the Fund. Dickens was disappointed, although he had been prepared for this defeat, telling Elwin before the meeting that 'our most unfortunate calling is to be defeated by agglomerated Humbug'; and, never one to give up easily, he kept the argument going long after the votes had been counted against him.[38]

He had been running a parallel campaign in the Royal General Theatrical Fund, attending its meeting on 2 April to champion the right of amateur actors to financial help, and using the occasion to gibe at the lamentable conduct of the war in the Crimea. When the Haymarket Theatre staged a battle, he declared, it did not find it impossible to fire a shot because the ammunition had been left somewhere it was not wanted.

The war continued to enrage him. He wrote angrily to Captain E. E. Morgan, an American merchant seaman who had become friendly with many English artists and men of letters, complaining that 'we have got involved in meshes of aristocratic red-tape to our unspeakable confusion, loss and sorrow'.[39] As the immensity of the scandal emerged, Dickens became a strong supporter of the campaign mounted by Sir Austen Layard, the archaeologist who had excavated Nineveh. Layard, now Radical M.P. for Aylesbury, had been out to the Crimea and returned with a list of frauds and miseries he had witnessed at first hand; for all his agitation, however, he was out-manœuvred by the Palmerston government, and when his censure came to a vote in Parliament he was defeated by 359 votes to 46. Such a setback in the House of Commons was no deterrent to Dickens, who was full of contempt for what in *Household Words* on 26 May he called 'the House of Parler and Mentir'. A better job could be done by a 'half dozen shopkeepers taken at random ... and shot into Downing Street out of sacks' than by the 'Red-Tapers and Sealing-Wax Chafers' who so cruelly mismanaged government. Dickens had no hesitation about using his paper in such a cause. 'If you ever see any new loophole, cranny, needle's-eye, through which I can present your case in *Household Words*,' he wrote to Layard on 3 April 1855, 'I most earnestly entreat you ... to count upon my being Damascus Steel to the core.'[40] What galled and alarmed him, he told Layard, was 'the alienation of the people from their own public affairs'.

In phrases which revealed his emotional tension he went on to describe the unhappy situation. 'I believe the discontent to be so much the worse for smouldering instead of blazing openly, that it is extremely like the general mind of France before the breaking out of the first Revolution, and is in danger of being turned by any one of a thousand accidents .... into such a devil of a conflagration as never has been beheld since.... And until the people can be got up from the lethargy which is an awful symptom of the advanced state of their disease, I know of nothing that can be done beyond keeping their wrongs continually before them.'[41]

When Layard's agitation led to the formation of an Administrative Reform Committee Dickens promptly joined it, telling Miss Coutts that he had decided 'to give (as a kind of example to a large class), Twenty Pounds' to its subscription. Miss Coutts disapproved: Layard's denunciations of the government and its incompetent and ageing commanders, she insisted, was setting class against class. Dickens stood by his defence of the 'disgusted millions'.

'You assume that the popular class take the initiative,' he replied on 15 May. 'Now as I read the story, the aristocratic class did that, years and years ago, and it is *they* who have put *their* class in opposition to the country—not the country which puts itself in opposition to *them*.... The people will not bear for any length of time what they bear now.'[42]

Dickens was unable to attend the first meeting of the Administrative Reform Association at the Drury Lane Theatre on 20 June, but a week later he was among the speakers at what Palmerston sneeringly called 'the private theatricals at Drury Lane'. Telling the audience that he had some experience of public and private theatricals he gibed back at Palmerston in parliamentary fashion. 'I will not say that if I wanted to form a company of Her Majesty's servants, I think I should know where to put my hands on "the comic old gentleman"; nor, that if I wanted to get up a pantomime, I fancy I should know what establishment to go to for the tricks and changes.... We have seen the *Comedy of Errors* played so dismally like a tragedy that we really cannot bear it. We are therefore making bold to get up the School of Reform.' The speech went beyond bitter jokes. The country's rulers, Dickens insisted, were inflicting far worse damage than its enemies. Palmerston might jeeringly tell Layard to find a day for himself when he asked for a debate. 'Name you the day, First Lord,' Dickens said ominously, 'and History may then—not otherwise—find a day for you.'[43] His indignation against the war broke out on social as well as political occasions. One evening at dinner with Lord Russell, for instance, he expressed his opinions so forcefully that it 'was like bringing a Sebastopol battery among the polite company'.[44]

His troubled state of mind persisted all through the spring and early summer. His restlessness, he told Angela Coutts on 8 May, was 'impossible to be described—impossible to be imagined.... I sit down of a morning, with all kinds of notes for my new book ... get up and go out, and walk a dozen miles—sit down again next morning—get up and go down a railroad—come back again and register a vow to go out of town instantly, and begin at the feet of the Pyrenees'.[45] He toyed with the notion of going to Constantinople with Layard. 'Tomorrow', he wrote to Maria Winter, 'I shall probably discuss with somebody else, the idea of going to Greenland or the North Pole.'[46] He wandered about London at all hours, made engagements and felt too distraught to keep them. 'I feel as if nothing would do me the least good but the setting up of a Balloon,' he told Wilkie Collins on 11 May.[47] He was going through the difficult preliminaries to starting a new novel. 'All my symptoms are very bad,' he reported to Angela Coutts on 24 May.[48] He had, however, at last begun the story he called 'Nobody's Fault' until he changed the title to *Little Dorrit* just before the first number was published in December 1855.

With the new tale started he needed to plan his distractions more carefully and focus his energies. He had already decided to rent a house at Folkestone for the summer and then to spend the autumn and winter in Paris, where he could press on with his writing and 'complete the polishing of Mary and Katey'. Before leaving London, as he told Clarkson Stanfield on 20 May, he had 'a little lark in contemplation' with Collins—who had written 'an odd Melodrama' called *The Lighthouse*—which, still hankering for dramatic success, Collins hoped would get a professional production by Benjamin Webster at the Adelphi Theatre. Meanwhile, Dickens put on a production in the schoolroom theatre in Tavistock House, and Stanfield was invited to provide the scenery for the one set. He did so in two days; it took up so much room that only twenty-five spectators could get into the schoolroom. Dickens made some minor changes in the text, wrote a prologue in verse and a song for Mary to sing, arranged for the invitations, and took the leading role of Aaron Gurnock, the lighthouse keeper haunted by the belief that he had murdered a man. Collins, Egg, and Lemon played the other main parts, and joined Dickens in a revival of *Mr. Nightingale's Diary*. There were four performances, including a special preview for the tradespeople. 'Such an audience!' Dickens wrote to Stanfield the morning after the last night on 19 June. 'Such a brilliant success from first to last!... Lemon and I did every conceivable absurdity, I think, in the farce; and they never left off laughing.'[49] There was a celebration supper, at which the cast, relatives, and friends danced the Scottish reels 'in the maddest way' until five in the morning. On 10 July there was a special benefit performance at Campden House in Kensington, whose owner had a fully equipped private theatre and offered the use of it to help the Bournemouth Sanatorium. A few days later, invigorated by the theatricals, Dickens took the family down to 3 Albion Villas, Folkestone, for the summer holiday: 'taking dives into a new book', he told Macready, 'and runs at leap-frog over Household Words'.[50]

16

A Dread Phaenomenon

WHEN Dickens began his new novel in May 1855 he told Mrs. Watson that he was struggling with 'an immensity', and the task proved so formidable that it took him three months to complete the first number. He knew what he wanted to do. The story of the demoralized debtor William Dorrit and his devoted daughter was relatively straightforward, and its development was carefully planned. His difficulty was more emotional than practical. The encounter with Maria Winter had stirred old feelings and left him more unsettled than ever. Ever since his family had been shut away in the Marshalsea the shameful and claustrophobic memory had haunted him; now, entangled in responsibilities from which he could see no way of escape, that enclosing shadow fell gloomily across his life and coloured *Little Dorrit*. At the same time he was outraged by the misery and mismanagement of the Crimean War. It seemed that the country was similarly caught in a web of frustration. The private and public distress fused into a sustained allegory.

Everyone within the system, it seemed to Dickens, is in some way a prisoner. The notion of living death, implicit in *Hard Times*, had become explicit in a series of images of imprisonment which succeed each other in the novel like a set of Chinese boxes. It begins in a prison, it is set in a prison, and it ends with the marriage of Little Dorrit and Arthur Clennam as they leave the Marshalsea. As the Tite Barnacles cling to their sinecures and places they become as much the prisoners as the masters of the Circumlocution Office; the greed of the financier Merdle traps him in a system which he is powerless to control; the neurotic Mrs. Clennam is locked in a world of fear and fantasy; and the inventor Doyce is manacled to his obstructed invention. Like the tragic William Dorrit, Father of the Marshalsea, who cannot escape his role even when he regains his inheritance and becomes free to travel in Europe, the characters of *Little Dorrit* are eager to escape their fate but they do not know what to do with their lives, and so carry their prison with them wherever they go and whatever they do. They are anxious, restless, and destructively irresponsible—the original plan to call the book 'Nobody's Fault' was to underline the point that where none are guilty, all are guilty. Little Dorrit herself is the exception. Childhood is the only phase of life on which the shades of the prison house have not closed and its innocence is embodied in her unsullied goodness. Unlike Little Nell she has survived into adult life, caring for her selfish father like a child-wife. Disappointments had led Dickens to idealize women more strongly than ever; and for him innocence remained the clue to perfection.

As soon as he had settled his family in Folkestone, he immersed himself in the story. 'My thoughts have been upon my book since I came down,' he wrote to Wills on 22 July 1855.[1] On previous holidays he had taken the lead in organizing games, parties, and outings, but now there were fewer visitors and even the children were often a source of worry and annoyance as much as pleasure. He was relieved when, in September, a post was found for Charley in the banking firm of Baring Brothers at a salary of £50 a year. To this, he proudly told Macready, 'I graciously assented'.[2] Walter was home from the crammer at Wimbledon where he was preparing for a military career, Frank and Alfred had come across to Folkestone from their school in Boulogne, and there were three smaller boys running about as well as Mamie, Kate, and young friends. 'I find the elder little Lemon makes too much noise ... in eating biscuits', Dickens wrote half jokingly to Wilkie Collins, but when Walter clumped on the stairs his father asked querulously why the boy 'should seem to have on at all times, 150 pair of double-soled boots, and to be always jumping a bottom stair with the whole 150'.[3] The younger boys were still a source of pride and pleasure; he was so pleased with little 'Plorn' that he informed Mrs. Watson he was thinking of putting the boy up for public competition. Long walks were the only relief from his pent-up restlessness and late in August he reported to Beard that he had been 'swarming up the face of a gigantic and precipitous cliff'.[4] Peace of mind eluded him and Wills was given regular progress reports. 'I walk downstairs once in every five minutes, look out of the window once in every two, and do nothing else,' he told him on 11 September, but five days later things were going better. 'I am steeped in my story', he wrote, 'and rise and fall by turns into enthusiasm and depression.'[5]

Dickens was in a state of despairing indignation about the political scene. It was clear that Layard's reform movement was getting nowhere and his feelings spilled out in letters to friends. He wrote to Forster in September insisting that 'representative government is become altogether a failure with us, that the English gentilities and subserviences render the people unfit for it'.[6] A few days later he enlarged on the theme, telling Macready that 'I have lost hope even in the ballot'. The country was in a hopeless state. 'What with teaching people to "keep in their stations," what with bringing up the soul and body of the land to be a good child, or to go to the beer-shop, to go a-poaching and go to the devil ... what with flunkyism, toadyism, letting the most contemptible lord come in for all manner of places, reading the Court Circular for the New Testament, I do reluctantly believe that the English people are habitually consenting parties to the miserable imbecility into which we have fallen, *and never will help themselves out of it* ... we are on the down-hill road to being conquered, and the people WILL be content to bear it, sing "Rule Britannia", and WILL NOT be saved.'[7]

These feelings were so burnt into *Little Dorrit* that it became a scathing satire on political bureaucracy, and in the third number Dickens conceived the 'scarifier' he called the Circumlocution Office.[8] 'I have been blowing off a little of indignant steam which would otherwise blow me up,' he told Macready, 'and with God's leave I shall walk in the same all the days of my life; but I have no present political faith or hope—not a grain.'[9]

By the middle of October the family was on the move again. The plan was to spend the winter in Paris, but before Dickens took Georgina with him on 13 October to look for a suitable apartment there were obligations to be met. He gave a reading of *A Christmas Carol* for an educational charity in Folkestone, insisting that some of the five-shilling seats be made available for workingmen at threepence apiece; and on 11 October he went up to London to preside over a farewell dinner for Thackeray, who was leaving for a lecture tour of America.

Georgina had now assumed the routine management of the family and Dickens, while still affectionate to Catherine, increasingly treated Georgina as his intimate confidante and housekeeper. 'My dearest Catherine,' he wrote from Paris; 'We have had the most awful job to find a place that would in the least suit us.' He eventually took a set of apartments at 49 Avenue des Champs-Élysées. 'I think the situation itself almost the finest in Paris.'[10] The rooms, however, were ill-furnished and dirty, and at Georgina's instigation Dickens fell back on his skills as a stage manager to organize the owners, the porter, and various hangers-on into making the place habitable. As soon as it was cleaned and the furniture rearranged to suit his fancy he declared that it was 'exquisitely cheerful and vivacious', and sent for Catherine, Mamie, Kate, and the two smaller boys.

'You must be prepared for a regular Continental abode,' Dickens had written to Catherine. He fitted easily into the Parisian way of life. It offered just the blend of smartness, a lively literary milieu, and a theatrical Bohemia that suited his taste. 'You can not think how pleasant it is to me to find myself generally known and liked here,' he told Wills soon after his arrival.[11] His novels had sold well in translation and a standard edition was planned by Hachette; and *Chuzzlewit* was running in the *Moniteur*. He was, however, scarcely installed in his apartment when he had to return to London. Dr. Brown, the husband of the companion to Miss Coutts, died suddenly on 23 October when all three were together on holiday at Montpellier. Dickens felt that Miss Coutts was isolated from practicalities by her eminence and wealth, and he offered his help in this emergency, undertaking the unpleasant task of shipping the body back to England and arranging the funeral in the new church of St. Stephen's, Westminster, which Miss Coutts had financed at the cost of more than £100,000. It was, he wrote to Catherine from London, 'the vilest and most intolerable weather', and he was also troubled by conjunctivitis in the right eye. There were many difficulties, including a tussle with the Home Office officials who insisted that the prepared vault was too close to the novel central heating system in the new church; and Mrs. Brown complicated matters by trying to alter the date and place to ensure a more private ceremony. If the funeral were to be thus put off, Dickens told Catherine, 'I shall go distracted or at least turn grey.'[12] During the visit he caught up with his business at *Household Words*, and took the chance of dinners with Forster and Leech, Stanfield and Lemon. He did not return to Paris until after the funeral on 7 November, and he was then pressed to get on with *Little Dorrit*, in order to be three numbers ahead of the presses when publication began in December.

A week after his return Miss Coutts asked Dickens to find a suitable secretary, although she already had an accountant, a couple of charitable almoners, and several clergymen in her train. He was reluctant to surrender his advisory position, and as a compromise he suggested that his colleague Wills should take his place at an annual salary of £200 for the part-time services he was to render to Miss Coutts for another eleven years.

Back in Paris Dickens was soon complaining about the distractions that he had carelessly allowed to intrude upon his writing. He had begun to sit for his portrait to the noted artist Ary Scheffer. Dickens liked Scheffer and enjoyed the company of Scheffer's artistic friends, but he grew anxious when the sittings were prolonged through the winter. 'I can scarcely express how uneasy and unsettled it makes me', he told Forster, 'to have to sit, sit, sit, with *Little Dorrit* on my mind.'[13] Dickens was especially irritated, though he could not withdraw from the arrangement, because he could see no likeness to himself in what he called 'the nightmare portrait'. And he returned again to England in mid-December to give some promised readings of *A Christmas Carol*, for the benefit of the local mechanics' institutes at Sheffield, Birmingham, and Peterborough; the Peterborough reading was given as a mark of affection for his deceased friend Watson, and he stayed with the family at Rockingham Castle. *Little Dorrit* was off to 'a most tremendous start' Dickens declared, beating even the early sales of *Bleak House*.

Bradbury and Evans found the money accumulating so fast that they soon offered to increase the £200 they paid him each month, and before he left for Paris on Christmas Eve there was a party at Bradbury's house, with Evans, Lemon, and Forster. 'Afterwards we played Vingt-et-Un', he wrote to Catherine, 'and Lemon and I made a Bank against the company in the wildest manner.'[14]

There was a family party to greet him in Paris. 'On Christmas Day I had seven sons in the banquet hall of this apartment—which would not make a very large warm bath,' he told Edmund Yates.[15] There were many social invitations. He dined with the eminent playwright Scribe. He met composers, singers, and actors; he was complimented by Lamartine and puzzled by the 'chubby, matronly' George Sand: 'nothing of the blue-stocking about her', he commented, 'except a little final way of settling all your opinions with hers'.[16] And there were many English friends to see in Paris. The Brownings were living near by, in the rue de Colisée. Thackeray's daughters were staying with their grandmother while their father was lecturing in America. And there were visitors from England. An art exhibition in Paris that winter included work by Stanfield (who won a gold medal), Frith, Egg, and Landseer, and a number of his friends came over for it. He told Forster that he thought the English art made a poor show—niggling and insignificant compared with the French and with a horrid respectability 'strangely expressive to me of the state of England itself'.

For all his fame and fortune, and his efforts at cheerfulness, Dickens was still in a profound state of dissatisfaction. He described himself to Miss Coutts as 'prowling about the rooms, sitting down, getting up, stirring the fire, looking out of the window, tearing my hair, sitting down to write, writing nothing, writing something and tearing it up, going out, coming in, a Monster to my family, a dread Phaenomenon to myself, etc. etc. etc.'[17] Everything served to touch his temper. Harriet Martineau complained about an article in *Household Words* by Henry Morley which blamed the employers for factory accidents. Dickens was annoyed and himself wrote Morley's reply to strengthen it; he was always eager for safety measures and hard on mill-owners who neglected them. He also altered another article by Morley, which originally had criticized a strike in Manchester, to insist that the men had their reasons and their rights. His political views were now hardening into despair, and his only satisfaction lay in attack and mockery. 'I have a grim pleasure upon me tonight in thinking that the Circumlocution Office sees the light, and in wondering what effect it will make,' he wrote to Forster on 30 January 1856.[18] Carlyle was one who quickly responded to its sarcastic humour: 'recommend me to Dickens', he wrote to Forster, 'and thank him a hundred times for the "circumlocution office" which is priceless after its sort. We have laughed loud and long over it here; and laughter is by no means the supreme result in it—oh Heaven'.[19]

Throughout the first months of 1856 *Little Dorrit* absorbed his passions and, as he explained to Forster, there was only one way he could find relief from it: 'my head really stings with the visions of the book, and I am going, as we French say, to disembarrass it by plunging out into some of the strange places I glide into of nights in these latitudes'. In London one of his companions on nightly prowls had been Mark Lemon. 'I miss you, my dear old boy, at the play, woefully, and miss the walk home and the partings at the corner of Tavistock Square,' he told him early in the New Year. 'And when I go by myself I come home stewing Little Dorrit in my head.'[20] But nothing seemed to appease his 'horrible restlessness', and early in February he was back in London. There was business to attend to with the Theatrical Fund and with Urania Cottage, where there had been difficulties after a change of matron; henceforth, though Dickens attended committee meetings, he played little direct part in the affairs of the Home. He saw Charley, and was delighted with his progress at Baring Brothers. The essential purpose of his visit, however, was to press on with negotiations to buy himself a new home.

During the summer of 1855 Wills had casually discovered from the author Eliza Lynn Linton that she was the owner of Gad's Hill Place, a house on the London road near Rochester which Dickens had known as a boy, and that she might dispose of it to Dickens. His desire to possess it grew from a whim to rent it, when he first heard it might be available, to a plan to buy and greatly improve it. Mrs. Lynton wanted £1,800. Dickens, who had the house inspected by his brother-in-law Henry Austin, believed that it would cost a great deal to decorate and furnish it and he was reluctant to meet the price. Mrs. Lynton stood her ground, forcing him up from his offer of £1,500. 'We sold it cheap,' she recalled: '£1,700, and we asked £40 for the ornamental timber. To this Dickens and his agents made an objection so we had an arbiter who awarded us £90.'[21] Mrs. Lynton concluded that Dickens was an obdurate man. 'His will was as resolute as his pride was indomitable ... like a rod of iron in his soul.'[22] The protracted negotiations, Dickens told Wills on 2 March, seemed like 'a sort of Chancery suit which will never be settled', but the contract was eventually arranged on 14 March 1856 and Dickens was back in London to sign it.[23] Though he was chagrined at the extra cost of the shrubbery which lay across the London road, Dickens was delighted with the house. It was, he declared to Wills with typical hyperbole, a 'Giant Property', and Miss Coutts was more accurately informed that it was 'old-fashioned, plain and comfortable ... with a noble prospect at the side and behind, looking down into the Valley of the Medway....

To crown all, the sign of the Sir John Falstaff is over the way, and I used to look at it as a wonderful Mansion (which God knows it is not) when I was a very odd little child.'[24]

Dickens was increasingly relying upon Wills rather than Forster to look after general business arrangements of this kind, and the change was reflected in the financial structure of *Household Words*. Forster had written nothing for the magazine for the past two years, though he drew his one-eighth share of the profits; and when he failed to take up his option of buying that share for £1,000—in lieu of contributions—Dickens promptly assigned half of Forster's interest to Wills. Although Dickens was still intimate with Forster he no longer found him so companionable. Unlike Dickens, more rebellious and bohemian as he aged, Forster became more respectable and conservative, sensitive of his status as a man of letters. The distance between them was intensified when, as Dickens learnt in March, the 44-year-old Forster became engaged to marry the widow of Coulburn the publisher. 'Tell Catherine', he wrote at once to Georgina, 'that I have the most prodigious, overwhelming, crushing, astounding, blinding, deafening, pulverizing, scarifying, secret of which Forster is the hero, imaginable by the united efforts of the whole British population . . . after I knew it (from himself) this morning, I lay down flat, as if an Engine and Tender had fallen upon me.'[25] And he later reported sarcastically to Catherine what Maclise said about the bride-to-be and Forster. 'She has no blood Sir in her body—no color—no voice—is all scrunched and squeezed together—and seems to me in deep affliction—while Forster Sir is rampant and raging.'[26] She was, however, wealthy. Dickens reported to Miss Coutts that this 36-year-old widow had 'as many thousand pounds as she is of age'.[27] Forster now gave up his editorship of the *Examiner*, and took instead an agreeable public post as Secretary to the Commissioners of Lunacy.

Wilkie Collins, the best of companions for low-life jaunts, now provided the kind of friendship that suited Dickens. Collins had long planned a visit to Paris to see him, but Collins had been ill and he did not get across until Dickens had returned from his visit to London. He moved into a small pavilion near by which resembled, said Dickens, a private dwelling-house in a pantomime. He was, however, soon taken ill again with a rheumatic chill which kept him indoors for a fortnight; when he was able to go about Dickens took him on a tour of the catacombs, to see the guillotine demonstrated at the Roquette prison—'it can be got set up in private, like Punch's show', he told Collins before he arrived—to dine with literary friends, to a round of galleries, and to what he called a bachelor perspective of 'theatrical and other-lounging evenings'.[28] When Collins returned to London at the beginning of April Dickens wrote nostalgically about some 'Haroun Al

Rachid expedition' or other. 'On Saturday night I paid three francs at the door of that place where we saw the wrestling, and went in, at 11 o'clock to a Ball,' he told Collins in a typical report on his wanderings through the seamier haunts of Paris. 'Some pretty faces, but all of two classes—wicked and coldly calculating, or haggard and wretched in their worn beauty. Among the latter was a woman of thirty or so, in an Indian shawl ... I mean to walk about tonight and look for her. I didn't speak to her there, but I have a fancy I should like to know more about her.'²⁹

Jaunts of this kind fed his dissatisfaction with staid family life. The arrival of Macready in Paris in April confirmed his mood. It was a happy visit with outings to the theatre and dinners with friends like Scribe and Scheffer, but Dickens was struck by Macready's age and isolation, pitying him in that 'lonely Sherborne place', and he poured out his feelings to Forster. 'I have always felt of myself that I must, please God, die in harness, but I have never felt it more strongly than in looking at, and thinking of, him. However strange it is to be never at rest, and never satisfied, and ever trying after something that is never reached, and to be always laden with plot and plan and care and worry, how clear it is that it must be, and that one is driven by an irresistible might until the journey is worked out! It is much better to go on and fret, than to stop and fret. As to repose—for some men there's no such thing in this life. The foregoing has the appearance of a small sermon; but it is so often in my head these days that it cannot help coming out. The old days—the old days! Shall I ever, I wonder, get the frame of mind back as it used to be then? Something of it perhaps—but never quite as it used to be. I find that the skeleton in my domestic cupboard is becoming a pretty big one.'³⁰

By the end of April Dickens was more than ready for the move back to London. 'The tents are striking here', he wrote to Lemon on 27 April, 'and I can't work in the distracted apartments.'³¹ He and Georgina went over to England while the family stayed in Paris before moving on to Boulogne for the holiday season; but Dickens stayed in a hotel at Dover for several days because the Hogarths were still in occupation at Tavistock House until 3 May. As his wretchedness increased he became noticeably more outspoken about its causes. He explained to Wills that he could not 'bear the contemplation of their imbecility any more (and I think my constitution is already undermined by the sight of Hogarth at breakfast)'. He felt that he had been as generous to his wife's parents as his own and found them nearly as troublesome and irritating. He claimed that when he let them stay in his house while the family was away they left it dishevelled and dirty; that when he allowed them credit they ran up bills to his accounts; and that when he protested they assumed an air of injured innocence. 'I am dead sick of the

Scottish tongue in all its moods and tenses,' he had told Collins after the Hogarths had stayed in the house in March 1855, and by 1856 he was coming to the end of his patience.[32] Georgina was now the only member of the Hogarth family who did not try Dickens into a temper. Always singled out for praise, Georgina became more perfectly admired as her relatives sank into contempt. Dickens now etched his feelings about Georgina into the portrait of Little Dorrit herself, whose indestructible moral strength, purity of mind, and physical frailty all embodied his ideal of womanhood. For him she was 'the little Mother'. The hero of the novel, Arthur Clennam, only realizes the nature of his true feelings for her when he ceases to think of Little Dorrit as a child.

Dickens returned to a London that was preparing to celebrate the end of the Crimean War, and although he went to the top of St. Paul's to watch the firework display on 29 May 1856 he was as soured about politics as he was about his life. He was more interested in a new plan for theatricals. On 6 April he had reported to Wills from Paris that 'Collins and I have a mighty original notion (mine in the beginning) for another Play at Tavistock House. I purpose opening on Twelfth Night the theatrical season of that great establishment.'[33] And though the play was not yet written—it was prompted by a recent Admiralty report on the fate of Sir John Franklin's lost expedition to the Arctic—while he was in London he began to plan the scenery. 'Mr. Stanfield', he wrote to Miss Coutts on 13 May, 'has already been hanging out of the centre back-window of the schoolroom at the risk of his life, inventing wonderful effects and measuring the same.'[34]

In June Dickens was reinstalled in the Château des Moulineaux at Boulogne. By now he was well accustomed to this holiday routine, and even the children were neatly controlled. They had their own cottage in the rose-filled garden, and Dickens seized the chance to turn a moral. 'I have established (by way of a lesson in Common Things) a regular code of laws for the administration of that Institution,' he told Mrs. Brown, as if it were a copy of the regime at Urania Cottage. 'The washing arrangements and so forth are conducted on the strict principles of a Man of War. Nothing is allowed to be out of its place. Each in his turn is appointed Keeper for the week and I go out in solemn procession (Georgina and the Baby—as we call him—forming the rest of it) three times a day on a tour of inspection.'[35]

Boulogne put him in a good mood. He always enjoyed the country walks and the garden: it was, he wrote to Lemon on 15 June urging him to visit, 'a burst of roses'.[36] And in July he told Mrs. Brown that 'as I came from town yesterday the luxuriant hayfields were so beautiful that I felt as proud of them as if they were all mine';[37] and he boasted to Miss Coutts that the sweet peas were nearly seven feet high and that 'their blossoms rustle in the sun like Peacocks' tails'.[38] But too soon the summer began to fade. Early in August he sent an elegaic note to Mrs. Brown: 'the berries are turning red, and we have already begun to talk sometimes of our return home early in October'.[39] In fact, a cholera epidemic in Boulogne sent them packing much sooner. Before the end of the month Catherine had taken the children to England whilst Dickens and Georgina packed up and closed the house.

Dickens fulfilled his obligations for *Little Dorrit*, though he confessed to Miss Coutts on 26 September that he had not been 'in a quick vein'. His interest lay with Collins, now on the regular staff of *Household Words* at a salary of five guineas a week, who was pressing on with the play. Dickens was delighted with it, telling Collins that 'the strength of the situation is *prodigious*; and if we don't bring the house down with it I'm a—Tory'.[40] He was eager to see the plot worked out in detail. 'Immense excitement was occasioned here last night by the arrival of Mr. Collins in a breathless state, with the first two acts of his play,' Dickens wrote to Miss Coutts on 3 October. 'It is called *The Frozen Deep* and is extremely clever and interesting—very serious and very curious.'[41] Three weeks later it was finished and read to the assembled players. It was a melodramatic tale. Dickens was to play the part of Wardour, the disappointed lover of the heroine; Collins took the role of Aldersley, her betrothed, lost on an Arctic expedition and rescued by the rejected Wardour at the cost of his own life. To get up this substantial part Dickens went off for a twenty-mile tramp through the villages beyond Hampstead, declaiming his speeches 'to the great terror' of the villagers.

As soon as the play was finished it was cast—with parts going to Georgina, Egg, Lemon, Charley, and the two girls, and Forster enlisted to speak a prologue—and the rehearsals were held on each Monday and Friday from mid-October until the New Year. As usual Dickens drove everyone and supervised everything. Tavistock House, he declared, became like Chatham dockyard, with 'a painter's shop in the schoolroom; a gasfitter's shop all over the basement; a dressmaker's shop at the top of the house; a tailor's shop in my dressing-room'.[42] And yet he was able to continue with his writing. 'Calm amidst the wreck,' he wrote to Macready, 'your aged friend glides away on the Dorrit stream, forgetting the uproar for a stretch of hours, refreshing himself with a ten or twelve miles' walk, pitches headforemost into foaming rehearsals, placidly emerges for editorial purposes ... again calmly floats upon the Dorrit waters.'[43] The first performance was on 6 January 1857, to celebrate Charley's twentieth birthday; and it was repeated on three nights in the following week. The little theatre was packed on each occasion with about a hundred friends and notables, and Dickens made such a business of Wardour's death that he brought both cast and audience to tears. 'I certainly have never seen people so strongly affected by theatrical means,'[44] he proudly wrote to Mrs. Brown; and Macready, in a letter to Lady Pollock, confirmed that the acting was 'uncommonly good'.

'O reaction, reaction', Dickens wrote to Collins when it was all over and it was not long before he was focusing his despondency on to the political scene.[45] He told Macready that the family was again 'tranquil and domestic' with 'fire-eyed radicalism in its master's breast',[46] and he began to dispatch critical letters about public affairs. 'See what you are all about down at Westminster at this moment with the wretchedest party squabble,' he wrote to Sir Joseph Paxton that spring, 'and consider that poor Workingmen's meeting about Emigration, within a few yards of you all, the other night.'[47] And six weeks later he wrote to the Viceroy of Ireland, Lord Carlisle, that the 'signs of the times' were 'just as bad as the spirit of the people will permit of their being'.[48]

That gloomy note ran through the closing chapters of *Little Dorrit*, which Dickens finished early in May 1857. Forster thought that, like *Bleak House*, it showed a 'droop in his invention' and noted 'the want of ease and coherence among the figures of the story, and of a central interest in the plan of it'.[49] The critics were mixed in their reaction. One declared it to have 'all the supremacy of genius' and found the whole picture 'quick and warm with life', but most reviewers shared Forster's view. One thought it 'decidedly the worst' of Dickens's novels. Another talked of 'the wilderness of *Little Dorrit*'. 'We don't want him to be a politician, of whom there are plenty,' declared E. B. Hamley in *Blackwood's*; 'we want him to be a humourist, and painter of passion and life, where he stands almost without a peer.' The 'fire-eyed radicalism' which burned even more strongly in *Little Dorrit* than in his earlier novels was beginning to evoke a reaction. 'Who is this man', asked James Fitzjames Stephen early in January, 'who is so much wiser than the rest of the world that he can pour contempt on all the institutions of his country?' Stephen thought Dickens had a 'most lachrymose and melodramatic turn of mind' and that his subversive opinions would 'result in the purest despotism'. It was becoming clear that Dickens's satire was as much a reflection of his own state of mind as it was of the state of the nation. Walter Bagehot made the pertinent comment that Dickens 'began by describing really removable evils in a style which would induce all persons, however insensible, to remove them if they could: he has ended by describing the natural evils and inevitable pains of the present state of being in such a manner as must tend to excite discontent and repining'.[50]

Dickens, indulging as Bagehot saw in 'vague strivings and restless changes', unable to accept the fact that confinement is part of the human condition, desperately sought release, and turned again for comfort to the company of Collins. He had taken a brief trip to Brighton with his fellow novelist in early March, and Collins was now a regular companion on evening prowls, visits to theatres and to low haunts of the kind they had toured together in Paris. 'Any mad proposal you please will find a wildly insane response,' he wrote to Collins on 11 May.[51] Less than two weeks later he sent a similar appeal. 'Tomorrow I am bound to Forster; on Sunday to solemn Chief Justice's . . . on Monday to Geographical Societies . . . on Wednesday—if the mind can devise anything sufficiently in the style of Sybarite Rome in the days of its culminating voluptuousness, I am your man. . . . If you can think of any tremendous way of passing the night, in the meantime do. I don't care what it is. I give (for that night only) restraint to the Winds!'[52]

Another form of release was found in the alterations and decoration of Gad's Hill Place, of which Dickens formally gained possession in February 1857. In March he took Catherine, Georgina, and the two small boys down to an hotel in near-by Gravesend, when he could go daily to harry the builders who had to be 'squeezed out by bodily pressure'. There was a house-warming party on 17 May for an army of guests, and on 1 June the family moved down from London. In the spring months, moreover, Dickens was taken up in the usual round of public activities, attending dinners for the Royal Theatrical Fund, the Royal Hospital for Incurables, and the Royal Geographic Society. He was one of the best and most sought after speakers for such occasions, and he had a reputation of support for the sick, the poor, and the ill-educated. In March, too, he was engaged in another battle with the committee of the Royal Literary Fund, with whom he had been at odds since the failure of the reform group in 1855. 'God knows this institution to be a Satire as it stands,' he had written in *Household Words* in 1856, and he had attacked it again at the annual general meeting that year. Now he led the reformers in an assault more bitter than the last. 'I beg to report that I have my war-paint on,' he wrote to Dilke on 19 March, 'that I have buried the pipe of peace, and am whooping for committee scalps.'[53] And he told Macready that he was resolved to reform it or ruin it. The more bitterly he denounced it, however, the less support he received. His case for the 'dignity of literature' had so fused with his general state of anger that it had degenerated into personal abuse. The *Literary Gazette* talked of the 'pretentions and bad taste of such speeches as those of Mr. Dickens and Mr. Forster'.[54]

His energies, however, were diverted to a less contentious cause that summer. On 8 June Douglas Jerrold died suddenly. This 'acrid philanthropist', as Carlyle called him, had been a close associate though not an intimate of

Dickens; only a few days before he died Dickens had carried him off on a steamer to attend a dinner at Greenwich given by William Howard Russell, who had made his name as *The Times* correspondent in the Crimea. Jerrold was neither poor nor a spendthrift, and there was certainly no need for charity. Yet Dickens impulsively proposed to raise a Jerrold Fund of £2,000; the chance to revive the excitement of public readings and theatricals was too good to miss. Dickens was full of ideas. There would be a performance at the Adelphi of Jerrold's own play, *Black-Eyed Susan*; Thackeray would give a lecture; Dickens would read *A Christmas Carol*, and gather his troupe together to put on *The Frozen Deep*.

A committee was soon formed and it arranged to present the play on 8 July at the Gallery of Illustration in Regent Street. It also sought royal patronage, for there had been rumours that the Queen was interested in the play and had thought of inviting the company to Windsor. When she was asked to attend she at first declined, on the grounds that she could not lend her name to private subscriptions, but she offered Dickens a room in Buckingham Palace for a command performance. It was then his turn to object, telling the Queen that he 'did not feel easy as to the social position of his daughters' if they attended the Palace under such circumstances: the status of actresses, even if they were genteel amateurs, was scarcely respectable. The Queen then accepted his suggestion of a private performance for guests of her choosing at the Gallery of Illustration a week before the subscription night.

As soon as the details were settled Dickens threw himself into the preparations with customary vigour. 'There is a great deal at stake,' he wrote to Collins, 'and it *must be* well done.'[55] And he had to find time to entertain Hans Christian Andersen when he came to England as his guest. Andersen was an almost childish and excessively sentimental man, who could be both charming and trying; the family, Dickens reported, was 'suffering a good deal from Andersen'.[56] There was a brief break when Angela Coutts and Hannah Brown visited Gad's Hill and then invited Andersen to spend a short time in London, where he had been overwhelmed by the magnificent house of his 'straightforward, kind and good-natured' hostess. But for much of his visit it fell to Catherine to look after him. She took him to the Crystal Palace to hear the *Messiah* and to the theatre to see *Macbeth*. And he was one of the select group which attended the royal performance of *The Frozen Deep*. 'The Queen and her party made a most excellent audience,' Georgina reported to Maria Winter; 'so far from being cold, as we expected, they cried and laughed and applauded and made as much demonstration as so small a party ... could do.'[57] It was after midnight when the curtain fell, but the Queen had asked to see the accompanying farce as well and in the

interval she sent for Dickens to thank him. He again obdurately refused
the royal invitation. 'I replied that I was in my Farce dress and must beg
to be excused,' he told Forster the next day. The Queen pressed the point,
sending a message back that the dress could not be so ridiculous. Dickens
could not be moved; he would not appear before his sovereign in theatrical
costume. 'I was mighty glad to think, when I woke this morning,' he
remarked to Forster, 'that I had carried the point.'[58]

The Jerrold benefits went on, though Jerrold's son was said to be complaining at 'the hat being carried round' as if his father had died without
means. There were three public performances of the play; Dickens read
the *Carol* to an audience of over two thousand people at St. Martin's Hall;
and there was a request for the play to be taken up to Manchester. Amidst
so much bustle it was a relief to see Andersen go. He had much overstayed
his invitation and after he left Dickens put a card on his dressing-table:
'Hans Christian Andersen slept in this room for five weeks which seemed
to the family AGES.' There was a sadder parting, too, five days after
Andersen had taken the boat-train to Folkestone. Walter Dickens was only
sixteen, but Miss Coutts had used her influence to secure him a cadetship
in one of the East India Company's native regiments. Neither forceful nor
talented he had, nevertheless, been taught to ride, swim, fence, and shoot,
and he had been topped up with a smattering of Hindustani. His departure,
Dickens wrote to Edmund Yates on 19 July, was like having 'great teeth
drawn with a wrench';[59] and the following day he and Charley saw Walter
sail from Southampton on the *Indus*.

The Manchester performances still lay ahead. The great Free Trade Hall
was booked for 21 and 22 August, and Dickens felt emotionally excited by
the prospect of a vast audience. The reading from one of his books, or one
of his theatrical evenings, he confessed to Maclise, 'enables me, as it were,
to write a book in company instead of in my own solitary room, and to feel
its effect coming freshly back upon me from the reader'.[60] He felt, however,
that in such a large auditorium the female parts should be played by professional actresses, for Georgina and his daughters were too inexperienced
to project their voices. On the advice of Alfred Wigan, who managed the
Olympia Theatre, he offered the parts to the well-known actress Mrs. Ternan and two of her three daughters, Maria and Ellen Lawless Ternan.

The Ternans were a prominent theatrical family. Thomas Ternan, who
killed himself in a lunatic asylum in 1846, had been a tragedian. Macready,
who acted with him, said that he was opinionated, jealous, and small-
minded, and not in the first rank; but he thought better of Mrs. Ternan,
helped her career after her husband's death, and lent her small sums of
money when she was in difficulties. She had put all three of her daughters

on the boards as soon as they could walk and talk, for the family had to make a living as Thomas Ternan went downhill. Fanny, the eldest, was something of an infant prodigy, and in later life—when she was married to Thomas Trollope—her talent turned to writing novels. Maria was also a competent actress. The youngest daughter, Ellen, who had been born in Rochester on 3 March 1839, appeared on the stage for the first time at the age of three in Sheffield, when she played a child's role to her mother in *The Stranger*. At eighteen she was a small, pretty girl, with blue eyes and fair hair, and agreeably high-spirited. Although she had less of a theatrical vocation than her sisters, she had been accustomed to acting with them and she had made her own début as an adult actress in April 1857 in Talfourd's *Atalanta* at the Haymarket Theatre.

When Dickens approached the Ternans for the Manchester production they were members of Charles Kean's company at the Royal Princess's Theatre in Oxford Street, and he secured their release for the special performances. After he had spent three days rehearsing them at Tavistock House (where Catherine thought Mrs. Ternan 'pushing' and the girls too familiar), the whole company set off for Manchester. The theatricals for the Jerrold Fund had so raised his spirits that Dickens was once more the life of the party, making up conundrums and jokes to entertain the party on the train journey.

The theme of *The Frozen Deep*—redemption through self-sacrifice—precisely suited the sentiments of the Victorian middle class; and Dickens threw so much into the part that it moved his fellow actors as much as it affected the audiences. At the climax of the play Maria Ternan nursed the dying Dickens in her arms: 'her tears fell down my face, down my beard . . . down my ragged dress—poured all over me like rain, so that it was as much as I could do to speak for them', he wrote to Mrs. Watson on 7 December.[61] This performance, before three thousand people, Collins remarked afterwards, was 'the finest of all the representations of *The Frozen Deep*. . . . The trite phrase is the true phrase to describe that magnificent piece of acting. He literally electrified the audience.'[62]

Dickens was touched by the dramatic response he had evoked from Maria Ternan—it was still on his mind when he described the climax of the play to Mrs. Brown three weeks later—but his own emotions had been aroused by the younger sister, Ellen. He had met her earlier in the year when she was appearing in Talfourd's play and he had then been attracted by her youthful simplicity. The close quarters of rehearsal and travel confirmed that first impression. She fascinated him, for she fitted precisely into the ideal of lost innocence which had been so frustratingly evoked by Maria Winter.

17

The Skeleton in the Cupboard

'I AM horribly used up after the Jerrold business,' Dickens wrote to Henry Austin at the beginning of September 1857.[1] He was back at Gad's Hill and complaining of low spirits, low pulse, and low voice—all symptoms of an 'intense reaction' to the Manchester performance of *The Frozen Deep*. The change from the footlights to the harsher light of day, always an anti-climax, was worse than usual. The sudden infatuation with Ellen Ternan had exacerbated his dissatisfaction with Catherine and made his feeling of claustrophobia unendurable. In a fit of despair he sent a touching letter to Forster describing what had gone wrong. 'Poor Catherine and I are not made for each other, and there is no help for it. It is not only that she makes me uneasy and unhappy, but that I make her so too—and much more so ... we are strangely ill-assorted for the bond there is between us. God knows she would have been a thousand times happier if she had married another kind of man ... I am often cut to the heart by thinking what a pity it is, for her own sake, that I ever fell in her way. ... What is now befalling me I have seen steadily coming ... and I know too well that you cannot, and no one can, help me. Why I have even written I hardly know; but it is a miserable sort of comfort that you should be clearly aware how matters stand. The mere mention of the fact, without any complaint or blame of any sort, is a relief to my present state of spirits—and I can get this only from you because I can speak of it to no one else.'[2]

Forster had seen the Dickens household in all its moods and vagaries through the years and he sent a sympathetic answer, gently reminding Dickens that Catherine also had grounds for complaint. 'I claim no immunity from blame,' Dickens sorrowfully replied. He conceded that much of the trouble sprang from his volatile temperament and from the style of life which had followed from his rise to fame. 'You are not so tolerant as perhaps you might be', he told Forster, 'of the wayward and unsettled feeling which is part (I suppose) of the tenure on which one holds an imaginative life, and which I have, as you ought to know well, often only kept down by riding over it like a dragoon.' But even if he admitted such faults—'a thousand uncertainties, caprices and difficulties of disposition'—it would do no good: 'only one thing will alter that, and that is, the end which alters everything'.[3]

In this desperate mood Dickens needed distraction. Despite the physical exhaustion which followed each bout of theatricals, he felt, he told Mrs. Brown on 28 August, 'as if the scaling of all the mountains in Switzerland, or the doing of any wild thing until I dropped, would be but a slight relief'.[4] And the next day, writing to Wilkie Collins of his 'grim despair and restlessness', he proposed to 'go anywhere—take any tour—see anything—whereon we could write something together. . . . We want something for Household Words and I want to escape from myself. For when I *do* start up and stare myself seedily in the face, as happens to be my case at present, my blankness is inconceivable—indescribable—my misery, amazing.'[5]

Collins suggested a tour of Cumberland, and on 7 September he and Dickens set off, intending to work up a picaresque account of their travels for the magazine. On the second day, when Dickens dragged him up Carrick Fell in pouring rain, Collins slipped and badly sprained his ankle. Dickens broke the compass, the light failed, and the local inkeeper whom they had taken as a guide confessed that he was lost. For much of a bewildering and difficult descent, Dickens reported to Miss Coutts, he had to carry his friend '*à la* Richard Wardour'. While the adventure made good copy it spoiled the holiday. 'A man who can do nothing by halves', Collins concluded, 'appears to me to be a fearful man.'[6] They moved to 'a capital little homely Inn' at Allonby 'in rough wild country' near the sea, and Dickens told Georgina that it was 'what Broadstairs might have been, if it had not inherited a cliff, and had been born an Irishman'.[7] While Collins was confined to his room Dickens wandered disconsolately about the countryside, and as soon as Collins was well enough to hobble about they made their way to Doncaster; he was so short of copy that the five articles which described 'The Lazy Tour of Two Idle Apprentices' had to be padded out with a couple of macabre tales and an account of the 'saturnalia' in Doncaster during the St. Leger race-week. He had also been drawn to Doncaster by the presence of Mrs. Ternan and her three daughters in the town where her husband had once been manager of the theatre and a prominent Freemason. On 30 September, indeed, the local Masonic lodges arranged a benefit for the whole Ternan family. During this short season Maria played in *The Ladies Club*, a comedy by Mark Lemon, and Ellen—who returned to London in October to a succession of small parts with the Haymarket company—had a minor role in *The Pet of the Petticoats*. Dickens and Collins stayed in Doncaster for a week, attending rehearsals and performances as well as race-meetings before they went back to the south.

Dickens travelled straight through to Gad's Hill on 23 September. The

Hogarths were once again at Tavistock Square and he wished to avoid their company. He was still in a wretched state of mind, but during his tour and after seeing Ellen Ternan again, he had come to an important decision: he and Catherine might keep up the semblance of marriage, but in private at least there would be no pretence. On 11 October he wrote to Anne Cornelius, who had been a trusted servant for many years, giving instructions to convert his dressing-room at Tavistock House into a bedroom, and to close up the door leading to Catherine's bedroom with a set of bookshelves. The significance of such an activity could not be concealed either from the servants or from the Hogarths. Soon afterwards, when Dickens had to run up to town on business, he went to stay overnight at Tavistock Square. There was an altercation with the Hogarths, and he was so 'very much put out' by their 'imbecility' that he was unable to sleep; at two o'clock in the morning he got up and tramped the thirty-odd miles to Gad's Hill. He did not go back to his London home until the Hogarths were gone for good. When Forster heard of these dramatic gestures he pleaded for caution and forebearance. 'Too late to say, put the curb on, and don't rush at hills,' Dickens replied. 'I have no relief but in action. I am become incapable of rest. I am quite confident I should rust, break, and die if I spared myself. Much better to die, doing. What I am in that way, nature made me first, and my way of life has of late, alas! confirmed.'[8]

The more Dickens brooded on his plight the more he came to stress that the rift with Catherine had been implicit since the beginning of his marriage, and that it had widened steadily with the years. In mid-October he sent Emile de la Rue a letter very different in tone from the frank and affecting confession to Forster. 'Between ourselves,' he wrote to the old friends from Genoa, 'I don't get on better in these later times with a certain poor lady you know of, than I did in the earlier Peschiere days. Much worse. Much worse! Neither do the children, elder or younger. Neither can she get on with herself, or be anything but unhappy. (She has been excruciatingly jealous of, and has obtained positive proof of my being on the most intimate terms with, at least fifteen thousand women of various conditions of life, since we left Genoa. Please to respect me for this vast experience.) What we should do, or what the girls would be, without Georgy, I cannot imagine. She is the active spirit of the house, and the children dote upon her. Enough of this. We put the Skeleton away in the cupboard, and very few people, comparatively, know of its existence.'[9]

All through the autumn and winter the skeleton was kept in the cupboard. Dickens, morose and edgy, was busy with *Household Words* and his public engagements. On 5 November he went to the Warehousemen's and Clerks' School at Deptford to deliver a blast against the kind of education he had received at Wellington House; in December he gave a reading at Coventry in aid of the local Mechanics' Institute; and in January he lectured at Bristol. He found some distraction in alterations to Gad's Hill. 'I am improving it so much,' he wrote listlessly to Forster on New Year's Day 1858, 'yet I have no interest in the place.'[10] The whole household was affected by the dismal situation. For once there were no jolly plans for Christmas—the boys stayed at their school in Boulogne—or for the theatricals which had so often marked Charley's birthday on Twelfth Night. Catherine could do nothing right. When she wrote to Angela Coutts in February 1858 seeking help for her unemployed brother Edward, Dickens followed her letter with an angry apology. He was, he told Miss Coutts, 'inexpressibly vexed' that Catherine had acted without his knowledge: 'I hope you will forgive her more freely and more readily than I do.'[11]

Dickens had come to the crossroads of his life, and he did not know which way to turn. He had long assumed that there was no possible release from the marriage itself. It was only in 1857 that the Attorney-General, Sir Richard Bethel, pushed through the controversial Matrimonial Causes Act which permitted secular divorce, and even that required proof of adultery in the wife or adultery together with desertion or cruelty on the part of the husband. Dickens could not consider divorce for either reason. He was even unwilling to convert the private estrangement into a public separation, for he was acutely aware how much his readers treasured him as a celebrant of the family virtues. Any domestic scandal was bound to jeopardize his social position and damage his professional reputation. All the same, as he brooded on his unhappiness, so intensified by the image of the young and lively Ellen Ternan, he longed for some magical solution. 'I am weary of rest', he confessed to Mrs. Watson on 7 December 1857, 'and have no satisfaction but in fatigue. Realities and idealities are always appearing before me, and I don't like the Realities except when they are unattainable—*then*, I like them of all things. I wish I had been born in the days of Ogres and Dragon-guarded Castles. I wish an Ogre with seven heads ... had taken the Princess whom I adore—you have no idea how intensely I love her!—to his stronghold. ... Nothing would suit me half so well this day, as climbing after her, sword in hand, and either winning her or being killed!'[12]

Despite the attraction of such fantasy solutions, as he drifted uncomfortably through the winter he had to find some more practical way of releasing the accumulating tension. 'The domestic unhappiness remains so strong upon me that I can't write, and (waking) can't rest, one minute. I have never known a moment's peace or content, since the last night of The Frozen Deep,' Dickens wrote to Collins on 21 March; and in the same letter he told Collins of his plan to give public and paid readings from his works. 'In this condition, though nothing can alter or soften it, I have a turning notion that the mere physical effort and change of the Readings would be good, as another means of bearing it.'[13]

It was not a new idea, but the success of his recent readings for charity had been sensational enough for Dickens to think it was a good one.[14] It particularly suited his interests and style. 'Every writer of fiction', he suggested to the dinner of the Royal General Theatrical Fund on 29 March, 'writes in effect for the stage'; and this was especially true of his own work, which carried the humour, sentiment, and melodrama of the theatre into the novel.[15] No other novelist was so ardent for public appearances and performances, or for the sense of direct contact with his audience which these readings provided. He wrote to Forster at the end of March to insist that he had a 'particular relation (personally affectionate like no other man's)' with his public—a relationship which he had cultivated over the years through the part publication of his novels as well as in the pages of *Household Words*.[16] And he was a natural and superb soloist. When he was a stage-struck youth he had especially admired the great Charles Mathews, who would do a dozen characters in one evening, and when he turned entertainer himself he adopted the same style. Critics who saw both men considered that Dickens was the better and more versatile impersonator; and he had the advantage over Mathews that he could draw upon his own vocabulary of characters, already well known and well loved by his readers. No one doubted his talents. 'If Dickens does turn Reader he will make another fortune,' Wills had written after his triumph in Birmingham in 1853;[17] and when Thackeray saw him in *The Frozen Deep* he made a similar prediction. There was also the prospect of a fresh start, so appealing to a middle-aged man whose marriage was in ruins. Since Dickens was in no state to begin a novel, a series of paid readings offered an alternative and seemingly easy way of earning money; and it was an occupation which could absorb his restless energy and provide him with the flattering applause he craved.

Dickens had put the notion to Forster in September 1857 in the anticlimax after *The Frozen Deep*. 'What do you think of my paying for this place by reviving that old idea of some Readings from my books,' he asked in a letter from Gad's Hill. 'I am very strongly tempted. Think of it.'[18] Forster did think of it, and poorly. It was, he replied, 'a substitution of lower for higher aims; a change to commonplace from more elevated pursuits; and it had so much of the character of a public exhibition for money as to raise, in the question of respect for his calling as a writer, a question also of respect for himself as a gentleman'. Dickens was not so easily dissuaded. He turned to Miss Coutts as another arbiter of taste—she had, after all, disapproved of his theatrical enterprises—but neither she nor her companion Hannah

Brown objected. For a third opinion Dickens turned to his publisher Frederick Evans, who assured him that readings for profit would not damage his reputation as a writer. In March 1858 he went up to Edinburgh to read *A Christmas Carol* for the Philosophical Institute, and he had promised a charitable reading in April on behalf of the Hospital for Sick Children in Great Ormond Street. His enthusiastic reception in Edinburgh tipped the balance. 'My determination is all but taken,' he wrote to Forster when he returned. 'I must do *something*, or I shall wear my heart away. I can see no better thing to do that is half so hopeful in itself or half so well suited to my restless state.'[19]

Forster still disapproved. By such a relief from domestic misery, he believed, Dickens would destroy 'any hope of a better understanding' with his wife. This argument provoked another outburst. 'Quite dismiss from your mind . . . present circumstances at home,' Dickens wrote to him. 'Nothing can put *them* right, until we are dead and buried and risen. It is not, with me, a matter of will, or trial, or sufferance, or good humour, or making the best of it, or making the worst of it any longer. It is all despairingly over. Have no lingering hope of, or for, me in this association. A dismal failure has to be borne, and there is an end.'[20]

Edmund Yates was in St. Martin's Hall on Thursday 29 April when Dickens gave the first of his professional performances—organized by Arthur Smith, who had served as manager of the Jerrold fund-raising theatricals—and he recalled the impression Dickens made on the crowded gathering. 'Dickens', he wrote, 'stepped onto the platform, walking rather stiffly, right shoulder well forward, as usual, bud in button-hole, and gloves in hand. . . . He was received with a roar of cheering which might have been heard at Charing Cross.'[21] Before Dickens began to read the first item, from *The Cricket on the Hearth*, he briefly explained why he had decided to begin regular readings. 'I have long held the opinion, and have long acted on the opinion that in these times whatever brings a public man and his public face to face, on terms of mutual confidence and respect, is a good thing.' The great reputation he had already made in his charity performances ensured that each session was wildly successful; and no one suggested— as he had feared—that there was anything socially improper in a prominent author reading his work for profit. 'Mr. Dickens', the *Illustrated London News* declared in a typical comment, 'has invented a new medium for amusing an English audience, and merits the gratitude of an intelligent public.'[22] He had, in fact, found a new public for elevating but dramatic entertainment in much the same way as his early serials had created a new readership for fiction, for in his audiences there were many (especially Nonconformists and genteel ladies) who would never patronize the somewhat disreputable theatres or expose themselves to the risk of indecorous humour at other popular recitals.

While Dickens was evoking the family virtues with his admiring audience, he was putting them at risk at home; and an unlucky accident which provoked Catherine to jealous fury made matters worse. At the Manchester performance of *The Frozen Deep* Dickens and Ellen Ternan had played together in a farce called *Uncle John*, in which he took the part of an elderly man who falls in love with his young ward and makes her lavish presents of jewellery. The parallel was not lost on Catherine when a bracelet which Dickens had bought for Ellen Ternan was mistakenly delivered to Tavistock House. Kate Dickens said later that her mother bitterly resented the gift, which seemed to be proof of a clandestine love affair, though Dickens protested that he had often given such keepsakes to the ladies who had taken part in the theatricals; and the more hysterical Catherine became the more he defended Ellen as a wronged innocent. Catherine, he was determined, must concede she was in the wrong. Five years before he had insisted that Catherine should write a contrite letter to Augusta de la Rue, whom he considered she had similarly impugned. Now he demanded that she should make amends for her unworthy suspicions by paying a social call on Ellen and her mother. 'You shall not go,' her eighteen-year-old daughter Kate exclaimed when she found her mother weeping over the request.[23] Nevertheless Catherine was obliged to go on her humiliating errand.

It was not long before the Hogarths heard the whole sad tale, and Catherine found angry partisans in her mother and her younger sister Helen. Mrs. Hogarth, a more forceful personality than her husband, seems to have decided to treat Dickens as an errant son-in-law, and she urged Catherine to demand her maintenance in a separate household. It was becoming clear that some new arrangement would have to be made, and in the meantime— just as Dickens launched his first series of readings—he moved out of Tavistock House and into temporary quarters at the office of *Household Words*. In the midst of this upheaval he took steps to protect his reputation. 'I believe my marriage has been for years and years as miserable a one as ever was made,' Dickens wrote to Angela Coutts on 9 May, when he knew that a separation was unavoidable. 'I believe that no two people were ever created with such an impossibility of interest, sympathy, confidence, sentiment, tender union of any kind between them, as there is between my wife and me.... Nature has put an insurmountable barrier between us, which never in this world can be thrown down.' As this long letter gathered momentum Dickens began to speak far more harshly about Catherine, and more indulgently about his own failings, than he had in his desperate explanation to Forster in October. 'You know that I have the many impulsive faults which often belong to my impulsive way of life and exercise of fancy,' he told Miss Coutts; 'but I am very patient and considerate at heart, and would have beaten out a path to a better journey's end than we have come to, if I could.' Catherine, he again insisted, had neither loved nor been loved by the children, 'never presented herself before them in the aspect of a mother. ... No one can understand this but Georgina, who has seen it grow from year to year, and who is the best, the most unselfish and the most devoted of human Creatures. Her sister Mary, who died suddenly ... understood it as well in the first months of our marriage.' The indictment not only reached back to Catherine's deficiencies when she was a young bride; he went on to attack her long-standing depression. 'It is her misery to live in some fatal atmosphere which slays everyone to whom she should be dearest. It is my misery that no one can ever understand the truth in its full force, or know what a blighted and wasted life my married life has been.' With mounting rhetoric, he claimed that everyone found Catherine's presence unbearable: her mother could not live with her; her sister and younger brother could not live with her; even her personal maid, Anne, who had cared for Catherine 'like a poor child, for sixteen years', was apparently 'afraid that the companionship would wear her to death'. And though Dickens protested that he would do anything or spend anything that might be necessary for his wife's comfort, he could tolerate her no longer. As a final word he hinted that, besides her other failings, she was mentally unbalanced. 'I think she has always felt herself to be at the disadvantage of groping blindly about me, and never touching me, and so has fallen into the most miserable weaknesses and jealousies. Her mind has, at times, been certainly confused besides.'[24]

Catherine asked Miss Coutts to intervene, but her attempt at a reconciliation was useless. 'How I value your friendship and how I love and honour you, you know in part, though you can never fully know,' Dickens wrote to her on 19 May. 'But nothing on earth—no, not even you—no consideration, human or Divine, can move me from the resolution I have taken.... If you have seen Mrs. Dickens in company with her wicked mother, I cannot enter,—no, not even with you—upon any question that was discussed in that woman's presence.'[25] Catherine sent Miss Coutts a touching note of thanks for her 'kindness in doing what I asked. I have now—God help me—only one course to pursue. One day, though not now, I may be able to tell you how hardly I have been used.'[26]

Dickens hoped to come to some understanding with Catherine which would protect both her reputation and his own, and he asked Forster to act as go-between. Catherine dismissed him as too partisan; she preferred the kind-hearted Mark Lemon, who made a number of temporizing and face-saving suggestions. Catherine, according to one proposal, would keep her own room at Tavistock House but appear as hostess on formal occasions. Another scheme would allow her to remain at the London house when Dickens was at Gad's Hill, and to go down to Kent when he came up to town. In previous domestic crises Catherine had come to the verge of leaving; and now, encouraged by her mother, she tearfully but resolutely held out for public separation. Mrs. Hogarth took Catherine to Brighton while the settlement was arranged and by the middle of May the details had been worked out. Catherine was to have a house of her own and an allowance of £600 a year. She was free to visit the children or to receive them at 70 Gloucester Crescent, the more modest home near Regent's Park where she was to live; but with the exception of Charley, who was to accompany his mother at his father's request, they were all to remain in Georgina's care and under their father's control.

It was not long before reports of domestic trouble in the Dickens household spread through London society. There were 'all sorts of horrible stories buzzing about', Thackeray wrote to his mother, Mrs. Carmichael-Smith. One rumour had it that Mrs. Dickens was a secret drinker. Another claimed that Dickens had fallen in love with his sister-in-law and had turned his wife out as a consequence; and Thackeray, hearing some such tale at the Garrick Club, thought to correct it by declaring that the woman in question was an actress. He in fact knew of the Ternan family, and supposedly had used Mrs. Ternan as the model for Miss Fotheringham in his autobiographical novel *Pendennis*. But this well-meant remark was unhelpful, for it gave fresh currency to the very rumour that Dickens was at pains to suppress. When he heard of it he sent Thackeray a furious denial. 'We shall never be allowed to be friends,' Thackeray commented, but he did what he could to put matters straight. Dickens had written to him, Thackeray reported to his neighbour James Wilson, 'on the subject of a common report derogatory to the honor of a young lady whose name has been mentioned in connection with his. He authorizes me to contradict the rumour on his own solemn word and his wife's authority.' Dickens, Thackeray declared to his mother, 'says that it has been known to anyone intimate with his family that his and his wife's tempers were horribly incompatible and now the children are grown up—it is agreed they are to part.' Thackeray was sad at the news. 'To think of the poor matron after 22 years of marriage going away out of her house.'[27]

Dickens made every effort to quell the rumours and he was particularly incensed when he heard that Mrs. Hogarth and her daughter Helen were making scandalous imputations against him. He wrote at once to Frederic Ouvry, the solicitor from Coutts Bank to whom he had transferred most of his legal business. 'I received today, at first hand,' he told him on 26 May, 'from a very honorable and intelligent gentleman information of Mrs. Hogarth's having repeated these smashing slanders to him in a Concert Room, *since our negotiations have been pending*. I do not tell you this in anger, but simply that you may know the stern necessity of being relentless with her.' For the moment he diverted his attacks from Catherine, telling Ouvry to 'detach Mrs. Dickens from these wrongdoings *now*. I do not in the least suspect her of them, and I should wish her to know it. She has a great tenderness for me, and I sincerely believe would be glad to show it. I would not therefore add to her pain by a hair's breadth. It would be a pleasure to her (I think) to know that I had begun to trust her so far.'[28]

For all this kindly reference to Catherine, however, Dickens was determined to use her needs as a means of putting pressure on her mother. He insisted that he would not complete the financial settlement with Catherine until Mrs. Hogarth withdrew her discreditable suggestions. The Hogarths denied that they were responsible for slanders against Georgina and offered a statement on those lines. Dickens, through his solicitor, would not accept such a specific denial; it would not help matters. The Hogarths' solicitor then refused to hand over the statement until he had received the Deed of Separation. Dickens, however, refused to put himself in such a bargaining position. He was obdurate in his insistence and the Hogarths could not ignore the financial threat to Catherine. On 29 May Mrs. Hogarth and Helen Hogarth put their names to a formal disavowal. 'It having been stated to us that in reference to the differences which have resulted in the separation of Mr. and Mrs. Charles Dickens, certain statements have been circulated that such differences are occasioned by circumstances deeply affecting the moral character of Mr. Dickens and comprising the reputation and good names of others, we solemnly declare that we now disbelieve such statements. We know that they are not believed by Mrs. Dickens and we pledge ourselves on all occasions to contradict them, as entirely destitute of foundation.' On 4 June the formal settlement was delivered to Catherine in Brighton.

'The intense pursuit of any idea that takes complete possession of me is one of the qualities that makes me different—sometimes for good; sometimes, I dare say for evil—from other men,' Dickens had told Catherine years before; and now he proved the truth of his remarks.[29] His paper victory was not enough. He was still determined to impose his version of the truth at all costs. In this desperate mood he began to circulate copies of the Hogarth retraction: 'as I know Mrs. Yates's ears to have been abused,' he wrote to Edmund Yates in one such letter, 'I think it simply just that she should see it.'[30]

Georgina was also expected to play her part in stemming the tide of rumour. All through the quarrel she had unhesitatingly taken the side of Dickens against her sister and her parents. Still unmarried and only thirty-one, her position in the Dickens household after her sister had left was not formally improper but it was open to question, and in the eyes of her family it was obviously an act of disloyalty. Her aunt, Mrs. Thomson, writing to a friend, said that Georgina was an enthusiast who 'worships him as a man of genius, and has quarrelled with all her relatives because they dare to find fault with him saying "a man of genius ought not to be judged with the common herd of men" ... her vanity is no doubt flattered by his praise but she has disappointed us all'.[31] Georgina's role had waxed as Catherine's waned because—unlike Catherine—she accepted Dickens on his own terms, playing the role of the self-sacrificing sister so necessary to him. Abnegating any independent life for herself, she never married, and over the years (she lived to the age of ninety) she came to see all the domestic frictions as Dickens saw them and to accept his opinions as her own. She now wrote to Maria Winter, for instance, telling his version of the story. The separation, she insisted, was due solely to personal incompatibility, and Maria was not to believe 'the most wonderful rumours and wicked slanders which have been flying about the town'. She went on to tell Maria how Catherine had never got on with the children, using much the same phrases as Dickens himself had used. 'To a few of our *real* friends', she concluded, 'Charles wishes the *truth* to be stated, and they cannot show their friendship better than by quietly silencing with the real solemn truth any foolish or wicked person who may repeat such lies and slanders.'[32]

By now Dickens had worked himself up into a self-righteous frenzy. Friends were expected to take his side against Catherine. They were told nothing of his association with Ellen Ternan; instead they were given the impression that the Hogarths had been slandering their own daughter. 'The question was not I myself, but others,' Dickens wrote to Macready. 'Foremost among them—of all people in the world—Georgina!' The attack on her, he insisted, was the result of Catherine's 'weakness' and 'her mother's and her youngest sister's wickedness'.[33] Striking the posture of a much maligned innocent, Dickens complained of the 'strain and struggle' of the past month in a letter to Edmund Yates on 8 June.[34] 'Though I have unquestionably suffered deeply from being lied about with a wonderful recklessness,' he wrote, 'I am not so weak or wrong headed as to be in the least changed by it.' By this time, according to a critical outsider, the affair was being talked about 'at the corner of every street and in every social circle'. Dickens was still so determined to present himself in a favourable light and anxious for his reputation with his readers that he decided to publish an explanation in *Household Words*. The idea horrified Forster, Lemon, and Yates, and all three counselled him against it, but the only concession Dickens would make was to give an assurance that he would consult John Delane, the editor of *The Times*, with whom he was on friendly terms. Delane, surprisingly, agreed with Dickens, who at once drew up an extraordinary personal manifesto. Before he published it he sent the draft to Catherine. 'I will not write a word', he said, 'as to any *causes* that have made it necessary for me to publish the enclosed in *Household Words*.' And to an unforgiving gibe at Mrs. Hogarth he added the hope 'that all unkindness is over between you and me'.

The statement which appeared in *Household Words* on 12 June was so arch and ponderous that it was bound to cause more speculation than it allayed. 'By some means, arising out of wickedness, or out of folly, or out of inconceivable wild chance, or out of all three, this trouble has been made the occasion of misrepresentation, most grossly false, most monstrous, and most cruel—involving, not only me, but innocent persons dear to my heart, and innocent persons of whom I have no knowledge, if indeed, they have any existence.' This was strong stuff, more fitting for a sensational novel than a quasi-legal document, and Dickens rounded it off in the same style. Attacking 'all the lately whispered rumours', he concluded with an anathema: 'whosoever repeats one of them after this denial, will lie as wilfully and as foully as it is possible for any false witness to lie, before Heaven and earth'.

This statement, so confusing to anyone who was ignorant of the gossip and matrimonial situation to which it referred, was sent to the newspapers. Some editors published it, with critical comment. Others felt too embarrassed to do so. Mark Lemon, on whom Dickens had counted for support, refused to carry it in *Punch* on the grounds that it was unsuitable for a comic magazine. Both his staff and Bradbury and Evans took the same view; Dickens felt betrayed and he sent an angry note to the publishers. 'I have had stern occasion to impress upon my children that their father's name is their best possession,' he wrote, 'and that it would be trifled with and wasted by him if either through himself or through them he held any terms with those who had been false to it in the greatest need and under the greatest wrong it has ever known. You know very well why (with hard distress and bitter disappointment) I have been forced to include you in this class. I have no more to say.'[35] The quarrel marked the end of the long and close friendship between Mark Lemon and Dickens. Lemon could not condone such treatment of Catherine, for she too had been a good friend to his wife and children. He took the view that the applause at the amateur theatricals had spoilt Dickens; it was this that had turned his head and made him treat

Catherine so arrogantly. Others had similar opinions. 'Thinks himself God now,' acidly declared Shirley Brooks, the assistant editor of *Punch*. 'If he is, we are atheists, for I don't believe in him.'[36]

Dickens had lost control of himself, and in his fury and anxiety he continued to draw unwelcome attention to his domestic scandal. On 25 May he had written another long letter more explicitly rehearsing the miserable story of his marriage. He and Catherine, he claimed, had 'lived unhappily together for many years'. He spoke of 'her always increasing estrangement', of her previous suggestions 'that it would be better for her to go away and live apart', and of 'a mental disorder under which she sometimes labours'. He had hitherto believed, he asserted, that 'we must bear our misfortune and fight the fight out to the end' in the interest of the children and for the sake of appearances. In an extravagant eulogy of his sister-in-law, he said Georgina had sacrificed herself to be the 'playmate, nurse, instructress, friend, protectress, adviser and companion' to his children and had 'remonstrated, reasoned, suffered, and toiled again and again, to prevent a separation' from his wife. And he returned to his attack on 'the two wicked persons' who had 'coupled with this separation the name and honour of a young lady for whom I have a great attachment and regard'. In this veiled reference to Ellen Ternan he went on to declare: 'Upon my soul and honour, there is not on this earth a more virtuous and spotless creature than this young lady. I know her to be innocent and pure, and as good as my own dear daughters.'[37]

It was a formidable document, and in sending it and the Hogarth retraction to Arthur Smith, the manager of his public readings, Dickens gave explicit authority to use it to refute gossips. 'You have not only my full permission to show this but I beg you to show it to anyone who wishes to do me right, or to anyone who may have been misled into doing me wrong.' Smith was too zealous. He did not simply use the letter as Dickens intended but allowed it to reach the newspapers. Dickens was annoyed with Smith for this use of what he always thereafter called 'the violated letter', and he sent Catherine a shamefaced apology for the 'offensive' publication and declared that he was 'shocked and distressed' by it.[38] It was in fact published in full in the New York *Tribune* on 16 August, provoking a new wave of comment when it was copied back into English newspapers. Dickens, wrote *John Bull*, had 'committed a grave mistake in telling his readers how little, after all, he thinks of the marriage tie'. And one of those readers made the obvious comment: 'People will feel that they have been humbugged out of their idolatry.'[39]

Some comment was sad, some malicious, some light-hearted. Jane Carlyle reported a riddle. 'When does a man ill use his wife? When he gives her a Dickens of a time!' George Simpson of *Blackwood's* caught the general mood when he described Dickens as 'that fallen angel'.[40] The more frantically he tried to assert his innocence the more he revealed his guilt. His impetuosity had left a trail of wreckage—a broken home, blighted friendships, a tarnished respectability, and distress for all the family. 'My father was like a madman when my mother left home,' Kate Dickens said long afterwards; 'this affair brought out all that was worst, all that was weakest in him. He did not care a damn what happened to any of us. Nothing could surpass the misery and unhappiness of our home.'[41] The ladies concerned were suitably reticent. Ellen Ternan left the stage for good as the crisis broke. Her last appearance was in *Out of Sight, Out of Mind* at the Haymarket on 10 June, just two days before Dickens published his desperate statement in *Household Words*. Georgina simply repeated the version of the tragedy she gave to Maria Winter. And while Catherine made no attempt to defend herself in public, in private she dolefully continued to declare her devotion to Dickens. Not long after the separation, after seeing some of the children, she wrote to her aunt Helen Thomson. 'I still love and think of their father far too much for my peace of mind,' she said; 'my position is a sad one and time only may be able to blunt the keen pain that will throb at my heart but I will indeed try to struggle against it.'[42] And at the end of her life—she lived quietly at Gloucester Crescent until her death in November 1879—her one request was for the eventual publication of the letters which Dickens wrote to her before and during their marriage. They would show the world, she declared, that he had once truly loved her. It was understandable that Catherine should regard the letters which Dickens wrote to her over the years as proof of his devotion, for they were affectionate if dutiful: but, except for the way in which they revealed how powerfully Dickens had dominated their relationship from the first, they threw little light on the reasons for its later breakdown.

Although Kate Dickens described her mother as 'a sweet, kind, peace-loving woman, a lady', she recognized that despite her qualities she had her faults. A journalist named J. T. Danson, who worked with Dickens during the launching of the *Daily News*, described her as 'a commonplace, but not ill-disposed woman', and he suggested that she had been quite unable to cope with the way in which Dickens was so suddenly translated from a newspaper reporter into a celebrity. 'Where Dickens was great, she was small,' Danson wrote. 'His fame had, in fact, severed him from her; and had even acted upon her so as to make her seem no fit companion for him; and to leave her worse off than before.... Her dissatisfaction was incurable; and her mode of expressing it induced great and constant vexation to him.'[43] Catherine was a weak and self-pitying woman who found it difficult to make the best of life, and was certainly unsuited for the strains of the part in which her marriage had cast her. It is true that she had suffered five miscarriages and the birth of ten children over twenty years, yet from her first pregnancy she had seemed unable to enjoy motherhood. As a wife she had borne all the vagaries of her husband's difficult temperament without sharing in his fun and good humour. She had complained that a writer's life upset household routines and at the same time she showed little appreciation of the comforts brought about by its success. And when she was uprooted by her husband's pathological restlessness she did not seem to enjoy foreign scenes and new faces. She was known in the Macready household as 'a whiney woman' and her negative state of mind had done much to bring her marriage to breaking point.[44]

Dickens had a complementary habit of complaint—he was as eager to tell the public its faults as Catherine was to criticize him—and his resentment, frustration, and anger were fused into his novels or released in his theatrical performances. The mastery of make-believe was the solution of a genius to the bewildering problems of life; but while the displacement of his emotional energy into each novel or each burst of activity brought temporary relief, it did little to remove the conflicts which lay at the root of his restless anxiety. The euphoria of effort was always followed by the reaction of despair. Forster noted the paradox which made Dickens such a contradictory figure. He was, Forster said, kindly, generous, helpful, and well-meaning. He genuinely believed that only such simple New Testament virtues as love, charity, and forgiveness could change the hearts and minds of men, and he tried to practise what he preached. Yet the world of fancy and the world of fact were very different. It was easy, as Forster remarked, for him to impose 'an orderly arrangement of things' on his plots and to manipulate his characters to fit his sentiments. In everyday life, however, people were less tractable, and Dickens—whose personality, Forster said, made him 'rush at existence without counting the cost'—found it as hard as an eager and clever child to bear such frustration. In domestic matters, he added, Dickens 'had not in himself the resources that such a man, judging from the surface, might be expected to have had.... There was for him "no city of the mind" against outward ills, for inner consolation and shelter.'[45] It was this deficiency, so well observed by Forster, that had made it so difficult for Dickens to answer the question he had posed at the beginning of *David Copperfield*: 'Whether I shall turn out to be the hero of my own life'. For he could never resolve this conflict between his intentions and his feelings. It showed in public when he lost his temper with publishers, book pirates, American critics, politicians, and other targets of his scorn; Catherine and the children had plainly suffered from such bullying. Although he meant well, and could show pity and compassion for unfortunates, he could not overcome the deep-rooted and smouldering resentments that flared out whenever his sensitivities were touched. His own account suggests that it sprang from a profound and never-appeased antagonism to his mother, and when he became a man it carried over into his relationship with Catherine. His complaints that she neglected and rejected the children, that she was lazy and incapable in the home, and that she was spoilt and self-centred echoed his childish grievances against his mother; and he clearly felt that his own home might well have collapsed but for his self-sacrificing efforts to shore it up—as he believed he had shored up the home of his parents long ago, when their failure had made him feel himself a man before his time. The emotions of childhood had brilliantly served his art, but they were wholly inadequate for the demands of marriage.

18

Honour and Glory

'I CAN never hope that anyone out of my house can ever comprehend my domestic story,' Dickens wrote to William de Cerjat early in July 1858. 'I will not complain. I have been heavily wounded, but I have covered the wound up, and left it to heal.'[1] He had in fact been less successful than he claimed in concealing his hurt feelings. He had complained a good deal, in private and in public, and his disturbed temper broke out in other situations. In March, as he was denouncing Catherine for her suspicions, he flared out again at the Royal Literary Fund. He now proposed to rally his fellow reformers by presenting to the annual general meeting of the society on 10 March a pamphlet substantiating their argument with facts and figures about the society's affairs. In *The Case of the Reformers in the Literary Fund* Dickens attacked the Managing Committee with unconcealed hostility, asserting that £40 was squandered on administration for every £100 given in grants. This charge, the *Literary Gazette* declared, was 'the offspring of that fertile imagination which has deservedly placed Mr. Dickens in the foremost rank of living novelists'. Although the reform party had lost the initiative, and its case was overwhelmingly opposed by the meeting, the Committee was stung into a reply which tellingly noted that the salary of the secretary had been raised, and the lease of its expensive premises taken, at a time when Dickens and Dilke had both been members of the Committee; and that Dickens had seldom attended its meetings or shown much interest in its affairs. Dickens was not to be easily beaten and he quickly replied with another pamphlet, *Answers to the Committee's Summary of Facts*. 'It is a facetious facer I have given to those solemn imposters con amore,' he blithely told Collins when he sent him the proofs, and this exchange virtually finished the controversy.[2] In the following year, when Forster proposed to bequeath his library to the Fund if its constitution was reformed, the offer was rejected and Dickens and his allies resigned.

They had started with a reasonable case, but Dickens had handled it badly, allowing his criticism to degenerate into a grievance. When such a mood seized him he lost all sense of tactics, behaving as if revenge mattered more to him than reform; and his public tirades not only aroused resentment in his opponents, stiffening their resistance to his proposals, but came so closely before his private quarrel that they undermined the position of moral authority built up by years of success. He had undoubtedly laid himself open to the kind of abusive retort that came from Newton Crosland, a member of the Fund, after his self-justifying statement in *Household Words*. 'As long as your treacherous insinuations against the Literary Fund remain unretracted', Crosland wrote, 'you must excuse me if I decline to attach the slightest value to any assertions you may make concerning what affects your own interest ... I can believe anything that can be reasonably asserted against you.'[3]

Soon afterwards Dickens became involved in a needless and demoralizing quarrel with Thackeray. When Thackeray spoke at the Royal Academy banquet on 1 May he recalled their first meeting when, a young illustrator seeking work, he had called at Furnival's Inn to show Dickens some specimen drawings. And a few weeks before, when Thackeray had taken the chair at the Royal General Theatrical Fund dinner, Dickens had spoken warmly of his fellow novelist. They had much in common, politically and personally, and as sharp critics of the government during the Crimean War they were more in sympathy with each other than ever before: both had belonged to the Administrative Reform Association. Thackeray had often been a guest at Devonshire Terrace and Tavistock Square, their children were friendly, and they met socially at other houses, at the Garrick Club, and on public occasions. For all that, their friendship never warmed into intimacy. This was partly a matter of professional disagreement. Thackeray had objected when Dickens and Bulwer-Lytton had set up the Guild of Literature. He increasingly felt that his own work was slighted by comparison with the acclaim which greeted one Dickens book after another. 'Thackeray is so soured by the want of success which his writings of late have had', George Lewes wrote to William Blackwood, 'that he is sardonic and bitter against all who are successful.'[4] And his conception of the novel was in marked contrast to the humours and sentiments which Dickens wove into his fiction. It was partly a matter of temperament. Both men were proud and touchy; both were eager for praise; and these similar traits made them uneasy competitors. Now a trivial matter fanned the smouldering resentment into flame.

Thackeray had been piqued when he read a most unflattering profile of himself in *Town Talk* on 12 June 1858. He was the more upset because this disagreeable account had been written by Edmund Yates, whom Thackeray knew to be a protégé of Dickens and the author of a complimentary article on him in the previous issue. Yates had in fact been short of copy and had thoughtlessly scribbled the ill-considered column without meaning offence; Thackeray, however, saw the matter differently. 'No one meeting him could fail to recognise in him a gentleman,' Yates had written; 'his bearing is cold and uninviting, his style of conversation either openly cynical, or affectedly good-natured and benevolent; his *bonhomie* is forced, his wit biting, his pride easily touched ... there is a want of heart in all he writes which is not to be balanced by the most brilliant sarcasm.' Such adolescent gibes might be forgiven a stranger; Thackeray could not forgive them when they came from a fellow member of the Garrick Club. He had himself written wounding criticism as a young man, but he believed he had not broken the code of honour that anything said or done within a club was private—and in a stiff letter of protest to Yates he drew particular attention to that point. 'We meet at a club, where, before you were born I believe, I and other gentlemen have been in the habit of talking without any idea that our conversation would supply paragraphs for professional vendors of "Literary Talk".' In future, he told the youthful Yates, 'you will refrain from printing comments on my private conversations ... forego discussions, however blundering, upon my private affairs ... consider any question of my personal truth and sincerity as quite out of the province of your criticism'.

Yates was not crushed. He drafted a reply reminding Thackeray of the way he had caricatured fellow members of the Garrick Club—and such distinguished authors as Ainsworth, Bulwer-Lytton, and Disraeli—in his novels and his journalism. Before sending the letter he consulted Dickens, who felt grateful for the way Yates had recently rallied to the defence of his *Household Words* statement in the *Illustrated Times*. He thought that Yates had written an impertinent article, but Thackeray's high-handed reply ruled out an apology. So Yates sent a saucy answer. 'If your letter to me were not both "slanderous and untrue"', he told Thackeray, 'I should readily have discussed its subject with you, and avowed my earnest and frank desire to set right anything I have left wrong. Your letter being what it is, I have nothing to add to my present reply.' Thackeray appealed to the committee of the Garrick Club—where he spent much of his time and was a figure of some influence—to judge his complaint against Yates: publication of such articles, he insisted, was 'intolerable in a society of gentlemen'.

When the committee proposed to call a general meeting Yates replied that it had no standing in the matter; his article neither mentioned the club nor referred to any conversation on its premises. And Dickens took the same line. Yet the committee insisted on calling Yates to account, and Dickens thereupon resigned from it. Thackeray, meanwhile, exacerbated the dispute by a thinly disguised sneer at Yates in the current number of *The Virginians*: the 'witch's broth', Dickens declared, 'is now in full boil'. Yates and Thackeray both stayed away from the general meeting on 10 July, Yates sending a letter offering an apology to the club but refusing to concede anything to Thackeray. The meeting supported the committee by 70 votes to 46, telling Yates that he must apologize personally to Thackeray or resign. When he refused to do so he was expelled. He took legal advice and was told that he could bring an action against his forcible exclusion from the premises. Dickens was in the provinces while the wrangling continued, and after his return he wrote to Thackeray on 24 November saying that counsel thought the Garrick Club had acted illegally but suggesting that mediation was the best solution. He also conceded his part in the affair, but insisted that he had supported Yates because Thackeray's original reply had been too intemperate. Thackeray took the admission of support for Yates more seriously than the assurance that Dickens had acted without hostility. 'I grieve to gather from your letter that you were Mr. Yates' adviser in the dispute between him and me,' Thackeray wrote coldly; since Yates had threatened a lawsuit, he said, the matter was now out of his hands. When an acquaintance took him to task for quarrelling with an insignificant young man Thackeray gave a revealing reply. 'I am', he said, 'hitting at the man behind him.'

Dickens, though angered by Thackeray's condescending manner and irritated by his gossip about Ellen Ternan, could not risk an expensive Chancery action. 'By a series of Jew lawyer-like tricks', Yates wrote resentfully to a friend, 'the committee of the Garrick have got the best of me in my legal proceedings.' His only recourse was to publish a pamphlet, in which Dickens collaborated with him, and to include gibes at the Garrick committee in his satirical articles.[5] One of these provoked a reply from Charley Dickens, who had fallen out with his father and—like Thackeray—hit back through Yates. For Charley was engaged to Bessie Evans, the daughter of Frederick Evans, and he had persisted in the betrothal even when Dickens forbade his children to have any truck with Evans or his family. Thackeray saw the connection. 'I'm not even angry with Dickens now for being the mover in the whole affair,' he wrote to William Synge. 'He can't help hating me. ... His quarrel with his wife has driven him almost frantic. He is now quarrelling with his son.' But the rift remained. Two years later Thackeray found himself next to Dickens at a theatre and the two men shook hands without speaking; and the ice was not broken until a few weeks before Thackeray died in 1863.

Dickens had strained many friendships by his treatment of Catherine and by his insistence on unquestioning loyalty, and by the autumn of 1858 he had broken the old frame of his life beyond repair. Yet he clung tenaciously to the children; they were the proof that he was right and that Catherine was wrong—and their continuing presence in the house helped to refute gossip about his relations with Georgina.

In August Catherine visited Miss Coutts with some of the children, which prompted Miss Coutts to make another attempt to heal the breach. Much though Dickens valued her friendship he was not moved by her new appeal, sending her a feverish letter to say that reconciliation with Catherine was unthinkable. 'She does not—she never did—care for the children,' he wrote on 23 August; 'and the children do not—and they never did—care for her. The little play that is acted in your Drawing-room is not the truth, and the less the children play it, the better for themselves. ... As to Mrs. Dickens's simplicity in speaking of me and my doings, O my dear Miss Coutts do I not know that the weak hand that could never help me or serve my name in the least, has struck at it—in conjunction with the wickedest people whom I have loaded with benefits. I want to communicate with her no more. I want to forgive and forget her.'[6]

Although Miss Coutts continued to keep in touch with Dickens, she seemed unwilling to remain on the old terms of friendship and they saw little of each other. Dickens now turned to his new friends for comfort and patronage; he began to shower the Ternans with encouragement and gifts. He sent the eldest daughter Fanny to Italy to continue her musical education, chaperoned by Mrs. Ternan, and tried to advance Maria's career by introductions to such theatrical friends as Benjamin Webster. 'I have a great friendship for her', he told Edmund Yates, 'and know her to be one of the best and bravest of little spirits and most virtuous of girls.'[7] And he seems also to have provided financial help for Maria and Ellen, who had moved from Canonbury to a lodging at 31 Berners Street, off Oxford Street, which was more convenient for the theatres. Like many of his contemporaries— Wilkie Collins among them—Dickens began to lead a secret life, maintaining a second establishment where he could relax away from the public gaze and prudish conventions. Such patronage was not without risks. In October 1858 he was angered to discover that the 'domesticity' of the two young women was being 'looked after' by a policeman, and he sent Wills to Scotland Yard to protest against this 'unwarrantable conduct' and to insist that his proté-gées were 'in all things most irreproachable'.[8]

The claims on his purse were increasing, for Dickens now had to support Catherine, keep up Tavistock House and Gad's Hill, and subsidize the Ternan family. Arthur Smith was instructed to work up an extensive tour: in three months Dickens was to do 87 readings in 43 towns, and another 48 readings were planned to follow the first sweep through England, Scotland, and Ireland. Such a programme demanded an increase in the repertoire. *A Christmas Carol* was always a favourite. He chose scenes from *The Chimes* and *The Cricket on the Hearth*, worked up Paul Dombey, Mrs. Gamp, and Jonas Chuzzlewit, and made a triumph of the trial from *Pickwick*.

On 2 August 1858 Dickens started at Clifton, where the people 'were perfectly taken off their legs by *The Chimes*'.[9] The next night, at Exeter, was 'a prodigious cram'.[10] At Plymouth there was 'a shout all through'.[11] By the end of the first week, when Smith had collected nearly £400 in entrance money, Dickens was telling Miss Coutts of his 'immense success' and adding that 'it is a great sensation to have a large audience in one's hand'.[12] He went on to similar excitement at Worcester, Wolverhampton, Shrewsbury, and Chester. From Liverpool, on 21 August, he wrote ecstatically to Edmund Yates: 'A wonderful house here last night, the largest in numbers and the largest in money we have ever had. ... There were 2300 people and 200 guineas ... Arthur bathed in checks, took headers into tickets, floated on billows of passes, dived under weirs of shillings, staggered home faint with gold and silver.'[13] The audiences, Dickens realized, were overcome by his versatility. 'They don't quite understand beforehand what it is, I think,' he wrote to Wilkie Collins from Worcester, 'and expect a man to be sitting down in some corner, droning away like a mild bagpipe.'[14] What they were given was a brilliant series of carefully rehearsed impersonations, in which Dickens recreated the characters of his tales before their eyes. There was no precedent for such a thing, and he watched carefully for reactions which would tell him what went down well. He was particularly struck by the way the stories convinced and moved his audience as if they were real. 'It is very curious to see how many people in black come to Little Dombey,' he observed to Miss Coutts. 'And when it is over they almost uniformly go away as if the child were really Dead—with a hush upon them.'[15]

At the end of August Dickens took the boat from Liverpool for his first visit to Ireland, where he was to read at Dublin, Cork, Limerick, and Belfast. 'The Emerald press is in favour of my appearance, and likes my eyes,' he reported to Georgina—and he found the public equally enthusiastic. 'I wish you and the dear girls could have seen the people look at me in the street; or heard them ask me ... to "do me the honour to shake hands Misther Dickens, and God bless you sir ... for the light you've been to me this night ... for the light you've been in mee house sir (and God love your face!) this many a year".'[16] Dickens, equally eager for affection and for cash, revelled in such popularity. From York he told Forster that 'the intelligence and warmth of the audiences are an immense sustainment, and one that always sets me up'.[17] Writing to Mary Boyle on 10 September he confessed that he suffered from fits of gloom that left him 'utterly desolate and lost'. Restored by a reading, 'the sky brightened before me once more'.[18] At the same time his letters were stuffed with financial titbits. By the time he reached Edinburgh, as he gleefully informed Wills, he knew that his profits for September alone would exceed £1,000.

This drive for flattering response and financial reward was a tiring business; but, as Dickens admitted to Wilkie Collins in a letter in mid-August, it was also an anodyne: 'I cannot deny that I shall be heartily glad when it is all over, and that I miss the thoughtfulness of my quiet room and desk. But perhaps it is best for me not to have it just now, and to wear and toss my storm away—or as much of it as will ever calm down while the water rolls—in this restless manner.'[19] He got some relief by making short visits to London between engagements, and he enjoyed having Mamie and Kate with him to see his triumphs in Scotland. 'Hear Dickens, and die,' declared the *Scotsman*; 'you will never live to hear anything of the kind so good.'[20] Yet when he turned south the dates stretched away for another month, through the industrial cities to Oxford, Portsmouth, and a final night at Brighton on 13 November. Eleanor Emma Christian, who had danced with Dickens so long before at Broadstairs, saw her old friend in Southampton and she noticed 'his face lined by deep furrows, hair grizzled and thinned, his expression careworn and clouded'.[21] It was, however, a remarkable progress on which, as he proudly told Miss Coutts, he had made a great deal of money—and also found, in the 'personal affection' of his public, consolation in his misery. 'I consider it a remarkable instance of good fortune ... that I should in this autumn of all others, have come face to face with so many multitudes.'[22]

Such success restored his spirits. It also made him obdurate against those whom he considered as false friends because they had failed to rally to him in his distress. Bradbury and Evans were obvious victims. As soon as Dickens returned to London from his reading tour he sent Forster to tell them that he wished to buy out their interest in the magazine, and to announce that he was taking his printing and publishing business back to Chapman and Hall; though Chapman was on the point of retirement and Hall was dead, the firm was flourishing and willing to take Dickens back on any terms he cared to name. Bradbury and Evans, anxious to keep their stake in *Household Words*, refused to sell. Forster, armed with a power of attorney, brusquely told them that Dickens was in no mood for a compromise and that he was prepared to start a rival journal. While Bradbury and Evans went to law Dickens went to work. 'I have taken the new office; have got workmen in,' he wrote to Forster in February 1859; 'settled with the printer; and am getting an immense system of advertising ready.'[23] He had also chosen a title. He had first decided upon *Household Harmony*, which Forster understandably thought tactless in the circumstances, and he ran through a list which included *Home Music*, *Home*, *The Hearth*, *Change*, and *Good Humour* before he found a name which was comfortably distant from his domestic difficulties. He planned to start publishing *All the Year Round* on 30 April 1859.

When Bradbury and Evans got their hearing before the Master of the Rolls on 26 March they found themselves in the same difficulty as Bentley when, years before, Dickens proposed to break his contract for *Barnaby Rudge*. They could neither force Dickens to write for *Household Words* nor restrain him from writing under other auspices. The judge, dissolving the partnership which owned the magazine, put it up for auction; and on 16 May, two weeks before he closed the paper down, Dickens bought it for £3,550. Since he already owned five-eighths of the property it was a good bargain. He reckoned that he had got the stock at valuation and the goodwill for a few hundred pounds—and he had put Bradbury and Evans to the trouble of starting a new venture called *Once a Week* which had great difficulty in competing with *All the Year Round*.

Dickens got his paper off to a good start. By the fifth number it was already selling three times as well as *Household Words*. By July it had recouped all the costs incurred in launching it and made a profit as well, and its circulation climbed steadily. Dickens had learned his lesson from *Master Humphrey's Clock*, which started without the expected serial and had to be rescued by *The Old Curiosity Shop*. This time he began with a new story of his own and he commissioned signed serials from other notable writers—the first being Wilkie Collins, who contributed *The Woman in White*.

The need to meet a definite publication date provided the discipline that Dickens required to begin *A Tale of Two Cities*. He drew upon a French source for much of the plot; the new novel had many similarities to a play which the dramatist Watts Phillips worked up from the same source. It also relied heavily upon Carlyle's *French Revolution*—and on a parcel of books which Carlyle sent from the London Library when Dickens asked him for help—to show the terrible price that France paid for years of 'unspeakable suffering, intolerable oppression, and heartless indifference'. The indicting anger which had burned through *Hard Times*, *Bleak House*, and *Little Dorrit* had flared out again in *A Tale of Two Cities*, and Dickens used the Paris mob to point the same apocalyptic moral as the rioters who ran amok through London in the closing scenes of *Barnaby Rudge*: order will fail when human beings are denied their rights, and when order fails the terrifying forces of darkness will blindly destroy the innocent along with the guilty.

Dickens had never resolved his childhood ambivalence about violence. He was at once a defiant rebel against society, which in some moods he saw as a prison which crushed humanity out of normal shape; a secret sharer in the resentments of outcasts and criminals; and a man who had an obsessional fear of disorder. As he grew older he continued to rage against obvious injustice, but he became more fearful of the consequences of such rage. And when he began to write *A Tale of Two Cities* the atrocities of the Indian Mutiny were fresh in his mind. On 4 October 1857, soon after he heard of the massacre of women and children in Cawnpore, he wrote ferociously to Angela Coutts to say that were he Commander-in-Chief he would 'exterminate the Race upon whom the stain of the late cruelties rested'.[24] That Christmas, moreover, the *Household Words* story (written in collaboration with Wilkie Collins) was called 'The Perils of Certain English Prisoners', and *The Times* declared that in this 'short and slight' adventure Dickens had patriotically celebrated 'the great qualities displayed by our race in recent emergencies'.

There were personal as well as political echoes in *A Tale of Two Cities*. Dickens was still much affected by his performances in *The Frozen Deep* and the more recent stresses of separation from his wife. 'Sometimes of late, when I have been very much excited by the crying of two thousand people over the grave of Richard Wardour,' he told Angela Coutts on 5 September 1857, 'new ideas for a story have come into my head as I lay on the ground, with surprising force and brilliancy.'[25] The main idea, as he explained in his preface to the novel, was to have the self-pitying wastrel Sydney Carton lay down his life for Charles Darnay in the same way that Wardour had sacrificed himself for his rival Aldersley. 'A strong desire was upon me then', Dickens said of Carton's redeeming impulse, 'to embody it in my own person; and I traced out in my fancy the state of mind ... it has had complete possession of me; I have so far verified what is done and suffered in these pages, as that I have certainly done and suffered it all myself.' This gift of vivid identification, which Dickens could summon up on the stage and in his fiction, was vital to his art and a clue to the contradictions of his life—so strikingly personified in *A Tale of Two Cities* by the dualism of Carton and Darnay, twins in appearance and opposites in nature, symbols of death and resurrection.

The themes of guilt, suffering, death, and redemption ran more strongly through this novel than any of its predecessors as Dickens wove them around the hidden crime of the Evrémondes and the lust for revenge it engendered. He reached back to his memory of the solitary confinement system in Philadelphia for one of the possible titles he suggested to Forster: 'Buried Alive' was an appropriate phrase for the ordeal of Dr. Manette, the innocent prisoner in the Bastille recalled to life by the Revolution. He introduced Jerry Cruncher, in a parody of resurrection, to snatch bodies from the tomb. And as Carton stands in the shadow of the guillotine Dickens asserts the comforting promise of the New Testament—'he that believeth in me, though he were dead, yet shall he live'—and gives him a vision of expiation reaching down the years. Carton has transcended his infantile miseries and found his manhood at last.

PART FOUR

THE NATIONAL SPARKLER

1859–1870

19

Ashes of the Great

THE year 1859 was the watershed of the Victorian age. As the country recovered from the strains of the Crimean War its industry and trade were creating unprecedented wealth. The population was growing fast, and thanks to the spreading network of railways there was a new freedom of movement, and travel was cheap. The great landed interest was still powerful in politics, but the manufacturing districts were becoming large enough to tip the balance from a predominantly rural to an urban and industrial society. There was change in the world, and beyond it; in 1859, the liberating ideas of the new sciences about the nature of the cosmos and man's place in it, which had begun to shake the hold of revealed religion, found dramatic expression when Darwin published his evolutionary theory in his *Origin of Species*. And in the same year John Stuart Mill's essay *On Liberty* exemplified a similar change in political thought. The general election had brought in a triumvirate of reformers—the old champions of the Reform Bill under Russell, the new Liberals led by William Ewart Gladstone and John Bright, and their eccentric ally Palmerston—to fuse political reform and economic free enterprise. There was a sense that progress would march on to widening horizons of liberty and prosperity.

Dickens, at the crisis of his own life, was curiously ambivalent about these evidences of change. In many ways he was a man of his age with all the instincts of a Victorian entrepreneur, vigorously promoting his theatricals and his magazines, eagerly counting the profits from his public readings, and showing sharp business acumen in his dealings with his publishers. He was an inveterate and intemperate critic of the past. He had no use for what he called 'the Parrots of Society' who rasped out conservative and High Church versions of history, or for 'the Birds of Prey' who had thrived at the expense of ordinary men and women. 'If ever I destroy myself', he wrote to Douglas Jerrold when he was planning his *Child's History*, 'it will be in the bitterness of hearing those infernal and damnably good old times, extolled.'[1] And he was intrigued by mechanical inventions and social innovations. He once commented on the telegraph wire 'piercing, like a sunbeam, right through the cruel old heart of the Colosseum at Rome',[2] and he had written to Jerrold from Venice that those who complained of the railway being built out across the lagoon should be 'thanking Heaven that they live in a time when Iron makes Roads instead of Prison Bars'.[3] Dickens was interested in science and he was certainly an enthusiast for popular education and personal freedom. He had spoken up humanely for the sick, the poor, and the exploited, for reforms in factories, prisons, and Poor Law workhouses. He had, above all, the quality of sympathy which enabled him to touch the conscience of an age when philanthropy flourished as vigorously as reform.

Dickens was a part of his times and at the same time a man apart. For all his success he rejected the social and economic fabric and his books were purposeiy subversive. He was always scornful of Parliament and contemptuous of most politicians. He told Angela Coutts that Palmerston was 'the emptiest imposter and the most dangerous delusion, ever known'.[4] And he was always dubious about the will or the capacity of the people to improve their lot by political means. He distrusted the new capitalists, disliked the way they made their fortunes, and attacked the doctrines of political economy which justified their heartlessness; like Carlyle he was a moralist about money, and he sympathized with Carlyle's demand for a society regulated by relationships rather than cash, for a kinder world than that which was being pounded out by the steam engines; his work often exuded an appealing nostalgia for the days before the green fields were hidden by the smoke.

Such ambiguities also ran through his manner of life. No author ever knew London better or had a finer sense of its richly varied texture; yet he hankered for the Kentish countryside where he had grown up, and in later years he preferred Gad's Hill to anywhere. He came to see himself as a gentleman of the pre-industrial age, the life-style that he most admired. All the benevolent patriarchs in his stories inherited or achieved that desirable status, and all his heroes strove towards it. Gad's Hill, indeed, was the evidence of his success. His grandmother, who had been a housekeeper in a country mansion, had the pretensions of an upper servant, and his father had always given himself gentlemanly airs. Dickens, for all his misfortunes, had been brought up on the shaky margins of gentility; debt, after all, afflicted the best of families, and if it was shaming it was not quite as shaming as trade. The aspirations reached back over three generations to Crewe Hall, and all the traditional values that it seemed to represent. John Dickens had even found a tenuous claim to a coat of arms—a lion holding a Maltese cross—and by the middle of his career Dickens had adopted the device as a book-plate. He lived as a squire at Gad's Hill, comfortably supported on the rents of his talent as a writer and performer, cultivating his public like a conventional man of property cultivated his estate.

The contradiction between the impulse to reject society and the desire to be acceptable to it was always teasing Dickens, and he coped with it by breaking up his life into a series of roles and moving from one to another regardless of consistency. Now he was the radical editor, with a broken marriage and a clandestine relationship, now the famous novelist who celebrated the domestic virtues; now he was the actor-manager, hankering for the boards, now the country gentleman of leisure; and though he was a fierce critic of the getting of money he was also a man who drove himself to acquire it as a means to the independence he prized. He had turned himself into a public performer, and he was beginning to think of a reading tour in America.

His grievance against the American book trade was waning at last. A cash payment of £1,000 from an American newspaper for the story he called 'Hunted Down' was convincing evidence that U.S. publishers were willing to pay for his work; and there was reason to think that American readings would be even more profitable than those which had gone so well in England. In 1858 a journalist on the New York *World* named Thomas Coke Evans collected many testimonials from prominent clergymen, politicians, and editors, all assuring Dickens that he would again be welcomed in the United States. Evans sent these assurances with an offer to promote such a visit, and he followed up his proposal with a personal call in London late in January 1859. Dickens was hesitant, referring Evans to his manager Arthur Smith. He rightly suspected that Evans had no funds to back his lavish idea of eighty readings for a fee of £10,000 with all expenses paid, and would treat any contract as a negotiable property on which he would then raise the necessary money. On 9 August Dickens wrote to Bulwer-Lytton to tell him that Evans had 'no capital whatever, though there seems to be nothing against his character' and that he was simply 'an unaccredited agent'.[5] All the same Dickens had been sufficiently impressed to make one agreement with Evans on 17 March; in exchange for an annual fee of £1,000 he sent him plates of *All the Year Round* two weeks in advance of the London publication date, thus enabling him to print an edition in New York ahead of any competitors. And for a time Dickens was so attracted by the money Evans offered that his solicitor Frederic Ouvry felt it necessary to discourage him from signing a contract for a tour.

In the summer of 1859 Dickens was also urged to cross the Atlantic to give some readings by James T. Fields, who as a young man had admiringly followed him through the streets on the wintry night he arrived in Boston. Fields was now a partner in the Boston publishing firm of Ticknor and Fields, and when he visited Dickens he brought support for his proposal from Cornelius Felton and other American friends. Dickens was tempted, and yet reluctant. 'Several strong reasons would make the journey difficult for me,' he wrote to Fields.[6] Not the least of these was separation from Ellen Ternan. Dickens was a little more explicit on this point to Arthur Smith, saying that he was reluctant to go 'for a private reason, rendering a long voyage and absence particularly painful to me'.[7] And he admitted his uncertainty to Forster. 'I should be one of the most unhappy of men if I were to go', he wrote in July, 'and yet I cannot help being much stirred and influenced by the golden prospect held before me.'[8] A month later he had made up his mind. 'I have ... come to the conclusion *that I will not go now*!' he wrote to Fields on 6 August. 'A year hence I may revive the matter.'[9]

There were other reasons for delay. Dickens had recently appointed Frank Beard, a younger brother of his old friend Thomas Beard, as the family doctor; and he consulted him that summer, telling Wills at the beginning of July that he felt 'languid and short of starch'.[10] He needed a quiet routine. If he spent most of the summer at Gad's Hill he would sufficiently recoup his energies to tackle a second series of provincial readings in the autumn. He had, moreover, to devote himself to *A Tale of Two Cities*, which was moving so slowly that he complained to Forster that 'the small portions ... drive me frantic'.[11] He found it more difficult to condense a tale than to expand it; and between the first number at the end of April 1859 and its conclusion in November he had to compress the book into eight monthly parts and, at the same time, find an acceptable way of dividing these into the weekly instalments needed for *All the Year Round*. At the end of August he went to Broadstairs to visit Wilkie Collins, hoping that the bracing air and the sea-bathing would revive him as they had done so often in the past, and after his return he pressed on to finish the novel. 'I am very glad you like it so much,' he told Collins in October. 'It has greatly moved and excited me in the doing, and Heaven knows I have done my best and believed in it.'[12] He was even more positive to F. J. Régnier. 'I hope that it is the best story I have written,' he said when he sent proofs to Paris in the dubious hope that the censors appointed by Napoleon III might permit a stage version;[13] and he was so taken by its dramatic possibilites that he helped Tom Taylor put on a Lyceum production in 1860. Though he had told Régnier that the 'story is an extraordinary success here' and it had got *All the Year Round* off to an excellent start, the critics were cool and it attracted less comment than any of his previous novels. Even Forster, reviewing the novel anonymously in the *Examiner* when the bound volume came out in December, admitted that it lacked 'the quaint humour by which his reputation was first won'; its merit, he suggested, lay in the skill with which Dickens had fused private and public histories to conjure up the tempest of revolution.[14] By relying on incident rather than character, and story rather than dialogue, Forster recognized, the novel became a departure in style, an experiment which was not 'entirely successful'. There was a growing feeling among the critics that Dickens was sinking into a gloomy decline.

While Dickens was at work on the story his portrait was being painted by W. P. Frith, whose large-scale 'Derby Day' (which included a scene from *The Old Curiosity Shop*) had been the sensation of the Royal Academy in 1858. Frith, who had been urged to his task by Forster, was apprehensive; yet when he went for the first sitting at the end of January 1859 he found that Dickens 'sat delightfully' and talked most agreeably while he painted. His expression, Frith noted, was that of a man 'who had reached the topmost rung of a very high ladder and was perfectly aware of his position'.[15] The painter Edwin Landseer made a different comment. 'I wish', he remarked when he saw the finished portrait, 'he looked less eager and busy, and not so much out of himself, or beyond himself. I should like to catch him asleep and quiet now and then.'[16]

Dickens, however, scarcely knew the meaning of repose. As soon as the book was done in October he set off for a two-week reading tour of East Anglia and the Midlands. Once more he cheerfully reported large audiences and handsome profits. Arthur Smith 'turned away twice Peterborough';[17] Cambridge was 'beyond everything'; and the 'great doings' at Oxford included the 'Prince of Wales and what not'.[18] One night at Cheltenham gained him a clear £70: and there was more money to come from a set of readings in London over the Christmas season. *All the Year Round* was doing well with *The Woman in White*, which began to run in November as *A Tale of Two Cities* came to an end. Wilkie Collins had been determined to stagger the public into attention from the first gripping pages, and he had succeeded with a thriller that became the talk of London.

Professionally it had been a good year for Dickens. He had successfully launched his new magazine, written a shorter and a new type of novel, and proved that there was a continuing and most profitable market for his readings. It had also been a more peaceful year than 1858 when he had gone through the stormy separation from Catherine. Yet there were still problems with the children. Charley seemed to be doing well and he was about to sail for Hong Kong to buy tea in preparation for setting up as a merchant on his own account, but Dickens remained angry at his refusal to break his engagement with Bessie Evans. Though Walter had made a decent start in India, serving honourably in the Mutiny campaign and earning promotion to lieutenant, Dickens worried about him; and he worried more about Frank, afflicted with a stammer, recurrent deafness, and sleep-walking, who had no settled ambition and could do nothing right. Dickens thought he might use influence to get the boy into the Foreign Office. Alfred, who seemed to be the steadiest, was at the Wimbledon crammer, hoping to go on to an army commission. Sydney, always keen on the sea, was preparing to serve as a naval cadet. And the two smallest boys, Harry and Plorn, were at the Rochester grammar school.

The two girls, most exposed to the strains of Catherine's departure, had reacted differently to it. Mamie, now in her early twenties, had sided with her father; when he disapproved of a prospective suitor she meekly complied and contented herself as his companion and hostess at Gad's Hill. She did not see her mother again until after Dickens's death. Kate was more independent. She visited Catherine regularly and she was plainly uneasy at home. In 1860 she agreed to marry Charles Collins, the younger brother of the novelist. He was a painter—his close friends were Holman Hunt, Millais, and other members of the Pre-Raphaelite Brotherhood—and he had lately taken to journalism. Dickens thought well enough of his work to publish some of it in *All the Year Round*, but he thought less well of him as a son-in-law. Collins, too, was cool towards Dickens, telling Holman Hunt that he had always felt some impediment to entire intimacy between them. A dozen years older than Kate, Collins was an odd-looking fellow; he was irresolute, affectionate, and physically delicate, and an early infatuation with Maria Rossetti had left him with a streak of Anglo-Catholic asceticism. Kate, as Dickens suspected when he opposed the match, was marrying more to escape from home than for love; and Dickens was bothered by the Puseyite beliefs of Collins. After the wedding on 17 July, from which Catherine was conspicuously absent, Mamie found her father in Kate's room weeping into her wedding-gown. 'But for me', he sobbed, 'Katie would not have left home.'[19]

And there were other family troubles to distress him. His brother Frederick was as vigorous a sponger as his father. 'I have already done more for you than most dispassionate persons would consider right or reasonable,' Dickens had told him at the end of 1857;[20] but he was back again in 1858, cadging from Wills and Henry Austin and dunning Dickens for more. And in the autumn of that year, when Dickens came back from his speaking tour, he found that Fred had compromised Wills for a largish amount of money and had left his wife Anna. A year later the younger brother, Augustus, deserted his wife, who had gone blind, and went off to America with another woman. Dickens, forced to support another abandoned sister-in-law, complained bitterly about Augustus to Helen Dickens, the wife of his brother Alfred. 'He has always been, in a certain insupportable arrogance and presumption of character, so wrong, that, even when he had some prospects before him, I despaired of his ever being right.'[21] Alfred, who had been a hard-working civic engineer, had seemed more reliable. But when he died of pleurisy in July 1860 Dickens reported that Alfred was in a 'shattered condition' and had been 'habitually out very late at night'; and it turned out that Alfred had saved nothing to support his wife and five children. Once more Dickens had to assume responsibility. 'Day after day', he wrote on 19 August, 'I have been scheming and contriving for them, and I am still doing so, and I have schemed myself into broken rest and low spirits.'[22]

It was the responsibility which bothered him, not the cash: in 1859 his income was over £10,000, and for the previous decade it had usually run at more than £4,000 a year. The same sense of being exploited marred his relations with his mother; she, he wryly remarked, 'was left me when my father died (I have never had anything left to me but relations)'.[23] He had always been cool towards Elizabeth Dickens and she had become more difficult in old age, since she suffered from senility and delusions of grandeur. She was, Dickens said, 'a ghastly absurdity'. He paid a quarterly allowance of £25, but, visiting her one day towards the end of 1850, at the house in Hampstead which he maintained for her and the widowed Helen, he noted that 'the instant she saw me, she plucked up a spirit, and asked me for "a pound"'.[24]

Family and friendships decayed. In August 1859 Leigh Hunt died. Dickens regretted the caricature of Hunt as the feckless Harold Skimpole in *Bleak House*, and he tried to make amends by an anonymous but kindly notice of Hunt's *Stories in Venice*. This had not satisfied the friends of Hunt, and after his death they urged Dickens to make a public apology; the most he would do was to publish an article in *All the Year Round* which reviewed a new edition of Hunt's *Autobiography*—all he had done, Dickens said, was to copy Hunt's 'gay and ostentatious wilfulness' in the portrait of Skimpole, and he claimed that Hunt was as free from the 'imaginary vices of the fictional creature' as the model who sat for a painting of Iago was innocent of Desdemona's death.[25] A few months later the artist Frank Stone died of a heart attack. Dickens had known him since the early days of his success and remained on close terms, and Stone and his family—who were neighbours in Tavistock Square—had been keen participants in the amateur theatricals.

Dickens had also become estranged from his old illustrator, Hablôt Browne, who had accepted a position on *Once a Week*, the successor to *Household Words* which Bradbury and Evans devised when Dickens left them. Dickens was a man who demanded absolute loyalty and after a lifetime of professional co-operation *A Tale of Two Cities* was the last of Dickens's novels to be illustrated by Phiz. 'Confound all authors and publishers say I,' the melancholy Browne commented. 'There is no pleasing one or t'other. I wish I had never had anything to do with the lot.'[26] Frank Stone's son,

Marcus, replaced him as the Dickens illustrator. There was, however, brighter news of Macready, who had suffered sadly over the years, losing his wife, sister, and six children from tuberculosis. Dickens was delighted when he married again in April 1860. Some friends, Forster for one, disapproved because Macready was sixty-seven and his bride was merely twenty-three, but Dickens was more generous. 'God bless you, and God bless the object of your choice,' he wrote on hearing the news in March. 'I do not believe that a heart like yours was made to hold so large a waste-place as there has been in it.'[27] The couple moved from the gloomy house at Sherborne to Cheltenham and in May 1862 Cecile Macready gave birth to a healthy son.

As the months passed Dickens saw the collapse of his own marriage in a calmer light. There were no second thoughts. When Angela Coutts made another bid for a reconciliation with Catherine in the spring of 1860 he replied firmly. 'That figure is out of my life for evermore (except to darken it) and my desire is, Never to see it again.'[28] Looking back on twenty years of married life he said he believed that he had made 'a miserable mistake, and that the wretched consequences which might naturally have been expected from it, have resulted from it'. All the same, he assured Miss Coutts, 'I believe I am exactly what I always have been; quite as hopeful, cheerful and active, as I ever was. I am not so weak or wicked as to visit any small unhappiness of my own, upon the world in which I live.... As to my art, I have as great a delight in it as the most enthusiastic of my readers; and the sense of my trust and responsibility in that wise, is always upon me when I take pen in hand. If I were soured, I should try to sweeten the lives and fancies of others, but I am not—not at all.'[29] In this retrospective mood, when he was coming to terms with the new pattern of his life, Dickens decided to sell Tavistock House. He could now manage by turning some rooms at the office of *All the Year Round* into a *pied-à-terre* for routine visits and by renting a London house for a few months each year, when Mamie and Georgina wanted to be in town for the fashionable season. His real home was Gad's Hill.

He sold Tavistock House and much of its fittings and furniture to a Jewish moneylender named J. P. Davis. 'I strongly suspect that a good many people about town who have been there now and then during the last nine years', he jestingly remarked to Thomas Mitton in mid-August, 'will present themselves under the new administration in an entirely new capacity.'[30] And a few days later he went out of his way to assure Wills that 'the purchaser has behaved thoroughly well, and that I cannot call to mind any occasion when I have had money-dealings with anyone that have been so satisfactory, considerate and trusting'.[31] The remainder of the furniture and the personal effects accumulated over two decades were sent off down the turnpike to Gad's Hill. Dickens, who was shocked by the misuse of the private letters of public men, took the occasion to make a bonfire of all the letters he had kept. All the correspondence from Forster went into the flames; so did letters from such old intimates as Ainsworth, Macready, Maclise, Bulwer-Lytton, and Talfourd, as well as everything from Tennyson, Thackeray, Browning, Captain Marryat, and many other British and foreign men of letters. The plume of smoke, Dickens remarked, was 'like the Genie when he got out of the casket',[32] and the younger boys—Harry and Plorn—remembered that they had 'roasted onions in the ashes of the great'.[33] 'Would to God every letter I had ever written was on that pile,' Dickens reflected as he contemplated the holocaust.[34] He had burned his links to the past.

Dickens still turned to Forster for professional advice and occasionally for the kind of support that only a trusted friend could offer, but he now spent much of his time with younger companions and subordinates who were in no position to judge his behaviour and make him feel uncomfortable. He dined and went out with Wilkie Collins, Edmund Yates, and the young Irish writer Percy Fitzgerald whom he had met in Dublin and commissioned as a contributor to *All the Year Round;* he took up with the composer Francesco Berger, who had written the incidental music for *The Frozen Deep*, and the Swiss romantic actor Charles Fechter, who made his name on the Paris stage before settling in England with the help of Dickens. Fechter kept up a vivacious Bohemian style at his St. John's Wood villa: the gushes of merriment there, Wilkie Collins said, were as inexhaustible as the gushes of garlic. He was one of the few men with whom Dickens was able to relax in the convivial manner he had always enjoyed. All the members of this group, moreover, were men of the world, tolerant of the association between Dickens and Ellen Ternan. Berger recalled playing the piano while Dickens and his Nelly sang duets in the respectable five-floored house at 2 Houghton Place, in Ampthill Square off the Hampstead Road, which Dickens provided for the Ternan girls and their mother after Mrs. Ternan came back from Italy in 1861.

Dickens had thus shifted the focus of his social life. He was more sombre in spirit, more easily tired; and he preferred to spend as much time as he could at Gad's Hill and to entertain selected guests in a leisurely style. He kept a close eye on things. Before he started to write in the morning he made a tour of the rooms to see that everything was in its place—that meticulous obsession never left him—and then visited the dogs, the stables, and the kitchen garden. He always had labourers about, adding new rooms, remodelling the outhouses, excavating a tunnel beneath the London road to provide direct access to his shrubbery: 'when I get the workmen out this time,' he wrote to Forster after one such bout of improvement, 'I think I'll leave off'.[35] Yet he never did. He was proud of his alterations and he enjoyed showing friends round his country home. 'Life at Gad's Hill for visitors', Edmund Yates remembered, 'was delightful. You breakfasted at nine, smoked your cigar, read the papers, and pottered about the garden until luncheon at one.'[36] This was a substantial meal, though after a morning at his desk Dickens contented himself with bread and cheese and a glass of ale. In the afternoon, the energetic were often marshalled by Dickens for a walk of a dozen miles or more through the Kentish countryside at the cracking pace of four miles an hour; others were dispatched for a drive through neighbouring Cobham Park or taken to see the sights of Rochester or the views over the Medway marshes which had been his earliest horizons.

He had begun to mull over his memories of childhood again in some of the remembrances which he wrote for *All the Year Round* in 1860 and published as a book which he called *The Uncommercial Traveller*. He described his boyhood wanderings round Chatham dockyard and complained that Rochester, which he called 'Dullborough', seemed to have 'shrunk fearfully' from his boyish perspectives. 'All my early readings and imaginations dated from this place', he wrote, 'and I took them away so full of innocent construction and guileless belief, and I brought them back so worn and torn, so much the wiser and so much the worse!' He was working himself into the mood for another novel, which would soon be needed by his magazine.

The serial of *The Woman in White* was due to end in the summer of 1860, and Dickens was concerned to find a replacement. He first approached George Eliot, recognizing a woman's hand behind the male nom-de-plume, and telling her how warmly he had admired *Scenes from Clerical Life* and *Adam Bede*: 'if you should ever have the freedom and inclination to be a fellow labourer with me,' he wrote, 'it would yield me a pleasure that I have never known yet, and can never know otherwise; and no channel that even *you* could command should be so profitable'.[37] At first she accepted his proposal, merely asking for more time. It was not until February 1860 that she let him know that she could not provide what he wanted. She was, Dickens reported to the Irish novelist Charles Lever, 'terrified by the novel difficulties of serial writing: cannot turn in the space: evidently will not be up to the scratch when Collins's sponge is thrown up'.[38] Dickens had also been negotiating with Mrs. Gaskell, offering her two hundred guineas for a tale which would run in twenty-two weekly parts. She had similar difficulties. She had disliked her previous experience of serialization, and she was reluctant to see her work 'broken up into bits' again; and in any case she was not keen to collaborate with Dickens, for she felt that he had treated Catherine very badly. When she eventually wrote *Sylvia's Lovers* she gave it instead to Thackeray for publication in the *Cornhill Magazine*, a much more sober journal which he had launched just before Christmas 1859. Dickens thus had to fall back upon his third reserve, Charles Lever, who had followed his early success with *Harry Lorrequer* by a number of Irish genre novels. Lever had provided him with the opening chapters of *A Day's Ride: A Life's Romance*, and Dickens liked both the title and the text. Unfortunately, succeeding parts became verbose and so dreary that by October Dickens was compelled to send Lever news that wounded his considerable self-esteem. 'We drop', he wrote, 'rapidly and continuously', though he softened the blow by speaking well of the story, and blaming the difficulties of serialization.[39] The only solution was for Dickens to strike in himself with a story, and to push on with it so that the first part could appear before Christmas. He had told the Earl of Carlisle in August 1860 that he was 'prowling about, meditating a new book'.[40] His experiences with *A Tale of Two Cities* had increased his dislike of writing fiction for weekly publication, and his first intention was to write a large novel in twenty monthly parts; but now he felt that he had no choice if he was to save the magazine. 'I come in when most wanted', he told Forster, 'and if Reade and Wilkie follow me, our course will be shaped out handsomely and hopefully for between two and three years. A thousand pounds are to be paid for early proofs of the story in America.'[41]

Once started on the story he called *Great Expectations* Dickens worked steadily to have the first number ready to appear on 1 December 1860. The plot moved with smooth conviction, and from the first it sold well—it lifted the sagging sales of *All the Year Round* and quickly ran to several editions when the bound volumes appeared in August 1861. Dickens took a break from it in November 1860 when he went to Devonshire with Wilkie Collins and they worked on the Christmas story, 'The Message from the Sea', which was soon dramatized. It was an unusually cold winter: 'the water in the bedroom-jugs froze, and blew up the crockery', Dickens reported to Cerjat on 1 February 1861;[42] and during one walk his beard was frozen to his topcoat. He spent much of the winter in London, first at his apartment at the magazine office and then at 3 Hanover Terrace in Regent's Park, which he rented until the summer as a London base for Mamie and Georgina. He allowed himself sufficient leave from his novel to give six readings in London over Easter, clearing £500 after paying all expenses. 'A very great result,' he told Forster. 'We certainly might have gone on through the season, but I am heartily glad to be concentrated on my story.'[43]

Dickens had read over *David Copperfield* to avoid 'unconscious repetitions' before he started *Great Expectations*, and he reported to Forster that he 'was affected by it to a degree you would hardly believe'.[44] There was much in common between the two novels. They were both stories of an orphan boy who grows up feeling unwanted, and is forced into a struggle for survival. There was also a marked change in perspective. He wrote *Copperfield* at the climax of his breathless rush to fame, and young David naïvely exemplifies his acceptance by the genteel middle class and his success in his profession; he still saw his youthful heroes as romantic innocents whose innate good qualities emerge despite adverse circumstances. By the time he came to write *Great Expectations*, however, he was a chastened man, who saw far more deeply into the errors and trials of his early years. In this masterpiece of his maturity, Dickens actually reversed his theme to explore the sources of unhappiness rather than success. When Pip is released from the blacksmith's forge by a mysterious endowment, which he secretly feels to be his due, it is his less attractive qualities which come out as his material circumstances improve. He suffers from self-deception, false ambition, snobbery, and pride; and the more he suppresses the shaming facts about his youth the more his pride seems overweening—and the more he finds himself sport for manipulators. The chief of these is his unknown benefactor, the convict Magwitch, who makes him a 'brought-up London gentleman' and the instrument of his revenge against society. Miss Havisham, who has raised the beautiful but heartless Estella with a similarly vengeful purpose against men, plays on Pip's puppy love and his itch to be a social climber. The lawyer Jaggers teases him with hints and concealments about his inheritance, and Jaggers's clerk Wemmick is equally ambivalent about the secrets which bewilder Pip and corrupt him. Before he can come to himself he must lose his fortune, fall under the shadow of the gallows, be reduced to the point of death by fever, and feel the bitterness of Estella's frigidity: 'suffering has been stronger than all other teaching', she says when Pip finds her at the end of the tale. 'I have been bent and broken, but—I hope—into better shape.'

Pip can say the same as painful experiences strip him of his illusions, but his self-discovery turns upon his relationship with Magwitch. From babyhood, Pip confesses, he has sustained 'a perpetual conflict with injustice'; the death of his parents and the ill-usage of a sister who treats him as an encumbrance have left him without a sense of place in the world—and his personality is suffused by resentment and the guilt which accompanies it. The impulses of fear and attraction which gave Dickens himself an instinctive sympathy with outcasts prompt young Pip to help the fleeing convict, and persist even when the adolescent Pip is lured by the prospect of gentility. For Pip feels a profound identity with the man who becomes his substitute father; if, indeed, his feelings of hostility and abasement had been translated into actions he would be in prison with Magwitch, or in the hulks, or in a penal colony in Australia, or even on the scaffold. At the same time, in his acquired role as a gentleman he feels contaminated by his early contact with the man who covertly encourages his later snobberies and provides the tainted money to pay for them. Pip only resolves that paradox, and sets himself free to become a man, when he stands beside Magwitch in the Old Bailey and acknowledges the previously unspeakable truths of his life by holding the hand of the doomed criminal in the dock. Forgiveness and affection have come upon him together, and he no longer cares for the verdict of society. It is a sad yet loving deathbed reconciliation with the man who first incited his great but mistaken expectations; and it echoes the way in which Dickens had grown to accept his embarrassingly errant father—the prisoner in the Marshalsea who had encouraged the dream that his boy might grow into a gentleman and one day, perhaps, even come to own the house on Gad's Hill which they had admired when they walked out of Rochester together, long ago.

Dickens had not spared Pip his own agonies of spirit, and at the end of the novel as he originally wrote it Pip is left a wiser man among the complete ruin of his hopes. His false friends are lost to him, he is poor, he has loved a coldly condescending beauty—the essence of idealized and unawakened womanhood—and he has come to find the only anodyne for his sorrows in work. In June 1861 when Bulwer-Lytton suggested that the readers would dislike this doleful conclusion Dickens 'resumed the wheel' to turn a different ending in which, after the passage of years, a middle-aged Pip seems to find comfort with Estella. 'Upon the whole', he told Wilkie Collins, 'I think it is for the better.'[45] Yet the final effect of the novel was not substantially changed by this alteration to the closing paragraphs. In *Copperfield*, he had buried the child-wife Dora; and, still avoiding the difficult question of mature relationships with women, settled David with Agnes Wickfield as a companion-wife. In *Great Expectations*, after the miseries of the separation from Catherine, he traced the consequences of an adolescent love persisting into and destroying an adult life. He had come to accept that he would never know the fulfilment of a true-hearted love.

20

A Double Life

'I AM in the first desperate laziness of having done my book,' Dickens wrote to Forster from Gad's Hill at the beginning of July 1861.[1] He had driven himself hard to finish *Great Expectations* and his health had suffered. In May, as he was preparing the final numbers for *All the Year Round*, he had gone down to Dover in the hope that a few days by the seaside might relieve an attack of neuralgia; it had nevertheless persisted into June, and though he told Macready 'I have no doubt of very soon throwing off the little damage it has done me', he knew that he needed rest.[2] 'The subsidence of those distressing pains in my face the moment I had done my work', he wrote to Forster, 'make me resolve to do nothing in that way for some time.'[3]

Life was easier at Gad's Hill, where there was warm sunshine and he could amuse himself with games of cricket and rounders. At first he was busy with the proofs of *A Strange Story*, the new supernatural tale which Bulwer-Lytton was writing as a serial to succeed *Great Expectations*; in June he took Mamie and Georgina with him when he went up to Knebworth to see Bulwer-Lytton, whom he had always respected as a novelist and a playwright, and he wrote to tell Forster that his old friend had been 'talkative, anecdotal, and droll ... almost a new man'.[4] It was during this brief visit that Bulwer-Lytton persuaded him to alter the ending of *Great Expectations* as the last number went to press. Then, as the summer days wore on, Dickens conscientiously began to prepare for his next series of readings, for he planned to introduce some new items into his autumn repertoire. He devised five fresh pieces, three of them of considerable length. 'Every day for two or three hours', he told Forster in September, 'I practice my new readings, and (except in my office work) do nothing else. With great pains I have made a continuous narrative out of Copperfield, that I think will reward the exertion it is likely to cost me ... I have also done Nicholas Nickleby at the Yorkshire school and hope I have got something droll out of Squeers.... Also, the Bastille prisoner from the Tale of Two Cities. Also, the Dwarf from one of our Christmas numbers.'[5]

The plan was to give forty-seven readings, beginning at Norwich at the end of October, and Dickens was understandably distressed to hear at the end of September that his manager, Arthur Smith, was seriously ill. He had been so 'zealous and faithful' that Dickens was reluctant to replace him. 'You may imagine how anxious it makes me', he wrote to Forster, 'and at what a dead-stop I stand.'[6] In the event he had to make do with Smith's assistant, Thomas Headland, after Smith died at the beginning of October. Dickens told Mrs. Brown how severely he felt the loss: 'But we must all be brave as good soldiers are, and when the fast-thinning ranks look bare, must close up solidly and march on.'[7] Soon afterwards his brother-in-law Henry Austin died, and increased his anxieties, for Letitia had been left in poor circumstances.

The tour did not begin well. Dickens complained to Georgina after the first night 'that they were a very lumpish audience indeed'; above all, he missed Arthur Smith—'the sense I used to have of compactness and comfort about me while I was reading is quite gone'[8]—and although Headland did his best he was slow and incompetent. Posters and tickets went astray, bookings were mishandled, something went wrong at almost every reading. Dickens carried his own gas-lighting about the country, and at Newcastle a poorly fixed chandelier almost collapsed on him. His cool nerve averted a dangerous panic. At Edinburgh, where too many tickets had been sold, Dickens again calmed an overcrowded audience that was on the verge of disorder. He had achieved an unparalleled mastery over his public, and he was soon reporting success at every stop. 'Last night was brilliant ... we are full here tonight[9] ... we turned away half Dover and half Hastings and half Colchester';[10] and from Brighton he reported to Forster '1,000 stalls already taken here'.[11] He then went northwards in a triumphant progress through Newcastle, Berwick, Edinburgh, and Glasgow. It was the new *Copperfield* reading which particularly captured the audiences. It was 'without precedent in the reading chronicles', Dickens wrote to Wills from Edinburgh on 28 November. 'Four rounds when I went in—laughing and crying and thundering all the time—and a great burst of cheering at last ... I almost think it would have been better to have done Copperfield every night.'[12] He went south again through Carlisle, Lancaster, and Preston, with a good attendance even in the cotton town where 'the Mills are working half-time and trade is very bad',[13] and on to Manchester and Liverpool. There, in the middle of December, he broke off his planned itinerary as a mark of respect on the death of the Prince Consort. He came to think the national mourning exaggerated and prolonged, complaining about 'rampant toadyism'; but his immediate reaction was courteous.[14] 'I feel personally that the Queen has always been very considerate and gracious to me', he wrote to Wills on 15 December, 'and I would on no account do anything that might seem unfeeling or disrespectful.'[15]

In January 1862, after a Gad's Hill Christmas, Dickens set off to complete the tour, taking in Birmingham, Cheltenham, Plymouth, Exeter, and Torquay. Macready, now living at Cheltenham, went to hear the *Copperfield* reading. Dickens had made a point of visiting the town to see his old friend and he was touched by his praise. He wrote to Georgina describing the old actor's reaction: 'I swear to Heaven that, as a piece of passion and playfulness—er—indescribably mixed up together, it does—er—no, really, Dickens!—amaze me as profoundly as it moves me.... How is it got at—er—how is it done—er—how one man can—well? It lays me on my—er—back, and it is of no use talking about it!'[16] The readings improved as he repeated them. 'The brilliancy of the close—at Manchester and Liverpool—has been absolutely dazzling,' he told Thomas Beard.[17]

Dickens never flagged in front of an audience, but off-stage the frenzied pace began to take its toll. 'I am very much used up,' he told Georgina at the beginning of January.[18] By the end of the month he was sleeping badly, and complaining that he was 'dazed and worn by gas and heat'.[19] Nevertheless, he was so exhilarated by his success that he was able to go on to a series at St. James's Hall in London, starting in March and running through into June. Dickens had hoped that *Copperfield* would be a London sensation, but it surpassed all his expectations. 'It seems to take people entirely by surprise,' he told Forster. He was no less pleased with the financial success: 'Think of £190 a night!' he added.[20]

'I am trying to plan out a new book, but I have not got beyond trying,'[21] Dickens wrote to Cerjat in March 1862 and a month later he was telling Forster 'I have hit upon nothing for a story. Again and again I have tried.' Dickens was reluctant to blame the lucrative readings for his exhaustion and his inability to concentrate on anything else. He had taken a dislike to the house in Hyde Park Gate which he had exchanged with Gad's Hill for the season—this 'odious little house seems to have stifled and darkened my invention'.[22] The brilliant success of the readings had changed his ideas, and he was lured by the seeming ease with which he might earn very large sums of money, telling Forster on 28 June that 'it seems almost suicidal to leave off with the town so full'. He had long been accustomed to earning about £5,000 a year from his books and his journalism, but the readings so far had shown that a successful month could bring in £1,000, and in June he was dazzled by an even more rewarding prospect. 'A man from Australia is in London ready to pay £10,000 for eight months there,' he reported to Forster. Such a journey was a tempting substitute for the suggested tour of the United States, now postponed because of the Civil War. He took the idea seriously, and considered alternative bids. 'If the notion of these speculators be anything like accurate,' he remarked, 'I should come back rich.'[23]

He thought he might take Charles Collins as a companion, but Collins was in poor health and Dickens did not greatly care for his company. Then he put the idea to Thomas Beard. He thought he could write 'the Uncommercial Traveller Upside Down' as a series of reports for *All the Year Round*.

Throughout the summer of 1862 Dickens toyed with the scheme, and the more he thought of it the more uncertain he became. He was uncomfortable and distracted, telling Wilkie Collins in July 'I am become so restless that I cannot answer for anything'.[24] To add to his worries, Georgina, on whom he still relied, was ill that summer with a heart condition. 'No one can ever know what she has been to us', he remarked to Macready, 'and how she has filled an empty place and an ever-widening gap, since the girls were mere dolls.'[25] He planned to take her away for a holiday in the autumn. Meanwhile he went over to France and stayed awhile at a low rambling farmhouse among the poplar trees in the little village of Condette, a few miles south of Boulogne. It belonged to his old friend and landlord M. Beaucourt, and he had often walked to it during his earlier family holidays. He sought it as a retreat from the pressures of life at home, and he could take Ellen Ternan there—with her mother serving both as chaperon and as the third member of the triangular domestic pattern which he obviously found congenial. But, to judge from his behaviour, the relationship with Ellen was giving him little happiness or peace of mind; yet she had become a necessary part of his life, and his reluctance to be separated from her was one reason for hesitating about the Australian trip. During the late summer he talked much of his distress and uncertainty, telling Collins of the 'miserable anxieties' that have 'gathered and gathered'.[26] He was in no state to make headway with another novel and a reading tour was an easier solution. 'I can force myself to do at the reading desk what I have done a hundred times; but whether, with all this unsettled, fluctuating distress in my mind, I could force an original book out of it, is another question.'[27]

Dickens went to France again on 16 October, this time to set up in 'a most elegant little apartment' in the rue du Faubourg St. Honoré: although he complained about the high rent he told Wills that he had 'never seen anything in Paris, so pretty airy and light'.[28] Georgina and Mary followed him three days later and they settled down for the winter. Dickens found it an agreeable place to work on the Christmas number of *All the Year Round*. Yet in other respects he was far from comfortable. He lacked the heart for the cheerful social life he had led during his last long visit to Paris and he missed some of his old acquaintances. Scribe was dead and Victor Hugo in self-imposed exile in Jersey. His thoughts turned again to the Antipodes and he mulled over the problem in a letter to Forster. 'How painfully unwilling

I am to go', he wrote, 'and yet how painfully sensible that perhaps I ought to go—with all the hands upon my skirts that I cannot fail to feel and see there, whenever I look round. It is a struggle of no common sort, as you will suppose, you who know the circumstances of the struggler.' On the other hand he realized that he would be lonely and unhappy on so long a journey. 'The domestic life of the Readings is all but intolerable to me when I am away for a few weeks at a time merely,' he went on; he insisted that 'if I were to go it would be a penance and a misery, and I dread the thought of it more than I can express.'[29] Forster thought that such a venture would be 'little short of madness'. Dickens himself finally dropped the idea when Beard decided against it.

Dickens took Mary and Georgina back to Gad's Hill for Christmas. It was a family gathering. The boys were home from school. 'The house is pervaded by boys,' Dickens told Mary Boyle; 'and every boy has (as usual) an unaccountable and awful power of producing himself in every part of the house at every moment, apparently in fourteen pairs of creaking boots.'[30] Kate and Charles Collins were there too. Charley Dickens also came. Back from the East, and in partnership as a merchant in the City, he had married Bessie Evans in November 1861; but Dickens had stayed away from the wedding as he still was not reconciled to Evans, and had taken the marriage in bad grace. A year later he had come to accept it, and Charley brought his wife and what Dickens jokingly called his 'preposterous child' with him.[31]

By the middle of January 1863 Dickens was back in Paris finding consolation again in applause. He had gone to give a reading for charity at the British Embassy. His performance, he reported to Wills, 'so stuns and oversets the Parisians, that I shall have to do it again. Blazes of Triumph!'[32] He was pleased at finding new effects in *A Christmas Carol*—'so entirely new and so very strong, that I quite amazed myself and wondered where I was going next'.[33] But he was still very much at a loose end. At the start of the New Year he had written to Collins to say that at the end of February he might be open to any foreign proposal. 'Distance no object, climate of no importance, change the advertiser's motive.'[34] He idled in France for ten days, doing his best to put a brave face on things. On his birthday, an occasion they had so often spent together, he wrote to Forster from Arras, assuring him that 'I am as little out of heart as you would have me be—floored now and then, but coming up again at the call of Time'.[35]

The success of the Paris readings had inspired him to repeat his London programme. This time he chose the Hanover Rooms with their good acoustics and instructed 'Blockheadland'[36] to make the necessary arrangements for thirteen appearances between March and June 1863. It was rare to hear a critical voice about a Dickens reading, but Carlyle, invited by Dickens to attend the reading on 28 April, wrote thoughtfully to his sister on the following day: 'Dickens does it capitally such as *it* is; acts better than any Macready in the world; a whole tragic, comic, heroic *theatre* visible, performing under one *hat*, and keeping us laughing—in a sorry sort of way, some of us thought—the whole night.'[37] For all his success, Carlyle had sensed the underlying sadness of Dickens, who was constantly struggling against 'low spirits' and finding little satisfaction in his pleasures. Sometimes he could gossip with one of the group of writers at *All the Year Round*. 'What he liked to talk about', G. A. Sala recalled, 'was the latest new piece at the theatre, the latest exciting trial or police case, the latest social craze or social swindle, and especially the latest murder and the newest thing in ghosts.'[38] Sometimes he got up a party for a special occasion. In March the Prince of Wales married Princess Alexandra, and Dickens brought his two youngest boys up to town to see the illuminations; and he took them with Wills and his wife, Collins, the Forsters, and Robert Browning on a tour of the sights in a rented van. The evening was a failure, for the van was blocked for hours in the traffic and they all walked home having seen nothing. 'It is curious to see London gone mad', he wrote to the actress Isabella Glyn, complaining of the patriotic hysteria.[39]

Dickens liked having the youngest boys at home in the summer, though their noise disturbed him at work—'they boil all over the house', he wrote to Collins—and he found their education and their prospects of employment a continual worry.[40] Plorn, a shy and agreeable lad, had been dispatched in his turn to the crammer at Wimbledon, but he was so miserable that he had been moved to a less demanding place at Tunbridge Wells. 'Why did the kings in the fairy tales want children?' Dickens asked with exasperation.[41] He turned with more pleasure to supervise yet another alteration to the house: the decision to build out beyond the drawing-room, he claimed to Forster, was 'the crowning ingenuity of the Inimitable'.[42]

He had now settled on *Our Mutual Friend* as the title for the novel he had long had in mind, but he told Collins in August that he was 'never beginning to do it'.[43] Family problems and bereavements beset him. In August Mrs. Hogarth died, and Dickens wrote to Catherine relinquishing the space he had reserved next to 'poor Mary's grave'. Mrs. Dickens died soon afterwards. 'My mother died quite suddenly at last,' Dickens wrote to Wills. 'Her condition was frightful.'[44] He had also lost a number of friends. In the previous year both Angus Fletcher and Cornelius Felton had died, and in the spring Augustus Egg had died while travelling in Algeria. 'Ah, poor Egg!' Dickens wrote to Collins. 'What a large piece of many years he seems to have taken with him. . . . Think what a great "Frozen Deep" lay close under those boards we acted on! My brother Alfred, Luard, Arthur, Albert, Austin, Egg. Even among the audience Prince Albert and poor Stone!... However, this won't do. We must close up the ranks and march on.'[45]

Work was the best solace. Dickens managed to write 'Mrs. Lirriper's Lodgings' as the Christmas story for the year; it was in his old comic vein and a great success, quickly selling over 200,000 copies. And at the end of September Dickens signed an agreement with Chapman and Hall giving the publishers a half share in the profits of the new book in return for a down payment of £6,000. He was now eager to get on with it. 'I see my opening perfectly, with the one main line on which the story is to turn,' he wrote to Forster in October; 'and if I don't strike while the iron (meaning myself) is hot, I shall drift off again, and have to go through all this uneasiness once more.'[46]

The gathering at Christmas that year was again a large one, for Charley and his family were there (Dickens later remarked that 'another generation begins to peep above the table').[47] Even so, it was a sad Christmas. A few days before, Dickens had said goodbye to Frank, who had gone out to India. Frank was twenty and had been with his father for the last year or so in the office of *All the Year Round*. 'If I am not mistaken, he has a natural literary taste and capacity, and may do very well with a chance so congenial to his mind, and being also entered at the Bar,' Dickens had told Cerjat in February 1861.[48] But he was mistaken: in the event Frank preferred a more active life, and Dickens arranged a commission for him in the Bengal Mounted Police. He shared the family extravagance with money, but he did well in his new job and stayed in India for seven years.

On Christmas Eve, moreover, Dickens learnt that Thackeray had died that day. Dickens had been estranged from him since the row with Yates, but Kate Collins, still in close touch with Thackeray and his daughters, had long urged that the foolish estrangement should cease. Dickens was a man of considerable pride, who did not find it easy to overcome such barriers, and it was Thackeray who eventually took the initiative. When they met in the lobby of the Athenaeum just before his last illness, he held out his hand in greeting. Dickens responded warmly, and at Thackeray's funeral Kate noticed his expression of 'indescribable grief'.[49]

Thackeray's death was quickly followed by a greater shock. On his own birthday in February 1864 Dickens heard that his second son, Walter, who had been ill and was being invalided home from India burdened by debts, had died in a Calcutta hospital of an aneurysm on New Year's Eve. Dickens was deeply moved, but even in this family extremity he was unable to share his sorrow with Catherine. Her grief, her friend Sir William Hardman wrote, 'was much enhanced by the fact that her husband has not taken any notice of the event to her, either by letter or otherwise'. If, he added, anything were wanted 'to sink Charles Dickens to the lowest depths of my esteem, *this* fills up the measure of his iniquity. As a writer I admire him; as a man, I despise him.'[50] Dickens remained cold towards Catherine and he was still unyielding to Miss Coutts when she took this sad opportunity yet again to urge a reconciliation. 'Do not think me unimpressed by certain words in your letter concerning forgiveness and tenderness', he wrote, 'when I say that I do not claim to have anything to forgive—that if I had, I hope and believe I would forgive freely—but that a page in my life which once had writing on it, has become absolutely blank, and that it is not in my power to pretend that it has a solitary word upon it.'[51]

Not surprisingly, Dickens found it hard to settle to his new story. In February 1864 he moved back to London for the spring, renting 57 Gloucester Place. He had told Collins in January that it was difficult to get back to 'the large canvas and the big brushes'.[52] He was at work, he assured Miss Coutts a month later, 'though in a rather dull slow way for the moment'.[53] And he explained his failure to move more quickly to the understanding Forster. 'I have grown hard to satisfy', he said, 'and write very slowly. And I have so much—not fiction—that *will* be thought of, when I don't want to think of it, that I am forced to take more care than I once took.'[54] He was also so distracted by street noises that in May he promoted a letter of protest signed by Tennyson, Forster, Collins, Leech, Millais, Holman Hunt, and other eminent men who, he claimed, were driven nearly mad by grinders of organs and bangers of banjos.[55]

Nevertheless he made headway and the first number of *Our Mutual Friend* appeared as planned in the first week of May 1864. The serial started well, reaching 30,000 copies in three days, then the sales dropped; and Dickens, ever vigilant, told Wills to dive into the question of the falling-off. The circulation recovered, and with a number of parts in hand Dickens felt free to leave for what he called a 'Mysterious Disappearance'[56] to France at the end of June. These flying visits were often whims of the moment. 'My being on the Dover line, and my being very fond of France,' he told Cerjat, 'occasion me to cross the Channel perpetually. Whenever I feel that I have worked too much, or am on the eve of overdoing it, and want a change, away I go by the mail train ... I come back fresh as a daisy.'[57] Sometimes he went to Paris but more often to M. Beaucourt's agreeable house at Condette. In the gentle countryside of Picardy, reminiscent of the rolling wooded chalklands of Kent, he could walk and relax.

When he returned to Gad's Hill for the summer, however, he found it hard to pick up the threads again. 'Although I have not been wanting in industry', he wrote to Forster on 29 July, 'I have been wanting in invention, and have fallen back with the book. Looming before me is the Christmas work, and I can hardly hope to do it without losing a number. . . . This week I have been very unwell; and am still out of sorts; and, as I know from two days' slow experience, have a very mountain to climb before I shall see the open country of my work.'[58] At the beginning of August he was still lagging. 'I can't do it in this heat, though I make believe every day,' he wrote to Mrs. Wills; to cheer Wills, who was sick, he insisted that he was 'ready to do all office needful'.[59] He was fond of the loyal and competent Wills, on whom the publication of *Household Words* and then *All the Year Round* professionally depended. Dickens proposed, and Collins seconded, Wills for membership of the Garrick Club; in March 1865, when Wills was rejected because of his trade as a journalist, they both resigned in sympathy with their colleague—as Dickens had resigned twice before, once with Macready and the second time with Yates. They were supported by Charles Fechter who, Dickens told Wills, 'would trust himself to no community of men in which such things were done'.[60]

Dickens was a man to stand by friends who stood by him—and to mourn them warm-heartedly when he lost them. In September Walter Savage Landor died, now an old man of nearly ninety who had gone back to live in Florence during his last years. The death of John Leech a month later at the age of forty-seven was a greater shock. He was an old friend, working and sharing holidays together. 'I have not done my number,' Dickens wrote to Forster on hearing the news. 'This death of poor Leech (I suppose) has put me out woefully. Yesterday and the day before I could do nothing; seemed for a time to have quite lost the power; and am only by slow degrees getting back into the track today.'[61] He realized that he was losing his old resilience and must conserve his energies. Throughout the long winter he worked on down at Gad's Hill. There was no talk of another set of exhausting readings while the novel remained unfinished, and he refused invitations to dine. 'I always have given my work the first place in my life', he truthfully wrote to an old acquaintance, 'and what can I do now at 35!—or at least at the two figures, never mind their order.'[62]

Despite his setbacks Dickens kept to his routine. In the New Year of 1865 he was visited with a new affliction—a painful swelling of his left foot. The doctor said it was gout; Dickens thought differently. 'I got frostbitten by walking continually in the snow', he told Forster, 'and getting wet in the feet daily. My boots hardened and softened ... my left foot swelled, and I still forced the boot on; sat in it to write, half the day; walked in it through the snow, the other half; forced the boot on again next morning ... and being accustomed to all sorts of changes in my feet, took no heed. At length,

W. H. Wills

William Wilkie Collins, painted by his brother
Charles Allston Collins in 1853

Thomas Beard, journalist and lifelong
friend of Charles Dickens

The Ternan family.
Left to right: Frances, Mrs. Ternan,
Ellen with dog, Maria standing

Below: A family group at Gad's
Hill, which includes (left to right)
Wilkie Collins, Charles Collins,
Bessie Evans, Mamie Dickens,
Kate Dickens, Georgina Hogarth,
Charles Dickens Jr., Charles
Fechter and Charles Dickens

going out as usual, I fell lame on the walk, and had to limp home dead lame, through the snow, for the last three miles—to the remarkable terror, by-the-bye, of two big dogs.'[63] By the end of April his foot began 'to conduct itself amiably', he wrote to Macready. 'I can now again walk my ten miles in the morning without inconvenience, but am absurdly obliged to sit shoe-less all the evening.'[64]

It had now become his habit to spend the spring months in London and in March 1865 he rented 16 Somers Place, Hyde Park. 'I am working like a dragon at my book,' he told Macready cheerily. 'Gad's Hill is being gorgeously painted and we are here until the first of June.'[65] By the end of May, when he had almost completed *Our Mutual Friend*, he told Forster that 'work and worry, without exercise, would soon make an end of me' and that he was off to Paris for a short holiday. 'If I were not going away now, I should break down. No one knows as I know today how near to it I have been.'[66] Within a few days he felt better. He returned on 9 June and caught the 'tidal' train from Folkestone—since the Channel packet docked at the top of the tide the time of the train's departure changed from day to day. Further along the railway line, on the long straight stretch between Headcorn and Staplehurst, the foreman of a gang of platelayers had miscalculated the alteration in time; as the train approached almost fifty feet of track were still out of place and the driver could do nothing to avoid a wreck. 'Suddenly we were off the rail', Dickens afterwards wrote to Thomas Mitton, 'and beating the ground as the car of a half-emptied balloon might.' The engine, guard's van, and the first coach crashed over a small bridge into a stream. The next coach, in which Dickens was travel-ling, hung twisted over the ruined bridgework. Some of the following coaches had broken away, run down the bank, and overturned into the marshy ground; ten passengers in these coaches were killed and forty injured. 'No imagination can conceive the ruin of the carriages', Dickens wrote, 'or the extraordinary weights under which the people were lying, or the compli-cations into which they were twisted up among iron and wood, and mud and water.' He kept his head. He climbed out of the window of his compartment and with the help of a workman he rescued his travelling companions from their precarious perch. He then went to assist the casualties. One man, he said, had 'such a frightful cut across the skull that I couldn't bear to look at him. I poured some water over his face and gave him some drink, then gave him some brandy, and laid him down on the grass.'[67] Dickens was carrying a bottle and a half of brandy and he used it liberally as a restorative. As the immediate shock wore off he realized that he had left the manuscript for the next part of *Our Mutual Friend* in the compartment and he scrambled back into the wreckage to retrieve it. The characters of Mr. and Mrs. Boffin, he wrote in a postscript to *Our Mutual Friend* which described the accident, 'were much soiled, but otherwise unhurt'.[68]

Four months later Dickens had recovered sufficiently to make such a quip. At the time he was desperately unnerved by the experience. 'I could not have imagined so appalling a scene,' he told Miss Coutts;[69] and for some time he was in a state of distress. 'I am curiously weak, weak as if I were recovering from a long illness,' he commented to Forster.[70] Even as the shock passed he found that it had left a lasting effect. He was, thereafter, nervous about travelling in trains, and any unusual movement upset him; the physical sensation of the crash seems to have fused with the debility which was beginning to affect the left side of his body. 'A perfect conviction, against the senses, that the carriage is down on one side and generally that is the left, (and *not* the side on which the carriage in the accident really went over), comes upon me with anything like speed, and is inexpressibly distressing.'[71] And even four years later, when Mark Lemon was involved in a railway accident, Dickens said that the experience still had 'dreadful significance' for him. 'Be sure that you are right in being as quiet as you can,' he told Lemon. 'My watch (a chronometer) had palpitations six months afterwards, and I often wonder whether it would have escaped them if I had stopped it for rest.'[72]

The Staplehurst disaster was also an emotional shock for Dickens; it broke open his secret life. All that he had so carefully hidden was now at risk of discovery, for both Mrs. Ternan and Ellen were travelling back from France with him. In the scramble to escape Ellen lost her gold watch-chain, some trinkets, and a seal with her name engraved on it. On 12 June Dickens wrote anxiously to the station-master at the Charing Cross terminus to ask if these personal items had been found.

Dickens was clearly worried about publicity. 'I don't want to be examined at the inquest', he told Mitton, 'and I don't want to write about it.'[73] He had always been drawn towards mysteries and secrets; his plots depended upon the conventional concealments and surprises of theatrical melodrama and he had long suppressed much of his own childhood. By the time he wrote *Great Expectations* he had found the courage to cope with his complex feelings about his father; and the hidden childhood which had driven such early novels as *Oliver Twist*, *Nicholas Nickleby*, and *David Copperfield* had at last lost its force. But other secrets of adult life, which touched sexual springs of feeling within the family, remained to complicate his life and energize his fiction. The notion of parallel lives was a natural consequence of them and Dickens carried it into *Our Mutual Friend*, for its plot hinged on the two identities of the hero—John Harmon, apparently dead, and the heir to a fortune; and John Rokesmith, the impoverished secretary, who wants to be loved for himself, and courts the mercenary Bella Wilfer until pity and affection teach her that money matters less than love. This antithesis of wealth and poverty runs all through the novel. There are people who are spoilt by having money, or the semblance of it, such as the usurer Fledge-by, the Podsnaps, the Lammles, and the Veneerings; and there are people who are spoilt by the lack of it, such as Mrs. Wilfer and her daughter Bella, the covetous Silas Wegg and his ally Mr. Venus, the ambitious Bradley Headstone and his pupil Charley Hexam. All the characters, indeed, revolve about the great dustheap which is the tainted source of Harmon's inheri-tance, guarded by the ambiguous figure of the miser Boffin, and they are defined by their attitudes towards it. Money corrupts, Dickens demon-strates, so the story is populated by rogues, social parasites, and scavengers. Money is the root of avarice, which makes a bitter mockery of the affections. Money destroys, so the novel opens with a murder, half a dozen characters come to a bad end in the course of it, and the shadow of death, actual and metaphorical, haunts its pages. The survival of love in such circumstances is possible only for such humble persons as Betty Higden, Lizzie Hexam, and Pa Wilfer, or those who have been humbled by events—John Harmon, Bella Wilfer, and Eugene Wrayburn—and have changed their hearts and their scale of values.

The London in which Dickens set *Our Mutual Friend* was a sad and decay-ing society, from the waterfront which recalled the sleazy dens of *Oliver Twist* to the Harmon house in the lee of the dustheap and the evanescent prosperity of the Veneerings; and even his saving humour was turned to savagely sardonic purpose. The book which Mr. Boffin is forced to read to the briefly triumphant Wegg is Gibbon's *Decline and Fall*. As he aged Dickens increasingly despaired at what others made of the world. 'Every day of my life', he exclaimed to Bulwer-Lytton in July 1865, 'I think more and more what an ill-governed country this is, and what a pass our political system has got to.'[74] And *Our Mutual Friend* was an indictment to cap all those which had preceded it. In his postscript, indeed, Dickens went back to the first of all the social evils he attacked in his fiction. 'I believe there has been in England', he wrote of the Poor Law, whose rigours had driven the dying Betty Higden to flee the threat of the workhouse, 'no law so often infamously administered, no law so often openly violated, no law habitually so ill-supervised.'[75] He had laid the blame for the parlous state of things at many doors—on parish guardians, misers, moneylenders, speculators, political economists, lawyers, and politicians. But the connecting thread between them all was the curse of money, the need for money, the greed for money, money as the motive of life, money as the cause of death, and above all, money as the arid substitute for love.

For all these years Dickens had been obsessed by a problem which successive generations of his family had failed to solve. Mr. Micawber's celebrated dictum about a sixpence above solvency and a sixpence below it summed up the matter in a sentence. From his early years Dickens had suffered from the vain ambition, extravagance, and consequent poverty of his father; and as an adult he had seen the same improvident weakness afflict his brothers and most of his sons. He was the notable exception, for he had the wit and the ability to flee from the shadow of the Marshalsea. He was determined to remain solvent and stay free of the grip of the moneylenders and the costs and penalties of the law. The more his dependants proved financial liabilities, incapable of helping themselves and importunate for his aid, the more he felt the need to make and save large amounts. The habit of acquisitiveness had grown upon him, and he was being driven to the very soul-destroying behaviour which he had so brilliantly described and condemned in one novel after another. There was no simple solution, even in fiction, for the dilemma of a man who knew that both a lack and an excess of money could destroy the hope of happiness—and longed for love in place of it. In *Our Mutual Friend* the impoverished Rokesmith found the 'companionship I have never known', and the wealthy Harmon ensured that after all there was enough money to make it possible.

21

Powers of Evil

'I AM quite right again, I thank God,' Dickens wrote on 29 June 1865.[1] Although he had been badly shaken by the Staplehurst accident he was determined to take it lightly and he was in better spirits. Much of the summer was spent at Gad's Hill. Kate and Charles Collins were there, the two youngest boys were home for the holidays, and there were guests to receive and work to be done. On fine days he often sat writing in the small Swiss chalet assembled in the shrubbery across the main road from a kit of parts sent as a present by his actor friend Charles Fechter; and this was just one of the gifts which Dickens now received from friends and admirers. In 1864 Wills had given him a splendid brougham as a 'memorial of a happy intercourse'.[2] A black Newfoundland came from America to add to his collection of dogs, and Percy Fitzgerald gave him a mastiff bloodhound called Sultan which proved to be so destructive that it had to be shot a few months later.

One August day Fitzgerald went to Knebworth with Dickens, Mary, and Georgina, for Bulwer-Lytton was giving a banquet to celebrate the opening at long last of the residences built by the Guild of Literature and Art for retired artists and authors. 'Boz', Fitzgerald recalled, 'was in the highest spirits, gay as a bridegroom, with his flower, bright costume ... and hat set a little on one side.'[3] Dickens had maintained his interest, even when Parliament imposed a seven-year delay in the Act which established the Guild, yet the generous but ill-starred enterprise never served its purpose effectively. The scheme did not catch on and the property degenerated into a set of almshouses. In 1897 the Guild was dissolved, its remaining funds being distributed to the Artists' General Benevolent Institution and to the Royal Literary Fund, whose policies Dickens had so often and so angrily disputed.

Dickens was still a fighter for the causes in which he believed, although he had long begun to weary of the demands made upon him. Every worthy enterprise wanted him to speak on its behalf or at least to lend his name as a sponsor. 'For a good many years I have suffered a great deal from charities but never anything like what I suffer now,' he had complained to Edmund

Yates in the stressful days of his separation from Catherine. 'Benevolent men get behind the piers of the gates, lying in wait for my going out. ... Benevolent bullies drive up in hansom cabs. ... Benevolent area sneaks get lost in the kitchen and are found to impede the circulation of the knife-cleaning machine.'[4] He still thought of himself as a reformer—'think of my feelings as a Radical parent!'[5] he wrote to Percy Fitzgerald when Mary went campaigning for a Conservative friend—but his choice of targets was increasingly erratic and governed by personal techiness rather than by public principle. In a characteristic letter to Cerjat that autumn he fired off squibs on a set of disconnected irritations. He attacked the meat trade for holding the public to ransom after an outbreak of foot and mouth disease; he denounced the Americans for their 'swagger and bombast', worried about the Fenians in Ireland, objected to the 'muddle of railways in all directions possible and impossible', and harked back to the disasters of the Indian Mutiny. The immediate cause of his irritation was the campaign against Edward J. Eyre, the governor of Jamaica, who had just suppressed a native revolt and summarily hanged its leader—a black Baptist who had been a member of the island's House of Assembly. The critics of Eyre, led by John Stuart Mill, Charles Darwin, T. H. Huxley, and John Bright, demanded strong measures against him. Dickens was on the opposite side with Carlyle and Ruskin, and against the Liberals and dissenters: 'That platform-sympathy with the black—or the native, or the devil—afar off, and that platform indifference to our own countrymen at enormous odds in the midst of bloodshed and savagery, makes me stark wild.' Mill and his friends, he said, were 'jawbones of asses' who 'badgered about New Zealanders and Hottentots, as if they were identical with men in clean shirts at Camberwell'; and missionaries were 'perfect nuisances' who left every place worse than they found it. All such things, he declared in the tones of an intemperate squire, were simply visible evidences 'of our being ill-governed'.

For all his complaints, he told Cerjat, he was 'in the best of humours' and busy at work.[6] In September, when he had finished *Our Mutual Friend*, he spent ten days in France—'burnt brown', he told Forster, from walking by the sea. For the most part the novel had a sympathetic reception and the sales were good. Henry Chorley, the literary critic with whom Dickens had struck up a good friendship, declared in the *Athenaeum* that it was 'one of Mr. Dickens's richest and most carefully wrought books'.[7] Dickens was so taken by a review by E. S. Dallas in *The Times* that he presented him with the manuscript. Dallas, in his unsigned review, thought it was 'really one of his finest works' in which 'we see life in all its strength and seriousness and tenderness'.[8] At the same time, the novel provoked some sharp criticism. While the *Saturday Review* recognized that Dickens was unrivalled as a caricaturist, here he was 'not very witty or humorous'. The portrayal of the Veneerings, for example, 'seems to screech with ill-will and bitterness';[9] and the *Westminster Review* thought that the characters were 'a bundle of deformities'.[10] The same journals disliked the political overtones. The *Saturday Review* objected to the exploitation of Betty Higden's distress—'the vocation of making spiteful and clumsy attacks on Society is an uncommonly poor one';[11] and the *Westminster* wrote bluntly that the novel 'is not the place for discussions of the Poor Law'. The severest critic was the youthful Henry James, reviewing the novel in the New York *Nation*. He thought it was the poorest of Dickens's works—'the poverty not of momentary embarrassment but of permanent exhaustion'. It was a book 'so intensely *written*, so little seen, known or felt' which contained the letter of his old humour without the spirit. James felt that the cleverness of Dickens had triumphed at the expense of his humanity.[12]

Dickens had long ceased to be bothered by adverse criticism, and he now turned to his Christmas story for *All the Year Round*. 'Tired of *Our Mutual*', he told Forster, 'I sat down to cast about for an idea, with a depressing notion that I was, for the moment, overworked. Suddenly, the little character that you will see, and all belonging to it, came flashing up in the most cheerful manner, and I had only to look and leisurely describe it.'[13] In 'Dr. Marigold's Prescriptions' he produced a Pygmalion-like tale of a travelling cheapjack who adopts a deaf-and-dumb girl, teaches her to read, and falls pathetically but vainly in love with her. Its fairground humour and sentimentality harked back to the style of *The Old Curiosity Shop* and Dickens realized at once that it would greatly please his public. He decided to include it in his next repertoire of readings, and before he presented it he had worked up its effects by scores of rehearsals.

It was some time, however, before his plans were settled. 'I am doubtful whether to read or not in London this season,' he told Mary Boyle on 6 January 1866.[14] 'If I decide to do it at all, I shall probably do it on a large scale.' His health was the cause of some concern. Early that year he noticed that his pulse was irregular. 'There seems to be degeneration of some functions of the heart,' he reported to Georgina after he had consulted Frank Beard. 'It does not contract as it should. So I have got a prescription of iron, quinine and digitalis, to set it a-going, and send the blood more quickly through the system. ... I am not so foolish as to suppose that all my work can have been achieved without *some* penalty, and I have noticed for some time a decided change in my buoyancy and hopefulness.'[15]

It was apparently a penalty which Dickens was prepared to go on paying, for despite this medical warning he decided to go ahead with a new series of readings. He wanted a manager to replace Headland, who had proved so incompetent on the previous tour, and he had discussions with a number of concert and lecture agents. In the end he chose Chappell's of New Bond Street, who offered to cover all expenses and pay him £50 a night. He knew it was a demonic contract. 'I have just sold myself to the Powers of Evil for 30 readings,' he declared in March; and he tried to discount the daunting prospect of another round of uncomfortable journeys and overstimulating performances by pretending to Forster that Chappell's would relieve him of all strains. 'All I have to do is, to take in my book and read, at the appointed place and hour, and come out again.' Things were not so simple, as Forster realized. Dickens, he said, had undertaken 'labour that must in time have broken down the strongest man'.[16] But the agency was a great improvement on Headland, because it admirably handled the advertisements, hall-book-ings, and tickets, and it also provided Dickens with a most satisfactory assist-ant in George Dolby, a large bald-headed man with a stammer, whom Mark Twain described as a gladsome gorilla. Dolby quickly learned what 'the Chief' wanted, serving him on the reading circuit with a faithful competence that matched the service of Wills on *All the Year Round*. From 1866, in fact, Dickens depended upon these two reliable lieutenants to make his wear-ing life bearable.

Once more he took a London house for the season, settling Georgina and Mary at 6 Southwick Place, by Hyde Park. He began his own season of readings at the St. James's Hall on 10 April 1866, when he introduced 'Dr. Marigold's Prescriptions'. The printed version had sold over 250,000 copies in a few weeks, and Dickens had successfully tried out the reading on a small group of friends which included Forster, Collins, Fechter, and Browning. The next day he left for Liverpool, Manchester, and the main provincial and Scottish cities, taking Dolby and Wills with him, the latter being needed for company and also to get on with the work of the magazine. The pressures of the tour left little time for relaxation. Dickens, Forster said, was 'almost wholly in a railway carriage when not at a reading desk or in bed',[17] and to keep himself and his companions amused during the tedious hours he improvised word games, three-handed cribbage, charades, and similar non-sense. Dolby remembered whistling a sailor's hornpipe while Dickens danced, 'in spite of the frequent collapse of the orchestra in explosive laughter at the absurdity of the situation'. And Dolby became responsible for the substantial picnics which fortified the party along the way. 'With some salmon mayonnaise,' he wrote, 'a plain lettuce salad, some pressed beef, cold fowls and tongue, and a cold cherry tart, with a little *fromage de Rochfort* to finish, together with some coffee, made up by the aid of a spirit lamp, we contrived to pass the time very pleasantly.'[18] The tour went well and Dickens found Dolby an excellent companion; 'I made him laugh all the way,' he told Georgina.[19] He kept a close watch on his health and reported to Mamie or Georgina how he was feeling. 'Except that I cannot sleep, I really think myself in much better training than I had anticipated,' he wrote to Mamie. 'A dozen oysters and a little champagne between the parts every night, constitute the best restorative I have ever yet tried.'[20]

At the end of April Dickens raced back to London to give more of the eight planned readings there, went north again, returned to London in the middle of May, and after a final visit to Aberdeen wound up in Portsmouth—where he took Wills and Dolby on a hunt for his birthplace in Landport Terrace. Such an erratic itinerary, he believed, was good policy. There was no difficulty in selling tickets, especially the shilling seats which he required Chappell's to provide everywhere for the poorer public, but he thought it better to leave audiences in each city unsatisfied and eagerly awaiting his return visit. For all his hectic pace there was nothing slipshod about his work. Though Dickens confidently left all front-of-house business to Chappell's, in each hall he made as certain of the platform arrangements as an actor verifying his set. He always appeared in front of a maroon drop-curtain, standing at a table on which was placed a reading desk with two shelves, one for a glass and water-bottle, and the other for his handkerchief and gloves. And on either side of the stage he placed a battery of gaslights to illuminate his face and figure. These were the only properties he used to achieve his stunning dramatic effects, apart from the book from which he merely appeared to read, since he had memorized each phrase, inflection, and gesture.

As the tour drew to an end Dickens felt its strains. He was tired and unwell with a cold, but whatever his difficulties, his attitude to his readings was always strictly professional. One evening at Birmingham he was advertised to read the trial from *Pickwick* and in error gave his audience *Nickleby*. When he discovered his mistake he went back on stage to apologize and to give the *Pickwick* reading that had been promised.

When the tour ended on 12 June Dickens went down to the country again 'to rest and hear the birds sing' and to think over his plans.[21] The readings had brought in a total of £4,672 and the average takings had come out at over £150 a night. Chappell's, no less than Dickens, were delighted by such success, and they were quick to make a more ambitious offer for a series of fifty performances to begin in January 1867. Dickens, though tempted, delayed his reply. He was worried about his health, which had plainly suffered from the stress of five readings a week for six weeks on end. He had troublesome pains in his left eye, a persistent cold, and severe digestive discomfort. 'Twice last week', he wrote to Forster in September, 'I was seized in a most distressing manner—apparently in the heart; but, I am persuaded, only in the nervous system.'[22] He was determined to put these disabilities aside, for he could not resist the lure of the gaslit stage. He hoped to persuade Chappell's to raise his share to £70 for each reading, but by October they had settled for forty-two readings for a flat fee of £2,500.

The decision to make another reading tour was made by Dickens alone and the fee which he had secured was a good one. Yet there was an envious note in a letter he wrote to Collins, who was away that autumn on a foreign cruise: 'I am so undoubtedly one of the sons of Toil—and fathers of children—that I expect to be presently presented with a smock frock, a pair of leather breeches, and a pewter watch, for having brought up the largest family ever known with the smallest disposition to do anything for themselves.'[23] Dickens had no reason to be pressed for money. His bank account at this time usually ran to over £12,000 a year; his Christmas stories each earned more than most of his contemporaries could expect from a full-length novel; he had the income from reprints of his earlier works; he made a handsome profit from *All the Year Round*; and he had learned that he could make as much again from his readings. For all his complaints, he was not personally mean, and he lived up to the stories in which he extolled benevolence and satirized parsimony. A life begun as a flight from poverty was ending in a compulsive search for wealth.

His fear of fecklessness in the family, moreover, strengthened his innate tendency to stern discipline, convincing him that he had to correct inherited weakness by severity if his sons were to grow up manly and self-sufficient. Such an attitude only created the situation he feared. As one failure after another was sent out of the country with a lecture on the virtues of self-help and the evils of debt—Alfred had emigrated to Australia in May 1865— he felt more distressed and anxious; and the impulse to put money aside for his sons became stronger as each year brought him fresh evidence that they were unable to help themselves effectively.

The summer passed pleasantly at Gad's Hill with visits from Dolby and Forster and a cricket match between two local teams on the field next to the house. Dickens was busy with his Christmas story for 1866 and by the end of October he was reading part of 'Mugby Junction' to Mary Boyle (now one of the regular visitors at Gad's Hill), Georgina, and the two girls. It was received with 'such extraordinary peals and tears that I think I foresee a great success', he assured Wills. 'I don't think I ever saw people laugh so much under the prosiest of circumstances.'[24] The Christmas number of *All the Year Round* was a success with a sale of 250,000, and Christmas itself was celebrated at Gad's Hill by 'foot races and rustic sports on Boxing Day. 'Christmas Sports in Mr. Charles Dickens's Cricket Field' was the heading on a poster advertising the event, which had Charley as Clerk of the Course, Marcus Stone as the Starter, and Dickens himself as Judge. Over two thousand people turned up, and the road from Chatham looked as though there was a fair in town. Among the crowd, Dickens told Macready, 'were soldiers, sailors, navvies, and labourers of all kinds'. There was no disorder of any sort, he happily reported, 'and they went away at sunset rending the air with cheers'.[25]

Dickens started his reading tour in London on 15 January 1867, using part of 'Mugby Junction'; but it was poorly received and when he found a similar reaction in Birmingham and Leeds he dropped it from the repertoire. The familiar pieces went as well as ever, and the halls were crowded to capacity despite miserable weather. 'We have been reading in snow-storms and down-pourings of sheets of solid ice,' Dickens wrote to Wills on 24 January. 'At Chester it was such a night as one sees once in half a century',[26] and he told Mamie that the hall there 'was like a Methodist chapel in low spirits'.[27] The routine was punishing. 'Day after day we were doing the same things at the same time,' Dolby noted, 'packing our portmanteaus, travelling to a fresh town, unpacking the portmanteaus again, attending to the preliminary matters of business in connection with the readings, dining, and, after a rest for an hour or two, making for the hall, where the audience sat expectant.'[28]

Dickens showed signs of strain from the first. At Liverpool he had to rest on a sofa after the reading. 'I have been fainter of a night, after leaving off, than I like,' he wrote to Wills after two such attacks.[29] He dashed back to London in mid-February 1867, then left for Scotland. The shaking of the fast trains upset him; 'after the Staplehurst experience', he told Georgina, 'it tells more and more, instead of (as one might have expected) less and less'.[30] From Liverpool, where he stopped again on his way northwards, he was afflicted, he wrote to Mary, by a 'curious feeling of soreness all round the body', and he was not helped by an attack of nausea brought on by the white lead and arsenic in the new paint at the hotel in Glasgow.[31] All these symptoms were capped by a report to Frank Beard that he was suffering from piles and had lost 'a considerable quantity of blood'.[32] Dickens was clearly anxious about his health, but he was determined to go on and, for all his difficulties, his spirits were good. Dolby recalled that he 'invariably put the best construction on the discomforts he had to put up with, and in the most trying situation was always more cheerful and good-humoured than any other public man with whom I have ever been associated'.[33]

It was still bitterly cold in March when, joined by Wills, the party went over to Ireland, where there was a state of alert against a feared Fenian rising on St. Patrick's Day. Dublin was alive with constabulary and soldiery. All the same, Dickens reported to Forster, 'the Readings are a perfect rage at a time when everything else is beaten down'.[34] He returned to England for a last swing through East Anglia—the Cambridge colleges, he noted gleefully, 'mustered in full force'—and on to the West Country and up to Lancashire. Wherever he went he was rewarded by 'roars of welcome' and 'rounds of cheers', but the price for such applause was high.[35] He was becoming so tired that he could scarcely undress himself at night, yet he went on doggedly. His pocket diary for 1867 shows that in the first half of the year he spent 32 nights at Gad's Hill; he was in London for 31 nights and on a further 57 he was away on his readings.[36] It also recorded frequent and mainly week-end visits to 'N' at 'Sl'.

He was in fact going to see Ellen Ternan—he called her Nelly—who was living at Elizabeth Cottage in the High Street at Slough, then a small village near the Thames at Windsor. Now that he was so much in the public eye he was more than ever anxious to disguise this relationship. The rates on Elizabeth Cottage were paid by 'Charles Tringham', a pseudonym which Dickens also used in paying the rates on Windsor Lodge, the house which he subsequently provided for Ellen Ternan in Linden Grove, Peckham, on the south-east fringe of London. Elizabeth Cottage was on the verge of the country estate owned by the publisher Richard Bentley, with whom Dickens was now reconciled. He could use the footpath across Bentley's fields to reach Datchet station, more discreet and in some ways more convenient than the Great Western station at Slough itself, for the trains from Datchet took him to Waterloo, close to the office of *All the Year Round*. Despite the demands of the reading tour, Dickens spent 53 nights at Slough between January and July 1867.

There may have been other reasons for discretion. Kate Dickens declared that her father and Ellen Ternan had a child 'who died in infancy'.[37] If Ellen had been pregnant that spring a rural retreat such as Slough would have been a convenient place for concealment. There was in fact an exceptional and unexplained use of the word 'Arrival' in Dickens's diary for 13 April, and subsequent entries suggest that Ellen was unwell for a few weeks after that date. And despite the physical demands on his energies Dickens was in cheerful spirits. He had created a mystery of alternative identities in his own life of the kind which he had already used in *Our Mutual Friend* and to which he returned in the unsolved riddle of *Edwin Drood*. Such changes of role and name were clearly attractive to him; such an irregular and secret life was profoundly related to his lifelong sense of being an outsider. In this way he notionally separated his relationship with Ellen Ternan from the stresses of normal life and preserved its fairy-tale quality.

'If I look like some weather-beaten pilot when we meet', Dickens wrote to Clarkson Stanfield on 18 April, 'don't be surprised.'[38] By the time he saw Stanfield on a day in London between provincial journeys, his old friend was dying; and by the deathbed, at Stanfield's request, Dickens made up his quarrel with Mark Lemon. It was a sad occasion for he had known 'Stanny' since his first years of success. 'Poor dear Stanfield!' he remarked to Forster. 'I cannot think even of him, and of our great loss, for this spectre of doubt and indecision that sits at the board with me and stands at the bedside.'[39] What was troubling Dickens was the renewed suggestion, now the Civil War was over, of a series of readings in America. He was both attracted to the idea and fearful of it. 'I really do not know that any sum of money that could be laid down would induce me to cross the Atlantic to read,' he had written to James Fields in Boston on 2 May 1866. 'Why go through this wear and tear, merely to pluck fruit that grows on every bough at home.'[40] A year later he was beginning to think differently.

The fame of his readings had spread and Fields's original suggestion was now endorsed by speculators and admirers. He had been teased by many business propositions, including one from a syndicate of Boston enthusiasts who offered to guarantee him £10,000 and forgo all profits themselves. 'I am in a tempest-tossed condition', he confessed to Forster, 'and can hardly believe that I stand at bay at last on the American question. ... But the prize looks so large!'[41] One reason for an urgent decision, he told Forster, was that the presidential election was due in November 1868 and he did not wish to compete with it. Americans, he added, 'are a people whom a fancy does not hold long. They are bent upon my reading there, and they believe (on no foundation whatever) that I am going to read there. If I ever go, the time would be when the Christmas number goes to press.' He admitted to Georgina that the impulse to go was strong and to some extent irrational. He felt drawn to America, he said, 'as Darnay in the Tale of Two Cities was attracted to the Loadstone Rock, Paris'.[42]

Forster, Wills, and other friends tried to dissuade him. As he argued with them he implied that he was genuinely undecided, and while declaring that he didn't want more money he said that he was tempted only by the money. 'Have no fear that anything will induce me to make the experiment', he wrote to Forster, 'if I do not see the most forcible reasons for believing that what I could get by it, added to what I have got, would leave me with a sufficient fortune. I should be wretched beyond description there.'[43] But he wrote in a different tone on 3 June to Fields in Boston, saying that 'I am trying so to free myself as to be able to come over to read this next winter!'[44] And there was much special pleading in a letter he sent to Wills three days later. 'My idea of a course of Readings in America is, that it would involve far less travelling than you suppose ... and that the receipts would be very much larger than your Estimate. ... If you were to work out the question of Reading profits here, with Dolby, you would find that it would take years to get £10,000. To get that sum in a heap so soon is an immense consideration to me. . . . I shall never rest much while my faculties last, and (if I know myself) have a certain something in me that would still be active in rusting and corroding me, if I flattered myself that it was in repose.'⁴⁵

Since Forster remained adamantly opposed to the American enterprise, Dickens offered a compromise. On 13 June he wrote to Fields to let him know that Dolby was being sent across in early August in order to gauge the support for a tour and to look over possible halls and travel arrangements. It was also important for Dolby to judge whether there was any lingering hostility to Dickens from *American Notes* and *Martin Chuzzlewit* which might embarrass him. While James Gordon Bennett did suggest in his New York *Herald* that Dickens still owed Americans an apology, and reminded his readers of the original offence by publishing extracts from the original *American Notes*, other newspapers were more welcoming: 'there are tens of thousands', the *New York Times* declared, 'who would make a large sacrifice to see and hear the man who has made happy so many homes'. Dickens chafed for such news. 'Great reports from Dolby and also from Fields,' he told Wills on 2 September. 'But I keep myself quite calm and hold my decision in abeyance until I shall have book, chapter and verse, before me.'⁴⁶

Dolby was away for seven weeks and while he was gone Dickens had to face new uncertainties. One problem was Ellen Ternan; he was uneasy about leaving her for several months and he was toying with the idea of taking her with him. Then his health gave rise to such anxiety that it seemed he might be unfit to go. When he went up to Liverpool to see Dolby sail on 3 August his left foot had swollen up again and he could not wear a boot. 'I am laid up with another attack in my foot', he told Forster three days later, 'and was on the sofa all last night in tortures. I cannot bear to have the fomentations taken off for a moment.'⁴⁷ He consulted the eminent doctor Sir Henry Thompson, who decided that he was suffering from erysipelas, or a gouty condition. Dickens, anxious to play it down, ridiculed this diagnosis, and preferred that of an Edinburgh surgeon who had assured him that it was an affection of the delicate nerve and muscles, originating in cold. There were rumours that he was unwell, and these worried him; on the eve of a long and arduous venture he could not afford an impression that he was incapable of meeting his commitments, and he sent a facetious bulletin to a friendly journalist, F. D. Finlay of the *Northern Whig*. He insisted that he was suffering from nothing but 'periodical paragraph disease', that he was 'NOT in a *critical state of health*, and has NOT consulted *eminent surgeons . . .* is NOT recommended to proceed to the United States for *cessation from literary labour*, and has not had so much as a headache for twenty years'.[48] And letters in a similar vein were sent to other papers which hinted that Dickens was ailing. He was, he told one editor, 'combining his usual sedentary powers with the active training of a prize-fighter'; and he wrote a jocular note to Fields to pretend that Wilkie Collins and Charles Reade, who were visiting Gad's Hill, sent a stream of messengers to inquire how he was from one minute to the next. Buoyed up by the good reports from Dolby, he was determined to keep up his good spirits. 'I have given *my* feathers a shake and am all right again,' he told Wills on 2 September.[49]

Although no decision could be made until Dolby returned, Dickens was putting his mind to the American trip by the beginning of September. 'You can hardly imagine with what interest I shall try Copperfield, on an American audience,' he wrote to Fields, 'or, if they give me their heart, how freely and fully I shall give them mine.'[50] He was also bound to offer them other items that had proved immensely popular with his English audiences—the trial scene from *Pickwick* headed the list, closely followed by the *Christmas Carol*; the death of Paul Dombey, the tergiversations of Mrs. Gamp, and the dream of Trotty Veck were all firm favourites. What he had always called the '*Carol* philosophy' of Christmas came out strongly in his preferred selections. While he considered his possible repertoire he had other work in hand for America. Promises of a thousand pounds apiece had already induced him to write two stories. One of them, 'George Silverman', was an odd tale of a clergyman with an ambivalent personality, who seems both charitable and mean, kind and cruel. 'I feel', Dickens said of this unresolved character sketch, 'as if I had read something (by somebody else) which I should never get out of my head!'[51] In May he had suggested to Collins that they should collaborate on the next Christmas story. It was six years since they had worked together and Collins was deeply involved in writing *The Moonstone* for serial publication in *All the Year Round*, but he agreed. All through that summer he and Dickens met to discuss the plot and compare notes on their progress with 'No Thoroughfare'. They were so pleased with the tale that Collins was charged to convert it into a drama—the reverse process to that which translated *The Frozen Deep* into a story.

When Dolby returned with a favourable opinion Dickens at once accepted it, and presented his conclusions to Forster and Wills in a document which he called 'The Case in a Nutshell'. He proposed to go to America in the late autumn and to give eighty readings, Dolby preceding him to make the necessary arrangements; and from this tour, even when he allowed seven war-depreciated U.S. dollars to the pound, he expected to make a net profit of £15,500. 'Give me your opinion on it. To go or not to go?' he asked Wills on 24 September.[52] Wills remained adamantly opposed and this definite proposal upset Forster. In the course of an acrimonious interview with Dolby he made it clear that he had 'fully made up *his* mind that Dickens should *never go to America again*', and he gave Dolby one reason after another for this view.[53] Dickens was in poor health; more readings of this kind would damage his reputation as an author; the Americans, who had greeted Macready with a riot, might treat Dickens in the same way; there was no money to be made, or if there was it would be stolen or be lost in a bank failure. Dickens travelled up to Ross-on-Wye, where Dolby lived and Forster was staying, to rebut such arguments. Forster could do nothing. 'I have made up my mind to see it out', Dickens wrote to Georgina on 30 September, and on that day he sent a cable to Fields in Boston: 'Yes, go ahead.'[54] Forster, still unconvinced but defeated, wrote to John Bigelow in Boston that Dickens would sail on 9 November, 'and I heartily hope that all will go well with him'.[55] He raised no more objections, only earnestly imploring Dolby to take good care of Dickens.

There were, Wilkie Collins noted in his engagement book, 'dinners public and private to Dickens on his departure'. The most splendid was the farewell banquet in the Freemasons' Hall on 2 November, where over four hundred writers, actors, and artists sat down to the feast—and a hundred lady guests, including Georgina and Mary, watched the proceedings from the gallery. The occasion was a fantastic personal triumph for Dickens. 'Nothing like it has ever before occurred in London,' the New York *Tribune* reported. 'The company that assembled to honor Dickens represented humanity.' Dickens entered on the arm of the ageing Bulwer-Lytton, who was taking the chair, and in his train followed such notabilities as the Lord Chief Justice, the Lord Mayor of London, and a bevy of Royal Academicians. Around the hall hung scarlet panels, each carrying the name of a Dickens novel encircled with a golden laurel wreath, and the band of the Grenadier Guards played festive music. Lord Lytton, Edmund Yates bluntly remarked, spoke well, 'due allowance being made for his high-falutin' matter and manner'.[56] Dickens, Bulwer-Lytton said, had claimed 'his title-deeds to the royalty of genius while he yet lives ... a conqueror whom the conquered bless'. The audience gave a lively welcome to this and similar complimentary speeches, and when Dickens was called upon to reply 'the whole company rose in their seats and cheered again and again ... he was surrounded by a living wall of friends'. He was going to America, Dickens claimed, because he had so many requests expressing 'a kind of personal interest in me, I had almost said a kind of personal affection for me'.[57] For once he said little. 'I do not think I ever heard him to less advantage than on an occasion when most was expected of him,' Yates remarked.[58] Dickens explained next day to Wills that when he got up to speak 'but for taking a desperate hold of myself, I should have lost my sight and voice and sat down again'.[59] His brevity was none the less effective; one member of the audience felt 'that the real eloquence of the evening reached its climax in the silent tears of Dickens'.[60]

The next few days were taken up with family goodbyes and a reluctant separation from Ellen Ternan. Though she was going to Italy to stay with her sister Frances, now married to Thomas Trollope, Dickens had a lingering hope that he might call her to join him in America; he arranged to send a coded cable through Wills in which the words 'All Well' apparently would suggest that the risk seemed slight and 'Safe and Well' would be a signal to stay away.

On 8 November a party of friends went up to Liverpool to see Dickens sail next day on the *Cuba*. Wills and Yates were there and so were Wilkie and Charles Collins; and the group was completed by Charles Kent, the editor of the *Sun*, who had organized the dinner in the Freemasons' Hall. He had been a friend since his eulogistic review of *Dombey and Son*. Dickens was given the deck cabin of the second officer, which he said was 'big enough for everything but getting up in and going to bed in'.[61] The weather was favourable for most of the way, but even under the best of circumstances a winter passage was 'odious' he told Wills. But the *Cuba* had a good ten-day run to within fifty yards of the Boston dock, where the ship struck a mudbank and Dickens was taken off by the customs steamer *Hamblin*, on which Dolby and the newspaper reporters had come out to greet him. He arrived in Boston on a blustering evening in excellent spirits: 'was not sick for a moment—was highly popular on board—made no end of speeches after the last dinner of the voyage—sang no end of duets with the Captain ... and came over the side into the arms of Dolby (in a steam tug) illuminated with a blaze of triumph'.[62]

22

A Pile of Dollars

'GREAT excitement and expectation everywhere,' Dickens wrote to Mamie from Boston.[1] As soon as he arrived he realized that time had erased the mutual acrimony with which his visit had ended twenty-five years earlier. Everyone was kind and agreeable and he was delighted to find that he was not pestered in the streets and could take his daily ten-mile walk in peace, and that when strangers spoke to him they did so with politeness and discretion. 'The Bostonians having been duly informed that I wish to be quiet,' Dickens informed Georgina, 'really leave me as much so as I should be in Manchester or Liverpool ... it is a most welcome relief here, as I have all the readings to get up.'[2] Dickens had ten days in Boston before his first performance on 2 December and while he rested at the palatial Parker House, where the modern comforts included a bath with running hot water and central heating so powerful that the air was 'like that of a pre-Adamite ironing day in full blast', he noted other changes for the better.[3] Handsome streets now ran where there was formerly 'a black swamp' and there was 'more of New York in this fine city than there was of yore'.[4] He was glad to see old acquaintances like Oliver Wendell Holmes, R. H. Dana Sr., and Longfellow, who wrote to Forster on 23 November to express his pleasure at finding that Dickens had 'the same sweetness and flavour as of old and only greater ripeness'.[5] He was very much at ease with James Fields and his wife and their home was a comfortable retreat for him in Boston. He dined at Longfellow's house in Cambridge on Thanksgiving Day. He tried, however, to fend off casual callers and refuse unnecessary engagements. Dickens knew that he needed to conserve his energies, but he jocularly blamed Dolby for keeping him in seclusion. It was Dolby's belief, he claimed, that 'the less I am shown—for nothing—the better for the Readings'.[6]

The way in which Dickens kept aloof from invitations naturally provoked comment. Forster's friend John Bigelow, who was also staying at the Parker House, considered that Dickens drove himself too hard. 'He not only declined all proffers of hospitality ...' Bigelow remarked, 'but avoided visits of courtesy, even sometimes to rudeness, rather than allow his literary work to be interrupted.... I think myself that his lust for money made him un-consciously a suicide.'[7] It was a harsh though prescient judgement. Emer-son, meeting Dickens at dinner, got much the same impression, telling Mrs. Fields afterwards that he had 'too much talent for his genius; it is a dreadful locomotive to which he is bound, and can never be free from it nor set at rest'.[8]

While Dickens fretted, anxious to get to work, Dolby was busy with pre-parations. Despite the freezing weather there had been day-long queues for tickets and the opening set of readings was sold out more than two weeks in advance. The eager Americans, Dickens wrote to his son Charley before the first performance, had little idea what to expect; 'as they are accustomed to mere readings out of a book, I am inclined to think that the excitement will increase when I shall have begun'.[9]

For the first night Dickens chose the most popular of all his readings, giving *A Christmas Carol* and then the trial scene from *Pickwick*. He was greeted with deafening cheers when he walked on the stage; then after a moment's silence as he stood before his desk he began to read the familiar lines. 'Success last night beyond description or exaggeration,' Dickens wrote next day to Charley. 'The whole city is quite frantic about it to-day, and it is impossible that prospects could be more brilliant.'[10] Similar messages were sent off to Mamie, Forster, Wills, and Mary Boyle, who as usual con-trived to send him a fresh flower for his buttonhole for every performance. 'Those marvellous characters of his come forth ... as if their original creator had breathed new life into them,' John Greenleaf Whittier remarked. 'But it is idle to talk about it: you must beg, borrow, or steal a ticket and hear him. Another such star-shower is not to be expected in one's lifetime.'[11] Dickens was delighted by his reception and equally pleased by the amount of money he earned so quickly and so easily. After his third reading he wrote gleefully to Wills: 'I am going on (between ourselves) at a *clear profit* of £1300 per week!'[12]

Dolby went ahead to New York, where he found even greater enthusiasm. On the night before the tickets went on sale at Steinway Hall a line of people stretched half a mile down the street, and many brought blankets and mat-tresses to protect themselves against the severe cold. By morning there were over five thousand in the queue, and waiters from near-by restaurants served breakfasts along the kerb. There was already squabbling in the crowd, and pushing for places—the first signs of a trouble which was aggravated by speculators and became an incurable affliction as the tour proceeded. Dolby did his best to be fair, limiting each purchaser to four tickets, but he was outwitted by the touts who pushed dummy buyers into the line; a two-dollar seat was fetching twenty dollars or more. At the same time he was abused in the press because, Dickens said, 'he can't get four thousand people into a room that holds two thousand'.[13] The tickets for the first four New York readings were sold in a few hours and Dolby had taken in $16,000. When Dickens opened with the *Carol* and *Pickwick* he was hailed as he had been in Boston. 'It is absolutely impossible that we could have made a more brilliant success than we made here last night,' he wrote to Wills on 10 December. 'The reception was splendid, the audience bright and perceptive. I believe that I never read so well since I began.'[14]

Despite the intense cold Dickens reported that he was in 'capital health and voice', though he admitted to Wills that 'my spirits flutter woefully towards a certain place at which you dined one day not long before I left, with the present writer and a third (most drearily missed) person'.[15] Soon after landing in Boston he had realized that it was quite impossible for Ellen to join him and he had sent Wills the negative 'Safe and Well' coded cable. He was otherwise in good humour. The Westminster Hotel where he stayed was comfortable; he was amused when there was a fire one evening, and while the fire brigade dealt with it the manager invited him into a smoke-filled office to drink a nightcap. New York had grown out of recognition. 'Everything in it looks as if the order of nature were reversed, and everything grew newer every day, instead of older,' he told Wills on 10 December.[16] And a week later he sent another triumphant report on his progress. 'Everybody sleighing. Everybody coming to the readings. There were at least ten thousand sleighs in the Park last Sunday. Your illustrious chief—in a red sleigh covered with furs, and drawn by a pair of fine horses covered with bells, and tearing up 14 miles of snow an hour—made an imposing appearance.'[17] While Dickens amused himself with drives about the town, with an evening at the theatre, and with visits from the Fields, Horace Greeley, Bigelow, and William Cullen Bryant, the energetic and still maligned Dolby was at work stamping and selling tickets. When he came back to the hotel, Dickens told Mamie, he 'put such an immense untidy heap of paper money on the table that it looks like a family wash'.[18]

Dickens caught a cold in New York, and it persisted after he returned to Boston to give a set of Christmas readings and to spend the holiday with the Fields family. 'The low action of the heart, or whatever it is,' he wrote to Forster on 22 December, 'inconvenienced me greatly this last week. On Monday night, after the reading, I was laid upon a bed, in a very faint and shady state. And on the Tuesday I did not get up till the afternoon.'[19] He was also feeling homesick, for he had begun to count the readings and to reckon that he had delivered almost a quarter of his programme; and he felt the absence of Ellen. 'Enclosed another letter as before, to your protection and despatch,' he wrote to Wills with a note for Ellen. 'I would give

£3000 down (and think it cheap) if you could forward *me* for four and twenty hours only, instead of the letter.' On New Year's Eve, writing to Wills again with 'another letter for my darling enclosed', Dickens admitted that he was unwell and had called in a doctor, but he put a brave face on things.[20] He was, he declared, 'very greatly better—all right in fact',[21] and he failed to add that the physician had wished to forbid his readings until he was fully recovered. When he insisted on continuing the performances the strain was evident. 'Last Friday ... I was again dead beat at the end,' he told Georgina after he had returned to New York, where more than forty thousand people heard him read and he was recognized as he went about the streets.[22] 'I can scarcely exaggerate what I undergo from sleeplessness,' he wrote to her a week later.[23] All his letters to England now contained disquieting comment on his condition. 'I have tried allopathy, homeopathy, cold things, warm things, sweet things, bitter things, stimulants, narcotics,' he informed Forster early in January, 'all with the same result.'[24] He was living on an invalid diet. For breakfast he took nothing but an egg and a cup of tea. 'My dinner at three, and a little quail or some such light thing when I come home at night, is my daily fare. At the Hall I have established the custom of taking an egg beaten up in sherry before going in, and another between the parts. I think that pulls me up.'[25]

The New York readings included four appearances at the Plymouth Church in Brooklyn, where the minister was Henry Ward Beecher, the celebrated preacher and brother of the author of *Uncle Tom's Cabin*. Though Dickens found himself in a 'comically incongruous position', with the audience 'in veritable pews', he decided it was 'a wonderful place to speak in'.[26] There was the usual scramble for tickets. Because of the severe cold the waiting crowd lit an immense bonfire in a narrow street of wooden houses and nearly set them on fire. While the police dealt with the blaze, there was a general fight from 'which the people farthest off in the line rushed bleeding when they saw a chance of displacing others near the door, and put their mattresses in these places, and then held on by the iron railings'.

Dickens was cheered to hear from Wilkie Collins that the stage version of 'No Thoroughfare' at the Adelphi had made a hit and that Charles Fechter had been 'magnificent' in the part of the villain. Dickens reported to Collins that literary pirates, who had been the cause of so many disagreeable exchanges during his first American visit, were still profiting from his work; there was no hope of an authorized production of the play as 'it is being done, in some mangled form or other, everywhere'.[27] And, as he informed Fechter, piracy was not confined to the latest play: 'wherever I go, the theatres (with my name in big letters) instantly begin playing versions of my books'.[28] He was now more resigned to such annoying exploitation, not least because he was himself making money in America. 'Well,' he remarked to Forster, 'the work is hard, the climate is hard, the life is hard, but the gain is enormous.'[29]

From New York he went on to Philadelphia, Baltimore, and Washington. All went well, he wrote to James Fields, despite the fact that 'the cold remains just as it was (beastly) and where it was (in my head)'.[30] While the audiences remained 'ready and bright' Dickens thought they were surprised by his simple presentation. 'They seem to take it ill that I don't stagger on to the platform over-powered by the spectacle before me, and the national greatness,' he wrote from Philadelphia. 'They are all so accustomed to do public things with a flourish of trumpets, that the notion of my coming in to read without somebody first flying up and delivering an "Oration" about me ... is so very unaccountable to them, that sometimes they have no idea until I open my lips that it can possibly be Charles Dickens.'[31] In Baltimore it snowed for a day and a night, and Dickens realized that he lacked the strength to complete the original itinerary through Chicago and Canada in weather so bitterly cold. George Childs, the publisher of the Philadelphia *Public Ledger*, warned him that 'the people will go into fits' if he failed to go to Chicago. 'I would rather they went into fits than I did,' Dickens pointedly replied, and he bore in silence the gibes of Chicago newspapers which claimed he avoided the city because his brother Augustus had left a common-law wife and three children without support when he had died in Chicago a year before.[32] Dolby and James Osgood, who was loaned from the staff of Ticknor and Fields to assist Dickens, were 'lashed into madness' by the unjustified taunts. They knew that Dickens had long supported his brother's abandoned wife, and also sent money to his Chicago dependants. 'I have imposed silence upon them,' Dickens wrote to Georgina, 'and they really writhe under it.'[33] He valued the loyalty and companionship of his assistants all the more because he refused social invitations to conserve his energy for the readings, and Dolby and Osgood were his main resource against loneliness. As a distraction he promoted a walking match between them, to take place on 29 February when they would all be back in Boston.

Dickens arranged the affair with mock seriousness, drawing up an elaborate set of rules while snowbound in Baltimore. The contestants were given professional names, Dolby being described as the Man of Ross and Osgood as the Boston Bantam; Fields, as one umpire, was called Massachusetts Jemmy, and Dickens was the other.[34] Noting his 'surprising performances (without the least variation) on that truly national instrument, the American catarrh', Dickens took the title of the Gad's Hill Gasper. He immediately put the men into training. 'I gave them a stiff one', he wrote to Georgina, 'of five miles over a bad road in the snow, half the distance uphill.' He disregarded his own debility, setting heavy Dolby and the diminutive Osgood a cracking example. 'I took them at a pace of four miles and a half an hour, and you never beheld such objects as they were when we got back; both smoking like factories, and both obliged to change everything before they could come to dinner.' Whenever there was a chance of exercise Dickens kept them at it, with 'busters' and 'breathers' of eight miles or more. And the men were seized by the competitive spirit. 'They have the absurdest ideas of what are tests of walking power,' Dickens wrote, 'and continually get up in the maddest manner and *see how high they can kick* the wall!'[35]

All through his life Dickens was a man of resilient temper, able to work himself into a cheerful mood though he was weary and unwell. As he told Georgina in early February it was this ability to 'come up to scratch' which enabled him to cope with the rigours of winter journeys and the demands of the platform. He was in Washington for his fifty-sixth birthday. 'It was observed as much as though I were a little boy,' he happily told Mamie. 'Flowers and garlands ... bloomed all over the room; letters radiant with good wishes poured in'; and there were gold and silver presents on the dinner-table. Early in the day he was received by President Johnson, 'a man with a very remarkable and determined face', who had booked a whole row for his family at each of the Washington readings.[36] In the afternoon, when the politician Charles Sumner called on him, Dickens was prostrate and voiceless, and Dolby was applying a mustard plaster. It seemed impossible for him to read that night. All the same, he reported to Mamie, after five minutes at the reading-desk he was not even hoarse, and 'the whole audience rose and remained (Secretaries of State, President's family, Judges of the Supreme Court, and so forth) standing and cheering until I went back to the table and made them a little speech'.[37] He had come to rely upon such bursts of effective energy. 'The frequent experience of this return of force when it is wanted saves me a vast amount of anxiety,' he confided to Mamie, 'but I am not at times without the nervous dread that I may some day sink altogether.'[38] Among other stimulants he had been fortified by 'Rocky Mountain Sneezers', which he described to Fechter as 'compounded of all the spirits ever heard of in the world, with bitters, lemon, sugar and snow'.[39]

While he was in Washington Dickens dined with Sumner and Edwin M. Stanton, the Secretary of War, a great admirer of his novels who claimed to have read a nightly passage from them to calm his nerves during the Civil War—and stood up well when Dickens quizzed him with quotations. Soon afterwards President Johnson dismissed Stanton, a strong advocate of a punitive policy towards the defeated South, and precipitated a political crisis. 'It is well that the money has flowed in hitherto so fast,' Dickens wrote to Forster after he returned to Boston, 'for I have a misgiving that the great excitement about the President's impeachment will damage our receipts.'[40] Dickens in fact decided to cancel the readings planned for the first week in March and to take a holiday, for February had been an exhausting month and he was due to swing out through New England to Niagara Falls and back again. There was, moreover, continuing trouble about the ticket allocations. Kelly, a clerk whom Dolby had brought out from England to assist him, was caught speculating in seats and taking bribes from would-be purchasers. Dickens himself had to run down to Providence to make an appeasing speech, and in New Haven there was a riot at the box-office and the city's mayor presided over a protest meeting. In this case Dickens refunded the money which Dolby had already taken and postponed the reading for six weeks.

On 28 February Dolby returned to Boston from Rochester and Buffalo, where he had been selling tickets in advance, and the walking match took place next day. Although Dickens was far from well, he and Fields had already gone over the thirteen-mile course to Newton Center and back to Boston 'at a tremendous pace', and they again walked much of the way with Osgood and Dolby. The ground conditions, Dickens said, were 'indescribable, from half-melted snow, running water, and sheets and blocks of ice'.[41] It was also very cold, Dickens telling Mamie afterwards that 'our hair, beards, eyelashes, eyebrows, were frozen hard, and hung with icicles'.[42] He had undertaken to report this endurance test in the style of a comic sporting narrative. The Boston Bantam was 'a young bird, though too old to be caught with chaff.... The man of Ross is a thought and a half too heavy and if he accidentally sat down upon his baby would do it to the tune of fourteen stone.... At about six miles the Gasper put on a tremendous spurt to leave the men behind and establish himself at the turning point.... Though both were breathed at the turn, the Bantam quickly got his bellows into obedient condition and blew away like an orderly blacksmith in full work ... the Bantam pegged away with his little drum-sticks as if he saw his wives and a peck of barley waiting for him at the family perch ... finally doing the whole distance in two hours and forty-eight minutes. Ross had ceased to compete three miles short of the winning post, but bravely walked it out, and came in seven minutes later.'[43] In the evening, to cap the occasion, Dickens gave a banquet in the Parker House for the contestants and his closest Boston acquaintances, including Holmes, Lowell, 'and an obscure poet named Longfellow'.[44] He took much trouble with the menu and the wines, and he told Mamie that the floral decoration on the table was such 'as was never seen in these parts'.[45]

The nights released by the cancelled readings provided an opportunity for such social occasions. Longfellow gave a dinner for him and Dickens reciprocated. 'It is the established joke that Boston is "my native place" and we hold all sorts of hearty foregatherings,' he wrote to Macready.[46] The weather was so foul, with gales and blizzards, that he left Boston on 6 March, a day earlier than intended, and travelled straight through to Syracuse. He described the town to Fechter as 'a most wonderful out-of-the-world place, which looks as if it had begun to be built yesterday and were going to be imperfectly knocked together with a nail or two the day after tomorrow'.[47] The hotel was bad in all respects—'quite a triumph in that way', he told Georgina—and the party sat up late playing whist and cribbage to stay out of their rooms as long as possible. 'We had an old buffalo for supper,' Dickens said, complaining that the menu was all the more grotesque for being written in French, 'and an old pig for breakfast.'[48]

Such experiences, coming after the pleasant days in Boston, brought on a fresh bout of homesickness. All along the way Dickens had kept closely in touch with Gad's Hill. He had written to Mamie about re-covering some of the furniture and buying new carpets; and he had sent Harry advice on the best means of rejuvenating the local cricket club without the appearance of patronage, 'one of the curses of England', and without depriving the men 'of their just right to manage their own affairs'.[49] By the time he reached Syracuse, however, his more intimate letters revealed feelings so jaded that even his natural ebullience could not freshen them. 'I am beginning to be tired,' he wrote to Fechter on 8 March, 'and have been depressed all the time (except when reading) and have lost my appetite. I cannot tell you— but you know, and therefore why should I?—how overjoyed I shall be to see you again, my dear boy, and how sorely I miss a dear friend, and how sorely I miss all art, in these parts. No disparagement to the country, which has a great future in reserve, or to its people, who are very kind to me.'[50]

Although the readings were simply produced, Dickens needed his own staff to cope with them. Apart from Dolby, who came and went about his ticket business, he was usually accompanied by Osgood, his valet and dresser Scott, George the gasman, who attended to the lighting, a couple of clerks, and a boy or two. At Niagara Falls, much impressed by his second sight of the chasm, he declared a two-day holiday for his team and sent them all sightseeing before they turned for home: 'it is nearly all "back" now, Thank God,' he wrote to Forster.[51] In Buffalo he heard that his old friend Chauncy Hare Townshend had died. 'It is not a light thing to lose such a friend, and I truly loved him,' he told Georgina,[52] but, as he explained in a long letter to Forster, his own discomforts had become an increasing distraction. On the days when he gave a reading he was 'pretty well knocked up' when he returned to his hotel; and the travelling conditions had deteriorated. He returned to Albany through deep floods which seriously delayed his train and marooned others. And at Albany he realized that the old trouble had broken out in his left foot and that it seemed to be spreading to the right one as well. He blamed it, as before, on walking in melted snow. It both pained and lamed him, but he went on through Boston to Portland and New Bedford. It was snowing again and his catarrh came back as severely as before. 'I have coughed from two or three in the morning until five or six,' he wrote to Mamie on 29 March, 'and have been absolutely sleepless. I have had no appetite besides, and no taste. Last night here I took some laudanum, and it is the only thing that has done me good.'[53] The next day he sent an equally distressed letter to Forster. 'I am nearly used up,' he admitted. 'Climate, distance, catarrh, travelling, and hard work, have begun (I may say so, now they are nearly all over) to tell heavily upon me. Sleeplessness besets me: and if I had engaged to go on into May I think I should have broken down.'[54]

Dickens knew that he was on the verge of collapse and that he had been wise to cut Canada out of his itinerary—though the compulsion to go on reading was so strong that, at the same time he was complaining to his family and friends, he was corresponding with Chappell's about an autumn tour in England. 'However sympathetic and devoted the people are about me,' he wrote to Mamie from Portland, 'they *can not* be got to comprehend that one's being able to do the two hours with spirit when the time comes round, may be co-existent with the consciousness of great depression and fatigue.'[55] He summoned enough energy to give his last set of readings in Boston, although plans for a farewell banquet had to be cancelled, and he was proud of the way he rose to the occasion. 'I not only read last Friday when I was doubtful of being able to do so,' he reported to Mamie from Boston, 'but read as I never did before, and astonished the audience quite as much as myself.'[56] He was helped, Dolby said, by James Fields and his wife, who did much to make him forget his sufferings; and Dolby himself had become indispensable, Dickens declaring that he was 'as tender as a woman, and as watchful as a doctor'.[57] Dolby now sat anxiously in the wings throughout each reading, and kept Dickens supplied with the succession of drinks which had replaced a normal diet. 'At seven in the morning, in bed, a tumbler of new cream and two tablespoonsful of rum. At twelve a sherry cobbler and a biscuit. At three (dinner time) a pint of champagne. At five minutes to eight, an egg beaten up with a glass of sherry. Between the parts, the strongest beef tea that can be made, drunk hot. At a quarter past ten, soup, and anything to drink that I can fancy. I don't eat more than half a pound of solid food in the whole four-and-twenty hours, if so much.'[58] At the final reading on 8 April, before an audience packed with Boston's notability, he gave 'Dr. Marigold's Prescriptions' and the 'Mrs. Gamp' sketch. When the applause died away he made a brief and touching speech. 'My gracious and generous welcome in America, which can never be obliterated from my remembrance, began here,' he said. 'My departure begins here too; for I assure you that I have never until this moment really felt that I am going away. In this brief life of ours it is sad to do almost anything for the last time, and I cannot conceal from you, although my face will so soon be turned towards my native land, and to all that makes it dear, that it is a sad consideration with me that in a few moments from this time this brilliant hall and all that it contains will fade from my view for evermore.'[59]

He was to sail from New York on 22 April, and he insisted on giving his promised readings in the city before he left. The effort and excitement so raised his blood pressure that each night he seemed likely to be struck down by apoplexy, and his right foot had become so painfully swollen that he had to lean on Dolby as he walked out to read. Dr. Fordyce Barker, the physician whom he had consulted earlier in the tour about his catarrh, made the same diagnosis of erysipelas that Dickens had been offered in England. By 18 April, when he was to be the guest of honour at a press banquet at Delmonico's, he was unable to wear his boot and his attendance seemed doubtful. Dolby drove about town looking for a gout bandage, and he eventually borrowed one which Dr. Barker used to patch Dickens up for the evening. He arrived at the restaurant an hour late and entered limping on the arm of Horace Greeley, who was to preside.

It was a magnificent feast, with dishes named for famous authors and confectionery models of the Dickens characters. 'Captain Cuttle blossomed out of the charlotte russe,' the New York *World* noted next day, 'and Tiny Tim was discovered in *pâté de foie gras.*' When Dickens rose to reply to the toast he made handsome amends for the critical mood in which he had last left the United States, saying that it was henceforth his duty 'to express my high and grateful sense of my second reception in America, and to bear my honest testimony to the national generosity and magnaminity'. He had seen great changes. 'Nor am I, I believe, so arrogant as to suppose that in twenty-five years there have been no changes in me, and that I had nothing to learn and no extreme impressions to correct when I was here first.' He had been overwhelmed 'with unsurpassable politeness, delicacy, sweet temper, hospitality, consideration, and with unsurpassable respect for the privacy daily enforced upon me by the nature of my avocation here and the state of my health'. This glowing testimony, he promised, would be published as an appendix in each future edition of *American Notes* and *Martin Chuzzlewit*. 'And this I will do and cause to be done, not in mere love and thankfulness, but because I regard it as an act of plain justice and honour.' There remained only a peroration on the common heritage: 'better for this globe to be riven by an earthquake, fired by a comet, overrun by an iceberg, and abandoned to the Arctic fox and bear, than that it should present the spectacle of these two great nations, each of which has, in its own way and hour, striven so hard and so successfully for freedom, ever again being arrayed one against the other'.[60]

When Dickens finished and the applause died away he excused himself, for he was in too much pain to stay for the remaining speeches. He had still to make his last appearance on 20 April, and before an audience of over two thousand people he ended his tour as he had begun it, with the *Carol* and *Pickwick*. 'I beg to bid you farewell,' he said when he was finished, 'and I pray God bless you, and God bless the land in which I leave you.'

Two days later, on a sparkling spring day, Dickens went through the crowd which waited outside the Westminster Hotel to the private tug which took him to the *Russia*, moored out by Staten Island. There was a farewell lunch with Mr. and Mrs. Fields and other friends; and Anthony Trollope, just arrived on the *Scotia*, was among the larger crowd that went out in the passenger tender to say goodbye before the steam tug pulled the *Russia* towards the ocean.

It was a rough passage home, but the rest and sea air were a much needed tonic. Within four days Dickens was free of his catarrh and able to put a shoe on his right foot; and when he arrived in Liverpool he looked bronzed and fit. 'My doctor was quite broken down in spirits when he saw me,' he wrote to Mrs. Fields. '"Good Lord", he said, recoiling, "seven years younger!"'[61] The pile of dollars amounted to a small fortune. The seventy-six readings had grossed $228,000, or an average of $3,000 a night. After the deduction of $39,000 for expenses, and the conversion of the dollars into gold, Dickens told Forster, his profit 'was within a hundred or so of £20,000'. He exultantly reminded Forster that from his first readings in England he had made £10,000 and another £13,000 from those organized by Chappell's. 'These figures are of course between ourselves,' he wrote, 'but don't you think them rather remarkable?'[62]

23

The Hunt is Over

DICKENS came back to a splendid reception. People turned out to greet him as he drove from the station at Gravesend, and there were flags on houses all along the road. Gad's Hill Place, he reported to Mrs. Fields, was so decorated 'that every brick of it was hidden'. On the next Sunday, the bell-ringers at Higham started a celebration peal as soon as the service ended 'and rang like mad until I got home'.[1] Dickens was delighted by such signs of public esteem. Yet for all his pleasure in his return and the superficial improvement which the voyage had worked in his appearance, he could not wholly conceal the ravages of the American journey. Forster was quick to notice a loss of 'natural force'. For once Dickens himself was prepared to rest at Gad's Hill. 'I feel the peace of the country beyond all expression,' he wrote to Mrs. Watson early in May and he saw his little estate with a pleasurably fresh eye.[2] 'Divers birds sing here all day, and the nightingales all night,' he told Mrs. Fields. 'The place is lovely and in perfect order.'[3] He was glad to entertain Longfellow and his three daughters who hastened from an audience with the Queen at Windsor to spend the remainder of 4 July celebrating the American national holiday with Dickens. 'I turned out a couple of postilions in the old red jacket of the old red royal Dover road for our ride; and it was like a holiday ride in England fifty years ago,' he wrote to James Fields. 'Of course we went to look at the old houses in Rochester, and the old cathedral, and the old castle.'[4]

Yet he could not relax for long. There was work to be done for both his intimate collaborators had run into trouble. Wilkie Collins was ill and worried by the final illness of his mother, who had lost her wits; and, as he struggled to finish the elegant mystery of *The Moonstone*, he was taking massive doses of laudanum to ease the pain of a chronic eye complaint. He had made a successful play of 'No Thoroughfare' from the scenario which Dickens had roughed out for Fechter before leaving for Boston, and it had run for two hundred nights, but he was in no state to accompany Dickens to Paris to supervise the production at the Vaudeville Theatre under the title of *L'Abîme*. Wills was also incapacitated. While Dickens had been away he had taken a bad fall in the hunting field and been so severely concussed that his doctor had insisted upon a long rest. Dickens had to take full responsibility for the editorial work of *All the Year Round* and look after the business side as well. Fortunately the magazine was thriving on the appeal of *The Moonstone*, which had caught the public fancy better than any serial since *Pickwick*. As its publisher Dickens was delighted to see crowds waiting in Wellington Street to buy the latest number of this gripping tale. As a rival author he was piqued and, though he had earlier declared the novel to be better than anything he had ever done himself, he was less than generous in his private comment. 'I quite agree with you about *The Moonstone*,' he wrote to Wills on 26 July. 'The construction is wearisome beyond endurance, and there is a vein of obstinate conceit in it that makes enemies of readers.'[5]

Dickens was genuinely fond of Collins, whose company had cheered him in the depressed period when he was separating from Catherine, but there had always been an element of patronage in their relationship. Dickens was ever a generous but possessive friend. He had come to depend upon the younger man as a congenial and talented acolyte in journalism, amateur theatricals, plays, and fiction, and he found it difficult to let him go his own way. Collins, however, was no longer dependent upon Dickens. The years of Bohemian jaunts lay behind them; and as a writer Collins had made such a mark with *The Woman in White*, which had earned him the staggering sum of £10,000 in one year, that he could now choose what he wanted to do and name his own terms for it. As a gesture of friendship to Dickens he had put his own work aside to write his share of 'No Thoroughfare', and he had such a craving for success as a dramatist that he had easily been persuaded to convert the novelette into a play. But he had lost his former eagerness for collaboration, and quite clearly in 1868 Dickens was worried about his ability to produce a Christmas story without the help of Collins. 'I feel,' he had written to Fechter from America, 'as if I had murdered a Christmas number years ago (perhaps I did!) and its ghost perpetually haunted me.'[6] By the summer, he told Wills, he was 'in a positive state of despair' about the Christmas issue of the magazine. 'I cannot get an idea for it which is in the least satisfactory to me.'[7] Five days later he wrote again to Wills to say that he had made some false starts and had 'offered £100 reward at Gad's to anybody who could suggest a notion to satisfy me'.[8] He ground at the problem for another week or so and then admitted defeat. That year there was no Christmas number of *All the Year Round*.

In its place Dickens laboured at an unwelcome obligation. From Chauncy Hare Townshend he had inherited a substantial sum of money and instructions to publish Townshend's religious and philosophical manuscripts. He did his best to shape these tedious documents into a book which he disparagingly nicknamed 'Religious Hiccoughs'—Dolby found him 'nearly distracted by the conglomeration of ideas'—and this work of piety fell drearily from the press in the following year.[9] That summer Dickens lost another old friend, whose illustrations had graced some of his early work and whose company had cheered so many convivial dinners. 'Poor George Cattermole is dead,' Dickens reported to Wills in late July. 'Very very poor. Family quite unprovided for; debt and distress.'[10] Dickens had once had the energy in such circumstances to promote a theatrical benefit or some other form of practical help for the widow, but the best he could now do was to sign a memorial asking for help from the Royal Academy.

He was more concerned with the money troubles of his own sons. 'I can't get my hat on in consequence of the extent to which my hair stands on end at the costs and charges of these boys,' he exclaimed to Dolby on 25 September. 'Why was I ever a father! Why was my father ever a father!'[11] Charley's latest business venture had ended in bankruptcy (since 1866 he had been running a paper mill with money borrowed from Miss Coutts), leaving him with a personal debt of over £1,000. Dickens declined to bail him out, for fear of deluding his creditors into 'the preposterous belief that I could and would make some kind of bargain with them'. All he could do was to take Charley into the office of *All the Year Round*. 'I must turn his education to the best account I can,' he explained to Wills on 27 September; 'he can certainly take the bag and report on its contents, and carry on the correspondence.'[12] Harry, the most energetic and steady of all the boys, who had won a scholarship at Trinity College, Cambridge, was sent severe paternal advice with a cheque for £25. 'We must have no shadow of debt,' Dickens told him at the beginning of term. 'You know how hard I work for what I get, and I think you know that I never had money help from any human creature after I was a child. You know that you are one of many heavy charges on me, and that I trust to your so exercising your abilities and improving the advantages of your past expensive education, as soon to diminish *this* charge.'[13]

He was a man who greatly valued family sentiment and yet he could not easily express it to his own children. A year later, when Harry had done well and come down from Cambridge full of excitement that he had won a second scholarship, Dickens at first received the news so coldly that Harry was deeply disappointed; and then, as they walked up to Gad's Hill from the station, he turned to his son with eyes brimming with tears and gripped his hand with a stammered 'God bless you!' He was equally aloof with Plorn when, in September 1868, he dispatched the boy to join his brother Alfred in Australia with £200 and a plaintive reminder of his own youthful hardships. 'I was not so old as you are now when I first had to win my food,' he wrote in his farewell letter. All the same, as he sternly urged the distressed boy to realize that 'this life is half made up of partings, and these pains must be borne', he was deeply moved.[14] 'He seemed to me to become once more my youngest and favourite little child as the day drew near', he sadly told Fechter after Plorn had sailed, 'and I did not think I could have been so shaken.'[15] But he made no more effort to share this sorrow with Catherine, or to sympathize with her, than he had done when Walter died. He had long ago hardened his heart towards her; and now the family they had raised together had been scattered to the winds.

It was ten years since Dickens had broken with Catherine and given the first of his professional readings. These two decisions had opened a rift in his life which had steadily widened through the subsequent decade. In private he had withdrawn from the social round he had once so much enjoyed into the refuge provided by Ellen Ternan at Peckham and the comfortable familiarity of Gad's Hill—indeed Ellen herself was now an occasional guest at the house and accepted by Georgina and Mamie. Even Forster and Collins were being dropped in favour of his working cronies Wills and Dolby. In public, however, he seemed a different man, at the peak of his popularity as the 'National Sparkler', finding the emotional stimulus he craved in the excitement of readings and the nightly identification with his own familiar characters.

Before Dickens left Boston he had begun to negotiate with Chappell's for a final series of readings in London and the provinces, and they had offered to pay £6,000 for seventy-five performances, with all expenses paid. Dickens then raised the proposal to £8,000 for a hundred appearances. In four months he would earn as much from reading as he would expect to make in three years as a writer. The increase reflected his growing fear that the old flow of imaginative invention had begun to run dry; he now felt obliged to earn as much money as possible while he was well enough to travel and effective enough to hold his audience.

The new commitment, Forster believed, was a 'fatal mistake', for the performer was steadily destroying the man. One day that summer Forster was particularly alarmed when Dickens, who had walked over from his office in Wellington Street to dine at Forster's imposing house in Palace Gate, announced that on the way over he had been able to read only the right-hand side of the shop signs—and blamed this worrying defect on the medicine he was taking. Dickens, Forster considered, had persuaded himself that poor health 'was to be borne as the lot more or less of all men; and the more thorough he could make his feelings of independence, and of ability to rest, by what was now in hand, the better his final chance of a complete recovery would be'.[16] The American tour had shown what Dickens would

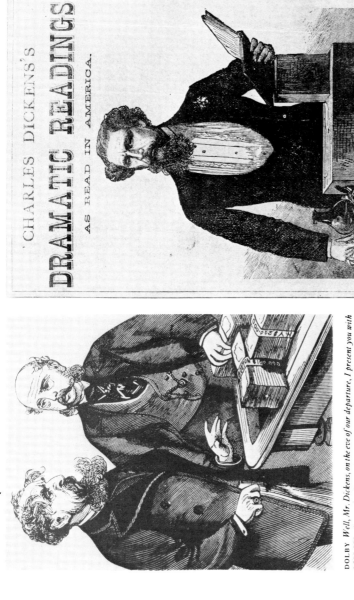

CHARLES DICKENS'S
DRAMATIC READINGS
AS READ IN AMERICA.

DOCTOR MARIGOLD.

BOSTON.
LEE & SHEPARD, Publishers.
1869.

DOLBY *Well, Mr. Dickens, on the eve of our departure, I present you with* **$300,000**, *the result of your Lectures in America.*

DICKENS *What! only* **$300,000?** *Is that all I have made out of these penurious Yankees, after all my abuse of them? Pshaw! Let us go, Dolby!*

Above: Cartoon of Charles Dickens and George Dolby at the end of the American lecture tour

Right: Title-page of a reading version of 'Doctor Marigold's Prescriptions', as given by Dickens during his American tour

Charles Dickens at the age of fifty

endure for money, and for the emotional stimulus of the readings; like an addict, he was willing to promise reform after a last bout of indulgence—and to pay any price in self-destructiveness to satisfy his craving.

That summer at Gad's Hill, as Dickens prepared for his autumn readings, he turned back to a sensational idea which he had considered and dismissed five years before. On 24 May 1863, when he had been reviewing possible additions to his repertoire, he had written to a friend of Thackeray: 'I have been trying, alone by myself, the *Oliver Twist* murder, but have got something so horrible out of it that I am afraid to try it in public.'[17] Now he was less squeamish and more responsive to the morbid appeal of the murderous Sikes. He was also concerned to provide some new excitement if he was to go on drawing large audiences. He worked at the text, though he told no one except Dolby. 'When you come to see me on Monday you shall look through the Murder as I have arranged it,' he wrote to him on 29 September. 'It is very horrible but very dramatic. If I decide on doing it at all, we will strike boldly for London.'[18]

While Dickens got ready for his tour, due to begin on 6 October 1868 at St. James's Hall, the country was plunged into a general election. William Ewart Gladstone, profiting from the recent extension of the franchise to many workingmen, became Prime Minister for the first time and the reformist wing of the Liberal party was greatly strengthened. Dickens had again been given opportunities to enter politics, for he had been approached to stand in both Edinburgh and Birmingham—where the Radical tide ran strong. Once more he refused, telling F. D. Finlay in Edinburgh that 'I am more useful and more happy as I am than I could ever be in Parliament'.[19] He was more outspoken to Thomas Trollope. 'The madness and general political bestiality of the General Elections will come off in the appropriate Guy Fawkes days,' he wrote on 10 September when the contest began: 'no consideration on earth would induce me to become a candidate for the representation of any place in the House of Commons. Indeed, it is a dismal sight, is that arena altogether. Its irrationality and dishonesty are quite shocking.'[20] A more resigned note sometimes crept into his invective. He wrote to Cerjat to say that 'the country is going to be ruined, and that the Church is going to be ruined, and that both have become so used to being ruined, that they will go on perfectly well'.[21]

The first evenings in Liverpool and Manchester went well 'notwithstanding election meetings'. But he quickly felt the strain. 'I have not been well,' he confessed to Forster after the tour had been running for three weeks, 'and have been heavily tired.' He was also upset by the death in Darlington of his last surviving brother, Frederick, and he sent Dolby off with Charley to look after the final arrangements. It was, he sadly declared to Forster, 'a wasted life, but God forbid that one should be hard upon it, or upon anything in this world that is not deliberately and coldly wrong'.[22] His health and his spirits were flagging, and he complained to Georgina of sleeplessness and sickness. 'I am perpetually counting the weeks before me to be "read" through,' he wrote to Wilkie Collins from Edinburgh, 'and am perpetually longing for the end of them; and yet I sometimes wonder whether I shall miss something when they are over.'[23]

He was more and more attracted to the idea of a new reading which would satisfy his need for a sensational climax. He wished, he admitted to Forster, to leave behind him 'the recollection of something very passionate and dramatic'. Yet he still held back from using the murder of Nancy for the fear that the effect might be too powerful. 'I have no doubt that I could perfectly petrify an audience by carrying out the notion I have of the way of rendering it,' he confessed to Forster when he first told him of the idea soon after the start of the tour. 'But whether the impression would not be so horrible as to keep them away another time, is what I cannot satisfy myself upon. What do you think?'[24] Forster's answer was that the subject 'was out of the province of reading'. Dolby objected that it would be too stressful. Dickens in fact admitted that the murder scene drove all the breath out of his body. But after he had consulted Chappell's he agreed, since the episode was so gruesome, that he would try it out on an invited audience at St. James's Hall on 14 November. He made it a gala occasion, providing an oysters and champagne supper afterwards for over a hundred guests, and Edmund Yates said that he excelled himself. As he 'flung aside his book and acted the scene of the murder, shrieked the terrific pleadings of the girl, growled the brutal savagery of the murderer, brought looks, tones, gestures simultaneously into play to illustrate his meaning,' Yates recalled, 'there was not one, not even of those who had known him best or who believed in him most, but was astonished at the power and versatility of his genius'.[25] When he was done, Dickens noted, his listeners were 'unmistakably pale and had horror-striken faces', and at the supper party his friends were divided on the desirability of a public performance. Dr. Priestley, a fashionable physician, cautioned him against the risk. 'You may rely upon it that if only one woman cries out when you murder the girl,' he said, 'there will be a contagion of hysteria all over this place.' Next day the noted Shakespearian scholar William Harness sent a letter to the same effect. The reading, he felt, 'was a most amazing and terrific thing but I am bound to tell you that I had an almost irresistible impulse upon me to *scream*, and that, if anyone had cried out, I am certain I should have followed'.[26]

Dickens was pleased by such testimony to his dramatic talent and the warnings did not deter him. He seemed to be seeking enough support from this private audience to justify the introduction of the *Oliver Twist* item into his programme, and he was delighted when the actress Mrs. Keeley urged him to do so. 'Having got at such an effect as that, it must be done,' she insisted; 'the public have been looking out for a sensation these last fifty years or so, and by Heaven they have got it!'[27] Dickens was also encouraged by the press comments. 'He has always trembled on the boundary line that separates the reader from the actor,' declared *The Times*; 'now he clears it by a leap.' As a final concession to his anxious friends Dickens agreed to try out the murder scene on normal audiences at the beginning of his New Year tour, first at St. James's Hall and then at Dublin, before he decided to use it regularly. Yet the emotions it aroused had already gripped him. Two days after the private reading he invited the painter W. P. Frith to the first public reading on 5 January. 'It is horribly like, I am afraid,' he said of the murder. 'I have a vague sensation of being "*wanted*" as I walk about the streets.'[28]

In the meantime he had made the script for the reading even more sensational than the version he had tried out in St. James's Hall. That had ended with the death of Nancy, which he had thought sufficient to strain the nerves of his listeners. In December, however, he reported to Collins that he had extended it and was 'trying it daily with the object of rising from that blank state of horror into a fierce and passionate rush for the end'.[29] The addition, which worked up to a pitch of morbid excitement, was not done merely for effect. The motives which had induced Dickens to revive this scene of telling violence had broken through the frame of fiction and were driving him to an exhausting obsession with its grisly detail. More than any other passage in his novels it starkly fused the themes of betrayed love, flight, and self-destruction which bound his life and work together; and there was no attempt to soften its brutal impact with humour or sentiment. He saw the last agony of Sikes through the eyes of the fleeing criminal, cornered at last and the victim of his own guilt and fear. 'Hark! A great sound coming on like rushing fire. What. Tracked so soon? The hunt was up already?' And each time Dickens appeared on the platform as Sikes, that diabolic embodiment of his own darkest feelings, some part of him felt the murderous rage against Nancy, some part ran away with Sikes and found no hiding place, and some part died each night as Sikes dropped in a public hanging as grim as those which Dickens once saw outside the London prisons.

The first-night audience was overwhelmed and the critics applauded. But success, at such a price, worried Dolby. 'The horrible perfection to which he brought it, and the novelty,' he noted, 'acted as a charm to him and made him the more determined to go on with it come what might.'[30] In Dublin, where the demand for seats was so great that mounted police were called out to control the crowd, Dickens was less pleased with his reading; and Percy Fitzgerald thought his performance strained and melodramatic. Yet the audience and the press were as enthusiastic as their London counterparts. The *Freeman's Journal*, hailing this 'masterpiece', declared that 'Mr. Dickens is the greatest reader of the greatest writer of the age'.[31] With such endorsement Dickens no longer felt inhibited and he began to read 'Sikes and Nancy' four times a week when he toured the West Country after his return from Ireland.

He made a point of going to Cheltenham so that the 'surprisingly infirm and aged' Macready could hear him read the murder scene. In the dressing-room afterwards, when Dickens waved away his old friend's praise, Macready insisted. '"No, Dickens—er—er—I will NOT", with sudden emphasis, "—er—have it—er—put aside. In my—er—best times—er—you remember them, my dear boy—er, gone, gone!—no"—with great emphasis again—"it comes to this—er—TWO MACBETHS!"' Then, Dickens told James Fields, 'he trailed off into a weak pale likeness of himself as if his whole appearance had been some clever optical illusion'.[32] The professional eye of Macready had noted the particular talent on which Dickens depended for success as a reader, and others recognized it too. 'He had the faculty,' recalled the Duke of Argyll, 'which many great actors have had, of somehow getting rid of their own physical identity, and appearing with a wholly different face and a wholly different voice. I never saw this power so astonishingly exerted as by Charles Dickens.'[33]

In the first weeks of 1869 Dickens coped fairly well with the strains of the tour, although the continued absence of Wills from the office meant extra work on *All the Year Round* and he was also writing more articles for the series collected under the title of *The Uncommercial Traveller*. By the middle of February, however, there were the first signs of a serious breakdown in his health. He was to give a reading in London on 16 February before going up to Scotland, but when Dolby called that morning he found that the old trouble had broken out in the left foot and that Dickens was lying in bed in great pain, and in great distress at the prospect of cancelling his performance that night. Frank Beard was summoned, with the surgeon Sir Henry Thompson, and they jointly signed a certificate forbidding his appearance. The doctors also made him postpone his journey to Scotland. 'It throws us all back,' Dickens wrote crossly to Forster, 'and will cost me some five hundred pounds.'[34] Four days later, despite the entreaties of his friends, he travelled up to Edinburgh. Although he was more comfortable and was soon back on the stage—'I think the Edinburgh audience understood the "Murder" better last night than any audience that has yet heard it,' he claimed to Georgina on 25 February—he had only been in the city two days before he felt it necessary to consult Mr. Syme, the celebrated surgeon. The new diagnosis pleased him, for Syme rejected Thompson's belief that the condition was due to gout and supported Dickens in his comforting theory that the trouble was simply due to walking with wet feet in the snow.[35] Rest, Syme said, was the only cure, though he gave Dickens some relief by providing a new surgical boot and Dickens cheerfully told Mamie that in all other respects he had been found in just perfectly splendid condition.

Dickens took no notice of the advice to rest and, using Syme's optimism as an excuse to ignore his illness, he planned his readings through March as though nothing were wrong with him. Dolby, disturbed to note that Dickens had begun to include 'Sikes and Nancy' in most of his programmes, urged him to choose less stressful items. Dickens was angered, smashing a plate and shouting at Dolby for his 'infernal caution'. Then, Dolby recalled, he relented and tearfully embraced him; and he came round to admitting that 'there was a little too much "murder" in our arrangements'.[36] He struggled through the winter weather to Glasgow, down to London and back to Manchester, and on to Wolverhampton, Hull, and York. Here, by cutting out the intervals in his reading, he managed to catch the night train to London for the funeral of the reformer Sir James Emerson Tennent, whom he had known in Italy in 1853 and to whom he had dedicated *Our Mutual Friend*. Forster saw him at the ceremony and thought him 'dazed and worn'.[37] Dickens admitted to fatigue but still tried to make light of his symptoms, reporting 'all well and brilliant personally' to Wills on 30 March. He took a box at the Adelphi for some of the family to see Charles Fechter in *Black and White*, a new play by Wilkie Collins: 'I have rarely seen Fechter to greater advantage,'[38] he told Wills charitably, although the play was poorly received and Collins was disappointed by its limited run. And then Dickens was off again to Birmingham, Manchester, and Liverpool, which was celebrating his last appearance in the town by a civic banquet in St. George's Hall on 10 April. The hall, Dickens told Fields, was 'less adapted to public speaking than Westminster Abbey', and the echoes had to be deadened with flags borrowed from naval ships in the Mersey.[39] Yet Dickens bore the many speeches well and returned to London with a lively party of friends.

After giving another reading at St. James's Hall Dickens again dashed northwards, meeting Edmund Yates in Leeds. Yates was shocked by the change in him. 'He looked desperately aged and worn; the lines in his cheeks and round the eyes, always noticeable, were now deep furrows; there was a weariness in his gaze and a general air of fatigue and depression about him.'[40] At long last his great virtue, that 'extraordinary elasticity of spirits', seemed to have gone out of him. He now lived from one reading to the next, cheered by every small evidence of success. 'They are selling my tickets here at a guinea apiece (original cost five shillings),' he told Frith from Leeds on 13 April. 'I wonder who gets the money. I know who don't and that is—Your illustrious friend, Charles Dickens.'[41] And Yates was soon justified in his anxiety. Dickens went on from Leeds to spend a restful weekend at Chester, and there he took a turn for the worse. 'I found myself extremely giddy, and extremely uncertain of my sense of touch, both in the left leg and the left hand and arms,' he told Forster a few days later.[42] He could not make up his mind whether to go on with the readings or to stop, and finally decided to send Frank Beard an account of his symptoms and ask for his advice. He forced himself to go through with two more readings at Blackburn, and then took a quiet day in Blackpool. From the seaside he sent Georgina a serious but seemingly reassuring note on 21 April: 'I am much better than I was on Sunday, but shall want careful looking to, to get through the readings. My weakness and deadness are all *on the left side*, and if I don't look at anything I try to touch with my left hand, I don't know where it is. I am in (secret) consultation with Frank Beard; he recognises, in the exact description I have given him, indisputable evidences of overwork, which he would wish to treat immediately.... My foot is greatly better too, and I wear my own boot.'[43]

In the morning of 22 April Dickens and Dolby went to Preston to be ready for that evening's performance, and they were soon joined by Beard, anxious to see Dickens and examine him. 'Beard has come down,' Dickens wrote to Mamie that afternoon, 'and instantly echoes my impression (perfectly unknown to him) that the readings must be *stopped*. I have had symptoms that must not be disregarded.'[44] And Beard warned Dolby that unless Dickens could be persuaded to rest 'I will not guarantee but that he goes through life dragging a foot after him'. All the same, Dickens wanted to give his Preston reading before he left for London. 'It will save so much trouble,' he pleaded, well aware that cancellation would make things difficult for Dolby and disappoint his audience.[45] As Beard was adamant, the reading was abandoned, and Beard took Dickens back with him to see Sir Thomas Watson. This distinguished physician confirmed Beard's diagnosis. Though Dickens *appeared* well enough, Watson declared after he had seen him, by his own account he 'had been on the brink of an attack of paralysis of his left side, and possibly of apoplexy'; and in a joint statement the two doctors attributed this dangerous state to 'extreme hurry, overwork, and excitement, incidental to his readings'.[46] They insisted that Dickens must take a long rest. He was reluctant to agree, because he had yet to give twenty-six of the hundred readings for which he was pledged to Chappell's, and he was keen to complete his contract—the more so because the firm had uncomplainingly written off the costs of the cancelled engagements. Yet he was clearly in a serious condition. 'Dickens, I find by Forster who was just here,' Thomas Carlyle wrote to his brother, 'has narrowly escaped *death* ... by rushing about "on his *readings*"—in chase of still other thousands of pounds which he needed so little!'[47]

Even in this extremity, however, Dickens still counted upon his much taxed capacity for recuperation. 'I told Dr. Watson,' he assured Chappell on 3 May, 'that he had no idea of the rapidity with which I should come up again.' All that was wrong, he claimed, was that 'the rapid railway travelling was stretched a hair's breadth too far', and he hopefully reported that 'the sense of exhaustion seems a dream already'.[48] Within a matter of weeks he had begun to badger Watson for permission to complete his programme. In the end Watson and Beard gave way, although they were worried about the consequences and imposed strict conditions. Dickens was to give no more than a dozen readings; he must not make any long railway journeys; and in any case the readings must be postponed until the spring of 1870. As he told Chappell, they were to be his 'London Farewells'.

24

Fallen from the Ranks

'I AM happy to report myself perfectly well and flourishing,' Dickens wrote to Macready on 20 July 1869, as the easy summer days at Gad's Hill restored the worst of the damage done by the last set of readings.[1] As his strength came back he even revived the idea of an Australian tour; it would give him a chance to see Alfred and the miserably homesick Plorn, who had left the sheep station where he had been sent. 'I was quite prepared for his not settling down without a lurch or two,' Dickens wrote to G. W. Rusden, the Clerk to the Parliament of Victoria, who was keeping an eye on Plorn. 'But knowing the boy, I want to try him fully.'[2] He still hoped for the best from his sons despite his disappointments, and he perked up when Henry did well academically at Cambridge, when the spendthrift Sydney was promoted to second lieutenant—'the youngest in the Service, I believe', he proudly observed to Macready[3]—and when Charley proved himself sufficiently at *All the Year Round* to manage the magazine with reasonable competence after Wills was injured. His family responsibilities, however, had been much on his mind when he had collapsed in April and he had decided to make a new will, which was signed on 12 May.

Without preamble Dickens first bequeathed 'the sum of £1,000 free of legacy duty to Miss Ellen Lawless Ternan, late of Houghton Place, Ampthill Square'. (She remained loyal to Dickens for some years and it was not until 1876 that she married a schoolteacher, the Revd. George W. Robinson, and brought up a family.) This gift to Ellen Ternan, large enough to attract notice after his death, came before some small legacies to his servants, the annuity of £300 which he provided for Mary so long as she remained unmarried, and the substantial bequest of £8,000 to Georgina. Georgina, who was fulsomely thanked for her 'ever useful self-denying and devoted' services to the children, was described as 'the best and truest friend man ever had'. And Catherine was predictably reproved. Dickens left her the interest on £8,000 while she lived, but he coldly put on record 'the fact that my wife, since our separation by consent, has been in the receipt from me of an annual income of £600, while all the great charges of a numerous and expensive family have devolved wholly upon myself'. The bulk of his large estate (for despite all his financial worries he eventually disposed of £93,000) was to be divided equally between his sons and daughters. The 'dear trusty friend' John Forster was to receive his gold watch, and all his manuscripts. A year later, after Wills had retired from *All the Year Round*, Dickens added a brief codicil leaving Charley his interest in the magazine.[4] Charley made no success of it; he started a printing firm which failed and went on to give readings from his father's work in America. When he died in July 1896— Mamie died three days later—he left a widow and five unmarried daughters penniless.

Dickens was cheered during his convalescence by the arrival of a group of his Boston friends on holiday. Apart from James Fields and his wife, the party included Dr. Fordyce Barker, who had attended him when he had been ill, Sol Eytinge, who had illustrated an American edition of his books, the Charles Eliot Nortons, and the daughter of James Russell Lowell, the Harvard man of letters who became a U.S. diplomat. When the Americans arrived in May Dickens took a suite in the St. James's Hotel to be conveniently near them, and brought Mary and Georgina up from the country to share in a round of entertainment that Dolby described as 'Brobdignagian in its proportions'.[5] One night he took Fields, Dolby, and Eytinge on a prowl through the East End haunts which he knew well; and with two detectives to guide and protect them they went down Ratcliffe Highway to the doss-houses and opium dens of dockland. In the same reminiscent mood Dickens took Fields to see the rooms at Furnival's Inn where he had lived when he first married and was writing *Pickwick Papers*. The party then decamped to the country. 'The red jackets shall turn out again upon the turn-pike road', Dickens had promised Fields in a letter on 9 April, 'and picnics among the cherry-orchards and hop-gardens shall be heard of in Kent.'[6] He indeed turned out two post-carriages with postilions to carry his friends down the Dover Road to Canterbury, where they made a mock search for Agnes Wick-field's house, and he showed them Rochester, Chatham, and Cobham Park, before winding up the visit with a grand dinner party and an evening recep-tion for friends and neighbours. Dolby was pleased to see Dickens so vigorous again, and brown with the walks, bowls, and croquet in the June sunshine. As the summer wore on there were other visitors. Wilkie Collins went down, and although he and Dickens were no longer on intimate terms, he noted that the visit was 'harmonious and pleasant'.[7] And after one of Ellen Ternan's visits, when she tried her hand at cricket, Kate Dickens cryptically remarked, 'I am afraid she did not play the game'.[8]

After the crisis in April Dickens seemed to be settling to a healthier and more leisured pace. On 30 August there was a rowing race on the Thames between Oxford and Harvard, and he proposed the main toast to the crews at a celebratory dinner and firework display at the Crystal Palace. Three weeks later he was at the Birmingham Institute, which had elected him its honorary president, opening the new term with an address which extolled the penny classes which the Institute ran for its artisan students. 'A man', he insisted, 'cannot really improve himself without in some degree improving his fellow men.' Then, replying to the vote of thanks, he concluded with a political epigram which was much misunderstood. 'My faith in the people governing, is, on the whole, infinitesimal,' he said; 'my faith in the People governed, is, on the whole, illimitable.'⁹ In both local and national papers the statement was taken as evidence that Dickens had become a Tory; *The Times* declared on 30 September that 'sentiments like these might be justifiable in the latitude of St. Petersburg'. All Dickens had done, in fact, was to repeat his lifetime scepticism of the nation's rulers, and to assert his confidence in the ordinary men and women whom they ruled. When he returned to the Institute on 6 January to preside over its prize-giving ceremony he was at pains to make his meaning clear, quoting Buckle's *History of Civilisation in England* to the effect 'that lawgivers are nearly always the obstructors of society, instead of its helpers' and reminding his audience of the Circumlocution Office. 'I was determined', he told Macready in thanking him for his support over this controversy, 'that my Radicalism should not be called in question. The electric wires are not very exact in their reporting, but at all events the sense was there.'¹⁰

It was four years since Dickens had published a novel—the longest gap since he started his literary career. In May, however, he saw a clear run of time before him, and by midsummer Dickens had an inkling of what he wanted to do. 'What do you think of the idea of a story beginning in this way?' he asked Forster in July, giving him an outline of a plot which followed the fates of a boy and girl pledged to marry by deceased parents: it was a notion very close to one he had jotted down years before in his 'Book of Memoranda'. Soon afterwards he again wrote to Forster. 'I laid aside the fancy I told you of, and have a very curious and new idea for my new story,' he reported in August. 'Not a communicable idea (or the interest of the book would be gone) but a very strong one, though difficult to work.'¹¹ Reverting to the system that had served so well when he was making his reputation, Dickens proposed that the serial version should come out in twelve monthly numbers with the familiar green illustrated wrappers; and he had no difficulty in negotiating favourable terms with Frederic Chapman, who had taken over the publishing firm from his cousin Edward and agreed to pay more than Dickens had asked for any previous novel. The price was £7,500 for the copyright, a half share of profits, and £1,000 for advance sheets sent to Boston for Ticknor and Fields to publish in their weekly magazine *Every Saturday*. The contract also contained an ominous though fair-minded clause which Dickens had apparently included in at least one earlier agreement. Should he die before the work was complete John Forster was to determine how much of the advance should be repaid to Chapman.

The title of the new novel was not settled until 27 September, when Dickens gave a dinner to mark his decision, but it had been included in the list of seventeen possibilities which Dickens had noted down on 20 August. He had thought of 'The Two Kinsmen', 'Flight and Pursuit', and 'One Object in Life' before working through 'The Loss of Edwyn Brood' to *The Mystery of Edwin Drood*. He was obviously much affected by *The Moonstone*; *Edwin Drood* involved a similar juxtaposition between England and the East, and depended equally upon hallucination as the key to the plot. In a phrase which precisely echoed the manner in which the jewel was hidden and found in *The Moonstone* Dickens wrote of 'two states of consciousness that never clash, but each of which pursues its separate course as though it were continuous instead of broken (thus, if I hide my watch when I am drunk, I must be drunk again before I can remember where)'.[12] Although the mystery remained unsolved, for Dickens had no completed plan for the book beyond the point where it breaks off, it was plainly not the simple matter of whether Drood is alive or dead, or even of who may have killed him. In this story, Kate Dickens said afterwards, her father intended the mystery to lie in the tragic secrets of the human heart rather than in the conventional concealment and detection of a crime. It lies, that is, in the divided personality of the opium-addicted Jasper, whose conscious and respectable self was apparently to pursue and unmask his unconscious, vengeful, and criminal self. Dickens had moved on from the theme of double identity in *Our Mutual Friend*, through the emotional obsession with Sikes in the later phase of his readings, to a book which explored the soul of a murderer.

From its opening scene, set in the opium den in Shadwell which Dickens had visited with Fields and Dolby and to which he returned in October to refresh his impressions, the novel relied upon disorientation for its effects. A reviewer in the *Academy* noticed 'the absence of all familiar boundaries and landmarks', and all through the twenty-three chapters which Dickens completed he reversed situations, values, and characters.[13] The cathedral at Cloisterham, far from being a reassuring symbol of Christian faith, is crumbling into decay, and its dean is an unprincipled trimmer. Property and the Law, epitomized by the egregious Mr. Sapsea, seem as stupid as ever to the Dickens who served his apprenticeship in Doctors' Commons and ridiculed his former masters in *Bleak House*. Mr. Honeythunder, the archetype of the intolerant reformer, is pilloried as a man whose 'philan-thropy was of that gunpowderous sort that the difference between it and animosity was hard to determine'.[14] These men are two-faced, like the ambi-valent Jasper, round whom the plot revolves; behind their conventional masks are images of moral corruption which reflect his evil. And even the more positive characters are ambiguously different from what they seem. Drood himself, giving his name to the book, is a very uncertain figure, and it is not known whether he is alive or dead. The strange brother and sister, Neville and Helena Landless, come unexplained from the East. Lieutenant Tatar comes from the sea. The fourth outsider, the mysterious Datchery, apparently comes from nowhere. A sense of illusion shimmers over the whole tale.

When it was published Wilkie Collins made an ungenerous comment. It was, he said, a 'last laboured effort, the melancholy work of a worn-out brain'.[15] It is true that Dickens had lost his old facility, and he confessed to Dolby as he started to write that he missed the pressure of earlier days. He also complained on more than one occasion that he was using up his plot too fast; and when the first two instalments were sent to the printer they were found to be uncharacteristically short of the necessary length for a monthly number. There were also rumours that in his eagerness to trump *The Moonstone* Dickens had written himself into a maze without knowing how to escape from it. Yet once he had got over what he described to Macready as 'the preliminary agonies' of a new book he began to compose smoothly and there was no flagging of invention.[16] The melancholy was another matter, for it was implicit in the life as well as the novel. As Dickens wrote its shadows were lengthening over Cloisterham—the near-by Rochester which provided his first and last models of society—and they fell darkly across the pages of *Edwin Drood*, conceived as a masterpiece by a man who had not left himself the time to execute it.

On Sunday 24 October, when James Fields was again staying at Gad's Hill, Dickens read him the first chapters of *Edwin Drood* from a manuscript 'scarcely dry from the pen';[17] and two days later, 'with great spirit',[18] he read them to Forster at Palace Gate. He was obviously glad to have made a good start, and the familiar work revived him into something like his old habits. In the course of the autumn he made a few trips to town to supervise Charley at *All the Year Round*, to dine out, or go to a theatre—one night he went with Forster to the Olympic to see a drama based upon *Copperfield*—and to meet Dolby over the plans for his final set of readings. Dolby, who had seen more of Dickens in his decline than anyone, rightly suspected that the recovery was superficial. For at the end of December the pain in the left hand and foot returned with such severity that Dickens was obliged to spend most of Christmas Day in bed, rising only to join the family after dinner. He was still suffering, though he made light of it, when he went to Forster on New Year's Eve to read the latest number of *Edwin Drood*. 'Dickens was very cheery,' noted Carlyle, who was a fellow-guest; 'he has got, I doubt, some permanent nervous damage from that conquest of £20,000 in Yankee-land, and is himself rather anxious now and then about it.... What a tragedy, and hideous *nemesis*.'[19] Railway travel, to which he had 'a now invincible dislike', quickly exhausted him. 'I am a little shaken by my journey to Birmingham,'[20] he wrote to Forster after he had been to the Institute's prize-giving on Twelfth Night; and one member of the audience noticed that while Dickens was bright-eyed and eloquent 'his face wore a hectic flush, his hair was greyer and thinner'.[21]

After the long rest there was much for Dickens to memorize and practise afresh before the readings began at St. James's Hall on 11 January. He was, however, cheered by the advance bookings. Despite a new scheme for collecting a year's income tax in one payment, which he said was having an adverse effect on the takings of concert halls and theatres, he was able to tell Forster that 'our "let" at St. James's Hall is enormous'.[22] To ease the expected stresses he once more took a London house, renting 5 Hyde Park Place, opposite Marble Arch, from his friend Milner Gibson; but he soon discovered that he had taken on more than he could properly manage. Forster was seriously concerned about the 'strain and pressure, which with every fresh exertion, he was placing on those vessels of the brain where the Preston trouble too surely had revealed that danger lay'.[23] And Frank Beard, whom Dickens had consulted before he started his twice-weekly readings, insisted on being present at every one of them and keeping a close watch on his condition. Dickens opened with two firm favourites, *Copperfield* and the trial scene from *Pickwick*. His normal pulse rate was 72 and that evening it went up to 96. On the second night, when he read 'Dr. Marigold's Prescriptions', it rose to 99. On 21 January, when he did the murder of Nancy for the first time it went to 112 and then, when he repeated the murder on 1 February, his pulse reached 118. Beard carefully noted each fluctuation. Apart from one occasion when the rate peaked at 124 after *Copperfield*, it was always highest when Dickens read 'Sikes and Nancy'. He often had to lie on a sofa for ten minutes before he could speak, and he would then go back to give a lighter number so that his audience should not leave on such a macabre note. 'I feel it was madness ever to do it continuously,' Dickens admitted to Wills in a letter on 23 January urging his friend to come and hear the 'Sikes and Nancy' reading 'before it is silent for ever'. He was already showing other symptoms. 'I have something the matter with my right thumb,' he reported to Wills, 'and can't (as you see) write plainly,'[24] and Forster noticed that he was carrying his arm in a sling and that his hand was painful and swollen well into February. On 21 March he told Forster that he was again suffering from partial loss of vision; and eight days later he said that 'the uneasiness and haemorrhage' from piles which had intermittently afflicted him for years had returned with 'aggravated irritability'.[25]

Dickens found it physically difficult to get through the twelve readings to which his doctors restricted him, but he was game to the end. He gave a special session one morning for actors and actresses who were not free to attend the evening performances, and he prided himself that he had carried away an audience of professionals bent on watching how the effects were got without scenery, costumes, or any other stage contrivances. Thackeray's daughter Annie, who was taken to the last reading of *Copperfield* by Kate Dickens, was similarly carried away. 'It was for all the rest of my life that I heard his voice,' she recalled. 'The slight figure stood alone quietly facing the long rows of people. He seemed to be holding the great audience in some mysterious way from the empty stage. Quite immediately, the story began; Copperfield and Steerforth, Yarmouth and the fishermen, and then the rising storm, all were there before us. It was not acting, it was not music, nor harmony of sound and colour, and yet I still have an impression of all these things as I think of that occasion.'[26]

Although in some of the later readings Dickens had trouble with his articulation, and mispronounced some familiar words, Forster noted that in his final appearance 'the old delicacy' came back, and Charley Dickens thought his father surpassed himself. It was a moving and simple occasion. More than two thousand people packed the St. James's Hall and hundreds stood in the street to pay homage. After Dickens had given the *Carol* and *Pickwick* readings, and after the cheers had died away, he spoke a few personal words. 'I have enjoyed an amount of artistic delight and instruction which perhaps it is given to few men to know,' he said; 'from these garish lights I vanish now for evermore, with a heartfelt, grateful, respectful, and affectionate farewell.'[27] As the applause broke out again he turned, with tears on his cheeks, and left the platform.

Dickens had given much in all his readings, and taken much for himself as well. The pleasure they had given him, Dolby remarked afterwards, could not be told in words; and he had besides made a small fortune from them. The profits from his 425 appearances over a dozen years amounted to more than £45,000. But when all the sums were done it was clear that Dickens had spent himself into physical ruin. He had driven himself too hard, his will sustaining him as his strength failed. But no amount of will, as Forster observed, could offset the 'disregard of such laws of life as were here plainly overlooked'.[28]

When the readings were finished Dickens stayed on for a time at Hyde Park Place, and at first he enjoyed the busy London scene. In March he was asked to Buckingham Palace.[29] The idea had come from Sir Arthur Helps, the Clerk to the Privy Council, who was the Queen's confidential adviser and a distinguished literary man to whom Dickens had sent some photographs from the American Civil War which had interested the Queen and served as a pretext for an audience. When she had asked to see him during the theatricals at Devonshire House, he told Helps he had refused because he was dressed for the farce in a ridiculous wig and dressing-gown and since he was not a professional actor he had thought such a costume incongruous. On this occasion, however, he gladly accepted, and he went to the Palace at half past six in the evening on 9 March, and despite his painful foot he stood gamely as protocol required through an audience which lasted for well over an hour. Helps, in his brief to the Queen, suggested that she might lead off with a reference to *David Copperfield*; but the conversation soon moved to weightier topics. Dickens, the Queen noted in her journal, spoke of the division of classes and his hope of a better feeling between them, and she was impressed by his 'large, and loving mind'. She hinted that she would like to hear him read, and he politely declined on the grounds that his latest series was the last and that in any case he needed a public audience to secure the necessary response. She presented him with a copy of her *Journal of Our Life in the Highlands*; and he undertook to send her advance copies of *Edwin Drood*, which was to begin appearing on the last day of March, and a uniform and specially bound set of his novels. As Dickens left, the Queen invited him to attend the next levee and to present Mary afterwards in the drawing-room. 'Don't faint with amazement if you see my name in that unwonted connection,' he wrote to Forster,[30] and he joked with Dolby about wearing the cocked hat of formal Court dress 'fore and aft'.[31]

On 5 April Dickens spoke at the annual dinner of the Newsvendors' Benevolent Association—an organization to which Dickens had often spoken and long supported—which helped the ragged boys and discharged servicemen who peddled newspapers in the streets. Two days later he gave a reception for his friends at Hyde Park Place, presenting the famous Hungarian violinist Joseph Joachim and two notable English singers. He dined one night with the American minister; on another he went to the Dean of Westminster; on a third he went to Lord Stanhope's to meet Disraeli; and Gladstone asked him to breakfast. The pace of social life, however, soon began to tell on him. 'I weary, at any season, of this London dining-out, beyond expression,' he told Charles Kent at the end of April; 'and I yearn for the country again.'[32] And his physical condition was deteriorating. 'I am sorry to report,' he wrote to Forster a fortnight later, 'that, in the old preposterous endeavour to dine at preposterous hours and preposterous places, I have been pulled up by a sharp attack in my foot. And serve me right ... I have cancelled everything in the dining way for this week.'[33] He could still jest about his disability. 'This appendage and I have been struggling together for some days,' he told William Ralston, 'and are still on the same ferocious terms.'[34] And on the next day he wrote to Charles Kent in similar terms of wry jocularity: 'Having viciously bubbled and blistered it in all directions, I hope it now begins to see the folly of its ways.'[35] Though he was taking doses of laudanum—'it hangs about me very heavily', he told Georgina[36]—the discomfort was too great for him to go to the Queen's Ball with Mary on 17 May, and he had to withdraw from the dinner of the General Theatrical Fund. He summoned his energies to attend a dinner given by Lord Houghton (his old acquaintance Richard Monckton Milnes) for the Prince of Wales and the King of the Belgians, but he was now so lame that he could not ascend the staircase for the reception and he had to be helped into the dining-room. One morning Douglas Jerrold's son saw Dickens limp into the office of *All the Year Round*, bent over and leaning on a stick, and so lined in feature and white-haired that he scarcely recognized him.

Dickens had a sense that time was running out for him. 'One can only work on, you know—work while it is day,' he said to a young woman with whom he was discussing the risk of dying while a serial novel was still uncompleted.[37] On 27 April he picked up a newspaper at Higham station and read that his 'old dear friend and companion' Daniel Maclise was dead. 'It has been only after great difficulty,' he wrote to Forster, 'and after hardening and steeling myself to the subject by at once thinking of it and avoiding it in a strange way that I have been able to get any command over it or over myself.'[38] Maclise had been withdrawn and depressed for some years, but Dickens remembered him as he had been when they were younger, and at the Royal Academy dinner on 30 April—his own last public engagement— he recalled Maclise when he replied to the toast of 'Literature'. On this grand occasion in the new premises at Burlington House, patronized by the Prince of Wales, Disraeli, and Gladstone, Dickens paid his tribute to 'the gentlest and most modest of men ... gallantly sustaining the true dignity of his vocation'.[39] A month later, on 22 May, when Dickens dined for the last time with Forster, they had just heard of the death of Mark Lemon. Apart from Macready, living in sad decline at Cheltenham, he and Forster were the last of the convivial set of men who had dined and joked together over so many years. That evening they recalled all those who, as Forster put it, 'had so fallen from the ranks since we played Ben Jonson together'. 'And none beyond his sixtieth year,' Dickens replied. When Forster said that it was no good to talk of the matter Dickens sadly responded: 'We shall not think of it the less.'[40] Macready lived on until 1873 and Forster died in 1876. His other lifelong friend, Thomas Beard, died a bachelor in 1891.

Before he left London Dickens had a final fling at his old favourite diversion. He had intended to take part in theatricals got up by neighbours in London, who had given roles to Kate and Mamie, and persuaded John Millais to paint the scenery. But he was too lame, and all he could do was to rehearse the actors and assume the duties of stage manager at the performance of 2 June. That afternoon, before the play, he added the codicil to his will which gave Charley his interest in *All the Year Round*, and said a rather tearful goodbye to Dolby. The next morning he went down to Gad's Hill to find the garden in the full bloom of early summer. The distractions of London society had impeded work on *Edwin Drood*, though he told Charles Kent that he had been 'most perseveringly and ding-dong-doggedly at work' and he had been delighted by the novel's immediate success:[41] the sale of 50,000 copies at the outset, he declared to Fields, had '*very, very far outstripped every one of its predecessors*'.[42] As soon as he was back at home he settled into the Swiss chalet to complete the due instalment.

On the following day, Saturday 4 June, Kate went down to Gad's Hill and her father proudly showed her the new conservatory which had been completed across the back of the dining-room during his absence. It was, he said, 'positively the last improvement'. On the Sunday evening, after Mamie and Georgina had gone to bed, he sat talking with Kate into the small hours about family matters—and in particular about a theatrical offer which she hoped might supplement her husband's modest income. Dickens knew that Kate and Charles Collins were hard up. He had recently commissioned him to illustrate *Edwin Drood*; but after Collins had drawn the wrapper he had again succumbed to the nervous debility which had spoilt his career as a painter, and his place had been taken by Luke Fildes. Telling Kate he thought her too sensitive for the stage, Dickens offered to make up what she would lose by rejecting the offer. And in this intimate mood he went on to confide to Kate that he felt his strength ebbing and that he feared he might never finish *Edwin Drood*. He wished, he told her, that he had been 'a better father, and a better man'.[43] The next morning, waking late, she went across to the chalet and interrupted him at work, and they parted with an affectionate embrace. That afternoon he walked into Rochester with his dogs to post some letters.

On Tuesday morning Mamie also went up to London, to stay with Kate. When Dickens had finished his writing for the day he felt too tired for his usual exercise, and he and Georgina merely took a gentle stroll under the great trees of Cobham Park. In the evening he strung some Chinese lanterns in the new conservatory, and they sat late by their glow talking sentimentally about his feeling for Gad's Hill. On Wednesday Dickens wrote hard all day, rather against his habit, for he was anxious to finish the number before he went to London on Thursday; he had to deliver his copy to the printer and to meet Luke Fildes, who was returning with him to look at local settings for the *Drood* illustrations.

When the work was done Dickens wrote a few letters and then walked back to the house for dinner at six. Georgina noticed that his colour and expression seemed odd, and that his eyes were full of tears. She asked if he was ill. 'Yes,' he said, 'very ill for the last hour.'[44] But he would not allow her to send for a doctor. As he sat at the table his articulation seemed impaired, and his conversation became disjointed. He talked about a nearby sale, about Macready's son, and of his desire to go at once to London. Then he complained of a toothache, put his hand to the side of his head, and asked for the window to be shut. Georgina went to him asking if he would like to lie down. 'Yes,' he replied, 'on the ground,' and he slipped down on his left side and lay unconscious, apparently stricken by an aneurysm in the brain.

The servants brought a sofa from the drawing-room and lifted him on to it, and he lay there breathing heavily. Mr. Steele, the local doctor, was called at once, and telegrams were sent off to the girls, to Harry, and to Charley. Mamie and Kate arrived that night, bringing Frank Beard with them; and the next morning Charley brought down another physician, Russell Reynolds. But there was nothing the doctors could do. Ellen Ternan was sent for and she arrived in the afternoon; and so did Mary Boyle, that constant friend who had often been at Gad's Hill and came at the last to sit quietly in the garden while Dickens lay dying within the house. At ten minutes past six on Thursday 9 June 1870, at the age of fifty-eight, and on the fifth anniversary of the Staplehurst railway crash which had so deeply affected him, Charles Dickens died with a tear on his cheek and a deep sigh.

'I am profoundly sorry for *you*, and indeed for myself and for us all,' Carlyle wrote two days later to Forster who, away in the West Country, was telegraphed the news. 'It is an event world-wide; a *unique* of Talents suddenly extinct; and has "eclipsed" (we too may say) "the harmless gaiety of Nations". . . . The good, the gentle, ever friendly noble Dickens.'[45] The Queen sent a telegram of regret and condolence. It was, Forster remarked, as if a personal bereavement had befallen everyone.

Dickens had hoped for a quiet burial in the graveyard of Rochester Cathedral, and in his will he had insisted that the ceremony was to be 'inexpensive, unostentatious, and strictly private', without black cloaks and mourning bands 'or other such revolting absurdity'. It was *The Times* which proposed his interment in Westminster Abbey, 'the peculiar resting place of English literary genius', and the Dean who offered it. Even so it was a simple affair. On 14 June the plain coffin was taken from Higham to London in a special train and placed in an equally plain hearse for the short journey from Charing Cross to Westminster. In the first of the three coaches were Charley, Kate, Mamie, and Harry. In the second were Georgina, Letitia Dickens, Charley's wife, and John Forster. And in the third were Frank Beard, Wilkie and Charles Collins, and the family solicitor Frederic Ouvry. The burial service was spoken, and an organ played a last elegy.[46]

For three days, while the grave was left open, an unending procession filed past the growing mound of flowers. 'I direct that my name be inscribed in plain English letters on my tomb,' Dickens had written in his will. 'I rest my claims to the remembrance of my country upon my published works, and to the remembrance of my friends upon their experience of me.'

References

Principal Sources

The following abbreviations have been used in the notes:

AF   Charles Dickens, Autobiographical Fragment in *Life* (see below)

CDE   R. C. Lehmann (ed.), *Charles Dickens as an Editor* (London, 1912)

CDML Walter Dexter (ed.), *Unpublished Letters of Charles Dickens to Mark Lemon* (London, 1927)

CDPR Philip Collins, *Charles Dickens: The Public Readings* (Oxford, 1975)

EJCD Edgar Johnson, *Charles Dickens: His Tragedy and Triumph* (London, 1953)

GHL   Georgina Hogarth and Mary Dickens (eds.), *The Letters of Charles Dickens* (London, 1882)

HCD   Edgar Johnson, *The Heart of Charles Dickens* (New York, 1952)

Life   John Forster, *The Life of Charles Dickens* (London, 1872–4)

MCDY William Toynbee (ed.), *The Diaries of William Charles Macready* (London, 1912)

MMCD Walter Dexter (ed.), *Mr. and Mrs. Charles Dickens* (London, 1935)

NSL   Walter Dexter (ed.), The Nonesuch Edition of *The Letters of Charles Dickens* (London, 1938)

PL   Madeline House, Graham Storey, and Kathleen Tillotson (eds.), The Pilgrim Edition of *The Letters of Charles Dickens* (Oxford, 1965, 1969, 1974, 1977)

RP   Charles Dickens, *Reprinted Pieces*

SB   Charles Dickens, *Sketches by Boz*

SCD   K. J. Fielding, *The Speeches of Charles Dickens* (Oxford, 1960)

TCH   Philip Collins, *Charles Dickens: The Critical Heritage* (London, 1971)

TLS   *The Times Literary Supplement*

UT   Charles Dickens, *The Uncommerical Traveller*

The authors have used the Oxford University Press edition of the novels of Charles Dickens, published in twenty-one volumes as *The Oxford Illustrated Dickens*.

Dates in brackets indicate attribution; a question mark indicates uncertainty.

1. A Child of Singular Abilities

1 Materials in Chatham Public Library: see also papers in UT and Christopher Hibbert, *The Making of Charles Dickens* (London, 1967)

2 The daughter married Richard Monckton Milnes, later Lord Houghton, a close acquaintance of Dickens in later life

3 Wrongly spelt Huffham in the register

4 *Dickensian*, Vol. XLIX, September 1953, '"The Old Lady" in *Sketches by Boz*' by William J. Carlton. Newnham declined to act as a trustee for the effects of John Dickens when he came before the Court for the Relief of Insolvent Debtors in 1824. His wife left small legacies to Fanny and Letitia Dickens

5 See 'Dullborough' and 'Nurses Tales' in UT, and Robert Langton, *The Childhood and Youth of Charles Dickens* (London, 1891)

6 Langton, op. cit.

7 'Dullborough' in UT

8 To Washington Irving, 21 April 1841, PL

9 Another boy, Alfred Allen Dickens, was born at Portsea in March 1814 and died that September; the brother named Alfred Lamert Dickens was born in 1822

10 Langton, op. cit.

11 *Life*; 'A Christmas Tree' in RP

12 Langton, op. cit.

13 *David Copperfield*; and *Life*

14 *Dickensian*, Vol. LIII, September 1957, 'Fanny Dickens Pianist and Vocalist' by William J. Carlton

15 AF

16 Ibid.

17 Ibid.

18 Ibid.

19 Ibid.

20 Ibid.

21 Ibid.

22 Ibid.

23 Ibid.

24 Ibid.

25 Ibid.

26 Ibid.

2. Rising Hopes

1 SCD: speech on 5 November 1857

2 SB: 'Our School'

3 AF

4 Robert Langton, *The Childhood and Youth of Charles Dickens* (London, 1891)

5 *Dickensian*, Vol. LIII, September 1957, op. cit.

6 *Life*

7 Langton, op. cit.

8 Henry Vizetelly, *Glances Back through Seventy Years* (London, 1893)

9 *Dickensian*, Vol. LVI, September 1960, 'The Strange Story of Thomas Mitton' by W. J. Carlton

10 SB: 'Doctors' Commons'

11 *Dickens Studies*, Vol. 1, No. 2, May 1965, 'Dickens' Literary Mentor' by W. J. Carlton

12 John Harrison Stonehouse, *Green Leaves* (London, 1931)

13 To Forster (?30–31 December 1844 and 1 January 1845) PL

14 (? July 1832) PL

15 SCD: speech on 20 May 1865

16 To Forster (? 15–17 August 1846) PL

17 SB: 'A Parliamentary Sketch'

18 To Maria Winter (Beadnell), 10 February 1855, NSL

19 (? 15 April 1833) PL

20 PL

21 PL

22 PL

23 6 June 1833, PL

24 Preface to *Pickwick Papers*

25 (3 December 1833) PL

26 (? 10 December 1833) PL

27 Preface to *Pickwick Papers*

28 *Dickensian*, Vol. LVIII, January 1962, ' "Boz" and the Beards' by W. J. Carlton

29 To Thomas Beard (29 November 1834) PL

30 (11 January 1835) PL

31 To Forster undated (1845) PL, Vol. IV, p. 460

32 SCD: speech of 20 May 1865

33 *Life*

34 (? 20 November 1834) PL

35 (16 December 1834) PL

36 N. P. Willis, *Dashes at Life with a Free Pencil* (New York, 1845)

37 (29 November 1834) PL

3. The Pilot Balloon

1 20 January 1835, PL

2 *Dickensian*, Vol. LXIII, May 1967, 'New Letters of Mary Hogarth and Her Sister Catherine'

3 Eleanor E. Christian, 'Recollections of C.D.', *Temple Bar* (1888)

4 (? late May 1835) PL

5 (? June 1835) PL

6 (? June 1835) PL

7 SCD: speech on 20 May 1865

8 (4 May 1835) PL

9 (9 July 1835) PL

10 (? July 1835) PL

11 (? August 1835) PL

12 (12 October 1835) PL

13 S. M. Ellis, *William Harrison Ainsworth and his Friends* (London, 1911)

14 W. O'Driscoll, *A Memoir of Daniel Maclise* (London, 1871)

15 (? 27 October 1835) PL

16 (5 November 1835) PL

17 (7 November 1835) PL

18 (1 December 1835) PL

19 (9 December 1835) PL

20 (18 December 1835) PL

21 PL

22 PL

23 (? 19 November 1835) PL

24 (25 November 1835) PL

25 (18 December 1835) PL

26 (? December 1835) PL

27 (? 30 November 1835) PL

28 (? 29 December 1835) PL

29 (21 January 1836) PL

30 (? 22 January 1836) PL

31 (? 18 January 1836) PL

32 (? 1 February 1836) PL

33 (9 February 1836) PL

34 To Macrone (11 February 1836) PL

35 *Morning Chronicle* 11 February 1836, cited in PL

36 *Court Journal*, 20 February 1836, cited in PL. See also J. Butt and K. Tillotson (eds.), *Dickens at Work* (London, 1957)

37 A. Waugh, *A Hundred Years of Publishing* (London, 1930)

38 (10 February 1836) PL

39 Preface to *Pickwick Papers*

40 W. Dexter and J. W. T. Ley, *The Origin of Pickwick* (1936)

41 PL

42 Preface to *Pickwick Papers*

43 PL

44 (21 February 1836) PL

45 (? 4 March 1836) PL

46 PL

47 (? 20 March 1836) PL

48 F. G. Kitton, *Charles Dickens by Pen and Pencil* (London, 1890–2)

49 PL, Appendix, Vol. I

50 (? mid-April 1836) PL

51 (14 April 1836) PL

52 PL

53 To J. P. Hullah (26 July 1836) PL

54 (? 27 July 1836) PL

55 G. N. Ray, *Thackeray* (London, 1955)

56 Butt and Tillotson, op. cit.

57 J. Sutherland, *Victorian Novelists and Publishers* (London, 1976)

58 (17 August 1836) PL

59 (? 18 August 1836) PL

60 (? 22 August 1836) PL
61 To J. P. Harley, December 1836, PL
62 (? 27 August 1836) PL
63 Henry Vizetelly, *Glances Back through Seventy Years* (London, 1893)
64 W. P. Frith, *My Autobiography and Reminiscences* (London, 1889)
65 TCH
66 PL

4. Asking for More

1 PL, Appendix, Vol. I
2 (? 29 September 1836) PL
3 PL
4 1 November 1836, PL
5 (29 September 1836) PL
6 (18 November 1836) PL
7 Ibid.
8 PL
9 (18 November 1836) PL
10 S. M. Ellis, *William Harrison Ainsworth and his Friends* (London, 1911)
11 (5 December 1836) PL
12 George Augustus Sala, *Charles Dickens. An Essay* (London, 1870)
13 PL
14 PL, Vol. I, p. 210 footnote
15 PL, Vol. I, p. 239 footnote
16 Richard Renton, *John Forster and his Friends* (London, 1912); and *Dickensian* special issue on Forster, Vol. LXX, September 1974
17 (? 23 March 1837) PL
18 (? December 1836) PL
19 To Bentley (7 January 1837) PL
20 (? 8 February 1837) PL
21 (? 18 January 1837) PL
22 Ivor Brown, *Dickens in His Time* (London, 1963)
23 (24 January 1837) PL
24 Queen Victoria's diary, 7 April 1839, from Viscount Esher, *The Girlhood of Queen Victoria* (London, 1912)
25 (24 January 1837) PL
26 *Dickensian*, Vol. LXIII, May 1967, 'New Letters of Mary Hogarth and Her Sister Catherine'
27 (? 21 January 1837) PL
28 PL, Vol. I, p. 253 footnote
29 *Dickensian*, Vol. LXIII, May 1967, op. cit.
30 To unknown correspondent (8) June 1837, PL
31 To George Thomson, 8 May 1837, PL
32 (12 May 1837) PL
33 (17 May 1837) PL
34 To Richard Johns (31 May 1837) PL
35 (17 May 1837) PL
36 *Dickensian*, Vol. LXIII, May 1967, op. cit.
37 (17 May 1837) PL
38 To unknown correspondent (8) June 1837, PL
39 (26 October 1837) PL
40 PL
41 (17 May 1837) PL
42 *Life*
43 Ellis, op. cit.
44 (? 14 June 1837) PL
45 To Bentley (? 17 June 1837) PL
46 *Life*
47 Alan S. Downe, *The Eminent Tragedian* (Cambridge, Mass., 1966)
48 *Dictionary of National Biography*
49 27 June 1837, MCDY
50 PL
51 14 July 1837, PL
52 (? 5 August 1837) PL
53 PL, Vol. I, p. 292 footnote
54 (? August 1837) PL
55 PL, Vol. I, p. 293 footnote
56 (14 August 1837) PL
57 18 August 1837, PL
58 PL
59 PL
60 PL, Appendix, Vol. I
61 (? 1 October 1837) PL

62 F. G. Kitton, *Charles Dickens by Pen and Pencil* (London, 1890–2)
63 *Life*
64 3 November 1837, PL
65 27 July 1837, PL
66 Ellis, op. cit.
67 16 August 1837 in PL, Appendix, Vol. I

5. Hard Bargains

1 The diary is in the Appendix to Vol. I, PL
2 To T. J. Culliford (6 December 1837) PL
3 To T. Beard (6 December 1837) PL
4 To Forster, 11 December 1837, PL
5 Diary, 1 January 1838, op. cit.
6 Diary, 6 January 1838, op. cit.
7 1 February 1838, PL
8 3 March 1839, PL
9 (? 26 July 1838) PL
10 Dickens told Talfourd on 4 October 1837 (PL) that the review 'contains a great deal I know to be true'
11 S. M. Ellis, *William Harrison Ainsworth and his Friends* (London, 1911)
12 (February 1838) PL
13 22 February 1838, PL
14 Preface to *Nicholas Nickleby*
15 (6 March 1838) PL
16 (? mid-December 1837) PL
17 (? 11 January) 1838, PL
18 (13 March 1838) PL
19 13 March 1838, MCDY
20 Ibid.
21 (? 19 November 1838) PL
22 11 December 1838, MCDY
23 PL
24 13 December 1838, MCDY
25 Lord Lytton, *Life of Edward Bulwer* (London, 1913)
26 Lord Ilchester, *Chronicles of Holland House* (London, 1937)
27 (? late March 1838) PL
28 To Forster, 23 June 1838, PL
29 To Bentley (29 August 1838) PL
30 (6 or 13 October 1838) PL
31 (2 October 1838) PL
32 PL
33 Ellis, op. cit.
34 30 December 1838 and 3 January 1839, diary: Viscount Esher, *The Girlhood of Queen Victoria* (London, 1912)
35 To Catherine Dickens, 1 November 1838, PL
36 PL, Vol. I, p. 451 footnote
37 To E. M. Fitzgerald, 29 December 1838, PL
38 PL
39 PL
40 PL, Vol. I, p. 495 footnote
41 (? 26 January 1839) PL
42 26 January 1839, PL
43 31 January 1839, PL
44 To J. P. Harley (7 February 1839) PL
45 PL, Appendix, Vol. I
46 PL, Appendix, Vol. I
47 (15 November 1838) PL
48 19 December 1837, PL, Vol. I, p. 44 footnote
49 PL
50 (5 March 1839) PL
51 5 March 1839, PL
52 6 March 1839, PL
53 (11 July 1839) PL
54 (13 March 1839) PL
55 PL
56 28 June 1839, PL
57 To J. P. Harley, 28 June 1839, PL
58 PL, Vol. I, p. 558 footnote
59 (11) July 1839, PL
60 9 September 1839, PL
61 Obituary in *All the Year Round*, 1 June 1867
62 5 October 1839, MCDY
63 (14 July 1839) PL
64 Ibid.

65 26 July 1839, PL
66 PL
67 PL
68 27 December 1839, PL
69 (4 November 1839) PL
70 (7 November 1839) PL
71 To James Hall, 19 November (1839) PL
72 To William Upcott, 28 December 1839, PL
73 To Forster (? 25 November 1839) PL
74 To Forster, 23 December 1839, PL

6. Flourishing Exceedingly

1 2 January 1840, PL
2 (13 February 1840) PL
3 PL, Vol. II, p. 23 footnote
4 (? 10 January 1840) PL
5 (10 January 1840) PL
6 13 January 1840, PL
7 *Dickens Studies Annual*, Vol. I, 1970
8 (? 7 April 1840) PL
9 G. N. Ray (ed.), *Letters and Private Papers of W. M. Thackeray*, Vol. 1 (Cambridge, Mass., 1945)
10 *Athenaeum*, 7 November 1840
11 22 March (1840) PL
12 To Forster (? 8 March 1840) PL
13 (1 February 1840) PL
14 Michael Sadleir, *Blessington d'Orsay* (London, 1933)
15 12 May 1840, PL
16 (22 May 1840) PL
17 1 June 1840, PL
18 2 June 1840, PL
19 (? May 1840) PL
20 PL
21 (17 June 1840) PL
22 (? 23 February 1840) PL
23 PL, Appendix, Vol. II
24 (8 July 1840) PL
25 Philip Collins, *Dickens and Crime* (London, 1962)
26 *Daily News*, 28 February 1846
27 To Macvey Napier, 28 July 1845, PL
28 F. Kaplan, *Dickens and Mesmerism* (Princeton, 1975)
29 To Dr. R. H. Collyer, 27 January 1842, PL
30 24 August 1841, PL
31 23 July (1841) PL
32 (? 7 August 1840) PL
33 31 July (1840) PL
34 (10 August 1840) PL
35 16 August 1846, MCDY
36 17 August (1840) PL
37 25 August 1846, MCDY
38 (? 20) August (1840) PL
39 2 September 1840, PL
40 Eleanor E. Christian, 'Reminiscences of Charles Dickens' in *Englishwoman's Domestic Magazine*, 1871
41 2 September 1840, PL
42 (? 8 or 9 September 1840) PL
43 2 October 1840, PL
44 Forster Collection, V & A
45 (3 November 1840) PL
46 3 November 1840, PL
47 (6 November 1840) PL
48 9 November (1840) PL
49 24 November 1840, PL
50 (? 21 December 1840) PL
51 To Ainsworth, 18 December 1840, PL
52 2 January 1841, PL
53 (? 8 January 1841) PL
54 PL
55 (? 22 December 1840) PL
56 (? 6 January 1841) PL
57 MCDY
58 (? 8 January 1841) PL
59 (? 17) January 1841, PL
60 Ibid.
61 30 January 1841, PL
62 PL, Vol. II, p. 187 footnote
63 *Christian Remembrances*, December 1842, cited in PL, Preface, Vol. II

64 PL, Vol. II, p. 210 footnote

65 PL, Vol. II, p. 215 footnote

66 PL, Vol. II, p. 233 footnote

67 To Thomas Latimer, 13 March 1841, PL

68 19 February 1841, PL

69 (8 February 1841) PL

70 (29 January 1841) PL

71 (4 February 1841) PL

72 8 April 1841, PL

73 8 April 1841, PL

74 9 June 1841, PL

75 (23 June 1841) PL

76 To Forster (26 June 1841) PL

77 To Forster (30 June 1841) PL

78 1 July 1841, PL

79 PL

80 PL

81 PL

82 (5 August 1841) PL

83 (11 September 1841) PL

84 Preface to *Barnaby Rudge*

85 (3 June 1841) PL

86 Thomas Carlyle to J. Sterling, 28 July 1837, in A. Carlyle (ed.), *Letters of T. Carlyle to J. S. Mill, J. Sterling and R. Browning* (London, 1923)

87 Thomas Carlyle to John Carlyle in J. A. Froude, *Thomas Carlyle. A History of His Life in London* (London, 1884)

88 (13 August 1841) PL

89 F. G. Kitton (ed.), *The Poems and Verses of Charles Dickens* (London, 1903)

90 15 December 1840, PL

91 E. Hodder, *The Life and Work of the Seventh Earl of Shaftesbury* (London, 1886)

92 Letter to W. H. Harrison, 6 June 1841, in *Works*, Vol. XXXVI

93 *Graham's Magazine*, February 1842

94 J. Butt and K. Tillotson (eds.), *Dickens at Work* (London, 1957)

95 23 August 1841, PL

96 PL, Appendix, Vol. II

97 1 September 1841, PL

98 (13 September 1841) PL

99 PL, Vol. II, p. 160 footnote

100 To John Wiley and G. P. Putnam, 31 August 1838

101 (13 September 1841) PL

102 21 April 1841, PL

103 PL

104 PL

105 (13 September 1841) PL

106 PL

107 (24 September 1841) PL

108 Quoted in EJCD; and 23 September 1841, MCDY

109 29 September 1841, PL

110 PL

111 John D. Sherwood, *Hours at Home*, (New York, July 1867)

112 18 November 1841, PL

113 (12 October 1841) PL

114 23 November 1841, PL

115 (25 October 1841) PL

116 *Life*

117 (25 October 1841) PL

118 To Angus Fletcher, 16 November 1841, PL

119 (late November 1841) PL

120 28 December 1841, PL

121 (mid-December 1841) PL

7. A Kind of Queen and Albert

1 To Frederick Dickens, 3 January 1842, PL

2 Forster to Maclise, on Dickens to Maclise (3) January 1842, PL

3 Ibid.

4 *American Notes*

5 3 January 1842, PL

6 Forster to Maclise, op. cit.

7 3 January 1842, PL

8 (17 January 1842) PL

9 To Fanny Burnett, 30 January 1842, PL, Appendix, Vol. III

10 21 January 1842, PL

11 R. H. Dana Sr. to Mrs. Arnold, 14 February 1842, PL, Vol. II, p. 34 footnote

12 (29 January 1842) PL

13 Ibid.

14 J. T. Fields, *Yesterdays with Authors* (London, 1874)

15 To Frederick A. Whitwell, 22 January 1842, PL

16 PL, Vol. II, p. 20 footnote

17 PL, Vol. III, p. 20 footnote

18 (29 January 1842) PL

19 30 January 1842, PL, Appendix, Vol. III

20 PL, Vol. III, p. 39 footnote

21 PL, Vol. III, p. 32 footnote

22 PL, Vol. III, p. 39 footnote

23 (29 January 1842) PL

24 PL

25 PL, Appendix, Vol. III

26 (? 4 February 1842) PL

27 31 January 1842, PL

28 (? 4 February 1842) PL

29 J. T. Fields, op. cit.

30 SCD

31 PL, Vol. III, p. 51 footnote

32 PL, Vol. III, p. 48 footnote

33 PL

34 SCD

35 W. Glyde Wilkins, *Charles Dickens in America* (London, 1911); and PL, Vol. III, p. 60 footnote

36 24 February 1842, PL

37 22 February 1842, PL

38 To Forster, 17 February 1842, PL

39 Wilkins, op. cit.

40 22 March 1842, PL

41 To Forster, 17 February 1842, PL

42 28 February 1842, PL

43 PL, Vol. III, p. 73 footnote

44 PL, Vol. III, p. 128 footnote

45 Wilkins, op. cit.

46 17 February 1842, PL

47 PL, Vol. III, p. 72 footnote

48 SCD

49 24 February 1842, PL

50 Wilkins, op. cit.

51 24 February 1842, PL

52 PL

53 22 February 1842, PL

54 24 February 1842, PL

55 27 February 1842, PL

56 PL, Vol. III, p. 75 footnote

57 24 February 1842, PL

58 13 March 1842, PL

59 Ibid.

60 To Charles Sumner, 13 March 1842, PL

61 24 February 1842, PL

62 14 March 1842, PL

63 15 March 1842, PL

64 *American Notes*

65 PL, Vol. III, p. 113

66 14 March 1842, PL

67 Wilkins, op. cit.

68 PL, Vol. III, p. 121 footnote

69 22 March 1842, PL

70 12 and (? 21) March 1842, PL

71 21 March 1842, PL

72 (15 March 1842) PL

73 Wilkins, op. cit.

74 To Charles Lanman, 5 February 1868, PL, Vol. III, p. 166 footnote

75 PL

76 PL

77 22 March 1842, PL

78 To Frederick Dickens, 4 April 1842, PL

79 1, 2, 3, and 4 April 1842, PL

80 15, 16, and (17) April 1842, PL

81 Ibid.

82 24 April 1842, PL

83 26 April 1842, PL

84 PL, Vol. III, p. 214 footnote

85 21 May 1842, PL

86 Ibid.
87 26 May 1842, PL
88 *American Notes*
89 26 May 1842, PL
90 31 July 1842, PL
91 MCDY
92 To W. H. Prescott, 31 July 1842, PL
93 3 August 1842, PL

8. Coxcombry and Cockneyism

1 31 July 1842, PL
2 Edwin W. Marrs (ed.), *Letters of Thomas Carlyle to his Brother Alexander* (London, 1968)
3 PL
4 8 July 1842, PL
5 11 July 1842, PL
6 31 July 1842, PL
7 (1 July 1842) PL
8 PL
9 To Miss Julia Pardoe, 19 July 1842, PL
10 PL
11 To Mrs. D. Colden, 15 July 1842, PL
12 31 July 1842, PL
13 31 July 1842, PL
14 Longfellow to Freiligrath, 6 January 1843, PL, Vol. III, p. 340 footnote
15 31 July 1842, PL
16 MCDY
17 8 May 1843, PL
18 H. P. Smith, 13 July 1842, PL
19 To H. P. Smith, 14 July 1842, PL
20 29 July 1842, MCDY
21 PL
22 8 September 1842, PL
23 To T. C. Grattan, 1 September 1842, PL
24 28 September 1842, PL
25 To C. C. Felton, 1 September 1842, PL
26 PL
27 PL
28 PL, Vol. III, p. 335 footnote
29 PL, Vol. III, p. 289 footnote
30 W. H. Gilman and J. E. Parsons (eds.), *Journals of R. W. Emerson*, Vol. VIII (Cambridge, Mass., 1970)
31 January 1843, PL, Vol. III, p. 348 footnote
32 PL, Vol. III, p. 348 footnote
33 31 December 1842, PL
34 PL, Vol. III, p. 348 footnote
35 (16 September 1842) PL
36 31 December 1842, PL
37 12 November 1842, PL
38 PL
39 The MS. is now in the Morgan Library. After Mitton's death in 1878 a box of family papers was passed to Georgina Hogarth; they 'revealed not only debt and difficulties but the most discreditable and dishonest dealing on the part of the father towards the son'. *Dickensian*, Vol. LVI, September 1960
40 4 April 1842, PL
41 20 February 1842, PL
42 31 December 1842, PL
43 (12 February 1843) PL
44 (? mid-February 1843) PL
45 28 February 1843, PL
46 (28 June 1843) PL
47 15 October 1843, PL
48 (28 June 1843) PL
49 13 June 1843, PL
50 To Talfourd, PL
51 PL, Vol. III, p. 575 footnote
52 28 September 1843, PL
53 Arthur A. Adrian, *Mark Lemon* (London, 1966)
54 Ibid.
55 G. N. Ray (ed.), *Letters and Private Papers of W. M. Thackeray*, Vol. 1 (Cambridge, Mass., 1945)
56 3 May 1843, PL
57 2 March 1843, PL
58 13 March 1843, PL
59 To C. C. Felton, 2 March 1843, PL
60 3 May 1843, PL
61 To C. C. Felton, 2 March 1843, PL

62 1 September 1843, PL
63 To Thomas Beard, 18 July 1843, PL
64 7 August 1843, PL
65 24 July 1843, PL
66 (13 August 1843) PL
67 PL
68 PL, Vol. III, p. 542 footnote
69 Ibid.
70 MCDY
71 PL, Vol. III, p. 542 footnote
72 (15 August 1843) PL
73 1 September 1843, PL
74 To Thomas Hood, 12 September 1843, PL
75 16 September 1843, PL
76 (24 September 1843) PL
77 Edna Healey, *Lady Unknown* (London, 1978)
78 16 September 1843, PL
79 To Macvey Napier, 17 October 1843, PL
80 2 January 1844, PL
81 To Mitton, 4 December 1843, PL
82 Peter Morgan (ed.), *Letters of Thomas Hood* (Toronto, 1973)
83 PL
84 2 January 1844, PL
85 Lord Jeffrey to Dickens, 26 December 1843, in TCH
86 *Fraser's*, February 1844
87 2 January 1844, PL
88 3 January 1844, PL
89 Jane Carlyle to Jeannie Welsh, 23 December 1843; Alan and Mary McQueen Simpson, *I Too Am Here* (London, 1977)
90 4 January 1844, PL
91 3 January 1844, PL
92 *Fraser's*, February 1844

9. Shadows in the Waters

1 (1 November 1843) PL
2 R. H. Horne, *The New Spirit of the Age* (London, 1844)
3 (1 November 1843) PL
4 To Forster (20 November 1843) PL
5 (2 November 1843) PL
6 (1 November 1843) PL
7 To Charles Smithson, 14 November 1843, PL
8 *Life*
9 PL
10 20 January 1844, PL
11 17 January 1844, PL
12 15 February 1844, PL
13 4 December 1843, PL
14 (11 February 1844) PL
15 12 February 1844, PL
16 PL
17 7 January 1844, PL
18 (18 January 1844) PL
19 To Forster (? August 1846) NSL
20 (? 15 March 1844) PL
21 To James V. Staples, 3 April 1844, PL
22 26 February 1844, PL
23 PL, Vol. IV, p. 54 footnote
24 28 February 1844, PL
25 To T. E. Weller, 1 March 1844, PL
26 11 March 1844, PL
27 13 March 1844, PL
28 PL
29 *Dickens Studies Annual*, Vol. II, 1972, 'Charles Dickens and the Weller Family' by D. H. Paroissieu
30 17 April 1844, PL
31 *Examiner*, 26 October 1844
32 (2 November 1843) PL
33 24 March 1844, PL
34 (May 1844) PL
35 To Forster (? 14–15 July 1844) PL
36 Thomas Carlyle to Forster, 6 June 1844, in F. G. Kitton, *Charles Dickens by Pen and Pencil* (London, 1890–2)
37 (? 20 July 1844) PL
38 (12) August 1844, PL
39 22 July 1844, PL
40 24 August 1844, PL

41 *Pictures from Italy*
42 (? 15–16 September 1844) PL
43 22 July 1844, PL
44 7 August 1844, PL
45 (? 10–11 August 1844) PL
46 (? 31 August 1844) and (? 30 September 1844) PL
47 22 July 1844, PL
48 (? 10 September 1844) PL
49 To Forster (? 15–16 September 1844) PL
50 *Pictures from Italy*
51 18 March 1845, PL
52 (? 6 October 1844) PL
53 (? 29 October 1844) PL
54 (? 6 October 1844) PL
55 (8 October 1844) PL
56 PL
57 To Forster (? 6 October 1844) PL
58 (? 30 September 1844) PL
59 (? 8 October 1844) PL
60 To Forster (8 October 1844) PL
61 Ibid.
62 (? mid-October 1844) p. 201, PL
63 (? mid-October 1844) p. 200, PL
64 (? 29 October 1844) PL
65 To Forster 3 and (4) November 1844, PL
66 5 November 1844, PL
67 (? 21 October 1844) PL
68 (? 1–2 November 1844) PL
69 3 and (4) November 1844, PL
70 8 November 1844, PL
71 (12 November 1844) PL
72 16 November 1844, PL
73 (12 November 1844) PL
74 16 November 1844, PL
75 PL
76 2 December 1844, PL
77 Maclise to Catherine Dickens, 8 December 1844, *Dickens Studies*, Vol. II, No. 1, January 1966, 'Two Sketches by Maclise' by K. J. Fielding
78 2 December 1844, PL

79 8 December 1844, PL
80 10 December 1844. R. R. Madden, *Literary Life and Correspondence of the Countess of Blessington* (New York, 1855)
81 8 December 1844, PL
82 10 March 1845, PL
83 To Forster (22 December 1844) PL
84 PL
85 To T. J. Thompson, 17 October 1845, PL
86 PL
87 27 January 1845, PL
88 4 February 1845, PL
89 To Emile de la Rue, 10 February 1845, PL
90 Ibid.
91 Ibid.
92 17 and 22 February 1845, PL
93 23 and 25 February 1845, PL
94 (? 2 March 1845) PL
95 To Sheridan Le Fanu, 24 November 1869, NSL
96 26 March 1845, PL
97 Thomas Trollope, *What I Remember* (London, 1887)
98 14 April 1845, PL
99 To Forster (13 April 1845) PL
100 9 May 1845, PL
101 9 May 1845, PL
102 To Forster (27 April 1845) PL
103 To T. Beard, 20 May 1845, PL
104 14 April 1845, PL
105 (15 June 1845) PL
106 18 March 1845, PL
107 (15 June 1845) PL

10. Battle of Life

1 2 November 1845, MCDY
2 (? early July 1845) PL
3 To Forster (? 26 July 1845) PL
4 (? 1 or 2 November 1845) PL

5 *Life*

6 Ibid.

7 (? 30–31 December 1844 and January 1845) PL

8 *Life*

9 PL, Vol. III, p. 502 footnote

10 17 August 1845, PL

11 To Augusta de la Rue, 27 September 1845, PL

12 Maclise to Forster in Forster Collection, V & A

13 PL

14 *Life*

15 To Augusta de la Rue, 27 September 1845, PL

16 To Mr. Head, 13 August 1845, PL

17 To Clarkson Stanfield, 15 July 1845, PL

18 15 November 1845, MCDY

19 To John Willmott (? 10 September 1845) PL

20 18 September 1845, PL

21 *Dickensian* special issue on Forster, Vol. LXX, September 1974

22 *Life*

23 30 September 1845 in Leonard Huxley (ed.), *Jane Welsh Carlyle: Letters to her Family* (London, 1924)

24 Elvan Kniten (ed.), *Letters of Robert Browning and Elizabeth Barrett Barrett, 1845–46* (Cambridge, 1969)

25 20 September 1845, MCDY

26 J. A. Froude (ed.), *Letters and Memorials of Jane Welsh Carlyle* (London, 1883)

27 27 September 1845, PL

28 PL

29 PL

30 Henry Reeve (ed.), *Greville Memoirs* (London, 1888)

31 Ibid.

32 PL

33 (28 October 1845) PL

34 Elvan Kniten, op. cit.

35 To Barton, April 1846, in F. R. Barton (ed.), *Some New Letters of Edward Fitzgerald* (London, 1923)

36 20 October 1845, PL

37 (31 October 1845) PL

38 (1 November 1845) PL

39 10 November 1845, PL

40 PL

41 20 October 1845, PL

42 To Bradbury and Evans, 28 October 1845, PL

43 PL

44 6 November 1845, PL

45 Joseph Crowe, *Reminiscences of Thirty-Five Years of my Life* (London, 1895)

46 *Dickens Studies*, Vol. I, 1965

47 Mrs. Oliphant, *William Blackwood and His Sons* (London, 1897)

48 27 December 1845, PL

49 Betty Miller (ed.), *The Unpublished Letters of Elizabeth Barrett to Mary Russell Mitford* (London, 1954); and to Mrs. Martin, *Letters of Elizabeth Barrett Browning* (London, 1898)

50 19 November 1845, PL

51 1 December 1845, PL

52 To William Empson, 28 November 1845, PL

53 1 January 1846, PL

54 *Morning Chronicle*, 24 December 1845

55 Macphail's *Edinburgh Ecclesiastical Journal*, February 1846

56 G. N. Ray (ed.), *W. M. Thackeray. Contributions to the 'Morning Chronicle'* (Urbana, 1955)

57 *The Times*, 27 December 1845

58 27 December 1845, MCDY

59 To C. Claxton, 8 January 1846

60 *Letters of Elizabeth Barrett Browning*, op. cit.

61 27 December 1845, MCDY

62 R. H. Horne, *The New Spirit of the Age* (London, 1844)

63 3 January 1846, MCDY

64 Florence Marryat, *Life and Letters of Captain Marryat* (London, 1872)
65 22 January 1846, MCDY
66 PL
67 V. Markham, *Paxton and the Bachelor Duke* (London, 1935)
68 *Dickensian*, Vol. LIII, January 1957, 'John Dickens, Journalist' by W. J. Carlton
69 J. B. Atkins, *The Life of Sir William Howard Russell* (London, 1911)
70 Elvan Kniten, op. cit.
71 22 January 1846, MCDY
72 Thomas Britton, quoted in A. W. Ward, *Dickens* (London, 1882)
73 *Dickensian*, Vol. 68, September 1972, 'Charles Dickens as J. T. Danson knew him' by K. J. Fielding
74 30 January 1846, PL
75 (30 January 1846) PL
76 12 February 1846, MCDY
77 26 February 1846, PL
78 PL, Vol. IV, p. 513 footnote
79 17 April 1846, PL
80 *Daily News*, 9, 13, 16 March 1846, and see further in Philip Collins, *Dickens and Crime* (London, 1962)
81 PL
82 PL
83 PL
84 PL
85 (? 17–20 April 1846) PL
86 17 April 1846, PL
87 1 April 1846, MCDY
88 Elvan Kniten op. cit.
89 1 June 1846
90 1 June 1846, MCDY
91 Elvan Kniten, op. cit.
92 PL
93 To Maclise, 14 June 1846, PL
94 (? 13 or 14 June 1846) PL
95 To Miss Coutts, 25 June 1846, PL
96 To Thomas Chapman, 3 July 1846, PL
97 Forster (? 28 June 1846) PL

98 26 May 1846, PL
99 (? 28 June 1846) PL
100 (25–26 July 1846) PL
101 Ibid.
102 Ibid.
103 *Dickensian*, Vol. XLVII, January 1951, 'Sidelights on a Great Friendship'
104 (? 15–17 August 1846) PL
105 To Forster (25–26 July 1846) PL
106 (30 August 1846) PL
107 To Forster (2 August 1846) PL
108 (9 & 10 August 1846) PL
109 (? 15–17 August 1846) PL
110 To Forster (24 and 25 August 1846) PL
111 24 October 1846, PL
112 To Mitton, 30 August 1846, PL
113 (18 July 1846) PL
114 PL
115 (30 August 1846) PL
116 (? 20 September 1846) and (30 August 1846) PL
117 PL
118 (? 20 September 1846) PL
119 (30 August 1846) PL
120 (? 6 September 1846) PL
121 25 September 1846, PL
122 (26 September 1846) PL
123 (30 September and 1 October 1846) PL
124 (3 October 1846) PL
125 (10 October 1846) and (26–29 October 1846) PL
126 30 November 1846, PL
127 To Thomas Chapman, 3 July 1846, PL
128 22 October 1846, MCDY
129 (11 October 1846) PL
130 24 October 1846
131 *Economist*, 10 October 1846
132 PL, Vol. IV, p. 642 footnote
133 16 February 1847, MCDY
134 Lord Cockburn, *Life of Lord Jeffrey* (Edinburgh, 1852)
135 (11 October 1846) PL
136 (20 October 1846) PL

137 (26–29 October 1846) PL

138 PL

139 To Forster (31 October 1846) and (4 November 1846) PL

140 *Dickensian*, Vol. LXVII, January 1951, op. cit.

141 (15 or 16 November 1846) PL

142 (13 November 1846) PL

143 PL

144 To Forster (13 November 1846) PL

145 PL

146 (? 30 November 1846) PL

147 To Forster (22 and 23 November 1846) PL

148 (? 30 November 1846) PL

149 (6 December 1846) PL

150 (? 12 December 1846) PL

151 PL

152 PL

153 See TCH

154 PL

11. Good Samaritan

1 HCD

2 *Life*

3 (26–29 October 1846) PL

4 NSL

5 28 January 1847, NSL

6 (? 30 November 1846) PL

7 February 1847 in *Life*

8 Ibid.

9 Lord Cockburn, *Life of Lord Jeffrey* (Edinburgh, 1852)

10 10 March 1847, MCDY

11 E. Hodder, *The Life and Work of the Seventh Earl of Shaftesbury* (London, 1886)

12 G. N. Ray (ed.), *Letters and Private Papers of W. M. Thackeray*, Vol. 1 (Cambridge, Mass., 1945)

13 John Ruskin, *Unto This Last* (London, 1862)

14 TLS, 19 September 1958, 'Thackeray and the "Dignity of Literature"' by K. J. Fielding

15 To Mrs. Carmichael-Smythe, 2 July 1847, in Ray, op. cit.

16 PL, Vol. IV, p. 643 footnote

17 24 October 1846, PL

18 9 March 1847, NSL

19 T. Chapman, 10 May 1847, NSL

20 Edna Healey, *Lady Unknown* (London, 1978)

21 27 June 1847, HCD

22 23 May 1847, HCD

23 26 August 1847, HCD

24 27 June 1847, HCD

25 Edmund Blunden, *Leigh Hunt* (London, 1930)

26 To Dr. Hodgson, 12 June 1847, NSL

27 To Alexander Ireland, 11 July 1847, NSL

28 Half the money went to Hunt; Dickens paid the remainder to Poole in instalments

29 11 August 1847 to unknown correspondent, NSL

30 10 September 1847, NSL

31 19 September 1847, NSL

32 2 September 1847, NSL

33 28 October 1847, HCD

34 HCD

35 SCD

36 NSL

37 NSL

38 29 February 1848 in EJCD

39 12 April 1848 in J. A. Froude, *Thomas Carlyle* (London, 1890)

40 10 April 1848, GHL

41 To Jane Carlyle, 10 April 1848, in Froude, op. cit.

42 To D. M. Moir, 17 June 1848, NSL

43 S. M. Ellis, *William Harrison Ainsworth and his Friends* (London, 1911)

44 5 December 1847, MCDY

45 October 1848

46 13 April 1848
47 2 April 1848, NSL
48 26 March 1848, MMCD
49 30 March 1848, NSL
50 To Revd. E. Tagart, 6 May 1848, NSL
51 CDML
52 Charles and Mary Cowden-Clarke, *Recollections of Writers* (London, 1878)
53 Ibid.
54 NSL
55 12 June 1848, NSL
56 Arthur A. Adrian, *Mark Lemon* (London, 1966)
57 NSL
58 27 July 1848, NSL
59 NSL
60 24 July 1848, MCDY
61 NSL
62 NSL
63 End September, NSL
64 Ibid.
65 14 October 1847, NSL
66 3 September 1847, NSL
67 End September 1848, NSL

12. Golden Harvest

1 MCDY
2 NSL
3 AF
4 NSL
5 12 January 1849, NSL
6 Ibid.
7 To Macready, 2 February 1849, Morgan Library MS.
8 1 February 1849, NSL
9 Wrongly dated 25 June 1849 in NSL
10 February 1849, *Life*
11 NSL
12 To Jeannie Welsh in J. A. Froude (ed.), *Letters and Memorials of Jane Welsh Carlyle* (London, 1883)
13 To Mrs. Brookfield, 4 May 1849, in G. N. Ray (ed.), *Letters and Private Papers of W. M. Thackeray*, Vol. 1 (Cambridge, Mass., 1945)
14 To Jeannie Welsh, op. cit.
15 W. Gérin, *Elizabeth Gaskell* (London, 1976)
16 Edna Healey, *Lady Unknown* (London, 1978), and HCD
17 7 September 1849, HCD
18 10 July 1849, NSL
19 MMCD
20 To Mrs. Brookfield, 24 July 1849, in G. N. Ray, op. cit.
21 28 July 1849, NSL
22 To Forster, September 1849, NSL
23 *Dickensian*, Vol. LXV, 1969, 'Thomas Talfourd and *David Copperfield*' by P. F. Skottowe
24 September 1849, NSL
25 September 1849, NSL
26 26 September 1849, NSL
27 October 1849, *Life*
28 5 October 1849, NSL
29 7 November 1849, NSL
30 12 November 1849, NSL
31 'Lying Awake' in UT
32 *The Times*, 13 November 1849, quoted in GHL
33 *The Times*, 19 November 1849, quoted in GHL
34 Philip Collins, *Dickens and Crime* (London, 1962)
35 17 November 1849, in Blanchard Jerrold, *Life and Memorials of Douglas Jerrold* (London, 1859)
36 D. Masson, *Memories of London in the Forties* (London, 1908)
37 NSL
38 7 October 1849, NSL
39 30 November 1849, NSL
40 29 January 1850, NSL
41 29 December 1849, NSL
42 To P. Cunningham, 12 May 1850, NSL
43 Gérin, op. cit.

44 Quoted in EJCD

45 12 April 1850, HCD

13. A Man of Parts

1 To John T. Lawrence, 10 December 1849, NSL

2 6 March 1850, HCD

3 Ibid.

4 13 August 1850, NSL

5 15 August 1850, NSL

6 NSL

7 To R. H. Horne, 6 July 1850, NSL

8 NSL

9 To Miss Coutts, 23 August 1850, HCD

10 MMCD

11 To Mary Boyle, 20 September 1850, GHL

12 Ibid.

13 NSL

14 NSL

15 CDE

16 NSL

17 December 1850

18 11 June 1851

19 26 July 1850, NSL

20 NSL

21 23 November 1850, NSL

22 15 January 1851 in EJCD

23 NSL

24 24 January 1851, NSL

25 8 December 1844, *Dickens Studies*, Vol. II, No. 1, January 1966, 'Two Sketches by Maclise' by K. J. Fielding

26 Forster Collection in V & A

27 PL, Vol. IV

28 PL, Vol. IV, p. 304 footnote

29 16 February 1846, PL

30 Forster Collection in V & A

31 8 July 1850 in MMCD

32 Quoted in SCD

33 Ibid.

34 To Miss Coutts, 23 March 1851, HCD

35 5 January 1851, NSL

36 TLS, 19 September 1958, 'Thackeray and the "Dignity of Literature"' by K. J. Fielding

37 *North British Review*, May 1851

38 To Lytton, 4 March 1851, NSL

39 5 January 1851, NSL

40 To Lytton, 23 March 1851, NSL

41 To Lytton, 25 March 1851, NSL

42 CDE

43 To Augustus Egg, 8 March 1851, in Kenneth Robinson, *Life of Wilkie Collins* (London, 1952)

44 To Dr. James Wilson, 8 March 1851, NSL

45 To Dr. Wilson, 11 March 1851, NSL

46 15 March 1851, NSL

47 23 March 1851, HCD

48 NSL

49 25 March 1851, MMCD

50 26 March, 1851, MMCD

51 4 April 1851, MMCD

52 SCD

53 15 April 1851, MMCD

54 17 April 1851, HCD

55 20 March 1851, HCD

56 NSL

57 Quoted in EJCD

58 13 May 1851, NSL

59 24 May 1851, NSL

60 Ibid.

61 1 June 1851, NSL

62 1 June 1851, NSL

63 11 July 1851, NSL

64 27 July 1851, CDE

65 *Life*

66 NSL

67 30 July 1851, CDE

68 CDE

69 11 September 1851, MMCD

70 To Henry Austin, 7 September 1851, NSL

71 8 September 1851, NSL

72 To Beard, 6 October 1851, NSL
73 HCD
74 (August 1851) NSL
75 CDE
76 2 October, MMCD
77 9 October 1851, HCD
78 7 October 1851, NSL

14. The Romance of Discontent

1 17 November 1851, HCD
2 13 January 1851, HCD
3 7 August 1843, HCD
4 John Lothrop Motley, *Correspondence* (London, 1889)
5 Gordon S. Haight (ed.), *Letters of George Eliot* (London, 1954)
6 Thomas Trollope, *What I Remember* (London, 1887)
7 Percy Fitzgerald, *Life of Dickens* (London, 1905)
8 E. Lynn Linton, *My Literary Life* (London, 1899)
9 Justin McCarthy, *Reminiscences* (London, 1899)
10 Mary Dickens, *My Father As I Recall Him* (London, 1900)
11 Gladys Storey, *Dickens and Daughter* (London, 1939)
12 To Miss Coutts, 25 October 1853, HCD
13 Harriet Beecher Stowe, *Memories of Foreign Lands* (Boston, 1854)
14 7 March 1852, NSL
15 16 March 1852, HCD
16 16 December 1851, NSL
17 16 October 1851, CDE
18 17 October 1851, CDE
19 W. Gérin, *Elizabeth Gaskell* (London, 1976)
20 Ibid.
21 15 November 1851, MMCD
22 GHL
23 15 February 1852, NSL
24 To G. Beadnell, 4 May 1852, NSL

25 To Lytton, 15 February 1852, NSL
26 HCD
27 25 July 1852, HCD
28 22 July 1852, NSL
29 Kenneth Robinson, *Life of Wilkie Collins* (London, 1952)
30 8 May 1852, NSL
31 NSL
32 1 August 1852, NSL
33 8 August 1852, NSL
34 *Life*
35 5 October 1852, NSL
36 *Life*
37 13 October 1852, NSL
38 19 October 1852, NSL
39 24 December 1852, NSL
40 22 November 1852, NSL
41 28 February 1852, CDE
42 NSL
43 SCD
44 NSL
45 5 May 1853, NSL
46 *Life*
47 (June 1853) NSL
48 Ibid.
49 18 June 1853, CDE
50 23 June 1853, NSL
51 18 June 1853, CDE
52 24 July 1853, NSL
53 27 August 1853, HCD
54 To Collins, 24 June 1853, in Robinson, op. cit.
55 NSL
56 24 September 1853
57 *Life*
58 Robinson, op. cit.
59 To Catherine Dickens, 5 October 1853, MMCD
60 25 October 1853, NSL
61 To Miss Coutts, 13 November 1853, HCD
62 25 October 1853, HCD
63 Robinson, op. cit.

64 To Catherine Dickens, 7 November 1853, MMCD
65 Ibid.
66 F. Kaplan, *Dickens and Mesmerism* (London, 1976)
67 5 December 1853, ibid.
68 14 January 1854, HCD
69 4 January 1854, HCD
70 UT
71 27 November 1853, HCD
72 13 January 1854, GHL
73 2 January 1854, HCD

15. Black and White

1 To Mrs. Watson, 1 November 1854, NSL
2 *Life*
3 9 March 1854, NSL
4 CDE
5 6 March 1854, NSL
6 Edmund Yates, *Recollections and Experiences* (London, 1884)
7 22 June 1854, CDE
8 To Miss Coutts, 22 June 1854, HCD
9 13 July 1854, CDE
10 14 July 1854, NSL
11 22 July 1854, NSL
12 13 July 1854, NSL
13 John Ruskin, *Unto This Last* (London, 1862)
14 G. O. Trevelyan (ed.), *Life and Letters of Lord Macaulay* (London, 1959)
15 To Knight, 17 March 1854, NSL
16 To Henry Coles, 17 June 1854, NSL
17 1 November 1854, NSL
18 20 August 1854, CDE
19 24 August 1854, CDE
20 14 October 1854, CDE
21 *Life*
22 26 October 1854, HCD
23 (October 1854) NSL
24 9 February 1855, HCD
25 25 January 1855, HCD
26 Edna Healey, *Lady Unknown* (London, 1978)
27 *Life*
28 10 February 1855, NSL
29 CDE
30 Kenneth Robinson, *Life of Wilkie Collins* (London, 1952)
31 15 February 1855, NSL
32 22 February 1855, NSL
33 Ibid.
34 Ibid.
35 AF
36 3 April 1855, NSL
37 19 March 1855, NSL
38 K. J. Fielding, TLS, 15 and 22 October 1954
39 (? November 1855) NSL
40 NSL
41 10 April 1855, NSL
42 HCD
43 SCD
44 To Collins, 8 July 1855, NSL
45 HCD
46 3 April 1855, GHL
47 NSL
48 HCD
49 20 June 1855, NSL
50 30 June 1855, NSL

16. A Dread Phaenomenon

1 CDE
2 4 October 1855, NSL
3 17 July 1855, NSL
4 23 August 1855, NSL
5 16 September 1855, CDE
6 30 September 1855, NSL
7 4 October 1855, NSL
8 To Collins, 30 September 1855, GHL
9 4 October 1855, NSL
10 16 October 1855, NSL

11 24 October 1855, CDE
12 3 November 1855, MMCD
13 (November 1855) NSL
14 21 December 1855, MMCD
15 2 January 1856, NSL
16 To Forster, 11 January 1856, NSL
17 19 February 1856, HCD
18 30 January 1855, NSL
19 Forster Collection in V & A
20 7 January 1856, CDML
21 E. Lynn Linton, *My Literary Life* (London, 1899)
22 See J. A. Hammerton, *The Dickens Companion* (London 1910)
23 CDE
24 9 February 1856, HCD
25 11 March 1856, NSL
26 9 May 1856, MMCD
27 15 July 1856, HCD
28 19 January 1856, NSL
29 22 April 1856, NSL
30 (April 1856) NSL
31 CDML
32 24 March 1855, NSL
33 CDE
34 HCD
35 5 July 1856, HCD
36 CDML
37 5 July 1856, HCD
38 13 August 1856, HCD
39 8 August 1856, HCD
40 12 September 1856, NSL
41 HCD
42 To Miss Power, 15 December 1856, NSL
43 13 December 1856, NSL
44 14 January 1857, HCD
45 19 January 1857, NSL
46 28 January 1857, NSL
47 1 March 1857, NSL
48 15 April 1857, NSL
49 *Life*
50 See TCH
51 NSL
52 22 May 1857, NSL
53 19 March 1857, NSL
54 K. J. Fielding, TLS, 15 and 22 October 1954
55 26 June 1857, NSL
56 To Miss Coutts, 10 July 1857, HCD
57 CDML
58 5 July 1857, NSL
59 19 July 1857, NSL
60 8 July 1857, NSL
61 Quoted in EJCD
62 Ibid.

17. The Skeleton in the Cupboard

1 2 September 1857, NSL
2 5 September 1857 in *Life*
3 Ibid.
4 HCD
5 29 August 1857, NSL
6 'Lazy Tour' in RP
7 9 September 1857, NSL
8 (October 1857) NSL
9 23 October 1857, F. Kaplan, *Dickens and Mesmerism* (London, 1976)
10 NSL
11 2 February 1858, HCD
12 Huntingdon Library MS.
13 NSL
14 See CDPR
15 SCD
16 (March 1858) NSL
17 Lady Priestley, *The Story of a Life Time* (London, 1908)
18 5 September 1857, NSL
19 *Life*
20 (March 1858) NSL
21 Edmund Yates, *Recollections and Experiences* (London, 1884)
22 31 July 1858, CDPR

23 Gladys Storey, *Dickens and Daughter* (London, 1939)

24 HCD

25 HCD

26 19 May 1858, HCD

27 G. N. Ray (ed.), *Letters and Private Papers of W. M. Thackeray*, Vol. 1 (Cambridge, Mass., 1945)

28 *Dickensian*, Vol. LII, 1956

29 5 December 1853, MMCD

30 31 May 1858, NSL

31 *Dickensian*, Vol. LII, 1956

32 MMCD, Appendix

33 28 May 1858, Morgan Library MS.

34 Yates op. cit.

35 MMCD, Appendix

36 Arthur A. Adrian, *Mark Lemon* (London, 1966)

37 MMCD, Appendix

38 5 September 1858, MMCD

39 In Ada Nisbet, *Dickens and Ellen Ternan* (Berkeley, California, 1952)

40 Gordon S. Haight (ed.), *Letters of George Eliot* (London, 1954)

41 Storey, op. cit.

42 *Dickensian*, Vol. LII, 1956

43 *Dickensian*, Vol. LXVIII, September 1972, 'Charles Dickens as J. T. Danson knew him' by K. J. Fielding

44 *Dickens Studies*, Vol. 2, May 1966, 'W. C. Macready and Dickens' by Philip Collins

45 *Life*

18. Honour and Glory

1 7 July 1858, NSL

2 29 April 1858, NSL

3 *Review of English Studies*, New Series, Vol. 6, 1955

4 Gordon S. Haight (ed.), *Letters of George Eliot* (London, 1954)

5 Edmund Yates, *Recollections and Experiences* (London, 1884)

6 23 August 1858, HCD

7 To Webster, 9 September 1861, NSL; to Yates, 3 April 1862, NSL

8 25 October 1858, Huntingdon Library MS.

9 To W. Collins, 11 August 1858, NSL

10 To Georgina Hogarth, 5 August 1858, NSL

11 To W. Collins, 11 August 1858, NSL

12 9 August 1858, HCD

13 Yates, op. cit.

14 11 August 1858, NSL

15 23 August 1858, HCD

16 29 August 1858, HCD

17 10 September 1858, NSL

18 Quoted in EJCD

19 11 August 1858, NSL

20 8 December 1858

21 *Dickensian*, Vol. LX, 1964, 'Who Was the Lady?' by W. J. Carlton

22 27 October 1858, HCD

23 21 February 1859, NSL

24 HCD

25 HCD

19. Ashes of the Great

1 3 May 1843, PL

2 *Pictures from Italy*

3 16 November 1844, PL

4 13 August 1856, HCD

5 See *Dickensian*, Vol. XCVIII, May and September 1952, 'Personal and Business Relations of Charles Dickens and Thomas Coke Evans' by Gerald G. Grubb

6 See James T. Fields, *In and Out of Doors with Charles Dickens* (Boston, 1876) and *Yesterdays with Authors* (London, 1874)

7 Ada Nisbet, *Dickens and Ellen Ternan* (Berkeley, California, 1952)

8 July 1859, NSL

9 Fields, op. cit.; and Grubb, op. cit.

10 1 July 1859, CDE

11 9 July 1859, NSL

12 6 October 1859, NSL

13 15 October 1859, NSL

14 10 December 1859

15 W. P. Frith, *A Victorian Canvas* (London, 1957) and *My Autobiography and Reminiscences* (London, 1889)

16 *Life*

17 To Frank Stone, 19 October 1859, NSL

18 To Georgina Hogarth, 21 October 1859, NSL; and to Wills, 16 October 1859, NSL

19 Gladys Storey, *Dickens and Daughter* (London, 1939)

20 12 December 1856, NSL

21 13 November 1859, NSL

22 To Mitton and to Frances Dickinson, 19 August 1860, NSL

23 Frances Dickenson, ibid.

24 To Georgina Hogarth, 27 November 1860, NSL

25 24 December 1859

26 *Dickensian*, Vol. LXV, 1969, 'Dickens and his Illustrators' by Nicolas Bentley

27 30 March 1860, NSL

28 5 April 1860, HCD

29 8 April 1860, HCD

30 16 August 1860, NSL

31 4 September 1860, CDE

32 Ibid.

33 Storey, op. cit.

34 Storey, op. cit.

35 *Life*

36 Edmund Yates, *Recollections and Experiences* (London, 1884)

37 10 July 1859, NSL

38 21 February 1860, NSL

39 6 October 1860, NSL

40 8 August 1860, NSL

41 6 October 1860, NSL

42 1 February 1861, NSL

43 28 April 1861, NSL

44 (October 1860) NSL

45 23 June 1861, NSL

20. A Double Life

1 1 July 1861, NSL

2 11 June 1861, NSL

3 (September 1861) NSL

4 1 July 1861, NSL

5 (September 1861) NSL

6 28 September 1861, NSL

7 3 November 1861, HCD

8 29 October 1861, GHL

9 To Wills, 30 October 1861, CDE

10 To Forster, 8 November 1861, NSL

11 Ibid.

12 CDE

13 To Wills, 13 December 1861, CDE

14 To Baylis, 1 February 1862, NSL

15 CDE

16 8 January 1862, NSL

17 1 February 1862, NSL

18 8 January 1862, NSL

19 To Georgina Hogarth, 28 January 1862, NSL

20 8 April 1862, NSL

21 16 March 1862, NSL

22 April 1862, NSL

23 28 June and 22 October 1862, NSL

24 22 September 1862, NSL

25 2 June 1862, Morgan Library MS.

26 20 September 1862, NSL

27 To Forster, 5 October 1862, NSL

28 24 October 1862, CDE

29 22 October 1862, NSL

30 27 December 1862, NSL

31 To Beard, 15 November 1862, NSL

32 19 January 1863, CDE

33 4 February 1863, CDE

34 1 January 1863, NSL

35 7 February 1863, NSL

36 4 February 1863, CDE

37 J. A. Froude, *Thomas Carlyle* (London, 1890)

38 G. A. Sala, *Things I Have Seen and People I Have Known* (London, 1894)

39 March 1863, NSL
40 9 August 1863, NSL
41 To Revd. W. Brookfield, 24 May 1863, NSL
42 (October 1863) NSL
43 9 August 1863, NSL
44 14 September 1863, CDE
45 22 April 1863, NSL
46 (October 1863) NSL
47 To Cerjat, 25 October 1864, GHL
48 1 February 1861, NSL
49 K. Perugini, 'Thackeray and my Father' in *Pall Mall Magazine*, August 1911
50 Sir William Hardman, *Letters and Memoirs* (London, 1925)
51 12 February 1864, HCD
52 24 January 1864, NSL
53 12 February 1864, HCD
54 29 March 1864, NSL
55 To M. T. Bass, May 1864, NSL
56 To Wills, 26 June 1864, CDE
57 25 October 1864, GHL
58 29 July 1864, NSL
59 7 August 1864, CDE
60 17 March 1865, CDE
61 November 1864, NSL
62 To Mrs. Proctor, 15 February 1865, NSL
63 3 March 1865, NSL
64 22 April 1865, NSL
65 Ibid.
66 (May 1865) NSL
67 13 June 1865, NSL
68 Postscript to *Our Mutual Friend*
69 11 July 1865, HCD
70 June 1865, NSL
71 Ibid.
72 16 April 1869, CDML
73 13 June 1865, NSL
74 20 July 1865, NSL
75 Postscript to *Our Mutual Friend*

21. Powers of Evil

1 To Mrs. Lehmann, 27 June 1865, NSL
2 To Wills, 30 November 1864, CDE
3 Percy Fitzgerald, *Memories of Charles Dickens* (London, 1913)
4 28 April 1858, NSL
5 7 July 1865, NSL
6 30 November 1865, NSL
7 28 October 1865, NSL
8 29 November 1865, NSL
9 11 November 1865, NSL
10 April 1866, NSL
11 11 November 1865, NSL
12 21 December 1865, NSL
13 (September 1865) NSL
14 6 January 1866, NSL
15 9 February 1866, NSL
16 11 March 1866, NSL; and *Life*
17 *Life*
18 G. Dolby, *Charles Dickens as I Knew Him* (New York, 1912)
19 17 April 1866, NSL
20 14 April 1866, NSL
21 To Miss L. Benzon, 18 June 1866, NSL
22 (September 1866) NSL
23 4 October 1866, NSL
24 21 October 1866, CDE
25 28 December 1866, NSL
26 24 January 1867, CDE
27 22 January 1867, NSL
28 Dolby, op. cit.
29 24 January 1867, CDE
30 15 February 1867, NSL
31 17 February 1867, NSL
32 18 February 1867, NSL
33 Dolby, op. cit.
34 22 March 1867, NSL
35 To Georgina Hogarth, 29 March 1867, NSL
36 See Felix Aylmer, *Dickens Incognito* (London, 1959), for a detailed discussion of this material

37 Gladys Storey, *Dickens and Daughter* (London, 1939)
38 18 April 1867, NSL
39 May 1867, NSL
40 James T. Fields, *In and Out of Doors with Charles Dickens* (Boston, 1876)
41 May 1867, NSL
42 10 May 1867, NSL
43 (May 1867) NSL
44 Fields, op. cit.
45 6 June 1867, CDE
46 CDE
47 6 August 1867, NSL
48 3 September 1867, NSL
49 CDE
50 3 September 1867, NSL
51 28 June 1867, CDE
52 CDE
53 Dolby, op. cit.
54 NSL
55 John Bigelow, *Retrospections on an Active Life* (New York, 1909)
56 Edmund Yates, *Recollections and Experiences* (London, 1884)
57 SCD
58 Yates, op. cit.
59 3 November 1867, NSL
60 Moncure Conway, *Autobiography* (London, 1904)
61 To Mary Dickens, 10 November 1867, NSL
62 21 November 1867, CDE

22. A Pile of Dollars

1 1 December 1867, NSL
2 25 November 1867, NSL
3 To Mary Dickens, 1 December 1867, NSL
4 To Wills, 21 November 1867, CDE
5 H. W. L. Dana, 'Longfellow and Dickens' in *Cambridge Historical Society*, Vol. 28, 1942 (Cambridge, Mass.)
6 To Wills, 21 November 1867, CDE
7 John Bigelow, *Retrospections on an Active Life* (New York, 1909)
8 Annie A. Fields, *Memories of a Hostess* (Boston, 1922)
9 30 November 1867, NSL
10 3 December 1867, NSL
11 Dana, op. cit.
12 6 December 1867, CDE
13 To Georgina Hogarth, 16 December 1867, NSL
14 CDE
15 Ada Nisbet, *Dickens and Ellen Ternan* (Berkeley, California, 1952)
16 CDE
17 To Wills, 17 December, CDE
18 11 December 1867, NSL
19 11 December 1867, NSL
20 Nisbet, op. cit.
21 To Wills, 30 December, CDE
22 12 January 1868, NSL
23 21 January 1868, NSL
24 5 January 1868, NSL
25 To Georgina Hogarth, 21 January 1868, NSL
26 To Wills, 30 December 1867, CDE
27 12 January 1868, NSL
28 24 February 1868, NSL
29 5 January 1868, NSL
30 15 January 1868, NSL
31 To Forster, 14 January 1868, NSL
32 G. Dolby, *Charles Dickens as I Knew Him* (New York, 1912)
33 8 March, Huntingdon Library MS.
34 Attached 31 January 1868, GHL
35 29 January 1868, NSL
36 To Mary Dickens, 11 February 1868, NSL
37 Ibid.
38 Ibid.
39 24 February 1868, NSL
40 25 February 1868, NSL
41 To Georgina Hogarth, 27 February 1868, NSL

42 2 March 1868, NSL
43 Dolby, op. cit.
44 Dolby, op. cit.
45 2 March 1868, NSL
46 21 March 1868, NSL
47 8 March 1868, NSL
48 To Georgina Hogarth, 8 March 1868, NSL
49 11 February 1868, NSL
50 NSL
51 16 March 1868, NSL
52 12 March 1868, NSL
53 29 March 1868, NSL
54 30 March 1868, NSL
55 29 March 1868, NSL
56 7 April 1868, NSL
57 Ibid.
58 Ibid.
59 SCD
60 Ibid.
61 25 May 1868, NSL
62 April 1868, NSL

23. The Hunt is Over

1   25 May 1868, NSL
2   11 May 1868, NSL
3   25 May 1868, NSL
4   7 July 1868, NSL
5   CDE
6   8 March 1868, NSL
7   26 July 1868, CDE
8   31 July 1868, CDE
9   G. Dolby, *Charles Dickens as I Knew Him* (New York, 1912)
10 26 July 1868, CDE
11 Berg MS.
12 CDE
13 15 October 1868, NSL
14 26 September 1868, NSL
15 (September 1868) NSL
16 *Life*
17 To Revd. W. Brookfield, 24 May 1863, NSL

18 Dolby, op. cit.
19 4 October 1868, NSL
20 Thomas Trollope, *What I Remember* (London, 1887)
21 26 August 1868, NSL
22 24 October 1868, NSL
23 8 December 1868, NSL
24 October 1868, NSL
25 Edmund Yates, *Recollections and Experiences* (London, 1884)
26 To Mrs. Fields, 16 December 1868, GHL
27 Ibid.
28 W. P. Frith, *My Autobiography and Reminiscences* (London, 1889)
29 8 December 1868, NSL
30 Dolby, op. cit.
31 14 January 1869, CDPR
32 To James Fields, 15 February 1869, NSL
33 CDPR
34 15 February 1869, NSL
35 To Forster, 2 March 1869, NSL
36 Dolby, op. cit.
37 *Life*
38 30 March 1869, CDE
39 9 April 1869, NSL
40 Yates, op. cit.
41 Frith, op. cit.
42 22 April 1869, NSL
43 21 April 1869, NSL
44 22 April 1869, NSL
45 Dolby, op. cit.
46 *Life*
47 28 April 1869, Alexander Carlyle (ed.), *New Letters of Thomas Carlyle*, Vol. II (London, 1904)
48 3 May 1869, NSL

24. Fallen from the Ranks

1 NSL
2 18 May 1869, NSL

3 18 October 1869, NSL

4 Appendix in *Life*

5 G. Dolby, *Charles Dickens as I Knew Him* (New York, 1912)

6 9 April 1869, NSL

7 Kenneth Robinson, *Life of Wilkie Collins* (London, 1952)

8 Gladys Storey, *Dickens and Daughter* (London, 1939)

9 SCD

10 2 March 1870, NSL

11 *Life*; and 6 August 1869, NSL

12 *Edwin Drood*

13 22 October 1870

14 *Edwin Drood*

15 *Pall Mall Gazette*, 20 January 1890

16 18 October 1869, NSL

17 James T. Fields, *Yesterdays with Authors* (London, 1874)

18 *Life*

19 Quoted in *Dickensian*, Vol. 69, May 1973, 'Carlyle and Dickens or Dickens and Carlyle' by K. J. Fielding

20 9 January 1870, NSL

21 SCD

22 9 January 1870, NSL

23 *Life*

24 CDE

25 29 March 1870, NSL

26 Anne Ritchie, *From the Porch* (London, 1913)

27 SCD

28 *Life*

29 3 March 1870, NSL

30 26 March 1870, NSL

31 Dolby, op. cit.

32 25 April 1869, NSL

33 16 May 1870, NSL

34 16 May 1870, NSL

35 17 May 1870, NSL

36 11 May 1870, NSL

37 EJCD

38 29 April 1870, NSL

39 SCD

40 *Life*

41 25 April 1870, NSL

42 To Fields, 18 April 1870, NSL

43 Storey, op. cit.

44 Ibid.

45 Quoted in TCH

46 *Life*

Index